Mass Media
and
American Politics

Mass Media
and
American Politics

FOURTH EDITION

Doris A. Graber
University of Illinois at Chicago

CO
PRESS

A Division of Congressional Quarterly Inc.
Washington, D.C.

Cover design: Ben Santora

Printed in the United States of America

Library of Congress Cataloging-in-Publication Data

Graber, Doris A. (Doris Appel)
  Mass media and American politics / Doris A. Graber. -- 4th ed.
    p.   cm.
  Includes bibliographical references and index.
  ISBN 0-87187-699-X
  1. Mass media—Social aspects—United States.   2. Mass media—Political
aspects—United States.   I. Title.
HN90.M3G7   1993
302.23'0973—dc20   92-38447
                                                                CIP

To
Jack, Jim, Lee, Susan, Tom—
my very special students

CONTENTS

TABLES AND FIGURES

Tables

PREFACE

The mass media play a central and ever-growing role in the conduct of American politics. The primary reasons are the growth of new media technologies such as cable and satellite television transmission; business mergers involving the electronic media and newspaper chains; and the deregulation of the communications industry during the Reagan and Bush administrations. Last, but by no means least, the battle between journalists and politicians for control over news content has escalated sharply.

To report and analyze these major continuing changes and their impact on politics and political news requires revision of this book at frequent intervals. The 1993 edition, besides describing the current media scene, incorporates important advances in the study of the influence of the media. It also analyzes media content in previously unexplored areas of politics. Many of the new data come from my own research on the media's impact on politics, particularly through television news. Political events and research findings have been updated, and fresh examples have replaced older ones throughout the book.

Although much has changed since the original publication of *Mass Media and American Politics* in 1980, the basic features of the interrelation between mass media and American politics have remained the same. This stands as a testimony to the maturity of the relationship. Therefore, the basic organizational structure of the book has been retained, albeit with some rearrangement of the chapter order. While the book discusses all of the mass media, the primary emphasis remains on news produced by television and newspapers because these are the chief sources of current information for people both in public and private life. Magazines and radio play a distinctly subordinate role.

In the past, most research has been limited to the relationship between media and politics during elections. This pattern continues, although it has become less pronounced. As the references in the text and in the suggested readings at the end of each chapter indicate, the scope of research has broadened over time. However, most of these recent studies are specialized, focusing on single segments of the total picture. Hence, the need still exists for a comprehensive, up-to-date college level textbook that provides an overview of the entire media field from a primarily political perspective. The fourth edition of *Mass Media and American Politics* serves that purpose.

Chapters 1 and 2 examine the mass media as institutions in the American political system and show how the media are both influenced by and reflect that system. Chapter 3 completes the discussion of the legal and political framework in which American media operate. It describes the legal rights of ordinary citizens, public officials, and newspeople to obtain and publish information and to be protected from damaging publicity.

Chapters 4 and 5 deal with newsmaking under ordinary and extraordinary circumstances, such as natural disasters and wars. Media structures, personnel, and operations are analyzed, and the impact they have on media content is explained and assessed. Investigative reporting and its influence on public policy is discussed in Chapter 6. The wealth of new information about political learning and opinion formation is explored in Chapter 7, along with new theories about media-induced asocial and prosocial behavior. Much of this material is based on my own research and on research undertaken jointly with Maxwell E. McCombs, currently at the University of Texas at Austin, and David H. Weaver, currently at Indiana University.

The powerful influence of the media in a variety of political situations is the subject of Chapters 8 through 11. These situations include media coverage of elections (Chapter 8), and the interplay between the media and major political institutions such as the presidency and Congress (Chapter 9). A new chapter covers the media's role in the judicial system more extensively than before and adds information about state and local news (Chapter 10). Chapter 11 details the steadily growing part that media play in the conduct of foreign policy. The book concludes with a discussion of policy trends and the new technologies and political forces shaping them (Chapter 12).

Besides the relentless march of political and technological events that dictated changes, the shape of the new edition owes much to colleagues and students who have commented on the book and to the scholars whose research has provided new insights. Their contributions are deeply appreciated. Special thanks are due to Edie N. Goldenberg, University of Michigan, and William C. Adams, George Washington University, for reading the original manuscript with exceptional care and making very constructive comments. The fourth edition was improved by the careful critiques by Robert Sahr, Oregon State University; Herbert Waltzer, Miami University of Ohio; and an anonymous reviewer. These scholars will surely recognize that most of their suggestions have been implemented.

I am also indebted to my research assistants, especially Laurent Pernot and Leta Dally. They tracked down many elusive references and data and contributed to the new research presented in the book. Whatever errors have crept into this new and heavily revised edition are my responsibility, of course—although the proverbial gremlins really did it. That there are not more mistakes is due to the watchful eyes of Debbie Hardin and Ann O'Malley who edited the final version of the manuscript. Brenda Carter, acquisitions editor for CQ Press, and the team she heads provided invaluable support that greatly eased the many chores entailed in book production. The concern and friendship of the CQ crew have been real morale boosters.

The time required to write books or complete extensive revisions is usually taken from the category labeled "family time." When it is willingly and even cheerfully surrendered by those who hold claim to it, research and writing progress with a minimum of emotional strain. Family time donated to a book is a generous, treasured gift. I am grateful to my family for this indispensable contribution to my work and for the love and understanding that it represents.

Doris A. Graber

CHAPTER 1

Media Power
and Government Control

On March 3, 1991, after a high-speed chase, several officers of the Los Angeles police stopped an African-American motorist for traffic violations. An angry confrontation ensued that ended with the white officers severely beating the motorist. A resident of a nearby apartment building, alerted by the noise, videotaped scenes of the beating. Over the course of the next year, the shocking footage was broadcast thousands of times throughout the nation, creating a widespread consensus among citizens of all races that the police had used excessive force. Police brutality and racism became simmering public issues, kept alive by the repeated airing of the taped scenes.

When news reports informed Americans at the end of April 1992 that an all-white jury had exonerated all but one of the Los Angeles officers on the charges of brutality, protest demonstrations pockmarked the country. In Los Angeles those demonstrations turned into one of the ugliest urban riots in decades, complete with shootings, beatings, massive arson, and looting. Fifty-three people were killed, and more than 2,000 were injured. Millions of dollars worth of property was destroyed, leaving sections of the city an economic wasteland. In the wake of the rioting, the focus of the ongoing presidential campaign turned to the hitherto neglected problems of urban decay and the alienated, impoverished underclass.

Political Importance of Mass Media

The impact of television on racial harmony and the fate of America's cities is but one example of how mass media, in combination with other political factors, can influence American politics. How journalists cover stories often plays a crucial part in shaping the perceptions of reality of millions of people in all walks of life. News stories, as seen through the eyes of reporters, take Americans to the battlefields of the world in Central America or the Middle East. They give them ringside seats for space shuttle launches or Arctic submarine patrols. They provide the nation with shared political experiences, such as watching presidential election debates or congressional investigations, that then form a basis for public opinions and for uniting people for political actions.[1]

The media often serve as attitude and behavior models. In the process of image creation, the media indicate which views and behaviors are acceptable and even praiseworthy in a given society and which are unacceptable or outside the mainstream. Audiences can learn how to conduct themselves in ordinary social and work situations, how to cope with personal crises, and how to evaluate major social institutions like the medical profession or the police. Media stories also indicate what is deemed important or unimportant by various groups of elites, what conforms to prevailing standards of justice and morality, and how events are related to each other.[2] In the process the media present a set of cultural values that their audiences are likely to accept in whole or in part as typical of American society. The media thus help to integrate and homogenize American society.

Attention to the mass media is all-pervasive among twentieth-century Americans. The average high school graduate nowadays has spent more time in front of a television set than in school, much of it during preschool and elementary school days. Even in school much learning about current events is based on information provided by the media. As adults, Americans spend nearly half of their leisure time watching television, listening to the radio, or reading newspapers and magazines. Averaged out over an entire week, this amounts to more than seven hours of exposure per day to some form of mass media news or entertainment. Television occupies three-fourths of this time.[3] With access to cable and satellite television, as well as video recorders that can store programs for delayed viewing, these figures are rising. Despite considerable dissatisfaction with the quality of television programs, television is the primary source of news and entertainment for the average American. It is also the most trusted source of information.

On a typical evening 98 million people, nearly half the country's population, are watching television between 8:00 and 9:00 P.M. If a "special" is broadcast, as many as 75 million to 80 million people may watch it.[4] In 1988 the debates between presidential candidates Michael Dukakis and George Bush were watched by 160 million Americans, not to mention millions of foreign viewers. The ability to attract such vast audiences of ordinary people, as well as political elites, constitutes a major ingredient in the power of the mass media. Mass media provide a nationwide forum for both individuals and groups and the important aspects of the nation's political and social life that the media choose to cover. People rely on mass media for this information and use it to identify their own interests.

The mass media are powerful guardians of political norms because the American public believes that a free press should keep it informed about the wrongdoings of government. Media images are especially potent when they involve aspects of life that people experience only through the media, rather than directly in their own neighborhoods. The personal and professional lives of politicians, revolutions in distant lands, frenzied trading at stock exchanges, heart transplants, and space shuttle landings are not generally experienced firsthand. Rather, popular perceptions of these activities are shaped largely by the images portrayed in news and fictional stories in print and electronic media. For example, prime time television exaggerates the likelihood of becoming a victim of crime. Heavy viewers, therefore, fear crime more and take more protective measures than do light viewers.[5]

Politically relevant information is often conveyed through stories that are not explicitly concerned with politics. In fact, since most people are exposed far more to nonpolitical information, make-believe media, such as movies and entertainment television, have become major suppliers of political images.[6] Entertainment shows on television, for example, picture social institutions, such as the police or the schools, in ways that convey esteem or heap scorn on them. They also express social judgments about various types of people. For instance, in the past television often depicted African-Americans and women as socially inferior and limited in abilities. This type of coverage conveys messages that audiences may accept at face value, even when they distort real-world conditions. The audience may think that social conditions and judgments shown on television are widely accepted and socially sanctioned and therefore ought to be maintained.

Not only are the media the chief source of nearly every American's views of the world, but they are also the fastest way to disperse information throughout the entire society. News of the assassination of President John F. Kennedy and the attempt on the life of President Ronald Reagan spread with incredible speed. In both cases more than 90 percent of the American people heard the news within ninety minutes of the event, either directly from radio or television or secondhand from other people who had received mass media messages.[7]

All of the mass media are politically important because they can reach large audiences. However, their impacts vary, depending on the characteristics of each medium, the nature and quantity of the political messages that it carries, and the size of the audience that it reaches. Print media need readers who are literate at appropriate levels. These readers enjoy the luxury of choosing what portion of content they wish to read and to review at will. By contrast, users of electronic media find it difficult to exclude portions of undesired content. Aside from recording and replaying the broadcast, or hearing a repeat broadcast, they cannot review what has been presented. However, many people who cannot enjoy print media because of reading difficulties have adequate listening and viewing skills so that they can extract meaning from broadcasts. That even includes very young children. The intonations available from the spoken word and meanings conveyed by nonverbal sounds, and the visual information in telecasts provide additional information that is largely lacking from printed messages.

One can generalize and say that print media excel in providing factual details and explanations involving abstract ideas. Electronic media, especially television, provide a greater sense of reality, which may explain why some audiences find electronic media more credible than print media.[8] Electronic media also convey physical images, including human body language and facial expressions, much more effectively than print media, and they are especially well suited to engage the viewers' emotions. Furthermore, it is easier for many people to gather insights on events and issues through the electronic media.

The nature of each technology has implications for the political purposes for which it is useful. Television is most likely to feature stories that are visually rich, stressing the pictorial aspects of the story and avoiding stories that deal with abstract concepts. By contrast, print media favor stories that can best be told through an ample number of words. Therefore, many political images transmitted by different types of media vary substantially in substance, manner of presentation, appeal to different audiences, and the political consequences they are likely to generate.

Functions of Mass Media

What major functions do the mass media perform? Three functions mentioned by political scientist Harold Lasswell are (1) surveillance of the world to report ongoing events, (2) interpretation of the meaning of events, and (3) socialization of individuals into their cultural settings.[9] To these three, a fourth function should be added: deliberate manipulation of politics. The manner in which these four functions are performed affects the political fate of individuals, groups, and social organizations, as well as the course of domestic and international politics. Let us look at each function in turn.

Surveillance

Surveillance involves two major tasks. For the political community at large, "public" surveillance throws the spotlight of publicity on selected people, organizations, and events. This publicity may then make them matters of concern to politicians and to the general public. It may determine which political demands are exposed and which are kept hidden. It also may force politicians to respond to situations on which their views would not otherwise have been aired. For individual citizens in their private capacities, "private" surveillance informs them about current events. While it may lead to political activities, its primary functions are gratification of personal needs and quieting of anxieties. The media, as Marshall McLuhan has observed, are "sense extensions" for individuals who cannot directly witness most of the events of interest to them and their communities.[10]

Public Surveillance. Because it arouses civic concerns and stimulates action, public surveillance is politically significant. Newspeople determine what is "news"—which political happenings will be covered and which will be ignored. Their choices affect who and what will have a good chance to become the focus for political discussion and action.[11] Without media attention the people and events covered by the news might have no influence, or reduced influence, on decision makers. Conditions that may be tolerated while these people or events remain obscure may quickly become intolerable in the glare of publicity. This is why politicians, who seek to garner or avoid publicity, time and structure events with media coverage in mind.

The following example illustrates the power of publicity to produce public action. In 1988, the *Chicago Tribune* published the story of Dale Bakker, Jr., a worker in a meat packing plant, whose fingers, wrist, and shoulder were left damaged from the pressures of performing his high speed meat-cutting job. Rather than changing the working conditions that had left the 36-year-old father permanently disabled, company officials suggested that he look for other types of work—even though there was little chance that he could find work given his physical disabilities.

The *Tribune* article accused major meat packing firms of unreasonably raising the production quotas of their workers over the past fifteen years to increase profits. It also charged the Reagan Administration with contributing to dangerous working conditions by slashing the numbers of safety inspectors and thereby weakening the Occupational Safety and Health Administration (OSHA). The story produced important changes. An industry trade group allotted $500,000 for research into ways to ease the physical strain on meat packing workers, and the nation's largest meat company adopted a more effective industrial safety program. At the federal level, fines for safety violations increased sharply.[12]

The events reported in this story were not unique. Disabling working conditions are not uncommon in large industrial plants in a variety of major industries. Yet very little is done about them by profit-sensitive industries or overworked regulatory agencies. The key for taking action in the Bakker case was the public surveillance provided through media coverage. Not all media publicity is as beneficial, of course. In many instances, misperceptions and scares created by media stories have undermined confidence in good policies and practices, good people, and good products. The human and economic costs have been vast. For example, a few years ago stories of dubious validity questioned the safety of chemically treated apples and cranberries; these stories caused millions of dollars of losses in the affected industries.

Fear of publicity can be as powerful a force in shaping action as actual exposure. Politicians and business leaders know what damage an unfavorable story can do and act accordingly, either to hide the story or to atone for their misdeeds by public confessions of guilt and regrets. Thus, when marijuana use became an issue during the 1988 and 1992 presidential election campaigns, a parade of officials openly confessed to similar sins or vowed publicly that they had never indulged. Major effects of public surveillance may arise indirectly from impressions created by news stories. If media stories dwell on crime and corruption in the inner city, residents may move to the suburbs, leaving the inner city deserted and even less safe and depriving it of tax revenues. Speculation that international conflicts or oil embargoes are in the offing may scare investors and produce fluctuations in domestic and international stock markets and commodity exchanges. Serious economic (and hence political) consequences may ensue.

The media not only bring matters to public attention; they also can doom people and events to obscurity by inattention. Lack of coverage may spring from the necessity to limit publication because the information supply exceeds the media's capacity to transmit it. Newspapers have only limited amounts of space available for news; time constraints on television and radio newscasts are even more stringent. The media also ignore matters that do not seem newsworthy by accepted journalistic criteria or that fail to catch their attention. Conscious attempts to suppress information for ideological or political reasons are another, less frequent reason for lack of coverage.

For many years left-wing social critics have faulted mainstream American journalists for using their news selection power to strengthen white middle-class values and suppress socialist viewpoints. They claim that these choices are made deliberately to perpetuate capitalist exploitation of the masses, in line with the ideological preferences of media owners. Critics also claim that the media have intentionally suppressed the facts about dangerous products, such as alcohol and tobacco, and about the socially harmful activities of large corporations, which may be responsible for water and air pollution or unsafe consumer goods.[13] On the other hand, right-wing critics complain that the media give undue attention to the views of the enemies of the established social and political order in hopes of undermining it. Each camp can cite a long list of stories to support its contentions.[14]

Media people deny these charges. They disdain political motives in news selection and defend their choices on the basis of general criteria of newsworthiness (treated more fully in Chapter 4). Like the social critics, they can muster a lot of evidence from news stories to support their claims. At the heart of controversies over the ideological bias of the media lie two basic questions that cannot be answered conclusively. The first concerns people's motivations. How can one prove what motivates journalists to act in certain ways? And is it fair to ascribe motivations to them in the face of their denials? The second question relates to story effects. To what degree can media stories produce the goals owners of print and electronic media and news professionals are allegedly seeking?

Besides calling attention to matters of potential public concern, the media also provide cues to the public about the degree of importance of an issue. Important stories are covered prominently—on the front page with big headlines and pictures or as a major television or radio feature. Less important matters are buried in the back pages or given very brief exposure on television or radio. However, nearly all coverage, even though it is brief and comparatively inconspicuous, lends an aura of significance to publicized topics.

Through the sheer fact of coverage the media can confer status on individuals and organizations. They "function essentially as agencies of social legitimation—as forces, that is, which reaffirm those ultimate value standards and beliefs, which in turn uphold the social and political status quo." [15]

Television made African-American civil rights leaders and their causes household names. Martin Luther King, Jr., and Jesse Jackson became national figures in part because of television. A political candidate whose efforts to win an election are widely publicized, a social crusader whose goals become front-page news, or a convicted murderer or terrorist who wins a hearing on radio or television often becomes an instant celebrity. Their unpublicized counterparts remain obscure and bereft of political influence.

Because the attention of the media is crucial for political success, actors on the political scene deliberately create situations likely to receive media coverage. Daniel Boorstin has labeled events arranged primarily to stimulate media coverage "pseudo-events." [16] They may range from news conferences called by public figures even when there is no news to announce, to physical assaults on people and property designed to dramatize grievances. Newspeople who cover such events may feel manipulated and resent it. Nonetheless, they cover many such stories.

Decisions about what to publish and thereby put on the agenda for public discussion and possible action are also beyond the discretion of media personnel when events are exceptionally significant or have become widely known already, or when the story is reported by competing media. For example, news about prominent persons and major domestic or international events must be reported.[17] But beyond such unavoidable events, there remains an extremely wide range of persons and events for which coverage is optional.

The power of the media to set the civic agenda is a matter of concern because it is not controlled by a system of formal checks and balances as is power at various levels of government. It is not subject to periodic review through the electoral process. If media emphases or claims are incorrect, remedies are few. Citizens can be protected from false advertising of consumer goods through "truth in advertising" laws, but there is no way in which they can be protected from false political claims or improper news selection by media personnel without impairing the crucial rights to free speech and a free press. Media critic Jay Blumler expresses the dilemma well:

> Media power is not supposed to be shared: That's an infringement of editorial autonomy. It is not supposed to be controlled: That's censorship. It's not even supposed to be influenced: That's news management! But why should media personnel be exempt from Lord Acton's dictum that all power corrupts and absolute power corrupts absolutely? And if they are not exempt, who exactly is best fitted to guard the press guardians, as it were? [18]

Private Surveillance.   Average citizens may not think much about the broader political impact of the news they read, hear, and watch. They use the media instead to keep in touch with what they deem personally important. The media are their eyes and ears to the world, their means of surveillance, which tell them about economic conditions, weather, sports, jobs, fashions, social and cultural events, health and science, and the public and private lives of famous people.

Being able to stay informed makes people feel secure, whether or not they remember what they read or hear or see. Even though the news may be bad, at least they feel that there will be no unsettling surprises. News reassures them that the political system continues to operate in the face of constant crises and frequent mistakes. Reassurance is very important for people's peace of mind. It tends to keep them politically quiescent because there is no need to act if political leaders seem to be doing their jobs. In turn, this has significant consequences for the stability of the political system and the ability of government to function.[19] For good or ill, the public's quiescence helps to maintain the political and economic status quo.

Other significant private functions that the mass media fulfill for many people are entertainment, companionship, tension relief, and a way to pass the time with minimal physical or mental exertion. The mass media can satisfy these important personal needs conveniently and cheaply. Through the media, people who otherwise might be frustrated and dissatisfied can participate vicariously in current political happenings, in sports and musical events, in the lives of famous people, and in the lives of families and communities featured in the news.[20]

Interpretation

Media not only survey the events of the day and make them the focus of public and private attention, but they also interpret their meanings, put them into context, and speculate about their consequences. Most incidents lend themselves to a variety of interpretations, depending on the values and experiences of the interpreter. The kind of interpretation that is chosen affects the political consequences of media reports. For example, since 1962 the way in which the media interpret the legal and social significance of abortions has changed considerably. Abortion used to be interpreted almost universally as murder. The emphasis was on the abortionist as the villain and the pregnant woman as an accomplice in the heinous crime. Now abortion is often cast into the frame of women's rights, although the older interpretations are still cherished by a portion of the public. Most Americans believe the pregnant woman has the right, with certain limitations, to protect her physical and mental health or the welfare of an infant likely to be born to a life of physical and mental suffering. The key situation that brought about the switch in media interpretation, and eased the change in public attitudes toward abortion, involved a television personality, Sherri Finkbine, who had taken thalidomide during her pregnancy before the drug's ill effects on infants were known. Fearing a severely malformed baby, she underwent an abortion in 1962.

Instead of reporting the action as murder, as had been the custom, news media throughout the country defended Sherri Finkbine's action. To steer clear of the negative connotations of the word *abortion*, journalists used a new vocabulary to put the act into a different light. They talked of "surgery to prevent a malformed baby," of "avoiding the possibility of mothering a drug-deformed child," and of the necessity of inducing a miscarriage to spare a child from loathing "its own image and crying out against those who might have spared it this suffering." [21]

Numerous circumstances influenced the type of interpretation that the Finkbine story received, but the primary factor was the reporters' or editors' decision, made independently or in response to pressures from the community or the news organization itself, to stress a particular image and to choose available informants and facts accordingly. Such journalistic choices play a large role in determining the political consequences of various situations.

By suggesting the causes and relationships of various events, the media may shape opinions even without telling their audiences what to believe or think. For example, linking civil strife in El Salvador to the activities of Soviet and Cuban Communist agents ensured that the American public would view the situation with considerable alarm. Linking the hostilities to poverty and social oppression would have put the problems into a far less threatening light. No explicit media warnings would be required to produce these diverse reactions.

There are countless ways in which news presentations can predetermine the conclusions that people are likely to draw, as political scientists Lance Bennett and Murray Edelman point out:

> We [journalists] can attribute any social problem to official policies, the machinations of those who benefit from it, or the pathology of those who suffer from it. We can trace it back to class or racial inequalities, to ideologies such as nationalism or patriotism, or to resistance to the regime. We can root the problem in God, in its historic genesis, in the accidental or systematic conjuncture of events, in rationality, in irrationality, or in a combination of these or other origins. In choosing any such ultimate cause we are also depicting a setting, an appropriate course of action, and sets of virtuous and evil characters, and doing so in a way that will appeal to some part of the public that sees its own sentiments or interests reflected in that choice of a social scene.[22]

The items that media personnel select to illustrate a point or to characterize a political actor need not be intrinsically important to be influential in shaping opinions and evaluations. During the 1988 presidential election campaign, the *Miami Herald* reported that a young woman had spent the night at the home of Gary Hart, then the front-runner among Democratic candidates, while his wife was absent. Although the story shed little light on Hart's political capabilities, five days after it was published nationwide Hart abandoned the race. A brief, unsuccessful re-entry into the campaign several months later demonstrated that his chances for winning the presidential nomination had been damaged beyond repair.

Socialization

The third major mass media function mentioned by Lasswell is political socialization (discussed more fully in Chapter 7). It involves the learning of basic values and orientations that prepare individuals to fit into their cultural milieu. Prior to the 1970s, socialization studies largely ignored the mass media because it was thought that parents and the schools were the primary agents. Studies conducted in the 1970s finally established that the media play a crucial role in political socialization.[23] The bulk of information that young people acquire about the nature of their political world comes from the mass media. It reaches them either directly through exposure to the electronic and print media or indirectly through exposure to the media of their families, teachers, acquaintances, and peers. Mass media information presents to the young specific facts as well as general values. It teaches them which elements produce power, success, and dominance in society, and it provides them with models for behavior. Young people make heavy use of such information to develop their opinions because they lack established attitudes and behavior patterns.

Public opinion polls show that most of the new orientations and opinions that adults acquire during their lifetime also are based on information supplied by the mass media. People do not necessarily adopt the precise attitudes and opinions that may be suggested by the media. Rather, mass media information provides the ingredients that people use to adjust their existing attitudes and opinions to keep pace with a changing world. The mass media must be credited, therefore, with a sizable share of continuing adult political socialization and resocialization. Examples of resocialization—the restructuring of established basic attitudes—are the shifts in sexual morality and racial attitudes that the American public has undergone since mid-century and the changing views on relations with mainland China and with the United Nations.[24]

Manipulation

In the post-Watergate era direct manipulation of the political process by the media has become increasingly common. Many journalists are powerful participants in the game of politics, rather than acting primarily as chroniclers of information provided by others. Media manipulation often takes the form of investigative journalism. Major print and electronic media now operate their own investigative units. Feature articles and television shows devoted exclusively to revealing the results of investigations have become highly popular. "Sixty Minutes," the CBS weekly collection of minidocumentaries, has reached and maintained top audience ratings for many years.

The purpose of these investigative shows, like that of their predecessors early in the century, is to *muckrake*. The term comes from a special rake designed to collect manure. President Theodore Roosevelt was the first to apply it to journalists who conducted their own investigations into corruption and wrongdoing to stimulate governmental action to clean up the "dirt" they had exposed. Muckraking today may have several different goals.[25] The journalist's primary purpose may be to write stories that expose misconduct in government and produce reforms. Alternatively, the chief purpose may be to present sensational information that attracts large media audiences and enhances profits. Other manipulative stories may be designed primarily to affect the course of politics in line with the journalists' political preferences. The various forms that manipulation can take are discussed in Chapter 6.

Effects of Mass Media

The public believes that the media have an important impact on the conduct of politics and on public thinking. Politicians act and behave on the basis of the same assumption. But many studies conducted by social scientists fail to show substantial impact. Why is there such a discrepancy between many social science appraisals of mass media effects and the general impression, reflected in public policies, that the mass media are extremely influential?

There are three major reasons. To begin with, many studies, particularly those conducted during the 1950s and 1960s, have taken a narrow approach to media effects, looking only for a few, specified effects, rather than all possible effects. Second, theories about the ways in which people use newspapers, television, radio, and other mass media have enhanced the belief in "minimal effects" because these theories suggest that people are disinclined to learn from the media. Finally, social scientists have encountered great difficulties in measuring effects because media stimuli make their impact as part of a complex combination of social stimuli.

Early Studies

Focus on Vote Choices. Eager for neat, readily quantifiable research designs, American social scientists began to study the effects of the mass media primarily in one narrow area: vote change as a result of media coverage of presidential elections. Among these early studies, several are considered classics. The first is *The People's Choice* by Paul Lazarsfeld, Bernard Berelson, and Hazel Gaudet of Columbia University. It reported how people made their voting choices in Erie County,

Pennsylvania, in the 1940 presidential election. Sequels followed in short order. The best known are *Voting: A Study of Opinion Formation in a Presidential Campaign,* by Columbia researchers Bernard Berelson, Paul Lazarsfeld, and William McPhee; *The Voter Decides,* by University of Michigan researchers Angus Campbell, Gerald Gurin, and Warren E. Miller; and the Michigan group's *The American Voter,* by Angus Campbell, Philip E. Converse, Warren E. Miller, and Donald Stokes.[26]

The early voting studies were based on the assumption that media influence could be ascertained by measuring its impact on voting choices. A well-publicized campaign presumably changed votes. If it did not, this indicated that the media lacked influence. Subsequent studies have shown that this reasoning is incorrect. There may be measurable media influence even when vote choice remains stable. Besides, media effects vary, depending on the office at stake and the historical period. At the time of the early voting studies, change of vote choice was quite uncommon because most voters adhered closely to partisan lines, regardless of media coverage. In recent years party allegiance has weakened substantially among many voters, so that the opportunities for media influence on vote choice are far greater.

Had the investigators concentrated on other settings, such as judicial or nonpartisan elections (for which few voting cues outside the media are available), they might also have discovered greater media-induced attitude change. Substantial media influence might have been found even in presidential elections if changes in people's trust and affection or knowledge about the candidates and the election had been explored. The early studies largely ignored these other types of media influences because they did not result in easily measurable behavior and attitude changes. Yet such changes constitute important media influences that are crucial components of a variety of political behaviors, quite aside from voting decisions.

The early voting studies focused almost exclusively on the individual citizen and failed to trace the linkages between effects on individuals and effects on the social groups to which they belong and through which they influence political events. Farm workers in California might not change their votes after hearing a candidate charge that illegal Mexican immigrants were taking jobs from American workers and depressing wage scales. But they might well use their union to testify against legislation permitting illegal immigrants to remain in the United States. They might even participate in violence against farmers who hire large numbers of alien workers. In turn, these activities might affect U.S.-Mexican relations and harm the worldwide image of the United States. Yet the early studies of media effects totally ignored such impacts on the entire political system and its component parts.

The findings that media effects were minimal were so pervasive in early research that, after an initial flurry in the 1940s and 1950s, social science research into mass media effects fell to a low ebb. Social scientists did not want to waste their time studying inconsequential effects. Despite seemingly solid evidence of media importance, they did not care to swim against the stream of established knowledge. Consequently, in study after study dealing with political socialization and learning, the mass media were hardly mentioned as important factors.

Learning Theories. The early findings were all the more believable because they tied in well with theories of persuasion. Mass media messages presumably miss their mark because they are impersonal. They are not tailored to the needs of specific individuals, as are the messages of parents, teachers, and friends. They do not permit immediate feedback, which then allows the sender to adjust the message to make it more suitable for the receiver. Furthermore, there is no compulsion to listen to mass media messages and no need to answer. Hence it is easy to ignore them.

Although there is a lot of truth to these claims, they fail to consider that television can simulate intimate personal settings. Audiences frequently interact with the television image as if what appears on screen were actually present in front of them. They may look on television commentators and actors as personal friends or enemies. Children often imitate people and situations seen on television, making them a part of their direct personal experiences.

Further support for the "minimal effects" findings came from various cognitive consistency theories. They postulate that average individuals dislike being presented with information that is incompatible with cherished beliefs. To avoid this painful experience and the necessity to change established beliefs, people expose themselves very selectively to the media. Social scientists have evidence that people are indeed selective in their use of the media and search for information that reinforces what they already believe and know. But, as will be discussed more fully in Chapter 7, the phenomenon is quite limited.

Recent Research

When researchers resumed their investigations of mass media effects in the wake of persistent evidence of strong media impact, they cast their net more broadly. They looked beyond media effects on voting to other effects during elections and in other types of political events. In this vein, researchers examined media impact on factual learning, on opinion formation, and on the satisfaction of a variety of human needs. They have also looked beyond the individual to effects on political systems and subsystems, a search that promises to be highly rewarding. But despite improvements in research designs and techniques, research into mass media effects has remained hampered by serious measurement problems.

Measuring Complex Effects. Mass media effects are difficult to measure, both at the level of the individual and at the societal level, because they are highly complex and elusive. The most common measuring device at the individual level—self-assessment of impact elicited during a poll—is notoriously unreliable. Researchers lack tools to measure the substance of human thinking objectively. Even when thoughts lead to overt behavior, they cannot accurately judge the nature of the thought. Moreover, actions spring from a variety of motivations so that it is difficult to isolate the part played by media.

Assessing mass media impact is especially difficult because mass media audiences already possess a fund of knowledge and attitudes that they bring to bear on new information. Since researchers rarely know precisely what this information is, or the rules by which it is combined with incoming information, they cannot pinpoint the exact contribution that particular mass media stories have made to an individual's cognitions, feelings, and actions. To complicate matters further, the impact of the mass media varies depending on the subject matter. For instance, media impact is greater on people's perceptions of unfamiliar issues than on their perceptions of issues that they have personally faced.

Ignoring Unanticipated Effects. Measurement of media effects has also suffered because unanticipated effects are frequently ignored. For example, when ABC television broadcast a highly publicized television drama about the horrors of nuclear war in 1984, it was widely either hoped or feared that many of the 80 million viewers would become more concerned about nuclear war. When the anticipated reaction did not occur, surprised observers of the impact of the broadcast reported that there were no effects. Most researchers failed to notice several totally unexpected important consequences of the broadcast. The percentage of people who had previously criticized President Reagan for pursuing policies likely to lead to war dropped sharply from 57 percent before the broadcast to 43 percent afterwards. In political terms, this amounted to decreased opposition to the military policies of the Reagan administration. At the same time, the broadcast also made people more conciliatory toward the Soviet Union and more supportive of general arms limitation agreements between the superpowers.[27]

A Case Study: Did Media Coverage Kill the Neutron Bomb? Assessments of the role of the media in the demise of plans for building a neutron bomb illustrate the problems faced in proving media impact. On June 6, 1977, the *Washington Post* published a front-page story about a new nuclear weapon, a neutron bomb, that "cuts down on blast and heat and thus total destruction, leaving buildings and tanks standing. But the great quantities of neutrons it releases kill people." Over the next ten months, the *Post* story caused consternation among executive branch officials, senators, Western European leaders, and political activists. As National Security Adviser Zbigniew Brzezinski commented quite accurately, "The *Post* article touched off a political explosion that reverberated throughout the United States and Europe." [28]

The idea of enhanced radiation bombs was not really new. Research and development had been conducted for twenty years. The objective was creation of a minimally destructive nuclear weapon to be used by Europeans on their own territory to repel invading armies. The U.S. Defense Department viewed the neutron bomb largely as an antitank weapon that would kill invading tank crews while sparing people and property in surrounding areas.[29]

The *Post* article forced high-level public officials to take action to repair the public relations damage. President Jimmy Carter ordered a delay in production of the bomb. Sen. Mark Hatfield of Oregon hurriedly introduced an amendment to the appropriation bill to ban further funding for neutron weapons. The prospective fight in the Senate then permitted the *Post* to justify follow-up stories and to publish anti-neutron bomb editorials. Gradually, other media began to pick up the story. On June 17, NBC ran a film clip showing the gruesome effects of neutron radiation on monkeys. ABC ran the clip a week later, and NBC then repeated it on the "Today" show. Meanwhile lurid *Post* front-page stories continued to unearth additional disquieting facts about the effects of neutron radiation, and other papers picked up the coverage. Little attention was paid to the Defense Department's explanations of the purpose and effects of neutron bombs.

Early in July the Defense Department began a low-key media campaign on behalf of the weapon to head off the Hatfield amendment barring funds. Reporters were invited for background briefings, and top Defense Department officials made the rounds of news talk shows. President Carter asked for continued funding during a televised press conference. The next day the Senate defeated the Hatfield amendment but voted that funding for the bomb be suspended until the president certified that the national interest required constructing the bomb.

Meanwhile anti-neutron bomb forces in Europe had begun to mobilize and antibomb stories and articles began to multiply. The Soviet Union added its voice in a massive antibomb propaganda campaign. Most allied leaders in Western Europe favored deployment of the bomb, believing that it held promise of repelling a Soviet invasion without nuclear escalation and without the devastation of much of Europe. But, scared by media-whipped opposition, they wanted to deflect the anger of antibomb forces from themselves onto President Carter by claiming that the United States was pushing the bomb. The Carter administration, in turn, tried to deflect blame by claiming that the European allies were urging deployment of the bomb. When an information campaign to build public support for the bomb fizzled, the president abandoned the project. National Security Adviser Brzezinski explained that President Carter feared he would be stigmatized as leading an "administration which introduced bombs that kill people but leave buildings intact." The image created by the *Post* article had come to roost.[30]

The demise of the bomb has been blamed on the press, beginning with the initial *Washington Post* story and continuing with subsequent news stories by the *Post* and other media in the United States and Europe. Without such coverage, appropriations for the bomb might have continued, and it might have been deployed quietly, without vociferous public opposition. Neither the Carter administration, the Senate, nor the European allies had expressed concern over the production and deployment of neutron weapons before 1977. Even after the stories broke, government leaders in Europe and the United States considered the bomb a worthwhile weapon. Its abandonment made Carter seem weak and caused major strains in the North Atlantic Treaty Organization (NATO).

The role of the *Post* and other media is not as clear-cut as it may seem, however. Actual deployment of the bomb, as distinct from its development, probably could not have been kept quiet since the bomb represented an important new type of weapon. It also seems doubtful that the well-organized antinuclear movement in the United States and Europe would have accepted the new weapon without attempts to stir up public opposition. Ever eager to condemn NATO military efforts in Europe, the Soviet Union with its vast government-controlled press certainly would have stirred up protests that could have stopped production and deployment. Finally, a more determined president, more adept at public relations aspects of public policy, might have been able to control the debate over the bomb by preparing a more favorable image for it before the press could talk of "killer warheads" that destroyed people but left buildings intact.

It is impossible to prove conclusively how crucial the media were in the neutron bomb case. It is equally impossible to prove that the media played no role or merely a minor role. Inability to prove mass media impact beyond a doubt has made social scientists shy away from assessing media influence on many important political events. In fact, social scientists often go to the other extreme and deny that effects exist simply because these effects defy measurement. This is unfortunate since many effects that cannot be measured precisely can be observed in the field and studied in the laboratory.

Statistical versus Political Significance. Social scientists also have been rather rigid in interpreting the significance of media influence when it has been found. They have falsely equated statistical significance with political significance, despite the fact that media impact on a small number of individuals can have great political consequences.

For example, during an election only 1 or 2 percent of the voters may change their votes because of media stories. That is a very small, statistically negligible effect. Politically, however, it may be a major impact because many important elections, including several presidential elections, have been decided by a margin of 2 percent of the voters. If an extra 2 percent of the vote had gone to the losing candidate in the 1976 presidential race, Ford would have stayed in the White House, and Carter would have remained a peanut farmer. Two percent of the voters sounds like a small number, but it runs into thousands, and even hundreds of thousands, when translated into actual numbers.

On an even smaller scale, if a broadcast of details of a race riot attracts a few listeners to the riot site and stimulates some to participate, the situation may escalate beyond control. Similarly, the impact of a single news story may change the course of history if it induces one assassin to kill a world leader or convinces one world leader to make an important political decision.

Influencing Elites. Another major problem with social science research on mass media effects is that it has concentrated on measuring the effects on ordinary individuals, rather than on political elites. The average individual, despite contrary democratic fictions, is politically fairly unimportant. Mass media impact on a handful of political decision makers usually is vastly more significant than similar impact on ordinary individuals. In addition, the impact on decision makers is likely to be far more profound because mass media information relates more directly to their immediate concerns. They may pay close attention to stories in which the public is not interested and which it often fails to understand. And they may spend considerable time and effort, and even make behavioral changes so that media coverage promotes their interests.

One example of media influence on elite behavior involves a brief column that appeared in the *Washington Post* in the summer of 1983. In it a Carter cabinet member complained that there had been little public reaction to reports that a campaign briefing book prepared for President Carter had fallen into the hands of the Reagan campaign staff. The book allegedly had been used to brief Reagan for his debate with Carter, in violation of campaign ethics and, possibly, national security. Initially the story produced no noticeable political waves, even though it had reached a worldwide audience, but it caught the eye of two politicians who were in a position to act.[31] One was a member of the congressional subcommittee with jurisdiction over the Ethics in Government Act. He, in turn, called it to the attention of the subcommittee chairman, Rep. Donald J. Albosta, a Michigan Democrat. The upshot was a major congressional investigation into the entire affair.

In light of what we have discussed thus far, it seems totally unrealistic to deny that the media are important in setting the stage for ongoing political developments, in shaping the views and behaviors of political elites and other selected groups, and in influencing the general public's perception of political life. As Theodore White put it, albeit with some exaggeration:

> The power of the press in America is a primordial one. It sets the agenda of public discussion; and this sweeping political power is unrestrained by any law. It determines what people will talk and think about—an authority that in other nations is reserved for tyrants, priests, parties and mandarins.
>
> No major act of the American Congress, no foreign adventure, no act of diplomacy, no great social reform can succeed in the United States unless the press prepares the public mind.[32]

Even if one takes a totally negative position, arguing that the media are nothing but a conduit of information over which they have no control, one cannot deny that people throughout the world of politics consider the media to be powerful and behave accordingly. This importance, which is an effect of media coverage, is reflected in efforts by governments everywhere, in authoritarian as well as democratic societies, to control the flow of information produced by the media lest it subvert the prevailing political system.

Who Should Control Newsmaking?

Attempts by governments to control and manipulate the media have been universal for centuries because governments worldwide believe media are important political forces. This belief is based on the assumption that institutions that control public information can shape public knowledge and behavior and thereby determine the support or opposition of citizens and officials to the government and its policies. That is why Emperor Napoleon claimed that "Four hostile newspapers are more to be feared than a thousand bayonets." Through control over mass information institutions and the stories they produce, governments everywhere seek to preserve the political system as a whole as well as to regulate the media and other social institutions that depend on media publicity. Although control occurs in all societies, its extent, nature, and purposes vary.

Several major reasons account for these variations. Political ideology is one of them. In countries where free expression of opinion is a paramount value and where dissent is respected, the media tend to be comparatively unrestrained. The right of the press to criticize government also flourishes when the accepted ideology grants that governments are fallible and often corrupt and that average citizens are capable of forming valuable opinions about the conduct of government. Finally, freedom of the press, even when it becomes a thorn in the side of the government, is more easily tolerated where governments are well established and politically and economically secure. In Third World nations, for instance, where governments are unstable and resources limited, it may be difficult to tolerate press behavior that is apt to topple the government or retard its plans for economic development.

Nowhere are the media totally free from formal and informal government and social controls, even in times of peace. On the whole, authoritarian countries control more extensively and more rigidly than do nonauthoritarian ones, but all systems represent specific points on a continuum of control. There are also gradations of control within nations, depending on the current regime and political setting, regional and local variations, and the nature of news. Common types of control systems used in authoritarian and nonauthoritarian societies will be described without giving details about any particular country.[33]

Authoritarian control systems are of two types: those that are nonideological and simply represent a desire by the ruling classes to tightly control media output so that it does not interfere with the conduct of government and those that are based on a totalitarian ideology, such as communism. The latter type actively uses and controls the media to support ideological goals. Examples of nonideological authoritarian control can be found in states ruled by military governments, or where constitutional guarantees have been suspended. Examples of control based on communism are found in Cuba and the People's Republic of China.

There are also two types of *nonauthoritarian approaches to control,* although they are not linked to differences in political ideology. Rather, these types are linked to differences in philosophies about the role that the media ought to carve for themselves in countries where they enjoy a great deal of freedom. The two types of nonauthoritarian approaches have been labeled *libertarian* and *social responsibility.* When journalists in democratic societies subscribe to the libertarian philosophy, they feel free to report whatever they wish as long as public tastes are satisfied. By contrast, when social responsibility philosophies prevail, newspeople expect to contribute to the betterment of society, spurring media audiences to behave in socially responsible ways. Journalists in the United States and Western Europe furnish examples of both of these philosophies. Often libertarian and social responsibility journalism occur simultaneously, or they may alternate during successive historical periods.[34]

In today's world, authoritarian systems of media control prevail in the majority of countries although many governments profess a desire for democratization and are struggling to move in that direction. Nonetheless, attempts to control internal and external news flows persist. In sessions of the United Nations Educational, Scientific and Cultural Organization (UNESCO), several members have opposed freedom of reporting about their countries even when the stories are to be published in foreign media. The argument has been made that only news that supports the established regime should be permitted and that all newspeople should be subject to supervision by officials of the country whose affairs they report. This story is told more fully in Chapter 11.

Role of Media in Authoritarian Regimes

What basic assumptions underlie authoritarian and nonauthoritarian philosophies of media operation, and what types of governmental structures and practices have been invented to implement these philosophies?

As Table 1-1 suggests, Communist and other authoritarian systems operate on the assumption that the government knows and represents the best interests of the people. Therefore, the mass media must not interfere with the operations of the government or endanger its survival. The press may point out minor deficiencies or corruption of low-level officials and suggest adjustments in line with prevailing policies, but beyond that it is considered inappropriate to criticize the basic system or its rulers. The policy of *glasnost,* or openness, initiated by the Soviet leadership in 1987, increased the emphasis on critical stories, but the scope of permissible criticism remained narrow until the collapse of the Soviet Union in 1991.

In most authoritarian political systems the mass media must take positions that firmly support the government. News must engender support for major policies, such as economic development or literacy campaigns. It must echo official stands about who the country's domestic and international friends and enemies are. But the media are free to choose the stories they wish to publish, as long as the offerings do not hurt the state or interfere with public policies.

Table 1-1 Contrasting Assumptions about Press Mission

Authoritarian regime assumptions	Democratic regime assumptions
Government knows and respects people's best interests	Governments are fallible and often corrupt
Press should not attack the government and its major policies	Press should attack the government when officials and policies seem flawed
News should engender support for major policies	News should stimulate critical thinking about major policies
News and entertainment programs should be selected for their social values	News and entertainment programs should be selected for audience appeal

Source: Compiled by author.

In totalitarian societies the role of the media is more stringently defined. The likely political and social effects of a story—rather than its general significance, novelty, or audience appeal—determine what will be published and what will be buried in silence. For instance, news about accidents, disasters, and crimes may be suppressed because these matters are believed to be devoid of value in teaching citizens proper conduct. Newspeople are encouraged to select stories that contain socially useful information and are apt to strengthen the people's allegiance to the political system. Even entertainment programs must serve political purposes. Music and drama performances, and even cartoon shorts in movie theaters, must carry appropriate social messages or have historical significance. The government supports such entertainment financially because it serves the important public purpose of shaping people's minds in support of the system.

Role of Media in Nonauthoritarian Regimes

The basic assumptions underlying mass media control in democratic countries contrast sharply with those of authoritarian societies, as Table 1-1 indicates. In democracies, governments are viewed as fallible servants of the people. They are deemed to be potentially corrupt, stupid, or abusive of citizens. Consequently, they must be constantly watched and, if they misbehave, criticized.

The media are regarded as objective reporters of good and evil who scrutinize the passing scene on behalf of a public that can and must appraise the performance of its officials. Journalists serve as the watchdog fourth branch of government, which monitors excesses and misbehavior of the executive, legislative, and judicial branches. Through playing an adversary role, journalists provide the feedback that democratic systems need to remain on course. If, as the result of their scrutiny, governments fall and public officials are ousted, this is as it should be.

Broadly stated, this is the theory behind the role of media in democratic societies. The practice is less clear-cut. In the United States, for example, neither newspeople nor government officials are completely at ease with the media's watchdog role. The media usually support the political system and rarely question its fundamental tenets. They limit their criticism to what they perceive as perversions of fundamental social and political values or noteworthy examples of corruption and waste. But because they depend heavily on the high and mighty as their sources of news, their links to the existing power structures are strong. Newspeople may even share information with government agencies, including policing bodies such as the Federal Bureau of Investigation and the Central Intelligence Agency. At times, reporters in a democratic society withhold important news at the request of the government when disclosure might cause harm. This happened when American media withheld news about the whereabouts of Americans who were hiding in the Canadian embassy during the Iran hostage crisis in 1979. Government officials, in an effort to keep their images untarnished by media attacks, may try to control the media through regulatory legislation or through rewards and punishments. These tactics are described more fully in Chapter 9.

The chief obligation of the mass media in free societies is to provide the general public with information and entertainment. According to the libertarian philosophy, anything that happens that seems interesting or important for media audiences may become news. It should be reported quickly, accurately, and without any attempt to convey a particular point of view. Subjects with the widest audience appeal should be stressed, even if that means heavy doses of sex and violence. Audience appeal is then expected to translate into good profits for media owners.

Although audiences may learn important things from the media, libertarians believe that teaching is not the media's chief task. Nor is it their task to question the truth, accuracy, or merits of the information supplied to them by their selected sources. Rather, it is left to the news audience to decide what to believe and what to question.

By contrast adherents to social responsibility tenets believe that news and entertainment presented by the mass media should reflect social consciousness. Media personnel should be participants in the political process, not merely reporters of the passing scene. As guardians of the public welfare, they should foster political action when necessary by publicizing social evils, such as industrial pollution or child abuse. In a similar view, undesirable viewpoints and questionable accusations should be denied exposure, however sensational they may be. If reporters believe that the government is hiding information that should be made public, they should try to discover the facts and publish them.

The type of journalism advocated by social responsibility journalists and the type of journalism advocated by totalitarian journalists have philosophical resemblances. Adherents of both approaches advocate using the media to support the basic ideals of their societies and to shape people into more perfect social beings. They are convinced that their goals are good and would not be achieved in a media system dominated by the whims of media owners or audiences.

But the similarities should not be exaggerated. Social advocacy in nonauthoritarian systems lacks the fervor, clout, and single-mindedness it has in systems where media control is monopolized by the government. Social responsibility journalism rarely speaks with a single uncontested voice throughout the entire society. Nevertheless, it frightens and antagonizes many news professionals and news audiences. If one agrees that the media should be used to influence social thought and behavior for "good" purposes, it becomes difficult to determine which purposes deserve to be included in that category. Critics of social responsibility journalism point out that journalists do not have a public mandate to act as arbiters of social values and policies in a society without a single vision of truth and goodness. Newspeople lack the legitimacy that in a democracy comes only from being elected by the public or appointed by duly elected officials.

Whatever the merits or faults of these arguments may be, at the present time social responsibility journalism is popular with a sizable proportion of the news profession.[35] Pulitzer prizes and other honors go to journalists who have successfully exposed questionable practices in the interest of social improvement. The most prominent "villains" targeted for exposure are usually big government and big business.[36]

Models of the News-Making Process

Beyond the basic concerns reflected in the philosophies of libertarians and social responsibility advocates, there are many other differences about guiding principles for reporting events. Scholars have identified four models of the news-making process: *the mirror model, the professional model, the organizational model,* and *the political model.* Each represents a judgment of what the major forces behind news making are or ought to be, and each profoundly affects the nature of news and its political impact.

MIKE PETERS reprinted by permission of UFS, Inc.

Proponents of the *mirror model* contend that news is and should be a reflection of reality. Newspeople observe the world around them and report what they see as accurately and objectively as possible. "We don't make the news, we merely report it," proponents of this view claim. The implication is that newspeople reflect whatever comes to their attention; they do not shape it in any way.

Critics of the mirror model point out that this conception of news making is unrealistic. Millions of significant events take place daily, forcing journalists to make choices about the general categories and specific stories to be published. Events that are publicized inevitably loom larger than life, reshaping the picture that the real world presents. Events that are ignored routinely vanish into nothingness. Even films and photographs distort reality. A small group of demonstrators may look like an invading army when cameras zoom in on them.

In the *professional model,* news making is viewed as an endeavor of highly skilled professionals who put together an interesting collage of events selected for importance, attractiveness to media audiences, and balance among the various elements of the news offering. Since audience appeal is the most important consideration for economic reasons, the audience becomes the ultimate judge of which stories may pass scrutiny and which will be ignored.

The *organizational model* is based on organizational theory. Its proponents contend that determination of what items will become news emerges from the pressures inherent in organizational processes and goals. Pressures springing from interpersonal relations and professional norms within the news organization are important, as are constraints arising from technical news production processes, cost-benefit consider-ations, profit orientations, and legal regulations.

Finally, the *political model* rests on the assumption that news everywhere is a product of the ideological biases of individual newspeo-ple, as well as of the pressures of the political environment in which the news organization operates. High-status people and approved institu-tions are covered by the media; those who are outside the dominant system or remote from the centers of power are generally ignored. Supporters of the prevailing system are pictured as good guys, oppo-nents as bad guys.

None of these models can fully explain the news-making process because the process reflects all of them in varying degrees. Since the influences that shape news making fluctuate, one needs to examine individual news-making situations carefully to account for the factors at work. Organizational pressures, for instance, vary depending on the interactions of people within the organization. Audience tastes change or are differently interpreted. Perceptions of "facts" differ, depending on reporters' dispositions. Moreover, the precise mix of factors that explains news making in any particular instance depends to a large degree on chance factors and on the current needs of a particular news medium.

Control Methods

Four types of controls of the press are widely used: legal, normative, structural, and economic.[37] All governments have laws to prevent serious press misbehavior such as deliberate, serious falsehoods. All societies also have social norms that members dare not defy. For example, in a religiously conservative country, ridiculing sacred con-cepts would lead to social condemnation. The way media organizations are structured and operated also shapes their product, as is clear when one compares the policy discretion enjoyed by publicly and privately owned media. Finally, economic support in the form of direct and indirect subsidies can be used to influence media performance.

The combination of methods by which governments control the media varies and so do the major objectives of control. Authoritarian societies use legal, structural, and economic means to restrict access to mass communications to voices friendly to the regime and to ensure that news stories remain supportive of most government policies. By con-trast, nonauthoritarian regimes rarely make formal attempts to deny foes of the regime access to the media. However, they often use normative pressures to avert publicity that endangers the national defense or violates widely held social norms.

In many authoritarian societies control over media content is established by limiting entry into the media business. For example, the government may require franchises for entry and grant them only to select people who support the government in all its endeavors. Often such franchises bestow monopoly control. Control through franchising media entrepreneurs is quite common for electronic media, even in democratic countries, because the government assigns broadcast channels. But democratic countries use this power less frequently to shut out political opponents. Entry to the mass media business is usually open to people representing a wide spectrum of political views. Newspapers generally do not require licenses in democratic societies. In the United States, for instance, anyone who has sufficient money may start a newspaper or newsletter. No permits are necessary.

Other methods used primarily by authoritarian countries to control publications are subsidies to favorite publishers or favoritism in the allocation of tightly controlled paper stocks for printing newspapers and magazines. Newspaper publishers whose activities displease the government may find themselves out of business because they cannot obtain paper. These types of economic controls may be imposed quite openly through formal rationing and subsidy schemes, or they may be imposed informally. The government may merely inform a disliked publisher that paper stocks are insufficient to supply that particular enterprise.

Media also may be controlled through manipulating access to news. For instance, the government may release information only to favored publications, putting less favored ones effectively out of business. While such practices are common in authoritarian societies, they occasionally happen on a smaller scale in more open societies. Angered by press coverage of his presidency, President Nixon at one point barred *Washington Post* reporters from his press plane.[38]

In addition to controlling the news business through franchises and restraints on access to news, authoritarian governments often limit what information may be published. This may be done routinely or selectively. In some countries nothing can be printed or broadcast until it has been approved by the government censor, who can suppress any story that the government deems objectionable. At times deletions are made after papers or magazines have been prepared for printing or already printed. This leaves tantalizing white spaces or missing pages. Television and radio scripts are often written or edited directly by government officials and must be broadcast without editorial changes.

Authoritarian societies frequently use treason and sedition laws to control media output. Treason and sedition are usually defined broadly in these countries so that anything that is critical of the government is potentially treasonable or seditious. People judged guilty of these crimes may be removed from the media business, sentenced to prison, or even executed. Such severe punishments are extremely strong deterrents to publishing stories that attack the government. Accordingly, disobedience is rare. Most journalists avoid difficulties with the official censor and with treason and sedition laws by refraining from using material that is likely to be objectionable. Government censorship then becomes replaced largely by self-censorship, easing the job of the official censor considerably.

When authoritarian regimes are totalitarian, media control is simplified because the government owns and operates all mass media and fully controls their output. Additionally, totalitarian countries frequently block out all unapproved communications from abroad. This includes jamming of foreign broadcasts and prohibiting the import of foreign printed materials. The strictness with which these controls are applied waxes and wanes, depending on the country's relations with other powers. But even during friendly interludes, totalitarian regimes rigidly control any information from abroad that might undermine their political system. They view such censorship as an intellectual quarantine that must be imposed to keep evil influences from undermining a beneficial political system.

In democratic societies official control of the content of mass media is deemed largely unnecessary. In the United States the First Amendment to the Constitution, which provides that "Congress shall make no law . . . abridging the freedom of speech, or of the press," has given the media an exceptionally strong basis for resisting government controls. The courts have ruled, however, that the protection is not absolute and must give way on occasion to social rights that the courts consider to be superior.

Competition among privately owned papers, magazines, and television and radio stations presumably generates a variety of viewpoints. If some media attack the government, other media will support it. The underlying, intriguing, but questionable assumption is that positive and negative as well as right and wrong information will somehow balance out and that the audience will be able to extract the truth from these conflicting reports.

A limited number of controls, such as regulatory laws, court decisions, and informal social pressures, guard against excesses by the media. In the United States the courts have generally ruled that these controls may be enforced only after media misbehavior has occurred. Courts have been very loath to impose "prior restraint" such as granting injunctions that would stop publication of information on the grounds that it would cause irreparable harm. But informal social and political pressures and the fear of indictments after publication have restrained presentation of potentially dangerous stories.

Controls in nonauthoritarian societies generally fall into four categories: guarding state survival through treason and sedition laws, shielding sensitive governmental proceedings, protecting individual reputations and privacy, and safeguarding the prevailing moral standards of the community. All societies find it necessary to have treason and sedition laws that prohibit publication of information that would endanger the nation's survival. The difficulty is to determine the point at which secrecy is so essential that freedom to publish must give way. In democratic societies media and the government are in perennial disagreement about the exact location of this point. Governments lean toward protection; the media lean toward disclosure.

There is little argument that treason and sedition are beyond the boundaries of unrestricted publication, even in an open society. More controversial are curbs on publication of government secrets—so-called "classified information." Governments try to establish controls over the publication of material that may be harmful to themselves or to individuals. For instance, confidential reports about the performance of government agencies, records of bidding on public jobs, and conversations during closed meetings are generally shielded from publicity. Finally, most governments also have laws protecting the reputations of individuals or groups and laws against obscenity. The merits of these controls on publication are discussed more fully in Chapter 3.

Defining the limits of government control over information dissemination raises difficult questions for democratic societies. Does official censorship, however minimal, open the way for the destruction of free expression? What guidelines are available to determine how far censorship should go? What types of material, if any, can harm children? Or adults? Should prejudicial statements be prohibited on the ground that they damage the self-image of minorities? The answers are controversial and problematic.

In addition to formal control of potentially "dangerous" news in authoritarian and nonauthoritarian societies, many informal restraints exist. As we shall see in Chapter 9, all governmental units, and often many of their subdivisions, have their own information control systems by which they determine what news to release, how to present it, and what news to cover up.

The limitations on the freedom of publication even in nonauthoritarian societies raise questions about the actual freedom enjoyed by the media compared with their counterparts in authoritarian societies. Is there really a difference, for example, in the independence of government-operated television networks in France and in North Korea? The answer is a resounding "yes." The degree of restraint varies so sharply that the systems are fundamentally different. In authoritarian societies the main objective of controls is to support the regime in power. In democratic societies the media are usually free to oppose the regime, to weaken it, and even to topple it. While they rarely carry their power to the latter extreme, the potential exists. It is this potential that makes the media in nonauthoritarian societies a genuine restraint on governmental abuses of power and a potent shaper of governmental action.

Summary

The mass media are an important influence on politics because they regularly and rapidly present politically crucial information to huge audiences. These audiences include political elites and decision makers, as well as large numbers of average citizens whose political activities, however sporadic, are shaped by information from the mass media.

The mass media are more than passive transmission agents for available information. Decisions made by media personnel determine what information becomes available to media audiences and what remains unavailable. By putting stories into perspective and interpreting them, media personnel assign meaning to the information and indicate the values by which it ought to be judged. News shaping is unavoidable because space is limited and because facts do not speak for themselves. Hence the media select and shape much of the raw material needed by political elites and the general public for thinking about the political world and planning political action. At times, newspeople even generate political action directly through their own investigations or indirectly through their capacity to stimulate pseudo-events.

Although many social scientists have remained somewhat skeptical about claims of large-scale media impact on politics, governments everywhere are keenly aware of the political importance of the media. Governments therefore have developed philosophies about the political role to be played by the media in their societies and about the proper ways to control the impact of the media on government activities. These philosophies have been implemented by constitutional and legal rules as well as by a host of informal arrangements. In this chapter we have briefly described how the basic philosophies, constitutional arrangements, and legal provisions differ in authoritarian and nonauthoritarian regimes.

Notes

1. For a brief overview of current knowledge about mass media effects, see Leo W. Jeffres, *Mass Media Processes and Effects* (Prospect Heights, Ill.: Waveland Press, 1986), chaps. 6-9.
2. The clues that mass media stories supply to the culture of their societies are discussed by George Gerbner, "Toward 'Cultural Indicators': The Analysis of Mass Mediated Public Message Systems," in *The Analysis of Communi-*

cation Content, ed. George Gerbner, Ole R. Holsti, Klaus Krippendorff, William J. Paisley, and Philip J. Stone (New York: Wiley, 1969), 123-132.

3. W. Russell Neuman, *The Future of the Mass Audience* (New York: Cambridge University Press, 1991), 3.

4. A good though somewhat dated source for media statistics is Warren K. Agee, Phillip H. Ault, and Edwin Emery, *Main Currents in Mass Communications* (New York: Harper and Row, 1986). Also see Ray Hiebert, Donald Ungarait, and Thomas Bohn, *Mass Media VI* (White Plains, N.Y.: Longman, 1991), chap. 11.

5. George Gerbner, Larry Gross, Michael Morgan, and Nancy Signorielli, "Charting the Mainstream: Television's Contributions to Political Orientation," *Journal of Communication* 32 (1982): 106-107.

6. Michael Parenti, *Make-Believe Media: The Politics of Entertainment* (New York: St. Martin's Press, 1992); S. Robert Lichter, Linda S. Lichter, and Stanley Rothman, *Watching America: What Television Tells Us about Our Lives* (New York: Prentice Hall, 1991).

7. Walter Gantz, "The Diffusion of News about the Attempted Reagan Assassination," *Journal of Communication* 33 (Winter 1983): 56-65.

8. Harold Stanley and Richard Niemi, *Vital Statistics on American Politics,* 2d ed. (Washington, D.C.: CQ Press, 1990), 69.

9. Harold D. Lasswell, "The Structure and Function of Communication in Society," in *Mass Communications,* ed. Wilbur Schramm (Urbana: University of Illinois Press, 1969), 103.

10. Marshall McLuhan, *Understanding Media: The Extensions of Man* (New York: McGraw-Hill, 1964).

11. Chapter 4 gives a more detailed definition of news. Evidence that the media set the agenda for national issues is presented in Donald L. Shaw and Maxwell McCombs, *The Emergence of American Political Issues: The Agenda-Setting Function of the Press* (St. Paul, Minn.: West Publishing, 1977), and in sources cited there. See also the essays in Sidney Kraus and Richard M. Perloff, eds., *Mass Media and Political Thought* (Beverly Hills, Calif.: Sage, 1985); and Maxwell McCombs, Edna Einsiedel, and David Weaver, *Contemporary Public Opinion: Issues and the News* (Hillsdale, N.J.: Lawrence Erlbaum Associates, 1992).

12. David L. Protess et al., *The Journalism of Outrage: Investigative Reporting and Agenda Building in America* (New York: Guilford Press, 1991), 8-12.

13. Examples of such criticism can be found in W. Lance Bennett, *News: The Politics of Illusion,* 2d ed. (New York: Longman, 1988); and Michael Parenti, *Inventing Reality: The Politics of the News Media,* 2d ed. (New York: St. Martin's Press, 1986).

14. An example of a conservative Washington-based media analysis group is Accuracy in Media (AIM). It publishes periodic reports of its media investigations. For claims that journalists in the elite media are ultraliberal, see S. Robert Lichter, Stanley Rothman, and Linda S. Lichter, *The Media Elite* (New York: Adler and Adler, 1986).

15. Jay G. Blumler, "Purposes of Mass Communications Research: A Transatlantic Perspective," *Journalism Quarterly* 55 (Summer 1978): 226.

16. Daniel Boorstin, *The Image: A Guide to Pseudo-Events* (New York: Atheneum, 1971).

17. Criteria of what constitutes "news" are discussed fully by Bernard Roshco, *Newsmaking* (Chicago: University of Chicago Press, 1975), chap. 3.

18. Blumler, "Purposes of Mass Communications Research," 228.

19. The results of reassuring publicity are discussed by Murray Edelman, *The Symbolic Uses of Politics* (Urbana: University of Illinois Press, 1964), 38-43, reprinted 1985.
20. Robert Kubey and Mihaly Csikszentmihalyi, *Television and the Quality of Life: How Viewing Shapes Everyday Experience* (Hillsdale, N.J.: Lawrence Erlbaum Associates, 1990), chaps. 5 and 7.
21. Marvin N. Olasky and Susan Northway Olasky, "The Crossover in Newspaper Coverage of Abortion from Murder to Liberation," *Journalism Quarterly* 63 (1986): 31-37.
22. W. Lance Bennett and Murray Edelman, "Toward a New Political Narrative," *Journal of Communication* 35 (1985): 156-171.
23. The early writings include David Easton and Jack Dennis, *Children in the Political System: Origins of Political Legitimacy* (New York: McGraw-Hill, 1969); Fred I. Greenstein, *Children and Politics* (New Haven: Yale University Press, 1965); Richard Dawson and Kenneth Prewitt, *Political Socialization* (Boston: Little, Brown, 1969); and Robert D. Hess and Judith Torney, *The Development of Political Attitudes in Children* (Chicago: Aldine, 1967). Examples of the studies in the 1970s are Sidney Kraus and Dennis Davis, *The Effects of Mass Communication on Political Behavior* (University Park, Pa.: Pennsylvania State University Press, 1976); Steven H. Chaffee, "Mass Communication in Political Socialization," in *Handbook of Political Socialization*, ed. Stanley Renshon (New York: Free Press, 1977). Also see Ellen Wartella, ed., *Children Communicating: Media and Development of Thought, Speech and Understanding* (Beverly Hills, Calif.: Sage, 1979).
24. Evidence that the public links attitude changes to mass media information comes from successive public opinion polls. See Benjamin I. Page and Robert Y. Shapiro, *The Rational Public: Fifty Years of Trends in Americans' Policy Preferences* (Chicago: University of Chicago Press, 1992). Also see Shanto Iyengar and Donald Kinder, *News that Matters: Television and American Opinion* (Chicago: University of Chicago Press, 1987); and Doris A. Graber, *Processing the News: How People Tame the Information Tide*, 2d ed. (New York: Longman, 1988).
25. Fay Lomax Cook, Tom R. Tyler, Edward G. Goetz, Margaret T. Gordon, David Protess, Donna R. Leff, and Harvey L. Molotch, "Media and Agenda Setting: Effects on the Public, Interest Group Leaders, Policy Makers, and Policy," *Public Opinion Quarterly* 47 (1983): 16-35.
26. Paul Lazarsfeld, Bernard Berelson, and Hazel Gaudet, *The People's Choice* (New York: Columbia University Press, 1944); Bernard Berelson, Paul Lazarsfeld, and William McPhee, *Voting: A Study of Opinion Formation in a Presidential Campaign* (Chicago: University of Chicago Press, 1954); Angus Campbell, Gerald Gurin, and Warren E. Miller, *The Voter Decides* (Evanston, Ill.: Row, Peterson, 1954); and Angus Campbell, Philip E. Converse, Warren E. Miller, and Donald Stokes, *The American Voter* (New York: Wiley, 1960).
27. William C. Adams, Dennis J. Smith, Allison Salzman, Ralph Crossen, Scott Hiber, Tom Naccarato, William Vantine, and Nine Weisbroth, "Before and After *The Day After:* The Unexpected Results of a Televised Drama," *Political Communication and Persuasion* 3 (1986): 191-213. See also Stanley Feldman and Lee Sigelman, "The Political Impact of Prime-Time Television: 'The Day After,'" *Journal of Politics* 47 (May 1985): 556-578.
28. This story of the neutron bomb is based on the account in Martin Linsky,

Impact: How the Press Affects Federal Policymaking (New York: Norton, 1986), 21-39.
29. Ibid., 22.
30. Ibid., 32.
31. *New York Times,* July 13, 1983.
32. Theodore White, *The Making of the President, 1972* (New York: Bantam, 1973), 327.
33. The discussion is modeled on Fred Siebert, Theodore Peterson, and Wilbur Schramm, *Four Theories of the Press* (Urbana: University of Illinois Press, 1963).
34. For a brief account of media history in the United States, see Bernard Roshco, *Newsmaking* (Chicago: University of Chicago Press, 1975), 23-57; see also James K. Baughman, *The Republic of Mass Culture: Journalism, Filmmaking, and Broadcasting in America since 1941* (Baltimore: Johns Hopkins University Press, 1992).
35. A study of North American journalists in the early 1970s showed that only 35 percent believed in neutral reporting. See John Johnstone, Edward Slawski, and William Bowman, *The Newspeople* (Urbana: University of Illinois Press, 1976), 117-123. For a somewhat different perception see David H. Weaver and G. Cleveland Wilhoit, *The American Journalist: A Portrait of U.S. News People and Their Work,* 2d ed. (Bloomington: Indiana University Press, 1991).
36. See, for example, Bernard Rubin, *Media, Politics, Democracy* (New York: Oxford University Press, 1977); and Erik Barnouw, *The Sponsor: Notes on a Modern Potentate* (New York: Oxford University Press, 1978).
37. Michael Gurevitch and Jay G. Blumler, "Linkages Between the Mass Media and Politics: A Model for the Analysis of Political Communications Systems," in *Mass Communication and Society,* ed. James Curran, Michael Gurevitch, and Janet Woolacott (Beverly Hills, Calif.: Sage, 1979), 283.
38. This and many similar incidents are reported in William E. Porter, *Assault on the Media: The Nixon Years* (Ann Arbor: University of Michigan Press, 1976).

Readings

Barnouw, Erik. *Tube of Plenty: The Evolution of American Television,* 2d ed. New York: Oxford University Press, 1990.
Davis, Richard. *The Press and American Politics.* New York: Longman, 1992.
Graber, Doris A., ed. *Media Power in Politics,* 2d ed. Washington, D.C.: CQ Press, 1989.
Leonard, Thomas C. *The Power of the Press: The Birth of American Political Reporting.* New York: Oxford University Press, 1986.
Lichter, S. Robert, Linda S. Lichter, and Stanley Rothman. *Watching America: What Television Tells Us about Our Lives.* New York: Prentice Hall, 1991.
Nimmo, Dan, and James E. Combs. *Mediated Political Realities.* New York: Longman, 1990.
Protess, David, and Maxwell McCombs, eds. *Agenda Setting: Readings on Media, Public Opinion and Policymaking.* Hillsdale, N.J.: Lawrence Erlbaum Associates, 1991.
Tuchman, Gaye. *Making News: A Study in the Construction of Reality.* New York: Free Press, 1978.

CHAPTER 2

Ownership, Regulation, and Guidance of Media

The disintegration of the Soviet Union in 1991 produced a scramble for control of Soviet media. Boris Yeltsin, the new leader of the Russian Republic, immediately appropriated all printing presses hitherto owned by the Communist party and dismissed top-level media personnel whom he considered political opponents. He negotiated with Mikhail Gorbachev, who still headed the Soviet Union, to acquire a major U.S.S.R. television channel for Russian television. Yeltsin and Gorbachev jointly selected the new Russian media leadership from the ranks of their political supporters. *Pravda* and *Izvestia,* the country's leading daily newspapers, received new chief editors, chosen for their anti-communist political views.

When the new Russian-controlled media ran into serious economic difficulties a few months later, the Yeltsin government—despite its own fiscal problems—promptly came to their rescue. Government leaders knew that a friendly press was essential in a period of political and economic instability and wanted to make sure that their political allies in the media would remain in control. To emphasize the high priority given to media enterprises, the Russian minister of information, a former editor of *Moscow Pravda* and a close friend of Boris Yeltsin, was promoted to vice-premier.

The Russian government's strenuous efforts to put control of the media into the hands of political supporters is a contemporary version of the classic battle for control of the information communicated to political elites and the general public. Concern about who will wield media power has been a central issue in American politics since colonial days. It has become particularly important in the twentieth century because of the public policy issues raised by new technological developments and forms of business concentration. The pros and cons of public and private control and of big business influence in the media industry will be weighed in this chapter. The impact of internal and external pressures on the industry, including those arising from economic constraints and from citizen lobbies, is also assessed. The public policy issues involved in media control are so complex, so intertwined with political predispositions and preferences, that no approach stands out as clearly "best." It therefore is no wonder that attempts to legislate have produced clashes of views, litigation, and little agreement on what the laws should be.

Control and Ownership: Public, Semipublic, and Private

Control and ownership of the media take a number of forms, each of which affects the nature of media output. The authoritarian pattern of total government control and its effects have already been discussed. As noted, some nonauthoritarian countries also control and own media, particularly radio and television, but their control over content is much looser, and their penalties for violations are much lighter.

Forms of Control: Pros and Cons

One reason for concern about media control and ownership is expressed in the old adage, "He who pays the piper calls the tune." If you fear government and its policies, you are likely to disapprove of direct operation of the media by government. You will be leery about extensive government regulation of privately operated media. But if, instead, you are afraid of the business ethics of private individuals and corporations, you would not want media control in private hands or directly influenced by large corporate enterprises.

Public policy issues raised by the debate over the merits of public versus private ownership of television illustrate the pros and cons. When governments own and operate major television channels, programming tends to reflect governmental policies closely, even in democratic countries. France, Israel, and Sweden are examples. However, Britain's experiences with operating radio and television through the British Broadcasting Corporation (BBC) show that governments, if they wish, can keep programming reasonably free from direct political interference. Big business control of television, if divided among various large corporations, is likely to bring more conflicting interests into play than would government control. For instance, a conglomerate heavily involved in export industries will not share the same views on tariffs as a conglomerate interested primarily in domestic manufacturing. Even within conglomerates, the interests of various components may clash, thus moderating the stands of the general management and lessening the chances that specific business interests will dominate programming. Nonetheless, the prevailing values reflected in the choice of broadcasts are likely to be mainstream and middle class.

Although there is more chance for diversity of political outlooks when business rather than government controls programming, the pressures springing from profit considerations lead to homogeneous program types. Media offerings must be structured so that they yield financial returns to the owners of media enterprises. Governments are free from such pressures because they can use tax money to finance whatever programs they deem to be in the public interest. They must consider intragovernment power struggles, but they do not need to concern themselves with the size of their audiences. Private owners do because their income depends on small fees from audiences or on large fees from advertisers and other sponsors. The latter want to attract large numbers of viewers, particularly those in the eighteen- to forty-nine-year age group, who hold the bulk of purchasing power. Mass appeal, rather than any social or cultural concerns, becomes the primary goal.

Given the pros and cons of government and business control, which is the better system? The answer depends on one's assessment of the motivations of the public and private sectors and one's beliefs about the proper role of the media. Today, when distrust of government is high and people view "big media" as a counterfoil to "big government," private control is the option preferred by most Americans. In terms of programming, the choice of this option means that the bulk of television fare will be geared to simple, emotion-laden programming that attracts large, diverse audiences. It also means shying away from controversial or troublesome issues that may antagonize and deplete media audiences and subsequently diminish advertising revenues.

Although such programming draws the wrath of many people, particularly intellectual elites, one can argue that their disdain constitutes intellectual snobbery. Who is to say that the mass public's tastes are inferior to those of the elites? The argument that people would choose educational programs over fluffy entertainment, if they had the chance, is false. Proof is plentiful that the mass public does indeed *prefer* light entertainment to more serious programs.[1] In print news, for example, magazines featuring sex or violence far outsell journals that treat political and social issues seriously. In fact, scholarly political journals frequently require subsidies to remain in print. Huge crowds are willing to pay heavily in time and money to see movies featuring heinous crimes and explicit sex. The most popular pay television channels show what is euphemistically called "adult entertainment," while channels devoted to highbrow culture languish and often perish.

Related to the concerns about domination of the media by government or private business interests is the fear of undue concentration of power. Diversity of ownership presumably encourages the expression of a great variety of views, which, to many Americans, is the essence of democracy. There must be a wide open marketplace into which ideas and opinions flow freely. But there is no agreement on exactly how diverse ownership must be to ensure this adequate flow of information and the opportunity for freedom of expression.[2] The American public appears to be more concerned about the concentration of media ownership in comparatively few hands than about control of media by private enterprise. Social reformers, on the other hand, are more concerned about business control, claiming that it caters to the lowest levels of taste and suppresses discussion of pressing social problems.

Public Control

In the United States outright government ownership and control over media have been comparatively limited. However, they are growing as more and more local governments become involved in owning cable television systems or operating channels on privately owned systems. Government ownership raises serious unresolved questions about the limitations, if any, to be placed on the government's rights to use these outlets to further its partisan political purposes.[3]

The federal government is most heavily involved in broadcasting. Abroad it controls broadcasts to American military posts and owns various types of foreign propaganda outlets. Some of the programs put out by propaganda agencies such as the Voice of America are barred from broadcast on the domestic airwaves because members of Congress have been reluctant to expose American audiences to deliberate propaganda.

A substantial proportion of radio broadcast space, ranging from 50 percent in the pre-Carter years to 25 percent currently, belongs to the federal government, which uses it for radio services supplied by the executive branch. Another 40 percent of the space is shared by the government and private interests, leaving only 35 percent for the exclusive use of the private sector.[4] Altogether, foreign and domestic federal broadcasts equal the volume of commercial broadcasts produced in the United States.

Semipublic Control

Media operation by semipublic institutions is another control option. The public broadcasting system is one example. It represents a mixture of public and private financing and programming, and public and private operation of radio and television stations. Created through the Public Broadcasting Act of 1967, the public broadcasting system supports educational and public service television stations whose programs do not generally attract large audiences. These stations usually cannot find enough commercial sponsors to pay for their shows.

Roughly one-fourth of American television stations participate in the public broadcasting system. In 1989 members included 340 noncommercial television stations and 313 noncommercial radio stations, the latter linked together as National Public Radio (NPR).[5] The administrative arrangements for the public broadcasting system, regulated now under the Public Telecommunications Act of 1978, have been complex. A Corporation for Public Broadcasting (CPB), staffed by political appointees, has handled the general administration, but it has been kept separate from the programming side of the operation to insulate public broadcasting from political pressures. A separate Public Broadcasting Service (PBS) has produced television programs, often in collaboration with state-supported foreign broadcast systems, like Britain's BBC, or France's Antenne Deux, or Japan's NHK. The Independent Television Service created by Congress in 1991 has awarded grants to independent producers for programs that "reflect regional, racial, ethnic or cultural issues otherwise unavailable on public television and programs that successfully explore aesthetic values, formats and genres." [6]

The attempt to keep the Corporation for Public Broadcasting from influencing programming has failed. The corporation does not tell public television stations what specific programs they should feature. Instead, it has guided programming by paying for some types of programs and refusing to pay for others. This has constituted effective purse-string control of programming by government. In the field of radio, NPR was created both to produce and distribute programs. Since cost considerations made it impossible to include all noncommercial radio stations, only the largest, best-organized ones were included. Some 350 stations currently qualify and are eligible for CPB funding grants and participation in NPR programs.[7]

Private foundations and big business enterprises and large corporations have poured money into the public broadcasting system. As Table 2-1 shows, they currently contribute 20 percent of its income, up from 13 percent ten years earlier. Their influence over programming has been further enhanced because the Federal Communications Commission (FCC) during the Reagan years permitted the Public Broadcasting Service to engage in some commercial broadcasting of economic news and to accept a limited amount of advertising. The general public also has influenced public broadcasting through donations that constitute nearly one-quarter of the income of public broadcasting systems and

Table 2-1 Income Sources of Public Broadcasting Systems, 1989 (in millions of dollars; includes nonbroadcast income)

Income sources	Millions of dollars	Percent
Federal government	264	17.3
State/local government and colleges/universities	451	29.5
Subscribers and auction/marathons	347	22.7
Business and industry	241	15.8
Foundations	69	4.5
Other	156	10.2
Total income	1,528	100.0

Source: Bureau of the Census, *Statistical Abstract of the United States,* (Washington, D.C.: Government Printing Office, 1991), 559, preliminary data.
Note: Public broadcasting system includes 313 CPB qualified radio stations and 340 public television stations.

through community advisory boards. Nevertheless, securing adequate financing is an enduring problem.

Public television is distinguished from commercial television primarily by an emphasis on experimental programs, cultural offerings like classical music and ballet (which constitute 18 percent of program content), news, public affairs, educational programs (54 percent), and minority-oriented shows.[8] The nature and quality of programming varies widely because public television represents a decentralized bevy of local stations. The audience for public television, except for its children's programs (which represent 18 percent of public television's programming time), has been small. On an average day or evening only 7 percent of the television audience tunes in to public television or public radio.[9] Even minority groups, for whom a number of public broadcast programs are presumably tailored, prefer the entertainment provided by commercial stations. Because of the limited appeal of public broadcasting and pressures to reduce public expenditures, there have been demands to disband the system completely and reallocate its frequencies to commercial channels.[10] Some of its programs might then be shown on commercial stations with federal subsidies.[11]

Supporters of the system contend that audience size should not be a criterion in judging its merits. Rather, the system should be viewed as a provider of needed special services that are neglected by commercial television precisely because they lack mass appeal or are commercially unattractive. Innovations pioneered by public broadcasting have spread to commercial broadcasting. For example, it played a leading role in developing the system of captions for the hearing-impaired. Public radio and public television also were among the first to move to satellite distribution systems that made it possible to deliv⌐ multiple national program services to communities.[12]

Since its inception, and particularly since public funding has increased beyond the minute initial amounts, the public broadcasting system has been subjected to considerable political pressures. For example, President Richard Nixon tried to make the system more responsive to federal government wishes by shifting some control over local programming from Washington, D.C., to the more pliable local managers. As expected, this change led to more traditional programming. In recent years, conservative politicians and media lobbies have tried to impose some oversight on PBS, which they consider to be a cheerleader for liberal causes. Such maneuvers demonstrate that dependence on public funds, even when these funds constitute only a fraction of total funding (17 percent for the federal government), may mean subservience to government control, despite barriers to direct government influence.

The ultimate fate of public broadcasting is in doubt. As one communication expert has noted:

> It is likely that legislative and regulatory provisions regarding public broadcasting will continue to be influenced more substantially by the struggles among much larger political and economic forces than by the most careful analysis of the needs of the enterprise. There is considerable conflict among these external agendas, and to various degrees they all detract from a discussion of how the long-term broader public interest might be realized through public broadcasting.[13]

Private Control

Public ownership of the mass media as well as semipublic control, as exemplified by the Corporation for Public Broadcasting and National Public Radio, have been discussed. To round out the picture, one needs to consider the many arrangements in which control is in private hands, subject to the laws and regulations of different governmental agencies. Private control arrangements range from individual ownership, where one person owns a newspaper or radio or television station, to ownership by huge corporate conglomerates.

Patterns of Private Ownership

The facts about media control patterns are relatively simple to explain, but there is much disagreement about their consequences. The overarching feature of media control in the United States is that it is predominantly in private hands. Owners include small and large business enterprises, labor groups, religious and ethnic organizations, and many other types of interests represented in American society.

Business Configurations

The general trend in America toward diversification also characterizes the media business. Of course, there are *independents,* individuals or corporations that run a single media venture and nothing else. The publisher who owns one newspaper or one radio or television station is an example. However, their numbers are declining, except for the tiniest enterprises.

Multiple owners have become increasingly common. These are individuals or corporations who own several media of the same type—mostly radio or television stations, or newspapers. Since there are fewer than two thousand daily newspapers in the entire United States, fewer than five thousand AM and five thousand FM commercial radio stations, and fewer than six hundred VHF and six hundred UHF commercial television stations, one might question whether a chain of twenty or thirty of these media ought to be controlled by a single owner.[14] Nevertheless, this has been the trend.

Even more common than the trend toward multiple owners has been the trend toward *crossmedia ownership,* ownership by an individual or corporation of several types of media, such as newspapers *and* television stations or newspapers *and* radio stations. This ownership pattern is worrisome when one owner controls all media in the same location. For instance, the same person might own a town's newspaper and television and radio station, effectively monopolizing local information sources. This practice has been prohibited since 1975, except where it was already established.

A fourth pattern encompasses *conglomerates,* individuals or corporations who own media enterprises along with other types of businesses. The General Electric Company (GE) is an example. Figure 2-1 illustrates the diversity of GE's interests. Those who are wary about the public-mindedness of large corporations fear that their nonmedia business interests may color their news policies. If, for instance, there is a soundly based demand to reduce the defense establishment, or to oppose construction of a missile system, the management of a conglomerate such as GE, which holds many defense contracts, may not examine these questions open-mindedly.

In major urban centers most media are owned by individuals or corporations that fall into the multiple-owner, crossmedia, and conglomerate classifications. For instance, the *Chicago Tribune* is owned by

Figure 2-1   The Diverse Holdings of the General Electric Company

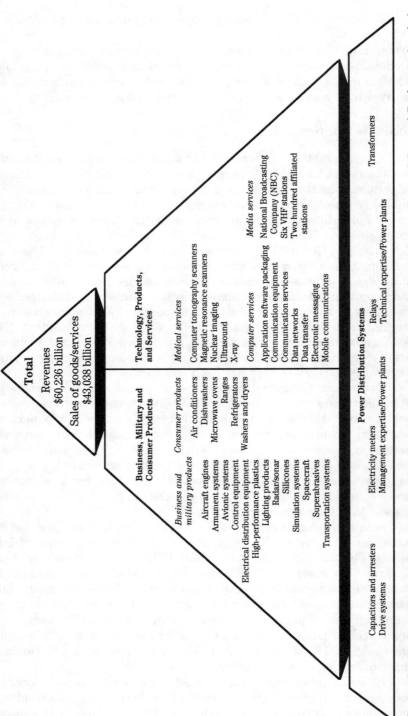

Total

Revenues
$60,236 billion

Sales of goods/services
$43,038 billion

Business, Military and Consumer Products

Business and military products

Aircraft engines
Armament systems
Avionic systems
Control equipment
Electrical distribution equipment
High-performance plastics
Lighting products
Radar/sonar
Silicones
Simulation systems
Spacecraft
Superabrasives
Transportation systems

Consumer products

Air conditioners
Dishwashers
Microwave ovens
Ranges
Refrigerators
Washers and dryers

Technology, Products, and Services

Medical services

Computer tomography scanners
Magnetic resonance scanners
Nuclear imaging
Ultrasound
X-ray

Computer services

Application software packaging
Communication equipment
Communication services
Data networks
Data transfer
Electronic messaging
Mobile communications

Media services

National Broadcasting Company (NBC)
Six VHF stations
Two hundred affiliated stations

Power Distribution Systems

Capacitors and arresters
Drive systems

Electricity meters
Management expertise/Power plants

Relays
Technical expertise/Power plants

Transformers

Source: Standard and Poor's Corp., *Corporation Records*, August 1991; General Electric, *Annual Report*, 1991; and Dun and Bradstreet, *America's Corporate Families*, 1991.

the Tribune Company, which owns nearly two dozen media enterprises and nearly a dozen companies outside the media field.[15] The major television stations in Chicago are owned by the national television networks and the Tribune conglomerate. Similarly, the major Chicago radio stations are owned by ABC, CBS, and NBC, the Tribune, Westinghouse, and other conglomerates or members of conglomerates. The radio and television stations in the nation's one hundred largest markets that remain under single ownership are mostly very small with comparatively weak signals.[16]

The number of media outlets controlled by individuals or corporations varies widely. In 1992 Cox Broadcasting Corporation owned eight radio stations, seven television stations, twenty-four cable television systems, and eight newspaper companies; the New York Times Company owned thirty-six newspapers, one radio station, five television stations, and twelve magazines. Capital Cities/ABC, besides owning the American Broadcasting Company Network, owned three cable television stations, eight television stations, seventeen radio stations, and eight daily and forty-six weekly newspapers, as well as six magazines and nineteen trade publications.[17] But one cannot judge the sweep of control exercised by any group merely by looking at the number of its outlets. Three additional factors need to be considered: *market size, competition within the market,* and *prestige of each media institution.*

Market Size

For purposes of assessing mass media performance and regulating electronic media, the country is generally divided into "markets" rather than states or regions. A market is the area in which a particular media enterprise attracts a substantial audience. For instance, each television station has a signal that can be clearly received by people living within a certain radius of the station. All of the people within that radius who can receive the signal are considered to be within the market. This means that they can be expected to respond to advertising for products and services provided by program sponsors.

Altogether, there are four hundred newspaper markets in the country and two hundred seventy broadcast markets. Their size varies widely. In major metropolitan areas such as New York, Chicago, or Los Angeles, a market with a fifty-mile radius may have a population of several million people. The same radius for a station in Wyoming might cover more cows than people.

The Federal Communications Commission considers market size only partially in its regulations designed to prevent concentration of ownership. To ensure that people throughout America are exposed to a wide variety of media voices, FCC regulations stipulate top limits for the numbers of stations that can be under the same ownership. Additional restrictions are imposed on multiple and crossmedia ownership within the same market. In recent years the FCC has also imposed some limits on the size of audiences that may be within the reach of a particular media owner, usually specifying that one owner may reach no more than 25 percent of the audience or of households in a market.

In 1992 the FCC increased the number of media enterprises that one owner may hold. The current limit is eighteen AM radio stations, eighteen FM radio stations, and twelve television stations. All of these may be very high frequency.[18] This means that an owner can be in forty-eight different markets (a few more if the owners belong to an ethnic minority), each reaching the homes of millions of people, as long as the 25 percent market share limit is honored. At present, four out of every five television stations in the one hundred most densely populated markets, which serve nearly 90 percent of the nation's households, belong to multiple-owner groups.

Newspapers can enter an unlimited number of markets. Consequently, newspaper chains can expand at will, up to the limits allowed by antitrust and antimonopoly laws.[19] By 1985 more than 68 percent of America's daily papers, boasting 78 percent of total circulation, were controlled by national and regional chains.[20] There are well over 100 such chains, but the majority control fewer than ten papers. However, the fourteen groups that owned twenty or more papers controlled 45 percent of all daily newspapers in the country. In terms of numbers of papers under its control, Thomson Newspapers was first, with 121 daily papers. Gannett held the number two spot, with seventy-eight daily newspapers, including *USA Today,* the country's first national newspaper. Donrey Media Group with fifty-two dailies and Park Communications with forty-two dailies were in third and fourth place. Most of these newspaper groups also own papers published less frequently, as well as radio and television stations. While ownership figures are constantly changing as papers are bought and sold, the relative rankings remain stable.

By 1990, the fourteen largest chains accounted for more than half of the total daily newspaper circulation (63 million copies) in the United States. This means that one-half of the papers read in the United States on any given day transmit news screened by personnel from only fourteen large business enterprises. Altogether, twenty-three corporations dominate all phases of mass media communication throughout the United States. The proportion of circulation controlled by chain-owned papers has been growing over the decades, but not by leaps and bounds. Although individual papers within chains generally enjoy editorial-page autonomy, they tend to be more uniform in political endorsements than are independently owned papers.[21]

Influence is even more concentrated for television. Instead of ten companies controlling one-third of the market, three huge conglomerate-owned networks—NBC, CBS, and ABC—dominate roughly two-thirds of the television households in the nation.[22] In addition, their parent companies—the General Electric Company, Columbia Broadcasting System, and Capital Cities/ABC—own other media enterprises such as recording companies, publishing houses, movie theaters, and radio and television equipment and supply companies, as well as unrelated ventures such as real estate firms, car rental companies, food supply houses, and home furnishing manufacturers.[23]

The networks produce a limited number of television and radio entertainment programs for their own use. The bulk of entertainment programming comes from other sources. Because production of programs is not regulated by government, this part of their business is not directly under FCC control.[24] However, the broadcast stations that each network owns are within the regulatory reach of the FCC, as are the "affiliates"—stations that regularly subscribe to the programs produced by a network.

The network-owned television stations are in the largest media markets. This means New York, Chicago, and Los Angeles for all three networks, supplemented by other major cities. In addition to producing and buying programming for its wholly owned stations, each network also supplies approximately 65 percent of the programming for its more than 200 affiliates. Even nonaffiliated stations make extensive use of network-selected programs following their initial runs. Because the vast majority of commercial stations are network affiliated, much of the televised information reaching American households is subject to choices and decisions made by network personnel. In addition, networks control radio outlets domestically as well as radio and television stations abroad.

To keep these figures in proper perspective, one must keep in mind that the three networks compete vigorously with each other for public favor and that they do not dominate programming completely for affiliates. The three networks are facing vigorous competition from the emerging fourth network, Fox Broadcasting Corporation, owned by media baron Rupert Murdoch. Fox owns and operates seven television stations, has 140 affiliates, and seems to be cornering the child, teen, and young adult audiences. It has arranged to have its programs carried by cable television.[25] Nearly 52 million households were served by cable television by 1990. Furthermore, nearly 63 million households owned video cassette recorders (VCRs) that permitted them to supplement over-the-air television fare.[26]

The capstone to the picture of narrowly held control over information outlets is supplied by the wire service companies. A huge share of the news stories appearing in nearly every newspaper in the country, and featured on television or radio news, originates from the wires of the Associated Press (AP) and United Press International (UPI). The roots of these two organizations go back to 1848, when six New York newspapers formed a cooperative association to share the cost of collecting foreign news. Out of this initial effort grew large organizations that employ reporters scattered throughout the world to collect and report news. News stories and bulletins are then transmitted electronically to subscriber newspapers and radio and television stations. Ninety-nine percent of the news sources in the United States that disseminate news on a daily basis have been served by either AP, UPI, or both. Associated Press has the lion's share of the market, while financially ailing UPI has been losing ground and seems to be on the verge of death. A handful of other wire services, such as those operated by the *New York Times*, the *Los Angeles Times*, and the *Chicago Tribune*, serve their own papers, along with a more limited clientele of subscribers.

News stories and bulletins supplied by the wire services are either used verbatim or rewritten by their clients. Depending on the resources available to a particular news organization for gathering and writing its own news, the proportion of wire service stories used directly or in rewritten form may vary from less than 10 percent to 80 percent or more of all stories. For many newspapers, a look at the mix of stories carried by wire services on any particular day will accurately foretell the mix of stories carried by the paper.[27] Wire service stories tend to predominate for foreign news and even for national news for smaller papers and stations that cannot afford their own correspondents. This means that a large share of news production in the United States is dominated by a small number of news-producing companies. However, none of the situations of limited competition that have been discussed involve monopoly controls. Even in one-newspaper towns, there is usually some inter-media competition from television and radio stations. Unfortunately, while carriers differ, the messages they present are likely to be very similar.[28]

Intramarket Competition

To preserve competition within each market, FCC rules now prohibit multiple and crossmedia ownership within the same market. However, this rule does not affect most radio and television combinations existing prior to 1970 or newspaper and broadcast media combinations existing before 1975. Since 1992, radio owners have been permitted to acquire a second station in markets with more than fifteen stations. To reduce dominance by the networks, the FCC also mandates that in markets with more than three television or radio broadcast stations at least one of every three stations must be reserved for owners who are not affiliated with any network.

Despite efforts to increase intramarket competition, limited competition (oligopoly) conditions prevail in the majority of markets. Electronic media are generally owned in pairs, limiting the total number of media owners in the community. Intramarket newspaper competition has also become rare. Ninety-eight percent of all American cities have only one daily newspaper.[29] Newspaper competition is rare outside the largest cities. Suburban dailies, which flourish in a few major cities, do not substantially alter the situation because their coverage of major news stories is usually limited.[30] In addition to a monopoly over local print news, newspaper owners frequently own a local television or radio station as well. However, the FCC has forced newspapers to relinquish broadcast properties whenever the combination enjoys a total monopoly within the market.

Prestige Leadership

Another reason for homogeneity in news supply is the consensus among journalists about the nature of news and the elements of good reporting. There are widely accepted standards of professionalism in journalism, just as there are in law or medicine or engineering. As part of this system of norms, certain members and products are widely accepted as models whose influence reaches far beyond their own organization. Critics call this the "jackal syndrome" or "pack journalism." [31] In the political news field the *New York Times* is the lion whom the jackals follow. In television Dan Rather and Tom Brokaw are models for the profession. Other news professionals watch what information these sources present, how they present it, and what interpretations they give to it, and they then adjust their own presentations accordingly.[32] The upshot is that the multiplication of voices in the media marketplace has contributed relatively little to meaningful diversity in news. The newcomers quickly join the old chorus and hum the prevailing tunes.

Small Business versus Big Business Control

The steady trend toward consolidation in the media industry has left control of information increasingly in the hands of a limited number of very large organizations. Because concentration has generally stopped short of infringing antitrust and antimonopoly laws, these laws have been of little help in halting or reversing it.[33] As will be pointed out in Chapter 4, economic factors are largely responsible for consolidation. Production of television programs and worldwide news gathering are very expensive. Only large, well-financed organizations, which are able to spread the costs over many customers, can provide the lavish media fare to which the American public has become accustomed.[34]

Even when there is no infringement of antitrust and antimonopoly laws, is it sound public policy to allow the rapid pace of consolidation of media enterprises to continue? Is there a danger that centralized control, besides bringing undesirable uniformity, also will lead to neglect of local needs? Does the absence of newspaper competition in American cities prevent diverse viewpoints from being presented to the public? The evidence lends little substance to these fears.[35] Neither does it sustain claims that the media giants routinely suppress diversity among the news outlets under their control, squelch antibusiness news, and stress anti-labor, pro-Republican, and jingoistic stories. It is true that many important stories are not published, including some that would be poor publicity for big business, but there is no hard evidence that the choices that are necessary to cope with an oversupply of news conform predominantly to a conservative political orientation.[36] In fact, many prominently featured broadcasts, movies, and magazine and newspaper articles in recent years have carried stories critical of conservative policies in general and of the business community in particular.

The charge that media owners pressure media personnel into supporting the existing political system also is not borne out. American journalists in large organizations, like their colleagues in small, independently owned enterprises, are interested in appealing to their audiences, and therefore their stories usually reflect the values of mainstream American society, regardless of the journalists' personal political orientations.[37]

What about the argument that small, individually owned enterprises would produce better programming, more suited to local needs? One way to test this assertion is to compare the amount of news and other public service programs offered by various types of television stations. By and large, news and public service programming have been more plentiful on stations owned by big business and by conglomerates than on stations owned by individuals.[38] Network stations do best of all. Similarly, radio stations and newspapers that have the best public service coverage, as judged by professional journalists, generally are controlled by large business enterprises or are part of a large network.

The contention that individually owned, small enterprises provide poorer public service than their larger, group-owned cousins is open to question. The measures of public service programming used by the FCC and most media studies are primarily quantitative. They gauge how much broadcasting time is spent on certain kinds of programs, but they do not analyze the quality of the programming. Small stations may make up in quality what they lack in quantity.

It is quite plausible, however, that big business control actually does mean qualitatively superior programs. Large enterprises are able to absorb the losses that are often incurred in the production of documentaries and public service programs. They have more money than do small enterprises to spend on talented people, research, investigations, and costly entertainment shows. They can send their leading reporters to all parts of the world to report breaking stories first-hand, even when it means losing money.

High costs explain why television programs produced in the United States fail to recapture their initial investment.[39] Hour-long episodes of prime-time programs often cost more than $1 million to produce. Even the news is lavishly produced. Networks use multiple crews to cover simple events like presidential news conferences. As many as ten crews have been sent abroad to report on fighting in the Middle East. On an average, each story broadcast on the NBC nightly news cost $63,000 in 1987. In that year top-rated news anchors commanded multi-million-dollar salaries, with Dan Rather leading the pack at CBS ($2.5 million), followed by Tom Brokaw at NBC ($1.8 million), and Barbara Walters and Peter Jennings at ABC (approximately $1 million). All in all, the costs of news production are staggering.[40]

On balance it seems that some of the arguments made against big business control of media are exaggerated. So are some of the arguments in favor of control by small enterprises. When FCC rules have forced small stations to spend time on non-network programs, the results generally have been poor. Unable to afford costly original programs produced locally, these stations have filled their non-network hours with cheap canned movies or syndicated quiz or talent shows. The arguments concerning the respective merits of big and small media enterprises cannot be settled definitively until more thorough comparisons of the quality of programs have been made. In the meantime it is important to recognize that current policies designed to reduce media concentration and encourage local programming rest on questionable assumptions and have failed to meet their objectives.

Curbs on Private Control of the Electronic Media

FCC Regulations

Even though the media business is largely in private hands in the United States, the federal government regulates some aspects of media management. The chief control agency is the FCC, a bipartisan body appointed by the president and confirmed by the Senate. It was a seven-member body until the summer of 1984, when its size was reduced to five commissioners to save money. In 1986 the appointment term was shortened from seven to five years, ensuring a faster turnover of commission personnel and greater control by the president. In theory, the commission is an independent regulatory body. In practice, congressional purse strings, public and industry pressures, and presidential control over appointment of new members, including naming the chair, have gravely curtailed its freedom of operation. The commission's independence is also weakened because its rulings can be appealed to the courts and have been overturned on a number of occasions. Conflicting political pressures from outside the agency as well as internal political pressures influence FCC policy making. As the authors of *The Politics of Broadcast Regulation* note:

> The broadcast policy-making system is usually modest in its goals, flexible in policy choices, sensitive to feedback, and prone to dealing with immediate problems through steps and options that are only incrementally different from existing policies.... A consequence of these characteristics is a reactive rather than an innovative system sluggish to respond to change in its environment, particularly to technological change that probably will be very rapid in the next decade or so. Clearly there are problems with this kind of policy-making system.[41]

Given the vagueness of its mandate under the Communications Act of 1934 to "serve the public interest, convenience, and necessity," the FCC has found it difficult to identify the objectives that should guide its regulatory powers. It has had to determine what social, economic, and technical goals the communications industry should achieve. It also has had to deal with conflicts over the adoption of various technologies and with the philosophical issue of regulation versus deregulation. On balance, the FCC's record of setting goals and enforcing its rules has earned it the reputation of being a benign and ineffective watchdog over the public interest at best and an industry-kept, pressure-group-dominated lapdog at worst.

The FCC's primary area of responsibility is control over the electronic media. The print media are essentially uncontrolled except for antitrust and monopoly laws that the Justice Department uses to curtail print media monopolies. However, the Justice Department has permitted economically weak newspapers to combine their business and production facilities, free from these restraints, as long as their news and editorial operations are separate. By 1987 twenty-one agreements for combining the business aspects of newspapers were in effect. It remains uncertain to what degree, if any, print media will be subject to the same controls as electronic media when they use electronic transmission, such as teletext or satellite transmission of newspaper copy.

FCC control has taken four forms: (1) rules limiting the number of stations owned or controlled by a single organization, (2) examination of the goals and performance of stations as part of periodic licensing, (3) rules mandating public service and local interest programs, and (4) rules to guarantee fair treatment to individuals and to protect their rights. While none of these rules deal directly with content, all of them increase the chances that content will be diverse and of civic importance.

Rules Limiting Station Ownership. As explained earlier, to prevent high concentrations of media ownership and ensure diversity of information sources, the FCC limits the number of stations that television and radio owners may control. In recent years, it has also limited the size of the audience that may be within the range of any one group of owners, allowing them no more than 25 percent market share. Nonetheless, networks with many affiliates, such as ABC, CBS, NBC, and Fox are within reach for more than ninety percent of the nation's audiences.

Since 1970 the FCC has had a one-to-a-customer rule that prohibits any party from acquiring more than one AM and FM radio station or more than one television station in the same market. This rule now also applies to cable systems. In line with the prevailing climate of reduced business control, it has been weakened through a series of exceptions. The rule has diversified station ownership, but it has not required the breakup of existing groups that violate the one-to-a-customer rule. Similar rules restrict newspaper-television, newspaper-radio, or newspaper-cable combinations. About one-third of all groups with television interests still have newspaper properties. Many of these multimedia combinations were formed at the urging of the FCC, which once thought that this type of arrangement would lead to better news services.

Station owners have been very eager to retain their licenses because station ownership has been enormously profitable. In 1980 the average television station was four times more profitable than the average Fortune 500 company, and the average network-owned station was six times more profitable.[42] Moreover, no investment is initially required to get a license from the government although pressures to change this are mounting. Licenses of profitable stations can be sold for millions of dollars since government controls have limited the total numbers of licenses issued so that the demand exceeds supply.

This picture of steady profitability changed in the late 1980s. Television news units were especially hard hit. They were forced to slash budgets and lay off several thousand employees. Partial deregulation of the television industry, the rise of new networks, such as media mogul Ted Turner's cable news network (CNN), and the development of new technologies generated fierce competition. Independent television stations multiplied, as did cable systems, television satellites, video recorders, and similar services such as teletext and microfiche. Affiliates reduced their reliance on network programming by producing their own news shows or importing satellite programs. Network audience share dropped from 93 percent in 1977 to 63 percent in 1992, producing a drop in advertising rates. Advertising revenues also declined because the pool of large advertisers shrank in the wake of business mergers.[43] The networks themselves caught the merger fever. ABC merged with Capital

Cities Communications, NBC was acquired by General Electric, and CBS barely fought off acquisition at great financial cost.

Today the FCC rarely uses its major power to lessen ownership concentration—refusal to renew a television license at the end of five years or a radio license after seven years. In the past shock waves pulsed through the media industry when the FCC refused a license. The landmark case involved Boston television station WHDH-TV, which was owned by a local newspaper company that also operated two local radio stations and held a controlling interest in a cable television company. Even though the station had performed well, the FCC in 1969 awarded the license to a competitor, Boston Broadcasting Inc., controlled by a citizens' group. This was the first time that a license was granted to a competing applicant on grounds involving the media concentration issue. Sen. John O. Pastore, then chairman of the Senate Communications Subcommittee, expressed fear that license withdrawal might henceforth be used capriciously for political reasons. His efforts finally led to new FCC rules that nearly guarantee license renewal to stations that perform satisfactorily.

In the past the FCC rarely encouraged new communications media in order to increase competition and diversity. It initially discouraged innovations such as FM broadcasting, VHF and UHF telecasting, and cable television. This attitude has changed in recent years, and the commission now encourages new entrants into the marketplace. For instance, it has fostered direct satellite broadcasting, pay television, and low-power television stations for small markets. It has also added frequencies for AM radio broadcasts.

Licensing as Performance Control. What is satisfactory performance? Television and radio must "serve the public interest, convenience, and necessity," but beyond requiring broadcasters to ascertain the community needs and interests by talking with community leaders, there are no guides for interpreting these rules. Even the requirement to keep in touch with community leaders was dropped in June 1984. This leaves the media and the FCC great leeway in determining what qualifies as good programming. The FCC has looked at the mix of programs, the proportion of public service offerings, and the inclusion of programs geared to selected groups. It has not scrutinized the subject matter of broadcasts in detail.

This hands-off attitude has applied to both program inclusions and exclusions. For instance, the FCC declined a viewer's request to order stations to provide information about Russian and Chinese political and military activities in North Korea. The viewer had argued that the American public needed this information to put into perspective reports about U.S. military activities in Southeast Asia. Similarly, despite concerted public lobbying the FCC has not ordered the networks to delay programming unsuitable for children until late evening and to reserve the early evening broadcast hours for "family" shows. However, the FCC has set limits on the amounts of advertising permitted in children's shows. Ads may not exceed twelve minutes per hour on week days and ten and a half minutes on weekends.

Through its licensing of news outlets, the FCC has tried to ensure the new licensees will meet the information needs of socioeconomic groups different from those already served by existing stations in a given area. When there are several qualified applicants for new broadcasting stations, the FCC is authorized to use a lottery to make the award. License award procedures have been designed to favor women, minorities, labor unions, and community organizations that are underrepresented in the ownership of telecommunications facilities. The FCC justifies these preferences as aids to diversity when they come periodically under attack. Once a license has been granted, the owners hold it for good and may even sell it with little government intervention. For stations that do not engage in discriminatory or fraudulent practices, and receive few or no complaints about poor programming, renewal has become automatic.

Since the 1970s numerous civic groups have entered renewal hearings to protest the type of programming offered or omitted by a particular station. As a result of such pressures, the FCC has reluctantly withdrawn licenses from a few stations over the years. The most recent case involved a Chicago station accused of neglecting informational programs and presenting obscene movies.[44] These withdrawals have made broadcasters more careful than in the past to avoid public opposition.

Compared with regulatory agencies in other countries, even in Western Europe, Canada, and Australia, the FCC controls the electronic media with a very light hand. It could, if it wished, rigorously define what constitutes "programming in the public interest." It could enforce its rulings more strictly and verify station performance records at license renewal time. The threat of license withdrawal for rule violations could be used as a much more powerful deterrent to misbehavior and as a much stronger lever to guide programming. Part of the problem is that the FCC staff, which numbers fewer than 1,900 people, is much too small to cope with all the duties assigned to the agency. In fact, it is chronically behind schedule, even for routine matters such as publication of its annual reports.

Public Service and Local Programming. In the past the FCC stipulated the minimum time that ought to be devoted to public service programs. Under the 5-5-10 rule, which is no longer enforced, 5 percent of programming had to be devoted to local affairs, 5 percent to news and public affairs, and 10 percent to nonentertainment programs. Beyond checking a television station's log to ascertain that it recorded the minimum amount of public service programming (the requirement had already been dropped for commercial radio broadcasts), the FCC did not examine the nature and quality of programs labeled "public service." In 1991, as part of its regulations of children's television, the FCC directed stations to maintain a record of educational and informational programs for children. But it set no standards, even though the record is a requirement for license renewal.[45]

To ensure that stations leave some time for programs of interest to local communities, the FCC requires that one prime-time hour between 7:00 P.M. and 11:00 P.M. is set aside for non-network programs. However, the "prime-time access rule" permits stations to fill all or part of the local programming slot with network news or public affairs programs, documentaries, or children's shows. The intent of the rule thus can be readily circumvented as long as the program choice was made by the local station. Obviously, the rule has not worked very well to promote genuinely local programming. As discussed earlier, most stations find it too costly to produce original programs. When they do, they prefer covering national and international news rather than local events that are less glamorous. Whenever groups of stations produce programs jointly, the strictly local focus also suffers.[46]

Fair Treatment Rules. The FCC has also made rules about access to the airwaves for candidates for political office and for people who have been the subject of media attacks. These types of controls are discussed in Chapter 3.

Control by Industry Associations and Advertiser Pressures

Industry lobbies are another means of controlling the mass media. Radio and television interests, especially the networks and their affiliated stations, are active lobbyists. Most belong to the National Association of Broadcasters (NAB), a powerful Washington lobby despite the diversity and often clashing interests of its members. The NAB has a membership of 5,400 radio and television stations. It has a staff of 140 people and an active Political Action Committee.[47] The networks have additional lobbying agents in Washington who are in continuous contact with the FCC. These lobbies are particularly concerned about guarding the freedom networks now enjoy in programming.

Besides the NAB, there are a number of other trade associations and publications, such as *Broadcasting* magazine, whose staffs engage in lobbying, often at cross-purposes to each other. For newspapers the

American Newspaper Publishers Association (ANPA), now merged with several other press associations, has been one of the most prominent. These organizations try to influence appointments to the FCC and to guide public policies affecting new technologies that may threaten established systems or practices. For instance, the network lobbies for many years tried to stifle cable television and to acquire control over domestic satellites.

To forestall regulation by outside bodies, the industry developed mechanisms for self-control. The NAB has had a radio code since 1929 and a television code since 1952 that set forth rules on program content and form. Both codes have been modernized periodically. The industry-wide codes are now superseded by individual codes in major broadcast enterprises and codes adopted by the Council of Better Business Bureaus. Print press self-policing has developed along similar lines. Scholars, too, have set forth codes of journalism ethics, most of which are quite vague, such as the five principles advocated by Edmund Lambeth. Ethical behavior, he contends, requires telling the truth and heeding humaneness, above all. It also requires striving for fairness, striving for independence from power holders, and acting as responsible trustees for the public's interests.[48] What these principles mean in practice is left for decision in specific cases.

The impact of industry-wide codes has always been limited. NAB codes, for example, applied only to NAB member stations that chose to subscribe to them. In 1977, a typical year, 25 percent of all television stations were not NAB members, and nearly one-half of the members did not subscribe to the codes.[49] Penalties for code violations were minimal. The worst penalty was withdrawal of a station's right to list itself as a subscriber to the code. Therefore, the code exerted only a limited amount of moral pressure on the industry. It did serve to blunt demands by pressure groups for government intervention to set and enforce standards.

Somewhat stronger pressures on program content arose in the 1970s from advertisers who actually withdrew their commercials from programs they considered to be obscene or excessively violent. Sears Roebuck was one of the earliest and largest advertisers to do so. McDonald's, American Express, and AT&T refuse to place commercials in such shows. Other companies, such as Procter and Gamble, the top television advertiser in the nation, retained consultants to seek out acceptable programs for their advertisements and avoid unacceptable ones. With thirty-second advertisements on top-rated shows like the Super Bowl yielding $850,000 in 1992, threats of withdrawal constituted tremendous economic pressures. In the wake of such pressures from advertisers, the number of programs featuring violence, particularly during prime-time hours, dropped temporarily. ABC, for example, canceled the sequel to a successful crime drama in 1989 after it failed to attract paid advertising. The program contained four re-enactments of crime, including two stabbings, a shooting, and a murder in which a husband set fire to his wife.

There is deep concern, however, that advertisers, spurred by pressure groups, could become unofficial censors. For instance, General Motors' sponsorship of an Eastertime program on the life of Jesus was canceled because evangelical groups objected to the content. There were crippling withdrawals of advertising from a CBS documentary on gun control, opposed by the gun control lobby, and from a series of interviews featuring ex-president Nixon, which aroused the ire of Nixon foes. In 1986 a number of public television stations refused to air a public television program on border disputes involving Israel because of strong objections by major Jewish groups. Subsequently, PBS revised the program to include pro-Israel commentary to balance the show's anti-Israel thrust. The television networks, although not shy about saturating the airwaves with uninhibited sex in television dramas, have refused advertising designed to instruct viewers about the use of condoms for protection against unwanted pregnancies and acquired immune deficiency syndrome (AIDS). Again, religious groups have been the unofficial censor. On the political front, "Amerika," a serial drama depicting life in the United States ten years after a Soviet takeover, aroused objections from so many groups in 1987, including the Soviet Union's government, that it was canceled. Protests over the cancellation then led to its reinstatement, though in a watered-down version.

Citizen Lobby Control

Citizens' efforts to affect the quality of broadcasting began in earnest in 1966 when the Office of Communication of the United Church of Christ, a public interest lobby, challenged the renewal of a TV license for a Jackson, Mississippi, station, WLBT-TV, because the station had discriminated against black viewers.[50] Blacks then constituted 45 percent of the Jackson population. The challenge failed, but it was the beginning of efforts by many other citizen groups to use pressure tactics to challenge license renewals.

A major victory was finally won in 1975 when the FCC refused to renew licenses of eight educational television stations in Alabama and failed to grant a construction permit for a ninth station because citizen groups had charged racial discrimination in employment at these stations. There also had been complaints that programs that dealt with affairs of the black community had been unduly excluded.[51] Since then, numerous stations have yielded to pressure for increased minority employment and programming rather than face protracted legal action.

By permission of Mike Luckovich and Creators Syndicate.

The National Citizens' Committee for Broadcasting (NCCB), headed by former FCC commissioner Nicholas Johnson, became widely known for sharp attacks on the shallowness of broadcasting and the weakness of governmental control. Besides watching and criticizing national media policy, the committee also aided the surveillance activities of local groups. It has now been absorbed into the Ralph Nader consumer protection organization. Other prominent national citizens' lobby groups include Accuracy in Media (AIM), a well-financed conservative media-monitoring organization; the Coalition for Better Television (CBTV), representing fundamentalist religious groups; Citizens for the American Way (CAW), a liberal media organization intent on blocking conservative lobbies; Action for Children's Television (ACT), which disbanded in 1992; the National Black Media Coalition (NBMC); and the National Latino Media Coalition (NLMC).

Despite the substantial impact of such groups on FCC rule making and licensing procedures, the 1980s saw a decline in citizens' national lobbying efforts.[52] One reason was the difficulty of sustaining citizen interest over long periods of time; another was lack of financial support and loss of leadership. The broadcast lobby defeated efforts to obtain public funding for citizens' groups, and foundation support dried up. Many groups were also discouraged by reversals in the appeals courts of substantial victories won in the lower courts. Some of the energies of citizen groups have been redirected into lobbying at the local level to ensure that the emerging cable system serves the interests of various publics.

In addition to the more than sixty organizations concerned exclusively with media reform, other organizations, such as the Parent Teacher Association, the National Organization for Women, and the American Medical Association, have lobbied on a variety of media issues. These include concern about stereotyping, access to media coverage and to media employment and ownership, advertising on children's programs, and enforcement of FCC program regulations. The groups' tactics include monitoring media content, publicizing their findings, and directly pressuring broadcasters, advertisers, media audiences, and government control agencies. Protest by PTA members has pressured advertisers, who, in turn, have succeeded in reducing the number of violent programs shown in the early evening hours. Legal maneuvers have ranged from challenges of license renewals to damage suits for the harmful effects of media content.[53]

It is difficult to assess the precise influence of these organizations because many of their goals overlap with other forces that affect media policy. The causes for which they have worked have prospered, however, over the years, and part of the credit undoubtedly belongs to them. Yet these groups, if they remain active, have a long road to travel before they can match the clout and resources enjoyed by the broadcast lobby and by public officials involved in media control.[54]

Summary

In this chapter we have examined the most common types of ownership and control of the media. The national government owns and operates vast overseas radio and television enterprises. At home it partially controls a far-flung system of public television and radio broadcasting that provides an alternative to commercial programming.

For the average American these government-controlled systems are peripheral, compared with privately owned print and electronic media enterprises. The major political problem in the private sector is concentration of ownership of media and concentrated control over news and entertainment programs. There has been great concern that the American public is ill-served because much of the media output is controlled by large business conglomerates, and newspaper competition is limited in most cities. Comparatively few, potentially biased minds thus shape the news and entertainment supply that undergirds public perceptions of political issues.

We have looked into the structure of the media business and government regulations designed to avert the potential dangers of concentration. We also have tried to evaluate the impact of the existing system on the form and slant of news and entertainment. Many prevailing views about the interrelation between media structures and functions appear to be wrong. Business ownership has not led to programming dominated by business perspectives. It has not shielded big business from harsh criticism. Coverage of local news has not withered, and large, rather than small, enterprises have excelled in providing news and entertainment. Since fears about the ill effects of the current structure seem misdirected, further research is needed to provide a sounder basis for public policies intended to ensure that American media serve the public interest.

Media operations and products are shaped not only by who owns them, but also by industry lobby groups and citizens' lobbies. Given the diversity of influences that are brought into play when news and entertainment are produced, it is as yet impossible to assess the precise impact that each of these influences has on media content in general or even on a particular story. In the next chapter we will focus on legal aspects of news production for additional clues to the mystery of the mix of influences shaping the news.

Notes

1. Examples of the types of shows that attract the largest audiences are "Roseanne" (comedy), "L.A. Law" (drama), and "60 Minutes," the popular investigative series that shares many qualities with popular detective shows. In addition, there are the ever-popular sports events such as the Super Bowl, entertainment industry awards presentations, and competitions such as the Miss America pageant.
2. Ben H. Bagdikian, *The Media Monopoly*, 3d ed. (Boston: Beacon Press, 1990), 3-26. For a negative view of the "marketplace of ideas" concept, see Benjamin Ginsberg, *The Captive Public: How Mass Opinion Promotes State Power* (New York: Basic Books, 1986), 98-148.
3. "Despite the expressed insulation of public broadcasters from federal editorial domination, case law specifically allows broadcast program decisions to be dictated by political officials when the state is licensee. Therefore, potential conflict exists between First Amendment and political interests." William Hanks and Lemuel Schofield, "Limitations on the State as Editor in State-Owned Broadcast Stations," *Journalism Quarterly* 63 (Winter 1986): 798.
4. Erwin G. Krasnow, Lawrence D. Longley, and Herbert A. Terry, *The Politics of Broadcast Regulation*, 3d ed. (New York: St. Martin's Press, 1982), 23, 74.
5. *Statistical Abstract of the United States* (Washington, D.C.: Government Printing Office, 1991), 559.
6. "TV Notes," *Chicago Tribune*, December 20, 1991.
7. Benjamin M. Compaine, Christopher H. Sterling, Thomas Guback, and J.

Kendrick Noble, Jr., *Who Owns the Media: Concentration and Ownership in the Mass Communications Industry*, 2d ed. (White Plains, N.Y.: Knowledge Industry, 1982), 342; and National Public Radio, *Annual Report*, 1986.

8. *Statistical Abstract of the United States, 1991*, 559.

9. The composition of this audience is analyzed in George Comstock, Steven Chaffee, Natan Katzman, Maxwell McCombs, and Donald Roberts, *Television and Human Behavior* (New York: Columbia University Press, 1978), 116-121. Also see Ronald F. Frank and Marshall G. Greenberg, *Audiences for Public Television* (Beverly Hills, Calif.: Sage, 1982).

10. Congress has been more eager to fund public broadcasting than the president. It approved a $1.1 billion three-year reauthorization of CPB in 1992 over presidential objections. A threatened veto did not materialize.

11. For example, see Bruce M. Owen, *Economics and Freedom of Expression: Media Structure and the First Amendment* (Cambridge, Mass.: Ballinger, 1975).

12. Willard D. Rowland, Jr., "The Federal Regulatory and Policymaking Process," *Journal of Communication* 30 (Summer 1980): 141. Education-based audience differences are discussed in W. Russell Neuman, "Television and American Culture: The Mass Medium and the Pluralist Audience," *Public Opinion Quarterly* 46 (Winter 1982): 478-481.

13. Rowland, "The Federal Regulatory and Policymaking Process," 149; see also Bill Carter, "Conservatives Call for PBS to Go Private or Go Dark," *New York Times*, April 30, 1992.

14. *Statistical Abstract of the United States, 1991*, 556, 562.

15. Besides media holdings, Tribune enterprises encompass the fields of energy, mining, trucking, paper, finance, and a major league baseball team. *Tribune, 1991 Annual Report*.

16. Herbert H. Howard, "An Update on TV Ownership Patterns," *Journalism Quarterly* 60 (Fall 1983): 395-400.

17. *Directory of Corporate Affiliations* (Wilmette, Ill.: National Register Publishing, 1992), 243-245, 343-345, 897-899.

18. AM (amplitude modulation) stations and VHF (very high frequency) stations reach the largest audiences. The newer FM (frequency modulation) and UHF (ultra high frequency) stations use different parts of the airwaves and reach fewer people. Their signals cannot be received by radio and television sets designed only for AM and VHF reception.

19. Antitrust regulations become operative when the eight largest firms in a particular type of business control more than 50 percent of the market, and the twenty largest firms control 75 percent or more of the market.

20. Phillip H. Ault, "Mass Ownership Takes over the Media," in *Main Currents in Mass Communications*, ed. Warren K. Agee, Phillip H. Ault, and Edwin Emery (New York: Harper and Row, 1986), 168ff; *Editor and Publisher International Yearbook 1991*.

21. Daniel B. Wackman, Donald M. Gillmor, Cecilie Gaziano, and Everette E. Dennis, "Chain Newspaper Autonomy as Reflected in Presidential Campaign Endorsements," *Journalism Quarterly* 52 (Fall 1975): 411-420. Media critic Ben H. Bagdikian claims that quality deteriorates when papers are acquired by a chain. *The Media Monopoly*, 6-7, 84-89.

22. Bagdikian, *The Media Monopoly*, 23.

23. Capital Cities/ABC interests include motion pictures, advertising, insurance, marketing, and tourism. For CBS, it is production and sale of musical instruments, toys, warehousing, consulting, packaging, and audio-video

products. The various holdings of NBC's parent company, General Electric, are diagrammed in Figure 2-1.

24. They are subject to operational regulations, however. For instance, one network may not operate a second network covering the same market. The amount of programming that may be produced is also limited.

25. Kenneth R. Clark, "Crazy Like a Fox," *Chicago Tribune*, June 1, 1992.

26. *Statistical Abstract of the United States, 1991*, 556.

27. Maxwell E. McCombs and Donald L. Shaw, "Structuring the 'Unseen Environment,'" *Journal of Communication* (Spring 1976): 18-22.

28. Benjamin M. Compaine, "The Expanding Base of Media Competition," *Journal of Communication* 35 (1985): 81-96; and Nancy Signorielli, "Selective Viewing: A Limited Possibility," *Journal of Communication* 36 (Summer 1986): 64-76.

29. Bagdikian, *The Media Monopoly*, 8-9.

30. In 1991, there were 1,781 daily newspapers, 574 semiweekly papers, and 8,546 weekly papers. *Statistical Abstract of the United States, 1991*, 561.

31. J. Herbert Altschull, "The Journalist and Instant History: An Example of the Jackal Syndrome," *Journalism Quarterly* 50 (Autumn 1973): 389-396.

32. For example, see J. Herbert Altschull, "Khrushchev and the Berlin 'Ultimatum': The Jackal Syndrome and the Cold War," *Journalism Quarterly* 54 (Fall 1977): 545-551.

33. David C. Coulson, "Antitrust Law and the Media: Making the Newspapers Safe for Democracy," *Journalism Quarterly* 57 (Spring 1980): 79-85; Ben H. Bagdikian, "Conglomeration, Concentration, and the Media," *Journal of Communication* 30 (Spring 1980): 59-64; and James N. Rosse, "The Decline of Direct Newspaper Competition," *Journal of Communication* 30 (Spring 1980): 65-71.

34. A brief comparison of media systems throughout the world is presented in John C. Merrill, *Global Journalism*, 2d ed. (New York: Longman, 1991). Also see Donald Wilhelm, *Global Communications and Political Power* (New Brunswick, N.J.: Transaction, 1990).

35. Compaine, "Media Competition," 88; Robert M. Entman, "Newspaper Competition and First Amendment Ideals: Does Monopoly Matter?" *Journal of Communication* 35 (1985): 147-165; and Stephen Lacy, "The Effects of Intracity Competition on Daily Newspaper Content," *Journalism Quarterly* 64 (Summer/Autumn 1987): 281-290. For a contrary view see Bagdikian, *The Media Monopoly*, 84-89.

36. For contrary views see W. Lance Bennett, *News: The Politics of Illusion*, 2d ed. (New York: Longman, 1988), chap. 4.

37. A scientific appraisal of the effects of owners on media output is presented in Frank Wolf, *Television Programming for News and Public Affairs: A Quantitative Analysis of Networks and Stations* (New York: Praeger, 1972).

38. Gary A. Hale and Richard C. Vincent, "Locally Produced Programming on Independent Television Stations," *Journalism Quarterly* 63 (Autumn 1986): 562-568.

39. Don R. Le Duc, "Deregulation and the Dream of Diversity," *Journal of Communication* 32 (Autumn 1982): 174.

40. Kenneth R. Clark, "Network Woes," *Chicago Tribune Magazine*, May 17, 1987, 28.

41. Krasnow, Longley, and Terry, *The Politics of Broadcast Regulation*, 284.

42. Compaine et al., *Who Owns the Media*, computed from pp. 33 and 397.

43. Bill Carter, "Television: The Networks Finally End Their Prime-Time Decline," *New York Times,* April 13, 1992.
44. Steven Morris, "FCC Denies WSNS-TV New Broadcast License," *Chicago Tribune,* September 20, 1990.
45. Many contradictory bills have been introduced in Congress to deal with news and public service programming requirements. Most of them die early in the game. *Congressional Quarterly Weekly Report* is an excellent source for tracking these legislative developments. See also Edmund L. Andrews, "F.C.C. Limits Ads on TV Shows Aimed at Children," *New York Times,* April 10, 1991.
46. Nancy R. Csaplar, "Local Television: The Limits of Prime-Time Access," *Journal of Communication* 33 (Spring 1983): 124-131; see also Edmund L. Andrews, "F.C.C. Limits Ads on TV Shows Aimed at Children," *New York Times,* April 10, 1991.
47. *Encyclopedia of Associations* (Detroit, Mich.: Gale Research Co., 1988), vol. 1, 76.
48. Edmund B. Lambeth, *Committed Journalism: An Ethic for the Profession* (Bloomington: Indiana University Press, 1986). See also Bruce A. Linton, "Self-Regulation in Broadcasting Revisited," *Journalism Quarterly* 64 (Summer/Autumn 1987): 483-490.
49. Joel Persky, "Self-Regulation of Broadcasting—Does It Exist?" *Journal of Communication* 27 (Spring 1977): 200-210.
50. *Office of Communication of the United Church of Christ v. FCC,* 359 F.2d 994 (D.C. Cir., 1966).
51. Krasnow, Longley, and Terry, *The Politics of Broadcast Regulation,* 54-62.
52. Ibid., 56-57.
53. These activities are summarized in Anne W. Branscomb and Maria Savage, "The Broadcast Reform Movement at the Crossroads," *Journal of Communication* 28 (Autumn 1978): 25-34.
54. Forrest P. Chisman, "Public Interest and FCC Policy Making," *Journal of Communication* 27 (Winter 1977): 77-84.

Readings

Besen, Stanley M., Thomas G. Krattenmaker, A. Richard Metzger, Jr., and John R. Woodbury. *Misregulating Television: Network Dominance and the FCC.* Chicago: University of Chicago Press, 1985.

Head, Sydney W., and Christopher H. Sterling. *Broadcasting in America: A Survey of Electronic Media.* 5th ed. Boston: Houghton Mifflin, 1987.

Horwitz, Robert Britt. *The Irony of Regulatory Reform: The Deregulation of American Telecommunications.* New York: Oxford University Press, 1989.

Krasnow, Erwin G., Lawrence D. Longley, and Herbert A. Terry. *The Politics of Broadcast Regulation.* 3d ed. New York: St. Martin's Press, 1982.

Merrill, John C. *Global Journalism.* 2d ed. New York: Longman, 1991.

Smith, Anthony. *The Age of Behemoths: The Globalization of Mass Media Firms.* Washington, D.C.: Brookings Institution, 1991.

Snow, Marcellus S., ed. *Marketplace for Telecommunications: Regulation and Deregulation in Industrialized Democracies.* New York: Longman, 1986.

Tunstall, Jeremy. *Communications Deregulation: The Unleashing of America's Communications Industry.* London: Basil Blackwell, 1986.

CHAPTER 3

Press Freedom and the Law

The American Constitution guarantees the freedom of the press from government control because it is deemed essential to safeguard American democracy. What does press freedom mean in practice and how do First Amendment guarantees affect what American mass media cover or neglect? Is television anchor Dan Rather correct in claiming that press freedom redounds to "the benefit of listeners and viewers and readers. The cause is America"? [1] Or has press freedom been the suit of armor that protects a powerful, privileged, and often arrogant press from taking responsibility for its frequent misbehaviors?

Conflicting perspectives on what press freedom has meant and should mean reflect perplexing dilemmas faced by democratic societies. How can freedom of the press to report all news be reconciled with protection of society from the dangers of unrestrained publicity? How can an unfettered media establishment be kept responsive and responsible?

We will begin to answer those questions by probing the problems that arise when a free press claims the exclusive right to decide what to publish and what to omit, a right that often clashes with demands by citizen groups for newspaper space and air time to publicize social and political causes. Then we will turn to difficulties the press faces in gaining access to information needed for a story when the government claims the right to conceal this information. Finally, we will examine barriers to publication that have been imposed by legislators and courts to safeguard private and public interests.

The First Amendment is the constitutional basis for most of the laws and court decisions about the right of access to the press and freedom to gather news and publish it. The amendment guarantees that "Congress shall make no law ... abridging the freedom of speech or of the press." This makes the fourth estate the only private business in America that is given a privileged status by the Constitution. The dimensions of this privilege, however, have fluctuated since the First Amendment was ratified in 1791. Moreover, similar clauses in state constitutions have often been construed in ways that differ from interpretations at the national level.[2]

The Founding Fathers granted this special status to the press because they believed that the right to collect and disseminate information and opinions free from government controls is the bedrock of a free society.[3] If restraints are needed to protect society from harmful publicity, they must come through the deterrent effects of fear of punishment after publication, not through "prior restraint." Publication can be prevented only if it "will surely result in direct, immediate, and irreparable damage to our nation or its people."[4] The belief in the political importance of a free press has stood the test of time and remains a cornerstone of American democracy. Therefore, anything that affects the interpretation or the scope of this basic right is a matter of major political significance.

Access to the Media

The notion of government "by the people" seems to imply that the people have a right to make their voices heard. Practically speaking, this means that they must have access to the mass media. Ralph Nader's consumer protection movement or the antismoking crusade that swept the country in the 1980s, to take two examples, could never have gathered widespread support without mass media publicity. What would have happened if the media had refused to tell these stories? Did the reformers have a right to mass media publicity for their views and for their organizing activities?

The answer is "no," making it very difficult for most people, other than journalists or major public figures, to gain access to the media. In his book *Freedom of the Press for Whom? The Right of Access to the Mass Media,* Jerome Barron, a lawyer interested in civil liberties, accused the media of fighting for broad rights of free expression for themselves while denying these same rights to the public.[5] Media personnel decide what stories to publicize and whose views to present. This leaves many who want to proclaim their views without a suitable public forum.

Barron argued that the First Amendment right to publish freely should be open to all individuals and groups, not only to news professionals. If individuals have a special cause or feel that some of the situations depicted by the mass media are not presented accurately, or that certain information is omitted, they should have an opportunity to use the mass media to state their views. Without this right, they may be doomed to political ineffectiveness.

Print Media

What rights of access to the mass media do individuals in private and public life have? To answer this question accurately, a distinction must be made between print and electronic media. American courts have usually held that the freedom of the print media to determine what they will or will not print, and whose views they will present, is nearly absolute. As long as the media stay clear of deliberate libel and slander and do not publish top-secret information, they may make publishing decisions unhampered by legal restraints. Even restraints on publishing false or misleading information are lacking.

The freedom of the press to publish or suppress information is delineated in the case of *Miami Herald Publishing Company v. Tornillo* (1974).[6] At issue was the constitutionality of a Florida statute that gave candidates for public office who had been personally attacked by a newspaper a right of reply. A candidate attacked on the editorial page had the right to reply on the editorial page in a format similar to that used by the accuser. If the attack appeared in the news pages, the candidate had the right to equal space, type, and position there. The law had been passed to deal with the problem of personal attacks published very late in a campaign, giving candidates little time for a rebuttal. The consequence might be loss of the election.

The case arose in 1972 when Patrick Tornillo, Jr., leader of the Dade County Teachers Union, was running for the Florida State Legislature. Just before the primary the *Miami Herald* published two editorials objecting to Tornillo's election because he had led a recent teacher's strike. Tornillo demanded that the paper print his replies to the editorials. The paper refused. After Tornillo lost the primary decisively, he brought suit against the paper.

The case went through the Florida court system, with lower court rulings overturned at higher stages. Finally, in 1974 it reached the U.S. Supreme Court, which ruled unanimously that newspapers can print or refuse to print anything they like. Editors have an unlimited right to decide what goes in or what stays out of the paper. No one, including a candidate whose reputation has been damaged, has the right to demand space in a newspaper. Therefore, the Florida statute granting a right to reply was unconstitutional. The decision reaffirmed what had been the thrust of the law all along. Private citizens may request that a story or response to a personal attack be printed and that request may be granted, but they have no right to demand publication.[7]

Electronic Media

The rules are different for the electronic media, based on the view that limited spectrum space makes them semimonopolies. Unlike the print media business, which is open to anyone, entry into the electronic media business requires a license from the government. In return for the privilege of broadcasting over the public airwaves, license holders are subject to government regulations. These include rules ensuring that the license holders do not prevent public access to the airways in specified situations.

The public's access rights to electronic media fall under three categories: the *equal time provision,* the *fairness doctrine,* and the *right of rebuttal.* These access rights are based on Section 315 of the Communications Act of 1934 and its amendments and interpretations. The equal time provision requires that broadcasters who permit a candidate for political office to campaign on their stations must give equal opportunities to all other candidates for the same office. Under the fairness doctrine, broadcasters who air controversial issues of public importance must provide reasonable opportunities for the presentation of conflicting viewpoints. The right of rebuttal requires that an attack on the honesty, character, or integrity of an identified person or group entitles the targets of the attack to a reply. The broadcaster must notify the targets about the offending broadcast and must supply a transcript or summary. Thereafter, a reasonable opportunity to respond must be provided. All of the regulations that mandate public access are subject to one very important implicit condition: the rights arise only after the station has broadcast the information in question.

The Right to Equal Time. If a station gives or sells time to one candidate for a specific office, it must make the same opportunity available to all candidates for that office. Even if there are fifteen candidates for the same office, they all have a right to equal time, including those with few backers. By the same token, whenever the station denies time to all candidates for the same office, none of them has a right to demand access under the campaign coverage provisions of Section 315. The rules exclude coverage provided through regular news programs and selected talk shows that have been specifically exempted.

Stations constrained by the all-or-none equal time rule often opt for "none," particularly for state and local offices. This keeps many viable candidates off the air who might otherwise have gained exposure. But it saves stations from cluttering their programs with numerous campaign broadcasts that would be of little interest to their listeners and costly to the station in lost advertising revenues.

To make it possible to stage lengthy debates among mainline candidates for major offices without running afoul of the equal time provisions, Congress suspended these provisions in 1960. This permitted Kennedy and Nixon to debate. A different tactic was used in 1976 and 1980. To facilitate the Carter-Ford and Carter-Reagan debates, the FCC permitted them to be staged as public meetings, which can be covered by the news media like regular news that is not subject to the equal time rule.

Billing the 1976 and 1980 presidential debates as public meetings arranged by the League of Women Voters and covered by the press like any newsworthy event was obviously a subterfuge to avoid the intent of the law. Several minor party candidates, eager to be included in the debates, sued in 1976 on the ground that this circumvention of equal time provisions was illegal. But the courts ruled against them. Finally, in November 1983, the FCC reversed its previous position by declaring that radio and television broadcasters were free to stage political debates at all political levels among candidates of their own choosing. The sole remaining restriction on debates is that broadcasters must not "favor or disfavor" any particular candidate. Candidates who feel that they have been unfairly shut out may appeal to the FCC.[8]

The curbs on political dialogue other than debates have led to widespread dissatisfaction with the equal time rule. Many observers believe that the rule has done more political harm than good. It has blocked the public from receiving many important messages by current and prospective public officials. For instance, when President Gerald R. Ford set forth his farm policy in a speech to the Future Farmers of America in 1976, the networks shied away from full-length coverage because it might involve them in an equal time allotment for the Democratic candidate. Normally, they would have broadcast a presidential speech outlining major policy proposals. Critics are also unhappy about public sanction of subterfuges to evade the rule and about piecemeal legalized exceptions.

The Right to Fair Treatment. The fairness doctrine has had a broader reach than the equal time provision because it is not limited to candidates for political office. Under the fairness doctrine reasonable time must be given for the presentation of issues of public concern and the expression of opposing views if a highly controversial public issue is discussed. What constitutes such an issue is a matter to be ultimately decided by the courts. In an average year fewer than 10 percent of the fifteen thousand charges of unfairness are sustained.

Like the equal time provision, the fairness doctrine has impoverished public debate by suppressing controversy. The media have frequently shied away from programs dealing with controversial public issues to avoid demands to air opposing views in place of regular revenue-producing programs.

When controversial programs have been aired, it has been difficult to decide who has the right to reply. For instance, when President Richard Nixon justified America's incursion into Cambodia during the Vietnam War, three groups immediately demanded time to broadcast counterarguments: a group of Democratic senators, the Democratic National Committee, and a group of business executives organized to oppose the war. The courts settled the problem of choosing among claimants by ruling that no group has the right to expound its particular brand of opposition. Rather, it is up to the media to decide which opposing group will be heard. This decision gives the media great control over the types of opposition views that will be aired. They usually select the most prominent groups who wish to be heard. Groups that hold unconventional views or whose politics are on the extreme right or left are also unlikely choices. This sharply reduces their chances for challenging the power structure. It is one of many ways in which media practices perpetuate the established social order.

The media can bypass fairness claims by including opposing views on controversial issues in their regular news programs. Generally, the FCC and the courts have sustained the media's contentions that these issues have been fully aired in regular newscasts. The courts have also ruled against an automatic right to oppose statements made during presidential news conferences, as long as the media air contrary views in news analyses immediately after the conferences.

The media thus retain control over the array of viewpoints that receive a hearing. Pressures and litigation, however, have made the media more receptive to featuring opposing views voluntarily. It has become traditional to allow spokespersons for the opposition to offer rebuttals after presidential, gubernatorial, and mayoral messages covering major policy issues. The temper of the times has thus curbed editorial freedom, even though legal rights remain unchanged.

Is there a right of reply to contentious statements made in business commercials? The oil industry, conservationists, and the drug industry, among other groups, have used commercials to raise questions about controversial public policies. Commercial firms and public interest groups have asked for time to respond. The question about response rights arises because First Amendment protections do not automatically extend to commercial messages. In fact, free expression in such messages has been severely constrained through truth-in-advertising laws administered by the Federal Trade Commission. If the media must make time available to respond to commercial messages, must it be free of charge? The answer is unclear.

A landmark case in 1969 seemed to indicate that there was a right to reply to commercial messages. It concerned television advertisements for cigarettes before such commercials were banned from television. John W. Banzhaf III, a young Manhattan lawyer and antismoking activist, accused the cigarette companies of promoting the perceived glamour of cigarette smoking without advertising its dangers. He demanded the right to present views opposed to smoking, a life and death public health issue. The networks countered that opposition to smoking had been adequately presented by commercials and publications from various health organizations concerned with cancer and heart and lung disease. The Supreme Court sided with Banzhaf. It supported the circuit court's decision that smoking involved such an extraordinarily important health issue that, contrary to usual rules, broadcasters must balance cigarette commercials with antismoking spots.[9]

This decision did not supply a yardstick to determine which issues are exceptional enough to warrant time for countercommercials. The case has turned out to be the exception rather than the rule. In all subsequent cases claims for countercommercial time have been refused. The law remains very unclear about the right to reply to commercial messages because the courts have spoken with forked tongues. The practice of media enterprises in allowing replies has also been quite mixed.

The Right of Rebuttal. Individuals who are assailed on radio or television in a way that damages their reputation have the right of rebuttal. The landmark case *Red Lion Broadcasting Co. v. Federal Communications Commission* (1969)[10] established a rather broad scope for the right of reply. The case arose because a book by Fred J. Cook, a very liberal journalist, about Barry Goldwater, a conservative senator, was attacked by the Rev. Billy James Hargis on a program conducted and paid for by the ultraconservative Christian Crusade. Fred Cook asked for broadcast time, free of charge, to reply. The station was willing to sell him reply time, but it refused to grant it free of charge, disclaiming responsibility for the content of programs for which various groups had bought television time. If the stations were forced to grant free rebuttal time for statements on such broadcasts, they could not afford to sell time to private broadcasters who might air controversial right- or left-wing views.

In the *Red Lion* case, to the delight of proponents of ready public access to the airwaves, the courts sided with the plaintiff. Cook was granted the right of rebuttal, at station expense, on the grounds that maligned individuals deserve a right to reply and that the public has a right to hear opposing views. The decision proved to be a hollow victory for supporters of free access, however, because it led to sharp curtailment of air time for controversial broadcasts.

The *Red Lion* case is one of many examples of political manipulation of the regulatory process. Cook's protest had been paid for and orchestrated by the Democratic National Committee as part of an effort to generate an avalanche of demands for rebuttals to conservative radio and television programs. The hope was that stations would then cancel these programs to avoid the costs of free rebuttal time.[11] This did, indeed, happen. By 1975 the Christian Crusade had been dropped by 300 of its 350 stations. Since 1969 the courts have retreated somewhat from their broad support for the right of rebuttal at station expense because of its chilling effects on controversial broadcasts. The flood of rebuttal requests also mired the FCC in a morass of claims and counterclaims that it could not process with its limited resources.

Reform Proposals. To halt the deleterious effects on programming and the flood of FCC proceedings, strong demands have been voiced by members of Congress and many broadcasters and communication scholars to do away with all the access provisions linked to Section 315 equal time, fairness, and right of rebuttal provisions. The pleaders contend that there is no longer any reason to consider electronic media as semimonopolies. In fact, print media, which are uncontrolled by government, face less competition in the age of one-newspaper towns than do electronic media with their competing networks and competition among multiple radio and television outlets. Besides, the distinction between print and electronic media is becoming increasingly blurred since newspapers now use electronic channels for many operations. Therefore, the argument goes, the electronic media should be just as free as the print media to make publishing decisions. The quality and fairness of programming decisions, and their success in presenting a wide array of viewpoints on controversial issues, should be judged from a long-range perspective at license renewal time rather than case by case. Renewal of a station's license should hinge on adequate performance over the entire five-year period. Such reforms, proponents claim, would encourage stations to air controversies and provide a balance of views over a period of time.[12]

Opponents of reform point to the airing of many controversial programs despite Section 315. They warn that removal of access protections will leave the public at the not-so-tender mercies of media gatekeepers. As Jerome Barron has lamented, "The myth says that if the press is kept 'free,' liberty of discussion is assured. But, in how few hands is left the exercise of 'freedom'!"[13] The vast influence of the electronic media on public perceptions requires safeguards stronger than ordinary market forces, others argue. If audience rights are paramount, as the *Red Lion* case affirms, shouldn't the audience be protected from media unfairness and misjudgment?[14]

To ensure survival of the fairness doctrine, Congress passed a bill making it law in the spring of 1987. President Reagan promptly vetoed the bill, and the FCC later ruled unanimously that the fairness doctrine is unconstitutional.[15] Although the doctrine's goal had been fairness, it had "in fact resulted in 'blandness' or 'nothingness.' " [16] Major media organizations were delighted with the ruling and prepared to battle for its support by the courts, should that become necessary. Meanwhile, Congress has tried repeatedly to revive the rule, leaving its ultimate fate uncertain. The effect on the airing of controversies has been minimal.[17]

Problems of the Status Quo

Apart from the right to reply to a personal attack, to request time to express opposing views when controversial matters of public interest are aired, and the right of rival candidates to equal broadcast time, there are no access rights for individuals. Short of getting into the media business, there is no way to bring messages to public attention through the mass media if the media are unwilling. Federal courts have ruled that public television enjoys complete editorial freedom as well. A group of citizens had sued the Alabama Education Television Network and the University of Houston because they canceled the film "Death of a Princess" in response to protests by Saudi Arabia's royal family and threats of economic boycott. The citizens had charged unfair denial of their right of access to information and claimed that the cancellation constituted political censorship. The court disagreed.[18]

Large news organizations increasingly guarantee exclusive broadcast rights to major events to a single media enterprise. This practice is another restraint on information dissemination. All news outlets, aside from the contract holder, are precluded from covering the event.[19] Exclusive contracts have been negotiated even for public spectacles such as the rededication of the Statue of Liberty during its centennial. The television networks have also been very restrictive in airing public information programs by professionals outside their own organization. Similarly, professional organizations have frequently restrained the flow of news to the general public. For instance, when scientists discovered a treatment that could cut pneumonia deaths by AIDS victims by half, they felt constrained to withhold the news for five months until the *New England Journal of Medicine,* a highly regarded professional publication owned by the Massachusetts Medical Society, had first published their reports. The power of the journal to act as the gatekeeper for major medical news springs from the fact that scientists prize the prestige derived from publication of their work in the journal. If they violate journal rules by releasing data to the lay public prior to publication in a medical journal, their story may be rejected for publication.[20]

People in public office who want access to the mass media to explain their views face problems quite similar to those of private individuals. Although the media are likely to be more sympathetic to their requests, on many occasions coverage is denied. Several speeches by Presidents Nixon, Ford, and Reagan, and a 1992 news conference by President Bush were not broadcast at all because the media considered them partisan political statements or claimed that they contained nothing new. Others were carried by only a few stations, forcing the president to compete against regular broadcasts, reducing his audience sharply. On still other occasions broadcasts of presidential speeches have been deferred until late evening, denying the president access to prime-time audiences. Carter and Reagan tried to prevent such problems by tailoring their requests for media time to the needs of the media. In particular, they avoided schedule conflicts with major sports events.

The question of access rights to the airwaves also has been raised in connection with population groups whose concerns are different from those of the general public. Several public interest groups have asked for more children's programs, even though they would be of little interest to the majority of listeners and viewers. The FCC has concurred that children constitute an important special audience whose needs for distinctive programming must be met. Stations have been reluctant to add children's programs because revenues from them are comparatively low, particularly after the FCC reduced the amount of advertising permitted on children's programs. Curtailment of advertising was intended to spare immature viewers from the temptations offered by advertising.

Other audiences whose right of access to special programs has been recognized sporadically include African-Americans, Hispanics, and lovers of classical music, to name a few. Occasional rulings have forced the electronic media to set aside time for broadcasts geared to such groups, whose needs might be ignored if the forces of the economic marketplace were allowed full rein. The FCC has further protected the interests of these groups by giving preference in license applications to stations whose output is likely to serve neglected clienteles. But in light of the growing number of cable, television, and radio outlets, making access easier for everyone, government protection of special interest groups is declining. In 1981 the Supreme Court freed the FCC from any obligation to weigh the effects of alternative program formats on various population groups when making licensing decisions. The Court's ruling arose from a series of cases in which radio stations had changed their format, for instance, from all news to all music.[21]

Other Approaches to Media Access

Attempts to gain access to the mass media through independently produced programs, individual requests for air time, and FCC rulings that support the interest of minority audiences have been only moderately successful. Other routes to access are even less satisfactory. Letters to the editor and op-ed essays are examples. Due to lack of space, most papers publish few letters and opinion pieces. The *New York Times,* for instance, receives more than sixty thousand letters a year and publishes 4 to 5 percent of them, limiting length strictly. Even with these stringent controls, space devoted to letters equals space for editorials in the *Times.* Editors select the letters and op-ed essays to be published, using a variety of criteria that discriminate against those from average people. Messages that are unusual or are sent by someone well known are most likely to be printed.

Another avenue to access is the use of paid advertisements. Labor unions, business enterprises, lobby groups, and even foreign governments have placed advertisements in newspapers, such as the *New York Times* and *Wall Street Journal,* and on the air to present their side of disputes and public policy issues. This route is usually open only to large companies, such as W. R. Grace and the Mobil Corporation, that can afford the steep purchase price, which may run into thousands of dollars for full-page advertisements and national broadcast exposure. Even then print and electronic media have occasionally refused to print advertisements or sell air time when messages seemed to them too controversial—on topics like the energy crisis and deficit spending, for example.

When the Republican National Committee wanted to buy three half-hour slots on national television in 1975 to explain the party's philosophy and goals to the public, the networks refused. The courts upheld the refusal as long as this policy was applied evenhandedly for all similar organizations. The courts have also upheld the right of newspapers to refuse to sell advertising space as long as refusal is not used to discriminate against particular groups. However, in some instances courts have ordered papers to accept controversial advertising as long as advertising space for miscellaneous announcements was for sale.

Most people who would like to publicize their views cannot afford the high cost of paid messages. Instead, they try to gain attention by creating a sensational event and inviting the media to witness it. A young Chinese dissident used the tactic in 1992 when he invited the media to watch his display of posters commemorating the brutal suppression of China's pro-democracy movement in Beijing's Tienanmen Square. The ensuing free publicity reached millions of people all over the world. Few protests meet with such success and many fail miserably, as happened to the man who invited the media to a self-immolation to protest unemployment in 1983. Camera crews filmed the action while the protester suffered life-threatening burns. The story received nationwide coverage, but the emphasis was on the callousness of the film crew that did not stop the burning. The unemployment issue was well-nigh ignored.[22]

The rise of lobby groups eager to ensure broad access rights to people with minority viewpoints, and the FCC's sympathy with their pleas, have made broadcasters more sensitive to pressures for access by political activists. But even if radio or television station management is willing to grant access to such people, especially when they have engaged in newsworthy activities, there still is the problem of insufficient time to air every claimant's views. Despite the multiplication of television and radio channels in the wake of technological advancements, there will never be enough channels or even newspaper pages to publicize all important views to large audiences. Nor do concerned citizens have the time or capacity to listen to all significant views and put them into proper perspective. In fact, the capacity to broadcast and publicize already far exceeds the audience's capacity to listen and assimilate. Studies of cable system users have shown that regardless of the number of channels available and the important stories that they may feature, the average viewer rarely taps more than six.

Access to Information

Special Access for the Media?

The right to publish without restraint means little if information cannot be obtained. This raises the question of whether the media do and should have a special right of access to places where they wish to gather information. Supreme Court decisions have denied the existence of special rights. In *Zemel v. Rusk* (1965), for instance, a citizen sued to claim his right to a passport to visit Cuba and learn about conditions there. The Court upheld the State Department's ban on Cuban travel and ruled that neither ordinary citizens nor media personnel have a right to gather information. In the Court's words, "The right to speak and publish does not carry with it the unrestrained right to gather information."[23] A similar ruling was handed down in *Branzburg v. Hayes* (1972), a case involving a journalist's right to refuse testimony before a grand jury because he wanted to protect his sources. "It has generally been held," noted the Court, "that the First Amendment does not guarantee the press a constitutional right of special access to information not available to the public generally."[24] The press had argued that its status as the fourth branch of government, surveying the political scene for the public, entitled it to special rights of access.

The decisions denying such rights exclude journalists from access to many politically crucial events and thus deprive the public of important, albeit sensitive, information. Closed White House and Camp David meetings provide examples. Other events that are often barred to the media are pretrial hearings and grand jury proceedings that determine the sufficiency of evidence of wrongdoing to justify indictments. Because grand jury proceedings frequently involve high political stakes, news about them has repeatedly been leaked to newspeople by participants. The press also has no right to attend conferences of the Supreme Court where the justices reveal why they decided to hear certain cases and refused to hear others. Media people may be barred from attending sessions of legislative bodies closed to the general public. Such sessions ordinarily deal with secret information that may require protection or with matters that might prove embarrassing to legislators.

Newspeople have no right to be admitted to sites of crimes and disasters when the general public is excluded. Nor do they have the right to visit prisons and interview and film inmates, even for the purpose of investigating prison conditions and rumors of brutality. In many cases where access has been denied, the Supreme Court has stressed that reporters could get the information they needed without special access privileges.[25] This may indicate that the Court is willing to grant access in situations where information about prison conditions is totally lacking.

Many of the Supreme Court's decisions in the early 1970s regarding access to information were highly controversial, as shown by 5 to 4 divisions in *Branzburg v. Hayes* (1972), *Pell v. Procunier* (1974), and *Saxbe v. Washington Post Co.* (1974).[26] This clash of views among the justices has made media access rights a very fluid and exciting area of legal development. A great deal of pressure has also been exerted on Congress to pass legislation that would clear up some of the uncertainties. Advocates of broadened access rights have been especially vocal.

By custom, although not by law, newspeople often receive preferred treatment in gaining entry to public events. Press passes ensure media access to the best observation points for inaugurations of chief executives, space shuttle landings, and political conventions. In many instances the media are admitted (for example, to the scene of accidents and crimes), while the general public is kept out. Access, however, is purely at the discretion of the public authorities in charge.

In wartime military officials often bar news personnel from combat zones. They keep them out by denying transportation to these areas or, as happened in Grenada in October 1983, by keeping invasion plans secret. Initial news accounts of American forces' invasion of this tiny Caribbean island were vague and often contradictory because the administration had banned the press. The closest reporters could get was the island of Barbados, some 150 miles away. Two days after the invasion, fifteen reporters were allowed to visit Grenada for a few hours under strict military supervision. On subsequent days two larger groups followed. Press restrictions remained in force for a full week. The situation was the same during the buildup to the Persian Gulf War in 1990-1991, and during the war itself. Despite press protests and a suit filed by news outlets against President George Bush and the Defense Department, the government effectively throttled free access to news. Such news blackouts clearly exemplify denial of access to news without any legal recourse. The Department of Defense has issued new regulations to ease media access in similar future situations. Past experience suggests that they will make little difference.

Access to Government Documents

General Rules. Government documents are another extremely important source of political information to which access is frequently obstructed. The Freedom of Information Act, signed by President Lyndon B. Johnson on July 4, 1966 and amended in 1974 to make the act more enforceable, ostensibly opened many government files to the news media and the general public.[27] Burdensome application requirements and the costs of duplicating information, however, have limited its usefulness for news personnel. In recent years, the intricacies of scanning computerized records that were programmed in unfamiliar ways have raised additional access hurdles. Nonetheless, the act has led to important revelations such as CIA involvement in political affairs in Chile and Cuba, illegal financial dealings by members of Congress, and the failure of government to protect the public from unsafe nuclear reactors, contaminated drinking water, and ineffective drugs. Most reporters, however, are content to cover readily available current news rather than use the Freedom of Information Act to dig into government files to unearth past misdeeds.

The act has been used by organized crime and narcotics traffickers to spot threats to their activities and by business firms to spy on competitors. To cope with these and other abuses, the act was amended again in 1986. Fees charged to businesses for information were raised to cover the full costs of inquiries. Fees were lowered for media enterprises to encourage their search for information. Although most of the changes garnered widespread approval, some First Amendment champions criticized provisions that broadened the right of government agencies to refuse requests for information.[28]

Many types of public documents remain unavailable to reporters despite the pervasiveness of freedom of information laws at all levels of government. Most laws provide for access to "public records," but political jurisdictions define public records differently. Laws obviously constitute a public record, but are citizens entitled to inspect the minutes of the meetings that preceded passage of a law, or tapes of the proceedings, or exhibits that a legislative committee considered before passing the law? In many states the term *public record* does not encompass any information about the genesis of laws and regulations.

Computerization of governmental records is raising many new issues about access. According to the congressional Office of Technology Assessment, "there is no common information dissemination policy within the executive branch and Congress which specifies how government information is to be disseminated in other than hard copy or microfiche format." [29] The courts have acknowledged that information stored in government computers constitutes a public record, but they have yet to decide definitively what access rights exist. For example, do journalists have the right to ask for specific data within a data base, or does such a request entail the creation of a new "record" that public agencies are not required to supply? Must government agencies facilitate computer access by installing user-friendly programs? The *Congressional Record*, for example, could not be searched effectively until full text-searching facilities were developed. What about data stored in now obsolete files that current personnel cannot retrieve? It will take many years to find satisfactory answers to such questions and to develop reasonably uniform policies.

Applicants for information often must demonstrate a special need for a particular set of data. A journalist or private citizen cannot go into a record center and say, "I would like to examine all your records on public health matters." Exactly what is wanted must be specified, which is difficult to do without knowing what is available. The kinds of interest that must be demonstrated and the degree of precision of information requests are determined by administrators.

A widely used rule of thumb about access to information is that disclosure must be in the public interest and must not do excessive harm. Access should be denied if the harm caused by opening records is greater than the possible benefit. Accordingly, if a reporter requested the records of welfare clients for a story on welfare cheating, this request would probably be denied because it is embarrassing to many people to have others know that they need public assistance. Because there are no precise guidelines for determining what is in the public interest and what degree of harm is excessive, the judgments of public officials who control documents are supreme. Many state legislatures are unwilling to leave access policies to the discretion of administrative officials. Therefore, they list the kinds of records that may or may not be disclosed. But that approach is unsatisfactory because legislators cannot possibly foresee all types of records that may be kept. Release of records may then be stopped simply because they are not specifically mentioned in the legislation.

Certain types of documents are routinely barred from disclosure. While the reasons are usually sound, closed access may not be in the public's best interest. For example, examination questions and answers for various tests given by government agencies are usually placed beyond public scrutiny. If questions and answers to civil service examinations were published, the value of these examinations might be totally destroyed. On the other hand, if the fairness and appropriateness of examination questions for public jobs are in doubt, public scrutiny of questions and answers might be beneficial. Favoritism in grading exams of the protégés of the powerful is a widely practiced tactic that also is difficult to expose without access to graded exams.

Other data frequently kept from media personnel are records that could give advantage to business competitors, such as bids for work to be performed for the government. In most states the law requires competitive bidding and mandates that contracts, with some exceptions, go to the lowest bidder. Because corruption is common in awarding government contracts, reporters often are very interested in what has been bid or what promises have been made in return for contract awards. Without access to the records, investigative reporting of suspected fraud or corruption is impossible. On the other hand, secrecy is warranted because publicizing the details of a bid would unfairly allow another firm to underbid by a few dollars and thus get the contract.

Clearly, some restraints on access are essential to protect individuals, especially now when access to computerized government information can make the average citizen's life an open book for anyone adept at using social security numbers to compile individual dossiers. Yet restraints may make betrayals of the public trust easier for potential offenders. The cloak of secrecy may conceal vast areas of corruption. Finding the right balance between protection of individuals and protection of the interests of the public through media access is an extremely difficult and controversial task.

Historical and National Security Documents. Access to the records that major public officials keep of their administration is limited. In the case of presidents, many of the records are kept at special presidential libraries scattered throughout the country. Records of public officials are usually unavailable to the media and the general public until thirty years after the death of the public official. The thirty-year limit was selected to spare possible embarrassment to people whose private and public lives were entangled with that of the official. Exceptions to the thirty-year rule arise when official papers are classified as public rather than private. Because the distinction between personal and public papers is not clear, exceptions frequently are contested in court. Former president Richard Nixon sued unsuccessfully to recover control of many of his records about the Watergate affair that had been released to the media.

The closure of the private records of public officials is part of the privacy protection afforded to all individuals, but it serves a public purpose as well. For uninhibited discussion in policy making, assurance of confidentiality is essential. Without it, people will posture for an audience rather than freely address themselves to the substance of the issues that are under consideration. The danger of inhibiting free discussion also explains why deliberations prior to legislative or judicial decisions are generally closed to public scrutiny.

Documents concerning matters of national security usually cannot be published. Examples are CIA intelligence data and information about prospective negotiations or sensitive past negotiations. News about specific new weapons adopted by the United States, or stories indicating that security devices are not operating properly, may also be restricted. In some cases, however, such information is available in open files and can be pieced together into a coherent story. Government efforts to stop the publication of this kind of story have been unsuccessful in recent years, except when prohibitions about publication were a matter of law. In 1982, for instance, it became a crime to publish the names of covert intelligence agents, even when they were taken from public documents.

In the absence of laws, the story may be different. Consider this 1979 case. The federal government was able to obtain an injunction to prohibit a Wisconsin magazine, *The Progressive,* from publishing descriptions, culled from open documents, of how a hydrogen bomb can be made. The injunction amounted to prior restraint contrary to the ruling in *Near v. Minnesota* (1931), in which Chief Justice Hughes had ruled that publication may be prevented for national security reasons only in time of war.[30] The injunction delayed publication for six months but was lifted when other publications disclosed most of the same information the magazine article had contained. Since the government's chances of ultimately sustaining the injunction in the Supreme Court were slim, it decided to drop its efforts to stop the story.

Of course, most instances of security censorship never reach the lawsuit stage, leaving an enormous number of documents outside the public domain. Federal officials estimated in 1982 that up to 1 million documents are labeled as *classified* annually. Another 16 million are placed beyond easy access because they contain information taken from previously classified documents. Added to these staggering statistics at the federal level are massive numbers of documents withheld by state and local officials.[31]

The main problem with security censorship lies in the determination of what information is truly sensitive and must be protected and what information should remain available to media personnel and the public. The media and, to a lesser degree, Congress have been trying to expand the range of information that is made available for publication. The president and executive agencies, charged with protecting national security, have bent over backward to protect information that might compromise security.

The most graphic illustration of this perennial battle is the *Pentagon Papers* case. Daniel Ellsberg, a former aide to the National Security Council, a high-level executive agency that plans security policy, testified in court that he had become disillusioned about U.S. military activities in Vietnam. He claimed that foreign policy information contained in a study commissioned by the Defense Department about America's gradual entrapment in the Vietnam War had been improperly classified as top secret. Its release, he thought, would turn people against the war. He copied the information surreptitiously and gave it to prominent newspapers for publication. Because the war was still in progress, the executive branch considered this a criminal breach of security and sued Ellsberg and the media that printed the information. In *New York Times Co. v. United States* (1971), the Supreme Court absolved the media, ruling that the government had been overly cautious in classifying the information as top secret.[32] In the Court's view publication did not harm the country. The case brought against Ellsberg for leaking the information was also dismissed because evidence had been collected through illegal means. While the case cleared Ellsberg and the media of the specific charges brought against them, it left the government's contention unchallenged that officials may be prosecuted for jeopardizing national security by disclosing classified information to the press. Accordingly, Samuel Loring Morison, a naval intelligence analyst, was convicted in 1985 on espionage charges for providing a British military magazine with intelligence satellite photographs.[33]

The Supreme Court decision in the *Pentagon Papers* case and subsequent lower court rulings did not end the public controversy. Analysts still disagree about whether the disclosures from the *Pentagon Papers* damaged the foreign interests of the United States. Those who concur with the Court point out that much of the information released had already been available. Dissenters counter that the information had never been compiled in a single document and published in prominent sources such as the *New York Times* and *Washington Post*. They also

refer to the dismay expressed by many European leaders about spot-
lighting events that they had deemed confidential.

Prior to the Nixon years, if a government agency decided that
certain information needed to be kept from the media, the courts
usually went along with the decision. This has obviously changed. Many
people still believe that the decisions to disclose or withhold security-
related information from the media and the public should be made by
the agencies that routinely deal with military and foreign policy security
information, since they are infinitely better qualified to assess matters
of public security than are judges whose training is narrowly legal. Wise
decisions about disclosure of national security information are particularly difficult because both the clamor of the media to obtain access and
the government's contention that the information requires protection
are often self-serving. What is dubbed "the public interest" may be
simply the reporters' interest in furthering their careers, or the publishers' interest in making money, or the government's interest in shielding
itself from embarrassment.

At times, security issues are resolved through informal cooperation
between the government and the media or through self-censorship. For
instance, during the Iranian hostage crisis, six American hostages were
sheltered in the Canadian embassy in Teheran for several weeks.
Prominent news organizations, such as NBC, CBS, *Time, Newsweek,*
and the *New York Times,* were privy to this information. Following
requests from the White House and State Department, they decided to
withhold the news to protect the hostages, even though it meant
foregoing an excellent story. The story surfaced early in 1980, after the
six hostages had been smuggled out of Iran.[34] Similarly, media have
refrained from providing the public with details in a number of
kidnapping incidents when news stories could have jeopardized delicate
negotiations between kidnappers and the would-be rescuers of the
victims.

Executive Privilege. The doctrine of executive privilege is deeply
intertwined with the question of the limits of secrecy. Chief executives
have the right to conceal information that they consider sensitive. This
privilege extends to all of their personal communications to their staffs
about public matters. Prior to the Nixon years the courts usually upheld
executive privilege, but decisions since then suggest that the scope of
the privilege is waning.

Silence by various government departments and agencies also
sharply restricts political news available to the media. Undisclosed
information frequently concerns failures, incidents of malfeasance,
malfunctions, or government waste. Agencies guard this type of news
zealously because disclosure might harm the agency or its key personnel.

Chief executives at all levels of government often issue directives restraining top officials from talking freely to journalists. In March 1983 President Reagan even directed that lie-detector tests be given to check compliance with disclosure rules. In the face of opposition, the directive was later rescinded. Although not usually enforceable, directives that muzzle public officials tend to reduce the flow of information to the press and the public.

Except for the ever-present opportunity to get information through leaks, reporters find it difficult to penetrate the walls of silence erected by publicity-shy agencies. It is far easier to rely on press handouts or publicity releases supplied by the agency or on secondary reports from agency personnel. Handout information usually reflects the sources' sense of what is news rather than the reporters' sense of what is news.[35]

Private Industry Documents

While the problem of government secrecy as a restraint on information collection is formidable, it is small compared with the problem of access to news stories covering the private sector of society. Many enterprises, whose operations affect the lives of millions of Americans as much or more than many government agencies, shroud their operations in secrecy. If General Motors or International Telephone and Telegraph or General Mills wants to exclude reporters from access to information about their business practices, they can do so with impunity. So can drug companies, repair shops, or housing contractors.

The Freedom of Information Act does not cover unpublished records of private businesses, except for the reports made to the government about sales or inventory figures or customer lists. As noted earlier, many of these reports are withheld from the public on the ground that business cannot thrive if its operational data are made available to its competitors.[36] Moreover, the chances that withheld information will be disclosed through leaks are infinitely less in business than in government because suspects in the private sector can be summarily dismissed.

Individual Rights vs. the Public's Right to Know

Thus far we have mainly considered barriers to the free flow of information imposed by the mass media to protect editorial freedom or by government or industry to shield potentially sensitive information. Next we will discuss barriers to circulation of information imposed by individuals or on behalf of individuals for the purpose of protecting the right to privacy, the right to an unprejudiced trial, the right to gather information freely, and the right to a good reputation.

"*Sorry, boys. I was told to keep my big mouth shut.*"

Drawing by Levin; ©1987 The New Yorker Magazine, Inc.

Privacy Protection

How much may the media publish about the private affairs of people in public and private life without infringing on the constitutionally protected right of privacy? How much is excluded from public scrutiny because of privacy rights? The answers depend on the status of the people involved. Private individuals enjoy broad, though shrinking, protections from publicity; people who have become public figures because their lives are of interest to the public or because they are public officials do not.

In general, state and federal courts have been fairly lenient in permitting the media to cover details about the personal affairs of people whose lives have become matters of public record. The right to publish has been upheld more often than the right to privacy. This trend is epitomized by a 1975 Georgia case involving a young woman who had been raped and murdered. To protect its privacy, the family wanted to keep her name out of stories discussing the crime. The news media did not honor the family's request and published gruesome details of the crime, naming the victim. The family sued for invasion of privacy, claiming that there was absolutely no need to disclose the name and that Georgia law prohibited the release of the names of rape victims. The U.S. Supreme Court disagreed and overturned the Georgia law. It held that crime was a matter of public record, making the facts surrounding it publishable, despite protests by victims and their families.[37]

Circumstances may turn private individuals into public figures. This happened to Oliver Sipple, a young man in a crowd of people watching President Gerald R. Ford. Sipple prevented an assassination attempt on the president by grabbing the would-be assassin's gun. Newspeople who interviewed him checked his background and discovered that he was part of San Francisco's homosexual community. Although this had nothing to do with his impromptu action in protecting the president, it was publicized. The disclosure caused Sipple great personal difficulties. He brought suit for invasion of privacy, but the courts denied his claim, saying that he had become an "involuntary public figure" by seizing the gun and had thus forfeited his right to privacy.

Individuals may also lose their right to privacy when they grant interviews to reporters. Once the interview is given, reporters are free to round the story out with observations that were not part of the interview but that the journalists feel are "newsworthy." They are also free to publish those facts that were told to them in confidence except for publishing the name of a source to whom the reporter has promised confidentiality.[38] If reporters, without malice, misrepresent some of the facts, this, too, is tolerated. The rationale is that the public is entitled to a full story, if it gets any story at all, and that reporting should not be unduly inhibited by fears of privacy invasion suits.

Many privacy invasion cases involve unauthorized photographs of people in public life. Jacqueline Kennedy Onassis, the widow of President John F. Kennedy, went to court to sue one particularly obnoxious photographer for taking photographs of her private life. The court ruled that even though she was no longer the first lady, she remained a public figure. Therefore, pictures could be taken and printed without her consent. The court, however, ordered the photographer to stop harassing her.[39]

To strengthen privacy protection, the courts in recent years have permitted subjects of unsolicited investigative reports to use trespass laws to stop the media. An example is the trespassing judgment won by the fashionable restaurant, *Le Mistral,* against CBS in 1978 after reporters had entered the premises and filmed a story showing violations of New York's health code.[40] The courts also have been increasingly willing to protect people against willful infliction of emotional pain by news media. However, the Supreme Court ruled unanimously in 1988, in a case brought by the Rev. Jerry Falwell against *Hustler* magazine publisher Larry Flynt, that the work of satirists and cartoonists enjoyed full First Amendment protection.[41] Falwell's plea for privacy protection and for compensation for emotional injury was denied.

Because relatively few cases of invasion of privacy are taken to the courts for decision, privacy protection rests primarily on news media sensitivity. In recent years, it has not been finely honed. Even mainstream newspapers now feature columns devoted to celebrity gossip, while tabloid papers and television shows of the same genre revel in this type of journalism. When *USA Today* informed former tennis star Arthur Ashe in 1992 that it was investigating rumors that he was a victim of AIDS, Ashe knew that the story was destined to become front page news. Efforts to protect his privacy would be futile. Therefore, he chose to make a public announcement about his illness himself. Many journalists and members of the public condemned *USA Today* for the privacy invasion. But most agreed that in the current news climate it has become impossible to protect newsworthy individuals from the "feeding frenzy" of print and electronic tabloid journalists. Once the proverbial cat is out of the bag, all join the chase, including serious news professionals who do not want to ignore stories that titillate the public's fancy and consequently draw large audiences.[42]

Fair Trial and the Gag Rule

The broad scope of disclosure permitted about most people in public life could be contrasted with the limited scope of disclosure that the courts permit in their own bailiwick in criminal cases. The courts have zealously guarded the right of accused persons to be protected against publicity that might influence judge and jury and harm their case. This has been true even though scientific evidence demonstrating that media publicity actually influences the parties to a trial is scant and somewhat contradictory.[43]

The stern posture of the courts in censoring pretrial publicity is weakening, however. In 1983 two Supreme Court justices refused to block a nationwide television broadcast about a sensational murder case scheduled for trial three weeks later. The trial involved seven white New Orleans policemen accused of the revenge slaying of four black men suspected of participation in the murder of a white police officer. The trial had been moved from New Orleans to Dallas because of prejudicial publicity in New Orleans. In the same vein, a federal court refused in 1983 to prevent television stations from showing tapes of a cocaine transaction incriminating John DeLorean, a well-known automobile maker and jet-set celebrity. DeLorean's attorneys had argued that the pretrial publicity would make it impossible to impanel an impartial jury. In another case the courts ruled that incriminating tapes used in a corruption trial of several members of Congress could be publicly shown, even though some of the defendants had not been tried as yet, and the convicted defendants were appealing the case.[44] When prominent national political figures have asked to have their trials moved out of Washington because of prejudicial pretrial publicity, their requests have almost invariably been refused.[45]

The question of the permissible scope of media coverage of court cases was brought to wide public attention by two murder cases, *Shepherd v. Florida* (1951) and *Sheppard v. Maxwell* (1966).[46] In these cases the Supreme Court held that the defendants, convicted of murder, had not had a fair trial because of widespread media publicity. As Justices Robert H. Jackson and Felix Frankfurter put it in *Shepherd v. Florida,* "The trial was but a legal gesture to register a verdict already dictated by the press and the public opinion [it] generated." The convictions therefore were overturned.

Judges have the right to prohibit the mass media from covering some or all of a court case before and during a trial, even when the public is allowed to attend courtroom sessions. As discussed in Chapter 10, judges may make rules restraining filmed coverage or may bar it completely. No evidence need be brought that the information covered by the gag order would impede a fair trial. Gag orders may extend even to judges' rulings that tell the media to refrain from covering a case. Thus the fact of judicial suppression of information may itself be hidden.

Gag orders interfere with the media's ability to report on the fairness of judicial proceedings. They also run counter to the general reluctance of American courts to condone prior censorship. Nonetheless, the courts have upheld gag laws as a necessary protection for accused persons.

Numerous reporters have gone to jail and paid fines rather than obey gag rules because they felt that the courts were overly protective of the rights of criminal suspects and insufficiently concerned with the public's right to know. A 1976 decision, *Nebraska Press Association v. Stuart,* upholds to a certain degree the reporters' views.[47] In that case the Supreme Court reversed a gag order that had been in effect for several months concerning coverage of a murder trial. The Court declared that careless reporting that interferes with the rights of defendants should be forestalled by judicial maneuvers other than gag laws. For instance, trials can be moved to different jurisdictions if there has been excessive publicity locally. Suits also can be brought against media enterprises or individual reporters who have acted irresponsibly by publicizing testimony from closed sessions of the courts, taking unauthorized pictures, or bribing court personnel to leak trial testimony, for example.

The policy on gag laws is still unclear, however. Some lower courts have failed to comply with Supreme Court directives or have evaded the spirit of decisions. For example, instead of gagging the press, judges have placed gags on all the principals in a case, including the plaintiffs and defendants, their lawyers, and the jury, to prohibit them from talking about the case, particularly to members of the press. In an increasing number of cases, judges have barred access to information by closing courtrooms to all observers during pretrial proceedings as well as trials. This has not, however, stopped legal personnel, including prosecutors, from leaking information to the press when that seems advantageous.

The Supreme Court during the 1980s began to strike down a number of these restrictions, or limit their use by specifying the circumstances under which media access may be denied. In *Richmond Newspapers v. Virginia* (1980), the Court ruled that the public and the press had an almost absolute right to attend criminal trials.[48] In the same vein the justices declared in 1984 that neither newspeople nor the public may be barred from observing jury selection, except in unusual circumstances.[49] The Supreme Court appears to be moving closer to the notion that the public's access to judicial proceedings is part of the First Amendment rights guaranteed by the Constitution.

Shield Laws

Digging into the affairs of public officials and other prominent citizens or exposing the activities of criminals or dissidents often requires winning the confidence of informants with promises to conceal their identity. Newspeople are hampered in their prepublication research if a court or legislative body has the right to know the identity of their sources, to examine unpublished bits of information, and to issue subpoenas for them. If reporters disclose such information, they break their word. Their sources are likely to dry up, whether these sources are public officials who have leaked confidential information or underworld informers.

On the other hand, failure to disclose information may allow criminals to go unpunished and innocent victims to be denied justice. This is why media organizations at times agree to comply with subpoenas fully or partially. For instance, the networks in 1985 agreed to surrender portions of unused film scenes from the hijacking of a TWA airliner that they deemed relevant for the prosecution of the hijackers.[50] In 1992, seven local television stations, the *Los Angeles Times,* and a *New York Times* photographer received federal grand jury subpoenas for unpublished pictures of crimes committed during the Los Angeles riots. They were expected to refuse; however, they were willing to surrender pictures that had already been published.[51]

Shield laws that protect reporters against inquiries have become particularly urgent whenever law enforcement agencies find it difficult to penetrate dissident and deviant groups. At such times these agencies are tempted to use subpoenas to compel testimony from journalists, making them unwitting agents of the government. Shield laws are also needed to protect the physical safety of sources who disclose the activities of organized criminals or terrorists.

The Supreme Court has ruled that newspeople, like ordinary citizens, generally do not have the right to protect their sources in the face of a subpoena. They have no special right to be warned about a court-approved search of their premises to uncover evidence that might reveal their sources and the information provided by them.[52] Nor may they shield records or editorial deliberations from judicial scrutiny if these records are needed to prove deliberate libel. However, if the needed information is available from unshielded sources, the judges have often excused journalists from disclosure.[53]

Recognizing the ill effects of these common law-based compulsory disclosure rules on investigative reporting of crime and corruption, more than half of the states have passed shield laws to protect reporters from forced testimony. Shield laws give journalists most of the rights enjoyed by lawyers, doctors, and clergy to shield their sources' identity and information. Shield laws also may bar searches of news offices to discover leads to crimes. The Privacy Protection Act of 1980 prohibits government authorities at all levels from conducting surprise searches of newsrooms, except in a few, clearly specified situations.[54]

Shield laws usually do not ensure absolute protection. For example, when the right of reporters to withhold the names of their sources clashes with the right of other individuals to conduct a lawsuit involving serious matters (such as gathering evidence for a murder or conspiracy trial or a libel suit), state shield laws and common law protections must yield. In 1978 *New York Times* reporter Myron Farber was fined and jailed for thirty-eight days for disobeying a court order to provide information to a murder defendant. Farber's story about a series of deaths in a New Jersey hospital had led to the trial of the physician charged with murdering the patients. In 1983 the Maryland Supreme Court ruled that Loretta Tofani, a *Washington Post* reporter, must testify about prisoners in a suburban jail who had told her about committing rape and being rape victims. The reporter's articles had won a Pulitzer Prize.[55] Likewise, CBS News was required to give Gen. William Westmoreland the text of its in-house investigation of a 1982 television documentary that had allegedly libeled the general. The documentary on the Vietnam War had charged West-moreland with falsifying enemy troop figures. In his libel suit West-moreland contended that producers of the documentary had deliberately omitted information that exonerated him. The U.S. District Court in New York City rejected the network's contention that its in-house report was protected by First Amendment guarantees; the network had referred in court to findings contained in the report.[56]

Some journalists advocate a federal shield law to protect all newspeople throughout the country. Others, fearing that such a law would provide conditional shielding only, prefer to do without shield laws of any kind; they contend that the First Amendment constitutes an absolute shield. These differences of opinion have taken steam out of the pressure for a federal shield law.[57] Members of the judiciary also deny that shield laws are needed, but for different reasons. In the words of Justice Byron R. White, "From the beginning of our country, the press has operated without constitutional protection for press informants and the press has flourished." Hence absence of shield laws has "not been a serious obstacle to either the development or retention of confidential news sources by the press." [58]

The power of congressional committees to compel testimony is equal to the power of the courts in this regard. A prominent 1992 case involved reporters from *Newsday* and National Public Radio (NPR). They were subpoenaed by a Senate committee created to investigate how charges of sexual harassment, made by a former colleague of then Supreme Court candidate Clarence Thomas, had been leaked to the media. The reporters refused to answer questions about their sources, as predicted, claiming First Amendment protection. The Senate, in line with past behavior in similar cases, decided against contempt citations, thereby avoiding a constitutional confrontation over reporters' right to refuse to name sources when requested to do so by a congressional committee.[59]

Libel Laws

Libel laws are designed to provide redress when a person's reputation has been tarnished unjustly by published information. To win a libel suit, a plaintiff must prove that the defendant's negligence or recklessness led to publishing information that exposed the plaintiff to hatred, ridicule, or contempt. For years libel suits, even when they were lost in court, had a dampening effect on investigative reporting. Then in 1964 that changed substantially for cases involving public officials. An action for libel was brought by the police chief of Montgomery, Alabama. An advertisement in the *New York Times* had charged him with mishandling civil rights demonstrations. The Supreme Court absolved the newspaper, ruling in *New York Times v. Sullivan* that a public official who claims libel must be able to show that the libelous information was published "with knowledge that it was false or with reckless disregard of whether it was false or not." [60]

The "Sullivan rule" has made it very difficult for public officials to bring suit for libelous statements made about them. Malicious intent and extraordinary carelessness are hard to prove, especially since the courts give the media the benefit of the doubt. By the same token, the Sullivan rule has made it much easier for media to publish adverse information about public officials without extensive checking of the accuracy of the information prior to its publication.

Since its 1974 decision in *Gertz v. Robert Welch*, the Supreme Court has applied more restrictive interpretations of the meaning of "public figure." [61] In that case the Court held that a prominent lawyer, whose name had been widely reported in the news, was not a public figure and could therefore sue for libel. A person who had not deliberately sought publicity, the Court ruled, would be deemed a public figure only in exceptional circumstances. What these circumstances are remains unclear. [62] However, even a private figure, suing a news organization for libel, must prove that damaging statements are false if they involve "matters of public concern." [63] Otherwise, the burden of proof that the statements are true rests on the media.

The battle between freedom of the press and the right of individuals to be protected from harmful publicity is full of confusing developments. [64] The courts have pulled back from the position that made individual rights, except the right to a fair trial, largely subordinate. They have done so by distinguishing the rights of private individuals from those of public figures and by construing the category of "public figures" more narrowly. This leaves private individuals with substantial rights to bar the media from publishing potentially libelous or embarrassing facts, so long as those facts are not a matter of public record. Whether libel suits may be brought to challenge expressions of opinions remains controversial after the Supreme Court ruled that opinions could be libelous if proof of their falsity was possible. [65]

By and large, laws and court decisions protecting private individuals have not greatly benefited people in public life. The principle that full publicity for the activities of public officials and institutions is essential has been reaffirmed repeatedly, most recently in the *Hustler v. Falwell* case, which strongly reaffirmed the Sullivan rule. [66] The Supreme Court has even discouraged libel suits by public figures by requiring that such suits be dismissed by the federal courts before trial if the evidence fails to suggest libel with "convincing clarity." [67] The best protection for public figures from unscrupulous exposure by the media are the informal and formal codes of ethics by which most journalists abide most of the time. The increasing number of suits by public figures against media people have also become a damper on careless reporting because these suits are costly in time and money, even when the media are exonerated. By 1983 the investigative television show "60 Minutes" had successfully defended itself in 150 libel actions, but the costs were staggering. Financially weaker programs could not have paid them; neither could they have risked multi-million-dollar judgments against them, should they lose a libel suit.

The Libel Defense Resource Center, which tracks libel law, reported in 1991 that average libel awards in 1989 and 1990 ran just under $4.5 million. That was a tenfold increase over the average figures for the 1987 to 1988 period, when juries often failed to impose heavy fines. The Center estimates that 90 percent of all libel actions are dropped, settled, or dismissed prior to trial. When trials *do* occur, news organizations are the losers in two-thirds of the cases. Individual judgments have run as high as the $58 million awarded in a 1991 case against a Texas broadcast company, but such judgments have been routinely reduced sharply on appeal. Nonetheless, financially weak institutions cannot afford to risk multi-million-dollar judgments against them that would force them out of business.[68]

Other Restrictions on Publication

As discussed in Chapter 1, all governments prohibit the publication of certain information on the grounds that the public interest would be harmed. The United States is no exception. The areas where censorship is most prevalent are national security involving external dangers, national security involving internal dangers, and obscenity. In each category there is general agreement that certain types of information should not be publicized. There is very little agreement, however, about where the line ought to be drawn between permitted and prohibited types of material. We have already discussed the controversy surrounding the release of the *Pentagon Papers* as well as the government's efforts to prohibit publication of a magazine article detailing, on the basis of available but dispersed information, how a hydrogen bomb might be manufactured. Additional examples involving external security will be presented in Chapter 11.

Internal security news primarily entails investigations of allegedly subversive groups and reports on civil disturbances. Several relevant cases are discussed in Chapter 5. Such news also involves media portrayal of asocial behavior that might lead to imitation. Various attempts to limit the portrayal of crime and violence, either in general or on programs to which children have access, are examples. They are discussed in Chapter 7.

Closely related to restraints on the depiction of crime and violence are restraints on publication of indecent and obscene materials and broadcasts that include offensive language or portray sexual matters or human excretion. It is feared that such broadcasts may corrupt members of the audience, particularly children, and lead to imitation of undesirable behavior. Although reports of the Presidential Commission on Obscenity and Pornography have cast doubt on the claim that such broadcasts are socially dangerous, many foes of obscenity and "dirty" words remain unconvinced.

In addition, proponents of obscenity restraints argue that publication of indecent and obscene materials, particularly in visual form, offends community standards and should therefore be prohibited by law. This argument rests on the notion that the public, as represented generally by self-selected spokespersons and organized protest groups, should have the right to prohibit the dissemination of material that offends the sense of propriety of many citizens. Despite the popularity of pornography, as shown by the millions of citizens who read pornographic magazines, go to pornographic movies and stage shows, and rent pornographic videos, laws in many places bar free access to such information. Nationally, the FCC requires that indecent programming be featured only between midnight and 6:00 A.M., when children are unlikely to be watching television. Obscene programming is barred at all times. Indecent material has been defined by the FCC as "material that depicts or describes, in terms patently offensive by contemporary community standards for the broadcast medium, sexual or excretory activities or organs." Obscenity has been defined by the Supreme Court as "something that, taken as a whole, appeals to the prurient interest; that depicts or describes in a patently offensive way sexual conduct, and that lacks serious artistic, political and scientific value." [69] The Supreme Court has repeatedly upheld these types of restrictions.

Another example of protective censorship is the ban since 1971 on cigarette advertising on radio and television. It is designed to protect susceptible individuals from being lured into smoking by seductive advertisements. Pressures for additional areas of protective censorship have been considerable and range from pleas to stop liquor, sugared cereal, and casino gambling advertisements to requests to bar information dealing with abortion or drug addiction. Legislatures and courts have rejected most of them except when advertising on children's programs was involved. But the future is unclear. Some of these matters have become election issues. If candidates have committed themselves to censoring abortion or drug information, for example, they may be compelled to follow through on their promises by working for appropriate laws after being elected.

So-called "hate" broadcasters also remain a gray area in broadcast law. Contrary to the expressed public policy of the nation, many small stations or individual programs routinely attack racial, ethnic, and religious groups. Like broadcasts with obscene language, these attacks violate the sense of propriety of many citizens. Nevertheless, the FCC has been reluctant to withhold licenses from the offending parties because genuine freedom of expression includes "freedom for the thought we hate," as Supreme Court Justice Oliver Wendell Holmes said long ago.

The case of KTTL-FM, a small country-music station in Dodge City, Kansas, illustrates the dilemma. The station has attacked African-Americans, Asians, Roman Catholics, Jews, public officials, the courts, and the Internal Revenue Service. It has suggested hanging public officials, "cleansing the earth" of "black beasts," and preparing militarily for an impending racial Armageddon. But despite protests to the FCC from Kansas lawmakers and members of the public, KTTL-FM's license is unlikely to be revoked as long as no actual violence can be linked to its broadcasts.[70] While formal restraints remain few, informal restraints have mushroomed. Television and radio stations have disciplined or dismissed reporters and commentators who made comments offensive to sensitive groups such as African-Americans, women, and homosexuals.

Summary

In a democratic society citizens have the right and civic duty to inform themselves and to express their views publicly. The press, as the eyes and ears of the public, shares these rights and must be protected against restraints that could interfere with its ability to gather information and disseminate it freely. In this chapter we have seen how these important basic principles have been modified to meet the realities of political life in the United States. Despite legislation such as the Freedom of Information Act of 1966, a great deal of information about government activities remains unpublished. Either it has been classified as secret for security reasons, or it is not released to the public because it could embarrass individuals or lead to undesirable business practices. The public and press also are excluded from many executive sessions of legislatures, grand jury sessions, pretrial proceedings in the courts, and other official meetings if the participants so desire.

Nearly all of these exclusions have been challenged in the courts because they constitute restrictions on the right of access to information that may deserve publication. The courts have ruled that most of them are compatible with constitutional guarantees of free speech and press. They also have ruled, for the most part, that news professionals enjoy neither greater rights of access to information than does the general public, nor, in the absence of shield laws, greater freedom to protect their access to information by refusal to disclose their sources.

The right to publish information is also limited. Here the public is most seriously restricted because newspeople claim the exclusive right to determine what to publicize and what to omit. The power of print media to refuse a forum to most citizens is nearly absolute, aside from social pressures mandating that stories of widely recognized public concern be published. Under current rules and regulations the electronic media must grant equal access to the air to political candidates for the same office. The fairness rule mandates air time for people who hold opposing views on controversial issues that have been aired. Although put to rest for the time being, the rule remains a lively ghost that may well rise again. The right of rebuttal is likely to share the fate of the fairness rule—either death is in the cards, or a reincarnation in the form of congressional legislation.

Even when access to a media forum is ensured, the right to publish is not absolute. News has been suppressed because of public policy considerations, such as the need to safeguard external and internal security and the need to protect the moral standards of the community. The scope of permissible censorship has been the subject of countless inconclusive debates and conflicting decisions by the courts.

The right to publish also conflicts on many occasions with the rights of individuals to enjoy their privacy, to be protected from disclosure of damaging information, true or false, and to be safeguarded from publicity that might interfere with a fair trial. The courts have been the main forum for weighing these conflicting claims, and the scales have tipped erratically from case to case. Two trends stand out from the haze of legal battles: the right to a fair trial generally wins out over the freedom to publish, and private individuals enjoy far greater protection from publicity than do people in public life. Shifting definitions of what turns a private person into a public person have blurred this distinction, however.

When one looks at the massive restraints on the rights of access to information, the rights of access to publication channels, and the right to publish information freely, one may feel deep concern about freedom of information. Is there cause for worry? Taking a bright view, one can point out, as Justice Byron White did in the 1972 *Branzburg* case, that "the press has flourished. The existing constitutional rules have not been a serious obstacle" stopping the press from investigating wrongdoing.[71] The press as watchdog may be chilled by legal restraints, but it is not frozen into inaction. From the perspective of champions of First Amendment rights, that may be small comfort.

Many current political and judicial trends point toward greater restraints and greater public tolerance for restraints, especially when national security is involved. Constant vigilance is the price that will have to be paid to preserve the heritage of freedom of thought and expression.

Notes

1. Quoted in Lucas A. Powe, Jr., *The Fourth Estate and the Constitution: Freedom of the Press in America* (Los Angeles, University of California Press, 1991), 289.
2. Robert F. Copple, "The Dynamics of Expression under the State Constitution," *Journalism Quarterly* 64 (Spring 1987): 106-113.
3. For an analysis of how well these rights have been used, see Doris A. Graber, "Press Freedom and the General Welfare," *Political Science Quarterly* 101 (Summer 1986): 257-275.
4. Justice Potter Stewart in *New York Times v. United States*, 403 U.S. 713 (1971).
5. Jerome Barron, *Freedom of the Press for Whom? The Right of Access to the Mass Media* (Bloomington: Indiana University Press, 1973).
6. 418 U.S. 241 (1974).
7. For a full discussion of the case, see Fred W. Friendly, *The Good Guys, the Bad Guys and the First Amendment: Free Speech vs. Fairness in Broadcasting* (New York: Random House, 1977), 192-198.
8. Phil Gailey, "F.C.C. Lets Broadcasters Hold Political Debates," *New York Times*, November 9, 1983.
9. *Banzhaf v. Federal Communications Commission*, 405 F. 2d 1082 (D.C. Cir. 1968), *cert. denied*, 396 U.S. 842 (1969).
10. 395 U.S. 367 (1969).
11. Friendly, *The Good Guys*, 32-42.
12. Ibid., 199-236.
13. Barron, *Freedom of the Press*, 5.
14. For a discussion of these issues, see Jonathan W. Emord, *Freedom, Technology, and the First Amendment* (San Francisco: Pacific Research Institute for Public Policy, 1991); Hugh Carter Donahue, *The Battle to Control Broadcast News: Who Owns the First Amendment?* (Cambridge, Mass.: MIT Press, 1989).
15. See the March 28, June 27, and August 8, 1987, issues of the *Congressional Quarterly Weekly Report*.
16. "Excerpts from F.C.C. Statement," *New York Times*, August 5, 1987.
17. Patricia Aufderheide, "After the Fairness Doctrine: Controversial Broadcast Programming and the Public Interest," *Journal of Communication* 40 (Summer 1990), 47-72.
18. *Muir v. Alabama Educational Television Commission*, 688 F. Sec. 1033 (1982). First Amendment problems encountered when governments own media are discussed by William Hanks and Lemuel Schofield, "Limitations on the State as Editor in State-Owned Broadcast Stations," *Journalism Quarterly* 63 (Winter 1986): 797-801. The right of public broadcasters to editorialize was upheld in *League of Women Voters v. FCC*, 731 F. 2d 995

(D.C. Cir. 1984).

19. Paula J. Lobo, "First Amendment Implications of Exclusive Broadcast Contracts," *Journalism Quarterly* 60 (Spring 1983): 41-47.

20. "AIDS Panel Delayed News of Treatment," *New York Times,* November 14, 1990.

21. *FCC v. WNCN Listeners Guild,* 450 U.S. 582 (1981).

22. W. Lance Bennett, Lynne A. Gressett, and William Haltom, "Repairing the News: A Case Study of the News Paradigm," *Journal of Communication* 35 (Spring 1985): 50-68.

23. *Zemel v. Rusk,* 381 U.S. 1 (1965). See also Louis A. Day, "Broadcaster Liability for Access Denial," *Journalism Quarterly* 60 (Summer 1983): 246-261.

24. *Branzburg v. Hayes,* 408 U.S. 665, at 684 (1972).

25. See, for instance, *Pell v. Procunier* 417 U.S. 817 (1974); *Saxbe v. Washington Post Co.,* 417 U.S. 843 (1974); and *Houchins v. KQED,* 438 U.S. 1 (1978).

26. These and related cases are discussed more fully in John J. Watkins, "Newsgathering and the First Amendment," *Journalism Quarterly* 53 (Autumn 1976): 406-416. For more recent cases see Donald M. Gillmor, Jerome A. Barron, Todd F. Simon, and Herbert A. Terry, *Mass Communication Law: Cases and Comment,* 5th ed. (St. Paul: West Publishing Company, 1990), chap. 6.

27. The act was an amendment to the 1946 Administrative Procedure Act—5 U.S.C.A. 1002 (1946)—which provided that official records should be open to people who could demonstrate a "need to know" except for "information held confidential for good cause found" (sec. 22). The 1966 amendment stated that disclosure should be the general rule, rather than the exception, with the burden on government to justify the withholding of a document, if challenged in court (5 U.S.C.A. Sec. 552 and Supp. 1, Feb. 1975).

28. Linda Greenhouse, "Agencies Get New Power to Withhold Investigative Reports," *New York Times,* October 29, 1986.

29. Office of Technology Assessment, *Informing the Nation: Federal Information Dissemination in an Electronic Age* (Washington, D.C.: Government Printing Office, 1988), 183-207. State regulations are discussed in Council of State Governments, *A New Age: Electronic Information Systems, State Governments, and the Preservation of the Archival Record* (Washington, D.C.: Council of State Governments, 1991).

30. 283 U.S. 697 (1931). The other exceptions are "requirements of decency" and incitement to violence and forceful overthrow of a legitimate government.

31. Robert Pear, "Information Curb Assailed by Panel," *New York Times,* August 9, 1982.

32. 403 U.S. 713 (1971).

33. Stuart Taylor, Jr., "Federal Judge Rules Espionage Laws Apply to Disclosures to Press," *New York Times,* March 15, 1985; *United States v. Morison,* 844 F. 2d 1057 (4th Cir.), *cert. denied,* 109 S. Ct. 259 (1988).

34. Deirdre Carmody, "Some News Groups Knew of 6 in Hiding," *New York Times,* January 31, 1980. Also see Doris A. Graber, *Public Sector Communication: How Organizations Manage Information* (Washington, D.C.: CQ Press, 1992), 49-61.

35. Judy Van Slyke Turk, "Information Subsidies and Media Content: A Study of Public Relations Influence on the News," *Journalism Monographs* 100 (December 1986): 1-29. For comparative views of government secrecy, see

Itzhak Galnoor, ed., *Government Secrecy in Democracies* (New York: Harper and Row, 1977). Also see Doris A. Graber, *Public Sector Communication: How Organizations Manage Information* (Washington, D.C.: CQ Press, 1992), 49-61.

36. Richard B. Kielbowicz, "The Freedom of Information Act and Government's Corporate Information Files," *Journalism Quarterly* 55 (Autumn 1978): 481-486.
37. *Cox Broadcasting Corp. v. Cohn,* 420 U.S. 469 (1975).
38. *Cohen v. Cowles Media Co.,* No. 90-634 (1991). Also see Linda Greenhouse, "Justices Rule Press Can Be Sued for Divulging a Source's Identity," *New York Times,* June 25, 1991.
39. *Gallella v. Onassis,* 487 F. 2d 986 (1973).
40. *Le Mistral Inc. v. Columbia Broadcasting System,* 402 N.Y.S. 2d 815 (1978).
41. *Hustler v. Falwell,* 108 S. Ct. 876 (1988). See also Robert E. Drechsel, "Mass Media Liability for Intentionally Inflicted Emotional Distress," *Journalism Quarterly* 62 (Spring 1985): 95-99.
42. Alex S. Jones, "News Media Torn Two Ways in Debate on Privacy," *New York Times,* April 30, 1992.
43. Interestingly, the courts maintain the fiction that judges can command jurors to strike improper information presented in court from their memory. Presumably, judges are unable to do the same for media information that jury members might have received outside the courtroom. The issue is examined in Judith M. Buddenbaum et al., "Pretrial Publicity and Juries: A Review of Research," research report 11 (Bloomington: School of Journalism, Indiana University, March 1981).
44. See, for example, *U.S. v. Alexandro,* 675 F. 2d 34, *cert. denied,* 103 S. Ct. 78 (1982); *U.S. v. Jannotti,* 673 F. 2d 578, *cert. denied,* 457 U.S. 1106 (1982); *U.S. v. Myers,* 692 F. 2d 823 (1982); *U.S. v. Williams,* 705 F.2d 603 (1983); and *U.S. v. Kelly,* 707 F. 2d 1460 (1983).
45. A recent example is Michael K. Deaver, a Reaganl White House aide indicted for perjury. In his request for a change of venue, he presented the court with 471 hostile news clips from Washington, D.C., papers. Philip Shenon, "Like Others in the Past, Deaver Says Fair Trial Isn't Possible in Capital," *New York Times,* April 22, 1987.
46. 341 U.S. 50 (1951); and 384 U.S. 333 (1966).
47. 427 U.S. 539 (1976).
48. 448 U.S. 555 (1980). The implications for the right of access are discussed in Roy V. Leeper, "*Richmond Newspapers, Inc. v. Virginia* and the Emerging Right of Access," *Journalism Quarterly* 61 (Autumn 1984): 615-622. Subsequent cases are discussed in Ann L. Plamondon, "Recent Developments in Law of Access," *Journalism Quarterly* 63 (Spring 86): 61-68.
49. Glen Elsasser, "High Court Curbs Secret Jury Selection," *Chicago Tribune,* January 19, 1984. The controversy arose because the Riverside County, California, Superior Court closed jury selection in a rape and murder case. The Press-Enterprise Company of Riverside sued to gain access to the court proceeding and to the relevant transcripts.
50. Alex S. Jones, "CBS Compromises on Subpoena for Videotapes of Hostage Crisis," *New York Times,* July 27, 1985.
51. "Tapes and Photos of Riots Are Focus of Legal Struggle," *New York Times,* May 22, 1992.
52. *Zurcher v. The Stanford Daily,* 436 U.S. 547 (1978).

53. *Anthony Herbert v. Barry Lando and the Columbia Broadcasting System Inc.,* 441 U.S. 153 (1979).
54. The impact of the law is discussed in Tony Atwater, "Newsroom Searches: Is 'Probable Cause' Still in Effect Despite New Law?" *Journalism Quarterly* 60 (Spring 1983): 4-9.
55. *Tofani v. State of Maryland,* 297 Md. 165 (1983).
56. "Westmoreland/CBS Controversy," *Historic Documents of 1983* (Washington, D.C.: Congressional Quarterly, 1984), 401-412. See also *Westmoreland v. CBS, Inc.,* 596 F. Supp. 7170 (S.D.N.Y. 1984).
57. Jonathan Friendly, "Prosecutors Increase Efforts to Make Press Name Sources," *New York Times,* November 26, 1983.
58. *Branzburg v. Hayes, id.* at 699.
59. "Senators Won't Force Reporters to Reveal Thomas Hearing Sources," *Chicago Tribune,* March 26, 1992.
60. 376 U.S. 254, at 279-280 (1964).
61. 418 U.S. 323 (1974).
62. *Time Inc. v. Firestone,* 424 U.S. 448 (1976); *Hutchinson v. Proxmire,* 443 U.S. 111 (1979); *Wolston v. Reader's Digest,* 443 U.S. 157 (1979). Also see Robert L. Hughes, "Rationalizing Libel Law in the Wake of *Gertz:* The Problem and a Proposal," *Journalism Quarterly* 60 (Autumn 1985): 541-542.
63. *Philadelphia Newspapers Inc. v. Hepps,* 106 S. Ct. 1558 (1986).
64. On fact/opinion distinctions, see Harry W. Stonecipher and Don Sneed, "Libel and the Opinion Writer: The Fact-Opinion Distinction," *Journalism Quarterly* 64 (Summer-Autumn 1987): 491-498. The problem of proving damages is discussed in David A. Anderson, "Presumed Harm: An Item for the Unfinished Agenda of *Times v. Sullivan*," *Journalism Quarterly* 62 (Spring 1985): 24-30.
65. Hughes, "Rationalizing Libel Law"; Linda Greenhouse, "Ruling in Libel Case, High Court Says Some Opinion Isn't Protected," *New York Times,* June 22, 1990.
66. *Hustler v. Falwell,* 108 S. Ct. 876 (1988).
67. *Anderson v. Liberty Lobby,* 477 U.S. 242 (1986). Also see *Bose Corporation v. Consumers Union of United States,* 466 U.S. 485 (1984).
68. Alex S. Jones, "Libel Study Finds Juries Penalizing News Media," *New York Times,* September 26, 1991.
69. *Miller v. California,* 413 U.S. 5, at 15 (1973). Quoted in Irvin Molutsky, "F.C.C. Rules on Indecent Programming," *New York Times,* November 25, 1987.
70. Reginald Stuart, "F.C.C. Bars Penalty on Racism on Air," *New York Times,* April 29, 1985.
71. *Branzburg v. Hayes, id.* at 699.

Readings

Carter, T. Barton, Marc A. Franklin, and Jay B. Wright. *The First Amendment and the Fifth Estate: Regulation of Electronic Mass Media.* Mineola, N.Y.: The Foundation Press, 1986.
Chamberlin, Bill F., and Charlene J. Brown, eds. *The First Amendment Reconsidered.* New York: Longman, 1982.

Gillmor, Donald M., Jerome A. Barron, Todd F. Simon, and Herbert A. Terry. *Mass Communication Law: Cases and Comment*, 5th ed. St. Paul: West Publishing Company, 1990.

Kaplar, Richard T., ed. *Beyond the Courtroom: Alternatives for Resolving Press Disputes*. Washington, D.C.: The Media Institute, 1991.

Lewis, Anthony. *Make No Law: The Sullivan Case and the First Amendment*. New York: Random House, 1991.

Lichtenberg, Judith, ed. *Democracy and the Mass Media*. Cambridge, Mass.: Cambridge University Press, 1990.

Powe, Lucas A., Jr. *The Fourth Estate and the Constitution: Freedom of the Press in America*. Los Angeles: University of California Press, 1991.

CHAPTER 4

News Making and
News Reporting Routines

Was it politically relevant news when a tabloid newspaper, distributed in grocery stores, reported in 1992 that presidential candidate Bill Clinton had an extramarital affair? The story swept rapidly through tabloid newspapers and television shows, local television news and radio talk shows, and finally moved to mainstream dailies and prime-time television. By the time the story played itself out, it made headlines in the prestige press as well as on network television news. Was it politically relevant news that President Bush hates broccoli? That story, too, swept the nation's press and became a staple for countless political jokes.

On the other hand, was it politically relevant news that the Bush administration had backed Iraq's President Saddam Hussein, supplying him with arms and deadly chemicals, until he invaded Kuwait? The story was covered by a few elite media, such as the *Los Angeles Times,* the *New York Times,* the *Wall Street Journal, U.S. News and World Report,* and ABC's "Nightline." Except for a few regional newspapers, most of the press ignored it, until late in the presidential campaign.

Why are some events chosen for extensive nationwide coverage while others that seem equally or more politically significant are slighted? What explains the uniformity of story types in America's print and electronic media? What stories should the media cover and how should they cover them?

This chapter will focus on how routine news is usually manufactured and reported. The discussion of news making during various types of crises is left to the next chapter. Speaking about the "manufacture" of news does not mean that journalists concoct the stories they report. It does mean that they select events to cover and interpret from a myriad of events happening in a particular time period. What portions of the raw material they select and how they put it together determines the nature of the finished news product. It is a manufactured creation, therefore, and *not* a natural growth that journalists merely harvest.

There is no magical quality that makes something "news." What is publishable in one setting for one medium is not necessarily appropriate for another. Newsworthiness of individual stories will vary from country to country, audience to audience, and time to time. Thus in 1903, when Orville and Wilbur Wright invited the press to Kitty Hawk, North Carolina, to cover their attempts to fly an airplane, not a single reporter came. Only seven American newspapers considered the first controlled and sustained flight newsworthy enough to print stories about it, and only two papers gave the feat front-page play. Seventy-six years later all facets of aviation fascinated the public. Flocks of reporters came to see a lone pilot, using human foot power, pedal above the English Channel in a lightweight aircraft called the *Gossamer Albatross*. The story received worldwide press and television coverage.

A Profile Sketch of American Journalists

How do the people who produce the news and entertainment programs—reporters, writers, editors, and producers—go about their task? As William Small puts it: "This is the rubbing point, the actual confrontation with what is happening. It is also the point of greatest influence." [1]

What determines journalistic choices and thus shapes the flow of news and entertainment? The question can be answered from three perspectives. *Personality theory* can be used to explain newspeople's professional behavior in terms of personality and social background factors. A second approach is *organization theory*. Because newspeople operate within news production organizations, their behavior can be explained by examining organizational pressures and goals. Lastly, one can seek clues to the influence of media personnel in *role theory*. Depending on the professional role conceptions that media personnel adopt, the stories will vary. For instance, journalists who see themselves as impartial reporters of the news will behave differently from those who see themselves as partisan reformers.

Background and Personality Factors

Factors known to influence occupational performance include social background and traits that are idiosyncratic to particular individuals. Examples of background factors are level of education, race, and sex.

Their precise impact on professional orientations remains a matter of heated scientific and political controversy. Idiosyncratic factors, which include artistic tastes, emotional outlook, and intellectual interests, explain why newspeople who come from similar backgrounds will nonetheless prefer different stories or will give a different emphasis to the same news story or entertainment plot. Personality factors and organizational logic intertwine, with the latter setting the broad boundaries of what is acceptable news.

What are some of the personality and background factors that influence the substance and shape of news? Data collected by G. Cleveland Wilhoit and David H. Weaver for their study *The American Journalist* are helpful in answering this question. Other studies support these findings, which are based on telephone interviews with 1,001 randomly selected newspeople in the United States.[2] The sample was divided into journalists working in "prominent" news organizations— major networks, big city newspapers, and wire service organizations— and journalists working in small towns and relatively little-known news enterprises. Each group was further divided into supervisory (42 percent) and nonsupervisory (58 percent) personnel.

Wilhoit and Weaver found that the social profile of newspeople closely resembled the profile of other professionals in the United States. Ninety-five percent were white, 66 percent were male, 60 percent were Protestants, and 70 percent had graduated from college. Sixty percent had taken some college-level journalism courses. The vast majority (93 percent) had been brought up in a church-going family and claimed to derive their journalistic ethics from their upbringing (72 percent) or from their job environment (88 percent).

In 1982, the year of the survey, only 5 percent of the executives in the prominent media were African-American, as Table 4-1 indicates. At the staff level, African-Americans constituted 3 percent. In the less prominent organizations, 2 percent of the executives and 4 percent of the staffers were African-American, and most of them worked for organizations serving the African-American community. At a time when African-Americans, Hispanics, and Asian-Americans constituted nearly 14 percent of the population, they owned less than 1 percent of radio and television stations. This was true despite federal efforts to increase minority representation on the assumption that a heterogeneous country is best served when media owners and staffs mirror the nation's diversity. If demographically distinct groups are uniquely qualified to assess their own needs, then racial, ethnic, and cultural underrepresentation in the media is undesirable.

Likewise, if balanced presentation of information requires that media organizations have women staffers in proportion to their numbers in the population, the media do not measure up, even though conditions

Table 4-1 Selected Characteristics of Journalists (in percentages)

Characteristic	Prominent organizations		Nonprominent organizations	
	Executives	*Staffers*	*Executives*	*Staffers*
Female	28	23	28	41
African-American	5	3	2	4
College graduate	64	56	50	58
Democrat	33	51	38	40
Republican	9	4	22	20
Independent	58	44	38	39
Other	—	1	2	1
Left orientation [a]	31	33	22	25
Middle roader	57	55	57	59
Right orientation	12	12	21	17

Source: Adapted from G. Cleveland Wilhoit and David H. Weaver, *The American Journalist: A Portrait of U.S. News People and Their Work,* 2d ed. (Bloomington: Indiana University Press, 1991), 12-64.

Note: In prominent organizations, $N = 58$ for executives and 78 for staffers; in nonprominent organizations, $N = 413$ for executives and 450 for staffers.

[a] Designations are self-identifications and include people claiming the orientation or claiming to lean toward it.

have vastly improved in recent years. In the prominent organizations women made up 28 percent of the executives and 23 percent of the staff. In the nonprominent media 28 percent of the executives and 41 percent of the staffers were women. Newspeople are also generally younger, more urbanized, and have greater job mobility than the general population.

What effect do demographic characteristics have on the news product? The evidence is inconclusive. Women, for example, do report more frequently on social issues of special concern to women, but are no more inclined than male reporters to quote females.[3] It also may be debatable whether adequate coverage of the nation's problems requires media organizations that are a microcosm of the larger society. Nevertheless, there appear to be certain connections between the product and the demographic characteristics of the personnel. For example, most general media emphasize established white middle-class groups and values and neglect minorities and poor people and their concerns. They also stress urban rather than rural affairs and supply heavy doses of primarily male-dominated sports. These patterns suggest that news output reflects reporters' backgrounds and interests.[4] An alternative explanation is that the patterns cater to the tastes of the kinds of audiences that advertisers find most attractive.

Like other professionals, newspeople have far more formal education than the general population. In the group working for prominent organizations, 64 percent of the executives and 56 percent of the staffers were college graduates, as were 50 percent of the executives and 58 percent of the staffers in the less prominent organizations. Newspeople without college degrees usually had received no professional training as journalists and so were less likely to have been exposed to social responsibility norms so prevalent on American college campuses. When asked about their professional goals, they were more likely to stress neutral reporting of facts, rather than interpretation and social advocacy. In fact, education appears to be the single most important background characteristic that shapes newspeople's general philosophy of reporting. People with more schooling are likely to be more liberal and have a keener sense of social responsibility.[5]

Only a very small percentage of the working press in prominent news organizations were Republicans. Among executives, 33 percent were Democrats, 58 percent were Independents, and 9 percent were Republicans. Among the staffers, 51 percent were Democrats, 44 percent were Independents, and 4 percent were Republicans. The rest had other affiliations. Comparable figures for the general population were 44 percent Democrats, 30 percent Independents, and 24 percent Republicans.[6] The many who called themselves "Independents" were more likely to identify with Democrats than Republicans.

These data on party affiliations show that owners of prominent media hire Democrats and liberal Independents to operate their media properties although they themselves usually share the Republican leanings of the big business community.[7] The political orientations of the personnel are reflected in the overall tone of stories selected by the prominent media. Economic and social liberalism prevails, as does a preference for an internationalist foreign policy, caution about military intervention, and some suspicion about the ethics of established large institutions, particularly big business and big government. However, in deference to the greater conservatism of media audiences, reporters restrain their liberalism somewhat.[8] Media personnel also treat the major parties fairly in most election campaign coverage. Such even-handedness is encouraged by anticipation of scrutiny and criticism on that score. Media bias has rarely been investigated outside the election context. Hence the extent to which biased reporting is a problem in prominent media is not fully known.[9]

Among the nonprominent media, the patterns of party affiliation and political leanings were far more representative of political patterns throughout the United States. Among the executives, 38 percent were Democrats, 22 percent were Republicans, and 38 percent were Independents. Among the staffers, 40 percent were Democrats, 39 percent were Independents, and 20 percent were Republicans. A circular effect seems to be at work: people in small towns perpetuate their more conservative outlook because their media, taking their cues from the audience, are comparatively conservative. However, the strength of Republican influence is less than it appears on the surface because the majority of Independents lean toward the Democrats, as noted earlier.

Table 4-2 presents the results of a nationwide survey by the *Los Angeles Times* in which newspeople and members of the general public were asked about their political views. While the two groups agreed fairly closely on many issues, journalists were nearly always more liberal when they disagreed. The widest gaps occurred for social issues.

When newspeople were asked about their general political orientations, 22 percent claimed to be left or left-leaning and 18 percent right or right-leaning. Fifty-eight percent saw themselves as middle-of-the-road. Obviously, these political orientations are muted by organizational pressures. In fact, by newspeople's evaluations, 30 percent of the media for which they are working are right or right-leaning, only 12 percent are left or left-leaning, and 57 percent are characterized as middle-of-the-road.[10]

In recent decades journalists as a group, like the general public as a whole, apparently have become more conservative. However, these trends are less noticeable among the leaders of the profession, judging from surveys of media elites at the *New York Times*, the *Washington Post*, the *Wall Street Journal, Time, Newsweek, U.S. News & World Report*, the three major networks, and public television. These media elites, who have a disproportionately large influence on political elites, remain liberals with cosmopolitan, antibourgeois orientations. Fifty-four percent see themselves as left-of-center, compared with 19 percent who lean to the right. In their judgment seven out of every eight of their colleagues lean to the left.[11]

On the idiosyncratic level, a person who enters the journalism profession, compared with personnel in other business enterprises, is generally more idealistic and more humanistic and prefers nonroutine work.[12] Social psychologists have discovered that such people tend to be on the left end of the political spectrum, with a sense of mission about reforming the injustices of society. They are opposed to regimentation and fiercely protective of their personal and professional independence.

Reporters' unique life experiences are also important in shaping their views of the world. It matters what personal contacts they are able to make. Washington-based reporters, for instance, may be able to use friendships with well-connected government officials to get important scoops. But, as a result of close personal ties with these officials, they may become captives of their sources' perspectives on the world.

Table 4-2   Issue Positions of General Public and Journalists
(in percentages)

Issue	Public	Journalists
Pro business	33	27
Pro labor	32	31
Business regulation		
Pro	22	49
Anti	50	41
Government aid to poor		
Pro	83	95
Anti	11	3
Income leveling laws		
Pro	55	50
Anti	23	39
South Africa disinvestment		
Pro	31	62
Anti	27	29
Verified nuclear freeze		
Pro	66	84
Anti	22	13
CIA Nicaraguan contra aid		
Pro	19	17
Anti	44	76
Defense budget		
Raise	38	15
Maintain	51	80
Abortion rights		
Pro	49	82
Anti	44	14
School prayer		
Pro	74	25
Anti	19	67
Affirmative action		
Pro	56	81
Anti	21	14
Death penalty for murder		
Pro	75	47
Anti	17	47
Hiring homosexuals		
Pro	55	89
Anti	31	7
Hand gun controls		
Tighten	50	78
Maintain	41	19

Source: Adapted from William Schneider and I. A. Lewis, "Views on the News," *Public Opinion* 8 (August/September 1985): 7.

Note: $N = 2,992$ for public, 2,703 for newspeople, drawn from 621 newspapers. Figures exclude "neutral" and "don't know" responses.

Organizational Factors

Colleagues and settings strongly influence newspeople. Every news organization has its own internal power structure that develops from the interaction of owners, journalists, news sources, audiences, advertisers, and government authorities. In most news organizations today, the internal power structure is slightly left of middle America, yet predominantly supportive of the basic tenets of the current political and social system.

When asked how much their editors try to censor or influence their reports, two-thirds of the journalists claimed complete freedom. However, when top executives do exercise control, it usually involves politically crucial matters. Journalists in small organizations perceived greater autonomy than their colleagues in bigger enterprises.[13] Although editorial censorship is rare, the possibility exists and serves to tether reporters to organizational norms.

Organizational pressures begin to operate even before the job starts. Most people join news organizations and remain with them only if they share the organization's basic philosophy. To win approval, professional recognition, and advancement, reporters learn very fast which types of stories are acceptable and which are likely to be squelched. They behave accordingly. This is particularly true if morale is high within the organization and if, as is generally the case, newspeople feel that their organization is producing a good product (85 percent do).

Relationships with colleagues are particularly important within the large, prominent news enterprises, where newspeople receive their main social and professional support from coworkers, rather than from the community at large. The opposite holds true in small towns, where newspeople often interact quite freely with community leaders and receive their support.

Which news organizations are regarded most highly by the journalism community? If use of a medium is a gauge of respect, then, as Table 4-3 indicates, *Time* magazine, *Newsweek,* and the *New York Times* rank highest. They captured the attention of one-third to one-half of the journalists. The fourteen most widely used publications included six newspapers and eight magazines. In addition, journalists watch television, but they value it far less highly than they do print media. Fifty-three percent watch the local news, and 34 percent watch the national news regularly during the week.[14] Overall, 17 percent rank the media as doing a very good job, 78 percent give them a fairly good rating, and 4 percent think they do a bad job.[15]

All of the highly rated, influential news organizations give ample coverage to news and usually shy away from sensational treatment. Most of them have headquarters along the northeastern seaboard. This distribution supports the frequently heard claim that American journal-

Table 4-3 Most Frequently Read Newspapers and Magazines
(in percentages)

Publications	Readers	Publications	Readers
Time	52	*Washington Post*	15
Newsweek	48	*Atlantic Monthly*	10
New York Times	33	*New Yorker*	10
Wall Street Journal	25	*National Geographic*	9
U.S. News & World Report	16	*USA Today*	9
Regional/city magazines	16	*Boston Globe*	9
Sports Illustrated	16	*Chicago Tribune*	9

Source: Adapted from G. Cleveland Wilhoit and David H. Weaver, *The American Journalist: A Portrait of U.S. News People and Their Work,* 2d ed.(Bloomington: Indiana University Press, 1991), 34, 37.

Note: N = 994 journalists for newspapers, 939 journalists for magazines.

ism is intellectually dominated by the Eastern press, which accounts for roughly 8 percent of the news profession. These are the "generative" media that produce the news that "derivative" media distribute. These are the media staffed by elite journalists whose social perspectives are left-liberal in contrast to the views characterized as "middle America." [16] The heavy reliance by newspeople throughout the country on these eastern "elite" news sources is one reason why patterns of American news coverage are broadly similar throughout the country. Regardless of regional and local differences that shape social and political views, Americans share most of their news. This provides a basis for nationwide public opinions that bear, to a marked degree, the imprint of the pacesetter media.

Despite the substantial evidence of media influence on American politics, most newspeople refuse to take responsibility for the impact on the public of their choice and cast of news stories. These self-appointed watchdogs of government and other social institutions insist routinely and appropriately that government and business must take responsibility for the intended and unintended consequences of their actions, yet they refuse to do the same even while claiming to subscribe to social responsibility journalism. Instead, journalists commonly argue that journalism is a craft and not a profession. Those doing the crafting, they claim, are little more than conveyors of bits of information created by others for which these others are solely responsible.

Role Models

Although editors and reporters take many cues about story importance and interpretation from the eastern elite media, they shape their basic news policies according to their own views about the role that media should play in society. The effects of the social responsibility role compared with libertarian stances have already been considered (see Chapter 1). News products also vary depending on whether newspeople see themselves largely as objective observers who must present facts and diverse views voiced by others or as interpreters who must supply meanings and evaluations. In the United States and Great Britain, journalists value the role of "objective" reporter. Explicit expressions of reporters' opinions are kept out of news stories and relegated to editorial and feature pages. In France and Germany, by contrast, all news tends to be editorialized.[17] The style is akin to that used by American weekly news magazines like *Time* and *Newsweek.*

Obviously, journalists' perceptions of their proper role shape news and are politically significant. They also often lead to organizational conflict. This was graphically demonstrated when the Australian publisher Rupert Murdoch bought several American publications, including the *New York Post,* the *Village Voice,* the *New West* magazine, and the *New York* magazine. The staffs of these organizations brought suit to stop the sale because they were unhappy about the role model Murdoch had adopted for his other publications—namely, to entertain and shock the public. The courts declined to interfere, saying that the choice of a role model is an editorial function.[18] A number of key staff people then resigned, unwilling to work for a publication that followed a role model they disliked.

Readers who live in large cities or subscribe to out-of-town papers often can select the types of papers they want. They may choose a paper like the *Wall Street Journal,* which tailors its news to the tastes of businesspeople, or like the *New York Times,* which emphasizes broad general coverage. Most people, however, cannot pick and choose news sources representing particular role models so easily. They have only a single print source readily available and a few radio and television stations. They are, therefore, limited to the role models represented by these sources.

Gatekeeping

A small number of journalists make the final decisions about which stories will actually be published or aired. These decision makers are often called "gatekeepers." They include wire service and other reporters who initially choose stories, the editors who assign the reporters and accept or reject what they submit, disc jockeys at radio stations who present five-minute news breaks, and television program executives. On the average newspaper or news weekly fewer than twenty-five people are involved in the final decision of what news is used. On the three major networks the combined editorial personnel responsible for choosing news number less than fifty people.

These few, particularly those who make news choices for nation-wide audiences, wield a tremendous amount of political power because they have the last word in deciding what will be widely available "news." This is why in public opinion polls that rank the influence of various American institutions on public life, the news media routinely rank among the top ten. When pollsters asked a national sample of Americans which telephone call the president should answer first if a topnotch editor, business leader, church figure, and educational leader called simultaneously, most chose the newspaper editor.[19] As we saw in Chapter 1, news stories influence what issues ordinary people as well as political elites will think about. Of course, media gatekeepers are not entirely free in their story choices. Coverage of certain stories, such as wars, assassinations, and airline hijackings, is almost manda-tory. But within the limits set by news conventions, others can be included or omitted at will. On an average night somewhat more than half of the stories on each major television network represent unique choices. The same phenomenon holds for print media, though to a lesser degree.[20]

Those who make news choices also select the sources through whose eyes the public views the world. As Table 4-4 shows, government officials are the main source of the vast majority of political stories reported by the wire services and national and local media. This gives the officials whose views are presented an excellent chance to influence the slant of the news. However, when highly controversial issues are at stake, gatekeepers usually turn to unofficial sources as well.[21] Table 4-4 also shows that private individuals rarely are sources either individually or collectively, as expressed in public opinion polls.[22]

Basing the news on a narrow spectrum of sources can lead to biased reporting. A study of stories dealing with the controversial consequences of marijuana use and the need for laws to protect public health and safety revealed that the views of top scientists specializing in marijuana studies were rarely aired. Reporters gave widest publicity instead to the views of "celebrity" authorities in tangentially related fields and to administrative officials in government agencies such as the National Institute of Mental Health, the Food and Drug Administration, and the Department of Health and Human Services. Consequently, the issue was portrayed almost exclusively from the perspective of health admin-istrators with scant attention to the views of drug-use specialists.[23] Reporters' choices of sources also have led to one-sided presentations in stories about genetic engineering (recombinant DNA) research, the swine-flu vaccination program, and the development of an artificial heart.[24]

Table 4-4 Sources of Front-Page News Stories (in percentages)

Source	*Times/Post* staff stories	Local press staff stories	Wire services staff stories	Total stories
Government	54	48	60	55
U.S.	(32)	(16)	(36)	(31)
State	(5)	(15)	(6)	(7)
Local	(6)	(17)	(5)	(7)
Foreign	(11)	(—)	(13)	(10)
Group-linked person	25	36	19	24
Private person	4	6	4	4
Foreigner	4	—	7	5
Other	12	9	11	11

Source: Adapted from Jane Delano Brown, Carl R. Bybee, Stanley T. Wearden, and Dulcie Murdock Straughan, "Invisible Power: Newspaper News Sources and the Limits of Diversity," *Journalism Quarterly* 64 (Spring 1987), 49. Reprinted by permission.

Note: Based on content analysis of news stories attributed to staff or wire service writers and published in the *New York Times, Washington Post,* and four local papers in North Carolina from 1979 to 1980. $N = 2,363$ for *Times/Post* stories, 804 for local press stories, and 2,048 for wire service stories, for a total of 5,215 stories. "Group-linked" persons are identified as members of a group but are not necessarily official spokespersons for the group.

A study of sources used for stories about welfare reform, consumer issues, the environment, and nuclear energy concluded that journalists favor sources that reflect their own inclinations.

> On welfare reform, liberal sources predominate over conservative ones. On consumer issues they look to Ralph Nader, the public interest movement, and liberal activist groups. On pollution and the environment, they select activist environmental groups and, once again, liberal leaders. On nuclear energy, anti-nuclear sources are the most popular.... Journalists by no means depend exclusively on liberal viewpoints. They cite a mixture of public and private, partisan and nonpartisan, liberal and conservative sources. But the liberal side consistently outweighs the conservative.[25]

Sources who have gained recognition as "experts" through media publicity tend to be used over and over again. Newspeople may neglect other, less publicized sources.

When a variety of media cover the same story, as happens routinely, they often use sources representing different elites. When that happens, the thrust of the story may vary widely even though the underlying facts are the same. For example, when researchers looked at 167 stories about a major stock market crash in 1987, they found that the causes and effects of the crash were assessed in quite diverse fashion by CBS evening news, *Newsweek,* the *New York Times,* and the *Wall Street Journal.* The three print media had relied most heavily on experts from the financial sector, drawing 38, 52, and 65 percent of their sources, respectively, from this sector. Government sources and academics took second and third place, but were used far less frequently. For CBS, government sources came first, followed by business sector and financial sector sources. CBS was also unique in drawing heavily (44 percent) on unnamed sources.[26]

The use of different sources led to disparate appraisals of the meaning of the crash and hence different impressions about needed remedies. In *Newsweek,* the national debt and presidential policies were cited as the chief causes; in the *New York Times,* it was the debt and computerized trading. *Wall Street Journal* sources emphasized computerized trading and the foreign trade deficit. On CBS news, the national debt was the chief villain, with twice the emphasis it had received by other sources. Presidential policies and partisan politics were other important causes. When it came to estimating the effects of the crash, all but the *Wall Street Journal* mentioned improved cooperation between president and Congress as a likely outcome. Beyond that, speculations about probable effects diverged widely, presenting media audiences with clashing images about the country's economic problems.

A few, highly respected national newscasters also are extraordinarily influential in putting their versions of news events on the political agenda. By singling out news events for positive or negative commentary, they may sway public and official opinions. If anchors Peter Jennings, Tom Brokaw, or Dan Rather declare that income tax cuts will benefit the rich, or that an American military presence in the Middle East will risk war, popular support for these policies may plunge.[27] A sixty-second verbal barrage on the evening news or a few embarrassing questions can destroy programs, politicians, and the reputations of major organizations. Political leaders fear this media power, because they often are unable to blunt it or repair the damage.[28]

Because Americans like to view their media as effective guardians of the public interest, the positive consequences of news story choices are usually stressed. Negative or questionable consequences should not be overlooked, however. Peter Braestrup, chief of the Saigon bureau of the *Washington Post* during the Vietnam War, in his book *Big Story* claims that unwise story choices and interpretations about the conduct of the war misled the public and government officials. After an exhaustive study of news reports and commentary about the 1968 Tet offensive of the North Vietnamese, Braestrup concluded that poor story selections led to policies that changed the course of the war, even though the images they created were unrealistic. Walter Cronkite and other commentators had used available information to piece together a picture of defeat for the South Vietnamese and American forces when the information really indicated a defeat for the North Vietnamese.

These erroneous interpretations heightened existing antiwar pressures. They contributed to the collapse of public support for the war, produced a speedup of troop withdrawal, and encouraged President Lyndon B. Johnson's decision to abandon a second-term race.[29] Opinions may differ about the wisdom of the end result, but the great weight that is sometimes given to misleading media interpretations is indisputable.

General Factors in News Selection

As discussed earlier, what becomes news depends, in part, on the *demographics, training, personality, and professional socialization* of news personnel. In the United States this means, by and large, upwardly mobile, well-educated white males whose political views are liberal and who subscribe in ever larger numbers to the tenets of social responsibility journalism (discussed in Chapter 2).

News selection also hinges on the *intraorganizational norms and professional role conceptions* of newspeople and on *pressures of internal and external competition*. Within each news organization reporters and editors compete for time, space, and prominence of position for their stories. News organizations also compete with each other for audience attention, for advertisers, and, in the case of the networks, for affiliates. If one station or network has a very popular program, others often will copy the format and try to place an equally attractive program into a parallel time slot to capture its competitor's audiences and advertisers. Likewise, papers may feel compelled to carry stories simply because another medium in the same market has carried it. Story choices made by the *Washington Post,* the *New York Times,* or *Christian Science Monitor* become models to be followed.

News personnel operate within *the broad political context of their societies* in general and their circulation communities in particular. Most of them have internalized these contexts so that they become their frames of reference. There is "no fundamentally non-ideological, apolitical, non-partisan news gathering and reporting system." [30] If a reporter's political context demands favorable images of racial minorities, news and entertainment will reflect this outlook most of the time. If adverse criticism of minorities is encouraged, the same stories used elsewhere to praise minorities will be used to defame them.[31]

Political pressures also leave their mark. Media personnel depend on political leaders for much of their information and are therefore subject to manipulation by these sources. Politicians and other powerful elites flood the media with self-serving story materials that are often hard to resist. Intensive, frequent contacts and the desire to keep relationships cordial may lead to cozy relationships, which make critical detachment unlikely. For instance, newspeople admittedly were under the spell of Gov. Nelson Rockefeller of New York because he made himself and state political news interesting to reporters and their editors and then to the public. "Not only did he skillfully work to make news ... but he orchestrated it superbly and, whenever he could, tried to accommodate the professional necessities of newswriters." [32] The ability to use the media to political advantage without antagonizing newspeople is the mark of the astute politician. Reporters can rarely resist such pressures for fear of alienating powerful and important news sources.

Economic pressures are even more potent than political pressures in molding news and entertainment. Newspapers and magazines need sufficient income to cover their production costs. Except for those that are subsidized by individual or group sponsors, publications must raise this income from subscription rates, from advertisers, or from a combination of these sources. Most costs for television and radio programming are covered solely by advertising income. Therefore, media offerings must appeal to large numbers of potential customers for the products that advertisers sell. This means that programs and stories must be directed either to general audiences in the prime consumption years of life (roughly twenty-five to forty-five) or to selected special audiences who are key targets for particular advertiser appeals. For instance, toothpaste, laundry detergent, and breakfast cereals are best marketed to the huge nationwide audiences who watch the regular nighttime situation comedies or detective stories; personal computers, fancy foreign sports cars, or raft trips down the Amazon are most likely to find customers among a select few. Advertisers for these latter products are attracted to upscale circulation journals such as *National Geographic* or *Fortune* or to specialized television documentaries.

Because the bulk of programming is directed to the general public, television and radio must maintain a smooth flow of appealing programs throughout the prime evening hours. Many people watch television indiscriminately. As long as the program is unobjectionable, they will remain with the station. In fact, viewers preselect fewer than half of the shows they watch.[33] If boring or controversial programs come on, a sizable part of the audience will defect to another station and remain tuned to it for the rest of the evening. Such considerations deter producers in prime time from mixing serious audience-losing programs with light entertainment. Fears of losing the audience for an entire evening also are major reasons for opposition to expanding the nightly network news to a full hour.

The need to keep audiences watching a particular station even affects the format of news and public service programs. Newscasters are selected for their physical attractiveness. Informal banter is encouraged, and nearly every newscast contains some fascinating bits of trivia or a touching, yet inconsequential human interest story. Complicated stories are avoided for fear of confusing audiences. This is why the story of Bush administration support for Iraq was ignored by most media. However, media people occasionally underestimate the tastes of the public for serious presentations, as shown by the popularity of the televised congressional debates about American involvement in the Persian Gulf war, and by the massive attention given to presidential news conferences and addresses. But these are the exceptions rather than the rule. H. L. Mencken was probably right when he said that "nobody ever went broke by underestimating the public's taste." As one station manager reminded his staff somewhat condescendingly:

> Remember that the vast majority of our viewers hold blue-collar jobs. The vast majority of our viewers never went to college. The vast majority of our viewers have never been on an airplane. The vast majority of our viewers have never seen a copy of the *New York Times*. The vast majority of our viewers do not read the same books and magazines that you read. . . . In fact, many of them never read anything.[34]

Criteria for Choosing Specific Stories

In addition to deciding what, in general, is publishable news, gatekeepers must choose particular news items to include in their mix of offerings. The motto of the *New York Times,* "All the News That's Fit to Print," is an impossible myth; there is far more publishable news available to the paper than it can possibly use. Gatekeepers also must decide how they want to frame each item so that it carries a particular message. For instance, at the height of the Vietnam War, ABC camera crews were ordered to concentrate on bloody battle scenes. This led to a story emphasis on the loss of human lives. Later on the focus shifted to internal corruption in Vietnam, black-marketeering, political opposition, and the treatment of ex-Viet Cong—a change that prepared the home front for withdrawal of American troops from an unworthy battleground.[35]

The criteria newspeople use in story selection relate to audience appeal rather than to the political significance of the story, its educational value, its broad social purposes, or the newspeople's own political views. This holds particularly true for television, where viewer numbers, demographic characteristics, and viewer attitudes are constantly monitored by rating services, such as A.C. Nielsen and the American Research Bureau (ARB). For both radio and television, advertising rates are based on audience size. A 1 percent increase in audience size can mean millions of dollars in additional advertising income. In the same

Houston
Houston Chronicle

Reprinted with permission of C. P. Houston.

way, newspaper advertising rates are based on paid circulation, which is monitored by an independent agency, the Audit Bureau of Circulation. Audiences are rarely asked if they would prefer different programs to existing fare. The fact that they watch or listen to or purchase papers in large numbers is assumed to certify that they like what they get.

The emphasis on audience appeal, and the economic pressures that mandate it, need to be kept in mind when the totality of media output is evaluated. They explain why the amount and kind of coverage of important issues often are not commensurate with their significance in the real world at the time of publication. For instance, a single heinous crime may focus audience attention on crime stories and lead to an upswing in their number and prominence—giving the appearance of a crime wave at a time when crime rates actually may be going down. A crystallizing event, such as the death of a prominent actor from AIDS, may call attention to a longstanding problem that has not changed in substance. By the same token, a noteworthy issue, such as homelessness, that has received a lot of coverage in the past may be dropped from peak attention because the audience is getting bored, even though the significance of the story may be increasing.[36]

A ten-year comparison of media stories with statistics on escalation of the Vietnam War, crime rates, and urban riots revealed that the peak year for riots was 1968; the peak year for riot stories was one year earlier. In 1967 the ratio of riots to riot stories was 4 to 1; in 1968 it was 12 to 1. With riots no longer anything "special," the ratio went to 16 to 1 in 1969 and 65 to 1 in 1970.[37] Similarly, a twelve-year scan of terrorism stories shown on network television revealed "a cumulative pattern of coverage that bears scant relationship to actual trends of terrorism over time."[38] As shown in Table 4-5, the discrepancy between the frequency of a newsworthy event and its coverage is especially well illustrated by crime news reporting. Nineteen percent of all murders occurring in Chicago were reported by the *Chicago Tribune,* compared to three tenths of one percent of assaults. Accordingly, more than 42,000 assaults were covered by a mere 14 stories compared to 180 stories for fewer than 1,000 murders.

Five criteria are used most often for choosing news stories. First, stories must have a *strong impact* on readers or listeners. People want to read about things relevant to their own lives. Stories about health hazards, consumer fraud, or a poor family winning a million-dollar lottery prize influence people more than do unfamiliar happenings with which they cannot identify. To make stories attractive, newspeople commonly present them as anecdotes that show their effect on average people. Inflation news becomes the story of the housewife at the supermarket; foreign competition becomes the story of laid-off workers in a local textile plant. In the process of personalization, the broader political significance of the story is often lost, and the news becomes trivialized.

The second element of newsworthiness is natural or man-made *violence, conflict, disaster,* or *scandal.* Wars, murders, strikes, earthquakes, accidents, or sex scandals involving prominent people—these are the kinds of things that excite audiences. In fact, inexpensive mass newspapers became viable business ventures in the United States only when the publishers of the *New York Sun* discovered in 1833 that papers filled with breezy crime and sex stories far outsold their more staid competitors. Mass sales permitted sharp price reductions and allowed the "penny press" to be born.

People also remember dramatic behavior better than more standard fare. For instance, in 1978 the most widely followed and remembered news event in the United States was the murder of nine hundred members of an American religious sect in Guyana. Ninety-eight percent of the respondents to a Gallup poll knew of the event—a number matched only by those who remembered the attack on Pearl Harbor in 1941 and those who recalled the dropping of atomic bombs on Hiroshima and Nagasaki in 1945.

A third element of newsworthiness is *familiarity.* News is attractive if it pertains to well-known people or involves familiar situations of concern to many. This is why newspeople try to cast unfamiliar

Table 4-5 Police versus Newspaper Crime Reports: Chicago, 1991

Crime	Police reports of Chicago crime		*Tribune* reports of Chicago crime		*Tribune* reports of all crime	
Murder [a]	925	0.3%	180	64.0%	874	69.0%
Sexual assault	3,575	1.1	23	8.2	155	12.2
Assault	42,237	13.1	14	5.0	47	3.7
Theft/Robbery/Burglary	275,101	85.4	65	23.0	190	15.0
Total	321,838	99.9%	282	100.2%	1,266	99.9%

Source: Compiled from police crime reports and newspaper index.

[a] Murder includes attempted murder and manslaughter; sexual assault includes rape; theft includes auto thefts.

situations, like mass famines in Africa, into more familiar stories of individual babies dying from malnutrition. The public's keen interest in celebrities is demonstrated by the amazing amount of detail that people can retain about the powerful and famous. Three decades after the assassination of President John F. Kennedy in 1963, many Americans still remember details of the funeral ceremony, as well as where they were when they heard the news. The sense of personal grief and loss has lingered, bridging the gap between the average person's private and public worlds. People value the feeling of personal intimacy that comes from knowing details of a famous person's life.[39]

The fourth element of newsworthiness, particularly important for newspapers and local television, is that an event must have *proximity,* which means it occurs close to home. This heavy preference for local news rests on the assumption that people are most interested in what happens near them. Local media flourish because local events are their exclusive province, free from competition by national television and national print media. In fact, roughly 75 percent of the space in local media is used for local stories.[40] Because national television news must concentrate on matters of interest to viewers throughout the entire country, it cannot depict events close to everyone's home. The public receives so much news from Washington and a few major metropolitan areas that these cities and their newsmakers have become familiar to the nation. This, in a sense, makes them "local" events in what media analyst Marshall McLuhan has called the "global village" created by television.

Lastly, news should be *timely* and *novel.* It must be something that has just occurred and is out of the ordinary, either in the sense that it does not happen all the time, like the regular departure of airplanes or the daily opening of grocery stores, or in the sense that it is not part of the lives of ordinary persons.

Among these five basic criteria, *conflict, proximity,* and *timeliness* are most important, judging from a survey of television and newspaper editors who were given sixty-four fictitious stories by a team of researchers and then asked which they would use and their reasons for using them.[41] Conspicuously absent from their choice criteria was the story's overall significance. Significance does play a part, however, when a major event is communicated, such as the outcome of a national election, the death of a well-known leader, or a calamitous natural disaster. Nevertheless, most stories are selected and framed primarily to satisfy the five criteria mentioned earlier.

Gathering the News

News organizations establish regular listening posts, or "beats," in those places where events of interest to the public are most likely to occur. In the United States, beats at the centers of government cover political executives, legislative bodies, court systems, and international organizations. Places where deviant behavior is most apt to be reported, such as police stations and hospitals, are monitored. Fluctuations in economic trends are recorded at stock and commodity markets and at institutions designed to check the pulse of the nation's business. Some beats are functionally defined, such as the "health" or "education" beat. Reporters assigned to them generally cover a wider array of institutions on a less regular schedule than is true of the more usual beats.

Stories emanating from the traditional beats at the national level, such as the White House, Congress, the Pentagon, and the Justice Department, have an excellent chance of publication, either because of their intrinsic significance, the prominence of their sources, or because reporters stationed there have filed stories that have cost money and effort to produce. In the *New York Times* or *Washington Post,* for instance, stories from regularly covered beats outnumber other stories two to one and capture the bulk of front-page headlines.[42]

All major media tend to monitor the same places. Consequently, news patterns are stable and uniform throughout the country. On the nightly news the leading story is shared by at least two of the major networks 91 percent of the time. It is featured on the third network in only a slightly less prominent position.[43] As Table 4-6 documents, the media are "rivals in conformity."[44] The table is based on content analysis of two Chicago newspapers and six nightly television newscasts, half of them local to Chicago. It was compiled by analyzing news that appeared on fourteen randomly selected days, spread out over fourteen months and covering each day of the week two times. The table shows the proportionate frequency of mention of the news topics that were covered on the selected dates. It presents striking evidence that the same kinds of stories and story types—although not necessarily identical stories—are reported by all news outlets. When the proportions of various types of news are compared, the similarities are greatest among the members of each of the three types of media. National television patterns show heavier proportionate emphasis on stories about the national government and international news and a proportionate deemphasis of sports news compared to the other groups. The newspapers, with their ability to use more information, devote more space to nonpolitical news. In fact, it is noteworthy that nearly half of the newshole—the space available for news stories, rather than advertising, legal announcements, circulation information, and the like—is devoted to nonpolitical stories. But, though the proportions vary, the array of topics covered is remarkably uniform. This pattern is typical for media systems throughout the country.[45]

Table 4-6 Frequency of Mention of News Topics, July 1990-August 1991 (in percentages)

News topic	Sun Times (6323)	Chicago Tribune (5668)	National TV ABC (172)	National TV CBS (168)	National TV NBC (138)	Local TV ABC (210)	Local TV CBS (287)	Local TV NBC (228)
Government/Politics								
National government	3.7	4.2	22.7	21.4	19.6	7.6	8.7	6.1
Elections	1.0	1.5	.0	2.4	.7	2.8	2.4	2.6
State government	1.2	1.7	1.7	2.4	.7	.5	1.0	.4
Local government	2.1	2.1	.6	.0	.0	4.3	1.7	2.6
International news	5.9	6.8	17.4	20.2	21.7	8.1	4.9	7.0
National affairs news	2.3	2.1	4.6	10.7	11.6	2.4	3.8	6.6
Local affairs news	3.4	3.7	—	—	—	9.0	9.4	7.4
Total	19.6	22.1	47.0	57.1	54.3	34.7	31.9	32.7
Economic issues								
Economy	1.4	1.8	4.0	5.9	5.8	.5	.3	.4
Business	7.7	9.5	2.9	1.8	1.4	2.3	1.0	.9
Labor/Unemployment	1.4	1.3	3.5	.6	.7	.9	.7	.9
Savings and loan	.1	.4	1.2	1.2	2.2	.5	.3	.4
Transportation/Energy	2.2	2.3	2.9	1.2	2.2	1.4	1.4	2.6
Health care	.4	.7	2.9	2.4	.0	.5	1.7	.4
Total	13.2	16.0	17.4	13.1	12.3	6.1	5.4	5.6

Social issues								
Civil rights/Deprived groups	.8	.9	2.3	3.0	2.9	.5	1.4	1.3
Education	1.4	1.5	1.2	1.8	1.4	2.4	.5	.4
Media	.5	.7	.6	1.8	2.2	1.9	1.4	1.3
Religion	.4	.8	1.7	.0	.7	.5	1.4	1.3
Abortion/Contraception	.2	.3	2.9	1.2	.7	.5	1.4	.4
AIDS/Cancer	.7	.5	4.1	3.0	2.2	1.9	1.0	.4
Other health issues	1.3	1.0	2.3	2.4	.7	1.4	3.1	1.7
Disasters/Accidents	1.6	1.3	1.2	4.2	3.6	2.8	4.9	7.4
Environment	1.1	1.0	1.2	1.2	1.4	.5	1.0	.9
Justice system	.9	1.5	5.2	5.4	4.3	2.4	1.9	.8
Individual crime	3.6	4.6	2.9	2.4	1.4	14.7	12.9	6.6
Total	12.5	14.1	25.6	26.4	21.5	29.0	30.9	22.5
Other								
Obituaries	2.1	3.8	—	—	—	—	—	—
Weather	1.5	2.1	1.2	3.0	2.9	6.2	8.2	8.3
Sports	24.5	20.1	7.5	1.2	4.3	21.9	21.2	22.3
Entertainment	26.1	21.8	2.3	.6	2.9	2.4	3.8	9.1
Total	54.2	47.8	11.0	4.8	10.1	30.5	33.2	39.7

Source: Author's research.

News, as media scholar Leon Sigal has put it, is always "the standardized exceptional." [46] Each day's or week's news is like a familiar play with slight changes in the scenes and dialogue and with frequent replacements in the cast of minor players although not of major actors. News is exceptional in the sense that it does not portray ordinary events, like eating breakfast or washing clothes or taking the bus to work. It is standardized in the sense that it deals with the same types of topics in familiar ways and produces standardized patterns of news and entertainment throughout the country. Repeated coverage of the same familiar scenes conveys to the public the feeling that all is going according to expectations and that, even when the news is bad, there is little to worry about. It has all happened before, and people have managed to cope.

News organizations, including the giants in the business, cannot afford to have full teams of reporters and camera crews dispersed across the country. In fact, economic declines have forced them to contract their bases. Even in good times, national networks generally station teams in only half a dozen cities where the equipment, support staff, and news personnel are good. Locations are not selected with an eye to covering all parts of the nation equally well or to providing diverse settings. Chance thus determines which locations receive coverage for routine stories and which are neglected.

Table 4-7 shows the percentage of network news stories devoted to individual American states in broadcasts monitored from July 1990 to June 1991. The table also reports the number of electoral votes to which each state was entitled according to the 1990 census as a rough measure of that state's population and political significance. Coverage of news about the states is extremely uneven. Twenty-four states were covered by fewer than twenty-five stories annually, with Arizona, Delaware, Hawaii, Idaho, New Mexico, South Dakota, West Virginia, and Wyoming receiving fewer than ten stories during that time. Such sparse coverage denies their news and their problems a national audience. Overall, the thirty-six states covered by fewer than fifty stories annually represent 48 percent of the country in electoral votes, but receive only 29 percent of the state news coverage. At the other end of the spectrum, California, Florida, Illinois, New York, Texas, and the District of Columbia combined received slightly more coverage than the thirty-six lowest ranking states. They represent only 30 percent of the electoral vote.

Ninety percent of picture coverage comes from the cities in which camera crews are regularly stationed—Washington, D.C. (where 50 percent of all news originates), and usually New York, Cleveland, Boston, Chicago, and Los Angeles.[47] Of course, special events will be covered anywhere in the country. Every network reports presidential

Table 4-7 Network Coverage of State News, July 1990-June 1991

Annual number of stories	States		Percentage of mentions	Percentage of electoral vote
2-23	Alabama Arizona Connecticut Delaware Hawaii Idaho Kansas Kentucky Mississippi Montana North Dakota Nebraska	New Hampshire New Mexico Nevada Oklahoma Oregon Rhode Island South Carolina South Dakota Utah Vermont West Virginia Wyoming	12.5	24.0
25-48	Alaska Arkansas Iowa Indiana Maryland Maine	Minnesota Missouri New Jersey Pennsylvania Tennessee Wisconsin	16.5	24.0
56-73	Colorado Georgia Louisiana Massachusetts Michigan	North Carolina Ohio Virginia Washington	22.5	22.5
100-133	D.C. Illinois	Texas	13.0	10.5
229-458	California Florida	New York	35.5	19.5

Source: Data compiled for the author by Laurent Pernot from the Vanderbilt Television News Archive Index.

Note: $N = 2,607$ stories. The electoral vote is a surrogate for population figures.

nominating conventions, wherever they are held, and routinely follows presidential travels, whether the destination is tiny Plains, Georgia, former president Jimmy Carter's home town, or the Great Wall of China. In 1990 more than 250 reporters journeyed to tiny New Madrid, Missouri, and stayed for nearly a week when a climatologist predicted that a major earthquake was imminent. The quake never happened. Aside from a few exceptions, events in remote sites are most likely to be covered if they involve prominent people and are scheduled in advance so that plans can be made to have media crews available.

Prior planning is also important for more accessible events. Time is needed to allocate camera crews, move them into position, and process and edit pictures. The necessity of planning ahead leads to an emphasis on the predictable, such as formal visits by dignitaries, legislative hearings, or executive press conferences. The news output reflects this preference for formally scheduled events. The development of portable camera equipment producing videotapes that can be broadcast with little further processing has greatly eased this problem. "Spot news" can now be filmed and broadcast rapidly. This is only one example of the profound impact of technological developments on the content of the news.

News Production Constraints

Many news selection criteria reflect the need to process news rapidly and to publish it quickly. Time pressures explain the emphasis on pseudo-events—events created for easy reporting by the media or for the media. Pseudo-events constitute almost 70 percent of all television news stories.[48] For example, politicians frequently plan pictorially attractive happenings, like bridge dedications or county fair visits, to accommodate newspaper or broadcast deadlines. When newspeople need a quick story about a revolution in Central America or youth gang violence, they arrange interviews with familiar leaders, whose remarks, knowledgeable or not, then instantly become *the* Central America or *the* youth gang story.

Once stories reach media news offices, selections must be made extremely rapidly. Ben Bagdikian, a former *Washington Post* editor who studied gatekeeping at eight newspapers, found that stories usually are sifted and chosen on the spot.[49] They are not assembled and carefully balanced with an eye to the overall effects. The typical newspaper gatekeeper is able to scan and discard individual stories in one or two seconds. At such speeds, judgments are almost instantaneous. There is no time to reflect or to weigh the merits of one story over another. Stories are judged more by how they balance previously selected stories than by their intrinsic importance. If the gatekeeper has ideological preferences, these are served instinctively, if at all, rather than deliberately. Ordinarily, stories left over at the end of the day will not be used on the next day because newer stories will have replaced them. Accordingly, a late-breaking story, unless it is very unusual or significant, has little chance for publication. West Coast afternoon stories are frequent casualties because they generally happen too late to be incorporated into the network evening news, which is run on an East Coast schedule.

Only 2.5 percent of the stories in Bagdikian's study were rejected because the editor did not care for the substance of the story or objected to its ideological slant. Twenty-six percent were rejected because of lack of space. The remaining 71.5 percent were rejected because they were judged to lack some or all of the elements of newsworthiness discussed earlier. The published newspaper usually contains the same proportions of different types of news as the original pool from which the stories were selected.[50] Rejection rates varied for different types of stories. Overall, nearly all wire service news, human interest stories, and crime news were rejected, along with more than two-thirds of farm news and science news. Even though much of the human interest information was rejected, it still constituted the largest single news category—23 percent of total news. By contrast, science news took 5 percent of total space and farm stories 6 percent.[51]

Public relations managers know the deadlines of important publications, such as the *New York Times, Wall Street Journal, Time, Newsweek,* and network television news. They schedule events and news releases to arrive in gatekeepers' offices precisely when needed and in appropriate formats such as computer diskettes, electronic mail, or video-cassettes. Public relations firms distribute thousands of video releases annually. If they are attractively presented and meet newsworthiness criteria, journalists find it hard to resist using them. This is especially true for smaller publications that lack adequate resources to produce their own stories. They relish receiving information subsidies.[52] News providers, eager to gain publicity for their causes, thus can influence the news production process. If news sources want to stifle publicity, they can announce the news just past the deadlines, preferably on weekends when few newscasts are scheduled. Powerful elites in the public and private sector make ample use of these opportunities. Even though the bulk of public relations releases are discarded, a substantial portion of news stories is based on them, usually without identifying the source.

Publications with less frequent deadlines, such as weekly news magazines, have a lot more time to decide what to publish. News magazine staffs also have more resources than most daily papers to dig out background information and present stories in a context that helps readers to evaluate them. These magazines are ideal for people who want quick, interpretive news that concentrates on a limited number of events.

Television news staffs have even less time than newspapers to investigate most stories and far less time to provide background and interpretation. When background or investigative stories do appear on television, they frequently originate in the print media. The problem of insufficient time pertains not only to preparing stories but also to presenting them. The average news story on television and radio takes about a minute, just enough time to announce that an event has taken place and present a fact or two about it. Complex stories may have to be scratched entirely if they cannot be drastically condensed.

Print media have space problems as well, but they are less severe than time constraints faced by electronic media. The average newspaper reserves 55 percent of its space for advertising. Out of its 45 percent newshole, generally 27 percent goes for straight news stories, the remainder for features of various types. Some papers reserve a standardized amount of space for news; others expand or contract the newshole depending on the flow of news and advertising. But whether the paper is a slim eight-page version or five to ten times that size, there is rarely enough space to cover stories as fully as reporters and editors would like.[53]

Besides the need to condense a news story into a brief capsule, television reporters also want stories with visual appeal. Unfortunately, what is visually appealing may not be important. For instance, during political campaigns, motorcades, rallies, hecklers, and cheering crowds make good pictures. Candidates delivering speeches are visually dull by comparison. Television cameras therefore concentrate on the colorful scenes rather than on the speechmaker. If these happenings are flashed on the screen in competition with the speech, they often distract from what the candidate is saying. Events that make dull pictures may have to be omitted. Racial violence in South Africa, for example, disappeared from television news after the government had prohibited picture-taking.

Because picture production is expensive for television as well as for print, picture stories selected early are likely to be kept even if more important stories break later. Financial considerations, as well as personnel reasons, favor information originated by the staff. News organizations prefer stories by employees already on their payroll to wire service stories by unknown reporters or stories from outside sources for which additional fees must be paid. News executives also have personal relationships with their own staffs and do not want to disappoint them by rejecting their stories.

Effects of Gatekeeping

The gatekeeping influences that have been discussed give a distinctive character to the American news product. There are many exceptions, of course, when one looks at individual programs or stories. There are also noticeable differences in emphasis among the conservative rural press, more moderate papers in small- and middle-sized towns, and the liberal press in major metropolitan centers. For instance, a study of the women's page/lifestyle section of American daily newspapers showed that news about the women's movement and women's careers constituted 20 percent of the coverage in this section in rural papers and nearly double that amount in papers in metropolitan areas.[54] Despite these variations, several shared attributes of American news stand out. They will be discussed under four headings: people in the news, action in the news, info-tainment news, and support for the establishment.[55]

People in the News

The gatekeeping process winnows the group of newsworthy people to a very small cadre of familiar and unfamiliar figures. Herbert Gans's study of news magazines and network television news reported in *Deciding What's News* showed that familiar people appear in three out of every four news stories. Most are political figures. Fewer than fifty politicians are in the news regularly. The list is headed by the *incumbent president*. Other people receive coverage primarily for unusual or remarkable activities, but incumbent presidents are covered regardless of what they do. News about *leading presidential candidates* ranks next; in presidential election years it often outnumbers stories about the president.[56]

A third well-covered group consists of *major federal officials,* such as political leaders in the House and Senate, the heads of major congressional committees, and cabinet members in active departments. In the post-Watergate period major White House staff members are part of the circle. So are former officials who are asked to comment on the current scene. The Supreme Court is in the news only intermittently, generally when important decisions are announced. Agency heads rarely make the news except when they announce new policies or feud with the president. Some people, however, are regularly in the news regardless of their current political status merely because their names are household words. Members of the Kennedy clan and a host of "experts" like Milton Friedman or Henry Kissinger are prime examples.

Below the federal level, the activities of *governors and mayors from large states and cities* are newsworthy if they involve major public policy issues or if the incumbent is unusual because of race, sex, or prior newsworthy activities. *Notorious individuals* also receive frequent news attention if their deeds have involved well-known people. Presidential assassins, mass murderers, or members of extremist political groups fall into this category. Ample coverage also goes to targets of congressional investigations and politicians indicted for wrongdoing in office.

Among the many powerful people rarely covered in the news are economic leaders (such as the heads of large corporations), financiers, and leaders of organized business (such as the National Association of

Manufacturers or the U.S. Chamber of Commerce). A few colorful labor leaders, such as George Meany and James Hoffa, have been news figures, but this was probably due more to their personalities than to their jobs. Important military leaders also remain obscure unless they conduct major military operations, such as General Norman Schwarzkopf in the Persian Gulf war in 1991. Political party leaders surface during elections but remain in the shadows at other times. Political activists, such as civil rights leaders or the heads of minority parties, and consumer activists, such as Ralph Nader, come and go from the news scene, depending on the amount of visible conflict they are able to produce. The same holds true for the heads of voluntary associations, such as leaders of antiabortion groups or churches.

Most people never make the news because their activities are not unusual enough to command media attention. Ordinary people have their best chance for publicity if they protest or riot or strike, particularly against the government. The next best chance goes to victims of disasters, personal tragedy, and crime, and to the actors who brought about their plight. The grisly nature of crimes, disasters, or other human tragedies, rather than the identity of the people involved, determines their newsworthiness. Ordinary people also make the news if their lifestyles or social activities become highly unusual or if their behavior diverges greatly from the norm for persons of their age, sex, and status. Finally, ordinary people make the news in large numbers as nameless members of groups whose statistical profile is reported or whose opinions have been tapped through polls or elections.

Action in the News

The range of activities reported in the news is quite limited— conflicts and disagreements among government officials (particularly friction between the president and Congress about economic or foreign policies), violent and nonviolent protest (much of it about government activities), crime, scandals and investigations, and impending or actual disasters. When the nation is involved in war, a large number of war stories are reported.

Government policies also provide frequent story material. These stories generally report policy decision rather than policy execution. Government personnel changes, including campaigns for office, are another news focus. Finally, two aspects of the ever-changing societal scene receive substantial coverage from time to time: major national events, like inaugurations or moon landings, and important social, cultural, or technological developments, like the Olympics or advances in the fight against cancer.

Info-tainment News

The criteria for newsworthiness and the constraints on news production shape American news and its impact, regardless of the particular subject under discussion. Accordingly, American news stresses novel and entertaining events, familiar people and situations, and conflict and violence. While events are covered, the underlying causes and likely consequences and the major issues involved are ordinarily neglected.

Novelty and Excitement. The demand for dramatic stories often means that sensational and novel occurrences drown out news of more lasting significance. For instance, eight times as much space and time are devoted to sports news as to news about local community problems such as school finance or housing.[57] Dramatic events, such as airline hijackings or serial murders, preempt more consequential happenings. Preoccupation with a single striking event, such as the stock market crash of October 19, 1987, can shortchange coverage of other news, such as a punitive American airstrike against Iranian targets. Speculations about a religious broadcaster's strong prospects in the 1988 Iowa presidential caucuses drowned out a Soviet leader's announcement of plans to withdraw from the long and bloody Afghanistan war.

The emphasis on excitement also leads to stress on trivial aspects of serious stories. As noted earlier, complex issues are presented as simple human interest dramas. Inflation is likely to become a story about John and Jane Doe, working-class homeowners, who are struggling to pay their mortgage. Such personalized stories do not explain the larger issues involved in inflation. But, judging from attention patterns, they are far more likely to be noticed than learned discussions by economic experts.

The search for novelty and entertainment also produces news that focuses on the present and ignores the past. The here and now is what counts most. This leads to fragmented and discontinuous news. It is aired as it is received, so that the background needed to place a story into its context is often missing. Clarifications are usually buried in the back pages. On television, snippets of news may be presented together to drive home an easily understandable theme, such as "Washington is in a mess" or "the inner city is decaying." The theme may come through, but the individual news item is blurred.

Fragmentation makes it difficult for audiences to piece together a coherent narrative of events. More background and interpretation would help, but it would also increase the chance for subjective interpretation by news commentators. A few papers, such as the *Christian Science Monitor,* and a few news programs, such as the

McNeil/Lehrer News Hour, cover fewer stories and present them in more detail. People who carefully read *Monitor* stories or watch the McNeil/Lehrer news acquire a better background for understanding social issues, but they miss out on other news for which there is no space. They may also get skewed information if newspeople misinterpret the significance of complex events.

Familiarity and Similarity. The demand for stories about familiar people and events close to home produces circular effects. Familiar people and situations are covered minutely, which makes them even more familiar and therefore even more worthy of publicity. The reverse is also true. During the 1992 presidential election campaign, Gov. Mario Cuomo of New York, whose rousing oratory had made news during the 1984 Democratic National Convention, became a potential candidate in many people's minds even though he never entered the race officially. Meanwhile, official entrants, such as Democrats Bob Kerrey and Tom Harkin, received less media attention and remained unfamiliar. They were forced to abandon the quest.

Familiar people may become objects of prying curiosity. The details of their private lives may take up an inordinately large amount of time and space in the mass media. The marital trials and tribulations of even distant political figures, such as Princess Diana, wife of the heir to the British throne, may command front-page coverage for extended time periods. Tabloids and serious media alike cover such stories at length. Only rarely do they focus on the potentially significant political consequences that might ensue, such as a change in the British system of governance away from its aristocratic roots to a more populist form of government.

Another significant consequence of the criteria of newsworthiness is that American news is very parochial compared with news in other countries. This neglect of news about foreign people and cultures leaves Americans deficient in their understanding of international affairs, a subject explored more fully in Chapter 11. Again, the pattern is circular. For instance, if events in Peru are rarely covered, stories about Peru will require a lot more background to make sense to Americans. This may take more time and space than the media are willing to give to any story, except during a crisis. Therefore, foreign coverage in American media is usually about people to whom Americans feel culturally close and whose policies are somewhat familiar, like the English, the Canadians, and people of Northern European countries. Foreign news concentrates on situations that are easy to report, which often means violent events like revolutions, major disasters, and the like. This type of coverage conveys the faulty impression that most foreign countries are always in serious disarray.

Conflict and Violence. The heavy news emphasis on conflict and bad news, which is most prevalent in big city media, has three major consequences.[58] The first and perhaps most far-reaching consequence is the dangerous distortion of reality that emphasis on negative news events may create. Crime coverage provides examples. Media stories rarely mention that many neighborhoods are relatively free of crime. Instead they convey the impression to many people that the whole city, and particularly inner city areas, are dangerous jungles. This impression may become a self-fulfilling prophecy. In the wake of crime publicity, many people avoid the inner city. They even shun comparatively safe neighborhoods after a single, highly publicized crime. The empty streets then make crime more likely.

Studies of people's perceptions of the incidence of crime and the actual chances that they will be attacked indicate that their fears are geared to media realities. In the world of television drama, the average character has a 30 to 64 percent chance of being involved in violence; in the real world the average person's chance of becoming a crime victim is a small fraction of that number.[59] In the same way, heavy media emphasis on air crashes and scant coverage of automobile accidents have left the public with distorted notions of the relative dangers of these modes of transportation.

A second consequence is that emphasis on conflict may cause some people to believe that violence is an acceptable way to settle disputes. Even when exposure of the conflict ultimately promotes its resolution, highlighting a violent process often makes it worse.[60] The media usually dramatize and oversimplify conflict, picturing it as a confrontation between two clearly defined sides. It is the hawks against the doves in war, the victors or losers in a legislative battle, the Communists versus anti-Communists in a struggle abroad. Even when a situation is not actually confrontational, the media may present it as a feud or a fight, making agreement more difficult.

Average people, when presented with clashing claims, often feel confused and find it extremely difficult to determine the truth. They have neither the facts nor the time to explore the issues. They are also left with the disquieting sense that conflict and turmoil reign nearly everywhere. This impression is likely to affect people's feelings toward society in general. They may contract "videomalaise," characterized by lack of trust, cynicism, and fear.[61] Many social scientists believe that such feelings undermine support for government, destroy faith in leaders, produce political apathy, and generally sap the vigor of the democratic process.

Finally, the popularity of violence stories has encouraged groups who seek media coverage to behave violently or sensationally to enhance their chances for publicity. One example comes from a lengthy strike by a union of Chicano workers against a Texas furniture company. During the first year, the nonviolent strike received very little publicity. To attract media coverage the leaders decided to stage noisy marches to the Capitol on the first and second anniversaries of the strike. Moderate language in appeals to the company and city authorities was replaced by fighting words. City councilors were called "rednecks" and challenged to stop the union's marches. These inflammatory accusations created a confrontation, brought city police to the scene, and heightened tensions. Celebrities, including Sens. Edmund Muskie of Maine and Birch Bayh of Indiana and farm labor leader Cesar Chavez, were invited to enter the fray. These maneuvers broke the year-long dearth of media coverage. No longer peaceful, the strike finally received ample publicity. In turn, this created sufficient pressure to bring about a settlement.[62]

A taste for conflict is not the same as a taste for controversy, however. Fear of offending members of the mass audience, wire service subscribers, or affiliated station managers often keeps stories dealing with controversial subjects like abortion or corruption in the church out of the media, especially network television. If those stories are reported, the treatment is ordinarily bland, carefully hedged, and rarely provocative. In fact, the world that television presents to the viewer generally lags behind the real world in its recognition of controversial social changes. The civil rights struggle, women's fight for equality, and changing sexual mores were widespread long before they became common on the television screen or received serious attention in the print media. Compared with television, newspapers can afford to be more daring because normally there is no other daily paper in the same market. Moreover, the nature of the medium makes it easier for the audience to ignore stories they find offensive or distasteful.

Neglect of Major Societal Problems. Despite the ascendancy of social responsibility journalism, the constraints of news production still force the media to neglect serious societal problems, such as alcoholism, truancy, environmental pollution, and care of the elderly and disabled. The pattern changes after a dramatic event, such as a rash of deaths in nursing homes or a big welfare fraud case. If a reporter investigates and finds that six elderly people starved to death because of neglect, the spotlighted incident may then lead to a series of reports on food in retirement homes. The shocking deaths provide the element of novelty. After that novelty has worn off, interest dims and media attention flags, even if the problem remains unsolved. One commentator calls it "the Weekend Yawn Rule." When the 1992 Los Angeles riots raised the racism issue, 80 percent of the audience was likely to tune out following a weekend of saturation analytical coverage. When audience boredom sets in, media coverage evaporates.[63]

Another reason why social problems are neglected is that most media staffs are inadequately trained to cover them. Proper appraisal of the administration of nursing homes or prisons or pollution control programs requires technical knowledge. Specialized reporters with expertise in areas such as urban affairs, science, or finance are available, as yet, only in large news organizations. Moreover, a science reporter can hardly be expected to be an expert in all fields of science. Nor can a reporter skilled in urban problems be expected simultaneously to master the intricacies of a major city's budget, its transportation system, and its services to juveniles. Because most news organizations throughout the country lack the trained staffs needed to discuss major social problems constructively, politicians and all kinds of "experts" can easily challenge the merits of unpalatable media stories.

Judging from media use patterns, most of the public is not very interested in the intricacies of major societal problems. For those who are interested and might be in a position to find solutions, lack of adequate media coverage makes it more difficult to rouse public support and become newsworthy in the process.

Support for the Establishment

The gatekeeping process also yields news that basically supports political and social institutions in America. Although the media regularly expose the misbehavior and inefficiencies of government officials, and routinely disparage politicians, for the most part they display a favorable attitude toward political leaders and the American political system. Misconduct and poor policies are treated as deviations from the norms, thereby implicitly reaffirming the merit of prevailing norms. Assumptions that underscore the legitimacy of the current political system are routinely embedded in news stories. For instance, when police protect a factory from violence by workers, it is assumed that they are the legitimate guardians of public order engaged in an appropriate government activity. The possibility that workers should own the factories and have a right to wrest them from the control of capitalists is never raised. Similarly, stories discussing the plight of homeless children tacitly assume that they ought to be living in conventional family units. The fact that other arrangements might be preferable is largely ignored.[64]

American political symbols and rituals, such as the presidency, the courts, elections, and patriotic celebrations, are treated with a high degree of respect by the media, enhancing their legitimacy. By contrast, news stories cast a negative light on anti-establishment behavior, such as protest demonstrations that disrupt normal activities, inflammatory speeches by militants, or looting during a riot. Obscenity and profanity in public places usually are edited out of news events. When they are featured, they generate floods of complaints about disrespect, prying, and poor taste. This puts dampers on such exposés, at least temporarily.

Explicit and implicit support for the established system, as well as sugar-coating of political reality, sometimes help and sometimes hurt the public interest. They hurt if faults in the established system and prevailing political ideologies are allowed to persist when publicity might lead to correction. The fear of publicity can also have a salutary effect on errant public figures. There are, however, situations in which shielding the shortcomings of the political system and even individual misconduct may be helpful. For instance, at times of national or international crisis, when the nation's prestige is an important political asset, detrimental stories can severely weaken the country. Similarly, the ability of elected leaders to govern effectively can be seriously damaged by disclosures of flaws in their personal lives, such as extra-marital ventures.

Generalized support for the establishment and the status quo is not unique to the media, of course.[65] Most institutions within any particular political system go along with it if they wish to prosper. People on their staffs have been socialized to believe in the merits of their political structures. Moreover, financial concerns make it essential for the media to cater to advertisers and audiences who firmly support the American political system. Staff members whose personal ideologies differ usually conform with established norms to avoid conflict with their bosses, advertisers, or affiliated stations. People are socialized throughout life to support their country and its policies. They want to believe that their government is competent, honest, and working hard to solve the nation's major problems. They often resent exposés that call into question this comfortable sense of security. Media support for the establishment thus helps to maintain respect for it and perpetuate it.[66]

Establishment support is further strengthened by the media's reliance on government information and press releases. As pointed out earlier, in the United States the bulk of news, particularly news pertaining to activities beyond the local community, comes from officials and agencies of the government.[67] Official viewpoints are likely to be particularly dominant when reporters must preserve access to their special beats, like the Pentagon or Justice Department, or when story production requires government assistance in collecting or gaining access to data. For instance, when military personnel are needed to transport correspondents to war zones, or when film producers want demonstrations of moon-flight research, the resulting stories are apt to support official views.[68]

Government officials and agencies are also used routinely to verify information. Reporters generally equate official position and rank of sources with accuracy. The higher the official level and rank the better. The assumption that government sources, such as police departments, or Department of Agriculture spokespersons, or presidential press aides, are reliable is, of course, debatable, especially since the particular thrust given to a story may put agencies into a good or bad light. Many private groups have complained that nearly exclusive reliance on government sources deprives them of the chance to publicize their own, more accurate versions of stories and that it results in one-sided reporting, tilted toward support of the establishment.

Appraising the News-Making Process

Do newspeople do a good job in selecting the types of news and entertainment categories they cover? Do they allot appropriate amounts of time and space to each of these categories? Do they fill them with good individual stories? The answers depend on the standards that the analyst is applying. If one contends that news can and should be a mirror of society, faithfully reproducing a miniature version of life, the news-making process leaves much to be desired. With their emphasis on the exceptional rather than the ordinary, on a few regular beats rather than a wide range of news sources, and on conflict and bad news rather than the ordinariness of daily life, the media picture a world that is far from reality. Reality becomes further distorted because the process of shaping news events into interesting, cohesive stories often gives these events totally new meanings and significance. This is why critics claim that the news creates reality rather than reports it.[69]

If one adopts the classical albeit debatable American notion that the media should be the eyes and ears of intelligent and aware citizens who are interested primarily in news of major social and political significance to their community and country, one will again find fault with the gatekeeping process. Obviously, much space and time are given to trivia, and many interesting developments are ignored or reported so briefly that their meaning is lost. Often the human interest appeal of a story or its sensational aspects distract the audience from recognizing the story's real significance.[70]

Even if one tests the media by their professed story formulas, appraisal scores are not high. An analysis of 350 randomly selected television news reports, which yielded 209 "routine" average length stories, showed that only four of seven key story elements were well covered. As Table 4-8 indicates, the factual elements of various types of stories were included in most stories. Over ninety percent had adequate information about *who* the important actors in the story were, *what* factual situation was involved, and *where* and *when* the situation had happened. But only half (53 percent) of the stories explained *why* the

Table 4-8 Coverage of News Elements in National and Local Broadcasts (in percentages)

News elements	Who	What	Where	When	Why	How	Context	Number
Events abroad								
East bloc politics	100	100	100	94	35	29	59	17
West bloc politics	100	100	91	100	36	18	45	11
Mideast problems	100	100	100	93	57	36	71	14
Third World unrest	100	100	100	100	54	46	77	13
Foreign/Defense policies								
Foreign policy	100	100	93	86	64	29	71	14
Defense policy	100	100	95	95	63	47	74	19
Economic issues								
Economic conditions	87	100	80	80	60	33	47	15
Fiscal policies	96	100	92	92	60	4	72	25
Non-economic issues								
Public officials	100	100	100	100	47	47	82	17
Law enforcement	100	100	100	100	32	42	63	19
Other domestic issues	100	100	91	96	39	48	61	23
Private sector news								
Business news	90	100	90	90	70	30	50	10
Health/medical news	100	100	100	100	67	33	75	12
Average scores	98	100	95	94	53	34	65	209

Source: Author's research.
Note: Numbers represent the percentage of stories in each group that cover the question. End column = N's.

situation was occurring. In some news categories, such as law enforcement, only one-third (32 percent) of the stories provided reasons. On an average only one-third (34 percent) of the stories told *how* the situation developed, giving details about the process.

Stories become more meaningful if they are put into an appropriate context, such as comparisons with similar past events, or accounts of the impact of the events on various groups. On an average, 65 percent of the stories provided *contextual information.* Unfortunately, contextual data were often scarcest in stories needing them most, such as reports about the economy or America's relations with its Western allies.

To find fault is easy; to suggest realistic remedies is far more difficult. Few critics would agree on what is noteworthy enough to deserve publication. Gradations and ranks in significance depend on the observer's world view and political orientation. Much of the published criticism of the media consists of polemical works that take the media to task for omitting the critic's areas of special concern. But one person's intellectual meat is another's poison. Conservatives would like to see more stories about the misdeeds of America's enemies and about waste and abuse in social service programs. Liberals complain that the media legitimize big business and the military and neglect social reforms and radical perspectives. Frequently, there is the additional charge that political bias dictates the choices made about inclusion and exclusion of media fare and about story focus and tone. These charges have been particularly common when the media have featured controversial public policy issues, such as the dangers of atomic energy generation or the merits of a new weapons system, or when political campaigns or demonstrations have been covered.

A number of content analyses of such events definitely refute the charges of political bias, if bias is defined as deliberately lopsided coverage or intentional slanting of news. These analyses show instead that most newspeople try to cover a balanced array of issues in a neutral manner and do include contrasting viewpoints.[71] However, as mentioned, the prevailing political culture colors everything because it provides the standards by which events are judged and interpreted. Most studies of bias have involved situations, such as elections, in which bias charges could be anticipated. Media personnel therefore may have taken exceptional care to cover elections evenhandedly. But even in more general realms, such as the coverage of American business enterprises, there may be more evenhandedness than one might expect from the frequent charges of both pro- and antibusiness bias in the media. A team of investigators sampled more than two thousand households nationwide to analyze the public's perceptions of bias in business news coverage. It discovered that 61 percent of the respondents considered business news biased. But half thought the bias was probusiness, while the other half thought it was anti-business.[72]

When coverage is unbalanced, as happens often, the reasons generally spring from the news-making process itself rather than from politically or ideologically motivated slanting. For instance, when Alexander Haig bowed out of the presidential race in 1988 and endorsed Sen. Robert Dole, three networks led with the story. The reason for this media prominence was a snow storm in New Hampshire that forced cancellation of most other campaign events on that day. Geography also affects the news-making process. Events happening in Chicago are reported more fully nationwide than are similar events in Denver because the networks have a permanently leased wire from Chicago to New York but not from Denver to New York. The New Hampshire presidential primary receives disproportionately ample coverage because it happens to be the first one in a presidential election year.

Inevitably, the stories that are publicized represent a small, unsystematic sample of the news of the day. In this sense every issue of a newspaper or every television newscast is a "biased sample" of current events. Published stories often generate follow-up coverage, heightening the bias effect. Attempts to be evenhanded may lead to similar coverage for events of dissimilar importance, thereby introducing bias.

News can be evaluated not only as a mirror of society or as a reflection of socially and politically significant events, but also from the standpoint of audience preference. By and large the media gatekeepers appear to be doing well by that standard. A 1983 study showed that on a scale of 0 to 100, Americans rated the appeal of television shows at 73. More than 90 percent of all shows rated above 50.[73] People like the products of the mass media industry well enough to consume them on a scale unheard of in the past. Three out of every four adults say they read newspapers regularly; nearly all homes have radio and television and use them extensively. In the average household the radio is turned on for three hours a day and television for seven. Millions of viewers, by their own free choice, have switched from other pretelevision age sources of diversion to watching shows condemned as "trash" by social critics and often even by the viewers themselves. These same people ignore shows and newspaper stories with the critics' seal of approval.

If viewed simultaneously from all three perspectives, the media overall have developed a balanced approach. Most newspapers and broadcast enterprises try to mirror at least a portion of the world. Most of the large news organizations also see it as their function to present some serious political and social information and analysis. At the same time, most cater to the audience's appetite for easily digested entertainment and diversion. The end product cannot fully satisfy everyone.

Summary

What is news depends on what a particular society deems socially significant and/or personally satisfying to media audiences. The prevailing political and social ideology therefore determines what type of information will be gathered and the range of meanings that will be given to it. News collection is structured through the beat system to produce the desired information.

Beyond the larger framework, which is rooted in America's current political ideology, overt political considerations rarely play a major part in news selection. Instead, the profit motive and technical constraints of news production become paramount selection criteria. These criteria impose more stringent constraints on television than on print media because television deals with larger, more heterogeneous audiences and requires pictures to match word stories. Unlike newspapers, which rarely have competition in the local market, television must compete for attention with several other electronic outlets.

The end products of these various constraints on news making are news media that generally support the American political system, but emphasize its shortcomings and conflicts because journalists see themselves as watchdogs of public honesty and because conflict is exciting. News is geared primarily to attract and entertain rather than to educate the audience about politically significant events. The pressures to report news rapidly while it is happening often lead to presentation of disjointed fragments and disparate commentary. This leaves the audience with the impossible task of weaving the fragments into a meaningful tapestry of interrelated events.

If judged in terms of the information needs of the ideal citizen in the ideal democracy, the end product of the gatekeeping process is inadequate. This is especially true of television, which provides little more than a headline service for news and which mirrors the world about as much as the curved mirrors at the county fair. Reality is reflected, but it seems badly out of shape and proportion.

Most of us, however, only faintly resemble the ideal citizen, and most of us look to the media for entertainment rather than for enlightenment. From this perspective a different appraisal suggests itself. By and large, American mass media serve the general public about as well as that public wants to be served in practice rather than in theory. Entertainment is interspersed with a smattering of serious information. Breadth of coverage is preferred over narrow depth. In times of acute crisis, as we shall see in the next chapter, the media can and do follow a different pattern. Serious news displaces entertainment, and the broad sweep of events turns into a narrow, in-depth focus on the crisis. But short of acute crisis, superficiality prevails most of the time.

Notes

1. William Small, *To Kill a Messenger* (New York: Hastings House, 1970), 280.
2. G. Cleveland Wilhoit and David H. Weaver, *The American Journalist: A Portrait of U.S. News People and Their Work*, 2d ed. (Bloomington: Indiana University Press, 1991). Some of the data presented here are not included in the published study. For an example of other supportive studies, see S. Robert Lichter, Stanley Rothman, and Linda S. Lichter, *The Media Elite: America's New Powerbrokers* (New York: Adler and Adler, 1986).
3. James Warren, "Survey Finds News Still Has Male Face," *Chicago Tribune*, April 8, 1992; also see Dick Haws, "Minorities in the Newsroom and Community: A Comparison," *Journalism Quarterly* 68 (Winter 1991): 764-771.
4. Herbert J. Gans, *Deciding What's News: A Study of CBS Evening News, NBC Nightly News, Newsweek and Time* (New York: Pantheon, 1979), 39-69, 116-145, 182-213; Stanley Rothman, "The Media, the Experts, and Public Opinion," chap. 8 in *The Mass Media in Liberal Democratic Societies*, ed. Stanley Rothman (New York: Paragon House, 1992); Kevin M. Carragee, "News and Ideology: An Analysis of Coverage of the West German Green Party by the *New York Times*," *Journalism Monographs* 128 (August 1991).
5. John Johnstone, Edward J. Slawski, and William T. Bowman, "The Professional Values of American Newsmen," *Public Opinion Quarterly* 36 (Winter 1972-1973): 522-540.
6. Center for Political Studies, University of Michigan, 1982 surveys.
7. For a comprehensive analysis of media elites and a comparison with other elites, see Lichter, Rothman, and Lichter, *The Media Elite*, 93-165.
8. Gans, *Deciding What's News*, 39-69, 182-213. Frank J. Sorauf, "Campaign Money and the Press: Three Soundings," *Political Science Quarterly* 102 (Spring 1987): 25-42, demonstrates the neo-progressive outlook of the press using coverage of campaign finance news as a test case.
9. C. Richard Hofstetter, *Bias in the News: Network Television Coverage of the 1972 Election Campaign* (Columbus: Ohio State University Press, 1976), 187-207.
10. Wilhoit and Weaver, *The American Journalist*, 25-32.
11. Lichter et al., *The Media Elite*, chap. 2.
12. Wilhoit and Weaver, *The American Journalist*, chap. 9.
13. Ibid., 214. Twenty percent of the journalists in the Wilhoit and Weaver study believe in neutral reporting. However, 49 percent subscribe to both neutral and participant philosophies. These philosophies thus do not appear to be mutually exclusive; also see Janet A. Bridges, "Daily Newspaper Managing Editors' Perceptions of News Media Functions," *Journalism Quarterly* 68 (Winter 1991): 719-728.
14. Wilhoit and Weaver, *The American Journalist*, 32-38.
15. William Schneider and I. A. Lewis, "Views on the News," *Public Opinion* 8 (August/September 1985): 6-11, 58-59.
16. Thomas E. Patterson and Ronald P. Abeles, "Mass Communications Research and the 1976 Presidential Election," *Items* 2 (June 1975): 13-18.
17. See, for example, Michael Rice and James A. Cooney, eds., *Reporting U.S.-European Relations: Four Nations, Four Newspapers* (New York: Pergamon, 1982).
18. Charles Whelton, "Getting Bought: Notes from the Overground," *Village*

Voice, May 2, 1977, 51.
19. "Mr. President, Ben Bradley Calling," *Public Opinion* 9 (September/ October 1986): 40.
20. See Dominic L. Lasorsa and Stephen D. Reese, "News Source Use in the Crash of 1987: A Study of Four National Media," *Journalism Quarterly* 67 (Spring 1990): 60-63, and sources cited therein.
21. Jane Delano Brown, Carl R. Bybee, Stanley T. Wearden, and Dulcie Murdock Straughan, "Invisible Power: Newspaper News Sources and the Limits of Diversity," *Journalism Quarterly* 64 (Spring 1987): 45-54; and Sharon Dunwoody and Steven Shields, "Accounting for Patterns of Selection of Topics in Statehouse Reporting," *Journalism Quarterly* 63 (Autumn 1986): 488-496.
22. W. Lance Bennett, "Toward a Theory of Press-State Relations in the United States," *Journal of Communication* 40 (Spring 1990): 103-125.
23. R. Gordon Shepherd, "Selectivity of Sources: Reporting the Marijuana Controversy," *Journal of Communication* 31 (Spring 1981): 129-137. Also see Sharon Dunwoody and Michael Ryan, "The Credible Scientific Source," *Journalism Quarterly* 64 (Spring 1987): 21-27; and Stanley Rothman and S. Robert Lichter, "Elite Ideology and Risk Perception in Nuclear Energy Policy," *American Political Science Review* 81 (June 1987): 383-404.
24. Nancy Pfund and Laura Hofstadter, "Biomedical Innovation and the Press," *Journal of Communication* 31 (Spring 1981): 138-154.
25. Lichter et al., *The Media Elite,* 62. The study is reported on 54-71. Also see Hans Mathias Kepplinger, "Artificial Horizons: How the Press Presented and How the Population Received Technology in Germany from 1965-1986," chap. 7 in *The Mass Media in Liberal Democratic Societies,* ed. Stanley Rothman.
26. Lasorsa and Reese, "News Source Use in the Crash of 1987."
27. The impact of news stories attributed to highly credible sources is described in Benjamin I. Page, Robert Y. Shapiro, and Glenn R. Dempsey, "What Moves Public Opinion?" *American Journal of Political Science* 81 (March 1987): 23-43.
28. Barbara Matusow, *The Evening Stars: The Rise of the Network News Anchors* (Boston: Houghton Mifflin, 1983).
29. Peter Braestrup, *Big Story* (Garden City, N.Y.: Anchor Books, 1978).
30. George Gerbner, "Ideological Perspective and Political Tendencies in News Reporting," *Journalism Quarterly* 41 (August 1964): 495-508.
31. For a discussion of the social systems framework for mass communications analysis, see James S. Ettema, "The Organizational Context of Creativity," in *Individuals in Mass Media Organizations: Creativity and Constraint,* ed. James S. Ettema and D. Charles Whitney (Beverly Hills, Calif.: Sage, 1982), 91-106.
32. David Morgan, *The Capitol Press Corps: Newsmen and the Governing of New York State* (Westport, Conn.: Greenwood Press, 1978), 44-47.
33. Ron Powers, *The Newscasters* (New York: St. Martin's Press, 1977), 30.
34. Quoted in Powers, *The Newscasters,* 79. The evidence on whether editors and reporters assess their audiences' tastes properly is mixed. Ralph K. Martin, Garrett J. O'Keefe, and Oguz B. Nayman, in "Opinion Agreement and Accuracy between Editors and Their Readers," *Journalism Quarterly* 49 (Autumn 1972): 460-468, say they do. Leo Bogart, in "Changing News Interests and the Mass Media," *Public Opinion Quarterly* 23 (Winter 1968-1969): 560-574, holds to the contrary.

35. Edward Jay Epstein, *News from Nowhere* (New York: Vintage Books, 1974), 17-18.
36. G. Ray Funkhouser, "Trends in Media Coverage of the Issues of the '60's," *Journalism Quarterly* 50 (Fall 1973): 533-538. Also see Everett M. Rogers, James W. Dearing, and Soonbum Chang, "AIDS in the 1980s: The Agenda-Setting Process for a Public Issue," *Journalism Monographs* 126 (April 1991).
37. Funkhouser, "Trends in Media Coverage."
38. Michael X. Delli Carpini and Bruce A. Williams, "Television and Terrorism: Patterns of Presentation and Occurrence, 1969 to 1980," *Western Political Quarterly* 40 (March 1987): 45-64.
39. Somewhat similar feelings are harbored even toward the casts of soap operas. People whose lives are confined largely to their homes often adopt soap opera stars as part of their family. They avidly follow the trials and tribulations of these people and may even try to model themselves after them.
40. A study of 149 small and large newspapers reports the following news space allocations: local, 75 percent; sports, 6 percent; national, 4 percent; women's issues, 4 percent; international, 3 percent; editorial, 3 percent; state, 3 percent; financial, 2 percent. The measurements refer to space in column inches of total newshole. Dan Drew and G. Cleveland Wilhoit, "Newshole Allocation Policies of American Daily Newspapers," *Journalism Quarterly* 53 (Fall 1976): 434-440.
41. Robert W. Clyde and James K. Buckalew, "Inter-Media Standardization: A Q-Analysis of News Editors," *Journalism Quarterly* 46 (Summer 1969): 349-351. Various theories about news selection criteria are summarized and analyzed in Pamela Shoemaker with Elizabeth Kay Mayfield, "Building a Theory of News Content: A Synthesis of Current Approaches," *Journalism Monographs* 103 (June 1987).
42. Leon V. Sigal, *Reporters and Officials: The Organization and Politics of Newsmaking* (Lexington, Mass.: Heath, 1973), 119-130. Also see Leon V. Sigal, "Sources Make the News," in *Reading the News,* ed. Robert Karl Manoff and Michael Schudson (New York: Pantheon Books, 1987), 9-37.
43. The leading story is shared by all three major networks 43 percent of the time. Joe S. Foote and Michael E. Steele, "Degree of Conformity in Lead Stories in Early Evening Network TV Newscasts," *Journalism Quarterly* 63 (Spring 1986): 19-23.
44. The phrase is from Stanley K. Bigman, "Rivals in Conformity: A Study of Two Competing Dailies," *Journalism Quarterly* 25 (Autumn 1949): 127-131.
45. Daniel Riffe, Brenda Ellis, Momo K. Rogers, Roger L. Van Ommeren, and Kieran A. Woodman, "Gatekeeping and the Network News Mix," *Journalism Quarterly* 63 (Summer 1986): 315-321. For a discussion of variations in individual stories, see Norman R. Luttbeg, "News Consensus: Do U.S. Newspapers Mirror Society's Happenings?" *Journalism Quarterly* 60 (Autumn 1983): 484-488.
46. Sigal, *Reporters and Officials,* 66.
47. Joseph R. Dominick, "Geographic Bias in National TV News," *Journal of Communication* 27 (Fall 1977): 94-99.
48. Robert Rutherford Smith, "Mythic Elements in Television News," *Journal of Communication* 29 (Winter 1979): 75-82.
49. Ben Bagdikian, *The Information Machines* (New York: Harper and Row, 1971), 99-100.

50. Ibid; Dunwoody and Shields, "Statehouse Reporting," 488-496.

51. David M. White, "The Gatekeeper," *Journalism Quarterly* 27 (Fall 1950): 383-390, replicated by D. Charles Whitney and Lee B. Becker, " 'Keeping the Gates' for Gatekeepers: The Effects of Wire News," *Journalism Quarterly* 59 (Spring 1982): 60-65. See also Guido H. Stempel III, "Gatekeeping: The Mix of Topics and the Selection of Stories," *Journalism Quarterly* 62 (Winter 1985): 791-796.

52. Judy Van Slyke Turk, "Information Subsidies and Media Content: A Study of Public Relations Influence on the News," *Journalism Monographs* 100 (December 1986): 1-29.

53. Drew and Wilhoit, "Newshole Allocation Policies," 434-440. Also see Leo Bogart, "How U.S. Newspaper Content Is Changing," *Journal of Communication* 35 (Spring 1985): 82-91.

54. Harriet Engel Gross and Sharyne Merritt, "Effect of Social/Organizational Context on Gatekeeping in Lifestyle Pages," *Journalism Quarterly* 58 (Autumn 1981): 420-427.

55. The first two headings have been adapted from Herbert Gans's study of news magazine and network television news. Herbert J. Gans, *Deciding What's News*, 8-31. See also Gaye Tuchman, *Making News: A Study in the Construction of Reality* (New York: Free Press, 1978); and W. Lance Bennett, *News: The Politics of Illusion,* 2d ed. (New York: Longman, 1988), chaps. 2 and 4.

56. Karen S. Johnson, "The Portrayal of Lame-Duck Presidents by the National Print Media," *Presidential Studies Quarterly* 16 (Winter 1986): 50-65. For a broad discussion of the coverage mix at the federal government level, see Stephen Hess, *The Washington Reporters* (Washington, D.C.: Brookings, 1981), chaps. 3 and 5.

57. Sandra William Ernst, "Baseball or Brickbats: A Content Analysis of Community Development," *Journalism Quarterly* 49 (Spring 1972): 86-90.

58. Gerald Stone, Barbara Hartung, and Dwight Jensen, "Local TV News and the Good-Bad Dyad," *Journalism Quarterly* 64 (Spring 1987): 37-44.

59. George Gerbner, Larry Gross, Michael Morgan, and Nancy Signorielli, "Charting the Mainstream: Television's Contributions to Political Orientations," *Journal of Communication* 32 (Spring 1982): 106-107. Small-town newspapers are more apt to highlight the positive, telling what is good rather than what is bad, because conflict is less tolerable in social systems where most of the leaders constantly rub elbows.

60. Clarice N. Olien, George A. Donohue, and Phillip J. Tichenor, "The Community Editor's Power and the Reporting of Conflict," *Journalism Quarterly* 45 (Summer 1968): 243-252. See also Bruce Cole, "Trends in Science and Conflict Coverage in Four Metropolitan Newspapers," *Journalism Quarterly* 52 (Fall 1973): 465-474.

61. The term is Michael J. Robinson's. See Robinson, "American Political Legitimacy in an Era of Electronic Journalism: Reflections on the Evening News," in *Television as a Social Force: New Approaches to TV Criticism,* ed. Richard Adler (New York: Praeger, 1975), 97-139. Gerald C. Stone and Elinor Grusin, "Network TV as the Bad News Bearer," *Journalism Quarterly* 61 (Autumn 1984): 521, report that only 25 percent of nightly television news is "good news."

62. Stephen E. Rada, "Manipulating the Media: A Case Study of a Chicano Strike in Texas," *Journalism Quarterly* 54 (Spring 1977): 109-113. Also see Gadi Wolfsfeld, "Symbiosis of Press and Protest: An Exchange Analysis,"

Journalism Quarterly 61 (Autumn 1984): 550-555.

63. Mike Royko, "Fire Is Going Out of Los Angeles Riot Story," *Chicago Tribune,* May 8, 1992.

64. Klaus Bruhn Jensen, "News as Ideology: Economics Statistics and Political Ritual in Television Network News," *Journal of Communication* 37 (Winter 1987): 8-27; Bennett, *News: The Politics of Illusion.*

65. For a strong attack on status quo support, see Claus Mueller, *The Politics of Communication* (London: Oxford University Press, 1973); see also Edward S. Herman and Noam Chomsky, *Manufacturing Consent: The Political Economy of the Mass Media* (New York: Pantheon Books, 1988).

66. There is resistance to change, even in entertainment program formats. See Jay G. Blumler and Carolynn Martin Spicer, "Prospects for Creativity in the New Television Marketplace: Evidence from Program-Makers," *Journal of Communication* 40 (Autumn 1990): 78-101.

67. Sigal, *Reporters and Officials,* 119-130. On the use of government sources for economic news, see Stephen D. Reese, John A. Daly, and Andrew P. Hardy, "Economic News on Network Television," *Journalism Quarterly* 64 (Spring 1987): 137-144; also see Jarol B. Manheim, *All of the People All the Time: Strategic Communication and American Politics* (Armonk, N.Y.: M.E. Sharpe, 1991), 27-35.

68. A comparison of war movies made with and without Pentagon aid showed that aided movies depicted the military in a more favorable light. Russell E. Shain, "Effects of Pentagon Influence on War Movies, 1948-70," *Public Opinion Quarterly* 38 (Fall 1972): 641-647.

69. For a fuller exploration of this issue, see David L. Altheide, *Creating Reality: How T.V. News Distorts Events* (Beverly Hills, Calif.: Sage, 1976); Gaye Tuchman, *Making News;* Mark Fishman, *Manufacturing the News* (Austin: University of Texas Press, 1980); and Bennett, *News: The Politics of Illusion,* chaps. 3 and 5.

70. But sensational news often contains a great deal of information. See C. Richard Hofstetter and David M. Dozier, "Useful News, Sensational News: Quality, Sensationalism, and Local TV News," *Journalism Quarterly* 63 (Winter 1986): 815-820.

71. George Comstock and Robin Cobbey, "Watching the Watchdogs: Trends and Problems in Monitoring Network News," in *Television Network News: Issues in Content Research,* ed. William Adams and Fay Schreibman (Washington, D.C.: George Washington University, 1978), 53-55. Also see Neil J. Kressel, "Biased Judgments of Media Bias: A Case Study of the Arab-Israeli Dispute," *Political Psychology* 8 (June 1987): 211-226; and Lichter et al., *The Media Elite,* 293-301. The difficulties of defining "bias" are explained in Stephen Lacy, Frederick Fico, and Todd F. Simon, "Fairness and Balance in the Prestige Press," *Journalism Quarterly* 68 (Fall 1991): 363-370. Also see Todd F. Simon, Frederick Fico, and Stephen Lacy, "Covering Conflict and Controversy: Measuring Balance, Fairness, Defamation," *Journalism Quarterly* 62 (Summer 1989): 427-434.

72. Robert A. Peterson, George Kozmetsky, and Isabella C. M. Cunningham, "Perceptions of Media Bias towards Business," *Journalism Quarterly* 59 (Fall 1982): 461-464.

73. Ron Aldridge, "New TV Rating System Stresses Quality Viewing," *Chicago Tribune,* April 25, 1983. Also see William Schneider and I. A. Lewis, "Views on the News," *Public Opinion* 8 (August/September 1985): 8-11, 58-59. The authors report the results of a *Los Angeles Times* nationwide survey in 1985

in which the public gave their newspapers a 96 percent positive rating when "very good" and "fairly good" ratings are combined. Local television received a 95 percent positive rating, and network television news ratings were 91 percent positive.

Readings

Entman, Robert M. *Democracy Without Citizens: Media and the Decay of American Politics.* New York: Oxford University Press, 1989.

Frank, Reuven. *Out of Thin Air: The Brief Wonderful Life of Network News.* New York: Simon and Schuster, 1991.

Gaunt, Philip. *Choosing the News: The Profit Factor in News Selection.* New York: Greenwood Press, 1990.

Goldstein, Tom. *The News at Any Cost: How Journalists Compromise Their Ethics to Shape the News.* New York: Simon and Schuster, 1985.

Leonard, Thomas C. *The Power of the Press: The Birth of American Political Reporting.* New York: Oxford University Press, 1987.

Shoemaker, Pamela J. *Gatekeeping.* Newbury Park, Calif.: Sage, 1991.

Shoemaker, Pamela J., and Stephen D. Reese. *Mediating the Message: Theories of Influences on Mass Media Content.* New York: Longman, 1991.

Weaver, David H., and G. Cleveland Wilhoit. *The American Journalist: A Portrait of U.S. News People and Their Work,* 2d ed. Bloomington: Indiana University Press, 1991.

CHAPTER 5

Reporting Extraordinary Events

The Nature of Crisis Conditions

What common thread joins the Gulf War, the attempted assassination of President Reagan, the Mount St. Helens volcanic eruptions, and the Los Angeles riots of 1992? The answer is that all are *extraordinary natural or man-made events*. They happen rarely. They are dramatic and rich in pictures that tug at human heart strings. And they seem salient to the lives of media audiences because they threaten their shared values and peace of mind and often their lives and property. Such events receive an extraordinary amount of sustained media coverage and an extraordinary amount of audience attention because people expect to be informed and to be protected by the appropriate government agency.

What politically significant roles do media play when such extraordinary events occur, and how do they go about playing them? To answer that question, we will take a close look at the four situations just mentioned, along with brief glances at related events. Once the broad coverage principles have been explained and illustrated, we will turn to a number of pseudo-crises. These are events when crisis-type coverage has elevated a comparatively normal event to the status of an extraordinary one.

In times of crisis the media, particularly radio and, in recent years, television become vital arms of government. As usual, they select, shape, and report the news to people in and out of government. But, in addition, they provide government officials quick access to the public directly or indirectly through media personnel. These official messages keep endangered communities in touch with essential information and instructions. They also allow government authorities to shape perceptions of the crisis and its causes and appropriate remedies.

Besides its intrinsic importance, coverage of extraordinary events highlights major philosophical and policy issues that plague the government-media relationship. In times of crisis, citizens' sensitivity to media publicity becomes heightened. The media's responsibility to serve public needs and the government's responsibility to control, direct, and even manipulate the flow of news for public purposes become issues of major, immediate concern. The Olympian view of media performance yields to a vision of danger at eyeball distance.

Four Crises

In this chapter we will examine media coverage of four crises: the assassination attempt on President Ronald Reagan on March 30, 1981; the riots in Los Angeles that started April 30, 1992; the war against Iraq in the Persian Gulf area in January and February 1991; and the eruption of Mount St. Helens in the state of Washington on May 18, 1980.

The Attempted Assassination of President Reagan

On March 30, 1981, President Ronald Reagan was felled by gun shots as he left a Washington, D.C., hotel. His press secretary, a Secret Service agent, and a police officer were also shot. A bevy of photographers and journalists who had been waiting for the president outside the hotel witnessed the assault, including the capture of the gunman, John W. Hinckley, Jr. The extent of injuries to the assault victims was not fully evident as they were rushed from the scene. It was only after Reagan began to cough up blood in the escape car that it became clear that he needed immediate medical attention for what turned out to be a punctured lung and a bullet lodged within three inches of his heart. At the hospital, a plucky, wise-cracking president was rushed to surgery. He was discharged on April 12 and returned to the White House to continue an uneventful recovery.[1]

The Los Angeles Riots

The events that led to the Los Angeles riots of 1992 are recounted in full in the opening pages of this book. In brief, videotapes showing white police officers beating an African-American motorist after a traffic violation had persuaded millions of viewers of all races that the police had used excessive force. Police brutality and racially-motivated mistreatment of minorities became simmering public issues, particularly in urban ghettoes. These feelings were kept alive and even fanned by countless repeated showings of the taped scenes.

When an all-white jury exonerated all but one of the officers on the charges of brutality in April 1992, protest demonstrations erupted throughout the country. In Los Angeles they turned into several days of destructive riots, complete with shootings, beatings, massive arson, and looting. Whole sections of the city were virtually destroyed. Fifty-three people died and more than two thousand were injured. Several of the injured died within days. Property damage ran into many millions of dollars.[2]

War in the Persian Gulf

In the summer of 1990, hostilities erupted in the Persian Gulf region when Iraq invaded neighboring Kuwait, despite strong indications that the world community might take punitive action. When economic sanctions failed to bring a withdrawal, the United Nations community, with the United States in the lead, started military operations. The war lasted forty-four days. It began with bombing attacks on Iraq on January 16, followed by a ground attack on February 23. Half a million American troops were sent to the Gulf and a similar number were mobilized on the home front. While most people assumed that Iraq would lose the war, the outcome and the ultimate cost of the war in terms of people and property losses on both sides were uncertain. Scud missile attacks on Israel raised the possibility of large scale losses by Iraq's enemies.[3]

The Mount St. Helens Volcanic Eruption

Mount St. Helens, a long dormant volcano in mountainous country in the state of Washington, erupted violently on Sunday morning, May 18, 1980. The earth tremors and explosions could be felt and heard within a radius of two hundred miles. Volcanic ash and steam blew ten miles into the atmosphere, while mudslides destroyed the landscape below. Two major explosions followed within a few weeks, each spreading more lava, ash, and mud. More than two dozen people were known to be dead and many more were missing. Falling ashes and soot paralyzed nearby communities in Washington and Oregon, forcing normal activities to a standstill. Economic damage amounted to nearly $3 billion. Federal and state authorities were forced to declare a state of emergency to help the stricken communities. Though eruptions ceased in June, it was uncertain when volcanic activity might resume on a minor or major scale.[4]

Table 5-1 Principal Sources of Disaster Information
(in percentage of responses)

Sources of information	Site A	Site B	Site C	Site D
Electronic media	66	59	75	75
Newspapers	24	20	40	64
Magazines	3	7	8	15
Nonfiction books	10	10	11	4
Other persons	17	12	14	9
Direct experience	37	32	20	6
Public education	9	6	5	—

Source: Dennis E. Wenger, "A Few Empirical Observations Concerning the Relationship between the Mass Media and Disaster Knowledge: A Research Report," in *Disasters and the Mass Media: Proceedings of the Committee on Disasters and the Mass Media Workshop* (Washington, D.C.: National Academy Press, 1980), 244. Reprinted by permission.

Note: Multiple answers were permitted. $N = 290$ for Site A, hurricane disasters; 281 for Site B, tornado disasters; 209 for Site C, flood disasters; and 341 for Site D, disaster-free control.

Media Response and Role

During crises the public depends almost totally on the media for news and for important messages from public and private authorities that might be vital for its survival. The mass media are the only institutions equipped to collect this massive amount of information and disseminate it quickly. Therefore when people become aware of a crisis, they turn on their radios or television sets, often on a round-the-clock basis, to monitor developments.

Table 5-1 presents data on sources that people used for crisis information in three communities hit by natural disasters. The table demonstrates people's heavy reliance on electronic media and the comparatively small role played by interpersonal communication and direct experience. Community A, located on the Gulf Coast, had experienced numerous hurricanes. Communities B and C, in the Midwest, had suffered two tornadoes and two major floods, respectively. Community D had no experience with a major natural disaster. A sample of residents in each of these communities was asked, "From what sources have you obtained the greatest amount of information concerning natural disasters?" Several sources could be cited in response.[5] Respondents in the disaster-free control community were asked to speculate about what sources might be most useful.

The audience for crisis information is massive and loyal. When the Gulf War started, television sets everywhere remained turned on throughout the night and into the wee hours of the morning so that people could watch unfolding events. To keep up with the round-the-clock coverage by CNN, all the networks sharply increased news coverage of the war. More than one billion people in 108 nations watched CNN war coverage, making its largely undigested reports of breaking events their leading source of war news. When American audiences were asked in a Gallup poll about their main source of war news, 89 percent mentioned television, 8 percent mentioned radio, and only 2 percent mentioned newspapers.[6]

Besides information, the public looks to the media to explain and interpret the situation, since media personnel are often the first ones on the scene collecting reports and trying to fit them into a coherent story. Official investigations generally come much later. The media also guide the public to appropriate behavior during the crisis. They warn people to retreat to a shelter, announce which areas are unsafe to enter, describe purification of polluted food and water, and supply news of missing persons, or schedules to be maintained by schools and work places. News stories also explain what immediate steps government authorities are taking to cope with the crisis.

Stages and Patterns of Coverage

Stage One. The typical scenario of crisis coverage has three stages. During the first stage, the crisis or disaster strikes or is announced as impending. Media people, officials, and onlookers rush to the scene. This immediately produces a flood of uncoordinated messages, largely transmitted over the airwaves. Radio and television stations interrupt regularly scheduled programs with bulletins announcing the extraordinary event, or they may preempt the entire program for reports from the scene.

Minutes after the start of the Los Angeles riots, television and radio broadcast live from the scene. They showed buildings on fire and beating and looting scenes, usually without a single police officer within camera range. Later, such scenes were blamed for allegedly tipping off rioters about places where they might assault, burn, and loot with impunity. On the other hand, these same stories also helped police find locations where their forces were sorely needed. Media outlets rapidly became information collection centers. People would phone them with reports to be broadcast or call them for information. The most important broadcasts in the early hours of the disaster were messages describing what was happening, directing people to places where calm prevailed, summoning police and later National Guard units, and coordinating appeals for relief supplies, such as food, blankets, blood donations, and medical equipment.

In the early phase the number of news broadcasts rises steeply. During the Gulf War and the Los Angeles riots, radio and television doubled broadcast time with CNN on a twenty-four hour news schedule. Many regular programs were replaced with war-related news and interviews. News bulletins were issued throughout the day on radio and television. Following the Mount St. Helens eruptions, a steady stream of eyewitnesses was interviewed on radio and television. With little new to report, the same facts were rehashed endlessly.

Once the initial announcements have been aired, many people who have heard the broadcast will relay the information to others by word of mouth, either in person or by telephone. This in turn stimulates those who have been alerted to tune in to subsequent broadcasts. For instance, when the news of the attempted assassination of President Reagan was first broadcast, it reached a large daytime audience that was listening to radio or watching television. Each person who heard the news told it to three other people on the average. More than 90 percent of the American public—more than two hundred million people—received the news within ninety minutes after the shooting.[7]

The striking characteristic of this first stage of coverage of extraordinary events is the rapidity of communication. Television and radio, helped by satellite technology, can focus the public's attention almost instantaneously on the developing situation. In many cases news about the extraordinary event replaces most other stories. Whatever else happens in the world during the crisis period, regardless of its importance, may be totally blocked out in the affected area or even the entire nation.

At this early stage the media are the major source of information, even for public officials concerned with the crisis. Media reports serve to coordinate public activities and to calm the audience. During the 1964 Anchorage, Alaska, earthquake, for example, the radio stations that were able to function became the focal point for coordinating information on casualties, property damage, and supplies so that officials could determine priorities for relief work. At a later stage direct communication among officials and other affected parties may supplement or even supersede media communication.[8] After President Reagan was injured, White House aide Lyn Nofziger circulated Reagan's good-humored remarks so that press reports would suggest that the situation was not as serious as it might seem. Reagan had joked with his wife when she rushed to the hospital that he "forgot to duck" and he had asked whether his surgeons were staunch Republicans.

Next to reaching the disaster site, the chief problem for newspeople during the first stage is getting accurate information. Rumors abound. During the Gulf War, some of the early information was incorrect. For example, NBC and ABC reporters, with gasmasks seemingly substantiating their reports, told about chemical attacks on Israel that had not occurred. CBS reported wrongly that the Israelis had retaliated. Much of the news consisted of raw, unevaluated data and speculation and rumor, mixed with some hard news. During the Alaska earthquake, many buildings were evacuated unnecessarily because it was falsely reported that they had been condemned or were about to collapse. The number of dead and the extent of injuries were frequently exaggerated. In the volcano disaster, reports about the health hazards of breathing volcanic ash were exaggerated. Newspeople received many conflicting reports and lacked enough time to check their accuracy.

If highly technical matters are involved—as happens in explosions, structural failures, and nuclear radiation disasters, such as the Three Mile Island incident—it may be impossible to present a coherent story. Government officials, eager to allay the public's fears and prevent panic, usually minimize the dangers when communicating with newspeople. Reporters ordinarily lack the expertise to know when officials are concealing the truth. They cannot make sense out of baffling technical data nor simplify the information so that lay persons can comprehend it.[9] Imagine their puzzlement at one typical news conference when the Nuclear Regulatory Commission's chief spokesperson, Harold Denton, attempted to correct a false report that the hydrogen bubble in the reactor was about to explode. Here is what Denton said:

> The oxygen generation rate that I was assuming yesterday when I was reporting on the potential detonation inside the vessel is, it now appears to have been, too conservative. There's an emerging consensus of technical opinion that the—for situations such as this where there's high oxygen overpressure in a vessel, that the oxygen evolution rate is very low, and our numbers for the rate of oxygen yesterday—I think I quoted a number on the order of 1 percent a day—is very, very conservative, and the actual rate is much lower than that.[10]

If you are baffled about what he meant, so were the reporters.

To provide continuous crisis coverage, television and radio stations must suddenly produce a steady stream of interesting crisis-related stories to fill many hours of broadcast time. When Mount St. Helens exploded, reporters relied on geologists, meteorologists, foresters, police, and agricultural and crop insurance specialists. The unrelenting pressure for fresh accounts often tempts media personnel to interview inexperienced eyewitnesses and commentators, who may lend a local touch without clarifying the situation. They also may report information that has not been adequately verified or that is atypical.[11] By focusing on the destruction of a small section of Los Angeles, for instance, the audience was left with the wrong impression that the entire city was in ruins.[12] The pressure for news encourages reporters and public officials alike to speculate about what happened and why. At times they spin past prejudices into a web of scenarios that casts blame for the disaster or its aftermath on socially outcast groups. The Los

Angeles riots, which occurred during the 1992 presidential campaign, were blamed by Democrats on Republican inattention to urban blight. Republicans blamed them on the welfare programs of the Johnson administration. "Outsiders" in a community (ethnic minorities or political deviants, for example) often become the hapless scapegoats. The racial riots of the 1960s were routinely attributed to "outside agitators" who were depicted as common criminals, bereft of moral dignity and social consciousness.

Stage Two. During the second stage, the media try to make sense of the situation. At this point enough time generally has elapsed so that the chief dimensions of the crisis have emerged. For instance, in the St. Helens disaster, the extent of the damage had been ascertained. Names of most victims and their injuries were known. Plans had been made for repairs and reconstruction. In the Reagan assault, information about John Hinckley, the assailant, and his motives in the shooting became available. In the Los Angeles riots, the number of dead and wounded were reported. It also was announced that there had been 5,808 fire reports, that 11,656 arrests were clogging the courts, and that property damage amounted to an estimated $717 million.[13]

In general, print media are able to do a more thorough job than radio and television in pulling together the various events and fitting them into a coherent story. Print media have larger staffs for investigation and more room to present background details that make the events understandable. For instance, in the months preceding the outbreak of the Gulf War and in the days following the start of the air war and later the ground war, the *New York Times* and the *Washington Post* probed into the reasons for the hostilities, the cost in human lives and property, and ecological damage from oil well fires.

During this second stage, governments and their critics may try to shape political fall-out from the event in ways that support their policy preferences. Gulf War coverage, for example, while appearing to present reality, sanitized the war. Television showed precision bombings, targeted down chimneys or directly into doors. The air force later admitted that 70 percent of the bombs dropped on Kuwait and Iraq actually missed their targets. The smart bombs shown on television represented only a tiny fraction of air force bombings. Military censorship prevented showing the arrival of dead soldiers in body bags at Dover Air Force base or featuring casualties. Enemy losses were rarely shown.[14] The 1986 nuclear disaster at Chernobyl in the Soviet Ukraine also provides many examples. The explosion of the reactor forced the evacuation of ninety-five thousand people, left twenty-seven towns and villages uninhabitable, and produced fatal radiation sickness in thousands of people.[15] Government sources in the United States and in the Soviet Union pictured the event as an aberration that happened because of a series of readily avoidable mistakes. The accident, they contended, should not undermine confidence in the safety of nuclear power plants. Antinuclear groups throughout the world tried to use the story to support the opposite point of view. By and large, their interpretation did not prevail.

Stage Three. The third stage overlaps with the other two. It involves attempts by media personnel to place the crisis into a larger, long-range perspective and to prepare people to cope with the aftermath. Steps toward restoration of normal conditions may be discussed. In the Los Angeles tragedy, presidential candidates Bill Clinton and George Bush toured the damaged neighborhoods and discussed rebuilding plans. The media also announced restoration of suspended services, such as mail deliveries and bus transportation, and the start of clean-up efforts. In the Mount St. Helens area, the media reported how local authorities were trying to revive the tourist trade. Symbolically, "ferns poking through the ashes were shown and there were fresh tracks of elk undaunted by the recent devastation." [16]

A concerted effort may have to be made to sustain morale when crises are prolonged. Optimism that volcano-damaged regions can return to complete normalcy was spurred by reports about recovery from other major eruptions. Following President Reagan's hospitalization, the media featured assurances that government business was proceeding normally and that the vice-president and White House staff were fully informed about domestic and international affairs.

During the Three Mile Island incident in 1979, the federal government attempted to halt disquieting conflicting reports by centralizing news releases. All information furnished by government and plant officials about the disaster had to be cleared through a press center operated by the Nuclear Regulatory Commission near the site of the accident. Although officials of the damaged plant protested the censorship, they complied with President Jimmy Carter's order. Later a formal investigation of how forty-three newspapers and network evening newscasts reported the accident credited the media with providing balanced treatment in a highly confused and confusing situation. [17]

Positive Effects of Coverage

Information about crisis situations, even if it is bad news, relieves disquieting uncertainty and calms people. The mere activity of watching or listening to familiar reporters and commentators reassures people and keeps them occupied. It gives them a sense of vicarious participation, of "doing something." To maintain this quieting effect, media personnel may avoid showing gruesome details of the crisis. While this was not true of the Los Angeles riots, where vivid scenes of assaults and looting were filmed by helicopter crews and broadcast immediately, it was true in Chicago a few weeks later. When rioting youths smashed store windows and looted, causing millions of dollars worth of damage, the front page headline in the *Chicago Tribune* proclaimed "Two for Two: Bulls Still Champs!" Under the banner-size letters, a much smaller headline noted that "Celebration Breaks Out Repeatedly" and alluded to the disturbances in a single sentence: "In a few areas, victory begat broken windows and uninvited shopping." A few short paragraphs on inside pages carried further news of the looting.[18]

News stories may be able to reassure people that they do not bear their grief and fears alone. After seeing the same pictures and listening to the same broadcasts, people can discuss the crisis with neighbors, friends, and coworkers who have shared their experiences. This gives the feeling of mutual support. Watching military briefings on television during the Gulf War, particularly the masterful performance of the commanding general, Norman Schwarzkopf, made Americans feel that their leaders valued their support enough to keep them fully informed about the rationale behind military decisions.

If the news conveys the idea that the authorities are coping properly with extraordinary events, this, too, is reassuring. Scenes of lava pouring down a mountain side or city blocks put to the torch during a riot become less frightening if the police, firefighters, ambulances, and medical personnel are on the scene. Watching the mayor or governor tour a disaster site provides further reassurance. Finally, directions about appropriate behavior may save lives and property and ensure that the stricken community continues to function.

The benefits of coverage are readily apparent in most but not all disasters. During the Los Angeles riots, for example, showing scenes of looting may have caused copy-cat violence. Atlanta, Cleveland, Madison, Long Beach, and San Jose, among others, had disturbances. When Los Angeles police were criticized for not acting more decisively to protect the riot-torn areas, police chief Daryl F. Gates told reporters that, with cameras whirring overhead, "We did not want to make it appear that we were overreacting. We were very, very careful not to show that provocativeness." [19] The looters were not so camera shy.

Negative Effects of Media Coverage

Media coverage also may have adverse effects. It is this possibility that raises serious questions about the responsibility of media personnel to consider the societal consequences of freedom to publish. The government's responsibility to prevent harm-producing coverage, possibly by strict censorship, also becomes a major political issue.

Careless or even carefully prepared news messages may so disturb people that they cannot act rationally. Once informed of a crisis, people may panic, endangering themselves and others. For instance, a precipitous mass exodus of frightened people during an impending flood or wind calamity may clog roads and overcrowd shelters; it may lead to injuries and death for those caught beyond the safety of their homes and workplaces. Pictures of violence may lead to a terrifying multiplication effect. Audiences frequently believe that the violent act is merely one of many. One house on fire or the sight of one victim's body may lead to visions of whole neighborhoods on fire and scores of victims killed. Police may be ordered to shoot lawbreakers on sight, and citizens may resort to excessive violence to protect themselves.

Statements provoking unwise reactions are more likely to be publicized in times of crisis because the exceptionally large demand for news and guidance reduces gatekeepers' vigilance. Pack journalism may run rampant when all available news is shared to provide as much coverage as possible. If mistakes are made by news sources or reporters, they appear in all the media. During the Kennedy assassination crisis, Dallas police made many rash comments about Lee Harvey Oswald, Kennedy's accused slayer. The remarks were widely publicized and would have impaired Oswald's chances for a fair trial had he lived. After the nuclear mishap at Three Mile Island, workers complained that erroneous media reports, based on conflicting assessments by government officials about the explosiveness of a hydrogen bubble, frightened their families into needless evacuation of the area and threatened the survival of the plant and their job security. Such consequences are commonplace as long as crisis news routinely dwells on worst-case scenarios without providing perspectives on their likelihood.[20]

Crisis and disaster news frequently attract crowds of citizens and reporters to the site, impeding rescue and security operations. News coverage of physical disasters routinely draws looters to the scene. When the media reported the deployment of antiterrorist commandos in 1985 after a Trans World airplane had been hijacked and hostages taken, the commandos lost the chance to surprise their targets.[21]

Media coverage also may incite or prolong rioting. During the Los Angeles riots, police reported that the presence of television cameras seemed to escalate the violence. Rioters actually appeared to "perform" for the cameras. Sights of looters attracted other looters to the scene, particularly when the pictures revealed that no police officers were present. During racial rioting in Detroit in 1967, live coverage of looting and shooting seemed to so arouse viewers that some who had never resorted to lawlessness took part in the violence.[22]

Wide publicity for terrorist acts and heinous crimes (such as airline hijackings, poisoning of food supplies, or serial mass murders)

By permission of Mike Luckovich and Creators Syndicate.

may encourage such acts and lead to copy-cat crimes. Extensive media coverage has been called the lifeblood of terrorism because the perpetrators use their assaults to attract attention to their causes and gain sympathy and support. Though it is debatable whether such tactics are successful in gathering support, they are commonly used by political dissenters as well as criminals. At times, when dissenters are nonviolent, violence nonetheless ensues when government forces suppress them. The violence at Tiananmen Square in China in 1989 is a good example. The Chinese government used military action to suppress widely publicized demonstrations. It wanted to discourage further open dissent and its consequences, such as swelling the ranks of dissenters and winning world-wide sympathy for their cause. Hundreds were killed and thousands were wounded in the massacre that followed.

Economic crises, too, can escalate as a result of media images. When prices on the financial markets plunged precipitously on October 19, 1987, media accounts used highly alarming language. *Panic, carnage,* and *nightmare selling* were common descriptive terms. Moreover, the media frequently compared the crash to the 1929 stock market calamity and discussed the Great Depression that followed. Such gloomy news apparently fanned the growing panic and further weakened the markets.[23]

Planning Crisis Coverage

Because media play such a crucial role in keeping the polity going during crises, most media organizations have more or less formal plans to cope with crisis coverage problems. This is particularly true for electronic media. In one sample of seventy-two radio and television stations in twelve U.S. cities, 70 percent of the stations had plans for reporting natural disasters, and 73 percent had plans for reporting civil disturbances.[24] The plans generally were more detailed for natural disasters because needs are more predictable, and there is greater consensus about objectives. Nevertheless, much remains to be decided on the spur of the moment. Confusion inevitably reigns at the start of a crisis. Contradictory messages are likely to abound until coordination can be arranged. In addition to media-sponsored plans, most stations are tied into the federal Emergency Broadcast System (EBS), a network for relaying news during a national emergency.

Crisis coverage planning has two aspects: preparing for the crisis and deciding how to present ongoing events. Plans to forestall crises are rare, probably because media focus on short-range happenings and predicting a crisis is difficult. Nonetheless, the media often have been blamed for neglecting preventive coverage. The Public's Right to Information Task Force of the President's Commission on the Accident at Three Mile Island blamed the Commonwealth Edison Company, the Nuclear Regulatory Commission, and the media for ignoring problems at the plant prior to the accident and for overemphasizing the safety of nuclear power.[25] In 1968 the Kerner Commission condemned the media for their silence about the plight of blacks in the United States. Ample early coverage, it claimed, might have prevented violence in the mid-1960s. Similarly, the 1992 Los Angeles riots were blamed on inattention to the plight of inner cities by major institutions, including the media.

Most of the time it is difficult to argue the case for preventive coverage because there is disagreement about what social indicators herald a crisis. Besides, even if newspeople could accurately forecast an impending disaster, increased publicity might not prevent it. As we will see in Chapter 7, publicity does not necessarily produce behavioral changes, however easy and obviously beneficial they may be.

Coverage to prevent the government from involving the nation in dangerous hostilities, including war, raises several serious issues. For example, inadequate media attention to the Bush administration's support of Iraq's government immediately prior to the Gulf War has been cited as a major factor in the assault on Kuwait that led to the war. Had the media published the story, the assault might have been prevented. Alternatively, it might have taken place anyhow, but with greatly reduced chances for success. Would publication have been a patriotic act or undue interference in the nation's foreign policy? It is hard to tell.

In 1980 columnist Jack Anderson reported that an election-minded Carter administration was planning a military invasion of Iran to counteract the humiliation of the ongoing hostage crisis. The vast majority of papers that normally carry Anderson's column printed it. Most papers also printed government denials. One paper editorialized, "The recklessness of a politically motivated invasion would be far more dangerous than reckless journalism." [26] No major invasion ever took place. Whether none was planned, contrary to Anderson's claim, or whether the column thwarted the plans was never clarified.

Natural Disasters. Rodney Kueneman and Joseph Wright, who examined the seventy-two radio and television stations' plans to cover natural disasters, found that the plans were generally predicated on the assumption that people tend to panic and that coverage must be designed to forestall this. The management of 72 percent of the stations, particularly those that had previous experience with natural disasters, assumed that panic would occur.[27]

Preparation for predicted natural disasters may involve the publication of news tracing the path of a storm or reporting geological studies that forecast the likelihood of earthquakes in an area. Official warnings and plans in case of disasters may be publicized along with information about protective measures that individuals can take. Stories that are graphic enough to arouse a lethargic population to prepare for the disaster, however, may cause panic or may be so scary that people shut them out of their minds. Such "ostrich" inclinations may explain why, despite frequent warnings about the danger of serious earthquakes in southern California, most residents have not taken recommended precautions.

On the other hand, widespread warnings about an impending disaster may lead to costly, unnecessary preventive measures when the warnings turn out to be false alarms. That happened in the winter of 1990 when warnings about an impending earthquake in the New Madrid earthquake zone in the country's midsection caused residents to flee, public services to be shut down, and numerous business events to be canceled. Iben Browning, a climatologist with no formal training in geology or seismology, had indicated that chances for the quake were only 50 percent, and his credibility had been questioned by a panel of seismologists and geologists who examined his findings. They contended that the criteria by which Browning judged the imminence of earthquakes and had made earlier correct predictions were no better than "random guessing." [28] Nonetheless, the story had received so much publicity that it was widely believed. Reporters by the hundreds gathered in the presumed danger zone to report the event, which did not occur.

Civil Disorders. Interviewees at 83 percent of the stations in the Kueneman-Wright study assumed that broadcasts about civil disturbances would produce a contagion effect so that more people would flock to the riot scene to commit violent acts. Broadcasters with previous experience covering riots reported that "respected members of the community, who had jobs, who lived in pretty decent homes, joined the rioting and became looters and snipers because all of a sudden there was an unleashing of ... hatred." [29] By contrast, social scientists who study disasters deny that panic and contagion occur frequently.[30] Whether or not they are correct, the important fact is that media personnel expect these reactions and act accordingly.

Compared to other types of crises, there has been relatively little advance planning for coverage of civil disturbances, despite their prevalence. From the riots of the 1960s, media personnel learned that it is wise to de-emphasize media presence when violence occurs because the perpetrators are spurred by the chance to have their actions publicized. Accordingly, media personnel try to act unobtrusively. For example, they avoid bringing identified television trucks into areas where disturbances are taking place. As mentioned earlier for the Chicago riots in the spring of 1992, newspapers may keep stories and pictures about the events off their front pages. However, such precautions are largely wasted when, as in the Chicago case, television reporters broadcast live coverage from the scene.

It also helps to avoid inflammatory details or language in news reports. Calmer terms can be substituted for words like "carnage," "holocaust," "mob action," or "massacre." The general rule often is "when in doubt, leave it out." Tempers can be soothed by publicizing interviews with responsible public officials and civic leaders who urge calm behavior and who indicate that the situation is under control. In the Los Angeles riots, Mayor Tom Bradley and Governor Pete Wilson were shown and quoted repeatedly about progress made in quieting the city. Rodney King, the victim of the police beating that ultimately led to the disturbances, also made an impassioned appeal for ending the violence. When the mayor says that "Things are under control" and vows that "as much as possible, we want to return this city to normalcy. We want people to feel free, to feel secure," tensions are apt to ease noticeably.[31]

The Problem of News Suppression

In natural as well as man made crises, suppressing news, either temporarily or permanently, raises major policy questions. How much coverage should be presented immediately, at the risk of telling an inaccurate story, spreading panic, and attracting bystanders and destructive participants to the scene? What facts should be withheld initially or permanently? Eighty percent of the newspeople in the sample of radio and television stations mentioned earlier said that they would temporarily withhold information that might provoke troublesome reactions. Many would go further, indicating that they would withhold live coverage entirely, particularly in civil disturbances, because they believed that it would increase the intensity and duration of the crisis. Some news outlets delay live coverage until officials have the situation under control. Others believe that suppression of live coverage will allow the spread of rumors that may be more inciting than judicious reporting of ongoing events. We do not know which of these views is most correct or how different circumstances affect reactions to media coverage of crises.

Deciding whether to suppress coverage becomes particularly difficult when a crisis involves terrorists, prison rioters, assassins of political leaders, or maniacal mass murderers who crave publicity. Granting exposure to them by live coverage glamorizes violence and may encourage further outrages. "By transforming a killer into a celebrity, the press has not merely encouraged but perhaps driven him to strike again and may have stirred others brooding madly over their grievances to act." [32] As Rep. Edward Feighan, D-Ohio, pointed out after chairing congressional hearings on terrorism and the media, the television age poses new dilemmas for a responsible press. "Terrorism is a new form of symbolic warfare, and the television screen is the battlefield on which these wars will be fought in the future." [33]

Such claims highlight the dilemma the press faces. Publicity does play into the hands of individuals willing to spread terror through indiscriminate killings and other abuses of the rights of fellow human beings. On the other hand, if the press fails to cover the terrorist acts, it can be accused of infringing on the public's right to know. It also forgoes publishing a dramatic event with wide audience appeal and substantial financial rewards. If the press follows the government's official line in describing terrorists and their motives, it becomes a government propaganda tool.[34] If it dwells on either the human strengths or the frightful human frailties of the violent actors, it will be accused of making saints out of villains or villains out of hapless victims of society's malfunctions.

In the same way, the press faces difficult decisions about news suppression during international crises and in time of war. During the Gulf War, the military kept tight control over news stories by escorting small groups of reporters to the battle front and then requiring that their dispatches be cleared by military censors. A number of reporters resented such constraints and ventured forth on their own in defiance of official rules and at the risk of their personal safety. While their fellow journalists generally approved, a *Los Angeles Times Mirror* poll showed that 80 percent of the public felt that news censorship by the military was a good idea. When CNN reporter Peter Arnett interviewed President Saddam Hussein during the war and broadcast Hussein's claim, denied by American officials, that the American air force had bombed an infant formula factory, a number of prominent critics publicly questioned Arnett's patriotism. They felt that the press, in wartime, must avoid publicizing news that may hurt war goals, particularly when the news is broadcast worldwide, as is true of CNN.[35]

Muted coverage is problematic. It generally leads to presentation of the official story only and suppression of unofficial views. The perspectives of civilian and military public security personnel become paramount. As a result they stress security aspects rather than the causes of violent behavior and the political and social changes, including new public policies, that might prevent future violence.

In Los Angeles riot coverage, the initial stories were not about minorities who supported the riots as a social protest against unfair treatment by the white community. The media reports suppressed or failed to vent the feelings and ideas of militant leaders in the affected communities. Instead, they concentrated on portraying minorities who supported the policies of the local governing elites. In the short run this helped keep the situation under control, but the long-run effects of carefully limited coverage are more troubling. In terrorist incidents or prison riots, failure to air the grievances of terrorists and prison inmates deprives them of a public forum for voicing their grievances. Their bottled up anger may lead to more violent explosions. Needed reforms may be aborted. Wartime news suppression may cover up misdeeds and encourage their repetition.

Some observers feel that muted reporting reduces the potential for arousing hatred and unbridgeable conflicts. Delayed coverage, they feel, can be more analytical and thus more likely to produce reforms. Others argue that the drama of an ongoing crisis raises public consciousness much better and faster than anything else. People will act to remedy injustice only if the situation is acute. If the crisis has already passed, action may seem pointless. A permanent news blackout will make reforms highly unlikely. Those opposed to muted coverage or news suppression are willing to risk paying a very high price in lost lives, personal injuries, imprisonment, and property damage in hopes that immediate, complete coverage will shock the community to undertake basic social reforms. Most American political leaders, as well as most newspeople, have hitherto opted for muting violent conflict rather than bringing it to a head.

Finally, there is the unresolved philosophical question about the wisdom and propriety of news suppression in a free society. The true test of genuine press freedom does not come in times of calm. It comes in times of crisis when the costs of freedom may be dear, tempting government and media alike to impose silence. If a free press is a paramount value, then the die must be cast in favor of unrestrained crisis coverage, moderated only by the sense of responsibility of individual journalists.

Covering Pseudo-Crises

Thus far, we have discussed genuinely extraordinary events. But there are many other situations that receive similar press treatment because they make interesting news stories. These are the pseudo-crises that have become front page news for days on end as well as generating many hours of live television and radio coverage. As television critic Rick Kogan put it:

> Real life—not the facsimiles and fantasy versions of it once so persuasively (and successfully) purveyed by entertainment television—gave us the most compelling and, like it or not, engaging TV images of 1991.... The Clarence Thomas hearings, for all their import, also steamed hotter than your favorite soap. The [William Kennedy] Smith rape trial, even with its numbing forensic details, was more arresting than "L.A. Law." Add to that such almost-surreal details as Los Angeles police officers beating a motorist, a failed coup in the Soviet Union, and Henry Kissinger playing weatherman on "CBS this Morning," and you have the making of a TV mega-hit: "The Real World Show." [36]

The various scenarios that make up this "Real World Show" on television, as well as in the print media, cause two serious problems. They exaggerate the significance of events that are not extraordinary, usually dwelling on dramatic elements chosen for their appeal to audiences rather than their significance to the development of the story. Perhaps more importantly, they crowd out other events that need coverage. If the media had cut back on overblown coverage, their newshole would have been filled by other, possibly more significant stories.

A brief look at the news stories mentioned by Kogan should be instructive. The Clarence Thomas confirmation hearings were important because they involved questions of fitness of a nominee for a life-long position on the U.S. Supreme Court. Between July 1, 1991, when Thomas was nominated, and October 5, when the hearings took an unexpected turn, the hearings received extensive coverage. The networks, for example, ran thirty to forty stories each, collectively taking up more than four hours of airtime.[37] By comparison, in a three month span, the networks, on average, devote thirty-six stories to the Supreme Court's activities, taking up less than one and a half hours of airtime.

The unexpected turn that was played out for nine days starting on October 6 were public charges by Oklahoma University law professor Anita Hill that Clarence Thomas had subjected her to sexual harassment when she was working in the agency that he headed. Print as well as electronic media featured saturation coverage. Besides reporting the hearings in their entirety, the evening news shows on ABC, CBS, and NBC carried four hours and eight minutes of reports about the hearings, nearly as much as for the coverage of Thomas's qualifications during the preceding three month span. The centerpiece of the coverage was the allegations, presented in lurid detail. Thomas was eloquent in his denials and Hill was equally eloquent in proclaiming that she was telling the truth. The audience was left to judge who should be believed since neither party could present absolute proof.

Did the lengthy soap opera deflect attention from more important issues of the candidate's political philosophy and judicial capabilities? Did it displace other important news in the print and electronic press? Yes. However, the coverage was not without major political consequence. By making voters, particularly women, aware of the fact that the Senate Judiciary Committee was composed entirely of males and that several members seemed unsympathetic to sexual harassment charges, it contributed to primary election victories of several women candidates for Congress who turned the hearings into campaign issues.

While there were thus some features in the Thomas saga that made coverage less of a waste, this has not generally been common in pseudo-crisis news coverage. The many hours spent on live coverage of the Smith rape trial, which involved a member of the Kennedy clan, were a sorry loss for news coverage. In the case of the Rodney King beating, overly extensive coverage of an important news story had unfortunate consequences. It contributed to the frustrations that exploded in the Los Angeles riots. The main reason for repeating coverage so frequently was the fact that the pictures were extraordinarily graphic. By contrast, the 1992 trial of mass murderer Jeffrey Dahmer, who told in detail how he drugged, murdered, and cannibalized his young victims, received relatively little coverage, even in the tabloid press, because it offered few good pictures.[38]

Finally, one may take issue with Rick Kogan about whether the failed coup against Soviet President Gorbachev received exaggerated, overly dramatic coverage, or whether it was handled properly. These issues are often controversial. As for Henry Kissinger as weatherman, this author offers "no comment."

Summary

In American political culture the normal feuds of politics are suspended when the nation is in danger. Although this unwritten rule is mentioned most often in connection with foreign policy, where "politics stops at the water's edge," it applies to the types of domestic crises discussed in this chapter. When life and property are endangered, when sudden death and terror reign, when well-known leaders are assassinated, or when the nation goes to war, normal media coverage practices are suspended. During crises, the media tend to abandon their adversarial role. They become teammates of officialdom in attempts to restore public order, safety, and tranquility.

The media perform indispensable functions during crises: they diffuse vital information to the public and officials, interpret events, and provide emotional support for troubled communities. Radio is particularly helpful in major disasters because its technical requirements are most adaptable to makeshift arrangements. It can broadcast without regular electric power supplies to people who have only a pocket transistor radio and are otherwise isolated. Round-the-clock news coverage by CNN and others and satellite transmissions from around the world make it possible to observe extraordinary events wherever they occur.

Because the media play such a large part in public communication during crises, the way they discharge their responsibilities has been of great concern to public officials and to the community at large. Information gaps, misinformation, and the dissemination of information that makes the effects of the crisis worse have led to demands that the information flow be controlled to better manage each crisis. Many media institutions have formal plans that temporarily set aside the usual criteria for publishing exciting news in the interest of calming the public.

Muted coverage, particularly during civil disturbances and incidents of political terrorism, may be unwise because it may drown out explicit and implicit messages about unmet societal needs. The need to plan for crisis coverage, however, is certain. Modern society faces crises of various sorts so frequently that policy makers in the media and in government would be remiss to make no plans for emergencies. By the same token, they should strive to avoid news distortion and waste when titillating stories tempt them to indulge in excessive coverage.

Notes

1. For details of the Reagan story, see Brigitte Lebens Nacos, *The Press, Presidents, and Crises* (New York: Columbia University Press, 1990), chap. 5.
2. For details of the Los Angeles riots, see "Rage in L.A.," *Chicago Tribune,* May 1, 1992.
3. For details of the Gulf War coverage, see William A. Hachten, *The World News Prism: Changing Media of International Communication,* 3d ed. (Ames: Iowa State University Press, 1992), chap. 9.
4. For details of the Mount St. Helens eruption, see Dan Nimmo and James E. Combs, *Nightly Horrors: Crisis Coverage in Television Network News* (Knoxville: University of Tennessee Press, 1985), chap. 4.

5. Dennis E. Wenger, "A Few Empirical Observations Concerning the Relationship between the Mass Media and Disaster Knowledge: A Research Report," in *Disasters and the Mass Media: Proceedings of the Committee on Disasters and the Mass Media Workshop* (Washington, D.C.: National Academy Press, 1980), 242-244. For a discussion of news-gathering techniques during disasters, see Rahul Sood, Geoffrey Stockdale, and Everett M. Rogers, "How the News Media Operate in Natural Disasters," *Journal of Communication* 37 (Summer 1987): 27-41.

6. *Gallup Poll Monthly,* January 1991, 21.

7. Walter Gantz, "The Diffusion of News About the Attempted Reagan Assassination," *Journal of Communication* 33 (Winter 1983): 56-65.

8. Daniel Yutzy, *Community Priorities at the Anchorage, Alaska Earthquake, 1964* (Columbus: Ohio State University Disaster Research Center, 1969), 127; and "Watching the War: Patterns of Diffusion and Information-Seeking during a Crisis," International Communication Association, May 1991.

9. Mitchell Stephens and Nadyne G. Edison, "News Media Coverage of Issues during the Accident at Three-Mile Island," *Journalism Quarterly* 59 (Summer 1982): 199-204, 259.

10. Quoted in Casey Bukro, "How Accurate Was Press about Three Mile Island?" *Chicago Tribune,* March 30, 1980.

11. T. Joseph Scanlon, "Media Coverage of Crises: Better than Reported, Worse than Necessary," *Journalism Quarterly* 55 (Spring 1978): 68-72.

12. Wenger, "A Few Empirical Observations," 252-253.

13. David L. Paletz and Robert M. Entman, *Media Power Politics* (New York: Free Press, 1981), 114-117; Robert Reinhold, "Los Angeles Ends Curfew, but Tensions Remain High," *New York Times,* May 5, 1992.

14. Hachten, *World News Prism,* 155-156.

15. Timothy W. Luke, "Chernobyl: The Packaging of Transnational Ecological Disaster," *Critical Studies in Mass Communication* 4 (December 1987): 357. See also Sharon M. Friedman, Carole M. Gorney, and Brenda P. Egolf, "Reporting on Radiation: A Content Analysis of Chernobyl Coverage," *Journal of Communication* 37 (Summer 1987): 58-79.

16. Nimmo and Combs, *Nightly Horrors,* 122.

17. Deidre Carmody, "News Media Defended in Inquiry on Reports of Three Mile Island," *New York Times,* October 31, 1979; and Peter Sandman and Mary Paden, "At Three Mile Island," *Columbia Journalism Review* 17 (July/August 1979): 43-58.

18. Steve Johnson and Susan Kucza, "Two for Two: Bulls Still Champs!" *Chicago Tribune,* June 15, 1992; and Louise Kiernan and John Fountain, "Bulls Fans Stampede over City," *Chicago Tribune,* June 15, 1992.

19. Seth Mydans, "Los Angeles Darkness Fell on Neighboring City," *New York Times,* May 20, 1992.

20. Eleanor Singer and Phyllis Endreny, "Reporting Hazards: Their Benefits and Costs," *Journal of Communication* 37 (Summer 1987): 10-26.

21. Alex Jones, "U.S. Sees the Press Helping Hijackers," *New York Times,* June 20, 1985.

22. Benjamin D. Singer, "Mass Media and Communication Processes in the Detroit Riot of 1967," *Public Opinion Quarterly* 34 (Summer 1970): 236-245.

23. John Corry, "Network News Covers the Stock Market Frenzy," *New York Times,* October 21, 1987; and Alex Jones, "Caution in the Press: Was It

Really a 'Crash'? " *New York Times,* October 21, 1987.
24. Rodney M. Kueneman and Joseph E. Wright, "News Policies of Broadcast Stations for Civil Disturbances and Disasters," *Journalism Quarterly* 52 (Winter 1975): 670-677.
25. Sharon M. Friedman, "Blueprint for Breakdown: Three Mile Island and the Media before the Accident," *Journal of Communication* 31 (Spring 1981): 116-128.
26. Douglas A. Anderson, "Handling of Controversial 'Merry-Go-Round' Columns," *Journalism Quarterly* 59 (Summer 1982): 295-298.
27. Kueneman and Wright, "News Policies," 671.
28. Michael Tackett, "Quake Jitters: How a Man Shook Midwest," *Chicago Tribune,* December 2, 1991.
29. Kueneman and Wright, "News Policies," 672.
30. See the report on the work of the Disaster Research Center at Ohio State University in E. L. Quarantelli and Russell R. Dynes, eds., "Organizational and Group Behavior in Disasters," *American Behavioral Scientist* 13 (January 1970).
31. Reinhold, "Los Angeles Ends Curfew."
32. *New Yorker,* August 15, 1977, 21.
33. Edward F. Feighan, "After the Hostage Crisis, TV Focuses on Itself," *New York Times,* August 19, 1985.
34. Alex P. Schmid and Janny de Graaf, *Violence as Communication: Insurgent Terrorism and the Western News Media* (Beverly Hills, Calif.: Sage, 1982), 98. For an analysis of the symbiotic relationship of media and sources of crisis news, see Gadi Wolfsfeld, "Symbiosis of Press and Protest: An Exchange Analysis," *Journalism Quarterly* 61 (Autumn 1984): 550-555.
35. Hachten, *World News Prism,* 163.
36. Rick Kogan, "As the World Churns," *Chicago Tribune,* December 19, 1991.
37. S. Robert Lichter and Linda Lichter, eds., "The Trials of Clarence Thomas: Media Coverage of Judge Thomas' Confirmation Battle," *Media Monitor* 5 (October 1991): 1-6.
38. James Warren, "Media Gives Dahmer Trial Mild Coverage," *Chicago Tribune,* February 2, 1992.

Readings

Alali, A. Odasuo, and Kenoye Kelvin Eke. *Media Coverage of Terrorism: Methods and Diffusion.* Newbury Park, Calif.: Sage, 1991.
Disasters and the Mass Media: Proceedings of the Committee on Disasters and the Mass Media Workshop. Washington, D.C.: National Academy of Sciences, 1980.
Nimmo, Dan, and James E. Combs. *Nightly Horrors: Crisis Coverage in Television Network News.* Knoxville: University of Tennessee Press, 1985.
Paletz, David, and Alex P. Schmid, eds. *Terrorism and the Media.* Newbury Park, Calif.: Sage, 1992.
Schlesinger, Philip. *Media, State and Nation: Political Violence and Collective Identities.* Newbury Park, Calif.: Sage, 1991.
Taylor, Philip M. *War and the Media: Propaganda and Persuasion in the Gulf War.* New York: St. Martin's Press, 1992.
Walters, Lynne Masel, Lee Wilkins, and Tim Walters. *Bad Tidings: Communication and Catastrophe.* Hillsdale, N.J.: Lawrence Erlbaum, 1989.

CHAPTER 6

The Media As Policy Makers

In his autobiography Lincoln Steffens, who has been called "America's greatest reporter," tells how a history professor introduced him to an audience as "the first of the muckrakers." Steffens corrected the professor. "I had to answer first that I was not the original muckraker; the prophets of the Old Testament were ahead of me, and to make a big jump in time so were the writers, editors, and reporters (including myself) of the 1890s who were finding fault with 'things as they are' in the pre-muckraking period." [1]

Steffens was right. Public exposés of evil and corruption in high places have been common throughout recorded history. They rest on the assumption that exposure will shame the wrongdoers and lead to public condemnation of their deeds and possibly punishment. Ultimately, reforms may ensue.[2] Exposés have always been and will continue to be an important feature of social responsibility journalism in America. They are a major part of the deliberate manipulation of the political process mentioned in Chapter 1 as one of the media's chief functions.

In this chapter muckraking will be examined to show how it really works, with particular attention to the role played by public opinion. Agenda building, another widely used strategy for manipulating politics, will be examined in different situations, such as leadership crises driven by political scandal, the development of science policy, and the support of interest group goals. Next we will assess the political impact of nationally broadcast factual and fictional documentaries on current political issues. Our study of manipulative journalism concludes with reflections on the responsibility of newspeople to refrain from questionable methods in their zeal to reform society.

Like other manifestations of the social responsibility ethic, manipulative journalism raises philosophical, ethical, and news policy questions. Do newspeople jeopardize important professional values, like objectivity and neutrality, when they try to shape the events that they report? Do they create a witch-hunting climate that intimidates officeholders and deters capable people from careers in politics? [3] If newspeople fail to objectively report the passing scene, do they sacrifice credibility? Where can media audiences turn for a reasonably unbiased view of the complexities of political life if media sources, like government officials, are partisans? Claims by newspeople that their political activities reflect the wishes of their audiences are questionable as long as the selection and activities of journalists are not subject to control by the publics that they claim to represent. In fact, public opinion polls show mixed rates of approval for many tactics used in investigative journalism. [4]

Despite the concerns it raises, the role of the journalist as political actor is currently popular. This is demonstrated by the many instances of outright collaboration between official policy makers and media personnel. It is also shown by the widespread practice of "leaking," where dissatisfied insiders, rather than attempting reforms on their own, enlist media support to gain their ends. Moreover, citizens routinely contact the media with problems concerning public affairs. In fact, just as the media have taken over many functions formerly performed by political parties during elections, so they have assumed many of the ombudsman, reform, and law enforcement functions traditionally performed by other institutions in society. Whether this is the cause or consequence of the weakening of these other institutions remains a hotly debated question.

Manipulative Journalism in Perspective

The extent of the efforts of newspeople to participate in policy making has fluctuated as philosophies of news making have changed. The turmoil of the 1960s, which raised the public's social consciousness, the Watergate scandal, which forced President Richard Nixon to resign, and the shift toward advocating a social responsibility ethic in journalism schools have once again raised manipulative journalism from a position of disdain to a position of high esteem. Approval is not unanimous, to be sure, but it is widespread, especially in elite media circles. Reporters and media institutions whose investigations have led to important social and political reforms frequently win prizes for high journalistic achievement. Given the prestige accorded to investigative journalists and the political successes attributed to them, it is no surprise that investigative reporting began to thrive in major print and electronic media institutions during the 1970s.

Independent investigative organizations that collaborate with media institutions have flourished as well. The nonprofit, foundation-subsidized Center for Investigative Reporting, established in San Francisco in 1977, is an example. The center uses freelance reporters who collectively conduct investigations and who can be hired by various media to undertake projects that cannot be readily handled internally. The Community Information Project in Los Angeles and the Better Government Association in Chicago are other institutions that do similar investigative work. Investigative Reporters and Editors (IRE), a national organization, has been active in teaching its approaches to mainstream journalists.[5]

Collaboration between independent watchdog organizations and the media is mutually beneficial. It ensures that the investigations of interest to these institutions will be publicized, thereby increasing the chances for corrective action. Tapping into media resources also helps cover the costs of complex investigations that can run into hundreds of thousands of dollars. This added financial support can be crucial. The media, in turn, gain collaborators who are skilled in investigating public issues and who often have excellent connections in government and in the community. The prestige and credibility of the organization may also enhance the credibility of a jointly issued report.

The substance and style of most investigative stories reflect three major objectives. The first objective is to produce exciting stories that will appeal to media audiences. Second, investigative reporters hope to gain plaudits from the journalism profession. Third, in addition to these routine journalistic goals, many reporters want to trigger political action or be part of it. Even when political consequences are not initially envisioned, most reporters feel highly gratified when their stories lead to actions that accord with their political and social preferences.

Sometimes the line between deliberate attempts to produce political changes and incidental sparking of reforms is too fine to distinguish. For example, when the media follow up on a report of a series of deaths in nursing homes, and discover and describe deplorable conditions that led to these deaths, is this a case of muckraking designed to manipulate political events and bring about reform? Or does the idea that reform is needed arise naturally and purely incidentally from a routine news story? Was Steffens telling the truth when he claimed, "I did not intend to be a muckraker; I did not know that I was one till President Roosevelt picked the name out of Bunyan's *Pilgrim's Progress* and pinned it on us." [6] Could Steffens have specialized in writing sensational exposés of corruption in state and local government and in private business for the sheer joy of delving into the muck, with no thought given to the major reforms that followed in the wake of some of his stories?

From the standpoint of the political reformer, it may not matter whether reform was an intended or unintended byproduct of investigative reporting. The distinction matters, however, to newspeople because it raises controversial issues about the proper role of journalism in American society. Journalists, even when they favor social responsibility journalism in the abstract, do not like to admit that they wrote their stories to produce social and political reforms. Moreover, they do not call attention to the fact that investigative reporting, unlike normal story gathering, is designed to prove a preconceived notion. Sources are carefully selected to gain support for the reporter's hypothesis. Opponents are shunned, except as a counterforce to lend credibility to the investigation.[7]

Muckraking Models

There are three ways investigative journalism leads to political action. Journalists may write stories about public policies in hopes of engendering a massive public reaction that will lead to widespread demands for political remedies. On the other hand, journalists may write stories to arouse political elites who are officeholders or who have influence with officeholders. These elites, eager to forestall public anger, then may attempt to resolve the problems, often even before the media report is actually published. Finally, action may be the result of direct collaboration between investigative journalists and public officeholders. They may coordinate news stories and supportive political activities to bring about desired reforms. We will trace the rate of success in each of these different types of situations.

The process can be pictured in the form of three models: the simple muckraking model, the leaping impact model, and the truncated muckraking model. Social scientists Harvey Molotch, David Protess, and Margaret Gordon, and their coworkers who developed these models, tested them in investigative situations entailing muckraking—sensational exposés of corruption usually involving high status individuals. The models also illustrate other types of manipulative journalism.[8]

The simple muckraking model begins when journalists investigate a serious societal problem that could be ameliorated through political action. The investigation leads to published news that stirs the public. Aroused public opinion then mobilizes policy makers who act to solve the problem. Schematically, the process usually looks as pictured below, although the sequence of the elements in the model may vary:

Journalistic investigation $>$ Publication $>$ Public opinion $>$ Policy initiatives $>$ Policy consequences

When some elements in the model are skipped entirely, the leaping impact model is at work. For instance, following investigation and publication of the story, policy initiatives may be taken without prior public opinion pressure. Alternatively, a journalistic investigation may have policy consequences even without new initiatives in policy or publication of reports about the investigation. In the truncated muckraking model the muckraking sequence may be aborted at any point so that the investigation fails to lead to corrective policies. This occurs frequently and can happen in several ways. The investigation may not lead to published stories because the evidence is insufficient or too hot to handle. Published stories may not stir public opinion. An aroused public may not move public officials to act. Policy initiatives may not lead to any symbolic or substantive results.

Several examples of muckraking will illustrate these models. Most of the examples come from intensive studies of muckraking conducted by scholars who had arranged to be alerted to forthcoming media exposés. This permitted them to interview citizens and policy makers concerned with the issue under investigation, both before and after publication of the stories. The impact of the story could then be assessed far more accurately than is usually possible when stories come as a surprise and permit only ex post facto assessment. Actual changes in public policy also were monitored for a period of several months following the exposés. The journalists' motives and methods in conducting the investigations were judged as well.[9]

Simple Muckraking

A story about reform of a school for mentally retarded children in Staten Island, New York, illustrates simple muckraking: the media aroused the public, and the public then demanded and received action. Television commentator Geraldo Rivera presented a seven-minute report about shocking conditions that he had observed during a visit to the Willowbrook State School. After a station near the school had shown the report, some seven hundred viewers called to express their concern. Shocked parents later gathered at the school and solicited promises of help from local public officials. The Staten Island Chapter of the Society for the Prevention of Cruelty to Children began hearings and asked the state and federal governments to investigate.[10] But the flurry of activity was short-lived and largely unproductive. Only minor reforms in the school's handling of children resulted from these investigations.

Such modest outcomes are typical in situations that reflect the simple muckraking model. Researchers rarely find solid evidence that media-aroused public opinion is a strong force for change. There are several reasons why. Many Americans are complacent or cynical about the political status quo. It is therefore difficult to spur them to take action on public problems, even those directly affecting them. For example, extensive efforts to arouse public concern about energy shortages and the need for conservation have proved largely futile.[11] Because most Americans' interests lie outside of politics, they ignore or assign little importance to investigative news stories, or forget them quickly, except when they are extraordinarily dramatic and point the finger at identifiable villains. Accordingly, politicians often feel safe in ignoring swells in public opinion, believing that they involve relatively few people and that they will soon subside when new issues capture the public's fancy.

On the other end of the interest spectrum, media investigative stories may be about an issue that is already a matter of great concern to the public. Although the investigative story confirms that concern, it does not push the public across the barrier of reluctance to press for political action. For example, a five-part newspaper series in the *Chicago Sun-Times* in 1982 on "Rape: Every Woman's Nightmare" dealt with the incidence and consequences of rape in the Chicago area. Interviews conducted prior to the series had shown that the public was already greatly concerned about the problem. The series maintained that concern, but it did little to spur new action to fight crime. An interesting, unexpected byproduct of the rape stories was heightened sensitivity of the newspaper staff to the problem. Following the series, *Sun-Times* stories on rape more than doubled in number, and coverage became more insightful.[12] Investigators rarely notice such unexpected consequences or much-delayed consequences. Hence reports about the effects of investigative stories often understate their impact.

Although it is difficult for the media to arouse public opinion, some investigative stories do. The Willowbrook State School case is an example. The elements that brought about its success included an emotional issue—the treatment of disabled children in the audience's locality; a flamboyant, well-known reporter who dramatized the story; and a local group of citizens directly and profoundly affected by the alleged misbehavior of public officials. When such a story captures people's interest, and they have little prior knowledge about the situation, they may learn much and become highly concerned. As we have noted, however, major corrective action remains unlikely.[13]

Leaping Impact Muckraking

A media exposé called "Arson for Profit" that was aired by ABC's "20/20" in 1979 exemplified the leaping impact model. The investigation indicated that extensive fire damage in Chicago's Uptown neighborhood resulted from arson planned by a group of real estate owners. The group would buy dilapidated buildings, insure them heavily, and then burn them down to collect the insurance. Following the exposé, government elites voiced concern but failed to act. Nevertheless, corrections occurred. The arson-for-profit perpetrators, fearing further public exposure, decided to retreat. In the month following the broadcast, fires declined by 27 percent in the area where arson for profit had flourished. It was the first decline in five years. Insurance payments for arson also dropped by more than 20 percent in the year following the arson stories. No other metropolitan area showed comparable drops. The Illinois legislature responded belatedly with very minor policy reforms. There were no criminal indictments of the parties implicated in the insurance fraud. This story exemplifies the leaping impact model because the leap was from publication directly to correction; elite arousal and, by and large, elite action and public opinion pressures were nonexistent.

The most common "leaping impact" situation takes place when newspeople and public officials openly collaborate. This *coalition journalism* may be initiated by media or government personnel, or it may arise by chance without prior formal contacts between media personnel and policy actors. Newspeople are very eager to involve government officials in investigative stories because this lends credibility and significance to their stories and increases the chances of substantial policy consequences. Although it may jeopardize the media's zealous pursuit of the watchdog role, coalition journalism gets results.

A good example of coalition journalism concerns the events following an NBC "Newsmagazine" story, "The Home Health Hustle," broadcast May 7, 1981, which exposed fraud and abuse in home health-care programs. Public opinion polls showed that the broadcast aroused the concerns of many viewers who previously were unaware of problems with these programs. But public opinion apparently was not instrumental in Congress's decision to introduce appropriate reform legislation. In the fashion of leaping impact models, the legislative results seemed to flow directly from collaboration between investigative reporters and members of the U.S. Senate that preceded airing of the story by several months.

Journalists had met with officials of the Senate's Permanent Subcommittee on Investigations to plan a series of hearings on home health-care fraud and to coordinate their broadcasts with the Senate's activities. The hearings were then announced during the broadcast. Subsequently, senators credited media personnel with major contributions to the investigation of home health-care fraud. However, it is uncertain to what degree the knowledge that television would feature the story spurred the senators to collaborate with the media. The combined investigative activities of the media and the Senate ultimately led to a number of proposals for corrective legislation. Still, in the end, the bills failed to pass. Aside from the effects of increased vigilance by public officials and home health-care consumers, there were no major changes that could be directly linked to the investigative stories.[14]

Similarly, when the rape series appeared in the *Chicago Sun-Times,* newspeople had already alerted policy makers. This permitted the policy makers to time announcements of previously planned measures, such as creation of a rape hotline, to coincide with the investigative series. When a story about unnecessary and illegal abortions in state clinics was about to break in Illinois, the governor immediately associated himself with the media investigators prior to publication. This made it possible to make reform proposals part of the original story. It also enhanced the governor's image as an effective leader.

Truncated Muckraking

The truncated muckraking model is well illustrated by the "Mirage" investigation, conducted in 1977 by the *Chicago Sun-Times* and CBS's "60 Minutes" program with the help of Chicago's Better Government Association, a civic watchdog organization. Hoping to demonstrate extensive graft in the city's regulatory agencies, the partners in the investigation opened a bar in Chicago, appropriately named the "Mirage." The bar was wired to record transactions that might take place between its personnel and city officials. In a brief period of time, ample evidence of bribery and fraud was accumulated.[15]

After the story about the illegal transactions was published, public opinion polls recorded that many citizens were outraged. Nonetheless, they took no serious corrective action to prevent similar graft in the future. Schematically, the model ended with the arousal of public opinion, skipping elite arousal and action and final corrective activities. The failure to produce a correction does not necessarily mean that an official response never occurs. Symbolic responses are common, such as promises of reform by political leaders, or studies of the problem, including public hearings, but with no action follow-up. At other times policy makers may punish individual offenders but do nothing to correct the situation that is causing the problem.[16]

The Role of Public Opinion

These examples of muckraking suggest that the major role attributed to public opinion in producing political action is greatly exaggerated. More often than not, the media fail to arouse the public, even when investigative stories are written to produce public excitement. When stories do agitate the public, little happens as a rule. Politicians and journalists have learned that public anger is short-lived. It can be safely ignored or channeled to support reform movements that are already under way. Corrective action is more likely to come when publicity-shy wrongdoers mend their ways, when the stories arouse elites, or when journalists and political elites have arranged to collaborate. It also helps when there are follow-ups on the story in different media and over a prolonged period of time.

Even though publicity rarely causes a tidal surge of public opinion, fear that it might do so makes the media more successful than other pressure groups in gaining their reform objectives. Since public opinion is, in fact, largely irrelevant in generating political reforms, the media's claim that they are handmaiden to the democratic process becomes highly questionable. In fact, the media are using the facade of public opinion support to enhance their already powerful position as political movers and shakers.

The Muddying of Public Figures

Stories about Joseph Biden's plagiarism, Jesse Jackson's reference to New York City as "Hymietown," Dan Quayle's escape into the National Guard to duck regular Army service, Chuck Robb's attendance at parties where cocaine was used, Barney Frank's liaison with a male prostitute, Douglas Ginsburg's marijuana smoking—all of these are part of the epidemic of mudslinging that mars the American political landscape. In each case, incidents in the lives of these individuals were endlessly examined, interpreted, and judged, regardless of the story's significance or private nature. It is true that the people just mentioned are important political figures. At the time, Biden and Jackson were candidates for the presidency, Quayle became vice-president, Robb was governor of Virginia, and Frank a congressman. Ginsburg was a nominee for the Supreme Court whose nomination was withdrawn. While the American press is entitled to probe the lives and reputations of such public persons, and the American public has a right to know about matters that are politically relevant, there is widespread agreement that the press has become overzealous in such investigations, destroying reputations needlessly.

Political scientist Larry Sabato, who refers to mudslinging episodes as "feeding frenzies," puts the blame on increasingly stiff competition among media for attention and on the need for round-the-clock radio and television enterprises to fill long hours with emotional audience-bait.

In such situations any development is almost inevitably magnified and overscrutinized; the crush of cameras, microphones, and people com-

Reprinted by permission of Doug Marlette and Creators Syndicate.

bined with the pressure of instant deadlines and live broadcasts hype events and make it difficult to keep them in perspective. When a frenzy begins to gather, the intensity grows exponentially. Major newspapers assign teams of crack reporters and researchers to the frenzy's victims. . . . Television news time is virtually turned over to the subject of the frenzy. Republican vice-presidential nominee Dan Quayle was the subject of ninety-three network evening news stories over the twelve days of his frenzy in August, 1988—more coverage than twelve of the thirteen presidential candidates had received during all the primaries combined.[17]

The Reagan-Gorbachev summit meeting, eight months earlier, had generated a mere fifty-three stories over a ten-day span.

Such attack journalism raises a number of important ethical and political issues. From the perspective of the people whose reputations and careers are dragged through the mud and often ruined, it raises questions about the right of privacy of public figures and the ethics of journalists who publish such stories even when they consider them to be politically irrelevant. Some journalists justify giving inordinate amounts of publicity to such incidents by claiming that they might throw some light on the individual's character. But many others, including personnel at elite media, admit that they are merely jumping on the bandwagon of competition. They argue that if others exploit the story, they must feature it as well. That is hardly the epitome of ethical behavior.

Beyond injury to individual public figures, there are broader consequences. The risk of having long-past or more recent indiscretions exposed to public view, or having off-hand remarks elevated into major pronouncements, sharply reduces the pool of people willing to serve careers in politics. Many talented people are likely to prefer the safety of private life over the merciless glare of unstoppable publicity in the public sector. Finally, the extraordinary amount of media time and space devoted to mudslinging frenzies comes at the expense of other, more worthwhile news that may never be published. The old Greek admonition "everything in moderation" is relevant. Whenever attack journalism seems appropriate, it should be practiced. But there is never a need for feeding frenzies, joined by journalists in sorry exhibitions of pack journalism.

Beyond Muckraking: Power Plays and Surrenders

Direct media intervention in the government process may take a number of forms other than muckraking. Three types of situations are usually involved: media power plays, media acting as surrogates for public officials, and media acting as mouthpieces for government officials or interest groups.

Least common are media power plays in which newspeople bully government officials into action by threatening to publicize stories that officials would prefer to conceal. During the Watergate investigations in the Nixon administration, a number of stories about political misdeeds were aborted when warnings by newspeople about prospective coverage brought about reforms. Similarly, Gary Hart dropped temporarily out of the presidential race in 1987 when the *Washington Post* threatened to publish new reports about his marital infidelities. In addition to overt threats, which are rare, implied or anticipated threats may have major political consequences. Politicians may act or refrain from acting because they know that newspeople might publish damaging information. Adverse publicity from influential columnists is especially feared.

Even less frequently, news personnel may act as surrogates for public officials by actively participating in an evolving situation, such as a prison riot or a diplomatic impasse. The solution, developed with the assistance of news personnel or at their initiative, may then significantly shape subsequent government action. Walter Cronkite's impact on relations between Egypt and Israel, mentioned in Chapter 11, is a famous example of diplomacy conducted by journalists. More commonly, reporters often spark investigations of illegal activities by alerting law enforcement officials. For example, a Chicago television station alerted city officials to illegal storage of hazardous and flammable chemical waste on the campus of the University of Chicago. Hours later, city fire officials inspected the scene and cited the university for numerous fire code violations.[18]

To prevent impending tragedies and solve existing cases, journalists have also become involved in broadcasts about kidnapped children and in "crime stopper" programs that feature reenactments or recountings of unsolved crimes. The programs use media stories, coupled with financial rewards, to elicit information from citizens that may help in solving the crime. They are featured in nearly five hundred communities in the United States and Canada and have helped to clear up thousands of felonies.[19] In fact, the Federal Bureau of Investigation credits such programs with facilitating the capture of up to 30 percent of the criminals on its Most Wanted List.[20]

A far more common form of interaction occurs when the media become a mouthpiece for government officials or interest groups, either because of belief in their causes or in return for attractive stories and other favors. This type of interaction often involves leaks. Government officials who are disgruntled with current policies or practices for personal, professional, or political reasons may leak information to sympathetic journalists to enlist their support. Journalists may cooperate and publish the allegations, or they may investigate the situation, often with the cooperation of the individuals who leaked the information.

When newspeople and officials collaborate, the boundary between ordinary reporting and manipulative journalism can become blurred. It is difficult to tell when one merges into the other because a correct diagnosis of manipulative journalism requires establishing motivations. In many instances the available evidence strongly suggests that newspeople acted as political partisans who used their powers of publicity to foster preferred causes and to harm others. When the *Philadelphia Inquirer* was tipped off by a congressional committee staff member about shoddy treatment of kidney dialysis patients, the paper rushed to the aid of the patients. It was clear from the start that dialysis providers and a negligent federal government would be the outright villains in the news stories.[21] In other cases the main objective in publicizing leaked information is mercenary. Newspeople put their services at the command of anyone who promises to be a fertile source for future news or who can provide an attractive story, no matter what the merits of the story may be. The television networks are particularly eager to obtain exciting scoops during "sweeps," the periods when audience ratings are measured to determine how much money advertisers will be charged.

Exploitation of the media by public officials and political interest groups, as a tool to attain their political objectives, is often quite obvious. The videotaped plea for help by an American hostage in Lebanon in the summer of 1989 is a good example. CBS, CNN, and NBC repeatedly broadcast a 98-second emotional message by Joseph

Cicippo who urged release of an Arab leader kidnapped by Israel. According to the taped message, failure to pressure Israel to act would lead to the death of all American hostages held by Cicippo's captors. Although the networks clearly stated that Cicippo seemed to be reading his plea under duress, because they broadcast the message they were accused of acting as a propaganda conduit for terrorists.[22]

In the same way, when CNN reporter Peter Arnett provided a world-wide forum for President Saddam Hussein of Iraq to condemn U.S. military ventures during the Gulf War, Arnett was widely criticized by members of Congress. On the other hand, prominent journalists lauded his broadcasts and praised his courage and skills.[23]

Although the media are often quite willing to publish a good story, even at the expense of fostering an undesirable cause, they are loath to become unwitting government tools. In 1986, for example, officials of the Reagan administration were suspected of spreading false information about Libya in an attempt to forestall terrorist attacks. When rumors about the administration's deception surfaced, news executives expressed outrage. The comment of Roone Arledge, president of ABC News, was the epitome of the general reaction when he called it "despicable to tinker with the credibility of one of our most sacred and basic institutions, the press, for whatever reason." [24]

Agenda Building

In many instances the media manipulate the political scene by creating a climate for political action. This makes them major contributors to agenda building, the process whereby news stories influence how people perceive and evaluate issues and policies. Agenda building goes beyond agenda setting. The media set the public agenda when news stories rivet attention on a problem and make it seem important to many people. Media build the public agenda when they create a political climate that determines the likely thrust of public opinions.

Newspeople rarely stir up controversies when established elites agree on matters of public policy. They have been criticized for timidity on that score.[25] The absence of reported conflict makes it seem, often erroneously, that elites as well as the public approve the unchallenged policies.[26] But when an issue becomes a matter of controversy among political elites, the media frequently zero in on it. They "supply the context that ... gives people reasons for taking sides and converts the problem into a serious political issue. In this sense the public agenda is not so much set by the media as built up through a cycle of media activity that transforms an elite issue into a public controversy." [27] The agenda building role of the media in policy making thus is symbiotic. The media are an essential part of the operation, but ultimate success hinges on major roles played by other political actors as well.

Molotch, Protess, and Gordon make this clear in the conclusion of their study of the role of investigative journalism in the Watergate scandal. The resolution of the issue was not, as popularly believed, a triumph for unaided media power:

> We therefore disagree with those who would assign "credit" for the Nixon exposures to the media just as we would disagree with those who would assign it to the Congress. Nor should the credit go, in some acontextual, additive sense, to both of these sectors. Instead, the Watergate "correction" was the result of the ways in which news of the Nixon scandals fit the goals and strategic needs of important media and policy actors. All of these actors, each with some degree of "relative autonomy"..., are part of an evolving "ecology of games," ... part of a "dance" ... in which actors have, by virtue of their differential skills and status positions, varying access to participate. Because they so continuously anticipate each other's moves, their activities are, as a matter of course, mutually constituted.[28]

Political Scandal

Sociologists Gladys and Kurt Lang reached similar conclusions. Their study of the role of the media in Watergate traces the precise part played by the media in this "ecology of games" in which the disparate interests of various political actors are blended to create and develop political scenarios. The Langs outlined the steps through which political agendas are usually constructed.[29] A look at the steps makes it clear that there is ample opportunity and often strong temptation for newspeople to guide agenda building deliberately.

Agenda building begins when newspeople decide to publish a particular story. In most instances this is a matter of free choice since few stories are so blatantly significant that omission is unthinkable. The second decision concerns the degree of attention to be given to the story. This is the point where ordinary agenda-setting activities can most readily turn into deliberate agenda building. If newspeople determine that a story should become prominent, they must feature it conspicuously and often enough to arouse the attention of the elite media, including national television, and the attention of political elites. The Watergate story, for instance, received extensive and sustained publicity in the *Washington Post* before it finally caught on and gained nationwide publicity.

Capturing national attention usually requires several other media-controlled steps. Issues must be put into an interpretive frame that will interest media audiences. For instance, as long as the media framed Watergate as an election campaign story, it was discounted by media audiences as just another partisan squabble. Once the media, with the aid of members of Congress, were able to depict it as an issue of pervasive corruption and dishonesty at the highest levels of government, it generated widespread concern. Without this climate of public concern, severe penalties for the Watergate offenders, including the president, would never have been acceptable. In the course of putting issues into a conceptual framework, language becomes an important tool. When newspeople and politicians switched from writing and talking about the Watergate *caper* or the *bugging incident* and began to discuss the Watergate *scandal* and *tragedy,* what had been perceived as a fairly trivial incident became transformed into a very serious matter.

As the Langs noted, the particular sources that the media select to tell a story are important. Skewing inevitably takes place when newspeople tap one human mind, rather than another, for information and interpretation. In the case of major public policy issues, sources become symbols that indicate to media audiences whether a particular position is or is not meritorious. When the media featured prominent Republicans and members of the judiciary acknowledging the gravity of the issues at stake and the need for an investigation, Watergate became a political crisis justifying drastic action.

Scientific and Technological Innovations

Agenda building by the media is not limited to political scandals but includes many other types of issues. We will discuss two areas in which agenda building is of vast importance for American political life: science policy and social movements.

Government support and regulation of science operations have become highly controversial public policy issues in twentieth-century America.[30] The fate of nuclear energy in the United States provides a particularly interesting example because major shifts in public opinion have been recorded and can be compared with the thrust of media stories. Public opinion regarding the safety and desirability of nuclear energy dropped sharply before as well as after the Three Mile Island nuclear accident in 1979. While only 20 percent of Americans were opposed to locating a nuclear plant in their community in 1956, 56 percent were opposed in 1979. Since then opposition has risen. Sentiment for building more nuclear energy plants has dropped precipitously, and nuclear energy now is rated as the least preferred energy source.

Social scientists have attributed this loss of public support to perceptions among the general public, as well as portions of the scientific community, that scientists knowledgeable about nuclear power have lost faith in it. No one seemed to know for sure how this perception started and whether scientists were indeed disillusioned with nuclear power as an energy source. To find out, political scientists Stanley Rothman and S. Robert Lichter interviewed 72 nuclear specialists, 279 scientists who worked in nuclear energy-related fields, and 741 scientists with no special ties to the nuclear industry.[31]

All the nuclear experts wanted to continue nuclear development; 92 percent of them urged rapid rather than slow progress. Of the experts from related fields, 95 percent also urged continued development; 70 percent favored rapid progress. Among scientists with no special ties to the nuclear industry, 10 percent wanted development halted. Ninety percent favored proceeding with nuclear development, albeit at a somewhat slower pace. Clearly, the widespread perceptions of science community opposition to developing nuclear energy were wrong. A replication of the study in 1985 in the United States and in 1986 in Germany confirmed these conclusions.[32]

A probe of the reasons for the faulty impression that most scientists opposed nuclear energy pointed to mass media stories. When pro- and antinuclear statements were counted in newspapers and television news, antinuclear statements predominated. Although positive statements predominated slightly in the early 1970s, by 1976 negative articles outnumbered positive ones by a two-to-one margin.

The attitudes of journalists toward the issue of nuclear energy matched the tone of their stories. The vast majority of science writers, especially those working for elite media and television, objected to the use of nuclear energy. On a scale ranking support of nuclear energy from +9 (strong support) to −9 (strong opposition), nuclear experts ranked at +7.9 and scientists in related fields at +5.1. By contrast, science journalists at the *New York Times, Washington Post,* and the television networks ranked at +0.5. Rothman and Lichter's figures for television reporters as a group were in minus territory at −1.9. Public television journalists were most strongly opposed with an average score of −3.3.

As Table 6-1 shows, a major factor in the predominantly unfavorable coverage was the choice of sources, particularly in the case of network television.[33] The small corps of reporters who specialize in science writing drew much of their information from enemies of nuclear development. For instance, television broadcasts between 1968 and 1979 quoted the Union of Concerned Scientists more than any other source. The union, an organization of antinuclear scientists, represented only a tiny fraction of the scientific community. Ralph Nader, the consumer advocate, was the most widely quoted individual "nuclear expert" during the period in question. In the month following the Three Mile Island accident, pronuclear views were never featured prominently. Although the antinuclear views of newspeople may have been the main reason for searching out and featuring compatible views expressed by

Table 6-1 Source Orientation Regarding Nuclear Energy Stories, 1970-1983 (in percentages)

Source orientation	New York Times	Time, Newsweek, U.S. News & World Report	ABC, CBS, NBC
Pronuclear	9	17	11
Antinuclear	7	40	62
Neutral/balanced	84	43	27

Source: Adapted from Stanley Rothman and S. Robert Lichter, "Elite Ideology and Risk Perception in Nuclear Energy Policy," *American Political Science Review* 81 (June 1987): 393. Reprinted by permission.

Note: $N = 486$ for *New York Times,* drawn from 10 percent random sample; 213 for news magazines, drawn from full universe; and 582 from television networks, drawn from 50 percent sample.

scientists, other factors, many of them typical in news production, also played a part. Among them, the economies of news supply are very important. Journalists are more likely to select stories that are readily available to them with comparatively little effort. In the 1970s antinuclear information was more readily available in easy-to-use formats. This happened because most nuclear scientists did not publish their work in general circulation journals. The comparatively small number of scientists who frequently explained their views in lay terms in the popular literature were disproportionately inclined to oppose nuclear energy development.

When journalists who oppose nuclear development find that most stories published in general circulation sources support the views that they prefer, it is not surprising that they draw heavily on these sources. This allows them to develop an exciting theme—the danger of nuclear power and the inadequate safety measures of a major industry—and support it with views that can be designated as "expert." Relying on science articles in general circulation journals is far easier than delving into arcane scientific journals and making contact with scientific leaders who may be reluctant to supply the absolute statements of doom or salvation that make exciting headlines. In the words of David Paletz and Robert Entman, "When values are shared by source and press and probably readers too, there is no felt need on the part of reporters to seek countervailing information elsewhere." [34]

As yet no one has definitely proven that skewed selection of sources for nuclear energy stories accounts for the public's current hostility to nuclear energy. However, studies of public opinion polls on science issues show that extensive media coverage of scientific controversies is followed by increased public opposition to the highlighted technology, even when the coverage is not particularly hostile. When media coverage of the controversy diminishes, opposition diminishes as well. The public, it seems, opts against any technology when doubts are raised about its safety. It is especially sensitive to heavily negative safety reports. Political elites, in turn, are loath to challenge scientific findings that the media have labeled as "expert" opinion or to take actions that may alarm the country.[35]

Firm proof is also lacking that the current decline of the nuclear energy industry can be attributed in large part to this hostile opinion climate. But even without such proof, the evidence strongly suggests that the predominantly negative images of the nuclear industry featured in numerous media stories played a major part in undermining the growth of the industry.

The situation has been similar in other fields of science, including biomedical research.[36] Only a few scientists, distinguished by their controversial positions on public issues, are steady sources for news about new drugs, new medical procedures, and various aspects of genetic engineering. The rest of the scientific community has remained largely excluded, often by its own choice and sometimes because of its disdain for popularized stories. In the same way, only a few potentially risky technologies have been scrutinized by science reporters, with choices determined haphazardly or with stories mirroring the interests of selected pressure groups. Many other science topics have been ignored and thereby kept off the public agenda, even though they address significant aspects of public health and safety. This situation is improving with the addition of weekly science sections in many newspapers. However, in the process of popularizing highly technical matters, most media reports contain minor and major errors of omission, emphasis, or fact.[37]

Social Movements and Interest Groups

Just as the media regularly boost selected public policy issues, so too can they promote selected groups that are working for specific public causes. Whenever a group needs wide publicity to reach its goals, a decision by media personnel to grant or withhold publicity becomes crucial for the group's success. Many decisions about coverage are made without explicit political motivations to boost a movement or suppress it. But in some instances the sympathies of newspeople for particular causes guide their choices of news content in hopes of influencing the course of politics. This is what happened with Students for a Democratic Society (SDS), part of what came to be known in the 1960s as the "New Left." The story is particularly interesting because it demonstrates that attention from sympathetic newspeople may boomerang and produce unintended, highly destructive consequences.

SDS had received little media attention for its activities on American campuses until *New York Times* reporter Fred Powledge wrote a long, supportive story. It appeared in the *Times* on March 15, 1965, some five years after the birth of the movement.[38] Coverage by a national news medium amounted to symbolic recognition that student radicalism had become an important political issue. When SDS sponsored a Vietnam War protest march on Washington in the spring of 1965, the event received nationwide coverage. Major articles on the New Left appeared in national news magazines and in large circulation weeklies such as the *Saturday Evening Post* and the *New York Times Magazine.*

Although many newspeople sympathized with the gamut of left-liberal reforms advocated by SDS and knew that sensational publicity might be harmful, they decided, in line with media prescriptions for exciting stories, to focus on the movement's most radical leaders and goals. News stories pictured SDS as a single-issue group, dedicated to violent opposition to the Vietnam War, rather than emphasizing its concern with a broad array of issues ranging from civil rights to socialism and anti-imperialism. The framing chosen by the media, contrary to SDS wishes, proved disastrous.

Besides misleading media audiences, the distorted image also affected the self-perceptions of SDS members. Individuals singled out by the media as spokespersons for the organization became celebrities. With this new-found status, many no longer felt accountable to their rank and file. To maintain the flow of publicity that they deemed essential for their survival, SDS members stressed the radical left-wing elements in the organization that conformed to the media image. In turn, this attracted new Leninist and Maoist members who expected the organization to perform as pictured in the media. These new members took over the leadership of the organization and turned it away from its long-range reformist goals to short-range and violent antiwar activities.

Sociologist Todd Gitlin contends that the media's decision in 1965 to give wide publicity to SDS ultimately destroyed the movement and with it much of the power of the New Left. In his vivid metaphor, the media spotlight became a magnifying glass that burned everybody to a crisp. Media efforts to bestow legitimacy on the movement failed totally. As is true in other instances of agenda building, political forces other than the media contributed to the turn of events. Radicalization of the SDS movement was also enhanced by the Johnson administration's escalation of the Vietnam War and by the growing alienation from mainstream society that it produced among many Americans.[39]

Many critics of American media contend that the fate of SDS is typical for groups that challenge the established order. As Paletz and Entman argue,

Organizations that accept establishment rules, and pursue incremental goals discretely, benefit from journalists' needs and practices. Groups whose methods violate convention, whose objectives require a significant alteration of the structure of power, usually find their radical activities distorted or condemned, their radical analyses and proposals ignored or scorned. Any publicity they receive tends to isolate them from the mass of citizens, encouraging them to moderate their ways until they either fade from sight or shade into the establishment.[40]

Of course, many movements, interest groups, and lobbies have been helped by media coverage, as long as they did not deviate too far from mainstream values. The civil rights movement is a memorable case. The media framed civil rights protesters as victims of racism, as the protesters preferred, rather than as troublemakers and lawbreakers, as their opponents preferred. Sympathetic nationwide coverage of freedom marches and of battles fought for civil rights in Little Rock, Arkansas, Selma, Alabama, and Oxford, Mississippi, helped ready lawmakers and the nation for passage of the Civil Rights Act in 1964. Support for consumer organizations and environmentalist groups constitutes another success story. Media publicity has legitimized these organizations in the eyes of the public and in the eyes of political elites.[41] Their activities now are covered regularly and favorably. Ralph Nader has become a media celebrity and a respected, much-consulted guru. The concerns of consumer interest groups and of general public interest lobbies such as Common Cause have become the subject of legislation, implemented through newly created public agencies.

There seems to be a pattern in the role played by media on behalf of successful social movements. That is the conclusion of two German scholars who analyzed how media coverage helped change attitudes and laws in West Germany dealing with conscientious objectors to military service.[42] Their study, which covered a fifteen-year period from 1961 to 1975, revealed that a few newspapers took the lead in supporting the cause of conscientious objectors. The rest of the media largely ignored the movement initially. Uncontested favorable publicity served to legitimize conscientious objectors and their demands and attracted new supporters. By the time the establishment press began to criticize the movement in the wake of protest activities by conscientious objectors, the movement had become so well accepted that its political demands could not be stopped. The struggle for acceptance of the movement had taken fifteen years, but it seemed much briefer because of sparse coverage by the mainstream press during the initial seven years. Protest actions finally aroused opposition forces and moved the struggle to the center of political attention.

The model illustrated by the case, which appears to be typical for successful social movements, involves four steps. Legitimation of the incipient movement begins with favorable coverage by a few sympathetic journalists. Undisputed media praise then attracts support for the movement among segments of the public. The third phase is reached when the growing movement becomes strong and legitimate enough to make political demands and engage in protest activities. At that time opposing voices are raised in the hitherto silent mainstream media. They come too late, however, to stop the success of the movement in the legislative arena and among important publics.

Protest groups are active partners in the agenda-building game. If they consider publicity essential to the success of their causes, as most of them do, they initiate contacts with potentially sympathetic journalists and create newsworthy events in which to showcase their objectives. Attracting sustained media attention hinges on the *status of the group,* the perceived *social and political legitimacy* of the group and its goals, the *newsworthiness* of its story, judged by the usual criteria, and the *consonance of* the group's *ideology* with the journalists' inclinations.[43]

Journalists, then, prefer to cover groups of high status or prominence that are perceived as legitimate and in pursuit of worthy goals with which the journalists identify, and who have interesting stories to tell. When these requirements are met, a transaction takes place, as exchange theorists have pointed out. The journalists' ability to bestow publicity is exchanged for the group's ability to supply newsworthy stories.

Low status organizations whose goals encompass routine human concerns are least likely to attract helpful publicity.[44] Political scientist Edie Goldenberg studied the attempts of four citizen groups in Massachusetts to attract newspaper coverage to the problems of welfare mothers, senior citizens, low-income tenants, and people deprived of fair treatment by the courts. Finding that these groups had little success, she concluded, "There is bias in the system that consistently favors some and neglects others." The favored groups are "haves," those who possess the resources to make and maintain contact with the press and to arrange their operations so that they complement the needs of the press. The unfavored ones are those "most in need of press attention in order to be heard forcefully in the political arena" yet "least able to command attention and . . . least able to use effectively what few resources they do control in seeking and gaining press access." Goldenberg warns, "If intensely felt interests go unarticulated and therefore are unnoticed and unaffected by policy makers, one important aspect of rule of, for, and by the people is weakened." [45] In the eyes of social critics such as Goldenberg, a free press must use its agenda-building powers to benefit all segments of society.

Documentaries and Docudramas

To influence public policy, newspeople are not limited to straight news and feature stories. Fictional productions, such as docudramas shown to millions of viewers on prime-time national television, are used as well. Docudramas are especially compelling because they reconstruct events in highly dramatic, emotional ways. Unfortunately, the viewer cannot tell what part of the story is real and what part is dramatic frosting.[46]

The political goals of many documentaries and docudramas are obvious. As Oscar Gandy has pointed out, "Too frequently to be mere coincidence, serial dramas, or the made-for-television movies we describe as docudramas, have been aired simultaneously with the discussion of related issues in Congress." [47] An example of a widely publicized docudrama that coincided with related political events was "The Day After," a two-hour ABC dramatization of a nuclear attack on Kansas City and its aftermath. It was broadcast on Sunday, November 20, 1983, following an extensive prebroadcast advertising campaign that included an eight-page viewer's guide. The drama was replete with scenes of burnt bodies, faces with blinded eyes rotting from radiation sickness, smoldering rubble, and survivors reduced to preying on each other.

At the time of broadcast, nuclear weapons policy was in the limelight. The Reagan administration was attempting to gain support in the United States and in Europe for deploying American missiles in European NATO countries. Antinuclear groups at home and abroad were working feverishly to stop the deployment. The docudrama was aired a few days before the decision to place the missiles was to be approved by the West German legislature. Excerpts were made available to German television.

Supporters of missile deployment feared that the program would lead to massive public demonstrations designed to force a change in nuclear deployment policies. When the Reagan administration was invited to send a representative to participate in a postbroadcast discussion of the lessons of the docudrama, it showed its profound concern by sending Secretary of State George P. Shultz. Throughout the furor raised by the broadcast, ABC denied that the timing had been politically motivated. The November date was chosen, it claimed, to raise ABC's ratings during a "sweeps" month, when ratings would be reflected in advertising prices.

What, then, was the political impact of "The Day After," which was viewed by more than 100 million people in homes, schools, churches, and town halls? [48] It appears that the broadcast boosted the activities of antinuclear groups and engendered fears that "The Day After" might generate a defeatist attitude among Americans. But public opinion polls after the broadcast did not show massive shifts of public attitudes about nuclear missile policies. In Europe, where immediate drastic political consequences had been expected, the missiles were deployed without major obstacles.

A number of analysts ascribed the lack of impact to flaws in the docudrama, which left the reasons for the nuclear attack uncertain and failed to deal squarely with nuclear policy issues. Others felt that the public had gained knowledge and awareness from the film, but had learned to distance itself psychologically from fictional disasters. Therefore, the audience failed to empathize fully with the stricken residents of Kansas City.

While the apparent consequences of "The Day After" were less than expected, other docudramas may be more potent. "J.F.K.," a 1991 movie-docudrama, suggested that President Kennedy's assassination sprang from a massive conspiracy that involved the White House, the CIA, and the FBI, among others. Polls subsequently showed that numerous viewers accepted the film's premises.[49] Concern or hopes remain high that prime-time broadcasts and the associated media coverage and public discussions may have major political consequences in the long or short run.[50] This potential impact obligates a responsible press to take greater pains to present all sides of an issue and to be more accurate in its depiction, even in a fiction program. Critics of "The Day After" felt that the drama understated the likely consequences of an atomic attack. Moreover, the appropriate background for appraising various policy options was lacking. Viewers were not told that the possibility of negotiating a nuclear freeze was severely constricted by the unwillingness of other world powers with nuclear arsenals to reciprocate and to permit verification of compliance.

Methods: Fair and Foul

The fairness and accuracy of news presentations and the appropriateness of news-gathering techniques become important issues when one considers the media as actors in the political process. The role they play, in combination with other political actors, defines political reality and guides political action.[51] In recent years the media have frequently been accused of improper methods. Lawsuits filed against them have multiplied.

Confirming Prejudgments

A famous, $120 million libel suit illustrates concerns about the legitimacy of some media tactics. The suit was brought by Gen. William C. Westmoreland against CBS for statements made about him in a ninety-minute documentary on the Vietnam War called "The Un-counted Enemy: A Vietnam Deception." The principal message of the documentary was that the general, while commander of American forces in Vietnam, had deliberately manipulated information about the strength of Viet Cong troops before the 1968 Tet (or Vietnamese New Year) offensive. Allegedly, he was trying to show the president and Congress that American troops under his command were winning the war. The Viet Cong offensive demonstrated that the enemy's strength and tenacity had been badly underestimated.

The case is ideal for examining questionable media practices because the results of an internal CBS review of production methods were made public. The network's own investigation indicated that the producers of the documentary believed in Westmoreland's guilt from the very start and organized the production to support their preformed conclusions. According to the internal report, CBS personnel made eleven major errors while putting together the documentary. These included failing to adequately support the charge that a conspiracy was involved, choosing to interview mostly people who supported the program's overall conclusions, reshooting unsatisfactory testimony after allowing a witness to hear what others had said, and "coddling sympathetic witnesses." [52] The report, which was prepared by senior CBS producer Burton Benjamin prior to the Westmoreland suit, contained portions of unedited transcripts of interviews in which sources were apparently coached by interviewers. At times interviewers asked loaded questions such as whether the respondent agreed that there had been "a full-fledged conspiracy to fake intelligence reporting." If respondents failed to agree, their remarks were omitted from the final broadcast. Materials that might have undermined the documentary's principal conclusions about General Westmoreland's activities ended up on the cutting room floor.

In the final documentary eight of the ten persons whose testimony was featured sided against Westmoreland. One of the two who did not, Lt. Gen. Daniel Graham, was given a mere twenty-one seconds of air time, even though he had been the chief of the army's current intelligence and estimates division in Vietnam in the late 1960s. Overall, Westmoreland and his supporters spoke for only five minutes and fifty-nine seconds, while his accusers were given nineteen minutes and nineteen seconds, a ratio of better than three-to-one for the accusers.

Van Gordon Sauter, then-president of CBS News, acknowledged that CBS policies and standards had been violated during the making of the documentary, but he argued that these flaws did not undermine the editorial integrity of the broadcast. According to him, it was an accurate account of the distorted estimates of enemy strength by the American military in Vietnam.

After several years of legal sparring, Westmoreland dropped his libel suit. Despite extensive exploration, the substantive issues remain unsettled. The issues of media policy are clearer. There is little disagreement about the standards of fairness and accuracy that should be applied in broadcasts on important public issues. The standards by which CBS judged its own conduct make this apparent. But—and this is the disturbing aspect—these standards continue to be breached all too often. Such breaches raise questions about the sense of responsibility of high-level media personnel. When important public matters are at stake, are the media, especially the influential electronic media, exercising sufficient care to make sure that the preconceptions of media personnel do not taint their stories and mislead media audiences?

With investigative journalism growing in popularity, the problem of inaccurate reports has mounted. Television networks increasingly are using videotapes shot by amateurs with portable equipment. The networks cannot be sure that the pictures are bona fide. In 1989, for instance, charges surfaced that a freelance camera man had faked and restaged battle scenes in film used in CBS newscasts and documentaries about the war in Afghanistan. It was alleged that scenes of sabotaging electric supply lines for Kabul, the capital of Afghanistan, were reenacted days after the event. The location of refugees was misstated to make the story more dramatic, and a Pakistani jet was misidentified as a Soviet plane.[53]

In many instances inaccurate reports have permanent economic, professional, and social consequences for the individuals and institutions whose story is told. In the Westmoreland case, for example, the reputation of a prominent general was at stake. In another case, one involving the Kaiser Aluminum and Chemical Corporation, business losses could run into millions of dollars. An investigative report had accused the company of knowingly selling dangerous household electrical wiring under false pretenses. In yet another case a partially fictionalized documentary about the mass murder of black youths in Atlanta suggested that the killer might still be at large. It raised doubts about the fairness of the trial of the man convicted as the murderer. The broadcast prompted the mayor of Atlanta and civic leaders to launch a public information campaign to blunt the anticipated ill effects.[54]

The serious injuries inflicted when publicity is careless or biased have become a deep concern for civil libertarians. As Ira Glasser, executive director of the American Civil Liberties Union, has warned, "Justice by press release and summary political punishment are methods we should have by now learned to avoid." [55] The problem is made worse by the fact that rebuttals, if permitted at all by the networks, have been subject to their editorial control. Network representatives have argued that documentaries, unlike ordinary news, are edited productions so that uncensored rebuttals need not be permitted.[56]

Entrapment

Serious ethical issues are also raised when newspeople undertake undercover operations or bogus enterprises created to entrap potential and actual wrongdoers. The story told earlier about the "Mirage," the tavern set up to elicit and record bribery by city officials, illustrates the practice. A far more massive crime trap was set by Canadian media to expose organized crime in North America. The investigation resulted in a three-and-a-half hour documentary broadcast by the Canadian Broadcasting Company (CBC) on March 27, 1979.

CBC reporters and agents who were planted inside organized crime circles used hidden microphones and cameras to obtain dramatic film footage of gangsters discussing their activities. In one instance a reporter arranged meetings with a woman suspected of helping gangsters to buy real estate in Atlantic City. The reporter pretended to represent a person in Italy who wished to export several million dollars from Italy to Canada. The money was then to be funneled into Atlantic City real estate under the guise that it belonged to legitimate Canadian investors. Through this initial contact, another meeting was set up between a disguised reporter, who had had previous experience as an informant for law enforcement agencies, and underworld dealers in illegal real estate. All of these meetings were taped, and some parts were filmed.[57]

Sting operations like these raise serious civil liberties issues even when they are conducted by regular law enforcement agencies, often under the watchful eyes of the courts.[58] The concerns about protecting the rights of suspects are even greater when the sleuths are acting without an official mandate and without supervision by a responsible public body. Quite aside from civil liberties issues, sting operations raise fundamental questions about the proper functions of the press. Should its watchdog role be carried to the point where it becomes a quasi-police force, tracking down selected offenders when a good story promises to be the likely reward?

Summary

In this chapter we examined direct involvement by journalists in the affairs of government. We began with an analysis of muckraking, comparing reality to a series of models of the process. The media's power to arouse public opinion with exposés of corruption is far less than is popularly believed. Even if the public becomes highly concerned, political action is not guaranteed. The belief that muckraking commonly produces reforms when journalists stir the public, and public opinion then pressures for political action, is wrong.

The most propitious road to reform is via direct liaisons between newspeople and government officials. When officials provide story leads in areas where they would like to produce action, or when newspeople can interest officials in taking action on issues that have come to the media's attention, successful political activities are apt to occur. On rare occasions the media are also able to produce action by using the club of potential unwanted publicity to force officials to act or by becoming participants in political negotiations.

The Watergate scandal illustrates how political action can emerge from the interplay of various political institutions. The media, through a series of agenda-building steps, created the climate in which it became possible to force the resignation of a president. Agenda-building examples from science policy and from the realm of interest group politics demonstrate the impact of the media on developments in these fields. The media serve as catalysts that precipitate the actions of other elements within the society. They enhance the influence of some political forces and weaken others, but the ultimate outcome may defeat their political purposes because it is beyond their control.

The media's public policy-making roles influence American politics in general as well as the lives of many individuals and institutions. How sensitively and accurately they are performed therefore become a matter of grave concern. News gathering and news production frequently are seriously flawed, even when media institutions profess to believe in high standards. How often the ethics and standards of the profession are violated, and what the costs are to people caught in the net of inaccurate publicity, is a matter for conjecture.

At the heart of most instances when newspeople allow themselves to be used as mouthpieces for politicians and interest groups lies the desire to produce exciting news stories. This is not surprising. Journalism requires telling stories that will attract audiences. That journalists are tempted to be good storytellers above all, even at the expense of other goals, should give pause to those who advocate that they should play the political game actively and regularly. One must ask whether their professional standards equip them to guide politics wisely and well. To put it another way: when issues are put on the crowded political agenda, should their newsworthiness be the controlling factor? If the answer is "no," then massive participation by the media in policy making may be very troubling.

Notes

1. Lincoln Steffens, *The Autobiography of Lincoln Steffens* (New York: Harcourt Brace, 1931), 357.
2. For a brief review of the history and tactics of muckraking and attack journalism, see Larry J. Sabato, *Feeding Frenzy: How Attack Journalism Has Transformed American Politics* (New York: Free Press, 1991), chap. 2; David L. Protess, Fay Lomax Cook, Jack D. Doppelt, James S. Ettema, Margaret T. Gordon, Donna R. Leff, and Peter Miller, *The Journalism of Outrage: Investigative Reporting and Agenda Building* (New York: Guilford Press, 1991), chap. 2.
3. Suzanne Garment, "Political Imperfections: Scandal Time in Washington," *Public Opinion* 10 (May/June 1987): 10-12, 60; Sabato, *Feeding Frenzy*, chap. 3.
4. David Weaver and LeAnne Daniels, "Public Opinion on Investigative Reporting in the 1980s," *Journalism Quarterly* 69 (Spring 1992): 146-155.
5. David L. Protess, *Muckraking Matters: The Societal Impact of Investigative Reporting*, Institute for Modern Communications Research Monographs Series (Evanston, Ill.: Northwestern University, 1987), 13.
6. Steffens, *Autobiography*, 357.
7. Protess et al., *Journalism of Outrage*, 214-227.
8. Harvey L. Molotch, David L. Protess, and Margaret T. Gordon, "The Media-Policy Connection: Ecologies of News," in *Political Communication Research: Approaches, Studies, Assessments*, ed. David L. Paletz (Norwood, N.J.: Ablex, 1987), 26-48. Protess et al. model the process somewhat differently in their more recent *Journalism of Outrage*. But the earlier version seems more explicit.
9. Protess et al., *Journalism of Outrage*, chaps. 3-6 details six investigations.
10. Robert Muccigrosso, "Television and the Urban Crisis," in *Screen and Society*, ed. Frank J. Coppa (Chicago: Nelson-Hall, 1979), 44-45.
11. Chris T. Allen and Judith D. Weber, "How Presidential Media Use Affects Individuals' Beliefs about Conservation," *Journalism Quarterly* 60 (Spring 1983): 98-104, 196.
12. Protess et al., *Journalism of Outrage*, chap. 4.
13. Often the chief point of a program is simply to alert the public to a problem; immediate action may not be expected. For example, PBS officials filmed their documentary "Crisis at General Hospital," to make the public aware of the inequity of a two-tier health system in which people of means are served by excellent private hospitals, while the remainder of the population receives second-rate care in inferior public hospitals. Kenneth R. Clark, "Hospital Dilemma: The System Sends Poor Home to Die," *Chicago Tribune*, January 17, 1984.
14. Protess et al., *Journalism of Outrage*, chap. 3.
15. The full story is told in Zay N. Smith and Pamela Zekman, *The Mirage* (New York: Random House, 1979).
16. Protess et al., *Journalism of Outrage*, 240-244.
17. Sabato, *Feeding Frenzy*, 53.
18. Protess et al., *Journalism of Outrage*, 134-135.
19. Wayne King, "Houston Finds that Dramatizing Crime Does Pay," *New York Times*, January 23, 1984.
20. Michael Killian, "New FBI TV Series Will Seek Viewer Help in Nabbing Criminals," *Chicago Tribune*, February 5, 1988.

21. Protess et al., *Journalism of Outrage*, 179-180.
22. "ABC Refuses to Telecast Taped Plea of U.S. Hostage," *Chicago Tribune*, August 4, 1989.
23. Barbie Zelizer, "CNN, the Gulf War, and Journalistic Practice," *Journal of Communication* 42 (Winter 1992): 73-78.
24. Robert D. McFadden, "News Executives Express Outrage," *New York Times*, October 3, 1986.
25. W. Lance Bennett, "Toward a Theory of Press-State Relations in the United States," *Journal of Communication* 40 (Spring 1990): 103-125.
26. Everett Rogers and James Dearing, "Agenda-Setting Research: Where Has It Been, Where Is It Going?" *Communication Yearbook 11*, ed. James Anderson (Newbury Park, Calif.: Sage, 1988); also see David Weaver and Swanzy Nimley Elliott, "Who Sets the Agenda for the Media? A Study of Local Agenda-Building," *Journalism Quarterly* 62 (Spring 1985): 87-94; Jane Delano Brown, Carl R. Bybee, Stanley T. Weardon, and Dulcie Murdock, "Invisible Power: Newspaper News Sources and the Limits of Diversity," *Journalism Quarterly* 64 (Spring 1987): 45-54.
27. Gladys Engel Lang and Kurt Lang, *The Battle for Public Opinion: The President, the Press and the Polls during Watergate* (New York: Columbia University Press, 1983), 58.
28. Molotch et al., "The Media-Policy Connection," 45, citing Peter Dreier, "The Position of the Press in the U.S. Power Structure," *Social Problems* 29 (February 1982): 298-310; also see Gadi Wolfsfeld, "Media Protest, and Political Violence: A Transactional Analysis," *Journalism Monographs* 127 (June 1991); William A. Gamson, *The Strategy of Social Protest*, 2d ed. (Belmont, Calif.: Wadsworth, 1990); and Clarice N. Olien, Phillip J. Tichenor, and George A. Donohue, "Media Coverage and Social Movements," *Information Campaigns: Balancing Social Values and Social Change*, ed. Charles T. Salmon (Beverly Hills, Calif.: Sage, 1989), 139-163.
29. Lang and Lang, *Battle for Public Opinion*, 59-60. Also see Michael Schudson, *Watergate in American Memory: How We Remember, Forget, and Reconstruct the Past* (New York: Basic Books, 1992).
30. Oscar H. Gandy, *Beyond Agenda Setting: Information Subsidies and Public Policy* (Norwood, N.J.: Ablex, 1982), 149-162.
31. Stanley Rothman and S. Robert Lichter, "The Nuclear Energy Debate: Scientists, the Media and the Public," *Public Opinion* 5 (August/September 1982): 47-48.
32. Stanley Rothman and S. Robert Lichter, "Elite Ideology and Risk Perception in Nuclear Energy Policy," *American Political Science Review* 81 (June 1987): 383-404.
33. For a more general discussion of the problem of sources of science information, see Hans Mathias Kepplinger, "Artificial Horizons: How the Press Presented and How the Population Received Technology in Germany from 1965-1986," *The Mass Media in Liberal Democratic Societies*, ed. Stanley Rothman (New York: Paragon House, 1992), 147-176; Kandice L. Salomone, Michael R. Greenberg, Peter M. Sandman, and David B. Sachsman, "A Question of Quality: How Journalists and News Sources Evaluate Coverage of Environmental Risk," *Journal of Communication* 40 (Autumn 1990): 117-130.
34. David L. Paletz and Robert M. Entman, *Media Power Politics* (New York: Free Press, 1981), 144.
35. Patrick Leahy and Alan Mazur, "The Rise and Fall of Public Opposition in

Specific Social Movements," *Social Studies of Science* 10 (1980): 191-205; and Alan Mazur, "Media Coverage and Public Opinion on Scientific Controversies," *Journal of Communication* 31 (Spring 1981): 106-115.

36. For a symposium on science news, see *Journal of Communication* 31 (Spring 1981): 84-189.

37. Renate G. Bader, "How Science News Sections Influence Newspaper Science Coverage: A Case Study," *Journalism Quarterly* 67 (Spring 1990): 88-96; Eleanor Singer, "A Question of Accuracy: How Journalists and Scientists Report Research on Hazards," *Journalism Quarterly* 40 (Autumn 1990): 102-116.

38. Todd Gitlin, *The Whole World Is Watching: Media in the Making and Unmaking of the New Left* (Berkeley: University of California Press, 1980), 25-26.

39. For models of the roles played by the media in fostering social movements, see Kevin M. Carragee, "News and Ideology," *Journalism Monographs* 128 (August 1991); Wolfsfeld, "Media Protest and Political Violence"; and Gamson, *The Strategy of Social Protest.*

40. Paletz and Entman, *Media Power Politics,* 146.

41. Gitlin, *The Whole World,* 284.

42. Hans Mathias Kepplinger and Michael Hachenberg, "Media and Conscientious Objection in the Federal Republic of Germany," in *Political Communication Research,* ed. David Paletz, 108-128. Also see Fay Lomax Cook and Wesley G. Skogan, "Convergent and Divergent Voice Models of the Rise and Fall of Policy Issues," *Agenda Setting: Readings on Media, Public Opinion, and Policymaking,* eds. David L. Protess and Maxwell McCombs (Hillsdale, N.J.: Erlbaum, 1991), 189-206.

43. Wolfsfeld, "Media Protest and Political Violence," 8-10.

44. Paletz and Entman, *Media Power Politics,* 144.

45. Edie Goldenberg, *Making the Papers* (Lexington, Mass.: Heath, 1975), 146-148.

46. The potential impact of docudramas is discussed by William C. Adams, Allison Salzman, William Vantine, Leslie Suelter, Anne Baker, Lucille Bonvouloir, Barbara Brenner, Margaret Ely, Jean Feldman, and Ron Ziegel, "The Power of *The Right Stuff:* A Quasi-Experimental Field Test of the Docudrama Hypothesis," *Public Opinion Quarterly* 49 (Fall 1985): 330-339.

47. Gandy, *Beyond Agenda Setting,* 88.

48. Sally Bedell Smith, "Film on a Nuclear War Already Causing Wide Fallout of Partisan Activity," *New York Times,* November 23, 1983.

49. Bernard Weinraub, "Hollywood Wonders if Warner Brothers Let 'J.F.K.' Go Too Far," *New York Times,* December 24, 1991; Jack R. Payton, 'J.F.K.' 's Premise Is Full of Holes—But So Was Warren Report," *Chicago Tribune,* December 24, 1991.

50. For a discussion of the subtle yet significant consequences that are often missed, see Stanley Feldman and Lee Sigelman, "The Political Impact of Prime-Time Television: 'The Day After,'" *Journal of Politics* 47 (May 1985): 556-578.

51. For a full discussion of the role of the media as political actors, see Timothy E. Cook, *Revisiting the Fourth Branch of Government: The News Media as Political Institutions.* Forthcoming.

52. Richard Bernstein, "CBS Releases Its Study of Vietnam Documentary," *New York Times,* April 27, 1983.

53. Bill Carter, "The Larger Issues Behind the Dan Rather Case," *New York*

Times, October 4, 1989.
54. William E. Schmidt, "TV Movie on Atlanta Child Killings Stirs Debate and Casts Doubt on Guilt," *New York Times,* January 31, 1985.
55. Quoted in Deirdre Carmody, "The Role of the Press in the U.S. Corruption Inquiry," *New York Times,* February 5, 1980.
56. For a typical case involving denial of the right to unedited rebuttal, see Sally Bedell, "ABC Backs Off Charge It Made against Mobil," *New York Times,* June 22, 1982.
57. Andrew H. Malcolm, "TV Film Links to Mob in Toronto," *New York Times,* March 28, 1979.
58. Bennett L. Gershman, "Abscam, the Judiciary, and the Ethics of Government," *Yale Law Journal* 91 (July 1982): 1565-1591.

Readings

Gitlin, Todd. *The Whole World Is Watching: Media in the Making and Unmaking of the New Left.* Berkeley: University of California Press, 1980.
Lang, Gladys Engel, and Kurt Lang. *The Battle for Public Opinion: The President, the Press and the Polls during Watergate.* New York: Columbia University Press, 1983.
Patterson, Margaret Jones, and Robert H. Russell. *Behind the Lines: Case Studies in Investigative Reporting.* New York: Columbia University Press, 1986.
Rotzoll, Kim B., and Mark Fackler, eds., *Media Ethics.* New York: Longman, 1987.
Schudson, Michael. *Watergate in American Memory: How We Remember, Forget, and Reconstruct the Past.* New York: Basic Books, 1992.
Smith, Zay N., and Pamela Zekman. *The Mirage.* New York: Random House, 1979.
Steffens, Lincoln. *The Autobiography of Lincoln Steffens.* New York: Harcourt Brace, 1931.
Zelizer, Barbie. *"Covering the Body": The Kennedy Assassination and the Establishment of Journalistic Authority.* Chicago: University of Chicago Press, 1992.

CHAPTER 7

Media Impact on Attitudes and Behavior

Murphy Brown, the star character of a popular prime time television situation comedy, had a baby out of wedlock in one of the show's episodes, broadcast in May 1992. In this day and age, unmarried motherhood on television is no earth-shaking event—or is it? The story was front-page news for newspapers around the country, including the *New York Times*. There was no dearth of important news at the time that might require filling space with any breaking story, however trivial. As the *New York Times* proclaimed in its story lead: "Thailand is in turmoil, the Federal deficit is ballooning and hot embers of racial resentment still smolder in the ruins of inner-city Los Angeles." [1] But today the high councils of government were preoccupied with a truly vexing question: Is Murphy Brown really against family values?

Why was Murphy Brown's pregnancy such big news? The reason was that Vice-President Dan Quayle had publicly denounced the show and its story line for eroding family values and glorifying unwed motherhood. President Bush had been peppered with questions about the make-believe birth during a news conference shared with the Canadian prime minister, who was also asked about it. White House spokesperson Marlin Fitzwater had flip-flopped on the issue in the course of a single day. In the morning, he condemned publicity for unwed motherhood; in the afternoon, he praised the fictional mother for foregoing an abortion.

The reason for all the commotion is the widely held belief that factual and fictional media stories shape the thinking and behavior patterns of countless Americans. What would the 38 million Americans of all ages who watched the show learn from it about family values in

America? This is just one of the many puzzling questions so often asked about the impact of mass media stories on children and adults. Are people's values and attitudes about society and politics really influenced by what they read and see? Does socially controversial behavior in television fiction and news programs produce imitation in real life? How much do people learn from the media and *what* do they learn?

In this chapter we will examine these questions, beginning with the assimilation of attitudes that occurs as an unintended byproduct of media exposure. By and large, newspeople do not try to teach political attitudes and values, nor do people try to learn them. Rather, exposure to individual, dramatic events or the incremental impact of the total flow of information over prolonged periods of time leads to "incidental" learning about the political world. We also will consider the ways in which people choose the media to which they will pay attention and the sorts of things they will learn. Finally, we will address the question posed at the start: To what degree does exposure to the mass media influence behavior in politically significant ways?

Differential Effects of Print and Broadcast News

Most Americans are exposed to combinations of all the media either directly or indirectly through contacts with people who have been exposed. We may know that American astronauts have walked on the moon. We may view this as a scientific miracle that raised the sagging prestige of the United States abroad and at home. And we may feel pride about the venture and yet some unease about its high price tag. But which of these thoughts and feelings come from television, or newspapers, or conversations, or from a combination of media? It is well-nigh impossible to disentangle such strands of information.[2]

Each medium, however, does make unique contributions to learning. For example, television, because of its visuals, is especially powerful in transmitting realism and emotional appeal. It does less well conveying the intended meanings of events. In one fairly typical study researchers asked viewers to relate the main points of specific stories; they failed on 72 percent of them. Miscomprehension rates for individual stories ranged from 16 percent to 93 percent.[3]

Print media excel in conveying abstract ideas and factual details. Since most tests of learning from the media focus on abstract knowledge or rote memory, print media are generally credited with conveying more knowledge than audio-visual media do.[4] In fact, media scholar Neil Postman warns that massive use of television will turn America into a nation of dilettantes who avoid serious thinking and crave only entertainment. He contends that television trivializes the problems of the world. It gives people the illusion of being knowledgeable when, in fact, they are distracted from probing issues in depth.[5]

The claim that the nature of the medium accounts for differences in knowledge gain is not as clear-cut as it may seem, however. Demographic differences among media users make it difficult to judge the significance of the finding that heavy newspaper users tend to be better informed than persons who do not read the paper. Newspaper devotees generally enjoy higher socioeconomic status and better formal education. Their status in life, therefore, provides above-average incentives for the kind of learning that is usually measured. Attitudes toward the media matter as well. Print media are viewed by most people as sources of information, while electronic media are viewed as sources of entertainment. However, when asked to choose either television or print news as an information source, most people opt for television for nearly all kinds of news. Television news is also deemed more credible than print news because "seeing is believing." [6] These additional differences, rather than the nature of each medium, may explain some of the differences in effects. Television becomes the most instructive medium if one abandons the conventional measures of knowledge gain and tests for information that is best conveyed audiovisually, such as impressions of people and the inferences they engender, or comprehension and long-term memory for highly dramatic events.[7]

Television's greatest political impact, compared with that of other media, is derived from its ability to reach millions of people simultaneously with the same images. Major broadcasts enter nearly every home in the nation instantaneously and simultaneously. Televised events become shared experiences. All of us were present vicariously when the *Challenger* spacecraft exploded, when a lone student defied armed might at China's Tiananmen Square, and when errant motorist Rodney King was bloodied by Los Angeles police. America's print media have never attained such a reach and the power that flows from it. Moreover, 23 million American adults are functionally illiterate and therefore are almost entirely beyond the reach of print media.[8] What the poorly educated now learn about politics from television may be fragmentary and hazy, but it represents a quantum leap over their previous exposure and learning.

In short, the research on the differential effects of various types of media reveals that different types present stimuli that vary substantially in nature and content. It would be surprising, therefore, if their impact were identical, even when they deal with the same subjects. However, "there is no evidence of *consistent* significant differences in the ability of different media to persuade, inform, or even to instill an emotional response in audience members." [9] Because current research does not provide adequate answers about the precise effects of these stimulus variations and about the processes by which individuals mesh a variety of media stimuli, we will focus on the end product—the combined impact of all print and electronic media stimuli.

The Role of Media in Political Socialization

Before considering the role that mass media information plays in shaping our attitudes toward society, the political importance of these attitudes must be assessed. Political socialization—the learning about structures and environmental factors and internalizing of customs and rules governing political life—is important because it affects the quality of interactions between citizens and their government. Political systems do not operate smoothly without the support of most of their citizens, who must be willing to abide by the laws and to support government through performing duties such as voting, paying taxes, or serving in the military.

Support is most readily obtained if citizens are convinced of the legitimacy and capability of their government and if they feel strong emotional ties to it. If political socialization fails to instill such attitudes, policies and laws that depend on public support, such as energy conservation or traffic regulations, may become unenforceable. If political socialization fails to provide citizens with sufficient knowledge, elections, at best, become a sham; people go through the motions of making a choice without understanding what this choice means. At worst, elections become a mockery in which clever politicians manipulate an ignorant electorate. Likewise, surveillance of government activities is impossible if people lack a grasp of the nature of government and public policies.

Childhood Socialization

Since political socialization starts in childhood, it is first conveyed by the small child's environment. From their families, and in recent decades from television, children usually learn basic attitudes toward authority, property, decision making, and veneration for political symbols. When children enter the more formal school setting, teaching about political values becomes quite systematic. At school, children also learn new factual information about their political and social world.[10]

The people who teach children rely heavily on mass media for much of the information and values that they transmit. Hence children receive a great deal of media-based information indirectly from the very beginning of their intellectual development. Children's direct contacts with the media are equally abundant.[11] In the United States millions of babies watch television. In the winter youngsters between two and eleven years of age spend an average of thirty-one hours a week in front of the television set—more time than in school. Between the ages of twelve and seventeen, this drops to twenty-four hours. Eighty percent of the programs children see are intended for adults and therefore differ substantially from the child's limited personal experiences. Children watch military combat, funerals, rocket launchings, courtships, seductions, and childbirth. If they can understand the message, its impact is likely to be great since, lacking experience, they are apt to take it at face value.

This strong impact of the mass media on children's political socialization has been convincingly demonstrated by research. When asked for the sources of information on which they base their attitudes about subjects such as economic or race problems, or war and patriotism, high school students mention the mass media far more often than they mention their families, friends, teachers, or personal experiences.[12] Comparisons of youngsters who use the media heavily with those who are light users confirm that school-age children who are heavy mass media users gain substantial information from the media and show greater understanding and support for basic American values, such as the importance of free speech and the right to equal and fair treatment.[13]

The finding that mass media strongly influence socialization runs counter to earlier socialization studies that showed parents and teachers as the chief socializers. Several reasons account for the change. The first is the increasing pervasiveness of television, which makes it easy for even the youngest children to be affected by mass media images. The second reason involves deficiencies in measurement. Much of the early research discounted all media influence unless it came through direct contact outside the classroom between the child and the media. That excluded indirect media influence, such as contacts with parents and teachers who convey media information to the child. These exclusions sharply reduced findings of media effects. Finally, research designs have become more sophisticated. In the early studies children were asked to make their own general appraisal of learning sources. A typical question might be: "From whom do you learn the most, your parents, your school, or newspapers and television?" The questions used in recent studies have been more specific, inquiring what children know about particular subjects, such as immigration policy, government in general, or education policy, and the sources from which their information came. In nearly every case the mass media were the chief sources of information and evaluations.

What children learn from the mass media and how they evaluate it depends heavily on their stage of mental development. According to child psychologist Jean Piaget, children between two and seven years of age do not independently perceive the connections among various phenomena or draw general conclusions from specific instances. Many of the lessons presumably taught by media stories therefore elude young children. Complex reasoning skills are fully developed only at the teen-age level. Children's interests in certain types of stories also change sharply with age, as do their attention and information-retention spans.[14] Children are likely to be highly supportive of the political system during their early years, but by their teenage years they have often become quite disillusioned about authority figures. This skepti-cism diminishes as education is completed and the young adult enters the work force. What role the media play in this transformation is unclear.[15] Knowledge is also slim about children's and adolescents' imitation of behavior depicted by media stories, the duration of memories, and the persistence of media effects.

Adult Socialization

The pattern of heavy media exposure continues from childhood to adulthood. The average American adult spends more than four hours a day watching television, well over two hours listening to radio, often while working or traveling by car, eighteen to forty-five minutes reading newspapers, and six to thirty minutes reading a magazine. Time spent with the mass media has jumped 40 percent since the advent of television, mostly at the expense of other leisure activities. Television alone now takes up nearly half of the leisure time of most Americans. On an average day, 80 percent of all Americans are reached by television and newspapers. On a typical evening, the television audience is close to 100 million people. This can double for extraordinary events, when more than 90 percent of the entire population may gather in front of the nation's television screens.[16]

This massive exposure contributes to the lifelong process of politi-cal socialization and learning. The mass media form

> the mainstream of the common symbolic environment that cultivates the most widely shared conceptions of reality. We live in terms of the stories we tell, stories about what things exist, stories about how things work, and stories about what to do.... Increasingly, media-cultivated facts and values become standards by which we judge.[17]

Once basic attitudes toward the political system have been formed, they usually stabilize, and later learning largely supplements and refines earlier notions. Established attitudes filter subsequent experiences. Major personal or societal upheavals may lead to more or less complete resocialization and revised political ideas. Short of drastic changes, the need to cope with information about new events and shifting cultural orientations also force the average person into continuous learning and gradual readjustments. But the basic value structure generally remains intact, even when attitudes are modified.[18]

Much of what the average person learns about political norms, rules, values, and events, and about the way people cope with these political happenings, comes of necessity from the mass media, including fictional as well as factual stories. Personal experiences are severely limited compared with the range of experiences that come to us directly or indirectly through the media about the social order and political activities. An accident report, for example, may suggest that police and fire forces respond too slowly and that emergency facilities in the local hospital are inadequate. When societal problems like poverty or pollution are framed as discrete events, such as one family's eviction or a particular oceanic oil spill, attention is likely to be focused on individual solutions, obscuring the larger societal problems.[19] Soap operas on radio and television may persuade audiences that most politicians are corruptible—after all, half of those shown on television are.[20] In fact, fictional stories are the most widely used sources for political information. Surveys show that only one-half to two-thirds of the adult public regularly consumes explicit political news.[21]

People's opinions, feelings, and evaluations about the political system may spring from their own processing of facts supplied by the media; from attitudes, opinions, and feelings explicitly expressed by the media in news or entertainment programming; or from a combination of the two.[22] Many people who use the media for information, and as a point of departure for formulating their own appraisals, reject or ignore attitudes and evaluations that are supplied explicitly or implicitly by media stories.[23] For example, the fact that independent presidential candidate Ross Perot financed his own campaign in 1992 was condemned by most media as "buying" the presidency. Nonetheless, most Americans viewed it as a praiseworthy effort to attain the office without entangling financial supporters.[24]

Most people are prone to accept newspeople's views in those areas where they have not had personal experience or guidance from social contacts. Rarely do they have enough information and understanding to form their own views about all national and international issues that confront them in bewildering succession. Even when people think that they are forming their own opinions about familiar issues, they often depend on the media more than they realize. If the media fail to supply adequate information, people's opinions may rest on unsound foundations. Extensive television exposure has been shown to lead to "mainstreaming," turning people into bland middle-roaders with a basically uniform outlook on political life that is "congruent with television's portrayal of life and society."[25]

When audiences have direct or vicarious experiences to guide them, and particularly when they have already formed opinions grounded firmly in their personal values, they are far less likely to be swayed by the media. In practice, this means that the least informed and least interested are most likely to reflect the viewpoints expressed in the media, particularly television. Parroting of viewpoints espoused by political commentators explains why people uninterested in politics often spout quite sophisticated opinions if they have been extensively exposed to news stories.[26]

The 1984 presidential debates between President Ronald Reagan and Sen. Walter Mondale, D-Minn., exemplify the effectiveness of the media in guiding opinions, even on comparatively simple matters. A telephone survey conducted immediately after the first debate showed that a slight majority of the viewers thought that the president had won the debate. After the media strongly attacked the president's performance, viewers' appraisals changed. Two days later, Mondale's winner ratings surpassed the president's by forty-nine points.[27]

Advertising research has documented how messages can affect consumers' perceptions of unfamiliar products and activities and thus change their behavior. Broadcasting may even lead to religious conversions. Radio and television evangelists attract more than 25 million Americans each week, and thousands phone program hosts to announce their conversion or financial support.[28]

Media's persuasiveness does not mean that exposure is tantamount to learning and mind changing. Far from it! Most media stories are promptly forgotten. Stories that become part of an individual's fund of knowledge tend to reinforce existing beliefs and feelings. Acquisition of new knowledge or changes in attitude are the exception rather than the rule. Still, they occur often enough to be highly significant.

Differences in Media Use and Socialization

Just as population groups differ in their cultural environment, economic interests, and psychological make-up, media preferences differ as well. We will outline some of these differences and assess the effects that they are apt to have on political socialization. The picture is extremely complex. For example, if we look at racial differences, we cannot simply talk about characteristic media exposure and impact patterns for nonwhites and whites; gender, age, education, income, region, and city size must also be specified. Additional variations come from commonly ignored factors such as lifestyle and social setting, family size, personality characteristics, and social and job pressures. Of course, the mere fact that individuals belong to a certain demographic category or social group does not mean that they necessarily share the media exposure characteristics of that category or group. For many individuals, group ties may be weak, with little impact on behavior. Group influence may also be weakened for people who are subject to conflicting group pressures. For instance, college students whose peer groups revel in left-wing literature may also be exposed by their families to conservative media fare. Predicting their media exposure and impact patterns from these different group affiliations would be hazardous.

Demographic Factors

Different media exposure patterns may be a partial explanation for knowledge and attitude differences among racial and ethnic groups.[29] For example, African-Americans rely less on the mass media for political information than do whites. Only 22 percent of African-Americans polled in a low-income Los Angeles neighborhood said that they relied on print media for most of their political information, and only 23 percent said that they relied on radio or television. Many named instead interpersonal sources such as their families or public agencies. By comparison, 40 percent of the whites mentioned print media as major sources of political news, and 43 percent mentioned radio and television. Hispanics found print and electronic media even less useful for keeping themselves politically informed than did African-Americans. Only 12 percent of the Hispanics said that they got most of their political information from newspapers, and only 5 percent called radio or television their most important sources. Such alienation from major sources of political information may hamper the political effectiveness of Hispanics and African-Americans in dealing with the majority culture.[30]

Nonwhites prefer to get their news from different papers and stations than whites, especially when media oriented to their racial group are available. Minority groups who primarily use ethnically oriented media are apt to live in different communication and socialization environments than do people in the majority culture. Substantial differences among racial groups in attitudes toward government agencies, and in trust in government and feelings of political efficacy, lend credence to the belief that diverse media images, combined with different life experiences, produce distinctive socialization patterns.

African-Americans and whites extract different information even when they use the same media. African-Americans are more apt than whites to believe that factual as well as fictional stories presented by the media are true to life. Therefore, the images that many African-Americans form about lifestyles or societal patterns are more likely to mirror the distortions found in media presentations.[31] A study of the diffusion of information about six assassinations showed that each racial group dwelled heavily on news that dealt with its own race. While all African-Americans and whites had heard about the deaths of Martin Luther King, Jr., and John and Robert Kennedy, many more African-Americans (10 to 24 percent more) knew about the assassinations of Medgar Evers and Malcolm X. Similarly, many more whites than African-Americans knew about the death of white Nazi leader George Lincoln Rockwell.[32]

There are many possible explanations for demographic variations in media use and socialization patterns. Despite the successes of the civil rights movement, most African-Americans still belong to different social groups than whites, and they lead lives quite unlike those of the white middle class to whose tastes most media cater. More African-Americans than whites fall into youthful age brackets where readership is generally lower. Fewer African-Americans than whites drive to work; hence fewer listen to radio news. For the many African-Americans whose schooling has been poor, deficient reading skills make newspaper reading unattractive. Television is an appealing alternative. Accordingly, African-Americans on an average watch about 15 percent more television than do whites.[33]

Some researchers have questioned whether the apparent differences between African-Americans and whites are based on race-linked cultural differences or spring instead from the fact that the African-American population is more frequently poor and educationally deprived. Bradley Greenberg and Brenda Dervin contend that within the subculture of poverty, African-Americans and whites use the media in similar ways.[34] They attribute differences in media habits and socialization to economic and educational differences. Other scholars argue that race and its cultural consequences are indeed important factors in media exposure and impact. Leo Bogart, for example, found racial differences in media-use patterns regardless of socioeconomic status.[35] The unresolved issues thus revolve around the causes of subcultural differences rather than their existence. If differences spring from race-linked cultural differences, they may be resistant to change. If they are linked to socioeconomic status, they may change readily with rising incomes, better education, and improved occupational status.

Gender, age, income, education, region, and city size also generate differences in newspaper reading, radio listening, and television viewing. For instance, men and women differ sharply in daytime television viewing; age has a bearing on newspaper reading; southerners listen to much less radio than do northerners. Program preferences vary as well. Women over fifty are the heaviest viewers of television news, followed by men over fifty. Twelve- to seventeen-year-olds are the lightest news watchers. Men far exceed women in following sports coverage, while women spend more time on television drama. Differences in media-use patterns are particularly pronounced between income levels. High-income families, who usually are better educated than poor families, use print media more and television less than the rest of the population. Upper income people also use a greater variety of media. Among the upper economic groups 57 percent are multimedia users compared with 27 percent in the lower economic groups. Thus the well-to-do potentially have much more information and a greater variety of information available to them. This helps them to maintain and increase their influence and power in American society.

In part, the poor pay less attention to print media because these media carry less information of interest to them. In fact, lack of interest in politics and disillusionment with government are the chief reasons given for failure to read newspapers. The urban poor need consumer information on prices, goods, and services more than coverage of new business regulations or city politics. Yet the print media rarely supply adequate consumer information. While print media are largely unattractive to the poor, television and radio programs appeal to them because these programs are easy to grasp and carry a great deal of light entertainment. They allow the poor to escape from the grim reality that surrounds their lives.

Unifying Forces

The notion of vastly different communications environments for various population groups should not be carried too far, however. The bulk of media entertainment and information is similar throughout the country and is shared by all types of media audiences. The same network television and cable programs are broadcast on the East Coast and the West Coast, in big cities and small towns. Differences among individual networks are slight. Hence television comes close to being a single, nationwide source of news and commentary. Radio is more diverse, but even many radio news programs are little more than national wire service reports. Insofar as newspaper stories are based on wire service information, they, too, are fairly uniform everywhere.

In Chapter 4 we saw that news media cover basically the same categories of stories in the same proportions. Specific stories vary, of course, depending on regional and local interests. Newspapers on the West Coast are more likely to devote their foreign affairs coverage to Asian affairs than are newspapers on the East Coast, which concentrate on Europe and the Middle East. Tabloids, such as the *New York Daily News,* put more stress on sensational crime and sex stories than does the staid *New York Times.* Nevertheless, news sources everywhere provide a large common core of information and interpretation that imbues their audiences with a shared structure of basic values and information.

Choosing Media Stories

Uses and Gratifications Theories

General patterns of media use do not reveal *why* people pay attention to specific stories, but a number of theories have been formulated to help explain how and why such individual choices are made. Currently, one of the most widely accepted of these theories is the "uses and gratifications" approach. Put most simply, proponents of this approach contend that individuals ignore personally irrelevant and unattractively presented messages and pay attention to the kinds of things that they need and that they find gratifying, provided the expenditure of time and effort seems reasonable.[36]

Uses and gratifications may be behavioral, emotional, or intellectual. Media scholar Lance Bennett groups them into three broad categories: curiosity and surveillance, entertainment and escape, and social and psychological adjustment.[37] For instance, people pay attention to stories that help them in making political decisions, such as voting or participating in protest demonstrations. They also use the media to gain a sense of security and social adequacy. Media stories help people to know what is happening in their political environment and to take part in discussions with friends and co-workers. They feel gratified if the media reinforce what they already know and believe. Finally, the media are used to while away time, reduce loneliness, participate vicariously in exciting ventures, and escape the frustrations of everyday life.[38] Audience studies show that people from all walks of life are most likely to view prime-time programs that are action-filled, humorous, and relaxing. Programs deemed informative or sophisticated are least likely to be chosen.[39] Of course, there is no guarantee that the gratifications that are sought are routinely attained. In fact, media may produce anxieties and fears as well as hatred and alienation. When radio and television were shut down by a long strike in Israel in 1987, the public reacted with relief rather than dismay. David Hartman, the Israeli philosopher, gave this explanation: "When television and radio become the prisms through which you look at reality, you come away saying, 'What an ugly place this is.' But when you take away those prisms and people's perceptions of reality are derived exclusively from their own daily experiences, which are for the most part prosaic, they inevitably become more relaxed and stable."[40]

Table 7-1, based on interviews with 6,564 adults in ten small cities throughout the United States, indicates the twenty-five newspaper content areas that are read most widely. People were asked to rate thirty to thirty-five common newspaper topics on a scale of 1 to 5. A score of 1 denoted that they always ignored the topic; a score of 5

Table 7-1 Rankings of Top Twenty-five Content Categories and Average Ratings Across Ten Markets

Rank	Rating
1. Natural disasters and tragedies	3.93
2. Stories and columns on the national economy (prices, unemployment, inflation)	3.87
3. News of the local economy	3.82
4. Column on local people and events	3.72
5. Stories about national politics and the president	3.72
6. Service information (TV listings, weather, movie listings, etc.)	3.71
7. News of international leaders and events	3.70
8. Stories on energy, conservation, and the environment	3.67
9. Stories on things to see and do in the area	3.66
10. Good Samaritan stories (people helping people)	3.60
11. Humorous stories and features	3.56
12. Accident and crime news	3.52
13. Health and medical advice	3.42
14. How fast the community is growing	3.33
15. Editorials and letters to the editor	3.32
16. Schools and education	3.31
17. City council and local politicians	3.30
18. News about the governor and state legislature	3.27
19. Consumer stories and advice	3.27
20. Stories about human psychology (the way we think and act)	3.22
21. Nature and outdoor stories	3.19
22. How-to advice on such things as crafts, auto and home repairs	3.19
23. News of record (births, deaths, weddings, etc.)	3.10
24. Space and exploration	3.10
25. Science and technology	3.08

Source: Judee K. Burgoon, Michael Burgoon, and Miriam Wilkinson, "Dimensions of Content Readership in 10 Newspaper Markets," *Journalism Quarterly* 60 (Spring 1983): 79. Reprinted by permission of the Association for Education in Journalism and Mass Communication, publishers of *Journalism Quarterly.*

Note: Ratings are based on a 1 to 5 scale. A rating of 1 means "never read"; a rating of 5 means "always read."

denoted that they always read it whenever it appeared. Presumably, the topics earning the highest scores supply the broadest array of gratifications.

Special subcultural needs may lead to significant variations in attention patterns. For instance, a Jewish person may be particularly attentive to news from the Middle East and other places that concern Israel. A person of Polish ancestry may look for news about food shortages and political developments in Poland. Women who favor increased job opportunities for women are apt to notice stories about women's expanding presence in the business world. What people actually select depends very much on their lifestyle and the context in

Table 7-2 Reasons for Attention or Inattention to News Stories

Reasons for attention	Percent	Reasons for inattention	Percent
Personal relevance	26	Missed	47
Emotional appeal	20	No interest	28
Societal importance	19	Too remote	10
Interesting story	15	Too busy	6
Job relevance	12	Doubt media	3
Chance reasons	1	Too complex	3
Miscellaneous	7	Redundant/Boring	2
		Doubt story	1

Source: Doris A. Graber, *Processing the News: How People Tame the Information Tide,* 2d ed. (New York: Longman Inc., 1988), 102. Copyright © 1988 by Longman Inc. Reprinted by permission of Longman Inc.

Note: N = 453 for reasons for attention, 1,493 for reasons of inattention.

which they are exposed to information. What is useful and gratifying in one setting may be less so in another. When people change their lifestyles, such as moving from daytime to nighttime work or trading a desk for a travel job, media patterns may change drastically to bring about closer accord with the people encountered in the new environment.[41]

Lifestyle also determines the time available for media use and hence the quantity of news that can be selected. In early adulthood when people begin their careers or raise children, the demands of home and job may leave little time for attention to the media. The cost of newspaper and magazine subscriptions may be prohibitive on a tight budget. Conversely, older people, whose home and job duties have become lighter and whose financial obligations are decreasing, frequently have much more time for reading or watching television. Lifestyle also determines what media are readily available. People may expose themselves to media that are of little intrinsic interest to them when this is convenient or socially appropriate. Table 7-2 shows the kinds of reasons people give when asked why they paid attention or failed to pay attention to particular news stories.

Other Selective Exposure Theories

Although people pick up what is personally useful and gratifying, they ignore many other bits of information, regardless of their political and social significance. Most of these omissions are random. People simply fail to notice certain information or have no time or inclination to pursue it, even when it comes to their attention. But systematic omissions occur as well. Various cognitive balance theories try to explain these omissions. According to these theories, people avoid information that disturbs their peace of mind, offends their political and social tastes, or conflicts with information, attitudes, and feelings they already hold. Social scientists explain selective exposure by pointing out that people are uncomfortable when they are exposed to ideas that differ from their own or that question the validity of their ideas. To avoid discomfort, people select information that is congruent with their existing beliefs.

Selectivity then leads to diversification of socializing influences and lays the groundwork for differential attitudes toward politics. It also reduces the already slim chances that an individual's beliefs, attitudes, and feelings will be altered once they have become established. Selective exposure therefore helps to explain the considerable stability that exists in cognitions and orientations such as party allegiance or isolationism or interventionism in foreign affairs.

Over the years scholars have repeatedly examined the various selective exposure phenomena and have modified their earlier theories in accordance with new findings. They now believe that selective exposure occurs to a lesser extent than was thought initially. Many people find it too bothersome to select news stories carefully, particularly when using electronic media. For instance, when television news carries stories that are objectionable to a viewer, there is no easy way to screen out the undesired stories and still watch the rest of the broadcast.

Many people are actually curious about discrepant information or pride themselves on being open-minded and receptive to all points of view. For instance, Democrats may want to hear what Republicans are saying to find out how the opposition is stating its case. They may also want to determine what counter arguments need to be formulated. Many people even enjoy news that contradicts their own ideas. At worst, exposure to discrepant information is not as universally painful as previously thought. It can be ignored, overlooked, or distorted. The source can be discredited and the message disbelieved.[42]

Much of the evidence for markedly selective exposure has come from settings in which available media supported the preferences of the audience. No choice was necessary; selection was de facto rather than deliberate. For example, unionized workers with friends and associates who are also in unions may encounter a lot of pro-union information at home and at work. They may not have to make a special effort to seek out pro-union information or reject anti-union opinions. In fact, anti-union information may be unavailable. Genuine rather than de facto selective exposure does occur, of course, but it operates more like a preference than a total exclusion rule. It appears to be most prevalent for those relatively few people who recognize dissonance and find it painful.

Agenda-Setting Theories

If selection of news items were entirely determined by personal needs and pleasures, news selection patterns would show infinite variations. This is not the case. Similarities in the political environment of average Americans and social pressures produce common patterns in the selection of news. As previously mentioned, gatekeeping practices largely account for the similarity in news supply, which is a powerful unifying force. Media also tell people in fairly uniform fashion which individual issues and activities are most significant and deserve to be ranked highly on the public's agenda of concerns.[43] Importance is indicated through cues such as banner headlines or front-page placement in newspapers, or first-story placement on television. Frequent and ample coverage also implies significance.

Many people readily adopt the media's agenda of importance, often without being aware of it, rather than selecting or rejecting news on the basis of what is personally gratifying or displeasing. We look at the front page of the newspaper and expect to find the most important stories there. We may watch the opening minutes of a telecast eagerly and then allow our attention to slacken. Consequently, agenda setting by the media leads to uniformities in exposure as well as in significance ratings of news items. When the media make events seem important, politicians are likely to comment about them and to take action. This enhances the perceived importance of these events and ensures even more public attention.

Numerous studies confirm the agenda-setting influence of the media.[44] In one intensive study of information processing, several thousand responses by small panels of voters showed that the panelists largely agreed on the current issues that were salient to their personal lives. The lists of issues mentioned by the panelists as most important to them personally, most talked about, and most salient to their community corresponded to cues in the news sources that they used in their communities.[45] However, agenda setting varied in potency. The audience followed media guidance but not slavishly.[46] Past and current experiences, conversations with others, and independent reasoning provided alternatives to media guidance.

Comparisons of media agendas with public opinion polls and reports about political and social conditions show that media guidance is most important for new issues that have not been widely discussed and for issues beyond the realm of personal experience.[47] Prominent media coverage does ensure that an issue will be noticed, but it does not guarantee that the audience will assign it the same relative rank of importance that media play has indicated. Likewise, information that is useful or gratifying to the audience will be noted, even if it is on the back pages, receives minuscule headlines, or is briefly reported at the tail end of a newscast.[48] The need for raw material for conversation with friends and associates is a particularly strong force in selecting stories.

Learning Processes

Media-Audience Interactions

The forces that make for diversity and for uniformity in the selection of news have been discussed. But what happens after the news has been selected? The early models that depicted a straight stimulus-response relationship have been disproven. There is no "hypodermic effect": information presented by the media is not injected unaltered into the minds of the audience. Rather, media and audience interact; the images conveyed by the media stimulate perceptions in audience members that reflect the media stimulus as well as each individual's perceptual state at the time the message was received.

Recent research indicates that from childhood on people develop ideas about how the world operates and feelings about various aspects of these operations. When these ideas relate to politics, they are usually grounded in information drawn from the mass media. Cognitive psychologists call these mental configurations by various names, including *schemata* and *scripts*.[49] As journalist Walter Lippmann explained seventy years ago:

> For the most part we do not first see, and then define, we define first and then see. In the great blooming, buzzing confusion of the outer world, we pick out what our culture has already defined for us, and we tend to perceive that which we have picked out in the form stereotyped for us by our culture.[50]

For instance, Marxists attribute most political events to economic forces. Accordingly, they interpreted stories about racial rioting in the United States in the late 1960s as signaling proletarian uprisings. Most Americans viewed them as stories about protests against racial injustice and its consequences.

Schemata serve as an organizing device that helps people to assimilate new information. If breaking news stories fit in with established schemata, they can be stored easily in memory as another example of a known concept. Numerous "knowledge-gap" studies show that political elites and other well-informed people who have appropriate schemata to process a wealth of information tend to absorb a great deal more from the mass media than do the poorly informed.[51] It is not functionally advantageous for the poorly informed to acquire knowledge that carries little meaning for them. This explains why information-poor population groups, although they are heavy consumers of the mass media, generally extract far less political information than do more politically sophisticated audiences. Thus during the course of a lifetime the knowledge gap between the privileged and underprivileged widens. Those with the least political knowledge are likely to remain politically unsophisticated and impotent. Moreover, the knowledge gap between the privileged and underprivileged makes mutual understanding of political views more difficult. Improved political education, which might shrink the gap, remains a distant goal.

Transient Influences

Many transitory factors impinge on news processing. A person's frame of mind may be accepting or rejecting. Attention may be focused totally on the news story or partly diverted. Up to half of the television audience eats dinner, washes dishes, reads, or talks on the telephone while watching television. Examination time at school, illness in the family, or the year-end rush at work may preempt the time normally devoted to media.

The other people present when news is received or discussed are also significant. For instance, if one watches or talks about a presidential inauguration with friends who are making fun of the way the president talks and acts, the occasion loses solemnity and becomes banal. If one watches or talks about the event with a group who admire the president, one comes away feeling inspired. Researchers cannot predict the effect of media messages without knowing the group context in which exposure or conversation took place.[52]

How a person interacts with information also depends on the format of that information. If news reports present conflicting facts or opinions, if they are overly long or overly short, if they are repetitious, dull, or offensive, their effect is apt to be diminished. Moreover, the total communications matrix affects the influence of its parts; the impact of print news may be blunted by prior presentations on television and radio that have removed the edge of novelty.[53]

Source credibility and appeal are other significant factors in news processing. People find television news more believable than comparable print news because they tend to trust anchorpersons after seeing them on their living room television screens.[54] Partisanship, too, may play an important role in source appraisal. It may cast a rosy glow over fellow partisans and a pall over the opposition.

Perceptual and Image Factors

When people receive new information they combine it with existing beliefs. But does the new reshape the old or the old reshape the new in the final images? Research has shown that images of political candidates are largely perceiver-determined for those aspects for which the audience already has developed complex schemata. For instance, people assume that Democratic presidential candidates will pursue policies typically associated with Democrats. They read or view the news in that vein, picking up bits of information that fit and rejecting, ignoring, or reinterpreting those that do not fit. The same is likely to hold true for information about big business or big labor, Mother Theresa or England's Queen. Average Americans are likely to interpret big business and big labor news negatively. Similarly, if reports about Mother Theresa or Queen Elizabeth permit a choice between favorable and unfavorable interpretations, the favorable image is apt to prevail.

Information about aspects of events or people that are not widely known or stereotyped leads to stimulus-determined images. How the media frame these political issues and depict people largely determines what the audience perceives. The personalities of newcomers to the political scene, assessments of their capabilities, and appraisals of the people with whom they surround themselves, for example, usually are stimulus-determined.[55] Likewise, when the media describe present-day China, when they cast doubt on the safety of nuclear energy production, or when they praise the merits of a newly developed drug, they create images that are likely to dominate people's schemata.

The general rule that media are most influential in areas where the audience knows least does not apply to specialized publications. Professional journals, for instance, often have a strong impact on their readers' images of professional matters. This happens because of the high credibility of the sources. The professionals who read these publications willingly subordinate their own views to those of the published experts.

Learning Effects: Knowledge and Attitudes

Measurement Problems

What kinds of politically relevant knowledge, attitudes, feelings, and actions spring from people's contacts with the media? Because of the limitations of measuring instruments, the answer is difficult. In Chapter 1 we pointed out the impossibility of isolating media influence when it is one of many factors in a complex environment.[56] For instance, the rising levels of cynicism about the U.S. government that occurred following the disclosure of the Watergate scandal in the Nixon administration cannot be directly and solely attributed to the disclosure stories. It is possible that cynicism was produced primarily by the experience of paying higher prices in the grocery store, facing motor fuel shortages at the gas station, or living through a public transit strike. Until researchers can trace an individual's mental processes and isolate the components that interact and combine to form mental images, the impact of media on knowledge and attitudes cannot be fully assessed. Nor can researchers understand completely just what is learned from media.

Research up to now has focused on very small facets of learning (for example, specific facts about political candidates or about a few public policies). Even within such narrow areas, testing has been severely limited, zeroing in on learning the substance of explicit messages rather than on assessing total knowledge gains. For instance, election coverage of a presidential candidate teaches more than facts about the candidate. It may also inform the audience about the role played by White House correspondents in campaign coverage and about living conditions in other cities. Because researchers usually ask only about learning campaign information, such ancillary learning, however important it may be, is overlooked. Much learning may even be subconscious. People may be unaware that they have learned something new and may not mention it when asked what they have learned. At times new information may be temporarily forgotten, only to reenter consciousness a short while later.[57]

Although many assumptions about learning that seem intuitively correct remain untested, media offerings continue to be judged as if these assumptions were true. The assumption that people deduce important social lessons from specific stories presented by the media is one example. For instance, media researcher Joshua Meyrowitz argues that television has radically changed social roles by stripping them of mystery and holding them up to continuous public scrutiny. Previously isolated housewives have learned about the attractive roles open only to males in American society, and the successes and failures of the women's movement have affected the behavior of these housewives. Television allows children to experience the adult world long before they are physically and emotionally prepared to cope with these experiences. In the age of television, political heroes have become ordinary mortals, and authority figures are no longer respected because the mystery of social distance has been stripped away.[58]

We believe that adults as well as children often model their behavior after characters they encounter in the media. We assume that unfavorable stereotypes will hurt the self-esteem of the groups so characterized, and so we urge newspeople to present these groups in a better light. Accordingly, the television image of African-Americans has changed dramatically since the 1960s, showing them frequently as mainstream middle class citizens and professionals.[59] News reports and dramatic shows supposedly teach people how lawyers or police officers or hospitals conduct their business. Presumably, impressionable people who watch these shows and like what they see will be motivated to aspire to these professions; conversely, distortions in the portrayal of these roles will mislead inexperienced people who regard them as accurate.

Although we assume these effects, and there is every reason to believe that many are quite common, most of them remain unmeasured. An important exception has been the Cultural Indicators project conducted since the mid-1960s at the University of Pennsylvania's Annenberg School of Communications. Using "cultivation analysis" the investigators studied trends in the dramatic content of network television and the conceptions of social reality produced in viewers. Their findings confirm that heavy viewers of television drama (more than four hours daily) see the world as television paints it and react to that world rather than to reality more than do light viewers of the same demographic background and similar circumstances. For instance, heavy viewers, exposed to large doses of crime in television drama, believe that the dangers of becoming a crime victim are far greater than they actually are.[60] They fear crime more and are more distrustful and suspicious than are persons who view television less often. They also are generally more pessimistic and tend to gravitate toward the middle-of-the-road "mainstream" politics depicted on television.

Like most research on mass media effects, these findings have been challenged on the grounds that factors other than mass media exposure account for the results. The characteristics of viewers rather than their exposure to television may be responsible for their images of the world and their addiction to television. The technical aspects of the Cultural Indicators project have also been challenged. Such scientific controversies indicate that research on mass media effects needs a lot more refinement before the findings can be considered definitive. This holds true, too, for a number of experimental studies that have found, for example, that television news coverage of specific events "primes" audiences to appraise politicians in light of these events, narrowing their political perspectives so that single phenomena deflect attention from broader problems.[61] Until such findings have been tested in natural settings to appraise under what conditions and for what time periods they apply, they must be considered tentative and incomplete. For example, it is not surprising that experiments indicate that President Bush's popularity ratings fare better when the audience has been primed with questions about Persian Gulf victories rather than the nation's financial troubles.⁶² But thus far experiments have failed to tell us how long the priming effects persist in natural situations and their likely political impact.

A neglected research sphere concerns forgetfulness. Much that is learned from the media is evanescent. When Iran is engulfed by revolution or Philadelphia rocked by a patronage scandal, the salient names and facts are on many lips, but after the crisis has passed, this knowledge evaporates rapidly. How rapidly seems to depend on a number of factors, most importantly of which is the ability to store and retrieve information. After three months of neglect, most ordinary stories have been forgotten, even by people with good memories. If stories are periodically revived with follow-ups or with closely related stories, memory becomes deepened and prolonged. In fact, a few crucial incidents are so deeply etched into human memory that they become permanent. The Great Depression, World War II, and the assassination of President John F. Kennedy are examples.⁶³

Factual Learning

Given these limitations on initial learning and on remembering, what can be said about the extent of political learning from the mass media? The data that follow come from a research project in which the information supply and political learning of four small panels of adults living in Midwestern and Eastern communities of various sizes were monitored intensively throughout an entire year.⁶⁴ When asked about topics covered by their news sources, these panelists could identify many, but the mix of topics varied from person to person. Seven broad topic areas were recognized by nearly every panel member as receiving "a lot of coverage" during the interview year. The list was dominated by economic and foreign policy issues. Sixteen other topics were recalled by a somewhat smaller majority of the panel members—all in all an impressive array of politically important topics to be remembered by an average mass media audience.

However, people do not seem to gain much specific knowledge from the media. They recognize information if it is mentioned to them, but fail to recall it without such assistance.⁶⁵ For instance, when panelists were asked open-ended questions at the height of the 1976 presidential campaign about the positions of presidential candidates Gerald R. Ford and Jimmy Carter on the issues of inflation and unemployment, specific knowledge was abysmally small, as Table 7-3 indicates. Half of the answers were "don't know's," even though these issues were personally important for the panelists and had been discussed with friends and associates. Specific information about each policy was contained in less than 10 percent of the answers on unemployment and less than 5

Table 7-3 Recall of Specific Information on Unemployment and Inflation (in percentages)

	Unemployment							
	Ford				Carter			
	Women		*Men*		*Women*		*Men*	
Responses	O	Y	Y	O	O	Y	Y	O
Statistics	0	0	0	2	4	0	2	11
Policy data	12	8	9	12	3	4	3	5
General information	41	38	44	43	43	41	48	35
Don't know	47	55	47	43	50	55	46	48

	Inflation							
	Ford				Carter			
	Women		*Men*		*Women*		*Men*	
Responses	O	Y	Y	O	O	Y	Y	O
Statistics	1	0	1	0	0	0	1	0
Policy data	1	2	2	0	3	2	6	6
General information	38	34	39	42	34	29	29	27
Don't know	59	63	59	58	63	69	64	67

Source: Doris Graber, "Agenda-Setting: Are There Women's Perspectives?" in *Women and the News,* ed. Laurily Keir Epstein (New York: Hastings House, 1978), 22. Copyright © 1978 by Laurily Keir Epstein. Reprinted by permission.

Note: $N = 1,716$ replies. O stands for older women and men (over age forty). Y stands for younger women and men (age forty and under). *Statistics* means that the respondent was able to cite precise figures for unemployment and inflation rates and/or rate changes. *Policy data* means that the respondent was able to refer to specific proposals made by Ford or Carter to cope with the inflation or unemployment problem. *General information* means that the respondent knew whether general trends were changing or stable, and knew whether action was planned, without being able to give specifics.

percent of the answers on inflation. Women, especially those forty years of age and under, recalled much less information than did the men. Age, education, and even prior knowledge and exposure to several news sources did not produce major differences in learning scores.

In the same way, when John Robinson and Dennis Davis tested comprehension of the main facts of thirteen television news stories within hours of viewing, the results were quite uniform. As Table 7-4 shows, comprehension scores hovered around 40 percent, with only minor differences among various age groups. Use of additional media boosted fact retention only slightly. Education and prior information

Table 7-4 Television News Comprehension Scores

Viewer characteristics	Group size	Score
Age		
18-29 years	97	42.3%
30-44 years	110	41.4
45-59 years	98	43.7
60 and older	82	38.8
Education		
Grade school	42	34.4
High school graduate	119	40.8
Some college	119	42.4
College graduate	107	45.6
Information base (name recognition test)		
Low	145	34.7
Medium	150	44.6
High	82	48.5
Additional news media use		
Newspaper		
Nonreader	185	40.7
Reader	202	42.3
Radio		
Nonlistener	274	41.8
Listener	113	41.3
News magazine		
Nonreader	249	40.5
Reader	128	43.7

Source: Adapted from John P. Robinson and Dennis K. Davis, "Comprehension of Single Evening's News," in *The Main Source: Learning from Television News,* ed. John P. Robinson and Mark R. Levy (Beverly Hills, Calif.: Sage, 1986), 122-126.

Note: Score is the percentage of a perfect score for the entire broadcast. A perfect score of 8 points for the thirteen stories amounts to 104 points. It required comprehending the central point of each story, as identified by the researchers, plus three or more important details. There were 387 viewers selected through national probability sampling.

levels produced the largest variations in scores, with the best informed scoring 13.8 percentage points higher than the poorly informed; people whose education terminated in grade school and college graduates' scores were separated by an 11.2 percent gap.

The paucity of factual learning by average individuals has disturbed many people who believe that story meanings cannot be extracted without memorizing factual details. Political scientists Scott Keeter and Cliff Zukin, for example, titled their intensive study of voter knowledge gains during the 1976 and 1980 presidential elections *Uninformed Choice.* They argued that most citizens are too uninformed to make intelligent political choices.[66] Earlier studies had registered even less factual knowledge than Keeter and Zukin's research. These judgments may be unduly harsh when knowledge is gauged largely by a citizen's ability to recall facts such as the names of prominent office-holders and figures about the length of their term of office or the growth rate of budget deficits. Such factual information tests are inappropriate for judging political knowledge and competence. What really matters is that citizens understand what is at stake in major political issues, and what policy options are available for coping with various problems.

Are people aware of major political issues and their significance? Are they able to place them in the general context of current politics? When these genuinely important questions are asked, the picture of the public's political competence brightens considerably. People may not remember the content of political speeches very well, but, as mentioned already, they are aware of a wide range of current issues. Moreover, when interviewers probe for understanding, rather than for knowledge of specific facts, they often discover considerable political insight. For instance, people who cannot define either *affirmative action* or *price deregulation* may have fairly sophisticated notions about these matters. They know about government price controls on some goods and services and fully understand the burdens faced by people hampered in finding a job because of their race or gender.[67]

Learning General Orientations

Some media stories leave the audience with politically significant feelings that persist long after facts have faded from memory. Although many details of the 1986 explosion of the *Challenger* space shuttle have been forgotten, Americans still retain vivid feelings of horror, sympathy, grief, and disappointment. Often news that etches a few facts into people's memories may leave them with generalized feelings of trust or distrust. For instance, prominently featured stories of serious corruption in government may lower the public's esteem for the integrity of government. People who read newspapers severely critical of various actions taken by the government express significantly less trust in government than those exposed to favorable views. People who have not gone beyond grade school seem to be particularly susceptible to erosion of trust in the wake of mass media criticism.[68] A number of laboratory and field experiments demonstrate similar linkages, positive as well as negative. Favorable publicity enhances esteem for government; unfavorable publicity diminishes it. Cynical people, in turn, tend to participate less than others in civic activities such as voting and lobbying.[69]

As political scientist Murray Edelman has noted, media stories may produce an overpowering sense of a world out of control, or they may reassure the audience that all is going well. Feelings of both insecurity and security may make people quiescent because they become fearful of interfering with crucial government actions or else complacent about the need for public vigilance. Fear that dissension weakens the government may decrease tolerance for dissidents. Edelman also warns that political quiescence leads to acceptance of faulty public policies, poor laws, and poor administrative practices—significant political effects.[70]

On a more personal level, millions of people use the media to keep in touch with their environment. This helps to counter feelings of loneliness and alienation because information becomes a bond among individuals who share it.[71] Media may also arouse desires that can change the course of life of individuals and societies. The models of life depicted by the media create wants and expectations as well as dissatisfactions and frustrations. These feelings may become powerful stimulants for social change for the society at large or for selected individuals within it. Alternatively, they may bolster support for the political status quo and generate strong resistance to change. Whether media-induced orientations and actions are considered positive, negative, or a mixture of both depends, of course, on one's sociopolitical preferences.

Deterrents to Learning

Lack of motivation for acquiring political knowledge and distaste for media offerings, as well as deficiencies in the information supply deter the average individual from keeping up with politics through media exposure. Most people do not need detailed knowledge of current affairs for either their jobs or their social relationships. They do not expect to be quizzed about television news programs. Rather than discussing politics, which they see as a touchy topic, they prefer to talk about sports, or the weather, or the local gossip. In fact, as the level of abstract, issue-oriented content of political news rises, the size of the attentive audience shrivels.[72] People scan the news for major crises without trying to remember specific facts. However, when they sense that events will greatly affect their lives, or when they need information to make voting choices, political interest and learning perk up quickly and often dramatically.[73]

Occasionally, serious programs on radio and television become highly popular. Most of them involve themes of corruption, violence, or other wrongdoing, which may account for their popularity. Examples are "60 Minutes," which probes a variety of social ills; "The Winds of War," a made-for-TV movie that recapitulated World War II; and documentaries dealing with rape, child-snatching, and prison violence. Broadcasts of congressional hearings on the selection of controversial Supreme Court judges or on the legality of secret activities of the executive branch fall into this category. These are exceptions, however.

Like a straw fire, widespread public interest in most political crises flares up and then dies quickly. For instance, attention focused relatively briefly in 1987 on the Iran-contra scandal even though it involved highly dramatic events like hostages, secret weapons deals, and circumvention of congressional mandates. After a few weeks audiences began to complain that stories about illegal financing of Central American military ventures usurped too much media time. Attention spans are erratic and brief, even though most Americans believe that, as good citizens, they ought to be well informed about political news, and they feel guilty, or at least apologetic, if they are not.[74]

Learning is further inhibited by the alienation of many population groups from the media. Some white ethnics, such as Polish-Americans or Italian-Americans, and police and union members, for instance, consider most mass media to be opposed to them. They believe that the media lie and distort when they cast police as trigger-happy oppressors of the disadvantaged, or unions as corrupt and a barrier to economic progress.[75]

Public opinion polls in recent decades show considerable erosion over time of public confidence in the trustworthiness of the media. On a scale ranging from "a great deal of confidence in people running the media," to "only some," to "hardly any," a 1987 National Opinion Research Center poll recorded only 19 percent high confidence in the media. Low confidence stood at 25 percent. By comparison, the Supreme Court earned a 38 percent high confidence rating, major companies stood at 31 percent, and organized labor at 11 percent.[76]

How media information is presented also affects learning. The public is bombarded daily with more news than it can handle. Most of the news is touted as significant even though much is trivial. The constant crisis atmosphere numbs excitement and produces boredom. The presentation of stories in disconnected snippets further complicates the task of making sense out of them and integrating them with existing knowledge. This is especially true when stories are complex. People who feel that they cannot understand what is happening are discouraged from spending time reading or listening. Featuring conflicting stories and interpretations, without giving guidance to the audience because that might jeopardize objectivity, also hinders learning.[77]

Television news deters the kind of factual and conceptual learning that social scientists measure and prize. Instead, it concentrates on conveying the essence of personalities and a sense of witnessing places and events.[78] Moreover, the average half-hour television news program covers the equivalent in words of only one newspaper page. If several newscasts are watched, about half the material is repetitive. Even within a single newscast a large proportion of every story is background information that puts the story into perspective for viewers seeing it for

Table 7-5 Network Television News Characteristics

Story length (seconds)	Percentage	Picture exposure (seconds)	Percentage	Number of pictures	Percentage
Less than 60	29	1-10	47	1-4	38
60-179	47	11-20	29	5-10	13
180-299	16	21-30	12	11-20	26
300+	8	31+	13	21-54	23

Source: Author's research based on a sample of 149 news stories from early evening newscasts on ABC, CBS, and NBC.

the first time. Moreover, most television programs are primarily designed "to evoke stored information . . . in a patterned way" to make use of what the audience already knows.[79]

Viewing purposes are also important. Because most people read news largely to make sure that no unexpected threats have arisen, and because they watch television news to be entertained, audiences are not likely to try hard to learn a wealth of factual information. What they actually wish to learn may not match the lessons available from the media, anyway. "Happy-talk" television news formats and exciting film footage encourage the feeling that news should be viewed as light-hearted diversion. Of course, an entertaining format does not preclude learning; nevertheless, it reduces motivation to learn.[80]

The internal structure of television newscasts also impedes learning. Three-quarters of all news stories take up less than three minutes, yet they are crammed with information that cannot possibly be absorbed in that time (see Table 7-5). In addition to the abundance of pictures that is noted in the table, each news story contains verbal information. The average ratio is three factual statements for every two pictorial scenes. For the fifteen to eighteen stories that make up a typical newscast, viewers are asked to absorb an average of eighteen factual statements and eleven picture scenes per story. That amounts to 324 statements and 198 pictures compressed into 22 minutes of news exposure. Furthermore, in most news programs disparate items are tightly packaged without the pauses that are essential to allow viewers to absorb information. Hence it is not surprising that half the audience after the lapse of a few hours cannot recall a single item from a television newscast. Distracting activities do not help either. Many people watch television while cooking dinner or playing games.[81]

Despite all of the deterrents to learning that have been discussed thus far, compared with other people in the world, Americans still rank quite high in political information levels. They also are well socialized into the American system. They may be disappointed and cynical about particular leaders or policies, but relatively few question the legitimacy of the government, object to its basic philosophies, or reject its claims to their support. If one believes in the merits of the system, this finding is, indeed, cause for satisfaction with current political socialization. In this light, the dire predictions about television-induced deterioration of political life and a general decline in intellectual achievement have not materialized.[82] If the American population becomes better educated, and if the media improve their coverage of politics, then knowledge levels are likely to rise. However, since television has become the main provider of information, it is essential to restructure knowledge tests so that they reflect the unique contributions made by audio-visuals to comprehending the world.

Learning Effects: Behavior

Because the media shape people's knowledge, attitudes, and feelings, they obviously can influence behavior. To assess the extent of behavioral effects, two areas that have long been of great political concern will be examined: imitation of crime and violence, particularly among adolescents, and stimulation of economic and political development in underdeveloped regions. In Chapter 8 we will discuss the effects of media coverage on voting behavior and in Chapter 11 the impact of the media on the conduct of foreign affairs.

Crime and Violent Behavior in Children

Many social scientists believe that violence and crime portrayed in the media, particularly on television, lead to learning and imitation. Children and young adults are deemed to be particularly impressionable. Because crime and violence are serious problems in American society, the possible link between television exposure and deviant behavior has been thoroughly investigated. The Surgeon General's office has produced a bookshelf of information.[83] Congressional committees have spent countless hours listening to conflicting testimony by social scientists about the impact of television violence. Meanwhile, violent content, particularly in fiction programs, has escalated. In 1986 nine out of ten entertainment programs broadcast during prime time contained violence at an average rate of eight violent incidents per hour. Weekend children's programs topped this rate with twenty-seven acts of violence packed into each hour.[84]

What have studies of the impact of television violence revealed? Despite the strong inclination of many of the researchers to find that

1985 CHICAGO TRIBUNE LOCHER

Reprinted by permission: Tribune Media Services.

crime fiction causes asocial behavior, the evidence provides only modest support. Some children do copy violent behavior, especially when they have watched aggression that was left unpunished or was rewarded and when countervailing influences from parents and teachers were lacking.[85] But, aside from immediately copying television examples when tempted to do so, children do not ordinarily become violent after exposure to violence in the mass media. Most children lack the predisposition and usually the opportunity for violence, and their environment discourages asocial behavior. In fact, exposure to crime makes some children more sympathetic toward the suffering of crime and violence victims.[86] A crude cause and effect model is therefore invalid.

The percentage of imitation-prone pre-adolescents and adolescents in the population is not known at this time. However, the wide dispersion of television throughout American homes makes it almost certain that the majority of children susceptible to violence will be exposed. Even in the absence of television, many other triggers could arouse these young people to violence. Whatever the source of arousal, even if the actual number of highly susceptible pre-adolescents and adolescents is tiny and statistically insignificant, the social consequences can be profound.

Other confounding factors in assessing the impact of television on children are age-linked comprehension differences. Younger children may not be able to comprehend many of the events presented by the media in the same way that adolescents do. Several studies of preschool-age and early grade-school-age children suggest that much of what adults consider to be violent does not seem so to children. Cartoon violence is an example. When an enemy drops Donald Duck on his head, or pummels Mickey Mouse, or flattens Fred Flintstone with a boulder, most children view it as funny make-believe.[87] For them, it is not a behavior model for action in the real world. Many of the programs that adults consider to be dangerous actually may be harmless.

Children not only see things differently from adults, but they also are less adept at drawing inferences. The complex social reasoning that adults often ascribe to even young children does not develop until youngsters reach their teens. For instance, after seeing a series of shows with the implied message that the big bully who hits everybody always wins, children presumably conclude that similar behavior on their part will yield similar results. In actuality, they may not draw such a conclusion. Although young children often imitate what they have seen, they are rarely able to generalize or respond to implied messages. Without a better understanding of how the average child at various stages of development interacts with stories presented by the media, we cannot completely assess media effects on subsequent behavior. Nor can we plan program content with any assurance that it will encourage children of all ages and in diverse social settings to engage in approved behaviors and to abstain from undesirable activities.

Behavior Change in Adults

What about imitation of socially undesirable behavior by adults? The same broad principles apply. Imitation depends on the setting at the time of media exposure and on the personality and attitudes viewers bring to the situation. Widespread societal norms seem to be particularly important. For instance, the 1970 report of the Presidential Commission on Obscenity and Pornography noted that exposure to aberrant sexual behavior led to comparatively little imitation. In fact, there was some evidence that greater availability of obscene and pornographic materials reduced sex crimes and misdemeanors because vicarious experiences were substituted for actual ones.[88] By comparison, there was a great deal more evidence that exposure to criminal behavior encourages imitation. The difference may be more apparent than real, however, since crime is more likely to be reported, while sexual perversions remain hidden.

In sum, the precise link between exposure to media images and corresponding behavior remains uncertain. Legislative tampering with media offerings therefore appears premature. It will take a great deal more research and experimentation to determine how media fare can be presented to produce desirable results and avoid undesirable ones. Even assuming that this goal could be reached, it is questionable whether a democratic society should attempt to manipulate the minds of its citizens to protect them from temptations to violate social norms. It may be best to leave control of the content of entertainment programs to widely based informal social pressures. Whether social pressures should be allowed to interfere with reporting real-world violence poses even more difficult dilemmas. The possibly adverse effects on behavior must be balanced against the need to keep informed about the real world.

Socioeconomic and Political Modernization

The assumed potential of the media to guide people's behavior has led to great efforts to use the media as tools for social and political development. The results have been mixed; there have been some successes and many failures.

Psychic Mobility.   The hope of using the media to bring about industrialization, improved social services, and democratization ran very high at mid-century. The psychological key to human and material development was then assumed to be a personality characteristic that political scientist Daniel Lerner labeled *empathic capacity*. The media were thought to be the stimuli; when the media present new objects, ideas, and behaviors they presumably stimulate people to empathize and imagine themselves to be involved with these objects, ideas, and actions. For instance, when the media show how slum dwellers have built new housing, or how flood victims have purified their polluted water supply, audience members presumably wonder, "How could I make this work for me?"

Before mass media became widely available to average people, this "psychic mobility" was generated when people came into direct contact with strangers with different lifestyles and experiences. Because contacts usually were limited to relatively few people, changes spread very slowly. The mass media, however, made it possible for the first time in human history to reach millions of people with comparative ease and to expose them to developmental stimuli, either directly or through contact with others reached by the media. Transistor radios and satellite television have opened even remote and inaccessible regions to modern communication and brought news of current lifestyles to isolated communities.

Social scientists who credit the media with a major role in modernization and democratization have made three assumptions. First, the mass media can create interest and empathy for unfamiliar experiences. Second, the mass media provide graphic examples of new practices, which are then readily understood and copied. (For instance, films and videotapes can show people how to build a cinder block house, how to plant potatoes more efficiently, or how to run an honest election.) Third, development, once started, creates an incentive for people to increase their knowledge and skills. Where formal education is not readily accessible, the media provide information and enhance the capacity to learn. Proof of these assumptions is seen in the progress in urbanization, industrialization, living standards, and political advancement that has followed media development in many regions.[89]

Psychological Barriers to Modernization. While many technologically and politically underdeveloped regions have shown measurable progress, with the media apparently serving as catalysts, modernization, including political change, has been far slower and more sporadic than expected. A number of psychological and physical obstacles have kept the dreams of the development theorists from coming true. Most damaging has been outright hostility by individuals or communities to change and unwillingness to alter long-established patterns. Mass media may actually become a negative reference point so that people condemn the lifestyle depicted by the media. The various fundamentalist groups around the world—such as Ayatollah Khomeini's followers in the Middle East or ultra-Orthodox Jews in Israel—that have mobilized to stop social and political changes provide examples.

People who are not overtly hostile to change still may be totally uninterested in changing. They may doubt their ability to cope with changes and they may be reluctant to further complicate a difficult life. People exhibiting this mental state cannot be reached by the mass media without the intervention of a trusted person, such as a priest, physician, or family member. Mass media influence then becomes a "two-step flow" reaching its targets through selected opinion leaders.

Putting unaccustomed behaviors and skills into words and concepts that people with little formal education can understand has also turned out to be exceedingly difficult. For instance, teaching new ways to keep food pure, or to apply for aid from a government agency, or to mark a ballot in a multi-candidate election involves concepts that may require schooling to grasp. The disparity in social backgrounds between journalists and their audiences may further confound the problem of communication. *Heterophily* (a gap between social backgrounds) complicates communication; *homophily* (similarity in backgrounds) eases it.

Changes that require adopting new social values or abandoning old habits are the most difficult of all and the least likely to occur. For example, people who were taught to abhor capitalist practices find it difficult to become entrepreneurs even when the media praise new forms of economic enterprise. Ingrained habits, such as driving without seat belts or engaging in unsafe sexual behaviors, are difficult to break despite extensive mass-mediated public education campaigns. Even after people have become aware of the dangers inherent in their behavior, and even when they concede that behavioral change is in their best interest, most still forgo voluntary change.

Adoption of Changes. Despite the difficulties, many mass media campaigns do succeed in bringing about socially desirable changes. How do they do it? We will outline five steps involved in change and indicate how the mass media fit into the picture.

The first step is an *awareness of the possibility for change.* Here the media are especially helpful. Radio can inform people about new energy-saving devices or new child-rearing methods. Television and movies can show new technologies and new styles of political participation.

The second step is *understanding how to accomplish the suggested changes.* For example, people may be aware that public assistance is available, but they may not know how to apply for it. Mass media usually fail to supply detailed information. On the average, only one-third of all stories that might inspire action of various types, such as environmental protection or energy conservation, contain implementing information.[90] Unless this gap is filled, the chain leading to the adoption of innovations is broken.

The third step is evaluation. People *assess the merits of the innovation,* given their circumstances, and decide whether they want to adopt it. Innovations often fail to take root because prospective users consider them bad, inappropriate, too risky, or too difficult. Media messages alone may not be persuasive enough. It may be crucial to have a trusted person urge or demonstrate adoption of the innovation.

The fourth step is trial. The effect of the media in *getting people to try innovations* is limited. Factors beyond media control are more important, such as social and financial costs of the change as well as the audience's willingness to change. Generally, young men are most receptive to innovations; older people are most skeptical and cautious.

Finally, the fifth step is adoption. The media contribute most to this phase by *encouraging people to stick with the changes* that they have made part of their life and work styles. For example, adoption of birth control is useless unless it is continuous. The same holds true for many health and sanitation measures or improved work habits. To ensure continuity, mass media must cover a topic regularly, stressing long-range goals and reporting progress.

Predicting which media campaigns designed to change behavior will succeed and which will fail has proved to be difficult. The federal government spends millions of dollars each year on public service advertisements and consumer education programs, but it has reaped little from these efforts. Numerous carefully planned projects to motivate poor people and elderly shut-ins to listen to vitally needed information about nutrition, medical care, and social security benefits have failed. On the other hand, campaigns to get people to study pesticide labels more carefully, to learn about employment for the mentally retarded, or to win support for environmental protection programs have succeeded. The reasons why have thus far eluded researchers in most cases.[91]

Douglas S. Solomon, who studied health campaigns conducted by private and public institutions, believes that four factors account for success or failure. To succeed, campaigns must *set well-specified, realistic goals* that are tailored to the needs of various target groups. They must *carefully select appropriate media and media formats* and present them at key times and intervals. *Messages* must be properly *designed for greatest persuasiveness.* There also must be *continuous evaluation and appropriate readjustments.*[92]

In some instances the media's efforts to mobilize people have produced unanticipated attitudes and changes in behavior. For instance, when television was introduced in several Canadian Eskimo communities in the 1970s, programs were designed to show the viewers how to modernize their living conditions and to acquaint them with Canadian affairs generally. Rather than aspiring to modernize their lifestyles, Eskimo adults in the television communities turned their eyes to the past. They wanted to return to traditional Eskimo ways. This attitude was not apparent in localities without television. Whether it sprang from nostalgia for the past or aversion to the lifestyle changes foreshadowed by television is unclear. It is interesting that the adults who yearned for traditional ways aspired to a modern lifestyle for their children following the introduction of television.[93]

Above all, the success of the mass media in bringing about change hinges on the receptivity for change. Ongoing efforts to use the media to modernize underdeveloped areas, to turn former Communists into democratic citizens, or to bring socially helpful information to the poor, the elderly, and the handicapped must concentrate on identifying the specific circumstances most likely to bring success. Responding to requests initiated locally, rather than designing information campaigns from the outside, and integrating local traditions into new approaches seem to hold the most promise.[94]

Summary

The mass media play a major role in *political socialization,* the learning and accepting of norms and rules, structures, and environmental factors that govern political life. Contrary to earlier findings that indicated limited impact, the media are very influential and consequently a tremendously powerful political force.

However, the impact of the media on political socialization and other aspects of political learning is not uniform for all members of the media audience. The media affect individuals in different ways, depending on lifestyles and circumstances. Psychological, demographic, and situational factors influence perceptions and the ensuing political consequences. So do the manner of news presentation and the perspectives from which news is presented.[95]

Although many factors contribute to diversity in socialization and learning, there are also powerful unifying forces. Most Americans are exposed to similar information and develop roughly similar outlooks on what it means and ought to mean to be an American both politically and socially.

Various theories explain why and how individuals select particular information to remember. Learning of specific facts presented by the media is sparse. Nonetheless, people become aware of many political problems and appreciate their basic significance, even without remembering details about them. Equally important, exposure to the media produces apathy, cynicism, fear, trust, acquiescence, and support— moods that condition participation in the political process, which may range from total abstinence to efforts to overthrow the government by force.

The media may also produce or retard behavior that affects the quality of public life. In this chapter we assessed the role of the media in fostering socially undesirable behaviors, such as crime and violence, and in the political and social development of various population groups. Media influence is greatest in informing people and creating initial attitudes; it is least effective in changing established attitudes and ingrained behaviors.

Given the many largely uncontrollable variables that determine media influence, concerted efforts to manipulate media content to foster societal goals are risky at best. They could set dangerous precedents for inhibiting the free flow of controversial ideas or for using the media as channels for government propaganda.

Notes

1. Michael Wines, "Appeal of 'Murphy Brown' Now Clear at White House," *New York Times,* May 21, 1992.
2. Impact differences between print and electronic media are discussed in W. Russell Neuman, Marion R. Just, and Ann N. Crigler, *Common Knowledge: News and the Construction of Political Meaning* (Chicago: University of Chicago Press, 1992); Marion Just and Ann Crigler, "Learning from the News: Experiments in Media, Modality, and Reporting about Star Wars," *Political Communication and Persuasion* 6 (1989): 109-127.
3. Jacob Jacoby and Wayne D. Hoyer, "Viewer Miscomprehension of Televised Communications: Selected Findings," *Journal of Marketing* 46 (Fall 1982): 12-26.
4. John P. Robinson and Dennis K. Davis, "Television News and the Informed Public: An Information-Processing Approach," *Journal of Communication* 40 (Summer 1990): 106-119.
5. Neil Postman, *Amusing Ourselves to Death: Public Discourse in the Age of Show Business* (New York: Viking Penguin, 1985). For a good discussion of the differences between the effects of print and television news on people's behavior, see Joshua Meyrowitz, *No Sense of Place: The Impact of Electronic Media on Social Behavior* (New York: Oxford University Press, 1985), 94-106.
6. Harold Stanley and Richard Niemi, *Vital Statistics on American Politics,* 2d ed. (Washington, D.C.: Congressional Quarterly Press, 1990), 69. Also see Michael J. Robinson and Andrew Kohut, "Believability and the Press," *Public Opinion Quarterly* 52 (1988): 174-189; and Cecilie Gaziano and Kristin McGrath, "Measuring the Concept of Credibility," *Journalism Quarterly* 63 (Autumn 1986): 451-462.
7. Doris A. Graber, "Seeing is Remembering: How Visuals Contribute to Learning from Television News," *Journal of Communication* 40 (Summer 1990): 134-155.
8. W. Russell Neuman, *The Future of the Mass Audience* (New York: Cambridge University Press, 1991), 86-104; and Steven H. Chaffee and Joan Schleuder, "Measurement and Effects of Attention to Media News," *Human Communication Research* 13 (1986): 76-107.
9. Neuman, *Future of the Mass Audience,* 99 (emphasis added).
10. John E. Chubb and Terry M. Moe, "Politics, Markets, and the Organization of Schools," *American Political Science Review* 82 (1988): 1065-1088.
11. Bruce Watkins, "Television Viewing as a Dominant Activity of Childhood: A Developmental Theory of Television Effects," *Critical Studies in Mass Communication* 2 (1985): 323-337. Average high school graduates have spent 15,000 hours watching television and 11,000 hours in the classroom. They have seen 350,000 commercials.
12. M. Margaret Conway, Mikel L. Wyckoff, Eleanor Feldbaum, and David Ahern, "The News Media in Children's Political Socialization," *Public Opinion Quarterly* 45 (Summer 1981): 164-178; and Gina M. Garramone and Charles K. Atkin, "Mass Communication and Political Socialization: Specifying the Effects," *Public Opinion Quarterly* 50 (Spring 1986): 76-86.
13. M. Margaret Conway, A. Jay Stevens, and Robert G. Smith, "The Relations between Media Use and Children's Civic Awareness," *Journalism Quarterly* 52 (Autumn 1975): 531-538; Suzanne Pingree, "Children's Cognitive Processes in Constructing Social Reality," *Journalism Quarterly* 60 (Fall 1983):

415-422. Also see Judith Torney-Purta, "From Attitudes and Knowledge to Schemata: Expanding the Outcomes of Political Socialization," in *Political Socialization, Citizenship Education, and Democracy,* ed. Orit Ichilov (New York: Teachers' College, 1990), 98-115; and Judith Torney-Purta, "Cognitive Representations of the Political System in Adolescents: The Continuum from Pre-Novice to Expert," International Society for Political Psychology paper, 1991.

14. Jean Piaget, *The Language and Thought of the Child,* 3d ed. (New York: Harcourt Brace, 1962). See also Torney-Purta,."From Attitudes and Knowledge to Schemata"; and Pamela Johnston Conover, "Political Socialization: Where's the Politics?" in *Political Science: Looking to the Future; Political Behavior,* vol. 3, ed. William Crotty (Evanston, Ill.: Northwestern University Press, 1991), 125-152.

15. A study of prime-time values on television showed that fewer than 4 percent concerned citizenship values such as patriotism or citizen duties. Gary W. Selnow, "Values in Prime-Time Television," *Journal of Communication* 40 (Summer 1990): 69.

16. Neuman, *Future of the Mass Audience,* 89-91.

17. George Gerbner, Larry Gross, Marilyn Jackson Beeck, Suzanne Jeffries Fox, and Nancy Signorielli, "Cultural Indicators: Violence Profile No. 9," *Journal of Communication* 28 (Summer 1978): 178, 193. See also George Gerbner, Larry Gross, Michael Morgan, and Nancy Signorielli, "Political Correlates of Television Viewing," *Public Opinion Quarterly* 48 (Summer 1984): 283-300. The media's role in changing social attitudes is discussed in Hans Mathias Kepplinger, "Artificial Horizons: How the Press Presented and How the Population Received Technology in Germany from 1965-1986," in *The Mass Media in Liberal Democratic Societies,* ed. Stanley Rothman (New York: Paragon House, 1992), 147-176.

18. W. Lance Bennett, "Perception and Cognition: An Information-Processing Framework for Politics," in *The Handbook of Political Behavior,* vol. 1, ed. Samuel L. Long (New York: Plenum Press, 1981), 101. The importance of pre-adult political learning for subsequent political orientations is discussed in Paul Allen Beck and M. Kent Jennings, "Pathways to Participation," *American Political Science Review* 76 (1982): 103-110. Also see Doris A. Graber, *Processing the News: How People Tame the Information Tide,* 2d ed. (New York: Longman, 1988), 184-188, 210-213.

19. Shanto Iyengar, *Is Anyone Responsible? How Television Frames Political Issues* (Chicago: University of Chicago Press, 1991), 136-143.

20. Stanley Rothman, S. Robert Lichter, and Linda Lichter, "Television's America," in *The Mass Media in Liberal Democratic Societies,* 221-266.

21. Paula M. Poindexter, "Non-News Viewers," *Journal of Communication* 30 (Autumn 1980): 58-65.

22. Entertainment programming can supply general information, such as problem-solving techniques, or specific information, such as the social roles of women and minorities. For examples see Gary W. Selnow, "Solving Problems on Prime-Time Television," *Journal of Communication* 36 (Spring 1986): 63-72; Selnow, "Values in Prime-Time Television"; G. Ray Funkhouser and Eugene F. Shaw, "How Synthetic Experience Shapes Social Reality," *Journal of Communication* 40 (Summer 1990): 75-87; W. James Potter and William Ware, "The Frequency and Context of Prosocial Acts on Primetime TV," *Journalism Quarterly* 66 (Summer 1989): 359-366, 529.

23. Graber, *Processing the News,* 90-93.
24. On an average, two-thirds of the people do not know their newspaper's position on specific economic, social, and foreign policy issues. Stephen D. Reese and M. Mark Miller, "Political Attitude Holding and Structure: The Effects of Newspaper and Television News," *Communication Research* 8 (April 1981): 182. William Schneider and A. I. Lewis, "Views on the News," *Public Opinion* 8 (August/September 1985): 5-11, 58-59.
25. Gerbner et al., "Political Correlates," 286.
26. Reese and Miller, "Political Attitude Holding," 182.
27. Michael J. Robinson, "News Media Myths and Realities: What the Network News Did and Didn't Do in the 1984 General Campaign," in *Elections in America,* ed. Kay Lehman Schlozman (Boston: Allen and Unwin, 1987), 149. For additional evidence of changes in political opinions produced by commentary, see Frederick T. Steeper, "Public Response to Gerald Ford's Statements on Eastern Europe in the Second Debate," in *The Presidential Debates: Media, Electoral and Policy Perspectives,* ed. George F. Bishop, Robert G. Meadow, and Marilyn Jackson-Beeck (New York: Praeger, 1978), 81-101.
28. Kenneth D. Wald, *Religion and Politics* (New York: St. Martin's Press, 1987), 209.
29. George Comstock, Steven Chaffee, Natan Katzman, Maxwell McCombs, and Donald Roberts, *Television and Human Behavior* (New York: Columbia University Press, 1978), 307-309. Also see Robert T. Bower, *The Changing Television Audience in America* (New York: Columbia University Press, 1985). Unfortunately, the book relies on 1980 data. For evidence that similarity in exposure leads to similar socialization, see Alexis S. Tan, "Media Use and Political Orientations of Ethnic Groups," *Journalism Quarterly* 60 (Spring 1983): 126-132.
30. Frederick Williams, Herbert S. Dordick, and Frederick Horstmann, "Where Citizens Go for Information," *Journal of Communication* 27 (Winter 1977): 95-99.
31. Comstock et al., *Television and Human Behavior,* 295-306. Also see Roger D. Masters, "Ethnic and Personality Differences in Response to TV Images of Leaders," American Political Science Association paper, 1991.
32. Sheldon G. Levy, "How Population Subgroups Differed in Knowledge of Six Assassinations," *Journalism Quarterly* 46 (Winter 1969): 685-698.
33. Leo Bogart, *Press and Public: Who Reads What, When, Where, and Why in American Newspapers* (Hillsdale, N.J.: Erlbaum, 1981), 76-79.
34. Bradley Greenberg and Brenda Dervin, "Mass Communication Among the Urban Poor," *Public Opinion Quarterly* 34 (Summer 1970): 224-235. Also see Bradley S. Greenberg, Michael Burgoon, Judee Burgoon, and Felipe Korzenny, *Mexican Americans and the Mass Media* (Norwood, N.J.: Ablex, 1983). For partly contradictory evidence, see Tan, "Media Use." See also Phyllis A. Katz and Dalman A. Taylor, eds., *Eliminating Racism* (New York: Plenum Press, 1988), 1-16.
35. The statistics in the next three paragraphs are from Bogart, *Press and Public,* 56, 66, 77. See also Leo Bogart, "Negro and White Media Exposure: New Evidence," *Journalism Quarterly* 49 (Spring 1972): 15-21; and George Comstock and Robin E. Cobbey, "Television and the Children of Ethnic Minorities," *Journal of Communication* 29 (Winter 1979): 104-115.
36. Karl Erik Rosengren, Lawrence A. Wenner, and Philip Palmgreen, eds., *Media Gratifications Research: Current Perspectives* (Beverly Hills, Calif.:

Sage, 1985). Also see Gina M. Garramone, "Motivation and Political Information Processing: Extending the Gratifications Approach," in *Mass Media and Political Thought,* ed. Sidney Kraus and Richard Perloff (Beverly Hills, Calif.: Sage, 1985), 201-222; David L. Swanson, "Gratification Seeking, Media Exposure, and Audience Interpretations: Some Directions for Research," *Journal of Broadcasting and Electronic Media* 31 (1987): 237-254.

37. W. Lance Bennett, *News: The Politics of Illusion,* 2d ed. (New York: Longman, 1988), 158-169; and Charles Atkin, "Information Utility and Selective Exposure to Entertainment Media," in Dolf Zillman and Jennings Bryant, eds., *Selective Exposure to Communication* (Hillsdale, N.J.: Erlbaum, 1985), 63-92.

38. Michael Morgan, "Heavy Television Viewing and Perceived Quality of Life," *Journalism Quarterly* 61 (Autumn 1984): 499-504; Philip Palmgreen, Lawrence A. Wenner, and J. D. Rayburn II, "Relations between Gratifications Sought and Obtained: A Study of Television News," *Communication Research* 7 (April 1980): 161-192; Robert W. Kubey, "Television Use in Everyday Life: Coping with Unstructured Time," *Journal of Communication* 36 (Summer 1986): 108-123.

39. Neuman, *Future of the Mass Audience,* 122.

40. Thomas L. Friedman, "No TV? Israel Is Savoring the Silence," *New York Times,* November 6, 1987.

41. Graber, *Processing the News,* 133-136. See also Stuart H. Schwartz, "A General Psychographic Analysis of Newspaper Use and Life Style," *Journalism Quarterly* 57 (Autumn 1980): 392-401.

42. The literature is reviewed in Zillman and Bryant, *Selective Exposure to Communication.*

43. Percy H. Tannenbaum, "The Indexing Process in Communication," *Public Opinion Quarterly* 19 (Fall 1955): 292-302. Also see Roy L. Behr and Shanto Iyengar, "Television News, Real-World Cues, and Changes in the Public Agenda," *Public Opinion Quarterly* 49 (Spring 1985): 38-57.

44. Donald L. Shaw and Maxwell E. McCombs, *The Emergence of American Political Issues: The Agenda-Setting Function of the Press* (St. Paul: West Publishing Co., 1977). See also Maxwell E. McCombs, "The Agenda-Setting Approach," in *Handbook,* 121-140; Shanto Iyengar and Donald R. Kinder, *News That Matters: TV and American Opinion* (Chicago: University of Chicago Press, 1987); Benjamin I. Page, Robert Y. Shapiro, and Glenn R. Dempsey, "What Moves Public Opinion?" *American Political Science Review* 81 (March 1987): 23-43; and Benjamin I. Page and Robert Y. Shapiro, *The Rational Public: Fifty Years of Trends in Americans' Policy Preferences* (Chicago: University of Chicago Press, 1991).

45. Doris A. Graber, "Agenda-Setting: Are There Women's Perspectives? " in *Women and the News,* ed. Laurily Keir Epstein (New York: Hastings House, 1978), 15-37.

46. For a relevant case study, see Tony Atwater, Michael B. Salwen, and Ronald B. Anderson, "Media Agenda-Setting with Environmental Issues," *Journalism Quarterly* 62 (Summer 1985): 393-397.

47. Harold G. Zucker, "The Variable Nature of News Media Influence," in *Communication Yearbook 2,* ed. Brent D. Ruben (New Brunswick, N.J.: Transaction Books, 1978), 227. See also James H. Watt, Jr., and Sjef van den Berg, "How Time Dependency Influences Media Effects in a Community Controversy," *Journalism Quarterly* 58 (Spring 1981): 43-50; Behr and

Iyengar, "Television News"; and Michael B. MacKuen and Steven L. Coombs, *More than News: Media Power in Public Affairs* (Beverly Hills, Calif.: Sage, 1981).

48. The importance of personal and contextual factors in news selection and evaluation is discussed in Lutz Erbring, Edie Goldenberg, and Arthur Miller, "Front-Page News and Real World Cues: Another Look at Agenda-Setting by the Media," *American Journal of Political Science* 24 (February 1980): 16-49; and David B. Hill, "Viewer Characteristics and Agenda Setting by Television News," *Public Opinion Quarterly* 49 (Fall 1985): 340-350. For a discussion of problems in measuring the relative impact of various factors, see Howard Schuman, Jacob Ludwig, and Jon A. Krosnick, "The Perceived Threat of Nuclear War, Salience, and Open Questions," *Public Opinion Quarterly* 50 (Winter 1986): 519-536. Also see Iyengar, *Is Anyone Responsible?*

49. Graber, *Processing the News*, 27-31, and, for details on learning processes, chaps. 7-9.

50. Walter Lippmann, *Public Opinion* (New York: Harcourt Brace, 1922), 31.

51. Phillip J. Tichenor, George A. Donohue, and Clarice N. Olien, "Mass Media Flow and Differential Growth in Knowledge," *Public Opinion Quarterly* 34 (Summer 1970): 159-170; and Cecilie Gaziano, "The Knowledge Gap: An Analytical Review of Media Effects," *Communication Research* 10 (October 1983): 447-486. For evidence of shared reactions to television programs, irrespective of educational level, see W. Russell Neuman, "Television and American Culture: The Mass Medium and the Pluralist Audience," *Public Opinion Quarterly* 46 (Winter 1982): 471-487.

52. Eliot Freidson, "Communication Research and the Concept of the Mass," in *The Process and Effects of Mass Communication*, rev. ed., ed. Schramm and Roberts, 197-208. See also Steven H. Chaffee, "Television and Social Relations, Introductory Comments," in *Television and Human Behavior*, 260-263.

53. Larry L. Burriss, "How Anchors, Reporters and Newsmakers Affect Recall and Evaluation of Stories," *Journalism Quarterly* 64 (Summer/Autumn 1987): 514-519. The impact of negative news is discussed in John E. Newhagen and Byron Reeves, "The Evening's Bad News: Effects of Compelling Negative Television News Images on Memory," *Journal of Communication* 42 (Spring 1992): 25-41.

54. Page and Shapiro, *Rational Public,* 35.

55. Roberta S. Sigel, "Effects of Partisanship on the Perception of Political Candidates," *Public Opinion Quarterly* 28 (Summer 1964): 488-496. See also Shanto Iyengar, "Television News and Citizens' Explanations of National Affairs," *American Political Science Review* 81 (September 1987): 815-831.

56. For example, when a sample of citizens was asked why their worries about nuclear war had increased, the following mixture of reasons was cited: increased media coverage (52%); Reagan administration policies (19%); new weapons/new technology/proliferation (19%); unrest in the Third World (13%); East/West tensions (11%); Soviet belligerence (4%); children/grandchildren's lives (4%); other reasons (2%); don't know/no answer/can't explain (5%). Michael A. Milburn, Paul Y. Watanabe, and Bernard M. Kramer, "The Nature and Sources of Attitudes toward a Nuclear Freeze," *Political Psychology* 7 (December 1986): 672.

57. An overview of hypermnesia research is presented in Robert H. Wicks,

"Improvement Over Time in Recall of Media Information: An Exploratory Study," School of Journalism, Indiana University paper, 1991.

58. Meyrowitz, *No Sense of Place.*

59. Ironically, the improved image may foster misconceptions and antagonize whites, fostering a new type of racism. Robert M. Entman, "Modern Racism and the Images of Blacks in Local Television News," *Critical Studies in Mass Communication* 7 (1990): 332-345; Paula W. Matabane, "Television and the Black Audience: Cultivating Moderate Perspectives on Racial Integration," *Journal of Communication* 38 (Autumn 1988): 21-31; S. Robert Lichter, Linda S. Lichter, Stanley Rothman, and Daniel Amundson, "Prime-Time Prejudice: TV's Images of Blacks and Hispanics," *Public Opinion* 10 (July/August 1987): 13-16. More cynical observers claim that improvement of the images of African-Americans reflects the desire to boost audience ratings by tapping the large audience of African-American viewers.

60. The chances of becoming a crime victim are small in real life, but 30 to 64 percent in TV life. See Gerbner et al., "Cultural Indicators," 106-107. For a critique of the work of Gerbner and his associates, see Paul Hirsch, "The 'Scary World' of the Nonviewer and Other Anomalies: A Reanalysis of Gerbner et al.'s Findings on Cultivation Analysis," parts 1 and 2, in *Communication Research* 7 and 8 (Winter 1980 and Spring 1981): 403-457 and 3-37; and Michael Hughes, "The Fruits of Cultivation Analysis: A Reexamination of the Effects of Television Watching on Fear of Victimization, Alienation, and the Approval of Violence," *Public Opinion Quarterly* 44 (Summer 1980): 287-303. Exposure to news about actual crime predicts salience of crime better than does personal exposure to crime. Edna F. Einsiedel, Kandice L. Salomone, and Frederick P. Schneider, "Crime: Effects of Media Exposure and Personal Experience on Issue Salience," *Journalism Quarterly* 61 (Spring 1984): 131-136. See also Hugh M. Culbertson and Guido H. Stempel III, " 'Media Malaise': Explaining Personal Optimism and Societal Pessimism about Health Care," *Journal of Communication* 35 (Spring 1985): 180-190.

61. Iyengar, *Is Anyone Responsible?* Iyengar and Kinder, *News That Matters.*

62. An example of corroborative research is Jon A. Krosnick and Donald R. Kinder, "Altering the Foundations of Support for the President through Priming," *American Political Science Review* 84 (June 1990): 497-512.

63. John Stauffer, Richard Frost, and William Rybolt, "The Attention Factor in Recalling Network Television News," *Journal of Communication* 33 (Winter 1983): 29-37. Also see Philip J. Hilts, "A Brain Unit Seen as Index for Recalling Memories," *New York Times*, September 24, 1991.

64. Graber, *Processing the News,* chap. 2.

65. Teun A. Van Dijk, *News as Discourse* (Hillsdale, N.J.: Erlbaum, 1988), 139-174; and John P. Robinson and Mark R. Levy, *The Main Source: Learning from Television News* (Beverly Hills, Calif.: Sage, 1986), 57-175. Also see Neuman, *Future of the Mass Media,* 92, for a brief review of relevant studies.

66. Scott Keeter and Cliff Zukin, *Uninformed Choice: The Failure of the New Presidential Nominating System* (New York: Praeger, 1983).

67. V. O. Key, with the assistance of Milton C. Cummings, Jr., *The Responsible Electorate* (Cambridge, Mass.: Harvard University Press, 1965), 7, reached the same conclusion. Also see Page and Shapiro, *Rational Public,* 383-390, regarding the wisdom inherent in public opinion.

68. Arthur H. Miller, Edie N. Goldenberg, and Lutz Erbring, "Type-Set

Politics: Impact of Newspapers on Public Confidence," *American Political Science Review* 73 (March 1979): 67-84.

69. Michael J. Robinson, "Public Affairs Television and the Growth of Political Malaise: The Case of 'The Selling of the Pentagon,'" *American Political Science Review* 70 (June 1976): 409-432. See also Garrett J. O'Keefe, "Political Malaise and Reliance on Media," *Journalism Quarterly* 57 (Spring 1980): 122-128. Also see Iyengar, *Is Anyone Responsible?*

70. Murray Edelman, *Politics as Symbolic Action* (New York: Academic Press, 1976); and Murray Edelman, *Constructing the Political Spectacle* (Chicago: University of Chicago Press, 1988).

71. Comstock et al., *Television and Human Behavior*, 289-309.

72. W. Russell Neuman, *The Paradox of Mass Politics: Knowledge and Opinion in the American Electorate* (Cambridge, Mass.: Harvard University Press, 1986), 137.

73. The desire to be politically informed varies widely. For details, see ibid. News selection criteria are discussed in Graber, *Processing the News*, chap. 4.

74. Doris A. Graber and Young Yun Kim, "Why John Q. Voter Did Not Learn Much from the 1976 Presidential Debates," in *Communication Yearbook 2*, ed. Brent D. Ruben (New Brunswick, N.J.: Transaction Books, 1978), 414-419.

75. Glasgow University Media Group, *Bad News* (London: Routledge and Kegan Paul, 1976).

76. *Public Opinion* 10 (September/October 1987): 25. Age differences in media appraisals are discussed in Michael J. Robinson, "An Absence of Malice: Young People and the Press," *Public Opinion* 9 (November/December 1986): 43-47.

77. Bennett, *News*, 44-63.

78. Daniel C. Hallin, "We Keep America on Top of the World," in *Watching Television*, ed. Todd Gitlin (New York: Pantheon Books, 1986), 9-41.

79. Tony Schwartz, *The Responsive Chord* (Garden City, N.Y.: Anchor Press, Doubleday, 1974), 25. For an excellent analysis of learning from television, see Robinson and Levy, *The Main Source*, chaps. 3-7:

80. C. Richard Hofstetter and Terry Buss, "Motivation for Viewing Two Types of TV Programs," *Journalism Quarterly* 58 (Spring 1981): 99-103; and Mihaly Csikszentmihalyi and Robert Kubey, "Television and the Rest of Life: A Systematic Comparison of Subjective Experience," *Public Opinion Quarterly* 45 (Fall 1981): 317-328.

81. Richard M. Perloff, Ellen A. Wartella, and Lee B. Becker, "Increasing Learning from TV News," *Journalism Quarterly* 59 (Spring 1982): 83-86.

82. For dire predictions see Jarol B. Manheim, *All of the People All the Time: Strategic Communication and American Politics* (Armonk, N.Y.: M. E. Sharpe, 1991), 204-209; Entman, *Democracy Without Citizens: Media and the Decay of American Politics* (New York: Oxford University Press, 1990), chap. 7. For a more positive view see Graber, *Processing the News*, 251-258; and Page and Shapiro, *Rational Public*, 383-390.

83. None of these studies focuses on the effects of exposure to nonfictional violence in the media since the First Amendment would be a strong bar to censorship of news. Surgeon General's Scientific Advisory Committee on Television and Social Behavior, *Television and Growing Up: The Impact of Televised Violence* (Washington, D.C.: U.S. Government Printing Office, 1971). For a critical review of the 1981 follow-up report, see Thomas D.

Cook, Deborah A. Kendzierski, and Stephen V. Thomas, "The Implicit Assumptions of Television Research: An Analysis of the 1982 NIMH Report on 'Television and Behavior,'" *Public Opinion Quarterly* 47 (Spring 1983): 161-201. See also Richard A. Dienstbier, "Sex and Violence: Can Research Have It Both Ways?" *Journal of Communication* 27 (Summer 1977): 176-188.

84. "Violent Family Hour," *Society* 24 (January/February 1987): 2.

85. George A. Comstock, *The Evidence on Television Violence* (Santa Monica, Calif.: Rand Corporation, P-5730, 1976); Jerome L. Singer, Dorothy G. Singer, and Wanda S. Rapaczynski, "Family Patterns and Television Viewing as Predictors of Children's Beliefs and Aggression," *Journal of Communication* 34 (Summer 1984): 73-89. The politics of research on the effects of television violence are discussed by Willard D. Rowland, Jr., *The Politics of TV Violence: Policy Uses of Communication Research* (Beverly Hills, Calif.: Sage, 1983).

86. James M. Carlson, *Prime Time Law Enforcement: Crime Show Viewing and Attitudes toward the Criminal Justice System* (New York: Praeger, 1985).

87. Robert P. Snow, "How Children Interpret TV Violence in Play Context," *Journalism Quarterly* 51 (Spring 1974): 13-21.

88. Presidential Commission on Obscenity and Pornography, *Report of the Commission on Obscenity and Pornography* (New York: Bantam Books, 1970). See also the *Attorney General's Commission on Pornography: Final Report,* published in 1986; and Dienstbier, "Sex and Violence," 177-180.

89. David O. Edeani, "Critical Predictors of Orientation to Change in a Developed Society," *Journalism Quarterly* 58 (Spring 1981): 56-64. The carefully measured impact of the introduction of television into a Canadian community is presented in Tannis MacBeth Williams, ed., *The Impact of Television: A Natural Experiment in Three Communities* (Orlando, Fla.: Academic Press, 1985).

90. James B. Lemert, Barry N. Mitzman, Michael A. Seither, Roxana H. Cook, and Regina Hackett, "Journalists and Mobilizing Information," *Journalism Quarterly* 54 (Winter 1977): 721-726.

91. Ronald E. Rice and Charles K. Atkin, eds., *Public Communication Campaigns,* 2d ed. (Newbury Park, Calif.: Sage, 1989).

92. Douglas S. Solomon, "Health Campaigns on Television," in *Television and Human Behavior,* 316-319.

93. Sheldon O'Connell, "Television and the Canadian Eskimo: The Human Perspective," *Journal of Communication* 27 (Autumn 1977): 140-144; and Gary O. Coldevin, "Anik I and Isolation: Television in the Lives of Canadian Eskimos," *Journal of Communication* 27 (Autumn 1977): 145-153.

94. Everett M. Rogers, "The Rise and Fall of the Dominant Paradigm," *Journal of Communication* 28 (Winter 1978): 64-69; and Wilbur Schramm and Daniel Lerner, eds., *Communication and Change: The Last Ten Years—and the Next* (Honolulu: University Press of Hawaii, 1976).

95. Stuart J. Sigman and Donald L. Fry, "Differential Ideology and Language Use: Readers' Reconstructions and Descriptions of News Events," *Critical Studies in Mass Communication* 2 (December 1985): 307-322.

Readings

Gamson, William A. *Talking Politics.* New York: Cambridge University Press, 1992.

Graber, Doris A. *Processing the News: How People Tame the Information Tide.* 2d ed. New York: Longman, 1988.

Gunter, Barrie. *Poor Reception: Misunderstanding and Forgetting Broadcast News.* Hillsdale, N.J.: Erlbaum, 1990.

Jensen, Klaus Bruhn. *Making Sense of the News.* Aarhus, Denmark: Aarhus University Press, 1986.

Kubey, Robert, and Mihaly Csikszentmihalyi. *Television and the Quality of Life: How Viewing Shapes Everyday Experience.* Hillsdale, N.J.: Erlbaum, 1990.

Meyrowitz, Joshua. *No Sense of Place: The Impact of Electronic Media on Social Behavior.* New York: Oxford University Press, 1985.

Neuman, W. Russell, Marion R. Just, and Ann N. Crigler. *Common Knowledge: News and the Construction of Political Meaning.* Chicago: University of Chicago Press, 1992.

Robinson, John P., and Mark R. Levy. *The Main Source: Learning from Television News.* Beverly Hills, Calif.: Sage, 1986.

van Dijk, Teun A. *News Analysis: Case Studies of International and National News in the Press.* Hillsdale, N.J.: Erlbaum, 1988.

———. *News As Discourse.* Hillsdale, N.J.: Erlbaum, 1988.

CHAPTER 8

Elections in
the Television Age

When ancient Greeks went to Apollo's temple at Delphi in search of answers to their questions, the oracle's response was often couched in vague, ambiguous language that lent itself to different interpretations. It was then the inquirer's task to proclaim the oracle's meaning. That meaning would be accepted as truth unless circumstances proved that the interpreter had erred. Modern day interpretations of the messages that voters convey through their votes are not unlike the ancient oracle: they are based on ambiguous evidence, yet they are widely accepted as truth. They are given sacred status because, in modern democracies, *vox populi, vox Dei*—the voice of the people is the voice of God.

So it happened in the 1992 senatorial primaries when two women won nomination contrary to political expectations. Election gurus interpreted their victories as an outcry by enraged voters against male arrogance and domination as symbolized by the television broadcasts of the Clarence Thomas confirmation hearings. The surprise victors were Carol Moseley Braun, who beat a powerful, long-term incumbent, Illinois Senator Alan Dixon, and Lynn Yeakel, a political novice, who defeated two strong contenders: Pennsylvania's lieutenant governor, her party's official candidate, and the District Attorney of Allegheny County.

Both women claimed that the nationally televised hearings into charges by Anita Hill, a law professor, that she had been sexually harassed by Supreme Court nominee Clarence Thomas, convinced them that more women must run for the Senate to correct the gender imbalance. Yeakel even used advertisements in her campaign that showed Pennsylvania Senator Arlen Specter at the hearings challenging

Anita Hill's testimony, followed by Yeakel's question "Did this make you as angry as it made me?" But do the candidates' motivations prove that the votes cast for them were protests against the symbolic meanings ascribed to the Thomas hearings?

The answer is "no." The feelings aroused by media coverage of the hearings may well have been the deciding factor. But, as in most election contests, many other factors could have produced the same outcome. For example, both women were involved in multiple-candidate races. In Braun's case, she was an African-American woman whose long-term political career in the state had made her familiar to many Illinois voters. She faced two white candidates, each concentrating on hurting the other's campaign. In such contests in Illinois, victory for the African-American candidate has been common. The Yeakel victory also involved a multi-candidate race, increasing the chances that an underdog would win. Five contenders were competing for the Democratic senatorial nomination. Yeakel, like Braun, won by a plurality of the votes. It is doubtful that she could have won in a two-person contest. It is interesting to note that Republican Arlen Specter, the chief target of Yeakel's ire, won his primary by a 2 to 1 margin.

Although the link between media and election outcomes has been studied more thoroughly than other media-politics linkages, the verdict remains unclear. Definitive answers are lacking for most cause and effect questions, such as those posed by the Braun and Yeakel upset victories in the Illinois and Pennsylvania primaries. Speculations about the meanings expressed through votes will continue to be plentiful, nonetheless, because these messages have great symbolic power, like the Delphi oracle. They constitute the mandates that politicians claim as justifications for their actions.

The State of Research

Understanding the role of the mass media in elections is hampered by imbalances in research. Presidential elections have been extensively studied, and congressional elections have drawn the attention of more and more scholars. Far less is known about the media's role in gubernatorial elections and practically nothing about their impact on local, judicial, or school board elections. The limited evidence available suggests that the role of the media varies substantially, depending on the particular office being contested, and the news appeal of a campaign. In congressional elections, for example, exciting campaigns are covered, while routine ones are ignored.[1]

Even at the presidential level little research has been done to point up differences in the role of the media as candidates and issues change from one election to the next.[2] High costs have discouraged researchers from studying media influences throughout the entire campaign from the preprimary period to the general election. The crucial early stages in the campaign when candidate selection takes place were largely ignored prior to Ronald Reagan's election in 1980.

The influence of factors such as incumbency, three-way competition, or major national crises has not been thoroughly investigated either. It stands to reason that the impact of the media will vary depending on the changing political scene, the type of coverage chosen by newspeople, and the fluctuating interests of voters. Comparable studies of media impact on elections in Canada, Great Britain, France, Germany, and elsewhere have been plagued by similar problems.[3]

Another serious obstacle to understanding is the dearth of media content analyses. Election news content and the context of general news in which it is embedded have been examined only rarely because content analysis is very costly. Without knowing the exact content of news, it becomes impossible to test what impact, if any, it had on viewers' perceptions. Another problem is failure to ascertain media exposure accurately. Investigators frequently assume that people have been exposed to media without checking precisely which stories have come to the attention of various individuals and what these individuals learned from these stories.

A shortage of good data also prevents researchers from isolating the effects of political advertising on political campaigns.[4] Candidates and their supporters spend a large share of their campaign budgets on political advertising displayed on bumper stickers and billboards, printed in newspapers, disseminated through video tapes, or broadcast with clockwork regularity on radio and television. The precise impact of these advertisements on target audiences is uncertain because it is difficult to untangle effects of commercials from the effects of other types of campaign publicity.

Apparently, ads that are entertaining do capture the attention of voters. Uncommitted voters, highly interested voters, and partisans of the advertised candidate are most likely to absorb the content.[5] Major campaign issues are often covered more extensively in television commercials than in network newscasts. For instance, during the 1972 presidential campaign, voters received four times as much issue information from advertising as from television newscasts.[6] Most viewers—particularly those who did not read newspapers and were poorly informed—remembered more from the commercials than from the television news. Simplicity of content, expert eye-ear appeal, and repetition of the message combined to produce this result.

Although people learn facts about campaign issues from commercials, most ads fail to influence viewers' evaluations of the candidates. Commercials are perceiver-determined. People see in them pretty much what they want to see—attractive images for their favorite candidates and unattractive ones for the opponent. If attempts to glamorize political actors and hide their weaknesses succeed, the effect lasts for only a short time. Commercials of opposing candidates, media exposés of deceptive messages, and people's cynicism about campaign propaganda see to that. By and large, commercials have not altered ultimate voting choices in recent presidential campaigns, although they seem to have had some impact during early primaries. The claims that television commercials can manufacture fairyland candidates and make them believable to credulous audiences apparently are vastly exaggerated whenever voters have alternative means to know the candidates.[7]

Whether commercials can inject crucial issues into a campaign remains debated. In the heat of campaigns, wins and losses are often attributed by the candidates to particular commercials or to the ability of the candidates to buy ample television time. The 1988 victory of the Bush campaign, for example, has been attributed to advertisements attacking the environmental and criminal justice policies of Bush's opponent. "Boston Harbor" and "Willie Horton" became famous election slogans. Scholarly corroborations are lacking for most of the claims that memorable ads produced election victories and defeats.[8] Nevertheless, the battle of the airwaves has been steadily increasing in recent campaigns, especially during primary contests. It has also begun to branch out from over-the-air television to cable outlets. Advertising rates are cheaper on cable television—an attractive medium because messages can be more readily tailored to the needs of the smaller cable audiences.

Television commercials often provide the only chance to gain attention for the many candidates who are ignored by the media.[9] At the lower levels of political office, where information is scant, the impact of commercials can be decisive. Indeed, wisely spent advertising funds can buy elections.[10] Michael Robinson concluded that commercials for congressional candidates "can work relative wonders," especially when they are not challenged by the other side. "A well-crafted, heavily financed, and uncontested ad campaign does influence congressional elections—1980 is substantial proof." [11]

The Consequences of Media Politics

The advent of television and its ready availability in every home, the spread and improvement of public opinion polling, and the use of computers in election data analysis have vastly enhanced the role of the mass media in elections. In this era of "media politics," what major changes have been wrought by the new technologies? Four consequences will be considered: a decline in party influence, an increase in the power of media personnel to influence the selection of candidates, the need for candidates to "televise well," and the importance of made-for-media campaigns.

Decline in Party Influence

Foremost among the changes is the declining influence of political parties, particularly in presidential elections. During the 1940s, when social scientists first investigated the impact of the mass media on the outcome of presidential elections, party allegiance was the most important determinant of the vote. It was followed by voters' feelings of allegiance to a social group, assessment of the candidate's personality, and consideration of issues, in that order.

Since the full flowering of the electronic age more than two decades later, the order has been reversed. The candidate as a personality has become the prime consideration at the presidential level. Second are issues associated with the candidate, followed by party affiliation and group membership.[12] When voters base their decisions on a candidate's personality or stand on issues, the media become more important because they are the chief sources of information about these matters.

Correspondingly, political parties take on less importance. When voters can see and hear candidates in their own living rooms, they can make choices that differ from those made by the party. Split ticket voting, that is, voting for candidates of different parties, has become common. Candidates can also defy and thereby weaken party control because radio and television give them direct access to voters. More candidates can enter the race and campaign on their own strengths, raising their own money and building their own organizations. New candidates with the aid of the media can gain a wide following rapidly. This new independence of voters and candidates makes primary and general election races more crowded and less predictable. Party regulars who have groomed themselves for years to attain positions of power may find themselves bypassed.

Party affiliation remains very important at the state and local levels where the average voter knows little about most candidates, and media information is scant, particularly on television. This is not true, however, when candidates run without overt or covert party designation and endorsement, or when candidates of the same party compete against each other in primary elections. When party choice criteria are lacking and personal experience or advice from opinion leaders is unavailable, voters turn to whatever guidance the media may offer. Some will follow expressed or implied media endorsements; others will take them as cues to vote the opposite way. In either case what the media say about the candidates influences the voting decision.

Media as King Makers

More than ever before, media personnel can influence the selection of candidates and issues.[13] Candidates, like actors, depend for their success as much on the roles into which they are cast as on their acting ability. In the television age media people usually do the casting for presidential hopefuls, whose performance is then judged according to the assigned role. Strenuous efforts by campaign directors and public relations experts to dominate this aspect of the campaign have been only moderately fruitful.

Casting occurs early in the primaries when newspeople, on the basis of as yet slender evidence, must predict winners and losers in order to narrow the field of eligibles. Concentrating on the front-runners in public opinion polls makes newspeople's tasks more manageable, but it often forces trailing candidates out of the race prematurely. As *New York Times* political writer R. W. Apple candidly admits, "Such early calculations are highly speculative. . . . But early calculations have a life of their own because they are the backdrop against which politicians and the media tend to measure the performance of the various candidates in their early confrontations." [14]

Perhaps the best example of this occurred in the 1976 Democratic primaries. Almost a dozen candidates were running, but the media covered Jimmy Carter, the little known former governor of Georgia, far more heavily and favorably than the other contenders. After the New Hampshire primary in February in which Carter received 30 percent of the Democratic vote, NBC's Tom Pettit called Carter "the man to beat." *Time* magazine labeled his campaign as the only one "with real possibilities of breaking far ahead of the pack." It featured him on its front cover, as did *Newsweek*. Along with the front-cover picture in *Time* went a 2,630-line feature story, compared with 300 lines devoted to all other Democrats in the race.

Sen. Henry Jackson of Washington and Rep. Morris Udall of Arizona did well in the early Democratic primaries, but between them received less than one-third of the television coverage that Carter received. Subsequent primary defeats, such as Carter's poor showing in Massachusetts in early March, were characterized as exceptions that merely slowed his momentum, rather than as disastrous defeats. Gallup poll ratings in early February that credited Carter with only 5 percent of the national vote were given little publicity.[15] As Figure 8-1 shows, coverage of the Republican contenders in the 1988 election is yet another example of uneven attention. George Bush received twice as much coverage in *Time* and *Newsweek* early in the campaign as Sen. Robert Dole and ten times as much as Rep. Jack Kemp.[16]

Figure 8-1 News Coverage of the Republican Contenders in *Time* and *Newsweek* in Early Stages of 1988 Nominating Contest

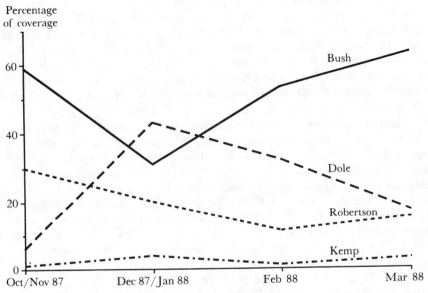

Source: Thomas E. Patterson, "The Press and Its Missed Assignment," in *The Elections of 1988*, Michael Nelson, ed. (Washington, D.C.: CQ Press, 1989), 99.

Note: Figure does not show coverage of Pierre DuPont and other possible Republican nominees who, together, received 3 percent or less of the coverage in each time period.

Candidates who exceed expectations in garnering votes win; candidates who fall short lose.[17] Carter won his prized "winner" status after less than 5 percent of the primary delegates had been selected. The Bush candidacy was prematurely declared dead when he finished behind Dole and Pat Robertson in a single early contest—the Iowa caucuses.[18] The emphasis that the media place on early victories creates psychological momentum that enhances a candidate's chances for winning successive primaries and getting the nomination. Media legitimation is particularly important for political unknowns such as Democratic hopeful Gary Hart in 1984. His second-place finish in the Iowa caucuses convinced newspeople that he was front-runner Walter Mondale's chief competitor. Extensive media attention, exceeding Mondale's coverage, propelled Hart to victory in New Hampshire.[19]

The winner or loser image often becomes a self-fulfilling prophecy because supporters and money, as well as media coverage, flow to the front-runner, especially when lesser contenders have dropped out of the race after poor showings in early contests. In Hart's case the money and support needed for a full-scale campaign in 1984 became available after his good shows in Iowa and several New England states had attracted press attention. Even then the boost was insufficient to match the resources of front-runner Mondale, whom news stories continued to designate as the likely winner of the presidential primary sweepstakes, albeit with lowered odds.

Media coverage and public opinion polls tend to move in tandem in the early months of a campaign. Candidates who receive ample media coverage usually do well in the polls. Good poll ratings bring more media coverage. Once the caucus and primary season has started in the spring of the election year, the outcomes of these contests become more important predictors of media attention. The winners and candidates whose scores seem surprising receive heavy media coverage; the media neglect the losers. One other pattern prevails. The substance of stories tends to be favorable for trailing candidates in the race and unfavorable for front-runners. Between January and June 1992, for example, more than 60 percent of the television comments about unlikely winners Ross Perot and Paul Tsongas were favorable. That compared to 41 percent for Jerry Brown and Bill Clinton, and 22 percent for President Bush.[20]

The media's role as king maker or killer of the dreams of would-be kings is often played over a long span of time. Image making for presidential elections now begins on a massive scale more than a year before the first primary. The "pre-pre-campaign," on a more limited scale, begins shortly after the finish of the previous election. By the end of 1981, for instance, thirty Democrats and fourteen Republicans had already been mentioned as potential presidential candidates for 1984.[21] Senators and governors who receive favorable publicity over many years may gradually come to be thought of as likely presidential nominees.

Captains of the media industry have often been able to use their personal influence and the power of the media under their control to support nominations for their favorites and to harm opponents. For instance, publisher Henry Luce enticed popular war-hero Dwight Eisenhower to run for the presidency in 1952. Luce put his publications, such as *Time* and *Life,* at Eisenhower's service. Kyle Palmer and the Chandler family, through their control of the *Los Angeles Times,* were instrumental in getting Richard Nixon a seat in the House of Representatives in 1946 and a U.S. Senate seat in 1950. Col. Robert McCormick used the powerful *Chicago Tribune* to defeat policies of the Roosevelt and Truman administrations and to put Republican politicians into office in Illinois.[22]

The power of the media also can be wielded to destroy candidacies. This happened to two Democratic candidates for the presidency in 1988, Senator Joe Biden of Delaware and Gary Hart. Biden was forced out of the campaign by widely publicized charges that his speeches contained plagiarized quotes from other political leaders. Hart withdrew after charges of philandering. Recurrent media references to the Chappaquiddick incident, a damaging personal event in Senator Edward Kennedy's past, also have dampened efforts by his supporters to draft him as a presidential contender. However, adverse publicity can be overcome. In the 1992 campaign, Democrat Bill Clinton was accused of adultery and draft dodging, causing his poll ratings and positive media appraisals to plummet. He recovered after winning major primaries despite the bad publicity.

Media images can also become vastly important during the general election campaign. For instance, the Kennedy-Nixon television debates of 1960, the Reagan-Carter debates of 1980, and the Reagan-Mondale debates of 1984 helped to remove public impressions that John F. Kennedy and Ronald Reagan were unsuited for the presidency.[23] Kennedy was apparently able to demonstrate that he was capable of coping with the presidency despite his youth and inexperience and Reagan in 1980 conveyed the impression that he was neither trigger-happy nor physically or mentally decrepit. Four years later, however, his inauspicious start in the opening debate made some viewers wonder whether advancing age had made him unfit for a second term. Demonstration of physical and mental vigor during subsequent debates helped reverse the unfavorable image that could have cost Reagan the election. No other medium could have equaled the reach and impact of television.[24] In fact, the risks of televised debates so awed presidential candidates after the 1960 encounter that a repeat performance did not occur for sixteen years. Since then they have become plentiful, with a veritable flood of debates during the 1988 and 1992 races. Their impact has fluctuated, ranging from inconsequential to decisive.

Presidents Lyndon Johnson, Jimmy Carter, and George Bush saw their chances for a second term diminish sharply in the wake of adverse media coverage.[25] Disapproval of Bush was directed mainly at his failure to solve major problems in the domestic economy. In Carter's case the media chose to commemorate the anniversary of a major foreign policy failure—the American hostages' prolonged captivity in Iran—just prior to the 1980 presidential election. In Johnson's case the media chose to publicize only certain statements from the full record of Johnson's public statements justifying his Vietnam policies, gutting the case the president needed to make in order to become a strong second-term candidate in 1968.[26] Johnson decided not to seek another term.

Media-operated public opinion polls are yet another weapon in the arsenal for king-making. The CBS-*New York Times* poll, the NBC-

Associated Press poll, the ABC-*Washington Post* poll, and the CNN-*USA Today* poll all conduct popularity ratings and issue polls throughout presidential elections and publicize them widely. During the final election week in 1984, the influential *New York Times* devoted one-third of its election coverage to poll reports.[27] These widely publicized poll results become bench marks for voters, telling them who the winners and losers are and what issues should be deemed crucial to the campaign. Depending on the nature and format of the questions asked by the pollsters and the political context in which the story becomes embedded, the responses spell fortune or misfortune for the candidates.

Polls may determine which candidates enter the fray and which keep out. Reagan was encouraged to enter the 1976 presidential race because President Gerald Ford's poll ratings were low prior to the Republican presidential nominating convention of that year.[28] With these low poll ratings as backdrop, Ford's subsequent rise in the polls was widely interpreted as a show of real political strength. Similarly, President Carter's poor poll ratings early in the 1980 campaign encouraged Kennedy's candidacy and gave Carter an image of political weakness that he was unable to shed even when his ratings improved. A Harris poll reported by ABC News in June 1980 boosted financial and volunteer support for Republican John Anderson when it showed that 31 percent of the respondents would vote for him "if the polls showed" that he had a real chance of winning the election. Ironically, poll predictions hastened Anderson's political downfall when he dropped below expected support in the crucial primary in his home state of Illinois.

Television-Age Recruits

A third important consequence of the new politics is the change it has wrought in the types of candidates likely to be politically successful. Because television can bring the image of candidates for high national and state office directly into the homes of millions of voters, political recruiters have become extremely conscious of a candidate's ability to look impressive and to perform well before the cameras. That requires the flair to act self-confidently and seemingly naturally in front of a bevy of cameras. People who are not telegenic have been eliminated from the pool of available recruits. Abraham Lincoln's rugged face probably would not have passed muster in the television age. President Harry S. Truman's "Give 'em Hell, Harry," homespun style would have backfired if presented to nationwide groups rather than small gatherings. Franklin D. Roosevelt's wheelchair appearances would have spelled damaging weakness. Roosevelt, in fact, was keenly aware of the likely harmful effects of a picture of him in a wheelchair and never allowed photographs to be taken while he was being lifted to the speaker's rostrum.

Actors and celebrities from other walks of life who are adept at performing before the public now have a much better chance than ever before to be recruited for political office. Reagan, a former actor; John Glenn, an ex-astronaut; and Jesse Jackson, a charismatic preacher, are examples of typical television-age recruits whose chances for public office would have been much smaller in an earlier era. As columnist Marquis Child has put it, candidates no longer "run" for office; they "pose" for office.[29]

In fact, good pictures can counterbalance the effects of unfavorable verbal comments. During the 1984 presidential campaign favorable pictures coincided with favorable poll results despite predominantly negative verbal commentary. When CBS reporter Leslie Stahl verbally attacked President Reagan for falsely posturing as a man of peace and compassion, the pictures accompanying her script told a different story. A Reagan assistant promptly thanked Stahl for showing four-and-a-half minutes of great pictures of the president, noting that "that's all the American people see." [30] Aware of the power of visuals, he was not in the least concerned about the scathing remarks. The pictures had shown the president

> basking in a sea of flag-waving supporters, . . . sharing concerns with farmers in a field, picnicking with Mid-Americans, pumping iron, . . . getting the Olympic torch from a runner, . . . greeting senior citizens at their housing project, honoring veterans who landed on Normandy, honoring youths just back from Grenada, countering a heckler, . . . wooing black inner-city kids. . . .[31]

Candidates who perform poorly on television now spend considerable time and money being coached by professionals. These television advisers have become year-round regular members of presidential and gubernatorial staffs. Names of media experts such as David Sawyer, Gerald Rafshoon, Tony Schwartz, David Garth, Roger Ailes, or Joseph Napolitan have become almost as well known as the names of the political bosses of yesteryear. These experts create commercials for the candidates and generate and handle general news coverage of the campaign.

In 1988 media expenses represented more than 60 percent of the general election budget spent by the major party nominees. Total presidential campaign spending was estimated at $500 million, with roughly half of the spending occurring prior to the nominating conventions.[32] Total spending for all 1988 elections at federal, state, and local levels amounted to $2.7 billion.[33] It will be higher for 1992 elections.

"WE CAN WATCH CLINTON ON MTV, BUSH ON 'LETTERMAN', PEROT ON 'ARSENIO'..... OR MADONNA ON 'MEET THE PRESS'...."

Reprinted with permission of King Features Syndicate.

Given the high cost of television commercials and of gaining news exposure, a candidate's ability to raise money remains an important consideration, even when federal funding is available. Wealthy candidates who can draw on personal resources have an advantage. Activities and statements likely to alienate donors are shunned. While there is evidence that the best-financed candidates do not always win, folklore says they do. Hence falling behind in the race for money to finance media exposure is a sharp brake on political aspirations. The political consequences in recruitment and postelection commitments that spring from such financial considerations are enormous.

Campaigning for the Media

A fourth major aspect of the new politics is the fact that mass media coverage has become the campaign's pivotal point. Campaigns are expressly arranged for the best media exposure before the largest suitable audience. To attract media coverage candidates concentrate on press conferences, talk show appearances, or trips to interesting locations.

As the cartoon suggests, appearances on various entertainment shows, once considered "unpresidential," have become routine. Maverick candidate Ross Perot started the pattern by first announcing his presidential aspirations on CNN's "Larry King Live" call-in show. The other candidates followed suit, preferring the lighter banter of talk shows and the respectful questions of callers to the pointed inquisition in interviews by the national press. Governor Clinton even bought television time to stage his own call-in show and, adorned with shades, played the saxophone on the hip Arsenio Hall show.

Even when candidates meet voters personally in rallies, parades, or shopping center visits, they generally time and orchestrate these events to attract favorable media coverage. In the 1992 campaign, candidates also made increasing use of videotapes to supply local television stations and various organizations with messages prepared and transmitted without the intervention of reporters. Given the tight finances of many stations, the expertly prepared tapes were most welcome. Candidate control over messages also increased through satellite interviews in which candidates chatted directly with local correspondents, most of whom were unlikely to ask hostile questions or limit the candidate's speech to sound bites of less than 10 seconds. All in all, the trend seems to be toward more direct contact by candidates with voters, and increased candidate control over campaign messages, all at the expense of campaign message control by the major media.

Incumbents have a distinct advantage over challengers. Although they may attract about the same number of campaign stories, incumbents receive additional attention through coverage of their official duties.[34] Incumbents may also be able to dictate time and place for media encounters. When a president schedules a meeting for reporters in the White House Rose Garden, ample coverage is ensured. There even is a quasi-incumbency status for promising challengers. Once they have attained wide recognition as front-runners, newspeople compete for their attention. Their power to grant or withhold it can be translated into influence over quality and quantity of coverage.

Candidates plan their schedules to dovetail with media coverage habits. They spend disproportionate amounts of time campaigning in Iowa and New Hampshire where media coverage is heavy, except when these races are essentially uncontested because a native or neighboring son is the candidate, as happened in Iowa in 1992. A survey of 1988 ABC, CBS, and NBC coverage showed that Iowa and New Hampshire, which have less than 3 percent of the U.S. population, received more media coverage during the 1988 primaries than all the other primaries combined.[35] During the 1984 campaign, Walter Mondale spent thirty days in New Hampshire. John Glenn spent thirty-two. Gary Hart topped this with fifty-two days, Ernest Hollings with sixty, and Reubin Askew with more than seventy.[36] Ample media coverage does not guarantee benefits at the polls. In 1988 Pete DuPont spent ninety-one days and $560,000 in Iowa, but he received only 7 percent of the Republican vote.

To keep a favorable image of their candidates in front of the public, campaign managers arrange newsworthy events to familiarize potential voters with their candidates' best aspects. Because most television producers do not like "talking heads"—shots of the faces of speakers—candidates may engage in staged activities merely to provide attractive, action-oriented pictures. Most of these pictures are deliberately packed with symbols to convey stock messages quickly and easily. For instance, showing candidates with old people, or African-American workers, or college students proclaims affinity for these groups. Reporter Leslie Stahl describes how Carter courted the voters in 1980:

> What did President Carter do today in Philadelphia? He posed, with as many different types of symbols as he could possibly find.
> There was a picture at the day care center. And one during the game of bocce ball with the senior citizens. Click, another picture with a group of teenagers. And then he performed the ultimate media event—a walk through the Italian market.
> The point of all this, obviously, to get on the local news broadcasts and in the morning newspapers. It appeared that the President's intention was not to say anything controversial.... Simply the intention was to be seen.[37]

Many campaign events are now staged as prime-time, live coverage television spectacles. Aside from occasional presidential debates, the conventions used to be the biggest single media event of presidential campaigns. Both major parties still select the convention cities with an eye to effective television coverage. Convention managers try to keep a tight rein on speakers and demonstrations. They want to make sure that desirable images are conveyed and that important speeches are made when the television audience is likely to be at a peak. For their part, media people who cover conventions try to structure the flow of words and pictures to cover unfolding events and still tell a coherent dramatic story. The difficulty of sustaining interest in nominating conventions when the identity of the nominee has already been firmly established has sharply reduced live prime-time coverage by the major television networks. The gap has been more than filled by gavel-to-gavel coverage by C-SPAN, CNN, PBS, and by assorted day-time and night-time programs.

Structuring and staging campaign activities such as conventions to make them newsworthy by the standards of modern American media has enhanced showmanship at the expense of substance. Because conflict is deemed attractive and memorable, journalists often goad campaigners into confrontations by asking questions that point up existing conflicts or that may lead to new battles. When journalists select the battlegrounds for the presidential contest, they shape the political agenda not only during the campaign but afterwards as well. Campaign statements coaxed from unwilling candidates may be subsequently construed as commitments to act.

Campaign stories are judged by general news criteria. Therefore minor candidates and newcomers whose chances for success are questionable do not get much coverage. Their efforts to attract the media are apt to fail since they simply are not "big news." Lack of coverage, in turn, makes it extremely difficult for them to become well known and increase their chances of winning elections. This is another example of unintentional media bias that redounds to the benefit of established politicians.

Media Content

What kinds of newspaper and television coverage have recent elections received? Did the media sufficiently cover the issues that would be likely to require attention from the new president? Were adequate criteria supplied to enable voters to decide which of several policy options would best suit their priorities? Were voters informed about each viable candidate's positions on the issues? Did they receive enough information about each candidate's personality, experience, and ability to evaluate the candidate's likely performance as president? We will now address these questions and assess the adequacy of the information supply for making voting choices in the manner that democratic theorists consider rational and desirable.

Any evaluation of how the media perform their task must also take their concerns into consideration. It is extremely difficult for the media to mesh the public's preference for simple, dramatic stories with the need to present sufficient information for issue-based election choices. Information that may be crucial for voting decisions often is too complex and technical to appeal to much of the audience. Hence newspeople feel compelled to feature exciting, humanly touching aspects of the election, even when they are trivial, without totally neglecting essential, unglamorous information useful for issue-based decision making.

Patterns of Coverage

Prominence of Election Stories. In a presidential election year election stories constitute roughly 13 percent of all newspaper political news and 15 percent of television political news. That puts them on a par with foreign affairs news or coverage of crime. Election news receives average attention in terms of headline size, front-page or first-story placement, and inclusion of pictures, but stories are slightly longer than average. Election stories, although quite prominent when primaries, conventions, and significant debates are held, do not dominate the news. Normally, it is quite possible to read the daily paper without noticing election news and to come away from a telecast with the impression that election stories are just a minor part of the day's political developments. Election news competes for audience attention with many other types of stories; this accounts, in part, for its limited impact.

Uniformity of Coverage Patterns. Patterns of presidential election coverage are remarkably uniform, regardless of a newspaper's partisan orientation. Media personnel at highly regarded papers everywhere select the same kind of stories and emphasize the same types of facts, despite the wealth of diverse materials available to them. The major difference generally is that small newspapers carry fewer election stories and that news stories vary in their evaluation of candidates, issues, and campaign events.[38] Television news patterns are also uniform.

Content analysis studies during congressional, state, and local campaigns show similar patterns. The political portraits that various media paint of each candidate match well in basic outlines and in most details.[39] For example, all major television stations and the three major local newspapers covered the 1983 mayoral campaign in Chicago in nearly identical fashion. One might expect that the need to compete against each other and the controversial nature of the race would have produced more diverse treatment.

Table 8-1 illustrates the similarity in patterns of coverage of the primary and general elections by the *Chicago Tribune* and *Chicago Sun-Times,* two major competing dailies in Chicago that are owned and operated by distinct enterprises, and the *Defender,* a paper owned and operated by African-American business leaders that caters to Chicago's large African-American community.

Election news patterns are quite stable in successive elections and uniform for all media covering a particular election. Thus Americans receive similar information on which to base their political decisions. Similarity of coverage of election campaigns has benefits as well as drawbacks. The large degree of homogeneity introduced into the electoral process is an advantage in a heterogeneous country, such as the United States, where it can be difficult to develop political consensus. But it also means uniform neglect of many topics and criteria for judging candidates. Shared knowledge is marred by shared ignorance. Uniformity throttles needed diversity.

A uniform information base obviously has not produced totally uniform political views throughout the country. Differences in political

Table 8-1 Distribution of Coverage Areas in the 1983 Chicago Mayoral Primary and General Elections (in percentage of story themes)

Coverage area	Primary election			General election		
	Tribune	Sun-Times	Defender	Tribune	Sun-Times	Defender
Campaign	43	46	53	42	41	44
Policy	28	24	19	20	21	23
Ethics	13	11	7	8	8	8
Qualities	11	14	19	19	19	14
Party	5	5	3	12	13	11

Source: Doris A. Graber, "Media Magic: Fashioning Characters for the 1983 Mayoral Race," in *The Making of the Mayor: Chicago 1983*, ed. Melvin G. Holli and Paul Green (Grand Rapids, Mich.: Eerdmans, 1984), 84. Reprinted by permission.

Note: For primary elections, $N = 639$ for the *Tribune*, 748 for the *Sun-Times*, and 303 for the *Defender;* for general elections, $N = 1,133$ for the *Tribune*, 1,288 for the *Sun-Times*, and 635 for the *Defender*.

evaluations, even among audiences that share the same news, must be attributed to news commentators' varying interpretations of the same facts and to the different outlooks that audiences bring to the news. As pointed out in the previous chapter, the impact of news frequently is perceiver- rather than stimulus-determined.

Of the factors that encourage uniform coverage, the professional socialization that is common to journalists appears to be the most important. As noted in Chapter 4, newspeople share a sense of what is newsworthy and how it should be presented. Pack journalism prevails with reporters covering identical beats in fashions that have become routine for election coverage. That means keeping score about who is winning and losing and reporting dramatic incidents and juicy personal gossip. It means avoiding dull facts as much as possible without totally ignoring essential information.

Coverage does not follow the *campaign model* of reporting.[40] In this model—the utopia of campaign managers—the rhythm of the campaign as produced by the candidates and their staffs determines what is covered. Reporters dutifully take their cues from the candidates. Press coverage conforms instead to an *incentive model*. Whenever exciting stories provide an incentive for coverage, they are published in a rhythm dictated by the needs of the media and the tastes of their audiences. The needs and tastes of the candidates may be ignored unless they manage to generate the kinds of stories and pictures that journalists find irresistible. This is why most campaigns now employ professionals who know how to attract desirable media coverage.

The incentive model is particularly noticeable in election coverage by specialized media. For instance, papers geared to ethnic audiences focus on the aspects of the campaign that are of primary concern to those audiences and ignore the rest. Business and labor publications put extraordinary emphasis on the campaign's relation to the economy, featuring stories ignored by general audience publications. In terms of timing of coverage, the incentive model explains why stories abound after the outcomes of contests are known and campaign activities have died down, rather than prior to such events when campaigning peaks.

Political and Structural Bias. Does election coverage give a fair and equal chance for all viewpoints to be expressed so that media audiences can make informed decisions? Are the perennial charges of bias leveled by disappointed candidates evidence that newspeople always show favoritism? Or are they merely reactions to coverage that did not advance their cause? Generally, media people try to produce balanced coverage for all major candidates for the same office. This holds true for print journalists, who have no legal obligation to keep coverage balanced, as well as for broadcasters, who are obliged to give equal coverage for special election programs but who are free to indulge in unequal exposure in regular news programs. However, there are no universally accepted standards of fairness and balance. Newspeople traditionally aim for rough parity in the number of stories about each candidate and rough parity in the balance of overtly favorable and unfavorable stories. Fairness does not mean discussing the candidates from the same perspectives, quoting their friends and enemies in equal proportions, or giving their stories similar time, space, or placement. It does not mean proportionate coverage of major political orientations. For example, during the 1984 Democratic National Convention, 85 percent of the interviews were conducted with liberal Democrats, although they constituted only 56 percent of the Democrats in Congress.[41]

Table 8-2 demonstrates the unfair imbalance that ensues when the media give the lion's share of coverage to those candidates who have the best chance for election. Republican contender Bernard Epton received practically no coverage during the 1983 Chicago mayoral primary elections. Most stories discussed Democratic contenders Jane Byrne, the incumbent, Cook County prosecutor Richard M. Daley (the son of the longtime mayor), and U.S. representative Harold Washington. Even during the general election, when Epton's chances for victory had risen dramatically because he was running against a black challenger in a racially polarized city, Epton lagged way behind his opponent. There also was imbalance in another coverage aspect—the choice of friendly and hostile sources. Typically, incumbents receive harsher treatment

Table 8-2 Source Orientation in the 1983 Chicago Mayoral Primary and General Elections (in percentage of story themes)

Source orientation	Primary election			General election		
	Tribune	Sun-Times	Defender	Tribune	Sun-Times	Defender
Jane Byrne						
Pro	17	27	12	9	9	2
Anti	29	26	17	11	14	7
Richard Daley						
Pro	23	24	10	1	1	—
Anti	8	2	6	—	—	1
Harold Washington						
Pro	20	21	52	34	38	72
Anti	2	1	3	19	11	2
Bernard Epton						
Pro	1	1	—	18	20	5
Anti	—	—	1	8	8	10

Source: Doris A. Graber, "Media Magic: Fashioning Characters for the 1983 Mayoral Race," in *The Making of the Mayor: Chicago 1983,* ed. Melvin G. Holli and Paul Green (Grand Rapids, Mich.: Eerdmans, 1984), 62. Reprinted by permission.

Note: For primary elections, $N = 639$ for the *Tribune,* 748 for the *Sun-Times,* and 303 for the *Defender;* for general elections, $N = 714$ for the *Tribune,* 828 for the *Sun-Times,* and 508 for the *Defender.*

than challengers because their records in office always provide targets for criticism. In the 1983 mayoral election, for example, the Jane Byrne story, with one minor exception, reflected predominantly the views of her enemies.

Completely fair and balanced reporting may be impossible because candidates' newsworthiness and willingness to talk to reporters vary. Incumbent president Reagan, dubbed "the Great Communicator," was far more newsworthy throughout 1984, thanks to his official position, than Walter Mondale, his challenger. In the Chicago mayoral campaign Harold Washington was a charismatic candidate, while his Republican challenger was lackluster. There was keen interest in exploring the changes that an African-American mayor might bring about for the city. No wonder the media found Washington far more newsworthy than his opponent.

One may even question whether it is fair to attempt to balance coverage when the situation surrounding candidates is not comparable. Reducing an incumbent's coverage to that accorded to a challenger seems unfair and inappropriate since the public needs to know what officeholders are doing. It would be equally inappropriate to automatically expand a challenger's coverage to an incumbent's proportions. Imbalanced coverage in these instances results from *structural bias,* which is caused by the circumstances of news production. This differs from *political bias,* which involves slanting the news for partisan reasons. Structural bias, although devoid of partisan motives, may profoundly affect people's perceptions about campaigns.[42]

At times it may be difficult to judge to what extent structural bias is fueled by political bias. In the Chicago election, for instance, newspeople could argue that the heavy emphasis on negative stories about incumbent Byrne was structural: there were many mayoral failures to cover. One could also claim that newspeople reveled in digging up negative news about her, while seeing and hearing comparatively little evil about her challengers. Editorials, of course, are intrinsically biased since their primary purpose is to express opinions.

As part of the editorial function, many news media endorse candidates. Republican candidates have received the bulk of endorsements for the presidency in this century; nonetheless, eleven Democrats have succeeded in the twenty-four presidential elections during this period. Endorsements for less exalted offices have been more influential, particularly in elections in which voters had little information to make their own decisions.[43] Influential papers, such as the *Los Angeles Times,* the *Washington Post,* or the late William Loeb's *Manchester Union Leader,* can be extraordinarily successful in promoting the election of candidates they have endorsed and in defeating unacceptable contenders. At the presidential level news coverage tends to be essentially evenhanded, regardless of the candidate endorsed. Below the presidential level the media tend to give more coverage to their endorsed candidates than to those they have not endorsed.

The effort to keep coverage balanced does not extend to third-party candidates. Anyone who runs for the presidency who is not a Republican or Democrat is out of the mainstream of newsworthiness and slighted or even ignored by the news profession. Especially newsworthy third-party candidates, such as George Wallace of the American Independent party, Robert La Follette of the Progressive party, John Anderson of the National Unity Campaign, and independent Ross Perot were notable exceptions. Newsworthiness considerations also account for the sparse coverage of vice-presidential candidates despite the importance of the office. Vice presidents frequently become president, but that possibility always seems remote until it happens. Ninety-five percent of the coverage in a typical presidential election goes to the presidential contenders and only 5 percent to their running mates.

Substance of Coverage: Candidates

Content analysis of major newspapers and of television network news broadcasts shows that the media discuss the qualifications of presidential candidates more amply than campaign events and issues. On an average, personal and professional qualifications of the candidates are referred to in 60 percent of the comments and issues in 40 percent (actually, a somewhat higher percentage since some of the discussion of professional qualities relates to ability to cope with issues).[44]

The qualifications highlighted by the media fall into two broad groups: those that are generally important in judging a person's character and those specifically related to the tasks of the office. Included in the first group are personality traits (such as integrity, reliability, and compassion), style characteristics (such as forthrightness or folksiness), and image characteristics (such as the ability to appear productive and level-headed). Professional qualifications at the presidential level include the capacity to conduct foreign and domestic affairs, the ability to mobilize public support, and a flair for administration. The candidate's political philosophy is also a professional criterion.

Over the years presidential candidates have been most frequently assessed in terms of their trustworthiness, strength of character, leadership capabilities, and compassion. As one wit has phrased it, the crucial question is, "Would you buy a used car from him?" For the media and the public as well, the question of trustworthiness has been paramount because American political executives, especially presidents, wield tremendous unchecked power. After trustworthy, the seven most frequently mentioned qualities are principled, compassionate, inspirational, forthright, strong, administratively competent, and capable in foreign affairs. Style and image characteristics, although important, pale before the prominence given to personality traits.

When it comes to professional capacities—the very qualities that deserve the fullest discussion and analysis—media coverage in recent presidential elections has been comparatively scanty and often vague even when an incumbent is running. Only a handful of professional qualifications have been mentioned with any frequency. These include general appraisals of the capacity to handle foreign affairs, which has been deemed crucial throughout the twentieth century, and the capacity to handle domestic affairs. The latter has primarily involved the capacity to sustain an acceptable quality of life for all citizens by maintaining the economy on an even keel and by controlling crime and internal disorder.

Although the same specific qualities reappear from election to election, treatment of individual candidates is dissimilar. For instance, in the 1983 Chicago mayoral campaign the *Chicago Tribune* devoted 42 percent of its discussion about candidate ethics to incumbent Byrne, compared with 21 and 9 percent, respectively, for her chief rivals, Washington and Daley. Each of the other papers had its unique

Table 8-3 Candidate Evaluations in Post-Labor Day Network
Television News, 1984

Candidate	Score	Candidate	Score
Ronald Reagan	−33	Walter Mondale	−10
George Bush	−55	Geraldine Ferraro	−28

Source: Data from Maura Clancey and Michael Robinson, "The Media in Campaign '84: General Election Coverage, Part I," *Public Opinion* 7 (December/January 1985): 53.

Note: Scores constitute the balance between all explicitly positive and negative references to the candidate. Neutral comments have been omitted. $N = 625$ news stories from ABC, CBS, and NBC early nightly news.

allotments of space: each treated the candidates unequally. Such disparate coverage makes it very difficult for the electorate to compare and evaluate the candidates on important dimensions. Effective comparisons are also hindered by contradictions in remarks reported about the candidates. Bound by current codes of objective reporting and neutrality in electoral contests, the media rarely give guidance to the audience for judging conflicting claims.

Verbal news commentary about political candidates is generally quite negative, especially for incumbents. Journalists speculate about the candidates' venal motivations, flawed characters, and sparse political talents. Choices therefore involve selecting the lesser evil. Table 8-3 shows the negative treatment 1984 presidential candidates received on the evening network news between Labor Day and the election. Comparable scores for Bush and Clinton in the 1992 primaries were −56 and −18, respectively. In 1988 the chief Democratic contenders were derisively labeled "the seven dwarfs." The lead paragraph in a *Time* magazine story at the end of the 1980 race between Reagan and Carter sums up the typical downbeat mood of recent presidential elections: "For more than a year, two flawed candidates have been floundering toward the final showdown, each unable to give any but his most unquestioning supporters much reason to vote for him except dislike of his opponent." [45]

Newspeople's comments are a comparatively minor reason for the negative cast of the news. The main reason lies in story selection and choice of sources to quote. As the 1983 Chicago mayoral campaign demonstrated so well, newspeople quote amply from hostile sources, dwelling on stories that make candidates look bad. Good news and good press are often considered "Pollyanna pap"; bad news and bad press and confrontations are deemed exciting drama. Such negative characterizations are hardly fair to capable candidates who often possess great personal strengths and skills that should be praised, rather than slighted.

On the whole, newspaper and television coverage are quite similar, except that the features are starker on television. If newspapers stress personality qualities heavily, television stresses them more. If newspapers concentrate on few qualities, television concentrates on even fewer. The usual one- or two-minute story gives little chance for in-depth reporting and analysis. It does permit creation of simple, graphic images that illustrate selected themes about the candidate and the campaign. Viewers can readily absorb and use such interpretive portrayals as a basis for making decisions.

To conserve their limited time, television newscasters create stereotypes of the various candidates early in the campaign and then build their stories around these stereotypes by merely adding new details to the established image. During the 1980 presidential campaign, Reagan was typecast as an amiable dunce stumbling into the presidency almost by mistake.[46] Reporters dwelled on his frequent misstatements of facts and mangling of names and statistics. They focused extensively on his much ridiculed comments that the trees in large forests and the volcanic eruption of Mt. St. Helens caused more pollution than cars and industries did. Carter, typecast in the 1976 race as the decent small-time loner who had ventured into a hostile Washington, by 1980 had become the J. R. Ewing candidate. He was constantly portrayed as mean, petty, and manipulative. During the 1992 campaign, Clinton became "slick Willy" and Bush an aimless shipwreck victim, incapable of guiding the ship of state.

The impact of television typecasting is vast because television reaches nearly every voter in national and state-wide campaigns. For instance, once Carter had been tagged as "fuzzy" in the 1976 campaign there was, according to his press secretary Jody Powell, "no way on God's earth we could shake the fuzziness question ... no matter what Carter did or said. He could have spent the whole campaign doing nothing but reading substantive speeches ... and still have had the image in the national press." [47] The general feeling in such cases seems to be that leopards do not change their spots.

Substance of Coverage: Issues and Events

Issues and events coverage usually lags behind coverage of personal characteristics in print and broadcast news. This imbalance bothers social scientists; they contend that the electorate ought to judge the candidates on their issue positions. It also runs counter to the common impression that the print media emphasize issues while television shows off personalities. Actually, electronic and print media display surprisingly similar patterns, although television lags behind print media in the range and depth of issue coverage.

The overriding consideration in choosing issues, as in other political coverage, is newsworthiness rather than intrinsic importance. This is why the changing record of happenings on the campaign trail, however trivial, receives extended coverage. Rather than exploring serious issues in depth, the emphasis is on brief, rapidly paced, freshly breaking events. In fact, the amount of coverage for particular issues often seems to be in inverse proportion to their significance. For instance, during the 1992 primaries, one out of every six campaign stories on the television networks referred to Governor Clinton's personal life. Sexual foibles, reputed drug use during college days, slips of the tongue, bad jokes, all make headlines and are repeated endlessly on various entertainment programs. In 1988, a staggering national debt and a crumbling Communist empire received less attention than did prison furloughs for convicted murderers and the pollution of a local harbor.

Three major features stand out in coverage of issues and events. First and most significantly, the media devote an inordinate amount of attention to campaign hoopla and the horse-race aspects of the contests. They slight political, social, and economic problems facing the country and say little about the merits of the solutions proposed, unless these issues can be made exciting and visually dramatic. Second, information about issues is patchy because the candidates and their surrogates try to concentrate on issues that help their campaigns and try to avoid issues likely to alienate any portion of the huge and disparate electorate from which all are seeking support. Third, newspeople, in turn, focus selectively on controversial issues that lend themselves to appealing stories. They rarely attempt systematic coverage of all-important issues. The issue positions of vice-presidential candidates remain virtually unexplored.

Table 8-4 shows the proportions of mentions allotted to various types of issues and events during the 1988 campaign, as covered by *Time* and *Newsweek*. It is based on content analysis of story paragraphs that appeared between October 1987 and November 1988, and is quite typical of election news coverage in other media.[48] Horse-race news predominated; along with various campaign issues and images, it accounted for 60 percent of the coverage. The policy issues that normally receive the heaviest coverage concern general domestic politics. These stories, which are available from regular beats, are usually tied to familiar names and widely salient domestic events. Therefore they require little background information, and pictorial coverage is easily arranged. Social problems, like poverty or the plight of the elderly, usually lack novelty and are complex to describe. They frequently involve highly controversial and emotionally charged policies about which candidates and media keep silent for fear of alienating large segments of the public. Therefore, they receive scant coverage in most election stories, except when they erupt

Table 8-4 Themes of 1988 Election News in *Time* and *Newsweek* (in percentages)

Themes	Proportion of news
Horse race (e.g., winning and losing, strategy and tactics, fund raising)	32
"Campaign" issues (e.g., facts and rumors of scandals, allegations of dirty or low-level campaigning)	13
"Campaign" images (e.g., candidates' styles of campaigning, posturing, likability)	15
"Governing" images (e.g., leadership ability, trustworthiness)	7
Policy issues (e.g., foreign policy, domestic economy)	17
Candidates' orientation (e.g., personal and political backgrounds, ideology, group support)	16
	100

Source: Thomas E. Patterson, "The Press and Its Missed Assignment," in *The Elections of 1988,* ed. Michael Nelson (Washington, D.C.: CQ Press, 1989), 98.

into violence. Coverage of economic issues, like unemployment, inflation, and taxes, is also limited because these issues are hard to explain and dramatize and rarely produce exciting pictures. Although these are issues of personal concern to the average voter, most people are unwilling to wrestle with a difficult subject that newspeople have not yet learned to simplify and dramatize.[49]

Candidates frequently complain about the media's reluctance to cover issues. As Carter put it in an interview in 1976:

> The traveling press have zero interest in any issue unless it's a matter of making a mistake. What they are looking for is a 47-second argument between me and another candidate or something like that. There's nobody in the back of this plane who would ask an issue question unless he thought he could trick me into some crazy statement.[50]

Nevertheless, candidates continue to emphasize issues. As Table 8-5 indicates, the comparatively limited attention to issue information should not be blamed on them. The table is based on a content analysis of the candidates' campaign rhetoric.[51] Issues made up more than 50 percent of the content of campaign oratory of presidential candidates Reagan, Carter, and Anderson, and of one vice-presidential candidate, Mondale. During the primaries, five of eleven major-party candidates devoted better than half of their rhetoric to issues. Reagan and Edward Kennedy topped 70 percent.

Table 8-5 Issue Mention by Presidential and Vice-Presidential Candidates During the 1980 General Election (in percentages)

Topic	Ronald Reagan	George Bush	Jimmy Carter	Walter Mondale	John Anderson	Patrick Lucey
Issues	71	44	59	65	61	37
Campaign events	5	27	14	16	15	53
Other	24	29	27	19	24	10

Source: Darrell M. West, "Rhetoric and Agenda-Setting in the 1980 Presidential Campaign" (Paper presented at the annual meeting of the Midwest Political Science Association, Milwaukee, Wisconsin, April 1982), 8. West's data are discussed more fully in *Mass Media and Elections: International Research Perspectives,* ed. Winfried Schulz and Klaus Schönbach (München: Verlag Olschläger, 1983), 290. Reprinted by permission.
Note: N = 549 for Ronald Reagan, 216 for George Bush, 574 for Jimmy Carter, 175 for Walter Mondale, 392 for John Anderson, and 19 for Patrick Lucey.

Media issue coverage is much narrower than party platforms. In recent elections, some twenty-five issues have usually surfaced in the press and some twenty on television. Typically, only half of these received extensive and intensive attention. Many important policy questions likely to arise during the forthcoming presidential term are totally ignored. While candidates like to talk about broad policy issues, such as war and peace or the health of the economy, newspeople prefer to concentrate on narrower, specific policy positions on which the candidates disagree sharply.[52] Comparisons of candidates' speeches with television newscasts show that two-thirds of the issues mentioned by candidates are broad, designed to attract wide support from an anxious electorate. By contrast, only one-quarter of the issues featured on television are broad. The rest deal with controversial matters like abortion, or busing, or military aid for a specific country.[53]

As is the case for coverage of presidential qualifications, issues discussed in connection with individual candidates vary. Voters thus receive little aid from the media in appraising and comparing the candidates on the issues. This makes it tempting to rest voting decisions on general personality characteristics, which are more amply presented and far easier to evaluate. Television images of the candidates can be judged by many of the same techniques that people use routinely to appraise the characteristics of persons whom they meet. Readers who find newspaper coverage confusing and depressing therefore tend to turn to television for a simpler and more encouraging image of the unfolding electoral scene.

Television news usually displays more uniform patterns of issue coverage for all the candidates and involves a more limited range of issues than does print news. The drama of campaigning receives even heavier emphasis than in the print media. Television stories are briefer, touch on fewer aspects of each issue, and contribute to the stereotypic images developed for particular candidates. Events are often fragmented and barren of context. Stripping information to its bare bones and covering what is left as a theatrical event apparently appeals to the public. Television news and commercials have become the primary sources of presidential election information for the majority of people, ranking well ahead of newspapers. In-depth election analyses in the press and on public television attract minuscule audiences.

Substance of Coverage: "Medialities"

Media coverage should be assessed not only in terms of the numbers of stories devoted to various topics, but also in terms of political impact. There are times when election politics is particularly vulnerable so that a few stories may carry extraordinary weight. Rapid diffusion of these stories throughout the major media enhances their impact. Michael Robinson calls such featured events *medialities*— "events, developments, or situations to which the media have given importance by emphasizing, expanding, or featuring them in such a way that their real significance has been modified, distorted, or obscured." [54]

During the 1988 presidential campaign, medialities included, typically, a policy scandal, an economic disaster, and personal foibles. They were:

- The Iran-contra hearings, which suggested that the Reagan administration was inept and contemptuous of the law. They tarnished the luster of several Republican contenders, especially George Bush, and their aftereffects lingered throughout Bush's administration.
- The stock market crash of October 19, 1987, which also called the capability of the administration into question. American voters are especially sensitive to pocketbook issues.
- The character tarnishing of several candidates, involving charges of premarital sex (Pat Robertson and Jesse Jackson), philandering (Gary Hart), plagiarism (Joseph Biden and, to a lesser degree, Jackson), and unfair campaign practices (Michael Dukakis, Bush, and others).

Such key stories can have a far more profound impact on the campaign than thousands of routine stories, and should be appraised accordingly.

Adequacy of Coverage

How adequate is current election coverage? Do the media help voters enough to make decisions according to commonly accepted democratic criteria? As coverage of the 1983 Chicago mayoral election and recent presidential campaigns demonstrate, appraisal of candidates and issues is not made easy for voters. In presidential contests information is ample about the personal qualifications of the major, mainstream candidates and about day-to-day campaign events. It is sketchy and often confusing about most professional qualifications, about substantive issues, and about the policy options involved in these issues. In the 1983 mayoral election, issue coverage was more complete and less confusing primarily because many issues at that level are less complex and closer to the voters' personal experiences.

Most primary contenders, candidates of minor parties, and vice-presidential candidates are largely ignored. This is not surprising because the field of candidates is usually much larger than most Americans realize. In 1984, for example, 229 persons were formal candidates for the presidency. The prevalence of negative information makes it seem that all of the candidates are mediocre or even poor choices. This negative cast appears to be a major factor in many voters' decision to stay home on election day. It also undermines the ability of newly elected officials to command essential support after the election, especially from members of the opposing party.

Coverage trends in congressional elections are similar to those in presidential contests, though total coverage is minimal by comparison. Challengers receive only a fraction of the coverage bestowed on incumbents. A count of newspaper coverage of forty-one incumbents and forty-one challengers in 1978 congressional races showed that challengers' share of total coverage was 28 percent in discussions of personal and political characteristics and 34 percent in issue discussions. In name mentions, challengers' share was 42 percent, and in positive commentary it was 30 percent.[55] As Table 8-6 shows, challengers' coverage is also inferior in quality. The table indicates the major content themes in fourteen tight congressional races in which an incumbent was running. The tone and focus of the stories tend to reflect the incumbents' campaign literature.[56]

In presidential contests the deficiencies of media coverage are most noticeable during the primary period, when a large slate of same-party candidates is running in each primary. The media solve the dilemma of covering a multitude of candidacies by giving uniformly skimpy treatment to all candidates except for those designated as front-runners. For instance, in 1980, 71 percent of all mentions of presidential contenders referred to the campaigns of Carter, Reagan, and Kennedy. The

Table 8-6 Median Number of Local Newspaper Paragraphs
Mentioning Selected Themes in Fourteen Tight
Congressional Races, September 27-November 7, 1978

Themes	Incumbent news	Challenger news
Campaign organization	22	27
Personal characteristics	10	13
Political attributes	49	4
Issues/Ideology/Group ties	29	12

Source: Peter Clarke and Susan H. Evans, *Covering Campaigns: Journalism in Congressional Elections* (Stanford, Calif.: Stanford University Press, 1983), 61. Reprinted by permission.

remaining 29 percent of the coverage was shared by seven second-tier contenders—John Anderson, George Bush, Howard Baker, Jerry Brown, John Connally, Philip Crane, and Robert Dole.

The balance between discussion of the candidates' qualifications and of campaign events and issues during the primaries is often the reverse of what it is in the general election. In 1976, for example, only 39 percent of all primary commentary referred to presidential qualities, despite the need to acquaint voters with a host of unfamiliar personalities. Horse-race and hoopla news predominated at the expense of substantive matters. As Thomas Patterson has noted, "Issue material is but a rivulet in the news flow during the primaries, and what is there is almost completely diluted by information about the race." [57]

Although the quality of coverage during the primaries may be thin, the quantity is substantial. A check of the *New York Times* in 1980 showed that 34 percent of all campaign stories appeared from January to March. The Iowa caucuses and the New Hampshire primary were especially well covered, making political events in these states disproportionately influential, considering their size and political unrepresentativeness. Only 30 percent of all stories covered the April-May-June period, despite the fact that twenty-five primaries, many of them in large states, occurred in this period. They thus received substantially less coverage than did the twelve earlier primaries.

The July-August time span, which follows the primary season, includes the nominating conventions. Approximately 25 percent of the voters usually make up their minds in this period, which received 31 percent of the campaign coverage in 1980. Most surprising was the dearth of coverage of the final campaign, following the Labor Day holiday in September. Although two presidential debates were held during the last two months of the campaign in 1980, this period garnered only 5 percent of the campaign coverage. What might have been a last-minute media blitz to rehearse the public for the political climax fizzled into a tired media anticlimax. Issue content did rise by 14 percentage points during the final campaign weeks, and election stories received slightly greater prominence in display as the campaign neared its end. This increased the likelihood that information on the candidates' positions on the issues would come to the voters' attention as the day of decision approached.

It would be unfair to blame low voter turnout in presidential primary and final elections entirely on inadequate election news. Many factors are involved, ranging from the excessive length and complexity of the campaign to the quality of the candidates, voter registration rules, and weather conditions. But interviews with voters show that poor coverage does play a significant part. Voters find election stories interesting, but not genuinely informative. The media depict campaigns as tournaments where winning and losing are all-important, rather than presenting what winning and losing mean for the political direction of the country in general or the observer's personal situation in particular. Taking its cues from the media, a detached audience accepts election news as just another story rather than as an important tale that will directly affect its own welfare in real life.

Media Effects

Learning about Candidates and Issues

What do people learn from campaign coverage? It varies, of course, depending on their interest in the campaign, prior political knowledge, desire for certain information, and political sophistication. But several general trends emerge from national surveys, such as those conducted biannually by the Survey Research Center at the University of Michigan, and from intensive interviews of smaller panels of voters, such as those conducted by the author of this book.

The foremost impression from interviews with voters is that they learn very little specific information in a presidential campaign. National surveys show that only 16 percent of the electorate reach genuinely high scores; 59 percent score below the mean in election knowledge.[58] These figures are based on the numbers of responses people are able to give when asked open-ended questions about parties and candidates. During the 1980 presidential primaries, an average of only 17 percent of the respondents in the National Election Survey increased their knowledge between February and June. An average of 10 percent actually lost ground over the course of the primaries.[59]

The interest that most citizens take in a campaign thus does not mean that they learn a great deal about it beyond who is winning and losing, how the candidates look, and how they go about fighting political battles. Interest in the campaign competes with interest in other events and issues. For instance, a panel of voters who kept diaries on the important news stories that came to their attention throughout a presidential election year devoted only 11 percent of their entries to election stories. When asked to name "major current events or issues," 38 percent of the panelists never named the primary election in the four interviews conducted during the primary season.[60] In the same way, during the early months of the 1988 campaign, 69 percent of the respondents to a national Gallup poll said that they had paid very close attention to news accounts about Jessica McClure, a Texas toddler who was trapped in an abandoned well for several days. Forty percent of the respondents said that they had followed the news of the 1987 stock market plunge closely, and 37 percent had done the same for accounts about the U.S. Navy's escort of Kuwaiti tankers through the Persian Gulf. The presidential campaign ranked lowest among the prominent news events about which the respondents were questioned. Only 15 percent claimed to have paid close attention to the Democratic race, and only 13 percent alleged close interest in the Republican contest.[61]

A comparison of election information supplied by the newspapers with information mentioned by survey respondents reveals roughly similar patterns, as Table 8-7 shows. A nationwide sample of people was asked to mention good and bad points about 1976 presidential nominees Ford and Carter that might affect their voting choices. The similarity between media content and the public's views was greatest for heavy users of newspapers. People also remember the content of campaign commercials. In fact, voters who know and care little about the election often have a better grasp of commercials than of the news.[62]

Media and public images, however, differ in emphases and richness of detail. The public mentions fewer issues and qualities and describes them less precisely. For instance, when asked about the reasons for voting for a candidate, a respondent may say, "I like him," but may be unable to name any specific reasons. A query about the issues that figured in the voter's appraisal of the candidates is likely to elicit a broad reference to foreign or domestic policy in general rather than to specific issues. Facts and figures are rarely recalled, and a good deal of misinformation surfaces when specifics are mentioned. Complex policy positions are remembered far less often than are positions involving simple yes or no choices.

Overall, three out of four answers people give when asked what they have learned about candidates and issues or why they would vote or refrain from voting for a certain candidate concern personality traits.[63]

Table 8-7 Presidential Qualities Mentioned by the Public and by Newspapers (in percentages)

Qualities	Likes		Dislikes		Newspapers
	Carter	*Ford*	*Carter*	*Ford*	
Personal suitability					
Personality traits	49	38	39	18	36
Presidential image	15	37	21	24	25
Style	5	4	16	10	16
Total	69	79	76	52	77
Professional competence					
Capacities	21	17	16	43	7
Relations with public	1	—	—	—	3
Philosophy	9	4	8	5	12
Total	31	21	24	48	22

Source: Survey data from 1976 Election Survey, Center for Political Studies, Survey Research Center, University of Michigan; newspaper data from author's research.

Note: The percentages are based on responses to the question, "Now I'd like to ask you about the good and bad points of the two major candidates for president. Is there anything in particular about (name of candidate) that might make you want to vote for him? Is there anything about (name of candidate) that might make you want to vote against him? What is that? Anything else?" $N = 2,182$ for Carter likes, 2,337 for Ford likes, 2,125 for Carter dislikes, and 1,747 for Ford dislikes. $N = 17,423$ mentions of qualities by newspapers.

People are interested in the human qualities of their elected leaders, particularly their trustworthiness, principled character, strength, and compassion. The media provide ample data on these traits. In many instances people apparently make their choice first, commonly on the basis of quick judgments about personality or vague feelings of party allegiance, and then later acquire information to justify that choice.

Much of the information the media make available is ignored. In a typical election, such as the 1976 presidential race, fully 43 percent of the people in a nationwide poll could comment on only one candidate's strengths and weaknesses. Less than 20 percent could state three or more likes or dislikes about either candidate. Appraisals commonly were limited to one or two statements. The issues people mentioned as important in the campaign represented a much abbreviated and imprecise version of media issue coverage. As Table 8-8 indicates, people stress economic and social issues much more than do the media. This is not surprising; these issues are personal. People do not need media coverage to know that inflation, unemployment, poverty, crime, race relations, and environmental pollution are serious problems requiring attention from presidents. Nor is it surprising that people put much less emphasis on campaign hoopla, covered so plentifully by the media.

Table 8-8 Comparison of Percentage of Mention of Issues and Events
by Newspapers, Television, and Survey Responses

Issues and events	Newspapers	Television	Survey responses
Campaign events	51	63	0
Domestic politics	19	14	5
Foreign affairs	14	10	5
Economic policy	11	9	75
Social problems	5	4	14

Source: Survey data come from the 1976 Election Survey, Center for Political Studies, Survey Research Center, University of Michigan; media data from author's research.
Note: Survey responses specify the most important national problem. $N = 11,027$ for newspapers, 1,355 for television, and 2,263 for survey responses.

Although they find these fleeting events entertaining, people make little effort to remember them long.

Knowledge Base for Voting

Many social scientists worry about the public's limited preparation for voting and fault the media for doing a poor job, particularly in covering issues. But the worry and blame are largely misplaced. Although election news definitely stresses personality traits over issues, it does supply a fair amount of issue coverage. Voters who want to base their decisions on the candidates' stands on specific issues can usually find that information. When voters are poorly informed about issues, it is chiefly because they do not consider elections important enough to take the time to learn about issues. Moreover, intensive studies of voters show that they often have a broad understanding of politics, even when they cannot recall specific details. This general knowledge equips them to draw sound inferences and make intelligent political decisions.[64]

Average voters concentrate heavily on personal qualities of the candidates—a choice that can be defended as sound and rational given the realities of politics. Forming opinions about complex issues like arms limitation or monetary policies is time consuming and difficult, particularly when experts' policy recommendations conflict. Moreover, voters do not know what issues will actually arise during a president's term and what obstacles the incumbent will face in implementing campaign promises. Therefore they ignore most issues, paying attention to only a few that are of major interest generally or personally.

The kind of thing that most people can judge best is a candidate's competence and integrity. People have learned through personal experience how to pick a doctor, minister, or mechanic without understanding medicine, religion, or machines. They know how to judge others in terms of trustworthiness and general ability. The information that media provide most plentifully is geared toward such evaluations of personal character.

Although most people gain little specific knowledge, they may retain conclusions drawn from long-forgotten facts. Voting choices often match approval of a candidate's policy positions, even when voters cannot recall the candidate's stands or the specifics of the policy.[65] Facts may condense into politically significant feelings and attitudes, which then may be remembered long after the facts have been forgotten. For instance, a general impression, developed during a series of elections, that one's party is fielding candidates of poor caliber may ultimately destroy party allegiance.

While the media furnish most people with more information than they are willing or able to use, the media fall short of supplying the needs of political elites. Opinion leaders, and the mass public that often relies on their guidance, would benefit from greater clarity of presentation in the daily press, more point-by-point comparisons of candidates and policies, and more ample evaluations of the political significance of differences in candidates and their programs. Where resources permit, journalists should research important topics neglected by the candidates and make the information available. More coverage should also be given to third party candidates and vice-presidential contenders, and less coverage to often meaningless polls.

Voting Behavior

Does campaigning via the media change votes? The answer to this perennial question so dear to the hearts of campaign managers, public relations experts, and social scientists hinges on the interaction between audiences and messages. Crucial variables include the voter's receptivity to a message urging change, the potency of the message, the appropriateness of its form, and the setting in which it occurs. A vote change is most likely when voters pay fairly close attention to the media and are ambivalent in their attitudes toward the candidates. Messages are most potent if they concern a major and unpredicted event, such as a successful or disastrous foreign policy venture or corruption in high places, and when individuals find themselves in social settings where a change of attitudes will not constitute deviant behavior. This combination of circumstances is fairly uncommon, which explains why changes of voting intentions are comparatively rare. Fears that televised campaigns can easily sway voters and amount to "electronic ballot box stuffing" are therefore unrealistic.

However, even small numbers of media-induced vote changes may be important. Many elections at all levels are decided by tiny percentages of votes, often less than 1 percent. The media may also have a crucial impact on election outcomes whenever they are able to stimulate or depress voter turnout. This is a more likely consequence of media publicity than changes in voting choices. It has led to concern about the changes in turnout that may be produced by broadcasts that predict election results before voting has ended. In the 1980 presidential election, for instance, NBC projected Reagan as the winner at 8:15 P.M. Eastern Standard Time, several hours before the polls closed on the West Coast. This could have reduced the late turnout on the West Coast, affecting presidential, congressional, and state contests. Despite several investigations of the problem, the precise impact of early forecasts on elections remains disputed. Current evidence indicates that the effects, if they do occur, have rarely been substantial.[66]

Attempts to stop immediate dissemination of projections of winners and losers have run afoul of First Amendment free speech guarantees. This may explain why the laws passed in more than half of the states to restrain exit polling are seldom enforced.[67] Congress has tried three times, starting in 1986, to pass a *Uniform Poll Closing Act*. While the measure has thus far failed to pass, prospects for ultimate success are good. The major television networks have pledged to refrain from projecting the outcome of a presidential election until the polls have closed. The concern about the impact of exit polls and early forecasts seems overdrawn. Voters are bombarded throughout the election year with information likely to determine their vote and turnout. Why should there be squeamishness on the very last day of the campaign?

The most important influence of the media on the voter does not lie in changing votes, once predispositions have been formed, but in shaping and reinforcing predispositions and influencing the initial selection of candidates. When newspeople sketched out the Jimmy Carter image and held him up as a potential winner during the 1976 primaries, ignoring most of his rivals, they made "Jimmy-Who?" into a viable candidate. Millions of voters would never have cast their ballot for the obscure Georgia politician had not the media thrust him into the limelight as a likely winner.

By focusing the voters' attention on selected individuals, their characteristics, and issue stands, the media also determine to a large extent the crucial issues by which the competence of the candidates will be gauged. Very early in the campaign, often long before formal campaigning starts, media interpretations of the significance of issues can shape the political and emotional context of the election.[68]

President Carter's chances for reelection in 1980 hinged on the images that the media resurrected from his four years in office. In the same way Watergate revelations created public moods that doomed many Republicans in the 1974 elections. Newspeople shape election outcomes by molding the images of political reality that lead to voting decisions rather than by suggesting voting choices to an electorate that prefers to make up its own mind. As Leon Sigal has noted, they "play less of an independent part in creating issues, sketching imagery, and coloring perceptions of the candidates than in getting attention for their candidacies. Newsmen do not write the score or play an instrument; they amplify the sounds of the music makers." [69] Although voters pay most concentrated attention to media coverage just before elections, the crucial attitudes that determine voting choices may already be so firm that the final vote is a foregone conclusion.

Summary

The role played by the media, especially television, in recent campaigns is powerful and pervasive. It has transformed election politics for high offices. Major changes are the weakening of the influence of political parties and other political actors, the domination of the campaign strategies and schedules by media demands, and the emergence of the media as king makers in political recruiting and promotion of candidates, particularly at the presidential level.

In this chapter we have scrutinized newspaper and television election coverage throughout the campaign. General coverage patterns, the substance and slant of coverage, and the manner of presentation were considered. The media emphasize personal rather than professional qualities of the candidates and campaign events rather than substantive issues. Stories are chosen for their newsworthiness, not their educational value. Structural biases abound and have important political consequences, but outright political bias is rare.

We also examined the effects of media output on the people who are exposed to it. Although the public complains about the skimpiness and shallowness of election coverage, it absorbs only a small portion of the considerable amount of information that is actually available. Nonetheless, the bits of information that people absorb create sufficient political understanding to permit sound voting choices based on appraisal of a chosen candidate's character. Minute changes brought about by the media in final voting decisions or voter turnout may alter the outcome of a close election and the course of political life.

Claims that the media influence elections very little rest on election studies in the 1940s and 1950s that have become obsolete. This early research preceded the age of television dominance and was concerned primarily with massive changes in individual voting decisions. More recent research has cast the net much wider to include media effects on all phases of the election campaign, from the recruitment and nomination stages to the strategies that produce the final outcome. In addition to media impact on the final voting choice, social scientists look at political learning during campaigns and at the information base that supports the voting decision. Television, in particular, has changed the election game rules, especially at the presidential level. Candidates and media have become inextricably intertwined. Those who aspire to elective office must play by the new rules of media politics.

Notes

1. For a good review of the presidential election process, see Herbert Asher, *Presidential Elections and American Politics: Voters, Candidates and Campaigns Since 1952,* 4th ed. (Homewood, Ill.: Dorsey Press, 1988); Stephen J. Wayne, *The Road to the White House 1992: The Politics of Presidential Elections* (New York: St. Martin's Press, 1992); and Nelson W. Polsby and Aaron Wildavsky, *Presidential Elections,* 7th ed. (New York: Scribner's, 1988). For reports on congressional campaigns, see Peter Clarke and Susan H. Evans, *Covering Campaigns: Journalism in Congressional Elections* (Stanford, Calif.: Stanford University Press, 1983); Edie N. Goldenberg and Michael W. Traugott, *Campaigning for Congress* (Washington, D.C.: CQ Press, 1984); and Jan Pons Vermeer, *Campaigns in the News: Mass Media and Congressional Elections* (New York: Greenwood Press, 1987). For state contests involving ballot issues, see Betty Zisk, *Money, Media, and the Grass Roots: State Ballot Issues and the Electoral Process* (Beverly Hills, Calif.: Sage, 1987). On gubernatorial contests see John W. Windhauser, "Reporting of Campaign Issues in Ohio Municipal Election Races," *Journalism Quarterly* 54 (Summer 1977): 332-340; Leonard Tipton, Roger D. Haney, and John R. Baseheart, "Media Agenda-Setting in City and State Election Campaigns," *Journalism Quarterly* 52 (Spring 1975): 15-22; and Jan Pons Vermeer, *"For Immediate Release": Candidate Press Releases in American Political Campaigns* (Westport, Conn.: Greenwood Press, 1982).
2. For comparisons of election coverage in various years, see John H. Kessel, *Presidential Campaign Politics: Coalition Strategies and Citizen Response,* 4th ed. (Homewood, Ill.: Dorsey Press, 1992); and W. Lance Bennett, *The Governing Crisis: Media, Money, and Marketing in American Elections* (New York: St. Martin's Press, 1992). Comparisons with election campaigns in foreign countries are presented in Edie N. Goldenberg and Michael W. Traugott, eds., "Mass Media in Legislative Campaigns," *Legislative Studies Quarterly* 12 (August 1987): 313-456; and Holli A. Semetko, Jay G. Blumler, Michael Gurevitch, David Weaver, with Steve Barkin and G. Cleveland Wilhoit, *The Formation of Campaign Agendas: A Comparative Analysis of Party and Media Roles in Recent American and British Elections* (Hillsdale, N.J.: Erlbaum, 1991).
3. For examples, see Winfried Schulz and Klaus Schönbach, eds., *Mass Media and Elections: International Research Perspectives* (München: Olschläger,

1983); and Semetko et al., *The Formation of Campaign Agendas,* and sources cited there.

4. Kathleen Hall Jamieson, *Packaging the President: A History and Criticism of Presidential Campaign Advertising* (New York: Oxford University Press, 1984); Dorothy Davidson Nesbit, *Videostyle in U.S. Senate Campaigns* (Knoxville, Tenn.: University of Tennessee Press, 1988); Richard Joslyn, *Mass Media and Elections* (Reading, Mass.: Addison-Wesley, 1984), chap. 7; and Diana Owen, *Media Messages in American Presidential Elections* (Westport, Conn.: Greenwood Press, 1991), 25-26; and Darrell M. West, "Television Advertising in Senate and Presidential Campaigns," Midwest Political Science Association paper, 1992.

5. Owen, *Media Messages,* 28.

6. Thomas Patterson and Robert McClure, *The Unseeing Eye* (New York: Putnam, 1976), 102-108; Leonard Shyles, "The Televised Political Spot Advertisement: Its Structure, Content and Role in the Political System," in *New Perspectives on Political Advertising,* ed. Lynda Lee Kaid, Dan Nimmo, and Keith R. Sanders (Carbondale: Southern Illinois University Press, 1986), 107-138; and Edwin Diamond and Stephen Bates, *The Spot* (Cambridge, Mass.: MIT Press, 1988).

7. Michael J. Robinson, "The Media in 1980: Was the Message the Message?" in *The American Elections of 1980,* ed. Austin Ranney (Washington, D.C.: American Enterprise Institute, 1981), 179-180; Owen, *Media Messages,* 25-60. For contrary views, see Joe McGinniss, *The Selling of the President, 1968* (New York: Trident Press, 1969).

8. West contends that ads made Dukakis seem electable and clinched his nomination. See West, "Television Advertising in Senate and Presidential Campaigns," 9.

9. Joslyn, *Mass Media,* chap. 7; and Michael J. Robinson, "Three Faces of Congressional Media," in *The New Congress,* ed. Thomas E. Mann and Norman J. Ornstein (Washington, D.C.: American Enterprise Institute, 1981).

10. Bruce E. Gronbeck, "Mythic Portraiture in the 1988 Iowa Presidential Caucus Bio-Ads," *American Behavioral Scientist* 33 (1989): 351-364; J. Gregory Payne, John Marlier, and Robert A. Baucus, "Polispots in the 1988 Presidential Primaries," *American Behavioral Scientist* 33 (1989): 365-381.

11. Robinson, "The Media in 1980," 186.

12. Walter DeVries and V. Lance Tarrance, *The Ticket Splitters* (Grand Rapids, Mich.: Eerdmans, 1972). Kessel, *Presidential Campaign Politics,* 260-266, defines *issues* very broadly. This leads him to the conclusion that issues are most important in voting.

13. For a well-reasoned argument questioning television influence, see Michael J. Robinson, "News Media Myths and Realities: What the Networks Did and Didn't Do in the 1984 General Campaign," in *Elections in America,* ed. Kay Lehman Schlozman (Boston: Allen and Unwin, 1987), 143-170. An equally well-reasoned argument supporting television influence is presented in Dean Alger, "Television, Perceptions of Reality and the Presidential Election of '84," *PS* 20 (Winter 1987): 49-57.

14. F. Christopher Arterton, "Campaign Organizations Confront the Media—Political Environment," in *Race for the Presidency: The Media and the Nominating Process,* ed. James David Barber (Englewood Cliffs, N.J.: Prentice Hall, 1978), 21.

15. Ibid., 22. See also Michael J. Robinson, "TV's Newest Program: 'The

Presidential Nominations Game,' " *Public Opinion* 1 (May/June 1978): 41-46.

16. Thomas E. Patterson, "The Press and Its Missed Assignment," in *The Elections of 1988,* ed. Michael Nelson (Washington, D.C.: CQ Press, 1989), 93-109.

17. Larry M. Bartels, "Expectations and Preferences in Presidential Nominating Campaigns," *American Political Science Review* 79 (September 1985): 804-815. The importance of the winner image is discussed in Henry E. Brady and Richard Johnston, "What's the Primary Message: Horse Race or Issue Journalism?" in *Media and Momentum: The New Hampshire Primary and Nomination Politics,* ed. Gary R. Orren and Nelson W. Polsby (Chatham, N.J.: Chatham House, 1987), 127-186.

18. Patterson, "The Press and Its Missed Assignment," 99.

19. William G. Mayer, "The New Hampshire Primary: A Historical Overview," in *Media and Momentum,* 23.

20. "The 1992 Elections—Primary Wrap-Up," *Media Monitor* 6 (June/July 1992): 5.

21. Richard Stout, "The Pre-Pre-Campaign-Campaign," *Public Opinion* 5 (December-January 1983): 17-20, 60.

22. Richard L. Rubin, *Press, Party and Presidency,* (New York: Norton, 1981), 129, 138.

23. For analysis of the impact of debates, see David J. Lanoue and Peter Schrott, *The Joint Press Conference: The History, Impact, and Prospects of American Presidential Debates* (Westport, Conn.: Greenwood Press, 1991); Sidney Kraus, *Televised Presidential Debates and Public Policy* (Hillsdale, N.J.: Erlbaum, 1988); and Kathleen Hall Jamieson and David S. Birdsell, *Presidential Debates: The Challenge of Creating an Informed Electorate* (New York: Oxford University Press, 1988).

24. The potency of visual information is discussed in Doris A. Graber, "Kind Pictures and Harsh Words: How Television Presents the Candidates," in *Elections in America,* 115-141; Shawn W. Rosenberg with Patrick McCafferty, "The Image and the Vote: Manipulating Voters' Preferences," *Public Opinion Quarterly* 51 (Spring 1987): 31-47; Shawn Rosenberg, Lisa Bohan, Patrick McCafferty, and Kevin Harris, "The Image and the Vote: The Effect of Candidate Presentation on Voter Preference," *American Journal of Political Science* 30 (February 1986): 108-127.

25. Michael J. Robinson, "A Statesman Is A Dead Politician: Candidate Images on Network News," in *What's News: The Media in American Society,* ed. Elie Abel (San Francisco: Institute for Contemporary Studies, 1981).

26. Walter Bunge, Robert Hudson, and Chung Woo Suh, "Johnson's Information Strategy for Vietnam: An Evaluation," *Journalism Quarterly* 45 (Autumn 1968): 419-425.

27. Thomas E. Patterson and Richard Davis, "The Media Campaign: Struggle for the Agenda," in *The Elections of 1984,* ed. Michael Nelson (Washington, D.C.: CQ Press, 1985), 124.

28. Anthony Broh, "Presidential Preference Polls and Network News," in *Television Coverage of the 1980 Presidential Campaign,* ed. William C. Adams (Norwood, N.J.: Ablex, 1983), 21.

29. Quoted in Edwin Diamond, *Sign-Off: The Last Days of Television* (Boston: MIT Press, 1982), 175.

30. Martin Schram, *The Great American Video Game: Presidential Politics in the Television Age* (New York: William Morrow, 1987), 25.

31. Ibid., 26.
32. Wayne, *The Road to the White House 1992*, 25, 48.
33. Herbert E. Alexander, "Financing the Presidential Elections, 1988," in *Quest for National Office: Readings on Elections*, ed. Stephen J. Wayne and Clyde Wilcox (New York: St. Martin's Press, 1992), 39-49.
34. James Glen Stovall, "Incumbency and News Coverage of the 1980 Presidential Campaign," *Western Political Quarterly* 37 (December 1984): 628. The effects of incumbency are similar at the congressional level.
35. Emmett H. Buell, Jr., " 'Locals' and 'Cosmopolitans': National, Regional, and State Newspaper Coverage of the New Hampshire Primary," in *Media and Momentum*, 66.
36. S. Robert Lichter, "How the Press Covered the Primaries," *Public Opinion* 11 (July/August 1988): 49.
37. Michael J. Robinson and Margaret Sheehan, "Traditional Ink vs. Modern Video Versions of Campaign '80," in *Television Coverage*, 18.
38. Buell found that two small New Hampshire papers differed in coverage from the *New York Times, Washington Post,* and *Boston Globe.* They gave minor candidates more equal coverage, had more features devoted to a single candidate, and covered issues more amply. See Buell, " 'Locals' and 'Cosmopolitans,' " 76-97.
39. See John Carey, "How Media Shape Campaigns," *Journal of Communication* 26 (Spring 1976): 50-57; Windhauser, "Reporting of Campaign Issues"; and Clarke and Evans, *Covering Campaigns.* For an exception in a senatorial campaign, see Jon F. Hale, "The Scribes of Texas: Newspaper Coverage of the 1984 U.S. Senate Campaign," in *Campaigns in the News*, 91-107.
40. C. Richard Hofstetter, *Bias in the News: Network Television Coverage of the 1972 Election Campaign* (Columbus: Ohio State University Press, 1976), 39-41.
41. William C. Adams, "Convention Coverage," *Public Opinion* 7 (December/January 1985): 45.
42. Wenmouth Williams, Jr., and William D. Semlak, "Structural Effects of TV Coverage on Political Agendas," *Journal of Communication* 28 (Autumn 1978): 114-119; and Hofstetter, *Bias in the News*, 32-36. For an interesting discussion of the special concerns involved in covering African-American candidates, see Jannette Lake Dates and Oscar H. Gandy, Jr., "How Ideological Constraints Affected Coverage of the Jesse Jackson Campaign," *Journalism Quarterly* 62 (Autumn 1985): 595-600.
43. G. Cleveland Wilhoit and Taik Sup Auh, "Newspaper Endorsements and Coverage of Public Opinion Polls in 1970," *Journalism Quarterly* 51 (Winter 1974): 654-658; and Byron St. Dizier, "The Effect of Newspaper Endorsements and Party Identification on Voting Choice," *Journalism Quarterly* 62 (Autumn 1985): 589-594.
44. The proportions are even more favorable for issues when in each story every single issue is coded rather than only three. Doris A. Graber, "Hoopla and Horse-Race in 1980 Campaign Coverage: A Closer Look," in *Mass Media and Elections*, 283-300.
45. Quoted in Anthony King, "How Not to Select Presidential Candidates: A View from Europe," in *The American Elections*, 305.
46. Typecasts have been extracted from Robinson, "A Statesman Is a Dead Politician," 178-182.
47. F. Christopher Arterton, "The Media Politics of Presidential Campaigns,"

in *Race for the Presidency,* 36.

48. Content analysis of 13 major newspapers and 5 television networks shows similar figures. Bruce Buchanan, *Electing a President: The Markle Commission Research on Campaign '88* (Austin: University of Texas Press, 1991).

49. Seymour Martin Lipset and William Schneider, *The Confidence Gap: Business, Labor, and Government in the Public Mind* (New York: The Free Press, 1983), chap. 5.

50. Quoted in Robert C. Sahr, "Energy as a Non-Issue in 1980 Coverage," in *Television Coverage,* 135.

51. Darrell M. West, "Rhetoric and Agenda-Setting in the 1980 Presidential Campaign," quoted in Graber, "Hoopla and Horse-Race," 289-290.

52. Benjamin I. Page, *Choices and Echoes in Presidential Elections: Rational Man and Electoral Democracy* (Chicago: University of Chicago Press, 1978), chap. 6.

53. Thomas E. Patterson, "Television and Election Strategy," in *The Communications Revolution in Politics,* ed. Gerald Benjamin (New York: The Academy of Political Science, 1982), 28.

54. Robinson, "The Media in 1980," 191.

55. Goldenberg and Traugott, *Campaigning for Congress,* 127-128. Also see Clarke and Evans, *Covering Campaigns,* 57-72.

56. Timothy E. Cook, *Making Laws and Making News: Media Strategies in the U.S. House of Representatives* (Washington, D.C.: Brookings Institution, 1989), 107.

57. Thomas Patterson, *The Mass Media Election: How Americans Choose Their President,* 3d ed. (New York: Praeger, 1988), 250. Also see Eric R.A.N. Smith, *The Unchanging American Voter* (Berkeley: University of California Press, 1989).

58. Kessel, *Presidential Campaign Politics,* 3d ed., 1988, 250. Also see Smith, *The Unchanging American Voter.* For contrary interpretations see Samuel L. Popkin, *The Reasoning Voter: Communication and Persuasion in Presidential Campaigns* (Chicago: University of Chicago Press, 1991).

59. Scott Keeter and Cliff Zukin, *Uninformed Choice: The Failure of the New Presidential Nominating System* (New York: Praeger, 1983), 80. The figures are based on Reagan, Kennedy, Bush, Brown, Connally, Baker, and Dole data. Learning data for 1984 are presented in Brady and Johnston, "What's the Primary Message?" 164-168.

60. Doris A. Graber, *Processing the News: How People Tame the Information Tide,* 2d ed. (New York: Longman, 1988), 140.

61. "The Girl in the Well Outpolls the Men in the Race," *New York Times,* November 19, 1987.

62. Owen reports that more than 90 percent of a sample of sophisticated voters remembered the major 1988 commercials. *Media Messages in American Presidential Elections,* 45.

63. Some scholars report that for making voting decisions issues are more important than the candidates' personality traits. For examples, see Kessel, *Presidential Campaign Politics,* 3d ed., 1988, 267-293. The disagreements are explained in part by different definitions of what constitutes either an issue or a personality comment and by different practices in the choice of items to be coded. Kessel reports that there has been a rise in issue emphasis since 1976. For 1984 his data show that 28.1 percent of the comments made by voters concerned candidates, 8.9 percent referred to

parties, and 62.9 percent related to issues. By contrast, pollster Richard Wirthlin reports that 29 percent of Reagan's voters cited issues, as did 44 percent of Mondale's voters. The Reagan/Mondale vote ratio was 59:41. Peter Hart and Richard Wirthlin Interview, "Moving Right Along? Campaign '84's Lessons for 1988," *Public Opinion* 7 (December/January 1985): 10.

64. Pamela Johnston Conover and Stanley Feldman, "The Role of Inference in the Perception of Political Candidates," in *Political Cognition: The 19th Annual Carnegie Symposium on Cognition,* ed. Richard R. Lau and David O. Sears (Hillsdale, N.J.: Erlbaum, 1986), 127-158. Also see Graber, *Processing the News.*

65. Graber, *Processing the News,* 85-89.

66. Paul Wilson, "Election Night 1980 and the Controversy over Early Projections," in *Television Coverage,* 152-153; Percy H. Tannenbaum and Leslie J. Kostrich, *Turned-On TV/Turned-Off Voters: Policy Options for Election Projections* (Beverly Hills, Calif.: Sage, 1983); and Paul J. Lavrakas and Jack K. Holley, eds. *Polls and Presidential Election Campaign News Coverage: 1988* (Evanston, Ill.: Northwestern University Press, 1988).

67. For a discussion of how state laws have fared in the courts, see Stephen Bates, "Lawful Exits: The Court Considers Election Day Polls," *Public Opinion* 8 (Summer 1986): 53-54.

68. Arthur T. Hadley, *The Invisible Primary* (Englewood Cliffs, N.J.: Prentice-Hall, 1976).

69. Leon V. Sigal, "Newsmen and Campaigners: Organization Men Make the News," *Political Science Quarterly* 93 (Fall 1978): 465-470.

Readings

Arterton, F. Christopher. *Media Politics: The News Strategies of Presidential Campaigns.* Lexington, Mass.: Heath, 1984.

Clarke, Peter, and Susan H. Evans. *Covering Campaigns: Journalism in Congressional Elections.* Stanford, Calif.: Stanford University Press, 1983.

Kaid, Lynda Lee, Dan Nimmo, and Keith R. Sanders, eds. *New Perspectives on Political Advertising.* Carbondale: Southern Illinois University Press, 1986.

Kern, Montague. *30-Second Politics: Political Advertising in the Eighties.* New York: Praeger, 1989.

Mickelson, Sig. *From Whistle Stop to Sound Bite: Four Decades of Politics and Television.* New York: Praeger, 1989.

Nesbit, Dorothy Davidson. *Videostyle in U.S. Senate Campaigns.* Knoxville: University of Tennessee Press, 1988.

Orren, Gary R., and Nelson W. Polsby. *Media and Momentum: The New Hampshire Primary and Nomination Politics.* Chatham, N.J.: Chatham House, 1987.

Owen, Diana. *Media Messages in American Presidential Elections.* Westport, Conn.: Greenwood Press, 1991.

Schram, Martin. *The Great American Video Game: Presidential Politics in the Television Age.* New York: William Morrow, 1987.

Semetko, Holli A., Jay G. Blumler, Michael Gurevitch, David Weaver, with Steve Barkin and G. Cleveland Wilhoit. *The Formation of Campaign Agendas: A Comparative Analysis of Party and Media Roles in Recent American and British Elections.* Hillsdale, N.J.: Erlbaum, 1991.

CHAPTER 9

The Struggle for Control: News from the Presidency and Congress

In the fall of 1991, the Soviet Union was in political and economic turmoil. A coup to displace President Mikhail Gorbachev had been followed by a counter coup and a struggle for power between Gorbachev and Boris Yeltsin, president of the Russian state. Yet, at this critical juncture in their political lives, both men devoted considerable time to interviews with American television journalists. For example, Boris Yeltsin invited ABC's Diane Sawyer and other television reporters to his office for an interview and later taped his position statements for immediate broadcast world-wide. Gorbachev, for his part, regaled CNN and the world's press with stories about his house arrest in the Crimea during the early days of the coup.

Why did they do it? Why do top level political leaders throughout the world expose themselves to frequently hostile interrogations by journalists who often write stories attacking them and their policies? The answer is that politicians desperately need the media to achieve their goals and the media covet access to politicians to get information for their most important stories.

American reporters in Moscow eagerly sought news about the historic changes that portended an end to decades of Cold War. Gorbachev and Yeltsin wanted to signify to their people and to the world that they, rather than the old-style Communists, were the country's acknowledged leaders, legitimized by international media attention. Despite their interdependence, the media and the government have a love-hate relationship. The two institutions have conflicting goals and missions and operate under different constraints. Therefore, they cannot live comfortably with each other, yet they dare not part company.[1]

The Adversary Relationship

To gain and retain public support and maintain their power, executives and legislators want to influence what information is passed on to the public and to other officials. They want to define situations and project images in their own way to further their objectives. Newspeople have different goals. They take special pains to expose wrongdoing by public officials. When they view the world from a different perspective than politicians, they describe the situation accordingly. They feel bound by the economics of the news business to present exciting stories that will attract large audiences. This often means prying into conflict, controversy, or ordinary wheeling and dealing—matters that government officials would like to keep quiet. Government wants its portrait taken from the most flattering angle, and at the least it wants to avoid an unflattering picture. The media, however, prefer candid shots that show government in awkward poses and compromising situations.

In this chapter we will take a closer look at the interrelationship of the media with the executive and legislative branches of government at the national level. The interface of the media and the court system and subnational levels of government are targeted in the next chapter. Casual as well as systematic observations readily establish that the media devote a great deal of attention to the affairs of the national government, particularly the presidency. As Table 9-1 shows, during the twelve-month span from July 1990 to June 1991, the early evening news broadcasts of ABC, CBS, and NBC ran an average of 131 network television stories per month about some aspect of the presidency. This amounted to roughly thirty percent of all political news stories. The numbers for Congress and the Supreme Court were considerably lower, with a monthly average of 92 Congress stories and a monthly average of 12 Supreme Court stories.

Table 9-1 indicates that coverage was unevenly distributed with several peaks and valleys for each of the branches of government. Compared to the Reagan presidency, the figures for the Bush presidency represent a sizable drop in attention to the president, a small decline in Supreme Court coverage, and a sharp rise in stories about Congress.

President Bush received roughly eight hours of television news coverage each month from the networks, compared with slightly less than five hours for Congress and less than one-half hour for the Supreme Court. Differences among the three networks in number of stories and time allotments were minimal, as Table 9-2 indicates. The president's share of television time amounted to roughly 60 percent, compared to 36.5 percent for Congress and 3.5 percent for the Supreme

Table 9-1 Evening Network News Coverage of the Three Branches of Government, July 1990-June 1991

Month	President N	President Time	Congress N	Congress Time	Supreme Court N	Supreme Court Time
1990						
July	124	6:00	136	6:15	26	1:42
August	135	13:26	67	4:21	2	0:01
September	146	8:44	107	5:10	13	0:26
October	160	8:35	150	7:48	14	0:23
November	129	9:32	88	5:29	6	0:09
December	115	7:07	71	4:03	1	0:01
1991						
January	117	10:11	72	6:18	9	0:11
February	146	11:55	47	3:07	2	0:01
March	96	4:18	67	2:58	16	0:24
April	100	5:31	91	4:21	6	0:08
May	172	6:07	107	4:34	15	0:24
June	132	5:28	100	4:21	38	1:31
Total	1,572	96:54	1,103	58:45	148	5:21
Monthly Average	131	8:04	92	3:06	12	0:27

Source: Compiled by the author from Vanderbilt Television News Archives Indexes.
Note: Three networks have been combined. Time is listed in hours and minutes.

Court. Newspaper coverage patterns resembled television but similarity in patterns does not mean that various media organizations project identical images of public officials. For example, when a local newspaper, an elite newspaper, and network television covered a proposal by President Reagan to cut taxes and the president's 1984 trip to Europe, researchers found three different sets of images in the stories.[2] The *Durham Morning Herald,* a local paper with limited resources for independent news analysis, presented accounts drawn largely from the wire services. These stories featured the themes, ideas, and perspectives provided by the White House and cast the president and the events into a favorable light. Although the elite *New York Times* reported the White House version of events, it subjected White House reports to critical analysis. The views of prominent foes of the president and his policies were given ample space. This created a much less rosy impression of the state of affairs. CBS evening news presented a more mixed picture. Verbal images were predominantly negative, whereas visual images, based on presidentially controlled photo opportunities, were highly favorable. Audiences for these three news sources thus were informed about the same events, but the tint of the interpretive lenses varied.

Table 9-2 Evening Network News Coverage of the Three Branches of Government in Percentage of Network Time

Network	President	Congress	Supreme Court
ABC	60.2	36.1	3.7
CBS	61.6	35.1	3.3
NBC	58.6	38.4	3.0

Source: Compiled by the author from Vanderbilt Television News Archives Indexes, July 1990-June 1991.

Note: N for ABC = 2,669 minutes; N for CBS = 3,642 minutes; N for NBC = 3,347 minutes.

The Media and the Executive Branch

Four Major Functions

The media perform four basic functions for government executives.[3] First, they *inform them about current events,* including developments in other parts of the government. This information sets the political scene for policies. When the media highlight problems, executive action often follows. Not infrequently, media furnish daily news faster than bureaucratic channels. President John F. Kennedy, for instance, would read the *New York Times* before beginning his official day because stories about foreign affairs often reached him twenty-four hours earlier through the *Times* than through State Department bulletins that had to be coded and then decoded.

Second, the media *keep executive branch officials attuned to the major concerns of the American people.* They do this directly by reporting on public opinion and indirectly by featuring the stories likely to shape public opinion. Public officials assume that newspeople keep in touch with popular concerns to be able to write stories that are meaningful to their readers and viewers. Readers and viewers, in turn, take their cues about what is important and worthy of discussion from the media.

Third, the media *enable executives to convey their messages to the general public as well as to political elites* within and outside of government. These channels of communication, to which presidents have ready access, provide unparalleled opportunities to explain administration policies, publicly attack opponents' positions, and force them to take stands they may want to avoid. Political elites need these channels as much as the public does because there is no effective communication system that directly links government officials who are dispersed throughout the country.[4]

Fourth, the media *allow chief executives to remain in full public view on the political stage,* keeping their human qualities and professional skills on almost constant display. Newspapers, television, and radio supply a steady stream of commentary about a president's daily routines. Coverage of personal life may be extensive. For instance, when President Ronald Reagan was recovering from gunshot wounds in 1981 several daily news briefings kept the public apprized of his progress. The media dutifully reported intimate details of the president's condition, including his mood, his tolerance of various medical procedures, and his daily diet. Beyond providing human interest tidbits, this coverage was intended to reassure the public that it was fully informed about the president's disability and his fitness to continue his official functions. Human interest stories help to forge close personal ties between people and their leaders and may contribute to the relation of trust that turns people into willing followers.

Media Impact

The political significance of the relationship between the media and the executive branch is greater than the few functions just described. As Rep. Newt Gingrich, R-Ga., put it: "If you are not in the *Washington Post* every day, you might as well not exist." [5] Media coverage is the very lifeblood of politics because it shapes the perceptions that form the reality on which political action is based. Media do more than depict the political environment; they *are* the political environment. Because direct contact with political actors and situations is limited, media images define people and situations for nearly all participants in the political process.

As we saw in previous chapters, the age of television politics that began in the 1950s has vastly enhanced media impact and hence media power. In the past a story might have caused ripples on the political seas when thousands of people in one corner of the country read it in the paper or heard it on the radio. Today that same story can cause political tidal waves when millions nationwide see and hear it simultaneously on television so that politicians feel compelled to react to it. Politicians now can visit with millions of potential followers in their living rooms, creating the kinds of emotional ties that hitherto came only from personal contact. An appearance on television may affect the political future of a member of Congress more than service on an important congressional committee.

By widening the circle of citizens who are routinely exposed to politics and by creating new types of politicians, television has tipped the political scales of power among the three branches of government in favor of the presidency. The first and second laws of "video politics"

YOUR TAX DOLLARS AT WORK : CONGRESS STARTS THE DAY WITH THE PLEDGE.

Reprinted by permission: Tribune Media Services.

explain why: "television alters the behavior of institutions in direct proportion to the amount of coverage provided or allowed," and "the more coverage an institution secures, the greater its public stature and the more significant its role." [6]

We have already described how strongly media in general, and television in particular, influence who becomes eligible for presidential office and how profoundly the media affect the conduct and outcome of elections. After elections the success of presidential policies, the length, vigor, and effectiveness of a president's political life, and the general level of support for the political system depend heavily on the images that the media convey. Changes in the president's approval ratings are highly correlated with the favorability of news stories. [7] For instance, support for the Vietnam War ebbed after television news showed and condemned American marines leveling Vietnamese villages and reported massacres of Vietnamese civilians by American troops. Television news generated "greater receptivity to darker news about Vietnam. . . . It was the end of the myth that we were different, that we were better." [8] Television also bestowed respectability on vocal opponents of the war by publicizing antiwar activities. President Lyndon B. Johnson considered it hopeless to try to recapture public support for the war after Walter Cronkite announced in 1968 that the war could not be won. As David Halberstam put it: "It was the first time in American history a war had been declared over by an anchorman." [9] Although it is difficult to prove conclusively that Vietnam War coverage had the massive effects that Halberstam claims, circumstantial evidence supports his verdict.

The media frequently raise issues that presidents and other public officials would prefer to keep out of the limelight. Budget deficits, crumbling highways and bridges, and inefficient veterans' hospitals are just a few examples. The Watergate scandal, which led to the resignation of President Richard Nixon, demonstrates how constant media prodding can put a damaging issue at the top of the public agenda despite massive presidential efforts to downplay it. The list of major and minor scandals that the media have highlighted to the government's dismay is seemingly endless—illicit dealings with Iran, corruption in regulating savings and loan associations, bounced checks at the congressional bank, tasteless jokes by members of the president's cabinet, and on and on.

Media coverage can increase as well as undermine public support for a president's policies. This is particularly important in national emergencies when backing by Congress and the public is vital. For instance, in August 1964 only 42 percent of the American public supported President Johnson's Vietnam policies. Many questioned his ability to continue to raise men and money for the war. After the president broadcast an explanation, however, these doubts were apparently dispelled; approval ratings of his Vietnam policies rose to a comfortable 72 percent. Similarly, President Nixon's dispatch of troops to Cambodia in April 1970 won a 50 percent approval rating after he explained it on television. Prior to the broadcast, only 7 percent of the public had approved. Favorable ratings for President Jimmy Carter's foreign policy jumped by 34 percentage points from 22 to 56 percent after the news media announced that the 1978 Camp David meeting had produced a peace settlement between Egypt and Israel. But such steep gains may be short-lived because memories fade quickly. President Bush's approval ratings during the Persian Gulf War in spring 1991 reached nearly 90 percent. Nine months later, they were below 50 percent and still dropping. Predictions that wartime success would sustain his popularity throughout the 1992 election campaign proved incorrect.

By highlighting problems, requesting government action, or reporting demands for action, media stories may spur new policies or change existing policies. In Chapter 6 we discussed the role played by investigative journalism in supporting proposed reforms, such as home health care regulation. To a lesser degree, ordinary stories that cover problems in the welfare system, environmental hazards, or consumer fraud also generate executive and legislative action. Sometimes the mere threat of publicity has been used by media personnel to force presidents and bureaucrats to act.

Sensational adverse publicity can kill as well as generate programs. For instance, the publicity following the accident at the Three Mile Island nuclear plant in Pennsylvania in 1979 predictably resulted in sharp curbs in the production of nuclear energy. Welfare programs, such as Head Start's prekindergarten training for underprivileged children or financial aid for minority businesses, were sharply cut in the wake of news about inefficient management and corrupt handling of money.

Media publicity can also be crucial in determining whether a presidential appointee will be confirmed by the Senate. During the Reagan administration, highly unfavorable media publicity was instrumental in killing the nominations to the Supreme Court of Robert H. Bork, attacked for his conservative legal views on civil rights, women's rights, and privacy; and Douglas Ginsburg, condemned for using marijuana at various stages in his life. In the same way, media stories about womanizing, heavy drinking, and other personal excesses by Senator John Tower were blamed in his failure to gain Senate approval for nomination as President Bush's Secretary of Defense. As television critic Tom Shales said about the Bork nomination: "Television may not have cooked 'his goose' but it certainly did some gourmet basting." [10]

Direct and Mediated Transmission

Audio-visual and print images about government are conveyed either directly or indirectly. Direct conveyance allows government officials to transmit their messages with a minimum of shaping by the media. President Harry S. Truman was the first to use the direct mode by broadcasting his entire State of the Union message in 1947 to a nationwide audience. In January 1961 President Kennedy further expanded direct coverage by allowing telecasts of news conferences to be broadcast live. Among public officials, presidents enjoy the greatest opportunities for uncontrolled access to the American people. As noted in Chapter 3, political leaders competing with the president for power and public support have tried for matching privileges with only moderate success.

Of course, even live television and radio broadcasts are not totally devoid of media influence because camera angles and other photographic techniques slant all presentations somewhat. For example, when President Reagan visited a military cemetery in Bitburg, Germany, to lay a wreath on the graves in 1985, CBS wanted to convey the essence of the controversy by filming the president against the backdrop of Nazi storm troopers' graves. The White House, disclaiming any intent to honor fallen Nazi soldiers, tried but failed to persuade the network to film the scene from a different angle.[11]

Instant commentary following presidential remarks has often blunted their impact. Likewise, print news stories describing a presidential news conference, even when they are followed by the full transcript, involve shaping by media personnel. Compared with the great leeway that newspeople usually have in choosing and interpreting information about the presidency, this type of control is minimal, however.

Indirect or mediated transmission—the shaping of news presentations by media personnel—lies at the heart of the tensions between media and government because it bestows more power on the media than governments like to surrender. Mediated transmission permits journalists to pick and choose from among the facts given to them. They routinely chop lengthy official statements into brief one- or two-sentence quotes and then weave them into an account often supplemented with information gathered from hostile sources. Television sound bites, which used to average 45 seconds in earlier decades, now average under 9 seconds. They rarely exceed 20 seconds. Thus the story is presented in a framework chosen and controlled by the media. By judiciously selecting spokespeople for specific points of view, and by structuring questions to elicit answers that fit neatly into the desired scripts, newspeople can evaluate public officials and policies at will. These appraisals are frequently negative, especially when the popularity of an administration is already falling. Newspeople are often accused of using mediated coverage deliberately, or at the least carelessly, to hurt public officials and their policies. Table 9-3 shows how various news sources quoted on the three major networks appraised President Bush's foreign and domestic policies during the first nine months of 1991. As has been common, the president received higher marks, albeit still predominantly negative ones, for foreign than for domestic policies. Eighty-nine percent of the ratings made by Republicans were positive, compared to 39 percent of ratings by the more numerous Democrats. In the previous year, without the image boost provided by the Gulf War, only 10 percent of the ratings by Democrats had been favorable.[12]

Media Goals and Tactics

Media personnel refute the charge that they go out of their way to show incumbent administrations in a bad light. They contend that they are looking for lively, significant stories that will earn them the respect of their colleagues and the acclaim of their readers and viewers. They see themselves as guardians of the public interest who help to

Table 9-3 How Sources Rated President Bush's Policies, January 1 to September 30, 1991

Policies	% Positive	% Negative	# of Sources
Foreign Policies			
Dealing with Soviets	58	42	33
Baltics	52	48	23
Persian Gulf	49	51	427
Israel and Palestinians	33	67	67
China	32	68	31
Aid to Kurds	24	76	37
Total foreign policies	46	54	744
Domestic Policies			
Environment	24	76	38
AIDS	19	81	36
Recession	15	85	26
Unemployment	14	86	29
Education	11	89	27
Total domestic policies	19	81	350
Total all policies	38	62	1,094

Source: Table compiled by the author with data taken from Robert and Linda Lichter, *Media Monitor* V: 9, November 1991, Center for Media and Public Affairs, Washington, D.C.
Note: Figures combine ABC, CBS, and NBC Nightly News.

make government more honest and efficient, and they believe that they have a duty to report the government's problems and wrongdoings. The actors who produced the unfortunate situation, not the newspeople who reported it, should be blamed, they argue. Politicians who attack the media for focusing on bad news are accused of resembling the ancient Greeks who often killed bearers of bad tidings. This is what reporter William J. Small had in mind when he entitled his book about government and the media *To Kill a Messenger.*[13]

As noted earlier, since news focuses on nonroutine aspects of political life, journalists cover many stories that deal with isolated instances of socially undesirable behavior that reflect badly on government. Media personnel assigned to the presidential beat regularly feature harsh criticism of presidential programs, particularly if it is voiced by politically influential opponents. Minor sins are often blown up as if they were major transgressions. For example, Martin Plissner, the political editor of CBS News, dug out from the back pages of the *New*

York Daily News President Carter's racially indelicate remarks that he saw nothing wrong with preserving the ethnic purity of neighborhoods. Then he asked one of his reporters to question the president about them at a press conference. Carter fell into the trap, and the story became front-page news, embarrassing a racially tolerant political leader.[14]

Managing a Rocky Marriage

All presidents profess to believe in a free press and to run an open government, but they rapidly develop a distaste for many of the reports about their administration. As President Kennedy told a news conference midway into his term in 1962, "[I am] reading more and enjoying it less." [15]

Presidents' displeasure with media coverage is readily understandable. Media coverage not only embarrasses them regularly and deprives them, to varying degrees, of control over the definition of political situations; it also forces them to talk in clichés that reporters find attractive and, in the process, to put themselves on record in ways that may narrow their options for future action. Media disclosures of secret activities, such as an impending military intervention or a planned price freeze, may actually force the president's hand. Bargaining advantages may be lost through premature publication of news; trivia, conflict, and public wrongdoing may receive undue emphasis.

In the rocky marriage between the press and the president, open battles are comparatively rare. Despite traded accusations that the government manipulates and lies and the press distorts and entraps, each side is fully aware that it depends on the other. If presidents refuse to talk to reporters, as happened often during the Nixon and Reagan years, or if they instruct their staffs and major departments and agencies to refuse interviews, important stories cannot be covered firsthand. Alienating the prime news maker and source of government news is a major catastrophe for any news organization. Reporters' eagerness to get the news firsthand gives the president a tremendous advantage in influencing the substance and spin of news stories.

The media, for their part, can withhold publicity that the president needs or force publicity that he does not want. They can stress the positive or accent the negative. They can give instantaneous live coverage or delay broadcasts until a time of their choosing. In 1987, for example, two of the three major networks refused a request for live coverage of President Reagan's speeches in support of his embattled nomination of Judge Robert Bork to the Supreme Court. All three networks refused to air his plea for additional funding for antigovernment forces in Nicaragua.

The upshot of such an even match between the press and the government is a good deal of fraternizing and cronyism between these two "enemies," often to the dismay of those who would have the press be "pure." Each side works hard to cultivate the other's friendship. They often collaborate in examining political issues and problems. At national party conventions, the leaders regularly provide the networks with live television feeds from different camera angles. Such coziness may reduce journalists' zeal to investigate government's misdeeds. Indeed, charges of collusion have been made when media time and again have suppressed news at the request of government departments or the White House. Many of these instances have concerned questions of national security. In 1980, for example, the press delayed publicizing plans for a U.S. invasion of Iran to rescue American hostages. In 1987 it suppressed technical data about eavesdropping devices designed to intercept information from Soviet marine cables.

The relationship between the media and the chief executive often displays three distinct phases.[16] Initially, there is a honeymoon period, a time of cooperation when the media convey the president's messages about organization of the new administration, appointment of new officials, and plans and proposals for new policies. At this early stage few policies and proposals have been implemented, so there is little opportunity for adverse criticism. Presidents and their advisers, eager to get their story across, make themselves readily available to the media and supply them with ample information.

Once the administration embarks on controversial programs and becomes vulnerable to criticism of its record, the honeymoon ends. This seems to be happening earlier and more abruptly now than in the past.[17] Such stories are attractive to the Washington press corps because they involve dramatic conflicts at the highest levels of government. They can be easily covered through interviews with Washington-based sources. The White House may retaliate by withholding news, by restricting presidential contacts with the press, and by increasing public relations activities.

If the rifts between media and the executive branch become particularly severe, there may be a third period in which both sides retreat from their mutually hostile behavior to a more moderate stance. Frequently, this phase coincides with a reelection campaign during which newspeople try harder to provide impartial coverage, and presidents are more eager to keep newspeople happy. The president may also be able to switch the focus of coverage to foreign affairs, knowing that this is the area least likely to generate hostile coverage. There is political magic in scenes of American presidents visiting China's Great Wall, meeting with world leaders in European capitals, or being welcomed in the Middle East.

Administrations' ability to get along with the media differ considerably. The president's interpersonal skills as well as the nature of the political problems faced by the administration account for much of the variation. In recent history the Kennedy and Reagan administrations have been particularly good at press relations, while the Nixon administration was especially bad. In fact, Nixon's Watergate problems might never have developed into a major scandal if he had been able to charm the press.

The relationship between the executive and media varies not only from one administration to the next but also from one part of the country to another. Frictions are greatest between the White House and the Washington press corps because they are most interdependent, and familiarity breeds a certain amount of contempt. The northeastern seaboard press has a reputation of being more critical than the press in the rest of the country. For this reason most presidents occasionally circumvent the eastern press by scheduling news conferences in other parts of the country and by making major policy announcements away from the East Coast. As Jeb Stuart Magruder, deputy director of Richard Nixon's reelection campaign, explained in his account of the Nixon years, "We were involved in media politics, and we were seeking not only to speak through the media in the usual fashion—press releases, news conferences—but to speak around the media, much of which we considered hostile, to take our message directly to the people." [18]

In the same way, presidents Carter, Reagan, and Bush arranged to visit small communities throughout the country to bask in the adulation of local audiences and local media for the benefit of nationwide television viewers. Taking advantage of new satellite technology, President Bush has made arrangements to be interviewed from his White House television studio by local television and radio stations throughout the country. Portable microwave transmitters beam videotaped signals to satellites 22,500 miles overhead, permitting the president to interact live with local anchors. As Clayton Yeutter, chairman of the Republican National Committee, put it, "You get him on there and he has this interchange with the broadcasters and he calls them all by their first names and he asks them what's going on out in west Texas and on and on. It just plays magnificently." [19]

The technique permits public officials to tailor their unedited, unfiltered messages for specific demographic groups and for single-issue groups, such as pro-life or pro-choice advocates in the abortion issue. The president has used the technology to lobby recalcitrant legislators personally, or through cabinet officials, by conducting briefings in their home territory. The 1991 trade treaty with Mexico is an example. Local anchors in southern California, Texas, and Florida were hooked up with cabinet officials like Labor Secretary Lynn Martin and U.S. Trade Representative Carla Hills to spread the president's appeal for support and counter opposition. Like his predecessor, President Bush also broadcasts a weekly Saturday afternoon radio program, hoping to attract front-page coverage in Sunday papers.

Presidential Communication Strategies

Besides circumventing the eastern press, presidents use an array of strategies to control the substance and tenor of news. Three approaches are particularly common. First and most important, presidents try to win reporters' favor. This is not difficult because presidents are constantly surrounded by people who must have fresh news to earn their pay. Second, presidents try to shape the flow of news to make good publicity more likely and bad publicity less likely. Third, they pace and arrange their work schedules to produce opportunities for favorable media coverage. Each of these strategies will be discussed in turn.

Winning Favor. To woo reporters, presidents offer good story material as well as occasional scoops that may bring distinction to individual reporters. They cultivate reporters' friendship by being accessible, treating them with respect, and arranging for their creature comforts. To keep reporters in line, presidents may threaten them directly or obliquely with withdrawal of privileges. These may include accommodations in the presidential plane, special interviews, or answers to their questions during news conferences. Presidents may attack individual reporters or their organizations for undesirable reporting, as President Kennedy did when he complained to *New York Times* publisher Henry Luce about reporters who had made inaccurate statements concerning the Bay of Pigs disaster. But the protest and requests that the offending reporters be punished were to no avail. No heads rolled in consequence.[20]

Shaping the News Flow. Presidents try to guide the flow of news by the thrust of their commentary and by controlling contacts with the press. For example, when publicity about illegal transfers of arms to Nicaragua had damaged President Reagan's administration, Thomas C. Griscom, the newly appointed director of the Office of Communications, managed to divert media attention from the affair. Reagan was persuaded to spearhead a drive for an "Economic Bill of Rights," including a balanced budget and line-item veto, to cast him into an attractive role. At the same time a monthly economic bulletin was

302 Mass Media and American Politics

distributed nationwide. It included camera-ready copy praising the economic successes of the Reagan administration, such as job growth and lowered inflation. To avoid questions about the Iran-contra affair, presidential contacts with the media were largely restricted to picture sessions. Marlin Fitzwater, the president's press secretary, was even kept in the dark about sensitive aspects of the situation so that he could honestly claim ignorance when reporters asked incriminating questions.[21]

To control news flow and assure that the administration speaks with a single voice, presidents may prohibit their staffs, on pain of dismissal, from publicly disagreeing with their policies. In addition, they may require administrative departments to clear interviews through the White House to avoid conflicting pronouncements on public policies. The Carter and Reagan administrations insisted that officials privy to sensitive information receive approval of their superiors prior to granting interviews to the press. Criticism by the eastern press has been averted by withholding advance copies of speeches or timing them late enough in the evening to preclude adequate coverage in the morning papers in the East.

Presidents also may space out releases so that there is a steady, manageable flow of news. If they want emphasis on a particular story, they may withhold competing news that breaks simultaneously. Sometimes a barrage of news is released or even created to distract attention from sensitive developments. For instance, at the end of the 1976 presidential campaign, Carter feared losses in California and New Jersey. To de-emphasize them, and to focus media attention on his expected victory in Ohio, he altered his travel plans to campaign primarily in Ohio. He also called Chicago's mayor, Richard Daley, just before a mayoral press conference to emphasize that Ohio would be the key state to win—a message Daley immediately passed on to the press. Carter's staff later claimed credit for deflecting media attention from the California and New Jersey primaries and making Ohio the critical state. As Pat Caddell, Carter's pollster, put it: "We orchestrated that. We were in trouble in New Jersey but we knew we were going to win Ohio. Then Daley did it. Of course, we orchestrated that too!"[22]

Orchestrating Coverage. Ways of arranging activities to create favorable publicity are numerous. They include creating newsworthy events, heightening suspense through news blackouts prior to major pronouncements, and staging public ceremonies as media spectacles at times when there are few competing events. Political successes may be coupled with political failures in hopes that publicity for the success will draw attention away from the failure. The Carter administration reportedly timed its announcement of the opening of formal relations with the People's Republic of China late in 1978 to buffer negative publicity if its attempts to clinch a peace settlement between Israel and Egypt failed. In the same way, the Reagan administration hoped that pictures of the American marines' successful military takeover of the tiny island of Grenada would counteract the images of the 1983 bombing of American marines in Lebanon.

News management may even go to the point of deceiving the press in order to present a smoke-screen message to the public. For instance, in 1961, the Kennedy administration told Miami reporters that five thousand U.S. troops had invaded Cuba's Bay of Pigs. This news was intended to encourage Cubans to rise up in support of a large invasion force. In actuality, only one thousand troops had been sent. After the troops ran into trouble, officials admitted that only a few hundred American troops had been involved and that their chief mission had been to land supplies for anti-Castro guerrillas in Cuba rather than to invade the country. When reporters discovered that they had been used to spread false stories, they were furious. The inevitable result was a credibility gap between the executive branch and the media.

Institutional Settings

On the President's Side. A president can shape the news indirectly through appointments to the Federal Communications Commission (FCC) and other public agencies concerned with the media and through informal contacts with personnel in these agencies. Financial lifelines can be controlled through the Office of Management and Budget, which screens the budgetary requests of all federal agencies, including those related to communications. Control can also be wielded through the Justice Department. For instance, the Antitrust Division challenged the FCC's approval of a merger between the American Broadcasting Company and the International Telephone and Telegraph Company. In that case the Justice Department carried a series of appeals through the courts and ultimately to the Supreme Court.

Presidents involve themselves directly in media policy making through various White House organizations, study commissions, and task forces. In 1970 President Nixon created the Office of Telecommunications Policy—the first permanent agency within the White House to plan communications policy. The Carter administration replaced this office with a less powerful organization within the Commerce Department, the National Telecommunications and Information Administration. By downgrading the agency, Carter gave the impression that the White House had distanced itself from communications policy questions and would leave the FCC free from White House pressure. However, a small policy planning staff remained in the White House to advise the president. This divorce of planning from operations still characterizes federal communications policy and has impeded strong executive leadership.

The White House Press Office and the Office of Communications. The Press Office, staffed by the press secretary and his or her deputies, supplies Washington-based reporters with news about the White House. By custom, the press secretary meets almost daily with the White House press corps to make announcements and take questions. These briefings supply reporters with the president's interpretation of events, which they then cast into perspectives of their own choice.

The Office of Communications, which has existed in various incarnations since the Nixon years, is concerned with long-range public relations management of the presidency. In consultation with the president, it determines the images that the administration needs to convey to gain and retain the approval of important constituencies in the public and private sectors, and to win support for desired policies. The office also coordinates the public relations activities of executive branch departments and agencies.

In the Bush administration, the work of the Office of Communications has been divided fivefold.[23] Media Relations involves dealing directly with media for matters such as scheduling public officials for talk show appearances. Public Affairs entails coordinating public relations activities throughout the executive branch. Public Liaison sets up bimonthly meetings between the president and groups of editors, publishers, and reporters outside Washington. The final two divisions are Speechwriting and Research. "The goal is to set the public agenda, to make sure that all parts of the presidential team (the White House staff, cabinet officers, and other executive branch officials) are adhering to that public agenda, and to aggressively promote the agenda through a form of mass marketing.... The ultimate goal is to influence—to the extent possible—what news will appear in the media about the administration and its policies."[24]

Modern public relations activities employ many different techniques. "Focus groups and polling data are used to fashion presidential messages; sound-bites are written into the public pronouncements of the president and his underlings to articulate those messages; public appearances are choreographed so that the messages are reinforced by visual images; and the daily line is enforced to prevent the articulation of conflicting messages."[25] To spread the messages throughout the country, the administration sends cabinet officers and others on speaking tours and arranges satellite interviews in local markets.

It is, of course, essential for a president to "sell" his policies by soliciting wide support for them and by presenting a united front within his administration. However, in the process democracy may be imperiled because, as John Anthony Maltese says in *Spin Control*, "Style is substituted for substance. Complicated issues are transformed into simple slogans and slick sound-bites ... timid, self-interested policymakers ... shy away from responsibility for their actions and delude themselves and their constituents with their own symbolic spectacle." [26]

On the Media's Side. The White House press corps consists of fewer than seventy newspeople who cover the president regularly. Many have considerable experience and reputations to match. The *New York Times, Washington Post, Los Angeles Times, Chicago Tribune, Philadelphia Inquirer,* and other major newspapers have full-time reporters exclusively assigned to the president. So do a number of newspaper chains, such as the Scripps-Howard papers, the Hearst press, and the Newhouse papers. Smaller papers may send their Washington bureau chiefs to the White House whenever there is news of special interest to their region.

Each of the major broadcast networks, as well as Cable Network News (CNN), has several reporters at the White House on a regular basis; smaller networks have one. The Cable Satellite Public Affairs Network (C-SPAN), a twenty-four-hour cable news operation with a staff of more than 150 people, provides White House coverage as well as gavel-to-gavel coverage of the House of Representatives. (C-SPAN sends its signal to more than 3,000 cable systems throughout the country. Although C-SPAN has the potential to reach more than 40 million people, so far the actual audience for government coverage has been quite small.) The White House also is covered by several other all-news cable services, weekly news magazines, and periodicals, as well as photographers and their supporting staffs. Hard economic times in the 1990s have forced cutbacks in personnel and have increased pooling of resources among media organizations. Even major events, such as presidential trips abroad or the national party conventions, are now often covered by a smaller corps of journalists, whose members report to several major news organizations.

Most of the country's dailies do not have a regular Washington correspondent or part-time "stringer" to cover the White House. The same still holds true for most of the country's television and radio stations. Inexpensive satellite time, however, has lowered news transmission costs and boosted the numbers of stations that can afford direct coverage of the Washington scene. Satellites have enabled many small stations to view the activities of the national government through the prism of local interests. News organizations without Washington staffs rely heavily on wire service news. Major domestic and foreign wire services have full-time reporters accredited to the

White House who cover the beat continuously, including presidential trips.

The White House press corps spends much of its time waiting for news from the president's staff. Reporters often find this frustrating and even humiliating. Their press passes give them unlimited access to the White House press room only. Other parts of the White House and executive offices are off limits except by special appointments, which are given out selectively. For public ceremonies in the East Room or Oval Office or Rose Garden, reporters usually are escorted as a group. Some have likened this to being herded like cattle. Many also object to the hero worship and protectiveness that they sense in the president's staff and the frequent occasions when presidents make personal or public moves without first alerting the press corps.

Forms of Contact

Press Releases and News Briefings. The release of news by chief executives or their aides takes a number of routinized forms. Most of these represent a concerted effort to control news output. The most common is the *press release,* a story prepared by government officials and handed to members of the press, usually without an opportunity for questions. It can be used verbatim, and officials hope that it will be. To make sure that the release appears at the most opportune time, it often has a date line that stipulates the earliest time when it may be published. If an administration wants to give the appearance of great activity or to distract reporters' attention from areas of undesired publicity, it may publish a flood of releases simultaneously. The Carter administration also initiated a program of taping thirty- to forty-second radio spots to be distributed to stations around the country on request. In this way stations receive the news in a ready-made version controlled by the White House. In a *news briefing* reporters have an opportunity to ask the press secretary about the news releases. But because executive officials furnish the news for the briefing, they control the substance and tone of the discussion. Although most press secretaries, as well as members of the press, believe that daily news briefings are unnecessary and could be covered just as well by press releases, the briefings have become traditional.

News Conferences. While a *news conference* may appear to be a wide-open question period, it is usually controlled tightly by the official being questioned. News conferences are a form of political theater, staged, directed, and partially written by top executives to cast themselves in praiseworthy roles. Seemingly spontaneous answers usually have been carefully prepared by experts on the executive's staff and rehearsed during extensive briefings that precede news conferences.

Since the days of Theodore Roosevelt, the first president to summon reporters to the White House regularly, presidents have initiated news conferences. Before John F. Kennedy's presidency, press conferences were not covered live, permitting the White House to make corrections before conference records were broadcast. Kennedy, who was a gifted extemporaneous speaker, stripped away this cloak of protection by allowing live filming of the conference. At the time, press critics called it "goofy" and likened it to "making love in Carnegie Hall." [27]

The live format remains controversial because it leads to posturing by the president as well as by members of the press. It also causes embarrassment for presidents who misspeak or suffer memory lapses. President Bush has lowered the risk by mostly holding informal news conferences on short notice, which makes it difficult to broadcast the live event without costly interruptions of scheduled programs. The informal format suits Bush's style, which is far less majestic than that of his former boss, Ronald Reagan.

Presidents often begin the event with a lengthy statement designed to set the conference's tone. The president may lead off with topics for which he wants headlines, or he may seek to divert media attention away from politically embarrassing issues. Presidents may generate questions by letting it be known ahead of time that certain types of queries will receive very interesting answers. They can often control the subject and tone of a news conference by recognizing friendly reporters for questions and avoiding follow-up questions. But no president has been able to squelch embarrassing questions entirely or to deny reporters the chance to use their questions as opportunities to express their own views about controversial issues.[28] Reporters revel in acting like prosecutors trying to extract a confession of major crimes from a hapless subject. Through posing leading questions, they try to force the president into making statements that he does not wish to make.

Backgrounders. Some news conferences are off-the-record *backgrounders* called by high officials to give newspeople important background information that they are honor bound to keep entirely secret or to publish only without revealing its source. Various forms of vague attribution are usually permitted, such as "government sources say," "it has been reported by reliable sources," or even more specifically, "the White House discloses" or the "Defense Department indicates."

Government officials like backgrounders because they are a relatively safe way to "test the waters." They permit officials to bring a variety of policy ideas before their colleagues and the public without openly identifying with them. Secretary of State Henry Kissinger used backgrounders to submit foreign policy options for public debate and to warn foreign countries that their behavior was unacceptable to the United States. To discourage the Soviet Union's support of India in a war with Pakistan, Kissinger told reporters in a backgrounder that Soviet policy might lead President Nixon to cancel a planned trip to Moscow. If the statement had been officially attributed to Kissinger, it would have constituted a threat that might have undermined détente with the Soviet Union.

Similarly, Secretary of Defense Caspar Weinberger summoned reporters to a secret briefing in 1982 to provide them with data on Soviet military capacity that would substantiate the administration's claim that the Soviet Union posed a grave military threat to the United States and Europe. The data—photographs produced by satellites and secret electronic systems—had been withheld because of fears that disclosure might alert the Soviet Union to U.S. surveillance tactics. Weinberger hoped that in the wake of a confidential viewing of these photographs, reporters would no longer publicly question the administration's claims of danger. Public support for Reagan's defense policies might then increase.

Unlike government officials, reporters are ambivalent about backgrounders. They like having access to news that might otherwise be unavailable, but they dislike being prevented from publishing all aspects of the story or from giving the source of the information so that the story can be placed in its proper perspective. At times reporters have evaded the prohibition on source disclosure by refusing to attend a background briefing and then reporting the story as told to them by reporters who attended. To prevent such leaks, government officials have occasionally solicited written pledges from reporters that they would not reveal information released during briefings. Usually reporters refuse to sign.

Ad Hoc Encounters

In addition to formal encounters, reporters and the president or White House staff meet informally in work or social settings. Frequently, the most probing stories about White House activities come from reporters not ordinarily assigned to cover the president. The regulars would be too vulnerable to retaliation by the White House if they wrote such penetrating reports.

Top government officials, and occasionally the president, may agree to be interviewed on programs such as "Nightline," "Good Morning America," the "Today" show, "Meet the Press," or "Face the Nation." Questioning on these shows can resemble a brutal inquisition. Executive officials participate anyhow because these programs provide excellent opportunities to present the administration's position to an interested nationwide audience. Besides, if questioning becomes excessively harsh, the audience often feels sorry for the targets and sides with them.

Leaks. An even less formal release of news occurs through *leaks,* the surreptitious release of information by government sources who wish to remain anonymous. Officials may leak information that they are not authorized to release or that they do not wish to release formally. Sometimes low-level officials leak information to gain attention from top officials.

Leaks are mixed blessings. They can destroy the timing of negotiations, alienate the parties whose secrets have been betrayed, and cause great harm by disclosing politically sensitive matters. They also may bring important suppressed issues to needed public attention, serve as trial balloons, and permit government officials to release information anonymously. Although presidents frequently leak confidential stories, they passionately hate news leaks by others. Because the source is hidden, personal confrontation and punishment are impossible. All recent presidents have therefore used federal investigative agencies such as the Federal Bureau of Investigation and the Central Intelligence Agency to find the sources of news leaks.

A typical leak occurred in 1991 during the Senate confirmation battle over the nomination of Judge Clarence Thomas to the U.S. Supreme Court. Confidential allegations presented to the Senate Judiciary Committee about sexual harassment by the nominee were leaked to the press. The leaks led to a second round of lengthy, acrimonious hearings before the nominee was confirmed. The episode did serious harm to Judge Thomas's reputation and undermined faith in the integrity of the confirmation process.

The harm that leaks cause must be weighed against their benefits. In a system in which the executive maintains tight control over the formal channels of news, leaks provide a valuable counterbalance. President Reagan's controversial budget proposals in 1983 are a case in point. Administration insiders, eager to bring their concerns to the public and Congress, resorted to almost daily leaks of economic appraisals that contradicted the president's views. An irate Reagan proclaimed, "I've had it up to my keister with these leaks," but he modified his budget plans nonetheless.[29]

The Media and Congress

According to political folklore, the presidency basks in the limelight of publicity at all times while Congress waits in the shadows. The television age has permanently altered the balance of political power, making the president dominant and the legislature inferior, political observers claim. As Sen. J. William Fulbright of Arkansas told Congress in 1970, "Television has done as much to expand the powers of the President as would a constitutional amendment formally abolishing the co-equality of the three branches of government." [30]

Image vs. Reality

If one probes beyond these impressions to the underlying facts, the situation appears less clear. When coverage of areas of legislative concerns is added to coverage that mentions Congress explicitly, Congress and the presidency receive roughly the same amount of national news attention. Moreover, it must be remembered that the bulk of coverage of Congress comes through stories about individual members published in their home states. Although local coverage does not generally attract national attention, it is politically crucial for each member.

In terms of substance, presidential coverage and congressional coverage did not differ noticeably. Table 9-4 presents a comparison of ten issues that emerged for television coverage of the president and Congress when issues were tallied on a monthly basis. The scores represent a combination of offerings by ABC, CBS, and NBC. The three networks showed almost identical patterns in the types of issues selected for stories about the presidency and Congress, with the Persian Gulf crisis and the budget receiving most coverage for both institutions. Placement of stories within the broadcast was also quite similar, further evidence of the uniformity of news judgment. However, the networks differed in the total amounts of time allotted to particular stories. Each network devoted considerably more time to presidential than to congressional stories, confirming that "435 members of the House and 100 members of the Senate compete for the crumbs of network time left after the president has got his share." [31]

The large proportion of time devoted to the Gulf crisis is a graphic example of the media's obsession with highly dramatic events at the expense of other important news. For the twelve-month time span covered by the table, the Gulf crisis constituted 34 percent of presidential news and 17 percent of congressional news. By contrast, news about the economy appeared in less than 1 percent of presidential and congressional stories.

Table 9-1 showed that Congress averages five hours of media coverage monthly on the nightly television news, compared to eight hours for the president. Why does Congress fare worse than the presidency? There are several reasons. Most importantly, the presidency makes a better media target because it is a single-headed

Table 9-4 Top Ten Issues on Network Evening News about the President and Congress, July 1990-June 1991

Issue	Story rank [a]			Time	n	% of N
	1	2	3			
President						
Persian Gulf Crisis	62	26	13	50:57	535	34.0
Budget	69	21	10	7:01	97	6.2
Soviet relations	53	25	23	5:58	80	5.1
Iraqi unrest/Kurds	75	20	5	4:40	61	3.9
Supreme Court	68	28	4	1:52	25	1.6
Civil rights bill	39	46	15	1:08	26	1.7
South American trip [b]	73	27	—	1:01	11	.7
Bush's health [b]	65	20	15	0:53	20	1.3
November election	33	58	8	0:53	12	.8
Economy [b]	57	36	7	0:52	14	.9
Average/total	60	31	10	75:15	881	56.2
Congress						
Persian Gulf Crisis	47	32	21	21:00	187	16.9
Budget	67	20	13	7:23	106	9.6
Supreme Court	62	28	10	1:51	29	2.6
Soviet relations	83	—	17	1:26	18	1.6
November election	33	52	14	1:22	21	1.9
Iraqi unrest/Kurds	64	29	7	1:15	14	1.3
Civil rights bill	33	52	15	1:10	27	2.4
Savings and loan [b]	43	38	19	0:59	21	1.9
Gun control [b]	54	15	31	0:41	13	1.2
Neil Bush and S & L [b]	40	50	10	0:26	10	.9
Average/total	53	32	16	37:33	446	40.3

Source: Compiled by the author from the Vanderbilt Television News Archives Index.
Note: N for President = 1,572; N for Congress = 1,108. The numbers are combined monthly scores for ABC, CBS, and NBC early evening newscasts. Stories are rank ordered by time. Time is in hours and minutes. Some percentages have been rounded.

[a] Expressed in percentage of number of stories on particular issue.

[b] Top-ranked issues not shared by Congress and the President.

institution readily personified, filmed, and recorded in the visible person of the chief executive. This gives the media and media audiences a familiar, easily dramatized focus of attention. Even stories originating from congressional sources frequently feature the president as the main actor. Stephen Hess reports that 71 percent of news stories about the president or Congress come from legislative sources, but Congress is the main actor in only 48 percent. Conversely, in the 29 percent of stories about the president or Congress that originate with the executive branch, 52 percent focus on the executive.[32]

The president is like a superstar surrounded by a cast of supporting actors. As the personification of the nation, the president can usually command national television or radio time, often at prime time and simultaneously on all major networks. During a recent ten-year period, three out of eleven congressional requests for television coverage were granted, compared with forty-four out of forty-five for the president.[33]

In contrast to the presidency, Congress is a many-headed hydra with no single widely familiar personal focus.[34] Its activities are conducted simultaneously in more than one hundred locations on Capitol Hill. No individual member can command nationwide media coverage at will. Even well-known senators and representatives are viewed as spokespersons for their own or their party's views, or as potential presidential candidates, not as spokespersons for Congress as an institution. Their celebrity status often has little to do with their legislative activity in Congress. In fact, there has never been a single spokesperson for Congress in general, or even for the Senate or House, because senators and representatives are loath to designate one of their number as *primus inter pares*. Consequently, most stories about Congress deal with individual members or legislative activity on specific issues rather than with the body as a whole.

Another reason why stories on Congress escape wide attention lies in the nature of its work. The legislative branch drafts laws, makes compromises among conflicting interests, forges shifting coalitions, and works out legal details. Stories about the executive branch that describe *what* is actually done are far more memorable than reports about *how* the laborious process of hammering out legislation works. Besides, the most interesting aspect of the legislative process, the shaping of broad guidelines for policy, is usually reported by the media as part of the work of the executive branch. Congress, to quote Chris Matthews, press secretary to Speaker Thomas P. O'Neill, is "the Hamburger Helper to the White House Story." [35]

Congressional coverage is frequently not as useful to the public as it could be because the media concentrate on readily available stories. In the early stages of the legislative process, when there is still time for citizens to influence a bill, congressional coverage has been least ample. Coverage usually focuses on final action that merely ratifies the work of committees and subcommittees. Citizens learn what the new policies are without being exposed to the pros and cons and the political interplay that led to the ultimate compromise.[36] Live television coverage of congressional sessions is changing this and is making Congress more vulnerable to constituent and interest group pressures.

Fearing that legislative floor sessions would present an unedifying, boring spectacle, Congress resisted live radio and television coverage of most sessions until the late 1970s. Prior to 1979 only selected committee hearings were televised, primarily those involving spicy topics such as labor racketeering, Communists in government, or high-level corruption. These televised sessions became highly dramatic morality plays, with casts of sinners brought to justice and congressional knights battling evil before the public. Senators such as Harry Truman and Estes Kefauver and beetle-browed Sam Ervin were catapulted into the national limelight by these hearings. Many of the targets of the investigations, on the other hand, were harmed by the damaging publicity, even when they were later officially exonerated of any misdeeds. Few ordinary congressional sessions could provide comparable drama. As the *Philadelphia Inquirer* noted after the hearings on organized crime conducted by Senator Kefauver's committee, there is simply "no show like watching people thrown to the lions." [37]

In 1979 the House of Representatives lifted the prohibition on televising its floor sessions. The action was prompted in part by the desire to counterbalance the political advantages reaped by the executive branch from heavy media attention. House sessions began to be telecast by a House-run closed circuit system. The rules for coverage are strict: only the member speaking may be filmed, *not* the listeners. This stipulation bars the public from seeing the typically near-empty House chamber and inattentive members. Commercial, cable, and public television systems have access to the House broadcasts but rarely cover them. The broadcasts have received their widest dissemination through live gavel-to-gavel coverage by C-SPAN.

In 1986 the Senate finally followed suit and permitted live coverage of its proceedings. It was prodded by the concern that the Senate was "fast becoming the invisible half of Congress," in the words of Sen. Robert Byrd, D-W.Va. Byrd thus phrased the political rationale: "We cannot hold our own with the White House and the House of Representatives when it comes to news coverage of the important issues of the day." [38] Sen. Robert Dole, R-Kan., called televised proceedings "an electronic bridge to the American people." [39] Apparently, other senators shared his view; an unusually large number of senators crossed that bridge dressed more nattily than usual and sporting well-polished rhetoric.

Televised sessions have not changed the publicity balance between the president and Congress. For the reasons outlined, Congress has not become a first-rate "show." A few interesting and unexpected results of congressional coverage have been reported, however. Representatives themselves are apparently among the most avid watchers of House coverage because the television cameras permit them to monitor sessions that they previously missed. Now they can keep up on floor action and issues reported by committees other than their own.[40] Members of Congress are generally unable to edit their videotaped remarks before they are broadcast, unlike their statements in the *Congressional Record.* This has made the legislators more cautious in their televised utterances. They do not wish to create images that may haunt their careers. Rather they try to use their appearances to create favorable images for themselves and their pet political projects.

Brief, quotable statements made by members in time to appear on the evening news have multiplied. Some members have claimed that recent sharp increases in the time spent to pass legislation are largely due to television coverage. More members want to be heard and they are likely to take more extreme positions because the media tend to focus on confrontations.[41] The added publicity also may make incumbent representatives even more unbeatable at the polls than they are now. In addition, broadcasting may make it more difficult for congressional leaders to keep the voices of dissident members muffled. It may be harder to reach legislative compromises once representatives have publicly committed themselves to definite positions. However, there is no solid proof thus far that television coverage has harmed consensus-building in the chamber.

Writing Congress Stories

Newspeople assigned to the congressional beat use general criteria of newsworthiness and gatekeeping to decide who and what will be covered and who and what will be ignored. Exciting, novel, or controversial topics that can be made personally relevant to the public and simply presented have precedence over recurrent complex and mundane problems, such as congressional reorganization or the annual farm bill. Orderly, dispassionate debate usually is passed over in favor of purple rhetoric and wild accusations that can produce catchy headlines. Heated confrontations are more likely to occur in the more intimate committee hearings than in full sessions. Accordingly, committee hearings attract most extensive coverage, particularly on television.

Since Congress is a regular beat, daily press briefings are conducted by the leaders of each chamber. Major media organizations such as the *Washington Post* and the *New York Times,* major newspaper chains such as Gannett, Hearst, and Knight, and the television networks and wire services have full-time reporters covering Congress. Some of these reporters are specialists in various policy areas. Some wire service reporters, for example, concentrate on news of interest to specific regions such as the West or South. There are also Washington "stringer" bureaus whose reporters serve assorted subscriber news services throughout the country. Specialized news services such as Congressional Quarterly cover the congressional beat in detail for professional audiences. In all, more than 3,500 correspondents are accredited to the press galleries in the House and Senate.[42]

Congressional press releases and written reports provide news sources without a regular reporter on Capitol Hill with much of their information about Congress. These documents are prepared and distributed by congressional press secretaries because wire service reporters are unable to attend the many hearings occurring simultaneously. Press releases enable members of Congress to tell their stories in their own words. They give an advantage to members whose offices can turn out interesting public statements. In 1970 only 16 percent of House offices reported that they had a staffer with press responsibilities; by 1986 that figure had risen to 76 percent.

Senators generally receive considerably more press coverage than do representatives, even though an equal number of reporters cover both houses. On network television, stories about senators outnumber those about representatives more than six to one, probably because senators have greater prominence, prestige, and publicity resources and their larger constituencies make them of interest to a wider audience. In general, high media visibility for senators as well as representatives hinges on serving in important leadership positions and being a congressional veteran. By contrast, sponsoring legislation or service on important committees matters little. Who one is obviously counts more than what one does. In practice, this means that more than half of the congressional membership receives no national television exposure at all. A mere twenty members of the Senate garner the lion's share of attention.[43]

Unlike the president, neither senators nor representatives enjoy automatic coverage of whatever they say and do, even though they issue frequent press releases and call occasional news conferences. However, on certain topics, such as tax policy or investigation of executive activities, congressional spokespersons, rather than the president, are routinely sought out. Additionally, many members of Congress receive regular local coverage through their own news columns or radio or television programs. They usually find their relations with the local media far more congenial than relations with a national press corps that cares little about focusing on the problems of particular congressional districts. Local media depend on senators and representatives for local angles to national stories because local slants make these stories more attractive to the target audiences. Since their Washington-based senators and representatives are ideal sources, newspeople are loath to criticize them.

Functions of Media

The functions performed by the national media for Congress and by Congress for the national media parallel press-presidency relations. However, there are major qualitative differences in the relationship. Neither Congress nor the media need the services of the other as much as the presidency needs the press. The national media can afford to alienate some legislators without losing direct access to congressional news. Similarly, except when passage of major controversial laws is involved, legislators can ignore national publicity and rely instead on publicity in their districts. News about national events and national public opinion is also somewhat less important to most members of Congress than to the president. The home media, rather than national news providers, are particularly important to legislators as sources of news relevant for their own constituents and as channels for transmitting messages to the home district while they are working in Washington.

National as well as local media provide senators and representatives with forums to express their views on political issues and to attract public support for themselves and their causes. Publicity is especially important for minority party leaders, who may need the media to pressure an unresponsive majority to accede to their concerns. However, frequent coverage is limited to a few stars whose names have become familiar because of their leadership positions in the House or Senate or because they headed dramatic congressional investigations. Most members cannot use "outsider strategies" because they rarely receive enough coverage to greatly enhance their legislative effectiveness or reelection chances. In an average year, a third of the Senate and half of the House receives no coverage at all in the national media.[44]

For a few members of Congress, national media attention may be a springboard to legislative effectiveness and to higher office, including the presidency. Once members achieve visibility, their fame often grows by its own momentum. They become regulars on interview shows, and their opinions are solicited when national issues are debated. However, members rarely receive the extensive personal coverage that presidents get. Even at best, when Thomas P. ("Tip") O'Neill became the most televised speaker in history because he personified the opposition to Reagan during his first two years in office, he still appeared on only 7 percent of the network evening news programs. By contrast, presidents nearly always (97 percent of the time) rate at least one story each day and usually two or three.[45] For most members media attention may do little more than make them visible targets for lobby groups. This may lead to reelection support from these groups or research support for pet projects. Publicity also may fuel support for the opposition. It may provide ammunition for rival candidates during the next election campaign.[46]

For members of Congress who are not aspiring to higher office and who do not need nationwide attention to achieve their legislative goals, national publicity may be practically irrelevant. By contrast, favorable media coverage in their districts is essential to let their constituents know what they are doing and to pave the way for reelection. A 1986 poll of press secretaries showed that they considered stories in local dailies, local weeklies, and press releases as the most valuable outlets. Televised floor proceedings, *New York Times* coverage, and network television news were deemed least productive.[47] As indicated, local publicity is usually easy for members to obtain. Several members of Congress have even owned mass media outlets, which ensured them ample favorable coverage. Lyndon Johnson is a prominent example. Many members also communicate through newsletters and individual letters sent to selected constituents. Some prepare cable television programs for their district or transmit carefully chosen video excerpts from committee meetings to home district media. Still others, eager to push their legislative agendas, write op-ed pieces for the local and national media. Nearly half of the senators use this strategy, as do 16 percent of the House members.[48]

In addition to full- or part-time media consultants, senators and representatives have studios available on Capitol Hill where they can produce low-cost video tapes, films, and audio tapes to distribute to their constituents.[49] Seventy-five percent of the House members and 80 percent of the Senate members use these facilities to make broadcasts for home-town distribution. Relationships between Congress members and journalists also benefit from the liaison services performed by the nonpartisan press galleries maintained by each chamber. In operation for more than a century, these galleries handle matters affecting the credentials and working facilities of the press.[50]

A Cautious Relationship

Just as the functions that media perform are similar for the executive and legislative branches, so is the love-hate relationship. But it, too, is less ardent for Congress, even though mutual recriminations are plentiful. Senators and representatives, competing with peers for media attention, bemoan lack of coverage of their pet projects and pronouncements. They complain that reporters treat them as if they were scoundrels conspiring to defraud the public. As Table 9-5 indicates, they have reason to lament the little positive coverage they receive. In fact, congressional coverage is considerably more negative than coverage of the presidency or the Supreme Court.[51] Members of

Table 9-5 An Evaluation of Press Coverage of Congress (in percentage of stories)

Newspaper	Positive	Negative	Neutral	Editorial ratio [a]
Atlanta Constitution	9	34	56	1:2.1
Boston Globe	14	32	53	1:1.8
Chicago Sun-Times	5	26	68	1:3.8
Dallas Morning News	5	18	78	1:1.8
Denver Post	12	32	57	1:1.1
Los Angeles Times	4	20	75	1:10
Miami Herald	6	27	67	1:2.4
Minnesota Star	5	29	66	1:2
Philadelphia Inquirer	8	40	53	1:3
Washington Post	5	21	75	1:2.4

Source: Adapted from Charles M. Tidmarch and John J. Pitney, Jr., "Covering Congress: An Analysis of Reportage and Commentary in Ten Metropolitan Newspapers," *Polity* 17 (Spring 1985): 480. Reprinted by permission.

Note: N = 2,299 stories, including news, analysis, editorials, op-ed items, and cartoons. The data in the table are based on content analysis of all Congress-related stories that appeared during thirty days spanning July and August 1978.

[a] Ratio of positive to negative editorials with neutral editorials excluded.

Congress resent the cross-examinations that reporters love to conduct with a prosecutor's zeal and with an air of infallibility. They charge and can prove that the media emphasize trivia, scandals, internal dissent, and official misconduct, but often ignore congressional consensus and passage of significant legislation. They blame the media for the declining prestige of Congress.

The media, in turn, complain with justification about legislators' efforts to manage the news through their professional publicity staffs. They point to members' lack of candor and to their exclusion of media personnel from many congressional meetings and executive sessions. Broadcasters also resent the strict controls placed on their coverage of congressional sessions. They are barred from taping their own stories and are limited in the subjects they can photograph.

But senators and representatives realize that they need the media for information and for the publicity that is crucial to passing or defeating legislation. They know that the media will discreetly ignore their personal foibles so long as no official wrongdoing is involved. Newspeople, in turn, realize that they need individual legislators for information about congressional activities and as a counterfoil and source of leaks to check the executive branch. Members are valuable for inside comments that can personalize otherwise dull stories. Congress often creates story topics for the media by investigating dramatic ongoing problems like auto or mine safety. A congressional inquiry may be the catalyst that turns an everyday event into a newsworthy item. The story then may ride the crest of publicity for quite some time, creating its own fresh and reportable events until it recedes into limbo once more. Newspeople do not want to dry up these sources; nor do media enterprises want to forgo the financial rewards generated by paid campaign commercials.

Congress and Communications Policy

The media, particularly radio and television, are aware of the power Congress has over regulatory legislation. In the past Congress made little use of its power to legislate communications policy, viewing it as a hornet's nest of political conflict best left alone. The major exception was passage of the Communications Act of 1934, which granted broad authority to the Federal Communications Commission (FCC), and of supplementary laws dealing with technical innovations. Periodic attempts to supersede the act have floundered, but the power to legislate communications policy remains. If and when strong, unified pressures from industry or consumer groups develop, Congress's powers to legislate communications policy could become important. Meanwhile, there is a vacuum in both policy formulation and oversight of administration that neither the president nor the FCC has attempted to fill.[52] Communications industry representatives have occasionally jumped into the breach. They are in a strong position to push their ideas because they enjoy a near monopoly over the basic information needed to make policy.

The communications subcommittees of the Commerce, Science, and Transportation Committee in the Senate and of the Energy and Commerce Committee in the House control communications policy largely through the power of investigation. The FCC has been investigated more frequently than most other regulatory bodies. In fact since 1970 more than fifty different congressional committees and subcommittees have reviewed various FCC activities. But there have been few dramatic results beyond spending a significant share of the commission's limited resources on responding to these investigations. Investigations have included reviews of specific FCC actions, studies of FCC operations and structures, examinations of broad policy issues such as the impact of television's portrayal of the aged or of alcohol and drug abuse, and studies of corruption in television game shows. The appropriations committees have wielded their power over the FCC's purse in a desultory way. They occasionally have denied funds for the commission or explicitly directed what particular programs should be funded.[53] However, monetary control may be stricter in the future because Congress switched the FCC in 1982 from the status of a permanently authorized agency to one requiring biennial renewal.

Although the Senate has seldom used confirmation hearings to impress its views on new FCC commissioners, this does not mean that the views of powerful senators have been ignored. Prospective commissioners are likely to study past confirmation hearings carefully and take their cues from them. Most presidential nominees have been confirmed. Appointments are usually made to reward the politically faithful.[54] While congressional control over the FCC has generally been light, there is always the possibility of stricter control. All the parties interested in communications policy, including the White House and the courts, pay deference to that possibility.

Congressional control over the media also includes matters such as postal rates and subsidies, legislation on permissible mergers and chain control of papers, and laws designed to keep failing newspapers alive. Copyright laws, which affect print and electronic media productions, are involved, too. So are policies and regulations about telecommunication satellites, broadcast spectrum allocations, and cable television. The vast, congressionally guided changes in the telephone industry are yet another area of major concern to media interests.

Laws regulating media procedures occasionally have a strong impact on media content and policies. For instance, FCC encouragement of diversification of radio programs was largely responsible for the development of a sizable number of FM rock music stations. These stations were able to provide alternatives to more conventional programs. Congressional scrutiny of documentaries may chill investigative reporting. Congress probed the circumstances surrounding a documentary on drug use at a major university because the events were allegedly staged, and it also looked into the accuracy of charges of illicit public relations activity by the Pentagon. Former Democratic senator John Pastore of Rhode Island, who was deeply concerned about television violence, helped create the Surgeon General's Advisory Committee on Television and Social Behavior, which has investigated violence in television shows in preparation for congressional action.[55] Congressional failure to act may also have far-reaching consequences for the mass media. For instance, as long as Congress did not regulate cable television, this medium was left under control of the FCC, the courts, and various state and local governments.

News Impact on Congress Members

On the whole, despite ample negative coverage, the media treat congressional leaders and Congress with a fair amount of deference and respect. Media critic Ben Bagdikian has even charged that the media are an effective propaganda arm for Congress that virtually guarantees the reelection of any incumbent who is willing to run. "Most of the media are willing conduits for the highly selective information the member of Congress decides to feed the electorate," he argues.[56] This claim is exaggerated; many factors unrelated to media coverage contribute to the high reelection rate of incumbents. Besides, the media often present incumbents in an unfavorable light, and do not publicize the bulk of their self-promoting press releases. A study of the Third Congressional District in Wisconsin showed that papers published only 7 percent of the available news release copy from their representative. Senatorial publicity fared even worse. Many papers did not publish any news releases; the most generous papers published no more than 30 percent of the news release copy they received.[57] Nonetheless, there is some truth to Bagdikian's charges of kid-glove treatment.

Michael Robinson's detailed analysis of the impact of media coverage on Congress revealed several major effects. The media have increased the reelection chances of incumbents, but only in the House of Representatives, where local coverage, which is generally favorable, is most important. In the Senate the negative tenor of the national media and the greater attention to challengers seeking Senate seats have reduced the reelection chances of incumbents. Newsletters, direct mail, and campaign brochures and advertisements partially fill gaps left by mass media coverage. They also serve as counterweights to the adverse news coming from newspapers and television. Skill in dealing with the media has become a crucial talent not only for presidents but also for would-be members of Congress. They must know how to "show-boat" to get coverage from newspapers and television.[58]

Compared with the presidency, the institution of Congress has suffered a decline in image and power. This springs partly from stories that usually picture it as lobby-ridden, incompetent, and fragmented and partly from the fact that the White House has provided more exciting copy.[59] However, individual presidents have been more bloodied by adverse publicity than have individual members of the House. Thus the media have fostered a stronger presidency, but weaker presidents, and a weaker Congress, but more durable representatives.

Summary

In this chapter we have examined the relationship between the media and the presidency and Congress. Coverage is ample, but the goals of the media differ from those of government officials. Officials want stories that report them and their work accurately and favorably. They also want to dominate the news-sifting process so that published news mirrors their sense of what is important and unimportant. Newspeople, on the other hand, want stories that are newsworthy, judged by the usual criteria. They believe that their publics are more interested in exciting events and human interest tales than in academic discussions of public policies, their historical antecedents, and their projected impact expressed in statistics. Newspeople also feel a special mission, like Shakespeare's Mark Antony, "to bury Caesar, not to praise him." And, like Brutus, they claim that their criticism is not disloyalty. They do not love the government less; they only love the nation more.

Each side in this tug of war uses wiles and ruses as well as clout to have its own way. The outcome is a see-saw contest in which both sides score victories and suffer defeats, but each is most attuned to its own failures rather than to its victories. The public interest is served in equally uneven fashion. If we equate it with a maximum of intelligible information about important issues and events, media presentations fall short. But coverage is good in that it is continuous, often well-informed, with sufficient attention to audience appeal to make dry information palatable. Investigative reporting has brought to light many shortcomings and scandals that otherwise might have remained hidden. The fear of exposure by the media has undoubtedly kept government officials from straying into many questionable ventures, although this effect is hard to document. On the negative side, fear of media coverage and publicity has probably inhibited desirable actions.

Because the contacts between officials of the national government and the media are so constant, a formal institutional structure has been established to handle these interactions. The fairly elaborate setup at the presidential level and the simpler arrangements for Congress have been described. We also have indicated some of the problems that newspeople face in covering a flood tide of complex news expeditiously, accurately, and with a modicum of critical detachment and analysis.

Problems in communications policy making remain. All three branches of government shape communications policy, but there is little coordination among them. Even within the executive and legislative branches control is dispersed among so many different committees and agencies that drift rather than direction has resulted. Few major policy decisions have been made except in times of crisis, and even then the weaknesses of government structures have made it easy for industry spokespersons to dominate decision making.

The government's weakness in this area may be a blessing in disguise and in the spirit of the First Amendment. Because the Constitution commands that Congress shall make no law abridging the freedom of the press, it may be well to keep all communications policy making to the barest minimum. As Chief Justice John Marshall warned early in the nation's history, the power to regulate is the power to destroy.[60] Policy making and regulation overlap. A uniform, well-articulated communications policy, however beneficial it may seem to many people, still puts the government imprint indelibly on the flow of information.

Notes

1. James Warren, "Media Used for Better, Worse in Coup," *Chicago Tribune,* August 25, 1991; Bill Carter, "Amid Crisis, Soviet Leaders Devote Prime Time to Television," *New York Times,* September 4, 1991. Joe S. Foote, *Television Access and Political Power: The Networks, the Presidency, and the "Loyal Opposition"* (New York: Praeger, 1990), 135, reports that just before President Carter publicly announced that he would recognize the People's Republic of China, he invited the anchors of the three major networks to Washington to break the news to them first. "This incident was tacit recognition that network anchors had assumed a status comparable to congressional leaders for whom this special type of briefing was usually reserved. The media stars had become a powerful force who deserved special handling."

2. David L. Paletz and K. Kendall Guthrie, "The Three Faces of Ronald Reagan," *Journal of Communication* 37 (Autumn 1987): 7-23.

3. Presidential communication in general is discussed by John Tebbel and Sarah Miles Watts, *The Press and the Presidency* (New York: Oxford University Press, 1985); and Barbara Hinckley, *The Symbolic Presidency: How Presidents Portray Themselves* (New York: Routledge, 1990). Also see Samuel Kernell, *Going Public: New Strategies of Presidential Leadership,* 2d ed. (Washington, D.C.: CQ Press, 1992). Books about the relations of individual presidents with the press include Kenneth W. Thompson, ed., *Ten Presidents and the Press* (Lanham, Md.: University Press of America, 1983); Frederic T. Smoller, *The Six O'Clock Presidency: A Theory of Presidential Press Relations in the Age of Television* (New York: Praeger, 1990); and Carolyn Smith, *Presidential Press Conferences: A Critical Approach* (New York: Praeger, 1990). Also see Mark J. Rozell, *The Press and the Carter Presidency* (Boulder, Colo.: Westview, 1988); and Robert E. Denton, Jr., *The Primetime Presidency of Ronald Reagan: The Era of the Television Presidency* (New York: Praeger, 1988).

4. As John Kenneth Galbraith has noted, "Nearly all of our political comment originates in Washington. Washington politicians, after talking things over with each other, relay misinformation to Washington journalists who, after further intramural discussion, print it where it is thoughtfully read by the same politicians. It is the only completely successful system for the recycling of garbage that has yet been devised." Quoted in William L. Rivers, *The Other Government: Power and the Washington Media* (New York: University Books, 1982), 19.

5. Quoted in Jarol B. Manheim, *All of the People All the Time: Strategic Communication and American Politics* (Armonk, N.Y.: M. E. Sharpe, 1991), 82.

6. Michael J. Robinson, "A Twentieth-Century Medium in a Nineteenth-Century Legislature: The Effects of Television on the American Congress," in *Congress in Change: Evolution and Reform,* ed. Norman J. Ornstein (New York: Praeger, 1975), 241, 256.

7. For President Bush the correlations between Gallup polls and good and bad press ratios were .73. S. Robert Lichter and Linda S. Lichter, eds., "The Postwar President," *Media Monitor* 5 (November 1991): 5.

8. David Halberstam, *The Powers That Be* (New York: Knopf, 1979), 49.

9. Ibid., 514. Also see Daniel C. Hallin, *The "Uncensored War": The Media and Vietnam* (New York: Oxford University Press, 1986).

10. Quoted in S. Robert Lichter and Linda S. Lichter, eds., "Bork: Decline and Fall," *Media Monitor* 1 (October 1987): 5.
11. Martin Linsky, *Impact: How the Press Affects Federal Policymaking* (New York: Norton, 1986), 37-38.
12. Lichter and Lichter, "The Postwar President," 2.
13. William J. Small, *To Kill a Messenger* (New York: Hastings House, 1970).
14. Jules Witcover, *Marathon: The Pursuit of the Presidency, 1972-1976* (New York: Viking, 1977), 302.
15. *Kennedy and the Press: The News Conferences* (New York: Crowell, 1965), 239.
16. Michael Baruch Grossman and Martha Joynt Kumar, "The White House and the News Media: The Phases of Their Relationship," *Political Science Quarterly* 94 (Spring 1979): 37-53. For a rhetorical analysis of presidential press images, see Roderick P. Hart, Deborah Smith-Howell, and John Llewellyn, "The Mindscape of the Presidency: *Time* Magazine, 1945-1985," *Journal of Communication* 41 (Summer 1991): 6-25.
17. Smoller, *The Six O'Clock Presidency*, 61-77.
18. Jeb Stuart Magruder, *An American Life: One Man's Road to Watergate* (New York: Atheneum, 1974), 101.
19. Timothy J. McNulty, "Bush Taking Direct Route to Viewers," *Chicago Tribune*, December 25, 1991.
20. William J. Small, *Political Power and the Press* (New York: Norton, 1972), 162.
21. John Anthony Maltese, *Spin Control: The White House Office of Communications and the Management of Presidential News* (Chapel Hill, N.C.: University of North Carolina Press, 1992), 211-213.
22. F. Christopher Arterton, *Media Politics: The News Strategies of Presidential Campaigns* (Lexington, Mass.: Heath, 1984), 181.
23. Maltese, *Spin Control*, 233.
24. Ibid., 2.
25. Ibid.
26. Ibid., 6.
27. Smith, *Presidential Press Conferences*, 41.
28. For a thorough analysis of presidential press conferences, see Smith, *Presidential Press Conferences*, and Blaire Atherton French, *The Presidential Press Conference: Its History and Role in the American Political System* (Washington, D.C.: University Press of America, 1982); and Frank Cormier, James Deakin, and Helen Thomas, *The White House Press on the Presidency: News Management and Co-Option* (Lanham, Md.: University Press of America, 1983).
29. Steven R. Weisman, "Reagan, Annoyed by News Leaks, Tells Staff To Limit Press Relations," *New York Times*, January 11, 1983. For a list of measures taken by the Reagan administration to stop leaks, see Ronald Berkman and Laura W. Kitch, *Politics in the Media Age* (New York: McGraw-Hill, 1986), 195-197. The Bush administration tried equally unsuccessfully to stop further leaks following the Thomas affair.
30. Robert O. Blanchard, ed., *Congress and the News Media* (New York: Hastings House, 1974), 105.
31. Kathleen Hall Jamieson, *Eloquence in an Electronic Age: The Transformation of Political Speechmaking* (New York: Oxford University Press, 1988), 14.
32. When presidential coverage on the networks was compared, ABC was the

briefest with twenty hours. CBS used twenty-nine and one-half and NBC twenty-six. Proportional allotments for individual stories were quite similar for all networks.

33. Stephen Hess, *The Washington Reporters* (Washington, D.C.: Brookings Institution, 1981), 99. The figures are based on 921 newspaper and 87 television stories.

34. For a more detailed description of bureaucracy coverage, see Rivers, *The Other Government*, 50-68.

35. Martha Joynt Kumar and Michael Baruch Grossman, "Congress: The Best Beat in Town" (Paper delivered at the annual meeting of the American Political Science Association, Washington, D.C., 1986), 8.

36. Hess, *The Washington Reporters*, 104-105; and Michael J. Robinson and Kevin R. Appel, "Network News Coverage of Congress," *Political Science Quarterly* 94 (Fall 1979): 410-411.

37. Gregory C. Lisby, "Early Television on Public Watch: Kefauver and His Crime Investigation," *Journalism Quarterly* 62 (Summer 1985): 242.

38. Quoted in Steven V. Roberts, "Senators Squint into a Future under TV's Gaze," *New York Times*, February 4, 1986.

39. Quoted in Dorothy Collin, "Senate Will Keep TV Plugged In," *Chicago Tribune*, July 30, 1986.

40. Stephen Frantzich, "Communication and Congress," in *The Communications Revolution in Politics*, ed. Gerald Benjamin (New York: The Academy of Political Science, 1982), 99.

41. Ibid., 100; also see Timothy E. Cook, *Making Laws and Making News: Media Strategies in the U.S. House of Representatives* (Washington, D.C.: Brookings Institution, 1989).

42. Stephen Hess, *Live from Capitol Hill: Studies of Congress and the Media* (Washington, D.C.: Brookings Institution, 1991), 117. On pages 33-61, Hess presents a content analysis of media coverage of Congress. Also see Cook, *Making Laws and Making News*, 57-70, and Robinson and Appel, "Network News Coverage of Congress," 407-418.

43. Timothy E. Cook, "House Members as National Newsmakers: The Effects of Televising Congress," *Legislative Studies Quarterly* 11 (Summer 1986): 203-226; and Stephen Hess, *The Ultimate Insiders: U.S. Senators and the National Media* (Washington, D.C.: Brookings, 1986). Also see Hess, *Live from Capitol Hill*, 55-58; and Mohamed Wafai, "Senators' Television Visibility and Political Legitimacy," *Journalism Quarterly* 66 (Summer 1989): 323-331, 390.

44. Cook, *Making Laws and Making News*, 59-69.

45. Hess, *Live from Capitol Hill*, 107.

46. Cook, *Making Laws and Making News*, 72.

47. Ibid., 83.

48. Hess, *Live from Capitol Hill*, 96-97.

49. For descriptions of these publicity efforts, see Berkman and Kitch, *Politics in the Media Age*, 230; and Michael J. Robinson, "Three Faces of Congressional Media," in *The New Congress*, ed. Thomas E. Mann and Norman J. Ornstein (Washington, D.C.: American Enterprise Institute, 1981), 55-96.

50. Hess, *Live from Capitol Hill*, chap. 2, has an excellent discussion of congressional press galleries.

51. Arthur Miller, Edie Goldenberg, and Lutz Erbring, "Type-Set Politics: Impact of Newspapers on Public Confidence," *American Political Science Review* 73 (March 1979): 70.

52. Daniel D. Polsby and Kim Degnan, "Institutions for Communications Policymaking: A Review," in *Communications for Tomorrow: Policy Perspectives for the 1980s,* ed. Glen O. Robinson (New York: Praeger, 1978), 501-514. See also Erwin G. Krasnow, Lawrence D. Longley, and Herbert A. Terry, *The Politics of Broadcast Regulation,* 3d ed. (New York: St. Martin's Press, 1982), 87-132; and Robert Britt, *The Irony of Regulatory Reform: The Deregulation of American Telecommunications* (New York: Oxford University Press, 1989), chap. 6.
53. Krasnow, Longley, and Terry, *The Politics of Broadcast Regulation,* 99.
54. Ernest Gellhorn, "The Role of Congress," in *Communications for Tomorrow,* ed. Robinson, 445-457.
55. For a full account of congressional investigations of television violence, see Willard D. Rowland, Jr., *Policy Uses of Communication Research* (Beverly Hills, Calif.: Sage, 1983).
56. Ben H. Bagdikian, "Congress and the Media: Partners in Propaganda," *Columbia Journalism Review* 12 (January-February 1974): 3-10. Also see Lou Cannon's discussion of "the cozy coverage of Congress" in his *Reporting: An Inside View* (Sacramento, Calif.: California Journal Press, 1977).
57. Leslie D. Polk, John Eddy, and Ann Andre, "Use of Congressional Publicity in Wisconsin District," *Journalism Quarterly* 52 (Autumn 1975): 543-546. Also see Jan Pons Vermeer, *For Immediate Release: Candidate Press Releases in American Political Campaigns* (Westport, Conn.: Greenwood Press, 1982).
58. Robinson, "Three Faces of Congressional Media."
59. Robinson and Appel, "Network News Coverage," 412. See also David L. Paletz and Robert M. Entman, *Media Power Politics* (New York: Free Press, 1981), 79-98.
60. *McCulloch v. Maryland,* 4 Wheaton 316 (1819).

Readings

Broder, David. *Behind the Front Page: A Candid Look at How the News Is Made.* New York: Simon and Schuster, 1987.
Cook, Timothy E. *Making Laws and Making News: Media Strategies in the U.S. House of Representatives.* Washington D.C.: Brookings Institution, 1989.
Denton, Robert E., and Dan F. Hahn. *Presidential Communication: Description and Analysis.* New York: Praeger, 1986.
Hess, Stephen. *The Government/Press Connection.* Washington, D.C.: Brookings Institution, 1984.
_____. *Live from Capitol Hill: Studies of Congress and the Media.* Washington, D.C.: Brookings Institution, 1991.
_____. *The Ultimate Insiders: U.S. Senators and the National Media.* Washington, D.C.: Brookings Institution, 1986.
Morgan, David. *The Flacks of Washington: Government Information and the Public Agenda.* Westport, Conn.: Greenwood Press, 1986.
Smoller, Frederic T. *The Six O'Clock Presidency: A Theory of Presidential Press Relations in the Age of Television.* New York: Praeger, 1990.
Tebbel, John, and Sarah Miles Watts. *The Press and the Presidency: From George Washington to Ronald Reagan.* New York: Oxford University Press, 1985.

CHAPTER 10

Covering the Justice System and State and Local News

In his classic study of media and public opinion, the renowned American journalist, Walter Lippmann, likened the performance of the media to "the beam of a searchlight that moves restlessly about, bringing one episode and then another out of darkness into vision." The media were not a "mirror on the world" as others had claimed. Lippmann concluded that "Men cannot do the work of the world by this light alone. They cannot govern society by episodes, incidents, and eruptions." [1]

What Lippmann observed and concluded in 1922 is as true today as it was then. The media provide spotty coverage, leaving much of the political landscape obscured. The institutions that will be covered in this chapter—the criminal justice system, including the courts, state governments and politics, and, to a lesser extent, local politics—have been in the shadows of media coverage. We know all too little about them, making informed citizenship difficult. Just like journalists, social scientists have largely ignored these backwaters of politics. Fortunately, that is beginning to change.

The Media and the Courts

Of the three branches of the national government, only the judiciary has been sparsely covered. As Table 9-1 in the previous chapter showed, this is the case even for the highest court in the nation. The pattern of sparse coverage is evident when one looks at individual networks, as Table 9-2 suggested, as well as when one scans major newspapers. For example, between July 1990 and June 1991, NBC devoted roughly 32.5 hours to presidential stories, 21.5 hours to Congress stories, and 1.5 hours to stories about the Supreme Court.

At the federal level, judges are rarely in the limelight. They infrequently grant interviews, almost never hold news conferences, and generally do not seek or welcome media attention, primarily because they fear their impartiality might be compromised. Remoteness enhances the impression that judges are a breed apart, doling out justice to lesser mortals. At the state and local levels, where many judges are elected rather than appointed to office, media coverage is somewhat more common, and the aura of judicial majesty recedes accordingly.

There is one major exception to the immunity from personal media scrutiny that Supreme Court justices enjoy. It is publicity for the hearings conducted prior to their appointment to the Court. At times, these hearings, and the public debate they engender, have been highly acrimonious. For example, a content analysis of media stories about the 1987 nomination of Judge Robert Bork, which covered the major networks and the *Washington Post,* showed an almost even split between favorable and unfavorable published commentary about the appointment. Prominent leaders were quoted for and against the appointment, making it a notable and noted media battle between political heavyweights.[2] Since dramatic hearings have great audience appeal, they are now often broadcast live, gavel-to-gavel, by "Court TV," a cable channel that specializes in reporting dramatic judicial proceedings, along with commentary by selected pundits.

Hearings also demonstrate how pressure groups often use the media to influence politics. For instance, during confirmation hearings for conservative justices Robert Bork and Clarence Thomas, liberal as well as conservative groups mounted a massive effort to gain media publicity for their perceptions of the merits of these appointments. Groups such as the American Civil Liberties Union, the NAACP, NOW, and the AFL-CIO spoke for the liberal camp, while conservatives lobbied through Pat Robertson's Christian Coalition and the Conservative Victory Committee. Tactics included television and radio advertisements, talk show appearances, essays appearing in the editorial opinion sections of newspapers, wining and dining media personnel, and careful research and coordination work.[3]

The courts as institutions also receive comparatively little coverage. There are exceptions, of course. The courts' difficulties in coping with the flood of legal actions, the problems of disparate sentencing policies, and the flaws in the correction system have all been the subject of sporadic media investigations. Speeches by Supreme Court justices to public bodies such as the American Bar Association have been telecast and reported nationwide. Chief Justice Warren E. Burger even allowed himself to be questioned routinely about his annual "State of the

Judiciary" speech. The news conference before the speech remained off the record, however, and the chief justice could not be quoted directly.

Although justices and court systems are not very newsworthy because they generally do not become embroiled in open battles about policies, their efforts—judicial decisions—do make the news. This is particularly true of U.S. Supreme Court decisions, which frequently have major consequences for the political system. For example, *Brown v. Board of Education* (1954) was widely publicized because it declared unconstitutional the separate schooling of children of different races, and *Roe v. Wade* (1973) received ample media attention because it involved the emotional issue of the right of a woman to have an abortion.[4] The Court continues to be in the news whenever it rules on issues that are likely to have an immediate pronounced impact on the lives of average Americans. But the focus of news stories is limited to the formal decision. The decision-making process remains largely shrouded in secrecy.[5]

Impact of Coverage

Publicity about Supreme Court decisions informs public officials at all government levels, as well as the general public, about the substance of selected decisions. A small corps of reporters is responsible for choosing the decisions to be covered. At the Supreme Court, full- and part-time reporters combined number about fifty people. Of these only the correspondents for the major wire services and for major newspapers are full-time.

Supreme Court coverage is difficult; the reporters must digest voluminous and often contradictory opinions supporting or dissenting from a given decision. This must be done quickly and without help from the justices who authored the opinions. Submission deadlines may be only minutes away and the news will be stale after more than twenty-four hours have elapsed. Advice from outside commentators, including legal experts, is usually unavailable initially since they are not allowed to preview the opinions. Leaks of advance information are very rare. The Supreme Court does have a press office, which provides some reference materials and bare-bones records of the Court's activities. But it refuses to provide interpretations of the justices' decisions in laypersons' terms, fearing entanglement in legal controversies. However, brief analyses of important pending cases are available to the media through publications sponsored by the legal profession.

Because of the shortage of skilled reporters, much court reporting, even at the Supreme Court level, is imprecise and sometimes even wrong. Justice Felix Frankfurter once complained that editors who would never consider covering a baseball game through a reporter unfamiliar with the sport regularly assigned reporters unfamiliar with the law to cover the Supreme Court. This situation has improved considerably in recent years, but it is far from cured. Many editors do not want to assign reporters whose knowledge of fine points of the law might make their stories too technical and incomprehensible.

Engel v. Vitale, a 1962 decision on school prayer, and *Baker v. Carr,* a decision requiring massive redrawing of electoral district boundaries, illustrate faulty reporting.[6] An analysis of stories about these two decisions in sixty-three metropolitan daily papers showed that headlines were misleading, and coverage was sketchy and uninformative.[7] Ill-informed statements by well-known people opposing the Court's decisions made up the major part of the stories. Several stories contained serious errors. For instance, the wrong clause of the Constitution was cited as the basis for the decision outlawing classroom prayer in public schools. Arguments made in lower courts were erroneously attributed to Supreme Court justices. Moreover, the media covered the prayer decision most heavily because it was relatively easy to grasp and presented an emotionally stirring story. They slighted the duller reapportionment decision, which was of far greater political significance because it forced states to reapportion legislative districts on a massive scale.

Many important decisions are completely ignored. The emphasis is on social policy issues, like civil rights, school prayer, and abortion, and little else.[8] During one typical Supreme Court term even the *New York Times* failed to mention one-quarter of all written opinions. In the stories about the remaining 112 opinions, 49 lacked essential information. The *Detroit News* failed to mention 70 percent of the written opinions.[9] However, when the print media decide to focus on a case coverage can be excellent, including commentary on legal issues and the long-range implication of the case.[10]

The thrust of judicial complaints about sketchy, inaccurate, out-of-context reporting is the same as for coverage of the presidency and Congress. However, reporting of court activities seems to be more superficial and flawed than its presidential and congressional counterparts.[11] The reasons are not difficult to understand. The volume of decisions is huge, frequently clustering near the end of the annual term. The subject matter is often highly technical, hard for reporters to understand and make understandable. With notable exceptions, stories about judicial decisions lack the potential to become exciting, front-page news. They are hard to boil down into catchy phrases and clichés. They rarely lend themselves to exciting visual coverage. The Supreme Court beat tends to be understaffed. All of these factors make it very difficult for assigned reporters to prepare interesting, well-researched accounts.

The information supplied to the public, though inadequate for providing important insights into the law and the judicial process, usually sustains respect for the judiciary and compliance with its rulings. Most people are poorly informed about the Supreme Court, but they still hold it in high esteem.[12] Occasionally Court publicity has the opposite effect, however. For instance, widespread adverse publicity about Supreme Court decisions outlawing prayer in the public schools has encouraged individuals and entire school systems to ignore that ban. It also has led to an abortive movement to pass a constitutional amendment to permit prayers in the public schools. Justice Tom Clark, one of the participants in the 1962 prayer decision, complained that misunderstanding of *Engel v. Vitale* made this ruling unpopular. He blamed inadequate reporting for the misunderstanding and lack of compliance.

Public reactions to Supreme Court decisions, in turn, may affect future decisions of the Court. Justices themselves are influenced in their work by what they read and hear from the media. Media reports of crime waves, or price gouging by business, or public opposition to aid for parochial schools are likely to influence Court decisions and set boundaries to judicial policy making.[13] This makes it tragic that much of the reporting leaves the public unprepared to make sound assessments of the Court's rulings. Recent research indicates that the amount of publicity given to a crime influences prosecutors at lower judicial levels. When there is little publicity, prosecutors are less likely to press for a trial of the case and more likely to agree to a plea-bargain settlement.[14] The effects of media coverage tend to persist for subsequent similar cases.

News about Crime and the Justice System

Publication of decisions by the Supreme Court and lower courts is by no means the only significant news about the judiciary. General news about crime and the work of the justice system is also important in creating images of the quality of public justice. Here a plentiful media diet is available, especially on local television news where 14 percent of the coverage is devoted to the topic. Health care issues receive less than half as much attention. Like stories about government activities, crime and justice system stories tend to focus on sensational events, often at the expense of significant trends and problems in the legal system that might benefit from greater public attention.[15]

The nature of crime news coverage and its prevalence in the media, particularly television, has long been a matter of concern to public officials and the public. It is widely believed that current coverage practices deflect attention from the social causes of crime and the policies needed to curb it. Sensational stories lead to exaggerated fear of crime because the focus is on the most violent incidents, which in real life constitute only a tiny portion of crime. As Table 4-2 showed earlier, 64 percent of the crime stories in the *Chicago Tribune* dealt with murder in a year when murder made up three-tenths of one percent of the actual crimes in the city. By contrast, white-collar crime, which is widely prevalent and often threatens public health and safety, received little coverage, concealing its seriousness as a social problem. Many experts on criminal behavior contend that extensive graphic coverage of crime can glamorize it and thereby encourage imitation by would-be offenders. News stories that focus selectively on sensational aspects of the case can also mislead the public—and possibly jurors—about who is guilty and who is innocent. When that happens, guilty defendants may escape justice and innocent ones may be convicted.

If there is widespread agreement that current patterns of crime news coverage are excessive and undesirable, why do they continue in daily newspapers and on national and local television throughout the country? There are several reasons. Most importantly, despite their complaints, audiences flock to crime news, partly as an issue of personal security but mostly to satisfy a hunger for excitement. Historically, this has always been the case since the birth of tabloid newspapers more than 150 years ago. When crime news makes huge front-page headlines, paper sales rise sharply. The local television news, with its heavy crime component, has eclipsed national news, which carries more serious political stories and less crime, in the battle for high audience ratings. In the entertainment world, crime shows are highly popular. Besides audience appeal, crime news has the advantage of ease of coverage. The police beat can supply a steady diet of new crimes for hungry reporters who prefer to mine a news-rich source rather than working leaner beats.

Judicial Censorship

Although crime and justice system news is amply covered by the media, there are important omissions. The Supreme Court bars reporters from all of its deliberations prior to the announcement of decisions. On the few occasions when information about a forthcoming decision has been leaked ahead of time, justices have reacted with great anger and have curtailed the contacts between newspeople and Court personnel. Television cameras are barred from the Supreme Court and other federal courts, and proceedings may not be broadcast directly. The Court allowed televising of oral arguments on a trial basis in 1988. But the practice was abandoned in 1989, based on an adverse vote by a majority of the justices.[16]

For years many state courts prohibited radio and television reporters from covering trials and other proceedings. This restriction was grounded in fears that electronic equipment might produce a carnival atmosphere that would intimidate participants, endanger witnesses, and harm the fairness of the proceedings. Sensational coverage of the Lindbergh kidnapping trial in 1935 spawned such bans. Now, however, they appear to be on the wane, prompted by a desire to allow citizens to watch how their courts operate. By 1988 most states permitted electronic coverage of judicial proceedings in their courts, but some of the permissions were on a trial basis. In most states, rules about coverage try to protect many of the actors in the judicial drama from undue invasion of their privacy.[17]

Restraints on live audio and video coverage are not the only limitations on judicial publicity. In the interest of ensuring fair trials, courts also limit the information that may be printed about court proceedings. These types of restrictions were discussed in Chapter 3.

Communications Law

Judges' views on communications law are also of interest to newspeople. The FCC's vague legislative mandate has given rise to numerous court battles, as has the interpretation of the First Amendment's free press provisions. From 1986 to 1991, for example, the Supreme Court judged 64 free expression cases. These represented only a tiny percentage of such cases judged by lower courts.[18] Since federal courts are frequently asked to interpret compliance with constitutional and statutory restraints, media lobbies have attempted to influence the appointment of federal judges and have often been parties in cases that involve communications law. They have tried to steer these cases to sympathetic judges during appeals from FCC rules and licensing decisions.

In an average year fifteen to twenty appeals involving FCC decisions about various aspects of communications policy are brought to the courts, most often to the Court of Appeals for the District of Columbia. The law permits any person who is "aggrieved" or whose interests are "adversely affected" by the orders of the FCC to seek a court review, and these provisions have been liberally interpreted. Such easy access has enhanced concern about the potentially large role of the courts in communications policy making.

The federal Court of Appeals has upheld the majority of FCC rulings, although this may be changing. In the late 1970s the court frequently substituted its own policy analysis and preferences for those of the commission.[19] In the limited number of cases that have reached the Supreme Court, usually because violation of First Amendment rights was alleged, the justices have generally upheld the FCC's rulings. While influence over the FCC itself thus seems more important for policy impact than the role played by the courts, it is difficult to gauge how much impact the prospects of judicial review have on FCC activities. Agencies frequently modify their behavior to avoid reversals by the judiciary.

The vagueness of the power granted to the FCC provides immense leeway to the courts as well as to the commission. As Daniel Polsby and Kim Degnan have observed, "If 'the public interest' leaves the FCC in a trackless normative wilderness in which it is free to make up the rules of the game, the courts' discretion to pass on those rules for reasonable or substantial correspondence with record evidence is not less broad." [20] Interpretation of the scope of the FCC's mandate therefore inevitably involves the courts in shaping communications policy.

Covering State and Local Affairs

It is an axiom of American politics that "All politics is local." Decentralized politics is essential and invigorating in a nation that spans a continent and embodies diverse political cultures and contexts. Since politics at the national level is glamorous and important, it is easy to ignore the grassroots that nourish and shape it. It is therefore not surprising that most research attention has been focused at the national level, despite the importance of coverage of local politics and local perspectives on national politics.

The Changing Media Grid

The Vanishing Metropolitan Focus. Mirroring the nation's political geography and culture, American newspapers and radio and television stations have been primarily structured to serve a multitude of local markets.[21] At the turn of the century, every large and medium-sized city and even many small towns had at least one newspaper and often more, geared to local political needs. When electronic media made their appearance they, too, were situated in nearly every city to serve local audiences. Technological changes and large-scale migration of former inner-city dwellers to the suburbs have taken their toll on the local focus of many American media enterprises. The numbers of newspapers have shrunk so that most cities are now served by a single newspaper and many communities no longer have a paper of their own. The electronic reach of radio and television has expanded so that these media are serving ever larger regions. When television stations and metropolitan dailies reach people in fifty counties, as is common, their domain includes some 1,300 governmental units, whose policies should be reported because they involve important public issues, including the power to tax. Numerous state legislators, as well as several national legislators, are elected within these counties. Given the many active political units that require media attention, media reporting, of necessity, is highly selective and superficial.

Because market areas and areas of political interest no longer coincide, reporting has turned away from strictly local problems to more generalized topics of broad interest to the entire market area. That has meant more focus on soft news like sports and entertainment and human interest stories. It has also meant less information about important local problems that face citizens and more non-committal coverage to avoid antagonizing a diverse audience. Lack of information about local politics and bland coverage translate into lack of concern and political apathy. As media critic Ben Bagdikian has put it:

> News distribution is no longer designed for individual towns and cities. American politics is organized on the basis of the 20,000 urban and rural places in the country, which is the way citizens vote. But the media have organized on the basis of 210 television "markets," which is the way merchandisers and media corporations sell ads. As a result, the fit between the country's information needs and its information media has become disastrously disjointed." [22]

The disjunction is likely to persist in the future, although the proliferation of audio-visual news programs transmitted via cable, microwave, videotex, and similar technologies may mean that some programs will again become more narrowly focused. Local governments now routinely use community access cable channels to allow their constituents to watch local government in action. City council meetings, committee hearings, court procedures, and more have become directly accessible to the public without the intervention of journalists. The suburbs, where such channels have been scarce in the past, are joining the parade, thereby providing more competition for suburban newspapers.

Umbrella Competition Patterns. In response to major population shifts from inner cities to sprawling suburbs, print media have developed a structure of "umbrella competition," where smaller units operate within the area covered simultaneously by the larger units.[23] Suburban newspapers have been thriving while metropolitan newspapers have shrunk in circulation, even when they have special sections targeted to different regions or communities in the metropolitan area and suburbs and when they present many features designed to lure suburban clienteles.[24] In Philadelphia, for example, the circulation of metropolitan newspapers dropped by nearly 50 percent between 1940 and 1988 (from 1,344,000 to 763,000).[25]

The umbrella pattern consists of four layers. The first layer is made up of large metropolitan dailies that provide substantial amounts of international, national, and regional coverage. The second layer is made up of smaller satellite dailies that resemble their larger cousins but carry more local news. The third layer contains suburban dailies. They emphasize local news, much of it nonpolitical, and are a rapidly growing sector. Between 1940 and 1988, suburban newspaper circulation in the Philadelphia area more than tripled (from 147,000 to 461,000).[26] Though still below the metropolitan circulation figures, suburban papers are profitable because they offer an attractive advertising opportunity to the many businesses whose customers now cluster in suburban areas. The fourth layer consists of weekly newspapers and "shoppers" that are distributed free of charge because they contain mostly advertising and only a sprinkling of news and feature stories.

The emphasis on local news increases as one moves through these layers. This has happened because newspapers with a narrower reach try to distinguish themselves from the metropolitan papers and thereby make themselves more attractive to their clientele. But, because of the lack of fit between media markets and political units, most of the local news avoids discussion and analysis of localized public issues, leaving them bereft of essential coverage. The fact that metropolitan papers now must share the advertising pie with suburban papers, as well as shoppers, has been a major factor in the death of dailies in multi-paper cities, leaving most of them without the kind of competition that invigorates political dialogue.

Television stations in smaller markets also tend to feature more local and less national and international news than their larger cousins.[27] Most radio news stations, which feature only news or a large amount of news, likewise devote more than half of their airtime to local news. However, stations in smaller radio markets tend to present fewer stories simply because there is less local news available.[28]

The Alternative Press. In addition to the four layers discussed, there is also an alternative press that tends to focus narrowly on issues of interest to people representing minority political cultures or people with distinctive life styles and cultural tastes. For example, many specialized media are targeted to various ethnic, racial, and religious groups. Some specialized media are published in foreign languages to meet the needs of immigrant groups. While they provide in-depth coverage of local, national, and international news of interest to their clientele, filling many gaps left by more superficial coverage in the general press, they omit news covering broader concerns. Unless they use other news sources as well, their readers may therefore live in a narrow communications ghetto that keeps them from fully understanding their surroundings. Specialized media also often try to generate support for issues favored by their audiences and may play a role in influencing local elections.

Media serving African-American and Hispanic communities are a good example. Approximately 300 African-American newspapers were published in the United States in 1989, mostly on a weekly basis. Many were small, but major cities, like New York and Chicago, had several such large, thriving papers. There also were five major daily Hispanic papers and hundreds of weeklies and monthlies. (Many English newspapers in areas with large Hispanic populations also have Spanish-language inserts.) Besides having their own print media, large subcultural groups in the United States are also served by electronic news media tailored to their special concerns. Television and radio stations geared to the needs of various subcultures exist throughout the country. For example, in 1989 there were 193 radio stations targeted to African-American listeners and 108 Spanish-language radio stations in the top 175 radio markets.

For audiences addicted to news broadcasts, there are also all-news cable television stations and all-news radio stations that feature a steady succession of newscasts, many of them repetitive. Call-in radio shows, where hosts of varying political persuasions will answer all sorts of questions, often engage in spirited discussions with guests and outside callers. In 1989, several call-in shows garnered the political limelight when they campaigned against a proposal for a 51 percent hike in congressional salaries. The proposal was defeated. Talk radio shows have also been able to encourage or discourage the passage of referenda and other issues important to local politics. Depending on whether listeners agreed or disagreed with the thrust of their advocacy, such political lobbying has been praised or condemned.

Government-Press Relations at Subnational Levels

Subnational news is important for state and local politics for the same reasons that make the media important on the national scene. Subnational news plays a significant role in setting the agenda for public policies. It helps or hinders politicians in achieving their goals. It influences the election and appointment of public officials. It informs the public and officialdom about political affairs and acts as a watchdog eager to foil political wrongdoing. However, there are differences in emphasis between national and subnational political coverage, largely because subnational politics operates on a much smaller scale and often performs different functions. Political scientist Delmer D. Dunn, who studied relations between public officials and the press in Wisconsin, identified several important distinctions between the national and subnational levels.[29]

How Officials Use the Press. At the subnational level, it is far easier for public officials to stay in touch with each other about their work. Therefore they use the media far less to discover what various organizations within the governmental structure are doing. The lesser need for media information also means that they make fewer systematic attempts to scan the media to extract information that has a bearing on their jobs. The fact that officials remain in closer contact with each other as well as with a comparatively tiny corps of reporters reduces the need for formal press conferences. Therefore it is not surprising that individual legislative leaders and department heads, while generally more accessible to reporters, are less inclined to call press conferences. Moreover, their news is rarely so exciting that they can feel assured of decent attendance at news conferences.

At the subnational level, fewer officials are experts in gaining publicity that will enhance the work that they are doing or even their own careers. Often their jobs are highly technical and difficult to explain to the lay public, discouraging reporters and officials alike from trying to report to the public. When officials do make the effort to tell their stories, reporters, who generally lack technical expertise, may be unable to judge whether they are receiving an accurate or a misleading account. When that happens, reporters are forced to tell the story just as it was told to them, allowing subnational officials to define the situation and often become unchallenged agenda setters. If the story relates to a policy decision involving major issues—for example, whether to start, continue, or stop a project, how to finance it, and similar matters—the official views are likely to prevail with little media scrutiny. However, because subnational officials often lack skill to use media effectively, they do not benefit from their control over news stories as much as might otherwise be expected. In fact, the public information and public relations materials they present to the media are often so poorly done that they generate stories that turn out to be detrimental to their agency's image.

Media scholar Phyllis Kaniss has identified six media styles that are commonly seen at the subnational level.[30] They occur at the national level as well, but less frequently because national officials are better prepared to handle their media relations expertly and more aware of the important consequences. The *paranoid media-avoider,* who abounds at the subnational level, fears the press and tries to avoid it as much as possible.[31] In the process, she or he antagonizes information-hungry journalists so that they are likely to retaliate with unfavorable publicity whenever an opportunity to do so presents itself. The *naive professional* supplies the media with information and talks freely with journalists without realizing that uncontrolled release of information will leave him or her at the mercy of reporters' whims. Reporters, rather than the official, then determine largely what will be published and the perspectives that will be reflected. The *ribbon cutter* is a media junkie who is heavily concerned with initiating events, however trivial, that are likely to attract journalists. The ensuing publicity may have few political payoffs. The *dancing marionette* takes her or his cues from media editorials and reports and takes action in areas suggested by newspeople, rather than initiating policies independently. The reward is likely to be favorable coverage because journalists like to see themselves as instigators of reforms. But the policy agenda favored by newspeople may be undesirable from the official's perspective. *Colorful quotables* excel in creating attractive sound bites and making sure that these come to the attention of reporters. Like ribbon cutters, their political rewards are apt to be small. Finally, *liars* conceal or slant information or distort it outright to put themselves in a favorable light. This is a dangerous strategy because it undermines their credibility.

In place of such unproductive strategies, Kaniss recommends that subnational officials, like their national counterparts, learn to understand the needs of local media so that they can structure the information they supply accordingly. This does not require deferring to journalists' preferences or sensationalizing news. Rather, it requires judicious choices of information for release and careful attention to the framing of stories.[32] For example, Avis LaVelle, press secretary to Chicago's Mayor Richard Daley, encouraged her staff to cover news stories themselves, like reporters, just as she was wont to do. When LaVelle met with reporters, she could then provide them with story materials selected and written from a reporter's perspective. In that way, she managed to control news flow in line with the mayor's goals while still pleasing the press.

The era of informal, inexpert handling of the press by subnational officials may be ending. Currently, all governors have press secretaries or public information offices. So do most big-city mayors. Like their counterparts at the national level, they try to use these offices to push executive programs through recalcitrant legislatures and to disseminate news about their activities to various political elites and the limited number of citizens who are interested in subnational news. However, as on the national level, these efforts often fail. The media may turn out to be powerful enemies rather than friends. The fact that a number of state legislatures—California, New York, Illinois, and Ohio, for example—now have their own press relations offices may be a factor.[33]

Eagerness for good media coverage is not limited to elected officials. Appointed officials, too, believe that they need good images to help them in their battles for funding and for support of the policies that their agencies try to pursue. A poll of high-level officials at the national level showed that 79 percent thought that positive coverage increased their chances of achieving major policy goals.[34] Legislatures rarely deny support to agencies that seem to enjoy high rates of approval. By the same token, bad publicity can hurt. When media frame stories in ways that suit media, rather than official goals, public officials may be forced to recast their own focus of attention. For example, city sanitation departments have been forced to concentrate on cleaning up lesser problems, and neglecting more serious ones, when publicity highlighted a particular situation.

As on the national level, strategies designed to win media attention from the subnational media include press conferences, press releases, staging events that media are likely to cover, writing op-ed pieces, and writing letters to the editor.[35] Press releases, the most common form of public relations, are also the least productive because they tend to be sparsely used by media. Rates of use may be as low as 5 percent, though that rate rises if the releases have interesting local angles.[36] Contacting media personnel directly seems to be the best and, apparently, a quite successful approach. Estimates are that more than half of the content of the print and electronic media originates with news sources, rather than springing from questions asked first by journalists. Government officials at all levels provide a large share of these so-called news subsidies.[37]

Most efforts to gain media coverage at the subnational level are directed at the print media, which are generally deemed the most effective transmitters of state and local political news. When governors, lieutenant governors, attorneys general, secretaries of state, and various legislative leaders in all states were polled, a majority named print media as most important in setting the political agenda, with wire services and television following.[38] Television stories are ranked below print press stories in effectiveness because they are too brief and too much skewed toward the sensational. Since state and local political news often lacks visual appeal, local television media tend to relegate such news to the tail end of the broadcast, giving it only cursory treatment.

However, more and more local officials seem to realize that television is the most important medium when it comes to mobilizing public opinion. They therefore watch closely how activities of interest to them are covered on local news to infer from the coverage what public reaction is likely to be. They have also increased their efforts to get television coverage for themselves and the agencies they represent.

How Reporters Operate at Subnational Levels.   Reporters are somewhat different at the subnational than the national level, also. Taken as a group, they have less formal education and considerably less job experience. Moreover, turnover rates are high and reporters are often forced to move to a different market when they switch jobs because of clauses in their contracts that forbid them to work for a competitor in the same area. In fact, judging from a comparison of reporters' and officials' level of education in New York's state capital, the officials' level of education may rank considerably above that of reporters.[39] Such disparities occasionally contribute to strained relations between reporters and officials when they disagree in their analyses of political events. However, most of the time, personal relations between reporters and officials tend to be more cordial at the subnational level because of their more frequent personal interactions. In fact, ties of friendship have been blamed for the dearth of press criticism of official conduct at subnational levels.

Aside from metropolitan newspapers, which often have many reporters, the press corps at the subnational level is usually considerably smaller than its national counterpart. It is therefore far less likely that reporters are assigned to a single beat. Rather, general assignment reporters prevail. While covering a broad range of events and people enhances their understanding of government in general, it also makes it more difficult for them to become experts in particular aspects of politics and to probe deeply into stories. Instead, such roving reporters depend more heavily on routine sources, such as daily inquiries at the police and fire departments, wire service stories and the wire service 'day books' that list major local events, local newspapers, assorted press releases, and tips from viewers.[40] As discussed in Chapter 4, and lampooned by the cartoon on the next page, stories with the best pictures and best sound bites tend to become leads, even when they are not necessarily the most important stories and when emphasis on the pictures may change the angle of stories and alter their impact.[41]

Because so few subnational stories are intrinsically interesting to media audiences, the pressure to make stories entertaining is heightened. That means featuring colorful, charismatic politicians who speak well in twenty-second sound bites and bypassing opportunities to receive more ample exposition of problems. Carefully calibrated, fact-rich pronouncements are generally deemed boring for most members of the audience. It also means covering key officials in major cities, such as big-city mayors, because they are among the few names familiar to people within a specific market, and ignoring officials, including the chiefs, of less well-known political units. The hunt for heartstring tugging coverage also leads to ambulance chasing by reporters, who haunt victims of various human tragedies and their families by intruding into their homes and hospital rooms to get stories.

Because timeliness is deemed so important for American media, late night newscasts try to present late-breaking events even when they are less important than earlier ones. Since most government business

By Dana Summers. ©1988, Washington Post Writers Group. Reprinted with permission.

stops in the early evening hours, this means that late night news broadcasts depend even more heavily than earlier ones on the staples supplied by police and fire department records. Kaniss's research showed that the proportion of serious political news on Philadelphia's television stations, on average, was cut in half during the late evening news periods.[42]

Since stories about government must compete with heart-wrenching tragedies, heinous crimes, and horrifying disasters, subnational television broadcasts, more so than national ones, concentrate on the sensational aspects of political stories. Knowing that stories that focus on people are more attractive than stories that concentrate on events, subnational television news emphasizes personalities. In the process of highlighting people, the importance of events and their broader and long-term consequences may be lost. For example, in a story on city council hearings on subway crime in Philadelphia, the facts and figures provided by various experts and government officials were downplayed while the testimony of the "Guardian Angels," an out-of-town volunteer patrol organization whose members were unfamiliar with the local scene, was highlighted.[43]

Compared to the much fuller, less sensationalist, and more analytical coverage in newspapers, Philadelphia's television stations were more likely to accept their sources' judgments without question. This meant that the views of public officials expressed in press conferences or press releases were more likely to be transmitted without passing scrutiny. When criticism of these views was aired, the emphasis was on brief, colorful sound bites, rather than on full exposition of the reasons underlying the criticism.

Journalists who work in large metropolitan areas tend to pay more attention to inner-city affairs than to outlying areas. In Philadelphia, the ratio was roughly two to one for newspapers. On local television, nearly all of the political stories related to inner-city politics, ignoring the suburbs.[44] Unfortunately, suburban reporters did not pick up the slack. A look at the contents of suburban news showed that 73 percent of the stories dealt with crime, accidents, disasters, and the like, slighting stories about other suburban concerns.

There are several reasons for "city myopia" by metropolitan media.[45] Among them is the fact that metropolitan newspaper offices usually are closer to the central city hall than to the suburbs. That makes inner-city officials and other news sources located in the inner city easier to reach. City officials are also more willing to make the trip to newspaper offices and radio and television studios that are located nearby than are their geographically distant colleagues in the suburbs. The multitude of small suburban jurisdictions are spread out over an extensive geographical area, making direct contacts time-consuming. Inner cities are also more likely to generate the kind of news that political reporters ordinarily cover, such as political wheeling and dealing, an ample pinch of corruption, and a heavy slice of crime. Spectacular fires are more common in inner-city neighborhoods, as are stories about ethnic and racial strife and protest demonstrations.[46] Most journalists find the city more exciting and relate its problems to events in the suburbs rather than the other way around. When reporters are assigned to suburban stories on a regular basis, they view it as akin to exile in Siberia. The smaller size of the press corps also accounts for the lack of coverage for many important subnational stories and for a strong dose of pack journalism, generated by the close contacts that often characterize smaller groups.

The Contents of Subnational News

When political scientist David Morgan classified political news in newspapers in New York state, he found that, on average, nine of the eleven papers that he examined devoted the least amount of coverage to state affairs (16 percent), followed by local affairs (19 percent). National news garnered the lion's share of attention (45 percent) and international news took the number two spot (20 percent). The balance between national and international news on one hand and state and

Table 10-1 Political News in New York State Papers

Paper locations	Local news	State news	National news	International news	Political news ratio of total
N.Y. State (General)	19%	16%	45%	22%	46%
Albany	15	45	32	8	42

Source: Adapted from David Morgan, *The Capitol Press Corps* (Westport, Conn.: Greenwood Press, 1978), 20-21.
Note: N = 9 general papers, 2 Albany papers.

local news on the other thus was two-to-one.[47] Table 10-1 tells the story. The table also shows that the patterns were different for papers in the state's capital, which was the only place where state news predominated (45 percent) and international news was minimal (8 percent). Overall, political news amounted to 46 percent of the newshole in the general press and 42 percent in the Albany papers.

State News: A Neglected Stepchild

The Local Emphasis. Why does state news receive the least attention when states play such important roles in politics? As we have seen, some media specialize in national news, like the national television networks, and other media specialize in local news, like many network affiliates. But few daily publications specialize in state news. Within states, the major media enterprises that have enough resources to cover more than local news are usually located in the state's most populous cities, rather than state capitals. The local scene offers them enough opportunities for good stories.

Moreover, since state legislatures have relatively brief sessions, and most state coverage has traditionally focused on the legislature rather than the governor, the flow of news from the capital is intermittent. Many daily papers therefore do not make the state capital a regular full-time beat. In some cases—New Hampshire is an example—the state's media markets overlap state boundaries so that news must appeal to residents of more than one state. That puts a damper on state news.[48]

The National Emphasis. State news is a double loser. The level of neglect of the state is even worse at the national level than it is locally. A content analysis of news broadcast on the major networks between July 1990 and June 1991 showed no signs that the new federalism, which assigns a vastly expanded national political role to the states, has focused national media attention on state issues. State news was

Table 10-2   Regional Focus of Network News Coverage

Regions	Percentage of mentions	Percentage of electoral vote	Discrepancy
Pacific (AK, CA, HI, OR, WA)	22.1	14.7	+7.4
South (AL, FL, GA, KY, MS, TN)	14.5	13.6	+0.9
Northeast (DE, MD, NJ, NY, PA, D.C.)	16.9	16.2	+0.7
New England (CT, ME, MA, NH, RI, VT)	6.4	6.5	−0.1
Plains (KS, NE, ND, SD)	2.4	3.1	−0.7
Mountains (AZ, CO, ID, MT, NV, NM, UT, WY)	6.5	7.4	−0.9
Middle Atlantic (NC, SC, VA, WV)	5.8	7.4	−1.6
Southwest (AR, LA, OK, TX)	8.4	10.2	−1.8
Midwest (IA, IL, IN, MI, MN, MO, OH, WI)	17.0	20.8	−3.8

Source: Author's research.

Note: N = 2,607 mentions in news stories during the period July 1990-June 1991. Figures for the three networks have been combined. The distribution of 538 electoral votes is based on 1990 census figures. Regions have been ranked from most to least advantaged.

extremely sparse on national television, constituting barely 1 percent of all nightly news stories. National television spotlighted a small number of states and neglected the rest. As Table 10-2 shows, some regions of the country received more ample coverage than one might expect, judged by the size of their populations (as reflected in their electoral votes), while others received considerably less. The concerns of midwesterners rated the least attention relative to their electoral votes, while the Pacific region dominated. The degree of discrepancy in regional coverage, favorable and unfavorable, is shown in the last column of the table. Table 10-3 provides a closer look at individual states. It shows the ten most covered and the ten least covered states and the degree of favorable and unfavorable imbalance.

From a political perspective, it is impossible to make sense out of the findings: some comparatively insignificant states, such as Colorado and Maine, bask in excess coverage while more important states, such as Pennsylvania and Ohio, are undercovered. The explanation lies in journalistic criteria. The states with the most ample coverage provided the best story materials at a place and time that was most convenient for

Table 10-3 State Distribution of Network News Attention: Ten Leaders and Trailers on the Advantage/Disadvantage Scale

State	Region	Overcovered states		
		Percentage of mentions	Percentage of electoral vote	Discrepancy
California	Pacific	18.3	10.1	+8.2
Florida	South	9.2	4.7	+4.5
New York	Northeast	9.1	6.1	+3.0
Colorado	Mountain	2.7	1.5	+1.2
Louisiana	Southwest	2.6	1.7	+0.9
Maine	New England	1.5	0.7	+0.8
Alaska	Pacific	1.4	0.6	+0.8
Massachusetts	New England	2.8	2.2	+0.6
Illinois	Midwest	4.5	4.1	+0.4
Georgia	South	2.7	2.4	+0.3

State	Region	Undercovered states		
		Percentage of mentions	Percentage of electoral vote	Discrepancy
Pennsylvania	Northeast	1.7	4.3	−2.6
New Jersey	Northeast	1.0	2.8	−1.8
Alabama	South	0.6	1.7	−1.1
Ohio	Midwest	2.9	3.9	−1.0
Tennessee	South	1.1	2.1	−1.0
Michigan	Midwest	2.5	3.4	−0.9
Oklahoma	Southwest	0.6	1.5	−0.9
Wisconsin	Midwest	1.3	2.1	−0.8
Connecticut	New England	0.7	1.5	−0.8
Arkansas	Southwest	0.3	1.1	−0.8

Source: Author's research.

Note: N = 2,507 mentions in news stories during the period July 1990-June 1991. Figures for the three networks have been combined. The distribution of the 535 electoral votes (D.C. was excluded) is based on 1990 census figures.

the media. States lacking in such attractions suffered from neglect, which could be costly to the state's economic and political welfare. Compounding such problems, state news coverage on the national networks also lacked political substance, focusing primarily on disaster, crime, and trivia stories. State economic, political, and social conditions and policies were ignored even when they had major national ramifications.

Print media coverage of state news, as judged by the *New York Times,* was considerably better.[49] Even when one excludes coverage of states within the New York region, more state stories were covered.

Table 10-4 News Choice Preferences

News choices	Very important	Important	Somewhat important	Not important
Local news	44%	40%	14%	3%
Weather reports	46	37	15	3
National news	52	31	12	6
World news	47	29	16	8
Statewide news	27	48	20	6
State legislative news	26	39	20	15
Regional news	17	40	31	13
University news	19	37	25	19
Sports reports	15	27	24	34

Source: Adapted from Carolyn A. Lin, "Audience Selectivity of Local Television News," *Journalism Quarterly* 69 (Summer 1992): 378.

However, there was regional imbalance as well in *New York Times* stories, with the Pacific area again gaining the lion's share of coverage and the Midwest the least. The fact that the *New York Times* found ample story materials suggests that the networks had the opportunity to report more state news, had they chosen to do so.

Complaints about inadequate coverage must always be tempered by the realization that media space and time are limited. What kinds of stories should the networks have omitted to make room for more news about the states? The answer is painful, given the fact that audiences love the entertainment and trivia stories that should be cut to make room for more politically meaty content. Nonetheless, the growing importance of state politics has made it essential to provide more adequate coverage for the benefit of interested publics, as well as political leaders.

As Table 10-4 shows, the public does realize the importance of state news, judging from a midwestern telephone survey conducted in 1987. The respondents were asked to rate the importance of various types of news in their choice of programs. Local news was in first place when one combines "very important" and "important" ratings.[50] State news, including news about the state legislature, while lower on the scale, still was ranked as "very important" or "important" by more than two-thirds of the respondents.

Local News Characteristics

Local news has become the biggest game in town. Sixty-seven percent of the adult population watches the local news daily, compared to the 49 percent who watch news on the national networks.[51] That means 6

Table 10-5 Television News Story Topics, July 1990 to August 1991

	National CBS (168)	National NBC (138)	National ABC (172)	Local CBS (287)	Local NBC (228)	Local ABC (210)
Governmental affairs	57	54	47	32	33	35
Economic issues	13	14	17	5	6	6
Social issues	26	22	26	30	23	29
Sports and Entertainment	2	7	10	25	31	24
Miscellaneous	3	3	1	8	8	6

Note: Based on author's content analysis of Chicago stations.

million more viewers for local than for national news. Local news has become a huge money maker, generating as much as 40 percent of a station's profits.[52] Stations first started to emphasize local news heavily in the 1970s because they could keep the advertising income. When local stations broadcast national news, most advertising revenue is remitted to the national networks.[53] Production of local news was also attractive because it was popular and far cheaper than most entertainment shows. Hence news programs multiplied in numbers as well as length, with some local news programs running as long as ninety minutes.

Primary Concerns.   As part of its mandate to assure that the electronic media serve the public interest, the FCC has insisted that local television and radio stations gear their programming to local needs, including coverage of local politics. That mandate has been honored more by lip service than by actual performance. Local stations do carry some local political news, and more than three-quarters of their stories originate locally. But many of these pertain to national and international affairs, rather than less glamorous local political events. The primary emphasis is on local crime and disasters and on entertainment, weather, and sports. This is hardly what the FCC had in mind when it called for "local" programming.

Table 10-5 presents a comparison of national and Chicago area local television news stories between July 1990 and August 1991. It shows that 90 to 95 percent of national television news dealt with governmental affairs, or assorted social and economic issues. By contrast, only 61 to 70 percent of local news dealt with substantive matters, with sports, entertainment, and a few miscellaneous nonpolitical issues making up the rest.

A content analysis of offerings by three local television stations in Philadelphia corroborates the Chicago findings. Kaniss found a heavy emphasis on features designed to entertain audiences at the expense of government and public policy stories.[54] Local television news allotted as much or more time to crimes, accidents, disasters, and fires than to stories about the national, state, and local governments and their policies. The pattern was the same for all three stations and seemed unaffected by the degree of importance of current political events. Within individual broadcasts, relatively minor incidents were often given preferred positions when they were dramatic, even if their general significance was low.

While these figures show a clear difference in the character of news, indicating that local news is far fluffier, one must keep in mind that there are generally more local newscasts. With more news time to fill, there is bound to be more filler material. Conversely, while the proportion of serious news may be smaller, the total amount of news may also be greater. But there is still another caveat—there may be more stories, but many of them are likely to be updates or outright repetition of earlier news. Moreover, despite the fact that there may be more news available, the majority of viewers are not glued to their television sets, eager to watch successive newscasts as the day develops.

Diversity. Just as one cannot lump all national media together for purposes of analysis, so one must differentiate local media along a number of dimensions. Size is one of them. Stations in the largest markets offered considerably more political news than stations in smaller markets.[55] Likewise, larger television stations devote a smaller percentage of news space to local news than smaller stations. Instead, stations in larger markets pay more attention to national and world events. The difference was roughly 6 percentage points for story count and 9 percentage points for newshole in a study of 14 stations in Michigan and Oregon when broadcasts were analyzed over a ten-day period.[56] This may mean that stations in larger markets are moving away from emphasizing local news as urged by the FCC's "localism doctrine."

National News on Local Media

One reason for growing attention to national and world news by local stations is greater ease of access. New satellite and microwave technology permits local stations to tap into the pool of national news at will and report it from a local angle. In addition, local stations are increasingly entering into cooperative news-gathering systems, such as Conus and Newsfeed, that allow member stations to send their stories to other members in the system via satellite. Consequently, local stations have become less dependent on network coverage for national and world events.

As we saw in Chapter 9, national newsmakers are eager to reach the hinterlands, where coverage tends to be gentler and more in tune with the newsmakers' agenda. Congress members rely heavily on publicity in their home states and make extensive efforts to supply local media with stories and videotapes. Washington also abounds with news bureaus that transmit national news, often presented from local angles, to member organizations or independent local clients.

Content analysis of Washington news presented locally shows that it has a distinctive flavor. With no nationwide audiences to please, local stations can put a more local imprint on the news and thereby make it more relevant to local audiences. Since happy news is preferred to tales of woe, the news can be more upbeat and less critical. Local reporters are also less likely to subject national political leaders to tough questioning because they are more distant from the scene and lack insider knowledge and Washington sources.

In contrast with national news, local newscasts analyzed between 1979 and 1985 covered executive and legislative branches in about equal proportions.[57] However, legislators were more often heard and seen than presidents, who were mentioned more frequently but not actually seen on-camera. As is true of national television, senators received considerably more coverage than House members. They were more likely to be judged favorably. Besides stressing local angles, stories on local television also highlight different organizations and issues. Coverage of Senate committees presented by Table 10-6 is an example that reflects a difference in priorities.[58] The table is the number of cameras dispatched by various national and local media organizations to the committee hearings, as recorded by the Senate Radio and Television Gallery.

Election Coverage at the Local Level

News about the Candidates. The entire American electoral system is organized to reflect local and statewide politics. All national officials—the president, senators, and representatives—are selected from state-based electoral districts, as are state officials, and the half million local officials who occupy legislative, executive, judicial, and administrative positions throughout the states. Candidates for most of these offices, including scores of positions on local government boards and committees, are of prime interest to geographically limited constituencies. They rarely attract the attention of nationwide radio and television broadcasts, or the few newspapers that have a nationwide circulation. Their political fate—and that of the areas that they serve—therefore depends to a major degree on the kind of coverage provided by local media.

The role of the local media in promoting candidates in state and local campaigns is similar to what was described in Chapter 8 for

Table 10-6 Senate Committee Coverage, 1979-1985, National versus Local Priorities

National priorities	Ranking	Local priorities	Ranking
Foreign Relations	1	Foreign Relations	3
Judiciary	2	Judiciary	1
Budget	3	Budget	13
Labor	4	Labor	2
Appropriations	5	Appropriations	8
Finance	6	Finance	4
Governmental Affairs	7	Governmental Affairs	7
Joint Economic	8	Joint Economic	11
Armed Services	9	Armed Services	12
Energy	10	Energy	6
Commerce	11	Commerce	5
Banking	12	Banking	10
Ethics	13	Ethics	15
Environment	14	Environment	9
Agriculture	15	Agriculture	14
Intelligence	16	Intelligence	21
Aging	17	Aging	16
Rules	18	Rules	19
Veterans' Affairs	19	Veterans' Affairs	17
Small Business	20	Small Business	18
Indian Affairs	21	Indian Affairs	20

Source: Adapted from Stephen Hess, *Live from Capitol Hill* (Washington, D.C.: Brookings Institution, 1991), 138.

Note: Coverage is based on counts of assigned cameras, February 1979-June 1985.

national campaigns. It is a growing role because state officials are spending more money on their media campaigns now than in earlier years. A large share of campaign spending goes to efforts to obtain general media coverage rather than relying only on advertisements. In the past, subnational officials relied heavily on radio coverage for their advertisements because of the high costs of television. The availability of cable channels is changing this; so is the ability to videotape messages and distribute them directly to interested parties.

While evidence is still spotty about the quality of election coverage at the local, compared to the national level, a study of the 1989 Virginia gubernatorial campaign found that local coverage was superior to national news media stories. The national media focused on the historic nature of the campaign, which pitted a white and an African-American gubernatorial candidate against each other in a southern state, and on the candidates' diverging stands on the abortion issue. Most of the coverage at the national level related to the African-American Democrat; the white Republican received little attention. The local papers excelled in providing profiles of both candidates and highlighting an array of issues facing the state.[59] However, both national and local media were one-sided in painting a highly favorable picture of one candidate (Democrat L. Douglas Wilder, incumbent lieutenant governor) and an unfavorable one of the other (Republican J. Marshall Coleman, a former state attorney general). In the same way a study of a race for chair of the Fairfax County (Virginia) Board of Supervisors found that "It appears that a different kind of press coverage occurs at the 'lower levels' of government—one in which more serious, substantive reporting is taking place." [60] Other studies have concluded that coverage characteristics and quality are similar for state and national coverage of gubernatorial races.[61]

Newspaper endorsements are also more important at the subnational than the national level. Most candidates for subnational offices are less familiar to the voters, who therefore turn more to the news media for guidance.[62] When viewers were asked to compare debates among presidential contenders at the national level with debates between candidates for state and local offices, they reported that they found the presidential debates more important and interesting, but learned more and were influenced more by the debates at state and local levels.[63] Seventy percent of the viewers in the local debate were undecided about their voting choices, compared to 40 percent of viewers in the presidential debate. If lack of information is a disease that plagues national elections, it apparently occurs in far more virulent form at the subnational level.

The fact that news media are now organized to serve larger markets often makes it difficult for candidates whose districts overlap several markets, or just a small slice of a large media market, to gain coverage. The media will not report about them as part of regular news coverage because limited time for news is reserved for stories of broader interest. Paid advertising coverage may be too expensive because rates are based on the numbers of people reached, not on the much smaller numbers that are constituents of the candidate. A state representative who serves a district of 50,000 voters rarely can afford to pay for access to many times that number just because the advertising "Area of Dominant Influence" (ADI) in which her or his district is located covers a multitude of urban, suburban, and rural counties.

News about Referenda. While elections at the national level involve the selection of candidates, albeit often in a context of voting for or against certain issues, elections involving local politics often are completely issue-centered. That happens when various referenda are on the ballot. Although these political contests have low visibility, their impact on the average citizen can dwarf that of the more publicized contests. Political scientist Betty Zisk, after studying 72 referenda in Massachusetts, Michigan, Oregon, and California between 1976 and 1982, concluded that they were well-covered. Despite the liberal stance of the papers under investigation (the *Boston Globe,* the *Detroit Free Press,* the *Portland Oregonian,* the *Los Angeles Times,* and the *San Francisco Chronicle*), there was little systematic bias in reporting these stories. All sides of each issue were amply discussed.[64] When the election was over, voters had agreed with the stance of newspaper endorsements about 68 percent of the time.[65] It is impossible to know with certainty whether this indicates media influence or merely an independently occurring concurrence of views.

Zisk contends that the side spending the most money, much of it to gain media coverage, won in three out of four cases (56 of the 72 campaigns, 78 percent). She believes that money purchased victory, rather than good causes attracting the most money. She faults newspeople for merely reporting charges and countercharges rather than analyzing the merits of proposals and unmasking misleading rhetoric and advertisements.[66]

On the good side, major regional newspapers provided comprehensive coverage of controversial issues. They carried extensive background features, pro and con articles and editorials, and news about campaign activities in the major urban centers, though not elsewhere in the jurisdiction covered by the referendum. By contrast, radio and television, the main sources of political information for average voters, carried little news about the referenda and few editorials. Thirty- and sixty-second television spot advertisements were totally inadequate to cover the important points of most of these complex issues. However, some radio talk shows gave extensive coverage to referenda, albeit often generating more heat than light.[67] When a poll tested voter knowledge about a nuclear power proposal for California, results showed that nearly 80 percent of the affected public, which had relied primarily on televised information, fell below the midpoint on a scale measuring knowledge about the proposal. Newspaper-reliant voters fared much better. However, comparisons between learning from newspapers and learning from television may be inappropriate when most survey questions reflect the type of information conveyed by newspapers, rather than television.

The Quality of Local News

Maintaining high-quality coverage is often more difficult for local than for national media. As mentioned, compared to most national television networks, local television has a far greater appetite for news because it usually has three or more daily newscasts. That puts a premium on broadcasting the latest news, rather than repeating more important stories that may have been broadcast earlier in the day. To maintain profitability through a wide audience reach, local television usually pitches its programs to a moderately educated middle-income audience that, presumably, is uninterested in sophisticated political analysis.

It is also more difficult for local newscasters to get high-quality news commentary for local political stories. Many local officials lack the skills and experience required to be good media information sources. Because their jobs are often technical—fire chiefs or health commissioners, for example—they are chosen for their technical abilities and managerial skills, with no regard for public relations expertise. The end result is a dearth of commentary on local stations. One content analysis of fourteen television stations of assorted sizes from five different markets found that only 43 (1.4 percent) of 3,037 stories that were examined included commentary.[68]

A further problem for local stations, as well as for local newspapers, is that they often lack economic resources. This may force them to apply an economy model of news selection. Rather than originating stories on their own and investigating them, they go after the cheapest stories. Usually, that is news based on handouts by various public relations practitioners or news based on rehashed reports by metropolitan newspapers—facetiously dubbed "plagiarism news." [69] In a study of three network affiliates in the western United States, 75 percent of the news at the small, economically weak stations came from handouts, 20 percent started with tips that were investigated, and 5 percent originated with reporters. For the largest, economically soundest station the figures were 50 percent, 36 percent, and 13 percent. As Ben Bagdikian has put it in his inimitable style, journalism is "a daily battle between God and Mammon. Too much of the time, it's Mammon 100 and God 5." [70]

However, larger local stations and newspapers, with greater financial resources, do somewhat better in seeking out important news and providing context for their stories so that they can be properly appraised.[71] They also find it easier to remain resistant to direct and indirect pressure arising from the dependency of news media on money from advertising. Smaller news outlets cannot afford to antagonize the advertising hand that feeds them. The same is true for print media, where larger papers are more immune—though not totally free—from the need to cater to advertisers.

The difficulties in maintaining high-quality news are all the more serious at the local level because there are few competing information sources when it comes to local politics. National problems and national politicians are widely scrutinized by a multitude of media, governmental investigating bodies, interest groups, and academicians. That rarely happens at the local level. Reporting by the local media may be the sole source of information available to interested citizens as well as government officials.

Critics of local news have often charged that local news does not perform the important watchdog functions of the press. These critics argue that it is soft on local politicians because it is not comfortable stirring up conflict among people who know each other personally. It is also soft when it comes to local projects and policies out of a sense of local boosterism. Reporters rarely question quantitative estimates of costs and benefits of local development projects. They tend to be upbeat in reporting about local business leaders and economic trends. They may examine local problems and report about the sad consequences, but they rarely turn to genuine investigative reporting. As Kaniss has noted: "... While there is much in the news and editorial columns that is critical of local officials, this criticism is limited when compared with the amount of information that is taken directly, and almost unquestioningly, from official bureaucratic sources."[72] There are, of course, major exceptions to these criticisms, particularly in large cities with well-staffed news media. But even there, whenever budgets get tight, investigative reporting is among the first casualties of malnourishment.

Summary

The media spotlight falls unevenly on various features of the body politic. In this chapter, we examined institutions that do not receive sufficient light so that the American public and political leaders can adequately assess these institutions and the roles they play in America's political life. Compared to other parts of government, the news covers national institutions best of all except for the judicial branch. We have explained the reasons for this lack of coverage and some of the political consequences, given the courts' importance in shaping American political life. We have also noted problems that do arise when the crime and justice system is in the news and the focus turns to sensational matters, rather than political substance. The controversy about the appropriateness of allowing cameras in courtrooms during various judicial proceedings highlights many of these issues.

The discussion then turned to media coverage of subnational news. Here we noted that state news is neglected by all media, except those located in state capital cities. Hence most citizens remain ignorant about state politics. However, coverage seems to be adequate for the needs of state-level politicians, who find it easy to use the media as an alarm bell for matters that they can then pursue directly in the limited setting in which state politics usually operates.

There is far more ample coverage of local news. Many regions within metropolitan areas, as well as suburbs and outlying communities, have local newspapers. But the quality of coverage of politics has deteriorated since the turn of the century. Markets reflect technological and merchandising conditions, rather than political needs. They design their offerings accordingly. Fewer cities now have their own daily newspapers and intra-city competition among major dailies has almost vanished. The political dialogue has suffered. However, it seems too early to mourn the death of solid local politics coverage. The new technologies that make it feasible to tailor broadcasts to the needs of small audiences may restore the vigorous publicity that is essential in a democracy.

Notes

1. Walter Lippmann, *Public Opinion* (New York: Free Press, 1965), 229.
2. "Bork Decline and Fall," *Media Monitor* 1 (October 1987): 5.
3. James Warren, "Bork Fight Paves Way for Thomas Ads," *Chicago Tribune,* September 6, 1991.
4. 347 U.S. 483 (1954); and 410 U.S. 113 (1973).
5. Richard Davis, "Lifting the Shroud: News Media Portrayal of the U.S. Supreme Court," *Communications and the Law* 9 (October 1987): 46; Bob Woodward and Scott Armstrong, *The Brethren* (New York: Simon and Schuster, 1979), claim to present an insider's view of court proceedings.
6. *Engel v. Vitale,* 370 U.S. 421 (1962). *Baker v. Carr,* 369 U.S. 186 (1962).
7. Chester A. Newland, "Press Coverage of the United States Supreme Court," *Western Political Quarterly* 17 (1964): 15-36. Also see Kenneth S. Devol, *Mass Media and the Supreme Court,* 2d ed. (New York: Hastings House, 1976).
8. Jerome O'Callaghan and James O. Dukes, "Media Coverage of the Supreme Court's Caseload," *Journalism Quarterly* 69 (Spring 1992): 195-203.
9. David Ericson, "Newspaper Coverage of the Supreme Court: A Case Study," *Journalism Quarterly* 54 (Autumn 1977): 605-607. See also Michael E. Solimine, "Newsmagazine Coverage of the Supreme Court," *Journalism Quarterly* 57 (Winter 1980): 661-664.
10. Stephanie Greco Larson, "How the *New York Times* Covered Discrimination Cases," *Journalism Quarterly* 62 (Winter 1985): 894-896; also see Stephanie Greco Larson, "Supreme Court Coverage and Consequences," Midwest Political Science Association Meeting paper, 1989.
11. David L. Grey, *The Supreme Court and the News Media* (Evanston, Ill.: Northwestern University Press, 1968). For additional examples of incorrect coverage, see Frank J. Sorauf, "Campaign Money and the Press: Three Soundings," *Political Science Quarterly* 102 (Spring 1987): 25-42.
12. Gallup polls taken on July 13, 1987, show that during the 1980s a majority of the public judged the Court's performance as good to excellent. See also Gregory Caldeira, "Neither the Purse Nor the Sword: Dynamics of Public Confidence in the Supreme Court, "*American Political Science Review* 80

(December 1986): 1209-1228.

13. Robert E. Drechsel, *News Making in the Trial Courts* (New York: Longman, 1983), 19-22.

14. David Pritchard, "Homicide and Bargained Justice: The Agenda-Setting Effect of Crime News on Prosecutors," *Public Opinion Quarterly* 50 (Spring 1986): 143-159.

15. A detailed account of coverage of crime and justice system news is presented in Doris A. Graber, *Crime News and the Public* (New York: Praeger, 1980). Also see Roy E. Lotz, *Crime and the American Press* (New York: Praeger, 1991); and Robert J. Griffin, *Interpreting Public Issues* (Ames: University of Iowa Press, 1991).

16. Richard Davis, *The Press and American Politics: The New Mediator* (New York: Longman, 1992), 185.

17. Susanna Barber, *News Cameras in the Courtroom: A Free Press-Fair Trial Debate* (Norwood, N.J.: Ablex, 1987), especially 18-19.

18. F. Dennis Hale, "Free Expression: The First Five Years of the Rehnquist Court," *Journalism Quarterly* 69 (Spring 1992): 89-103.

19. Erwin G. Krasnow, Lawrence D. Longley, and Herbert A. Terry, *The Politics of Broadcast Regulation,* 3d ed. (New York: St. Martin's Press, 1982), 65-66.

20. Daniel D. Polsby and Kim Degnan, "Institutions for Communications Policymaking: A Review," in *Communications for Tomorrow: Policy Perspectives for the 1980s,* ed. Glen O. Robinson (New York: Praeger, 1978), 513.

21. Ben H. Bagdikian, *The Media Monopoly,* 3d ed. (Boston: Beacon Press, 1990), 174.

22. Ibid., 288.

23. The term was coined by James N. Rosse. See note 4 in James M. Bernstein, Stephen Lacy, Catherine Cassara, and Tuen-yu Lau, "Geographic Coverage by Local Television News," *Journalism Quarterly* 57 (Winter 1990): 664.

24. Phyllis Kaniss, *Making Local News* (Chicago: University of Chicago Press, 1991), 5.

25. Ibid., 31.

26. Ibid.

27. Bernstein et al., "Geographic Coverage by Local Television News," 671.

28. Daniel Riffe and Eugene F. Shaw, "Ownership, Operating, Staffing and Content Characteristics of 'News Radio' Stations," *Journalism Quarterly* 67 (Winter 1990): 684-691.

29. Delmer Dunn, *Public Officials and the Press* (Reading, Mass.: Addison-Wesley, 1969): 150-163.

30. Kaniss, *Making Local News,* 175-179.

31. In a Wisconsin study in the late 1960s, 75 percent of executives, 36 percent of legislators, and 10 percent of administrators were media avoiders. Slightly more than a third of the legislators and administrators sought out the media. Mixed attitudes prevailed among the remainder of the sample. Dunn, *Public Officials and the Press,* 92.

32. Kaniss, *Making Local News,* 175-179.

33. Thad Beyle and G. Patrick Lynch, "The Media and State Politics," Midwest Political Science Association paper, 1991, 5. See Dunn, *Public Officials and the Press,* 131, for analysis of the public relations goals of executives, legislators, and administrators in Wisconsin in the late 1960s.

34. Martin Linsky, *How the Press Affects Federal Policymaking* (New York:

Norton, 1986), 236.

35. For usage patterns by Wisconsin executives, legislators, and administrators in the late 1960s, see Dunn, *Public Officials and the Press*, 143.

36. Dan Berkowitz and Douglas B. Adams, "Information Subsidy and Agenda-Building in Local Television News," *Journalism Quarterly* 67 (Winter 1990): 725.

37. Judy Van Slyke Turk and Bob Franklin, "Information Subsidies: Agenda-Setting Traditions," *Public Relations Review* 13 (1987): 29-41; Dan Berkowitz, "TV News Sources and News Channels: A Study in Agenda-Building," *Journalism Quarterly* 64 (Autumn 1987): 508-513.

38. Beyle and Lynch, "The Media and State Politics."

39. David Morgan, *The Capitol Press Corps: Newsmen and the Governing of New York State* (Westport, Conn.: Greenwood Press, 1978), 57-58.

40. Kaniss, *Making Local News*, 107.

41. As Kaniss, *Making Local News*, 108, notes: "Instead of an inverted paragraph order in the newspaper, where the most important information comes first, television news stories have the formula of a mini-drama, with rising action, climax and denouement. Television stories stress action, not background facts."

42. Kaniss, *Making Local News*, 118-120.

43. Ibid., 121.

44. Ibid., 126-127.

45. The term is used in Kaniss, 126.

46. Ibid., 76.

47. Morgan, *The Capitol Press Corps*, 20-21.

48. This discussion is based on Stephen Hess, "Levels of the Game: Federalism and the American News System," Hofstra University Conference paper, April 1992.

49. For the data base used for *New York Times* news, see Doris Graber, "Flashlight Coverage: State News on National Broadcasts," *American Politics Quarterly* 17 (July 1989): 277-290.

50. Carolyn A. Lin, "Audience Selectivity of Local Television Newscasts," *Journalism Quarterly* 69 (Summer 1992): 378.

51. *Washington Post Magazine*, May 13, 1990, 17.

52. Stephen Hess, *Live from Capitol Hill: Studies of Congress and the Media* (Washington, D.C.: Brookings Institution, 1991), 34.

53. Kaniss, *Making Local News*, 102.

54. Ibid., 113-130.

55. Hess, *Live from Capitol Hill*, 49.

56. Bernstein et al., "Geographic Coverage by Local Television News," 668, 670; for similar results, also see Stephen Lacy and James M. Bernstein, "Daily Newspaper Content's Relationship to Publication Cycle and Circulation Size," *Newspaper Research Journal* (Spring 1988): 49-57.

57. Hess, *Live from Capitol Hill*, 53.

58. Ibid., 138.

59. Mark J. Rozell, "Local vs. National Press Assessments of Virginia's 1989 Gubernatorial Campaign," *Polity* 24 (Fall 1991): 75.

60. Mark J. Rozell, "Campaign Press Coverage in the 'New Dominion': The 1991 Fairfax County (Virginia) Board of Supervisors Chairman Election," (Paper presented at the Eighth Citadel Conference on Southern Politics, Charleston, S.C., 1992), 18.

61. For a report on gubernatorial election studies in progress, see Beyle and

Lynch, "The Media and State Politics."

62. Byron St. Dizer, "The Effects of Newspaper Endorsements and Party Identification on Voting Choice," *Journalism Quarterly* 62 (Autumn 1985): 589-594.

63. A. Lichtenstein, "Differences in Impact between Local and National Televised Political Candidates' Debates," *Western Journal of Speech Communication* 46 (1982): 291-298; also see Dianne Bystrom, Cindy Roper, Robert Gobetz, Tom Massey, and Carol Beall, "The Effects of a Televised Gubernatorial Debate," *Political Communication Review* 16 (1991): 57-80.

64. Betty H. Zisk, *Money, Media, and the Grassroots: State Ballot Issues and the Electoral Process* (Newbury Park, Calif.: Sage, 1987), 28.

65. Ibid., 109.

66. Ibid., 246.

67. Ibid., 247-248.

68. James M. Bernstein and Stephen Lacy, "Contextual Coverage of Government by Local Television News," *Journalism Quarterly* 69 (Summer 1992): 338.

69. John McManus, "How Local Television Learns What Is News," *Journalism Quarterly* 67 (Winter 1990): 678.

70. Quoted in McManus, 672.

71. Bernstein and Lacy, "Contextual Coverage of Government by Local Television News," 339.

72. Kaniss, *Making Local News,* 90-91.

Readings

Hess, Stephen. *Live from Capitol Hill: Studies of Congress and the Media.* Washington, D.C.: Brookings Institution, 1991.

Kaniss, Phyllis. *Making Local News.* Chicago: University of Chicago Press, 1991.

Lotz, Roy E. *Crime and the American Press.* New York: Praeger, 1991.

Morgan, David. *The Capitol Press Corps: Newsmen and the Governing of New York State.* Westport, Conn.: Greenwood Press, 1978.

Surrette, Ray, ed. *The Media and Criminal Justice Policy—Recent Research and Social Effects.* Springfield, Ill.: Charles C Thomas, 1990.

Zisk, Betty H. *Money, Media, and the Grassroots: State Ballot Issues and the Electoral Process.* Newbury Park, Calif.: Sage, 1987.

CHAPTER 11

Foreign Affairs Coverage

How do the mass media shape the political dimensions of the world? What is the relationship between the new global media and U.S. foreign policy outputs? What, if any, are the links between the mass media and the process of creating foreign policy? How are the media used by the U.S. government to further its policy objectives around the world? Does television play any active roles separate from those of other media in the shaping of American foreign policy? [1] In this chapter we will try to answer these provocative questions, and several others, to shed light on the role played by the mass media in the shaping and conduct of American foreign policy.

To start the discussion, we will first focus on the overall significance that American media and American citizens assign to news about foreign countries. Then we will turn to the production of foreign news, noting how the process differs in significant ways from the creation of domestic news. We will consider the qualifications of foreign correspondents and the unique problems they face in collecting news and shaping it so that it meets mainstream approval and newsworthiness criteria, as well as the canons of journalistic ethics and independence. The task is extraordinarily difficult and we shall note how well it is currently carried out and give examples of past accomplishments as well as failures.

The Share of Foreign News

Newspeople commonly assume that the American public is highly ethnocentric, interested primarily in what goes on in the United States.

Reports about the public's often astounding ignorance about foreign countries and foreign affairs lend credence to these assumptions. When asked, Americans themselves profess somewhat greater interest, professions unmatched by their news consumption habits.[2] When given a choice, they do not seek out foreign policy news. For example, when NBC News broadcast a prime-time, hour-long interview with Soviet leader Mikhail Gorbachev in December 1987, just prior to a U.S.-Soviet meeting designed to reduce the danger of war, only 15 percent of the national audience tuned in. Half of the viewers who at that time ordinarily watch NBC's entertainment programs switched to other networks. They preferred "Kate and Allie," "Frank's Place," and "The World's Greatest Stuntman" to listening to the leader of a superpower. Public opinion polls have repeatedly shown that two-thirds or more of the public is often unaware of important foreign news, even when the situation has received ample and prolonged coverage.

Although foreign news lacks attraction for many Americans, it receives a considerable amount of coverage, especially on network television. In the content analysis reported earlier in Table 4-6, which covers July 1990 to August 1991, Chicago newspapers on average devoted 6 percent of the newshole to international news. The average for national television news was 20 percent and for local television news 7 percent.[3] Compared with major domestic news stories, foreign news normally receives brief space and time and modest display. Elite newspapers like the *New York Times* and the *Washington Post* are an exception. Selection criteria are also more rigorous. Foreign news must be more consequential for political, economic, or cultural concerns of the United States, it must involve people of more exalted status, and entail more violence or disaster.[4] During crises, particularly prolonged ones that endanger American lives, coverage often doubles or even triples. Then foreign news may drown out most other news.

Although Americans' interest in foreign affairs is limited, it does ebb and flow with the shifting political currents. It was high during the Vietnam War and various Middle East crises in the 1970s, 1980s, and 1990s. It also peaked in 1983 when the bombing of the U.S. Marine headquarters in Beirut, Lebanon, killed 241 American soldiers and later that year when U.S. troops landed on the tiny island of Grenada. The 1987 congressional hearings on U.S. weapons sales to Iran, the dissolution of the Soviet Union and the Soviet bloc in the 1990s, and the war against Iraq in 1991 marked other high points in public attention to foreign policy. Even during periods when interest is at a low ebb, television has made more Americans than ever before aware of foreign news. It provides a "reality that lives on ... in the memories of the millions who watched, rather than the few who were actually there."[5] Without television most people would have skipped such news if they encountered it in newspapers. Thus while exposure to foreign affairs information is massive, lack of interest still keeps learning at a relatively low level.[6]

When the spotlight shifts away from foreign news, the number of foreign correspondents usually declines. There were 637 accredited U.S. correspondents in South Vietnam in 1968. As American involvement in the war dwindled, the number dropped to 392 by 1970 and 295 by 1972. By mid-1974 only thirty-three remained. Even though this small corps of correspondents filed relatively few stories from Vietnam, editors often balked at running them in daily newscasts and papers because the public had presumably lost interest. When this happens, a spiral effect sets in. Presumed lack of interest leads to less coverage. Reduced coverage further lessens interest in foreign news. An upward spiral of domestic news takes up the slack. This pattern prevails in most of the country's newspapers and television newscasts whenever foreign crises subside.

The country's foreign policy elites, including government officials, depend heavily on prestigious media, as a State Department official attests: "The first thing we do is read the newspaper—*the newspaper*—the *New York Times*. You can't work in the State Department without the *New York Times*." [7] Members of the U.S. Congress, particularly those concerned with foreign affairs, and foreign officials in the United States have made similar comments. All feel that elite newspaper reports keep them informed faster and often better than their own official sources.

Making Foreign News

Although news making for domestic stories and for foreign stories differs substantially, there are many similarities. To make comparisons easier, our discussion of foreign news making will follow the organization of our discussion of domestic news making and news reporting in Chapter 4. First we will consider the gatekeepers—the corps of foreign correspondents who are the front-line echelon among gatherers of foreign affairs news. Then we will discuss in turn the setting for news selection, the criteria for choosing stories and the means of gathering them, the constraints on news production, and finally the effects of gatekeeping on foreign affairs coverage.

The Gatekeepers

Concentration of Control. A striking aspect of foreign news coverage is the high degree of concentration of the news-gathering process. Most news about events happening throughout the world is collected by four major wire services. They are the American Associated Press (AP), the British Reuters, the French Agence France-Presse (AFP), and, until 1991, the Soviet Tass.[8] Among these world class wire services, AP is by far the largest. It maintains eighty-four foreign bureaus in seventy countries from which it relays news by modern electronic means to subscribers in all parts of the world. For television, pictorial materials are collected by two television news services: Visnews and WTN. They are owned by British interests, primarily Reuters, the British Broadcasting Corporation (BBC), and Britain's Independent Television News.

The wire services station reporters in nearly half of the countries of the world. North American and Western European countries are most likely to have resident reporters; Africa and the Eastern bloc are least likely to have them, a decidedly uneven distribution.[9] The wire services ferret out the stories that make up the pool from which other gatekeepers select complete reports or find leads to pursue stories more fully. Because wire service reporters work for a vast variety of clients throughout the world, their news must be bland so that it does not offend people whose views span a wide political spectrum. Wire service news therefore emphasizes fast and ample reports of ongoing events, not interpretation, which then falls to other foreign correspondents.

Besides these worldwide organizations, the American market is also served by syndicated news collected by major American papers, like the *New York Times,* the *Washington Post,* and the *Los Angeles Times.* These papers have their own correspondents stationed abroad, a luxury enjoyed by barely 1 percent of all American dailies. Since the advent of television, the print press foreign correspondent corps has been joined by foreign correspondents from ABC, CBS, NBC, and CNN.

The major recent innovation in collecting and reporting international news is the rise of CNN, the 24-hour Cable News Network. By 1990, ten years after its birth, it had established eighteen overseas news bureaus to collect news round-the-clock, which was then relayed to 53 million homes in the United States and 200 million viewers in more than 100 other countries. The striking feature about CNN, besides the comprehensiveness of its newsgathering apparatus, is its continuous coverage of major crises such as the 1985 hijacking of a TWA jetliner or the 1991 war against Iraq. As is typical of live coverage, the reports are a mixed bag of events and interviews ranging from the trivial to the significant, with less time given to analysis and expert commentary than is typical for network television news.[10] The emphasis is on taping whatever is readily and inexpensively available so that viewers are the first to see a breaking news event at close range. Unique among international news reporting agencies, CNN also collects and broadcasts brief (usually under three minutes) uncensored reports submitted by sources throughout the world. They become part of its weekly two-and-a-half hour "CNN World Report." [11]

The stories gathered by the small corps of initial gatekeepers reach huge audiences. Although subscribers generally use only a limited portion of the coverage made available by these sources, what they do use mirrors the story patterns and interpretation of the initial gatekeepers. As Barry Rubin points out, "Once the main stories of the day have been identified and defined, the media can be like a stampeding herd, hard to turn toward a new interpretation of an issue." The stories chosen set the scene for follow-up stories. "The news of today sequels the news in the news of yesterday. Only a relatively small number of journalists are able or allowed to open up new areas of concern." [12] Stereotypes become fixed; countries and leaders whom gatekeepers depict as friendly or antagonistic to the United States may be characterized that way long after the reality has changed.

Surveillance of the Foreign Scene. The total number of full-time American foreign correspondents has fluctuated over the years, rising during international crises and falling afterward. Overall, the trend has been downward since its peak during World War II. Several reasons account for this. The ability to dispatch correspondents quickly from an American home base to foreign countries is one. Air travel has made it possible for each American correspondent to reach and cover many more countries than ever before. But physical mobility is not matched by the psychic mobility that would allow reporters to feel at home in more countries. Nor is it accompanied by sudden spurts in knowledge that would permit such "parachute" reporters to cover a new area with insight.

High costs also have forced a steady decline in the number of foreign correspondents. In the 1990s it cost up to $300,000 a year to keep one correspondent abroad, a steep price considering the limited demand for foreign affairs stories. Because it is much cheaper, many papers use stringers instead of regular employees and rely on reports produced by local foreign news media. Stringers, who are usually citizens of the country from which they report, are paid for each story they produce.[13] At best, they may have keener insight into local problems than American reporters sent to the country. But, like the reports gleaned from local news media, they often fail to meet the news-gathering standards prized by American media, and they may be unable to tailor news stories to the needs of American audiences.[14]

U.S. correspondents abroad are unevenly distributed. More are stationed in friendly locations than in neutral or hostile ones. Table 11-1 depicts the regions in which American foreign correspondents were stationed in 1991, and the regions whose correspondents were stationed

Table 11-1 Distribution of Foreign Correspondents, 1991
(in percentages)

Major regions	American correspondents abroad		Foreign correspondents in United States[a]		U.S./foreign comparison[b]
Western Europe	777	40%	687	45%	−5%
East Asia	313	16	307	20	−4
Latin America	249	13	140	9	+4
Middle East	187	10	116	8	+2
Southeast Asia and Pacific	125	7	62	4	+3
Soviet Union	90	5	39	3	+2
Sub-Sahara Africa	66	2	27	2	+1
Eastern Europe	50	3	28	2	+1
South Asia	41	2	28	2	0
Canada	28	2	45	3	−1
Other/International agencies	—	—	46	3	—
Total	1,926		1,525		

Source: For U.S. data, Ralph Kliesch, from the E. W. Scripps School of Journalism, Ohio University of Athens, Ohio; for foreign data, *Editor and Publisher International Yearbook, 1991* (New York: Editor & Publisher, 1991).

[a] The figure is for correspondents based in New York and Washington, D.C.

[b] The figure reflects distribution differences between the American and the foreign corps of correspondents, when column four is subtracted from column two.

in New York or Washington to report about the United States. The rank orderings of the two groups are mirror images. While numbers of correspondents have fluctuated from year to year, the proportions have remained fairly constant for regional distributions as well as locations in particular countries. Table 11-2 shows how four major news organizations allocate their correspondents. It demonstrates how thinly spread they are over relatively few capital cities, leaving huge gaps in coverage. Critics appropriately call this "hopscotch" journalism that leaps over vast, potentially important areas. However, the work of American reporters is supplemented through news from Reuters and Agence France-Presse, the British and French news agencies respectively, which have more ample representation in their former colonial regions where American reporters are especially sparse.

What kinds of people are these journalists who select the foreign news for American elites and publics? What are their biases? And how do they compare with the correspondents who cover the United States for the benefit of foreign nationals?

A typical American journalist abroad is a white male in his forties, college educated, with more than ten years of reporting news under his

Table 11-2 Distribution of U.S. Foreign Correspondents Serving Major News Outlets

Region	Cities	New York Times	Washington Post	Chicago Tribune	CNN
Asia	Tokyo	3	2	—	3
	Beijing	3	1	1[a]	1
	Manila	—	1	—	1
	New Delhi	1	1	—	1
	Bangkok	1	—	—	2
Subtotal		8	5	1	8
Middle East	Amman	—	—	—	2
	Jerusalem	1	1	1	1
	Cairo	1	1	—	—
Subtotal		2	2	1	3
Europe	London	3	1	1	4
	Paris	5	2	—	1
	Rome	1	—	—	1
	Berlin	1	1	—	1
	Bonn	1	—	—	—
	Warsaw	1	2	1	—
	Moscow	3	3	2	3
	Geneva	1	—	—	—
	Brussels	—	—	—	1
Subtotal		16	9	4	11
Africa	Johannesburg	1	1	1	—
	Nairobi	1	1	—	1
	Abidjan	1	—	—	—
Subtotal		3	2	1	1
North America	Toronto	2	1	1	—
	Mexico City	1	1	—	—
Subtotal		3	2	1	—
Central America	San Salvador	1	1	—	—
	Panama	—	—	1	—
	Managua	—	—	—	1
Subtotal		1	1	1	1
South America	Buenos Aires	1	1	1	—
	Rio de Janeiro	1	—	—	1
	Santiago	—	—	—	1
Subtotal		2	1	1	2
Total		35	22	10	26

Source: Personal communication.   [a] Also covers Manila.

Note: Figures as of February 1992.

belt. Aside from reporters and anchor persons flown in to cover special situations, many have remained at the same locations for several years, so that they are fully familiar with their area of coverage.[15] However, this does not necessarily mean the reporters possess language competence. In one survey, more than 80 percent of American reporters stationed in Western Europe and Latin America claimed to read and speak the native languages fluently or with easy facility. But in Eastern Europe and Africa, these figures were cut in half. The poorest showing was in Central and East Asia, where only 9 percent of American reporters could read the intricate written characters, and only 18 percent could speak the languages well. Deficient reading skills hamper American reporters in local interviews and investigations. They must depend on translated newspaper reports and on handouts to the foreign press. This sharply curbs their effectiveness as reporters. In some countries translators are supplied and controlled by the government. Presence of government officials during interviews is sure to dampen the free exchange of ideas that might otherwise take place.

Contacts with local people and personal ties that may supply good insights were also sparse, judging from the survey data. In Western Europe 33 percent of the correspondents said that most of their close friendships and social contacts were with nationals of the country. This was true for only 23 percent in Latin America, 16 percent in Eastern Europe, and 15 percent in Central and East Asia.[16] Although these figures double when more casual contacts are included, they still suggest that foreign correspondents are poorly integrated into the local setting.

Like staff people generally in prominent American news organizations foreign correspondents tend to be politically liberal, taking positions to the left of mainstream views. Nonetheless, they usually accept the government's assumptions about international affairs and its policies, except when major challenges are raised by prominent leaders. When that happens, the media rush to join the attack on the status quo.[17] (See Chapter 4.)

Public relations agencies hired by foreign countries to promote their images provide one very important, usually overlooked, source of news about foreign countries. Steadily growing numbers of countries are contracting for professional image management. In 1987, for example, 161 foreign political units spent an average of $800,000 annually on political messages directed at the United States.[18] By either stimulating or suppressing media coverage, public relations agencies can improve a country's media image. Presumably this then affects elite and mass opinion so that the country in question enjoys improved relations with American politicians and the American public.[19]

A good example of this kind of effect involved the government of Pakistan in 1989. It had hired Mark Siegel, a former director of the

Democratic National Committee and aide to President Carter, to orchestrate a political visit by Pakistan's new prime minister, Benazir Bhutto. Siegel decided to plan a five-day media blitz around the theme that Pakistan's move toward democracy was a triumph for American political values. He arranged for media exposure for the prime minister on "60 Minutes" and the McNeil/Lehrer News Hour, even before she reached the United States. During her visit, interviews were arranged on ABC and NBC news programs. Bhutto also gave a well-publicized address before Congress, a commencement address at Harvard University, and informal remarks at a White House dinner. The publicity was later credited with producing an increase in aid to Pakistan at a time when other foreign aid programs were slashed, and with decreasing resistance to supporting Pakistan's defense build-up.[20]

Surveillance of the American Scene. Altogether, 1,525 correspondents from foreign countries covered the United States in 1991. Just as Americans receive the most news about friendly foreign countries, so most news about America goes to its friends.[21] The foreign journalists stationed in the United States represent various regions and countries unevenly. In 1991 the corps included a mere 6 correspondents from Nigeria, Africa's largest nation, compared to 39 from Israel. Japan topped the list with 213 journalists compared to 39 for China and 22 for India, the world's most populous nations. Neighboring Canada had 45 and neighboring Mexico had 9. West Germany sent 129, while East Germany dispatched 5. Italy had an unaccountably large contingent of 117 correspondents while Belgium made do with 7.[22]

Foreign reporters are an extremely well-educated group. A survey conducted in the mid-1980s found that nine out of ten were university trained, and about half of these had advanced degrees. That included 22 percent who had earned a doctorate. Seventy-eight percent were fluent English speakers, and a majority were fluent in a third language as well. On the average, they spoke three languages. Nevertheless, close contacts with Americans were limited. Only 7 percent said that their best and closest contacts were Americans. In political orientation, foreign newspeople covering the United States were further to the left than most American reporters. Seventy percent claimed to be left-leaning, 14 percent preferred a middle position, and 17 percent leaned to the right.[23]

It is difficult for foreign reporters to cover the whole United States adequately. Most correspondents are kept busy in Washington and New York. They rarely travel to other parts of the country, except to cover special events such as major sports competitions or presidential nominating conventions. Thus the impressions that foreigners receive about Americans' opinions and politics are largely the views of official

Washington. The leftward orientation of most reporters from foreign countries produces a substantial amount of criticism of America's economic, military, and foreign aid policies and often makes the conduct of foreign relations rocky. Hostile coverage is only partially balanced by the influx of news from American media and government broadcasts, such as Voice of America (VOA) or, for several years, WORLDNET, a satellite program sponsored by the U.S. Information Agency (USIA). WORLDNET, which has been stopped for economic reasons, enabled reporters in foreign capitals to have direct access to top administration officials.

The Setting for News Selection

Cultural Pressures. American correspondents abroad, like domestic journalists, must operate within the context of American politics and American political culture. Although their personal leanings may be to the left of the political spectrum, they aim for the middle ground in their stories because that is what their audiences presumably want. Keeping in touch with the American scene is deemed so important that news organizations bring their reporters back to the United States periodically to refresh their feel for what is going on at home.

Stories not only must reflect the American value structure, but they also must conform to established American stereotypes. Accordingly, when U.S. correspondents in Peru accurately reported about the military government's reforms, the stories were rejected as lies because they contradicted the stereotype that military regimes support the status quo.[24] Similarly, the credibility of stories about the problems of foreign teenagers might be questioned unless these same problems were plaguing American youth.[25] On the other hand, U.S. correspondents abroad have greater leeway than their domestic counterparts to evaluate and interpret news because there is less likelihood that the domestic audience—ordinary citizens or powerful interest groups—will be offended.

Intra-organizational norms and pressures also influence news selection. Foreign news is gathered by a small enough group of reporters to allow for much personal contact and cooperation. Since the wire services perform the initial gatekeeping tasks for most newspapers and electronic media, topic selection is quite uniform nationally as well as internationally. Elite papers then take the lead in fashioning the norms for presentation and interpretation that editors and reporters throughout each country adapt for their media.

Political Pressures. Overt and covert political pressures to publish or suppress news stories play a greater role in foreign news production than on the domestic scene. As guests in the countries from which they are reporting, foreign correspondents often must do their hosts' bidding. Many of these hosts are dictators who safeguard their political survival by ensuring supportive publicity for their regimes and squelching unfavorable coverage. Foreign correspondents, like the native newspeople in that country, are heavily censored. If foreign correspondents want to remain in the country, they must write dispatches acceptable to the authorities. Otherwise they face severe penalties—expulsion, confiscation of their notes and pictures, closure of transmission facilities, refusal of contact by public officials, and the like. This has led to a strange phenomenon: the most undemocratic countries often receive the least criticism while more open societies are freely reproached.

Censorship can take the form of denying visas to bar entry to the country or restrictions on travel within the country. Scores of countries have barred foreign reporters from entering or have expelled them after entry. Cambodia, Laos, Vietnam, Nicaragua, El Salvador, Albania, the Soviet Union, and South Africa provide vivid examples in recent decades. When the Chinese city of Tangshan was destroyed by an earthquake on July 28, 1976, and more than 655,000 people were killed, reporters stationed in Beijing, barely one hundred miles away, were denied permission for more than a year to visit the scene.[26] Britain kept foreign reporters away from the embattled Falkland Islands in 1983. Israel repeatedly has imposed tight censorship on coverage of its activities in Lebanon and in the occupied West Bank and Gaza Strip. During the Iran-Iraq hostilities in the early 1980s, reporters were permitted at the front only whenever the host country thought it had won an engagement. Large areas of Central America have been closed to reporters, making it almost impossible to adequately cover hostilities there. South Africa has made it illegal to quote "banned" people, describe prison conditions, or film protest demonstrations.[27] In the Soviet Union reporters who interviewed dissidents were harassed.

Bureaucratic hurdles abound. In Moscow during the Soviet regime television reporters depended on the Novosti Press Agency for camera crews and access to various sites. Cameras were made available only after the Foreign Ministry's Press Department approved a story proposal. Once a proposal was filed, no deviations were allowed. Promised camera crews frequently arrived late or not at all. Pictures often were deliberately out of focus, and transmission equipment was disconnected if events did not proceed as planned.

Reporters in some countries face physical danger. Not infrequently, they have been jailed, assaulted, and sometimes murdered. During the Nicaraguan revolution of 1979, a national guardsman, angry over American support of revolutionary forces, shot and killed an American television reporter. Several murders of newspeople in Lebanon in the

1980s have been attributed to Syrian authorities angered by stories these journalists wrote.[28] The Helsinki Accords of 1975, in which many countries promised free and safe access to each other's newspeople, have done little to improve the situation.

When countries previously closed to foreign journalists suddenly open their borders, the newcomers may be totally unprepared for insightful coverage. The opening of the People's Republic of China in 1972 is an example. Reporters arrived with President Richard Nixon and Secretary of State Henry Kissinger. During their short stay in China, the reporters dutifully shot those pictures that the Chinese allowed them to shoot and reported those stories that the Chinese arranged for them to report. The resulting coverage was a romanticized travelogue rather than solid political analysis.

Media Diplomacy. A recent development in foreign news production is "television diplomacy"—attempts by television correspondents in the United States and abroad to inject themselves directly into the political process and attempts by U.S. and foreign leaders to use television to further their causes. The Middle East situation presents a number of dramatic examples. CBS anchor Walter Cronkite became a peacemaker on November 14, 1977, during a television satellite interview. At that time he drew from Egypt's president Anwar al-Sadat a public promise to go to Jerusalem if this would further peace. In a separate interview Cronkite secured a pledge from Israeli prime minister Menachem Begin that he would personally welcome Sadat at Ben Gurion airport, should he come. With such mutual commitments, the scene was set for the historic meeting.

When Sadat arrived in Israel on November 19, anchors from the three American networks were in his entourage. Among the welcoming crowds at the airport were an additional two thousand journalists from all over the globe. Again this was media diplomacy in the broadest sense. The event was covered live on American television and radio, giving the principals a chance to woo American audiences. In the weeks that followed, more than 30 million people in America and millions more worldwide watched and judged the peacemaking process. Television alone devoted twenty-four hours of broadcasts to the spectacle, supplemented by radio and print news.

When Arab-Israeli peacemaking moved to the United States the following spring, media diplomacy continued. President Sadat, fully aware of the importance of courting the American public, made himself available for a television interview immediately after arrival for the 1978 Camp David meeting. The next day in his address to the National Press Club, he accused the Israelis of stalling the negotiations. Israel countered this propaganda move by promptly dispatching Foreign Minister

Moshe Dayan on a ten-day speaking tour of major American cities to garner favorable publicity for the Israeli side.[29] The media reported it all with relish, proud of the role they had played in bringing about encounters between Israeli and Egyptian officials. Little thought was given to the political ramifications that ensue when foreign heads of state readily use the American press as their public relations tool.

The lessons learned by Sadat and Begin have not been lost on other world leaders. For instance, in 1979 Iran's revolutionary leader, Ayatollah Ruhollah Khomeini, rebuffed official emissaries from the United States who were sent to negotiate the release of the American embassy personnel held hostage by Iranian students. Khomeini preferred to discuss the situation with American television correspondents. A series of interviews was arranged. By requiring prior approval of questions, the Iranian government carefully controlled what was discussed. To ensure maximum exposure for the Ayatollah's views, Iranian leaders permitted an especially lengthy interview for the highly popular CBS program "60 Minutes." At the same time they assigned low priority to an interview to be aired on low-audience public television. The Iranian embassy also bought full-page advertisements in the *New York Times* and other American newspapers to acquaint the American public with Iran's version of the hostage story.

For their part, reporters used interviews with Iranian officials to suggest policies that might resolve the crisis and to elicit Iranian views and counterproposals. Placing these views before a worldwide audience made them part of the agenda of international politics. Media diplomacy facilitated negotiations that had broken down at the diplomatic level and generated a number of excellent proposals. Even when normal diplomatic relations exist, reporters often become part of the political process by publicizing interviews with political leaders in which the reporters determine and frame the issues to be discussed.

While media diplomacy is often helpful, it also is fraught with disadvantages and dangers. Government officials, who have far more foreign policy expertise than journalists, may be maneuvered into untenable positions. Foreign policy then may become incoherent and inexpert, with serious consequences for the nation. Another disadvantage of media diplomacy is that journalists may inadvertently provide a propaganda forum for foreign leaders. This is why CNN's Peter Arnett was so harshly condemned by many Americans when he engaged Iraq's president Saddam Hussein in a long television interview during the Gulf War. The interview permitted the Iraqi leader to broadcast accusations against his antagonists to a worldwide audience.

Economic Pressures.   Economic considerations, like cultural and political factors, strongly influence foreign news selection. First, there is

Don Wright, *Palm Beach Post*. Reprinted with permission.

the usual pressure to present appealing stories that attract big audiences and keep the media profitable. This pressure is even more burdensome for foreign correspondents than for their domestic counterparts because their stories must be exceptionally good to attract large audiences. Second, there is the pressure to avoid or minimize huge production costs. Reporting events such as President Nixon's trip to China or Israel's Yom Kippur War cost each network in excess of $3 million per event. Leasing cables for news transmission is expensive and so is telephone communication. Satellite transmission is also costly, especially for short messages. Some stories therefore may be shut out because they cannot be transmitted cheaply, while others may be included merely because transmission is comparatively inexpensive and convenient.

Gathering the News: The Beat

The international beat system is quite similar to local beats. Originally, newspapers established their foreign news bureaus in major capitals of the world, primarily in Western Europe. From there correspondents covered entire countries rather than particular types of stories; London, Paris, Bonn, and Rome were the main news-gathering spots. In the wake of the Vietnam War, Saigon, Tokyo, Hong Kong, and other Far Eastern points became important news centers. China moved into focus with the opening of diplomatic relations in 1972.

The average newspaper bureau abroad has one or two correspondents, one or two film crews staffed by foreigners, perhaps a radio correspondent, and a few stringers. Correspondents from these bureaus jet to spots within easy flying range whenever big stories break. For local news they rely heavily on national news services that exist in two-thirds of the countries of the world. Countries without such services, and without satellite transmission facilities, are far less likely to receive coverage than countries that have them.

The bulk of foreign affairs news for American media actually originates in Washington from various beats in the executive branch, especially the White House, the State Department, and the Pentagon. The president's views tend to dominate whenever situations are controversial. However, the media put their imprint on the news by featuring confrontational and hard-line views.[30] At times foreign policy stories may be hard to cover because officials are reluctant to talk whenever delicate negotiations or the prestige of the United States is at stake. A further common drawback to Washington stories is their lack of exciting pictures to dramatize them for television. Like domestic newspeople, foreign correspondents prefer to report predictable events, such as elections or summit conferences, so that coverage can be planned well in advance. The decision to film particular foreign stories abroad is usually made in the United States because the media's home offices consider themselves in closer touch with the interests of American audiences. Foreign bureaus do the actual filming.

Foreign news bestows unequal attention on various regions and countries of the world just as domestic news covers regions of the United States unequally. Neither is there any correlation between size of population and amount of coverage. In general, beats cover the countries with which the United States has its most significant diplomatic contacts. In recent years, that has usually meant England, France, West Germany, Italy, and the Soviet Union in Europe; Israel and Egypt in the Middle East; and, more recently, the People's Republic of China and Japan in the Far East. Africa and Latin America are covered lightly, except when Americans become concerned about humanitarian issues, like the treatment of people of color in South Africa, or civil strife involving charges of Communist influence, like the situation in Nicaragua in the 1980s. Asian coverage was light until the Vietnam War, when for several years it replaced stories from other parts of the world. Table 11-3 provides data on coverage of major regions of the world between July 1990 and June 1991.

The table has been divided into three time periods. The first column reflects television network news coverage for July 1990, a

Table 11-3 Network Coverage of World Regions, July 1990 to June 1991

Region	July 1990	August 1990 to February 1991	March to June 1991	Yearly total
Western Europe	26%	16%	12%	15%
Soviet Union	23	12	15	13
Eastern Europe	11	2	5	4
Middle East	8	57	45	51
Africa (Sub-Sahara)	8	3	6	4
South Asia	1	1	4	2
S.E. Asia and Pacific	7	2	4	3
East Asia	7	3	5	4
Latin America	7	2	4	3
Canada	1	1	1	1

Source: Compiled from Vanderbilt Television News Archives data.

Note: Pre-Gulf crisis, July 1990 $N = 520$; Gulf crisis, August 1990 through February 1991 $N = 4,029$; Post-Gulf crisis, March to June 1991 $N = 1,884$; Yearly total $N = 6,418$. Prior to German unification, East Germany was coded as Eastern Europe.

relatively normal month in foreign affairs. Attention on television, as well as in print news, was focused predominantly on Western Europe and the Soviet bloc, with somewhat more attention to the latter than in prior Cold War years. The middle column, covering August 1990 to February 1991, reflects the typical distortion that occurs when one area of the world moves into the limelight of attention. When attention became focused on the Middle East, most of the rest of the world dropped out of focus. However important problems were in other parts of the globe, they escaped the attention of most of America's political elites as well as the American public. The third column, extending from March through June 1991, shows the relatively slow return to the more usual patterns of coverage, with Middle East news diminishing and the slack distributed fairly evenly among the previously deprived regions.

Criteria for Choosing Stories

Foreign like domestic news is selected primarily for audience appeal rather than for political significance. This means that stories must have an angle that interests Americans. Sociologist Herbert Gans, who examined foreign affairs news in television newscasts and in news magazines, has identified seven subjects that are aired most often.[31] They include, first, American activities in foreign countries, particularly when presidents and secretaries of state visit, and, second, events that affect Americans directly in a major way (wars, oil embargoes, and other problems that transcend national boundaries, like unemployment and inflation).

A third area of interest concerns relations of the United States with totalitarian and formerly totalitarian countries. Internal political and military problems of these countries are emphasized. Elections in democratic countries with strong Communist or Fascist parties are also part of the routine coverage of the "totalitarian menace." Fourth, foreign elections in other parts of the world are covered if they involve a change in the head of state. There also is a sentimental attachment for following the major (and minor) activities of European royalty.

The fifth subject area entails stories about dramatic political conflicts. Most wars, coups d'état, and revolutions are reported; protests, as a rule, are covered only when they are violent. Left-wing coups receive more attention than right-wing coups. Disasters, if they involve massive loss of lives and destruction of property, are a sixth area of interest. There is a rough calculus by which severity is measured: "10,000 deaths in Nepal equals 100 deaths in Wales equals 10 deaths in West Virginia equals one death next door." [32] In general, the more distant a nation, the more frequently a newsworthy event must happen to be reported.

The seventh area of coverage involves the excesses of foreign dictators, particularly brutality against political dissidents (for example, the deeds of Uganda's former ruler Idi Amin and the leaders of Latin American death squads). Noticeably absent from American broadcasts and papers are stories about ordinary people and ordinary events abroad. These would be news to Americans, but, except for occasional special features, they are not *news* in the professional dictionary of journalists.

Foreign news stories also must have an appealing format. Emphasis on violence, conflict and disaster, timeliness or novelty, and familiarity of persons or situations are the major selection criteria. For instance, stories from Western Europe and other familiar areas are more likely to be published than stories from other parts of the world. When news from countries with unfamiliar cultures is published, the rule of "uncertainty absorption" comes into play. This unwritten rule requires that gatekeepers avoid foreign news of uncertain accuracy, coming from remote sources. Only plausible stories are acceptable, and they must be cast into a familiar framework, such as the battle against poverty and racism or the moral bankruptcy of military dictators. [33] Such biases make it very difficult to change images of culturally distant countries. Far-off parts of the world are rarely covered except when sensational events such as violence and disaster occur or there is negative news about top-level public officials. [34] Moreover, the high costs of covering news abroad force news organizations to limit the sites where they can maintain full-scale news operations.

The media's preference for news about current happenings has led to concentration on rapidly breaking stories in accessible places, regardless of their intrinsic importance. Long-range developments, such as programs to improve public health or reduce illiteracy or efforts to create new political parties, do not fill the bill if they lack a recent climax. Pressure for timeliness and novelty also fragments news presentation and usually precludes follow-through. This gives major events an unwarranted air of suddenness and unpredictability. They have neither a past nor a future—merely a brief presence in the parade of current events.

For example, when war-torn El Salvador held an election in March 1982, the press was there in full force, grinding out stories day after day. Coverage dwindled abruptly after the election, even though little had changed in El Salvador, and the Reagan administration continued to claim that the United States had important interests in that country. Most American media failed to explain the consequences of the election. When questioned about the exodus of newspeople, news executives said that other crises and events beckoned: the Falkland Islands War, fighting in Lebanon, and the foreign journeys of President Ronald Reagan and Pope John Paul II.[35]

At times coverage errs in the opposite direction. The story of Americans held hostage in Iran from November 4, 1979, to January 20, 1981, was vastly overcovered. Daily broadcasts featured dramatic visual scenes of young Americans held captive in a strange land, angry anti-American crowds, and anxious kinfolk at home. During the first six months of the crisis, nearly one-third of each nightly network newscast was devoted to the story.[36] Table 11-3 depicts a similar situation during the 1991 Gulf War with 57 percent of the news focused on the Middle East. Much of that coverage was repetitious and uninformative. With media attention riveted on one international trouble spot, most other foreign news tends to be slighted.

News Production Constraints

The problems of producing domestic news are magnified for foreign news making. Staffs are smaller, research facilities are more limited, language barriers are troublesome, and transmission difficulties may be enormous. Then, once the story finally reaches the audience, it may not be heard because of basic disinterest or ignorance of the setting in which it originated.

Production constraints are particularly severe for television news, which presents the bulk of foreign news to the average American. The quest for good pictures is often frustrated by restrictions on access or because facilities for taking and processing pictures are inadequate.[37]

Pictures are especially important for foreign news because they bring unfamiliar sights, which might be hard to imagine, directly into viewers' homes. Starvation in India or Nicaragua, the lifestyles of primitive tribes in New Guinea or Australia, or street riots in Spain or Hungary are better understood if they can be visually experienced. No words can make us feel the horrors of starvation as acutely as the picture of the starving child on the next page.

However, not even words and pictures combined can tell the whole story if the audience is unfamiliar with the setting in which the reported events are happening. Grisly street scenes of Israeli soldiers chasing and beating Palestinian protesters, rock-throwing youngsters confronted by armed Israelis, and overturned and burning vehicles created the image in 1988 of a brutal military and a country in the throes of an ugly civil war. These pictures profoundly affected the attitude of the American public, including the Congress, toward Israel. The sharp drop-off in affection resembled that suffered by Israel in the wake of reports about Israeli brutalities in Lebanon in the summer of 1982. Israeli pleas that the country's image was being distorted were of little avail. Most Americans were unaware that the riots were confined to a small section of the country. They failed to put Israeli reactions into the appropriate historical perspectives.[38] When gripping visuals constitute high drama, sans information, their impact can be overwhelming.

The need to keep news stories brief is particularly troubling for foreign correspondents because foreign news is often unintelligible without adequate background information or interpretation. Complexity therefore becomes a major enemy, and avoidance or oversimplification the defensive strategy. Stories must be written simply and logically even if the situation defies logic. Usually a single theme must be selected to epitomize the entire complex story.

The dominant theme of the Iran hostage stories was that innocent Americans were imprisoned by irrational anti-American terrorists—a gross oversimplification of a multifaceted situation. The complexities of Iran's internal politics received little attention because they could not be easily incorporated into a dramatic, visually appealing story. David Altheide, who studied coverage of the crisis, concluded that the reporting

> was consistent with criteria of production formats involving resolutions of practical concerns like accessibility, visual quality, drama and action, audience relevance, and encapsulation and thematic unity. The employment of these format considerations made newswork more predictable and manageable, but it also permitted the selection of themes resonant with cultural stereotypes and images already familiar to the journalists. In this way, cultural stereotypes, including political and ideological value judgments, found their way into news content.[39]

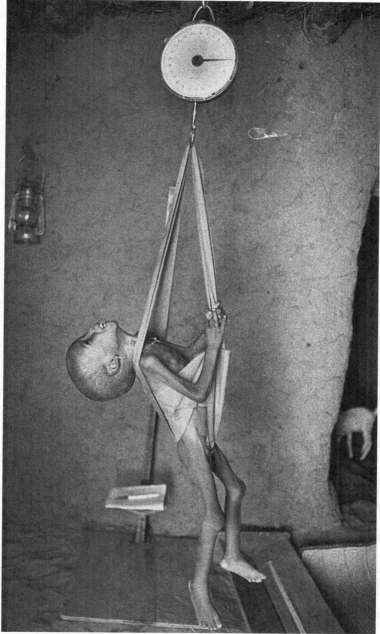

Magnum Photos. © Sebastiao Salgado

Starving child being weighed in a Third World country.

Effects of Gatekeeping

Foreign affairs coverage is ample, dramatic, and up to date, but it lacks depth and breadth, it stereotypes and oversimplifies, and it often distorts facts in the interest of timeliness. Accordingly, a twelve-year study of international terrorism stories led to the conclusion that "network coverage bore little relationship to actual patterns of occurrence. On the whole, the limitations of production and presentation, concerns over audience share, and the narrow focus of journalistic notions of professionalism result in coverage more notable for its erratic nature than for its systematic biases." [40] Officials and publics who rely on foreign affairs news may be misled, and faulty policies may ensue. The news about the Cold War is a good example.

Cold War Perspectives. Since relations between the United States and the Soviet Union were undoubtedly vastly important to Americans, as well as to the world in the period after World War II, one might expect the news media to devote a great deal of attention to this topic. What are the facts? Were American government officials and the public offered the broad picture, spanning all aspects of Soviet life and politics? Or was coverage narrowly focused on conflicting interests, provocations, and military power assessments? [41]

A study spanning the administrations of presidents Truman, Eisenhower, Kennedy, Johnson, Nixon, Ford, Carter, Reagan, and Bush shows that coverage was defective throughout the 1945 to 1991 time period. The study is based on analysis of every theme in presidential news conferences and in *New York Times* editorials during the forty-six-year period. This information was selected for analysis because presidential pronouncements, *New York Times* editorial stands, and the thrust of questions posed by the nation's top journalists in Washington tend to set the pattern for foreign affairs coverage.

As Table 11-4 shows, attitudes of American officials regarding the Soviet Union, such as fears about its intentions or the possibility for cooperation (21 percent), and specific events, such as summit meetings (14 percent) were well-covered. But only 6 percent of the themes explored during press conferences presented information about the actual status of U.S.-Soviet relations, mostly about military matters. Trade relations or scientific cooperation were largely ignored.

The Soviet Union's political influence and power were primarily assessed in terms of Soviet relations with other countries (23 percent), such as Vietnam, China, Poland, or regions like Western Europe and the Persian Gulf, or in military terms (18 percent), including defense spending, weapons systems, and troops stationed in satellite countries. While 41 percent of the themes dealt with these important matters,

Table 11-4 Soviet News Story Topics in the U.S. Press, January 1945 to January 1991

Topic	Press conference themes	Editorial themes
Soviet foreign relations	23%	14%
Soviet military policy	18	9
U.S. attitude about Soviets	21	33
U.S./Soviet meetings	14	5
U.S. military policy	5	6
Soviet attitudes about United States	4	7
U.S./Soviet comparisons	5	4
Human rights issues	3	11
Soviet leaders' quality	2	4
Communism as ideology	2	3
U.S. policy about Soviet Union	1	2
Soviet technology	1	1

Source: Author's research.

Note: $N = 2{,}636$ press conference themes and 5,310 editorial themes.

equally important internal Soviet conditions were slighted. Only 8 percent of the themes covered internal indicators that might have predicted the problems that led to the disintegration of the Soviet Union in the 1990s.

In line with the pattern of highlighting only a few topic areas, coverage of internal matters was also quite limited in scope. It focused on human rights issues (3 percent), such as the plight of dissidents, appraisals of the status of the Communist ideology (2 percent), the quality of the country's political leadership (2 percent), and on Soviet technology (1 percent). Comparisons between the United States and the Soviet Union were few (5 percent), even though they would have been useful in putting the Cold War into perspective. Though U.S. attitudes toward the Soviet Union were amply discussed (21 percent), there was little reciprocal analysis of Soviet attitudes and fears concerning the United States (4 percent).

One might argue that the topics that received attention seemed to be most important at the time and the ones on which information was most readily available. Even if we are willing to accept that justification, it is clear in retrospect that coverage was inadequate. The blame must be shared between journalists and presidents. Though journalists take the initiative in asking questions at news conferences, presidents have ample opportunities to weave information into their responses to reflect what they deem to be significant. In fact, analysis of all topics covered by news conferences shows that presidents frequently use this power so that their answers often have very little to do with the reporters' questions. Although press conferences aired important themes about the U.S.-Soviet relationship, over the span of years covered by this study it was possible to broaden out the picture and correct inaccuracies.

Coverage of the Soviet Union is an excellent example of drifting into coverage patterns with little planning or periodic reassessments. With minor variations, the same type of spotty, narrow coverage prevailed throughout all nine presidencies, regardless of the varying degrees of tension engendered by the Cold War during the 46-year span. The period encompassed three major Cold War confrontations when war was a distinct possibility, and three periods of partial thaw when peaceful relations seemed assured. The four most frequently mentioned thematic categories accounted for the bulk of commentary during each administration. In every case, more than two-thirds of the messages dealt with the top four themes, which cover a restricted array of topics. When it came to slighting certain topic areas, uniformity prevailed as well. With minor exceptions, topics like Soviet technology or the quality of Soviet leaders garnered little coverage.

Choosing Frames for Friends and Foes. The fact that foreign news reported in the American press is based primarily on American sources who stay closely to the mainstream line explains why pro-American perspectives dominate. As the saying goes, outcomes are judged by whose ox is gored. Coverage of the downing of two planes, one by Soviet fire and the other by American fire, illustrates the principle.

In 1983, a Soviet fighter plane shot down Korean Airlines flight 007 with a loss of 269 lives. Five years later, in 1988, the *Vincennes*, a U.S. Navy ship, shot down Iran Air flight 655 with a loss of 290 lives. The Soviets claimed that the shooting was justified because the plane had been identified as a hostile target; the Americans made the same claim for their action. Though the cases differed in detail and in the context in which they occurred, they were sufficiently alike to expect similarity in coverage. That did not happen, judging from coverage of the events in *Time, Newsweek,* the *New York Times,* the *Washington Post,* and the CBS evening news. The manner in which the news was framed, including the language and pictures used in the stories and the overall context into which the stories were placed, made the Soviet action a moral outrage and the American action a regrettable technological failure.[42]

For example, almost twice as much coverage was given to the tragedy caused by the Soviets than to its American counterpart, even though the loss of life was greater in the Iran Air case. Following the Korean Airlines crash, *Newsweek* proclaimed on its cover "Murder in the Air"; *Time's* cover read "Shooting to Kill/The Soviets Destroy an Airliner." *Newsweek's* cover on the 1988 crash was headlined: "The Gulf Tragedy: Why It Happened," omitting any reference to a suspected villain. Similarly, *Time,* in a small insert on its cover, said innocuously "What Went Wrong in the Gulf." The stories inside the magazines repeatedly accused the Soviets of knowingly destroying a civilian plane whereas the Americans' actions were excused as pardonable ignorance. The Soviets' action was characterized as typical behavior for that country and guilt was attributed to its leaders. Not so for the Americans.

The stories about the Korean airliner dwelled on the human tragedy encountered by the victims and their families; the Iranian airliner story de-emphasized that aspect. When Soviet actions were described, words like "atrocity," "crime," "massacre," and "murder" abounded. For the Americans, the emphasis was on the accidental nature of the event. When, during the investigation of the action of the *Vincennes,* some doubts were raised about the innocence of the American crew, these facts were generally buried in the back pages of the news magazines and newspapers. The same fate befell commentary that suggested the Soviet action might have been accidental, rather than deliberate.

There is no evidence that the distortions that spring from such chauvinistic framing are deliberate. Rather, the framing reflects the actual perspectives of the journalists, based on their choice of sources and the predispositions with which they approach stories involving countries identified as friend or foe. Nonetheless, this type of coverage has political consequences. In 1983, it heightened anti-Soviet feelings among members of Congress and the public, sharply reducing the momentum of the nuclear freeze movement that had been gaining ground.[43] In the Iran Air case in 1988, coverage defused potential pressure for withdrawal of American forces from the Persian Gulf region. Instead of seeing the incident as an example of harm caused by America's presence in the area, warranting reconsideration of the policy, the incident consolidated American support behind the Reagan administration's foreign policies in the Gulf.

Wars in the Television Age. In the wake of the Vietnam War, many politicians and other political observers believed that fighting lengthy wars had become nearly impossible for democratic societies in the age of full-color, battle-front television. When battle scenes are broadcast nightly in gruesome color in the nation's living rooms, public support for wars is likely to vanish. The depiction of Israel's invasion and siege of Beirut in 1982 presents a case in point. In the wake of footage of human carnage, Israel lost measurable amounts of support from its closest allies. This loss reduced its ability to pursue the war and undermined its bargaining position.

To avoid such circumstances, in the 1982 Falkland Islands War, Great Britain and Argentina both resorted to the kind of censorship usually associated only with authoritarian regimes. Like the Soviets in Afghanistan or the Syrians in Lebanon, the British and the Argentines curbed and delayed pictorial coverage of the war to reduce possibly adverse consequences at home. Similarly, no reporters were permitted to witness the first phases of the U.S. invasion of Grenada in 1983. The military is preoccupied with fighting during these initial stages and disinclined to take time out to deal with reporters. Moreover, it wants to keep its action plans secret. Journalists, on the other hand, want to be at the scene of action from the start with full access to the troops.

The press complained loudly about its exclusion from initial coverage in Grenada, which led to creation of a small rotating group of reporters who would be alerted about impending military operations so that they could be part of the initial operations. The system failed miserably when it was first tried in Panama in December 1989. The fourteen reporters in the pool reached Panama four hours after the fighting began and were not allowed to file stories until six hours later. Then their movements were restricted to tours under military escort. Government briefings were closely controlled by the military and generally uninformative. Neither the military nor the government was interested in having anyone question the soundness of the policy and the military phases of its execution. Even the press seemed disinclined to be critical in any way. Public support for the venture, as measured in public opinion polls, may have restrained the press. So may the fact that reporters had previously criticized President Bush for failing to take strong action against President Manuel Noriega who had been accused of a multitude of political misdeeds.[44]

As described in Chapter 5, the situation was not much better during the 1991 Gulf War, even though the rules had been revised again to permit journalists more freedom of movement. The pool system allowed only 100 of the more than 1,600 American reporters in the area access to some 500,000 troops. Reporters who went to the front without authorization were arrested and detained. The upshot was sanitized coverage of the war. Flawlessly executed precision maneuvers were shown but not failures or pictures of the dead and wounded, friend or foe. While military censorship was to blame for glamorizing the battlefield, journalists must share in the blame for inadequate coverage. Most of them failed to familiarize themselves with the history and politics of the peoples of the region and with the policies of various outside powers interested in the area, including the United States. Had they done so, their coverage could have been far more insightful.[45]

After the war, executives from the major American media filed a report with Defense Secretary Dick Cheney, complaining about the pool system and efforts to sanitize the news and delay it. "By controlling what reporters saw and when they saw it, the military exerted great power to shape and manage the news."[46] The complaints led to yet another revision of the rules, which was endorsed by the journalism community. Under the new rules, pools, which should be as large as possible, will be used only in the initial stages. They will be disbanded within twenty-four to thirty-six hours. While the military retains control over the rules, it will try to facilitate reporting, including facilitating transportation on military vehicles. The only area where the press and military could not reach agreement was on the right of the military to ask to review material for security purposes.[47]

It is unlikely that the time will ever arrive when the military and the press will be fully satisfied with each other's conduct. Their respective goals are much too antagonistic. War is a dirty business that will never be photogenic when shown in all its brutality. As long as "just" wars for "good causes" (whatever that may be) are condoned and even celebrated by the world community, full coverage remains a sensitive issue. If it does, indeed, discourage such military actions, the world community's ability to defend its interests will diminish. Ruthless members of the community can then use the threat of military action to advance their own goals. The price for such a peace may be too high.

Shortcomings and Distortions.   Just like domestic news, foreign news neglects major social problems, particularly political and economic development issues. The reasons are readily apparent. Social problems are difficult to describe in brief stories, visual materials are often lacking, and changes come at a glacial pace. Some social problems are extremely complex; most reporters are ill equipped to understand let alone describe them. When they do describe them, the focus is on their dramatic negative aspects: shortages, famines, conflicts, and breakdowns. As Rafael Caldera, former president of Venezuela, told a press conference at the National Press Club in Washington, D.C., "the phrase 'no news is good news' has become 'good news is no news.'. . . Little or nothing is mentioned about literary or scientific achievements" in American media or "about social achievements and the defense against the dangers which threaten our peace and development." Instead, "only the most deplorable incidents, be they caused by nature or by man, receive prominent attention."[48] It is small consolation for such ruffled feelings that news selection criteria for Third World events are typical for news everywhere.[49]

Negative and conflictual news is more prevalent in the U.S. media than in the media of many other societies, especially those of the Communist world. Comparisons of news coverage in the United States and in Canada, a society that is culturally close to America, furnish examples. The rate of violence on Canadian television news is half the U.S. rate.[50] When the people of Quebec voted in 1980 on the question of separatism from Canada, the *Washington Post* warned that civil war might erupt. American papers featured stories about serious rioting by separatists in English sectors of Montreal. By contrast, the *Toronto Globe and Mail* buried a small story about minor unrest in Quebec in the back pages. The prospect of civil war was never mentioned and was characterized as "ludicrous" by knowledgeable observers.[51] During the Iranian hostage crisis, *New York Times* coverage was dominated by stereotypical portrayals of Moslems and by tales of violence. Far more peaceful images emerged from reading the French paper *Le Monde*.[52]

By and large, Western news media feature more conflict than do media in authoritarian and totalitarian societies. In part this happens because government-controlled news organizations find it comparatively easy to shun dramatic negative news since government subsidies relieve them of the need to secure large audiences. Regardless of the reasons for the difference, the approach used by American news media draws attention to conflict rather than to peaceful settlement and makes much of the world outside of the United States seem chaotic. Although ordinary foreign news languishes in the back pages or is condensed into the briefest broadcast accounts, stories concerned with civil disorder and revolutions are featured prominently. Usually they are oversimplified and told from an American perspective that may be totally inappropriate. Instead of interpreting what the conflict means to the country and its people, the dominant concern ordinarily is whether the leaders are friendly or hostile to the United States and how this tilt will affect the international balance of power.

Distortions also plague domestic news coverage, but they are less deceptive because American audiences can see the situation more clearly; past experiences and socialization provide corrective lenses for viewing the domestic scene.[53] The foreign scene, by contrast, must be viewed without correction for myopia and astigmatism. Americans may be skeptical about the accuracy of the images, but they lack the means to judge the nature and degree of distortion.

Finally, the thrust of foreign news, like its domestic counterpart, provides support for government policies. The media routinely accept official designations of who America's friends and enemies are, and interpret their motives accordingly. Whenever relationships change, media coverage mirrors the change. Coverage of the Soviet Union's attack on Korean Airline flight 007 is a good example of the approach used for disfavored countries. In the same way, a comparison of *New York Times* coverage of strife in Cambodia and East Timor and of elections in Nicaragua and El Salvador showed that "Communist-tainted" Cambodia and Nicaragua were judged unfavorably. By contrast, comparable events in East Timor and El Salvador, countries deemed friendly to the United States, were cast in a favorable light.[54] Because the president and executive branch have remained the prime sources of foreign affairs news, they can, most of the time, set the agenda of coverage and frame stories to reflect official perspectives.[55]

If the media are generally supportive of government policy, how can their adverse comments about the Vietnam War be explained? The answer is that the media emphasized the government's positions until many respected sources voiced their strong dissent. At that point the media continued to give the administration's views on the war the largest amount of coverage. They coupled it, however, with coverage of the growing dissent in America about the merits of Vietnam policies, giving ample attention to antiadministration voices and to antiwar demonstrations. Even when protest was featured, the media gave voice primarily to "respectable" dissenters, not to political and social outcasts.[56]

Support of the Status Quo. News emphasis stabilizes perceptions about the international status quo. Preoccupation with the developed powers reinforces many Americans' beliefs about the importance of these nations. In the same way, portrayal of less developed countries as incapable of managing their own internal affairs makes it easy to believe that they do not deserve higher status and the media attention that accompanies it.

Newspeople usually are willing to withhold news and commentary when publicity would severely complicate the government's management of foreign policy. For instance, the media refrained from sharply criticizing Iranian leaders during the 1979 hostage crisis to avoid angering them and suppressed information about America's breaking of Japanese military message codes during World War II. Both are examples in which major political interests were at stake. Likewise, news of delicate negotiations among foreign countries may be temporarily withheld to avoid rocking the boat before agreements are reached. This has happened when East and West Germans have been engaged in discussions about border crossings and when the Soviet Union expressed willingness to negotiate arms limitations that it had previously refused to consider.[57]

The Unique Impact of Television

We have already mentioned that television has vastly broadened the American audience for foreign affairs coverage and that television anchors have repeatedly assumed roles formerly reserved for diplomats. But the medium has done even more.[58] With satellite transmission its audience has become global. Millions throughout the world, including government leaders, watched the 1987 hearings on U.S.-Iranian arms deals and coverage of the superpower summit meetings in 1987 and 1988. The fact that this international audience would be likely to react to these broadcasts constrained the behavior of the actors caught in the publicity glare. The political consequences were, no doubt, substantial.

Television changes the substance of important political events in ways that reduce the options of political leaders, as Zbigniew Brzezinski, President Carter's national security adviser, pointed out in a retrospective analysis of the Teheran hostage crisis:

> First, TV transforms essentially a political confrontation into a personal drama. The result is you cannot deal with it coldly in terms of the national interest but you must focus on the personal aspects. Secondly, as the confrontation becomes a personal drama, the bargaining capacity of the kidnappers is enhanced. Concentration on accommodation by the American government becomes more important. Thirdly, it humanizes the enemy. Therefore, you begin to make equations and equivalences, which dulls the sharpness of the possible response.[59]

One can argue that the influence of television in a hostage crisis is benign or that it is harmful. But few would argue with Brzezinski's claim that ample coverage alters the political situation.

Television may do three things in a crisis. First, it may dictate the national agenda by riveting public attention on the crisis to the exclusion of virtually all else. For example, during the stock market crisis of 1987, television slighted news about America's air attack on Iranian bases in the Persian Gulf and news about a domestic airline disaster. These would have been the top stories in calmer times. Second, televised crisis coverage may pressure the president to react hastily so that he does not appear weak and vacillating. As Lloyd Cutler, White House counsel to President Carter, put it: "If an ominous foreign event is featured on TV news, the President and his advisers feel bound to make a response in time for the next evening news program." [60] This may leave no time for investigation of the news report or for explanation of the event by officials of the foreign country. Normal diplomatic discourse becomes preempted by the media.

Third, television's impact on political elites and mass publics may narrow the president's freedom to bargain and maneuver. This happened during the Iranian hostage crisis. The Carter administration's poorly conducted hostage rescue mission has been attributed to pressures created by the prolonged television coverage of the hostages and publicized charges that President Carter was incompetent to resolve the situation.

Public officials are fully aware that television can affect their actions in major ways. In a survey of 95 officials serving in policy-related jobs, 81 percent indicated that they relied heavily on the media for policy-relevant information. Fifty-three percent attributed great influence to the media in the early stages of the policy cycle when the issues are initially framed.[61] Whoever controls this period—the American government, foreign governments, nongovernmental groups, or media personnel—is apt to have a powerful impact on the definition of the situation. Once the issue has been framed and a policy has been developed, media influence is far less potent.

Seventy-seven percent thought that positive and negative media attention enhanced the salience of an issue for the bureaucracy and the public. Seventy-eight percent thought that it was a bad idea for journalists to act on their own as diplomats.[62] Most (81 percent) agreed that television brings new players into the game of international politics, particularly nongovernmental groups. Most (71 percent) also believed that it speeds up the pace of policy decisions.[63] President Kennedy waited eight days in 1961 before commenting on the erection of the Berlin Wall; President Bush had to respond overnight to its destruction. As O'Heffernan puts it: "Television plays a special role in the American foreign policy process, but that role is limited and diffused. However, when it plays that role ... it exerts a power over events and decisions that surpasses all other media combined." [64]

However, the respondents cautioned against considering television as omnipotent. Impact hinges on the nature of the issue and the prevailing political environment, including official predisposition to act.[65] Thus pictures of starving Kurdish refugees in the mountains of Iraq would not have spurred relief missions by the Bush administration in 1991 if emergency food aid had not already been a policy alternative.

Appraising Foreign Newsmaking

In 1978, the United States, along with 145 other nations, signed a UNESCO Declaration on the Media. Among other things, the Declaration stated that "the mass media, by disseminating information on the aims, aspirations, cultures and needs of all people, contribute to eliminate ignorance and misunderstanding between peoples." The media also "make nationals of a country sensitive to the needs and desires of others," thereby ensuring "the respect of the rights and dignity of all nations, all peoples and all individuals." The media also foster "the formulation by states of policies best able to promote the reduction of international tension and the peaceful and equitable settlement of international disputes." [66]

Clearly, foreign news in the American press does not meet the high standards that UNESCO has set for it. It does not "eliminate ignorance and misunderstanding between peoples." It is too sparse and unbalanced, focusing on the wealthier and more powerful countries. It assesses foreign countries largely in terms of U.S. interests, with little attempt to explain their culture and concerns from their own perspective. It does not sensitize Americans to "the needs and desires of others" nor foster "respect of the rights and dignity of all nations." Rather, it reinforces Americans' preexisting assumptions and stereotypes.

These deficiencies must be assessed in light of the basic philosophy of news in a free society. As discussed in Chapter 1, American journalists by and large do not see themselves as extensions of the government, carrying out and keeping in tune with public policies. Although they may sympathize with UNESCO's goals, their first priority is to report exciting news to the American public. In a society that firmly believes in the independence of the press, this is a tolerable consequence.

Just as the press does not serve UNESCO's objectives, it fails to serve many objectives of the American government and many needs of the American public. Reporting of foreign news usually lacks a sense of history and a sense of the meaning of successive events so that it often confuses the public. A good example is the widely believed story that China turned to communism because of failures of American foreign policy. This interpretation ignores the long-range forces that made revolution in China inevitable. It vastly exaggerates the power of the United States to change the course of Chinese politics. The news does not provide sufficient information to permit most Americans to understand the rationale for major foreign policies such as support of the North Atlantic Treaty Organization (NATO) or the necessity for international economic cooperation.

Some stories, even those directly involving U.S. security, are ignored until events reach crisis proportions or until there is a precipitating incident. *New York Times* correspondent James Reston put the problem this way:

> We are fascinated by events but not by the things that cause the events. We will send 500 correspondents to Vietnam after the war breaks out . . . meanwhile ignoring the rest of the world, but we will not send five reporters there when the danger of war is developing.[67]

Phil Foisie, then-assistant managing editor of the *Washington Post*, adds, "We are surprised more often than we ought to be and need to be." [68] This leaves the country unprepared for twists and turns in foreign affairs that might have been foreseen.

If one assumes that better information leads to better policies, then deficiencies in news coverage are grave. When President Carter complained that he was ill informed about unrest in Iran prior to the overthrow of the shah in 1979, he intimated that American policy making and public support for policies would have benefited from more accurate news. In this case the CIA was blamed as well as the media, which perform what has been called a "massive overt intelligence operation." [69] Flawed coverage of the Vietnam War, also allegedly, misled the American public and misdirected foreign policy.[70] The media's stress on conflict—particularly on force as the solution for many international problems—contributes to feelings of insecurity.

Although the media are exceedingly important in providing the context for foreign policy and the print media are used widely as the information base for policy formation, explicit input into foreign policy making by journalists is muted. When journalists give policy advice or criticize ongoing policies, their influence is generally weaker than the influence of formal government agencies. In fact, *New York Times* columnist James Reston claims that press advice has great influence on American foreign policy only when things are obviously going badly, as they did in the Vietnam War.[71] When policy failures are not readily apparent and the president alleges that all is going well, contrary media claims are not likely to be believed by officials and the mass public.

Impact on Public Opinion

Because most Americans lack interest and knowledge about foreign affairs, they are easily swayed by what they see and hear on television, their primary source of foreign news.[72] Television is giving foreign news exposure to a new, impressionable public, highly susceptible to cues from the tube. Viewers are most readily influenced when stories reinforce or sharply challenge stereotypes, to the audience's surprise, and when they seem to relate to the lives of average Americans.[73] In the past, interest in foreign policy was largely confined to a newspaper-reliant elite whose education, interests, and experiences made them far more immune to media influence. Several decades ago "the public probably would never have heard of El Salvador, much less cared about it. Today the sheer volume of exposure to new information created by television assures a more involved public. Television has created a vast, inadvertent audience for news about foreign policy." [74]

Moreover, it has strengthened the president's hand when policies coincide with the tenor of news stories and limited the options when news and policies conflict. Public support for defense spending, for example, more than doubled between 1978 and 1980, jumping from 26 to 90 percent. Televised foreign news may well have been the explanation. It drove home the message that America's foes were gaining while the country was incapable of defending itself. The Iranian hostage crisis, the Soviet assault on Afghanistan, the upheaval in Poland, and the uncontrollable warfare in Central America were powerful scenes in this melodrama.[75]

As is true of most media effects, it is difficult to obtain convincing proof that public opinion about foreign countries mirrors the images media stories present. Nonetheless, available data suggest that it does. William C. Adams, on the basis of careful content analyses of television coverage of the Arab-Israeli conflict in the 1970s and 1980s, concluded that five important changes should have taken place in public opinion if it, indeed, reflected media coverage. Opinions should have become (1) more favorable to Egypt, (2) more sensitive to differences among Arab nations, (3) less favorable to Israel, (4) more sympathetic to Palestinians, and (5) slightly more pro-Arab overall. All of these changes occurred. Between 1976 and 1980 favorable opinion of Egypt rose by 25 percentage points, sizable differences in attitudes toward Arab countries developed, and opinions became more sympathetic to the Palestinians and more pro-Arab overall by 12 percentage points. By 1980 public sympathy for Israel had not yet dropped, in line with media coverage, but it began its downward trend shortly thereafter.[76]

Exporting News

Although the American public seems reasonably content with the foreign news it receives, Third World countries are unhappy with their coverage in the United States. Their disappointment about the world images presented to Americans is compounded by resentment that these images are exported to other countries throughout the globe. In the years since most of these nations gained independence, 80 percent of the non-Communist world's political and economic news has come from only four huge American enterprises: the Associated Press (AP), United Press International (UPI), the *New York Times* News Service, and the *Los Angeles Times-Washington Post* News Service. Most of the remainder has been produced by Britain's Reuters, France's Agence France-Presse, and the Soviet Union's Tass. Four countries thus have dominated the world's news supply.[77]

This concentration has given rise to charges of media imperialism—the dependence of domestic media systems on dominant foreign media systems.[78] Dependence on foreign news resources is particularly galling for developing countries because they believe that the flow of news is primarily one way—into the developing world but not out of it. Western news purveyors slight Third World happenings and the information needs of people in developing nations. Third World critics also decry the corrupting effects of Western news and entertainment programs that feature violence and sexually explicit episodes. Western programs allegedly damage the cultural identity of Third World nations, especially those that are vulnerable because colonialism has sensitized them to foreign values.[79] Imported news and entertainment offerings draw people away from their own heritage and create false expectations that it is easy to become rich. Third World people are tempted into materialism for the benefit of industrialists in the United States who are eager to sell their merchandise through television. Buyers of luxury goods then drain the Third World's resources.

Such interpretations of the motives and role of Western media are widely believed in the Third World. They seem quite plausible because the international news market is dominated by a few giant Western corporations that sell news, as well as more tangible goods, for profit. However, scientific proof is lacking that Marxist interpretations of the causes and consequences of Western dominance of Third World news and media entertainment are correct. As we noted in Chapter 7, people do not automatically learn new ways of life from the media, even when offerings are designed to educate. Certain conditions must first be met to provide an appropriate context. Hence claims that exposure to Western news automatically indoctrinates the audience are false.[80]

Content analyses of Western media, including wire service news, show that many of the charges of deliberate discrimination against the Third World are either groundless or exaggerated.[81] The emphasis on problems and failures in the Third World, rather than successes, and lack of attention to many small nations appear to be natural consequences of applying to the Third World the same criteria used for the more developed portions of the globe. The consequences may differ, but the treatment is the same.[82] The media's emphasis on disasters and conflicts in the Third World reflects the reality that Third World countries are undergoing major social changes and therefore bear a disproportionate burden of pain and suffering.

Elite newspapers in America, in sharp contrast to smaller, less prominent papers throughout the country, pay considerable attention to Third World news.[83] In the *New York Times, Washington Post,* and *Christian Science Monitor,* for example, an average of 65 percent of foreign news coverage is devoted to the Third World. The Third World also fares well in the proportion of front-page stories, editorials, opinion-page articles, and letters to the editor.[84]

Early entry into the media business has given the major news producers an economic edge of size and scale that makes it well-nigh impossible for developing nations to set up viable competing enterprises.[85] The high cost of television programming and the comparatively low cost of purchasing foreign television entertainment—roughly one-tenth of the cost of original programming—also have discouraged Third World countries from creating their own television industries. Many developing countries still lack facilities for producing television shows. Those that have them nonetheless import an average of more than half of their programs, particularly those shown in prime time.[86] In recent years local cultural programs have multiplied in Asia, Latin America, and Africa. They are often exchanged among Third World nations.

Current structures and patterns of telecommunications give price advantages to large producers and consumers. News transmission rates are cheaper when volume is high, making it extremely costly for poor countries to broadcast their messages. It also costs more to transmit news from underdeveloped countries than to receive it. In fact, all the economies of scale benefit the rich and hurt the poor.

Because they are dissatisfied with the status quo and see news as a powerful political force, Third World countries have lobbied in UNESCO for placing strict controls on the influx of foreign news. It has been largely a dialogue of the deaf. The United States and other Western countries have strongly resisted these attempts, deeming them infringements of the right to a free press guaranteed by the 1948 Universal Declaration of Human Rights. The trend toward controlled news in the developing world is making headway nonetheless. Even the European Community issued a directive in 1989 urging members to reserve the majority of their airtime for broadcasts originating in Europe.[87] UNESCO has been involved in planning for a code of journalistic ethics that would define *responsible* reporting. It also has investigated ways to make journalism a government-licensed profession. The United States withdrew from UNESCO in the wake of these efforts.

Third World countries are also contesting the control of the United States and other Western powers over world radio and satellite facilities. In the past, scarce international frequencies were allocated on a first-come, first-served basis. The developed nations received nearly 90 percent of the broadcast spectrum and the bulk of satellite facilities. Third World nations want to change this. They want to divide the spectrum equally among all nations and bar radio and television satellite transmissions across national borders unless the receiving country has given permission. They have also demanded more control over satellites. The United States has resisted Third World demands, believing that nations with current capability to use advanced telecommunications facilities should control these facilities.

The United States is the world's foremost international broadcaster.[88] International broadcast facilities are used to further important foreign policy objectives. The Voice of America broadcasts, for example, have been an integral part of the federal government's foreign information program, which is handled by the United States Information

Agency. It broadcasts from more than one hundred short-wave transmitters in the United States and abroad. Programs are beamed in some forty languages and reach more than 100 million listeners each week.[89] It has also operated WORLDNET, an international satellite television network. Additionally, VOA publishes magazines in different languages.

VOA broadcasts have portrayed American society and its problems and policies abroad and have provided Western news to countries unlikely to receive it in any other way. VOA's largest service used to go to the Soviet Union and Eastern European countries.[90] Radio Martí, added to VOA during the Reagan years, beams news to Cuba. It emphasizes developments in foreign areas where Cuban forces have been active, such as Central America and Africa.[91]

Summary

The quality of U.S. foreign policy and the effectiveness of U.S. relations with other countries are crucial to the welfare of people throughout the world. Sound policy and relations require a solid information base. As this chapter has shown, the foreign affairs information base on which Americans depend leaves much to be desired. The causes are complex and cannot be changed readily. They involve the structure of the foreign correspondent corps, the sociopolitical setting in which correspondents must work, and the audiences to whose world views and tastes the news must cater.

Foreign correspondents are a well-trained, able group. But there are too few of them to cover the world. They work within a narrowly controlled organizational structure consisting of a handful of giant news-gathering institutions that supply the news and entertainment needs of the United States and much of the rest of the world. If one distrusts giant information conglomerates that collect and shape the news for much of the world, the present situation is frightening.

Most Americans are reasonably well satisfied with the foreign news produced by these conglomerates. Live satellite television provides vivid images of breaking news, from tanks in Tiananmen Square, to Scud missiles striking Tel Aviv, to Lenin statues toppling in Moscow.[92] Many of the foreign clienteles, particularly political leaders in the Third World, are not. They complain that agents of monopoly capitalism are guilty of "electronic rape" of their people through decadent entertainment and Western political propaganda.

Foreign affairs news often must be produced under trying conditions. Strange locations and inadequate technological facilities can make a nightmare of the physical aspects of getting to the scene of the action, collecting information, and transmitting it. These technical difficulties are compounded by political difficulties. They include the reluctance of officials in the United States and abroad to commit themselves publicly on foreign affairs matters and the harassment of correspondents venturing into places where they are unwanted. Expulsion, imprisonment, and physical harm are common. With so much territory to cover and such limited personnel to cover it, newspeople frequently avoid areas where news is hard to get and devote their efforts instead to areas where public attitudes are supportive. This effectively removes many regions from media scrutiny and contributes to unevenness of news flow from various parts of the world.

How good is the foreign affairs news that reaches the United States and other clients of Western international news transmission facilities? The picture is mixed. Foreign correspondents must produce news that is at once timely, exciting, personalized, and brief, yet understandable for an American audience that is not intensely interested in most events abroad. Given the problems of foreign affairs news production, correspondents dwell heavily on negative and sensational news. They write stories from an American perspective that follows the current administration's foreign policy assumptions and the American public's stereotyped views of the world. They primarily cover the most important countries, keeping America's national interests and policy objectives in mind. Despite these shortcomings, Americans can obtain a reasonably accurate view of salient political events abroad, particularly if they turn to several elite newspapers that generally give thorough exposure to controversial American foreign policies. However, these papers rarely challenge the merits of foreign policies.

In recent years television commentators occasionally have become active diplomats through interviews that set the stage for subsequent political developments. Ted Koppel's "Nightline" television program, for example, has regularly featured electronic encounters between opposing leaders such as Philippine president Ferdinand Marcos and his successor Corazón Aquino or South Africa's president P. W. Botha and Nobel Peace Prize winner Bishop Desmond Tutu. Aside from these adventures, media influence on foreign policy has been largely indirect, exercised primarily through surveillance activities, the power to choose what to report and what to omit, and the ability to interpret the meaning of events. There has been little investigative or adversary journalism except when foreign affairs were obviously going badly, as happened toward the end of the Vietnam War. Political controversy has largely stopped at the water's edge.

Notes

1. Patrick O'Heffernan, *Mass Media and American Foreign Policy: Insider Perspectives on Global Journalism and the Foreign Policy Process* (Nor-

wood, N.J.: Ablex, 1991), xi-xiii.

2. In a nationwide survey conducted in March 1990, respondents who read newspapers (62 percent) or watched television news (59 percent) three or more times a week were asked if they paid a great deal or a lot of attention to foreign affairs. Twenty-three percent said yes when the question related to newspaper reading and 35 percent said yes about television watching. Holli A. Semetko, Joanne Bay Brzinski, David Weaver, and Lars Willnat, "TV News and U.S. Public Opinion about Foreign Countries: The Impact of Exposure and Attention," *International Journal of Public Opinion Research* 4 (1992): 27.

3. Depending on the definitions used by content analysts, these figures may vary. Michael Emery, who examined international news in ten newspapers between November 6, 1987, and January 6, 1988, reports an average figure of 2.6 percent. His figures for the *Chicago Tribune* are 1.8 percent. Only the *New York Times, Washington Post,* and *Christian Science Monitor* exceeded the mean. (Other papers in his sample were the *Los Angeles Times, Boston Globe, Philadelphia Inquirer, Miami Herald, St. Louis Post-Dispatch* and *Milwaukee Journal.* Figures in a 1984 National Advertising Bureau study are similar to the ones reported in Table 4-6. Michael Emery, "An Endangered Species: The International Newshole," in *Gannett Center Journal* 3 (Fall 1989): 151-164.

4. Pamela J. Shoemaker, Lucig H. Danielian, and Nancy Brendlinger, "Deviant Acts, Risky Business and U.S. Interests: The Newsworthiness of World Events," *Journalism Quarterly* 68 (Winter 1991): 781-795. The content of television network foreign news from 1972 to 1981 is discussed in James F. Larson, *Television's Window on the World* (Norwood, N.J.: Ablex, 1984).

5. Gladys Engel Lang and Kurt Lang, *Politics and Television Re-Viewed* (Beverly Hills, Calif.: Sage, 1984), 213.

6. Doris A. Graber, *Processing the News: How People Tame the Information Tide,* 2d ed. (New York: Longman, 1988), 104-107. For important distinctions between exposure to news and attention to news see Dan Drew and David Weaver, "Media Attention, Media Exposure, and Media Effects," *Journalism Quarterly* 67 (Winter 1990): 740-748.

7. Bernard C. Cohen, *The Press and Foreign Policy* (Princeton, N.J.: Princeton University Press, 1963), 164-165.

8. William A. Hachten, with the collaboration of Harva Hachten, *The World News Prism: Changing Media of International Communication,* 3d ed. (Ames: Iowa State University Press, 1992), 41-53. Other important international news suppliers are Germany's Deutsche Press Agentur (DPA) and Japan's Kyodo News Service, as well as China's Xinhua News Agency.

9. Robert H. Wicks and Douglas C. Walker, "A Day of Prime Time Televised War: Differences between CNN and the Broadcast Networks in Coverage of Breaking News in the Persian Gulf War," unpublished paper.

10. For an analysis of the contents of "CNN World Report" see Charles Ganzert and Don M. Flournoy, "The Weekly 'World Report' on CNN, an Analysis," *Journalism Quarterly* 69 (Spring 1992): 188-193.

11. Larson, *Television's Window,* 171-178.

12. Barry Rubin, "International News and the American Media," in *International News: Freedom Under Attack,* ed. Dante B. Fascell (Beverly Hills, Calif.: Sage, 1979), 214.

13. Rubin, "International News," 197-198. However, the fact that television news teams generally involve at least three people has produced some

increases in the foreign correspondent corps.

14. Daniel Riffe, "International News Borrowing: A Trend Analysis," *Journalism Quarterly* 61 (Spring 1984): 142-148.
15. Leo Bogart, "The Overseas Newsman: A 1967 Profile Study," *Journalism Quarterly* 45 (Summer 1968): 293-306. Judging from more recent profile studies of American journalists in general, these early profiles should still be reasonably accurate. See chapter 4.
16. Ibid., 299.
17. Nicholas O. Berry, *Foreign Policy and the Press: An Analysis of the New York Times' Coverage of U.S. Foreign Policy* (Westport, Conn.: Greenwood Press, 1990), xiii-xiv, 139-151.
18. Jarol B. Manheim, "Image Making as an Instrument of Power: The Representation of Foreign Interests in the United States," International Communication Association paper, 1991, 4.
19. Jarol B. Manheim and Robert B. Albritton, "Changing National Images: International Public Relations and Media Agenda-Setting," *American Political Science Review* 78 (September 1984): 641-657; Robert B. Albritton and Jarol B. Manheim, "Public Relations Efforts for the Third World: Images in the News," *Journal of Communication* 35 (Spring 1985): 43-59.
20. Jarol B. Manheim, *All of the People All the Time: Strategic Communication and American Politics* (Armonk, N.Y.: M. E. Sharpe, 1991), 125-126.
21. Shailendra Ghorpade, "Foreign Correspondents Cover Washington for World," *Journalism Quarterly* 61 (Autumn 1984): 667-671; and *Editor and Publisher International Yearbook, 1991* (New York: Editor & Publisher, 1991). As Table 11-1 shows, the regions most heavily covered by the United States send the most reporters to the United States.
22. *Editor and Publisher International Yearbook, 1991.*
23. Ghorpade, "Foreign Correspondents," 667.
24. Sophia Peterson, "International News Selection by the Elite Press: A Case Study," *Public Opinion Quarterly* 45 (Summer 1981): 159.
25. Robert M. Batscha, *Foreign Affairs News and the Broadcast Journalist* (New York: Praeger, 1975), 156.
26. Sean Kelly, "Access Denied: The Politics of Press Censorship," in *International News*, 249.
27. See Anne-Marie O'Connor, "Dateline: Honduras; Subject: the Contras," *Columbia Journalism Review* 26 (May/June 1987): 38-41; and John Grogan and Charles Riddle, "South Africa's Press in the Eighties: Darkness Descends," 39 *Gazette* (1986): 3-16.
28. John Kifner, "Reporter's Notebook: Fear Is Part of Job in Beirut," *New York Times*, February 22, 1982.
29. Bob Wiedrich, "Sadat Has Invented a New Diplomacy," *Chicago Tribune*, February 9, 1978.
30. For examples, see Berry, *Foreign Policy and the Press*. Also see Daniel C. Hallin, "The Media, the War in Vietnam and Political Support: A Critique of the Thesis of an Oppositional Media," *Journal of Politics* 46 (February 1984): 2-24.
31. Herbert J. Gans, *Deciding What's News: A Study of CBS Evening News, NBC Nightly News, Newsweek and Time* (New York: Pantheon Books, 1979), 30-36. See also Johan Galtung and Mari H. Ruge, "The Structure of Foreign News," *Journal of Peace Research* 2 (1965): 64-91; and Philip Gaunt, "Factors Affecting Foreign News Selection," Midwest Association for Public Opinion Research paper, 1989.

32. Edwin Diamond, *The Tin Kazoo: Television, Politics, and the News* (Cambridge, Mass.: MIT Press, 1975), 94.

33. Daniel C. Hallin, "Hegemony: The American News Media from Vietnam to El Salvador: A Study of Ideological Change and Its Limits," in *Political Communication Research: Approaches, Studies, Assessments,* ed. David L. Paletz (Norwood, N.J.: Ablex, 1987), 17; Robert M. Entman, "Hegemonic Socialization, Information Processing, and Presidential News Management: Framing the KAL and Iran Air Incidents," in *The Psychology of Political Communication,* ed. Ann Crigler and Shawn Rosenberg (forthcoming); W. Lance Bennett, "Marginalizing the Majority: Conditioning Public Opinion to Accept Managerial Democracy," in *Manipulating Public Opinion: Essays on Public Opinion as a Dependent Variable,* ed. Michael Margolis and Gary A. Mauser (Pacific Grove, Calif.: Brooks/Cole, 1989), chap. 15; and Hans Mathias Kepplinger, "Put in the Public Spotlight—Instrumental Actualization of Actors, Events, and Aspects in the Coverage on Nicaragua," in *The Mass Media in Liberal Democratic Societies,* ed. Stanley Rothman (New York: Paragon House, 1992), 201-219.

34. Galtung and Ruge, in "The Structure of Foreign News," have developed a much quoted scheme for rating the newsworthiness of various types of foreign affairs events. See also Elinar Ostgaard, "Factors Influencing the Flow of News," *Journal of Peace Research* 2 (1965): 39-63.

35. Jonathan Friendly, "El Salvador Overlooked as Most of Press Turns to Other Crises," *New York Times,* July 10, 1982.

36. William Adams and Phillip Heyl, "From Cairo to Kabul with the Networks, 1972-1980," in *Television Coverage of the Middle East,* ed. William C. Adams (Norwood, N.J.: Ablex, 1981), 26.

37. Rubin, "International News," 227.

38. Francis X. Clines, "In U.S. TV, Israelis Find an Unflattering Mirror," *New York Times,* February 1, 1988; and John Kifner, "Israeli Officials Object to U.S. News Coverage of Riots," *New York Times,* December 29, 1987. Also see O'Heffernan, *Mass Media and American Foreign Policy,* 29-36.

39. David L. Altheide, "Impact of Format and Ideology on TV News Coverage of Iran," *Journalism Quarterly* 62 (Summer 1985): 351.

40. Michael X. Delli Carpini and Bruce A. Williams, "Television and Terrorism: Patterns of Presentation and Occurrence, 1969 to 1980," *Western Political Quarterly* 40 (March 1987): 45-64.

41. This discussion is patterned on Doris A. Graber, *News and Democracy: Are Their Paths Diverging?* (Bloomington: Indiana University School of Journalism, 1992), Roy W. Howard Public Lecture No. 3, 11-16.

42. Robert M. Entman, "Framing U.S. Coverage of International News: Contrasts in Narratives of the KAL and Iran Air Incidents," *Journal of Communication* 41 (Autumn 1991) 6-27.

43. Ibid., 22-23.

44. David R. Gergen, "Diplomacy in a Television Age: The Dangers of Teledemocracy," in *The Media and Foreign Policy,* ed. Simon Serfaty (New York: St. Martin's Press, 1991), 47-63.

45. Stephen S. Rosenfeld, "In the Gulf: The Wars of the Press," in *The Media and Foreign Policy,* 241-255.

46. Hachten and Hachten, *World News Prism,* 165-166.

47. Robert Pear, "Military Revises Rules to Assure Reporters Access to Battle Areas," *New York Times,* May 22, 1992.

48. Quoted in Fernando Reyes Matta, "The Latin American Concept of News,"

Journal of Communication 29 (Spring 1979): 169.

49. Gary D. Gaddy and Enoch Tanjong, "Earthquake Coverage by the Western Press," *Journal of Communication* 36 (Spring 1986): 105-112. For a conflicting analysis, see William C. Adams, "Whose Lives Count?: TV Coverage of Natural Disasters," *Journal of Communication* 36 (Spring 1986): 113-122.

50. Benjamin D. Singer, "Violence, Protest, and War in Television News: The U.S. and Canada Compared," *Public Opinion Quarterly* 34 (Winter 1970-71): 611-616; and Chris J. Scheer and Sam W. Eiler, "A Comparison of Canadian and American Network Television News," *Journal of Broadcasting* 16 (Spring 1972): 156-164.

51. James P. Winter, Pirouz Shoar Ghaffari, and Vernone M. Sparkes, "How Major U.S. Dailies Covered Quebec Separatism Referendum," *Journalism Quarterly* 59 (Winter 1982): 608.

52. Edward W. Said, *Covering Islam: How the Media and the Experts Determine How We See the Rest of the World* (New York: Pantheon Books, 1981), chap. 2.

53. Hanna Adoni and S. Mane, "Media and the Social Construction of Reality: Toward an Integration of Theory and Research," *Communication Research* 11 (July 1984): 323-340.

54. Edward S. Herman, "Diversity of News: 'Marginalizing' the Opposition," *Journal of Communication* 35 (Fall 1985): 135-146.

55. John A. Lent, "Foreign News in American Media," *Journal of Communication* 27 (Winter 1977): 46-50. See also Jyotika Ramaprasad and Daniel Riffe, "Effect of U.S.-India Relations on *New York Times* Coverage," *Journalism Quarterly* 64 (Summer/Autumn 1987): 537-543; Hallin, "Hegemony"; and David Altheide, "Media Hegemony: A Failure of Perspective," *Public Opinion Quarterly* 48 (Summer 1984): 476-490.

56. Robert M. Entman and David L. Paletz, "The War in Southeast Asia: Tunnel Vision on Television," in *Television Coverage of International Affairs*, 181-201; and Hallin, "The Media." Also see Berry, *Foreign Policy and the Press* for many examples.

57. W. Phillips Davison, "Diplomatic Reporting: Rules of the Game," *Journal of Communication* 25 (Autumn 1975): 138-146.

58. The discussion that follows is based on James F. Larson, "Television and U.S. Foreign Policy: The Case of the Iran Hostage Crisis," *Journal of Communication* 36 (Autumn 1986): 108-130; and Joseph Fromm, "TV: Does It Box in President in a Crisis?" *U.S. News and World Report*, July 15, 1985, 23-24.

59. Quoted in John Corry, "The Intrusion of Television in the Hostage Crisis," *New York Times*, June 26, 1985.

60. Quoted in Ibid.

61. O'Heffernan, *Mass Media and American Foreign Policy*, 40.

62. Ibid., 49.

63. Ibid., 75.

64. Ibid., 77.

65. Ibid., 48. Berry, *Foreign Policy and the Press*, makes the same argument.

66. Article III, UNESCO Declaration on the Media.

67. James Reston, *Sketches in the Sand* (New York: Knopf, 1967), 195.

68. Quoted in Rubin, "International News," 216.

69. Rubin, "International News," 193.

70. Peter Braestrup, *Big Story: How the American Press and Television*

Reported and Interpreted the Crisis of Tet 1968 in Vietnam and Washington (Garden City, N.Y.: Anchor Press/Doubleday, 1978).

71. Rubin, *International News,* 182; Berry, *Foreign Policy and the Press,* concurs.

72. The influence of television on the perception of unfamiliar issues is discussed in Shanto Iyengar and Donald Kinder, *News that Matters: Television and American Opinion* (Chicago: University of Chicago Press, 1987).

73. William C. Adams, "Mass Media and Public Opinion about Foreign Affairs: A Typology of News Dynamics," *Political Communication and Persuasion* 4 (1987): 263-278.

74. William Schneider, "Bang-Bang Television: The New Superpower," *Public Opinion* 5 (April/May 1982): 13-14.

75. Larson, "International Affairs Coverage," 34-35.

76. Adams and Heyl, "From Cairo to Kabul," 16, 19-22. Also see Semetko et al, "TV News and U.S. Public Opinion," 30. Apparently print news has less impact on opinions than television news.

77. Mustapha Masmoudi, "The New World Information Order," *Journal of Communication* 29 (Spring 1979): 172-185. For an explanation of how international news services function, see Jonathan Fenby, *The International News Services* (New York: Schocken Books, 1986).

78. For a discussion of media imperialism, see Herbert I. Schiller, *Culture, Inc.: The Corporate Takeover of Public Expression* (New York: Oxford University Press, 1989); and René Jean Ravault, "International Information: Bullet or Boomerang?" in *Political Communication Research: Approaches, Studies, Assessments,* ed. David L. Paletz (Norwood, N.J.: Ablex, 1987), 245-265.

79. The impact of foreign television is assessed in Alexis S. Tan, Sarrina Li, and Charles Simpson, "American TV and Social Stereotypes of Americans in Taiwan and Mexico," *Journalism Quarterly* 63 (Winter 1986): 809-814.

80. Ravault, "International Information"; Glen Fisher, *American Communication in a Global Society* (Norwood, N.J.: Ablex, 1987), 15-18; and Michael B. Salwan, "Cultural Imperialism: A Media Effects Approach," *Critical Studies in Mass Communication* 8 (1991): 29-38. For a contradictory viewpoint, see Herbert I. Schiller, "Not Yet the Post-Imperialist Era," *Critical Studies in Mass Communication* 8 (1991): 13-28.

81. W. James Potter, "News from Three Worlds in Prestige U.S. Newspapers," *Journalism Quarterly* 64 (Spring 1987): 73-79.

82. Wilbur Schramm and L. Erwin Atwood, *Circulation of News in the Third World: A Study of Asia* (Hong Kong: Chinese University Press, 1981); and David H. Weaver and G. Cleveland Wilhoit, "Foreign News Coverage in Two U.S. Wire Services," *Journal of Communication* 31 (Spring 1981): 55-63. For a contrary view, see Daniel Riffe and Eugene F. Shaw, "Conflict and Consonance: Coverage of Third World in Two U.S. Papers," *Journalism Quarterly* 59 (Winter 1982): 617-626.

83. Coverage by smaller media is discussed in G. Cleveland Wilhoit and David Weaver, "Foreign News Coverage in Two U.S. Wire Services: An Update," *Journal of Communication* 33 (Spring 1983): 132-148.

84. Haque, "Is U.S. Coverage of News in Third World Imbalanced? " 523-524. Some confusion in dividing stories by country of origin has arisen from the fact that many Third World stories are transmitted through communications centers, such as London or New York. For example, most news from

402 Mass Media and American Politics

Latin America is relayed via New York. See Leonard R. Sussman, "Information Control as an International Issue," in *The Communications Revolution in Politics,* ed. Gerald Benjamin (New York: The Academy of Political Science, 1982), 183.
85. Oliver Boyd-Barrett, "Media Imperialism: Towards an International Framework for the Analysis of Media Systems," in *Mass Communication and Society* ed. James Curran, Michael Gurevitch, and Janet Woolacott (London: Arnold, 1971), 117, 129.
86. One exception is Brazil, which supplies its own domestic market and exports programs worldwide. Omar Souki Oliveira, "Brazilian Media Usage as a Test of Dependency Theory," *Canadian Journal of Communication* 13 (1988): 16-27.
87. Duncan H. Brown, "Citizens or Consumers: U.S. Reactions to the European Community's Directive on Television," *Critical Studies in Mass Communication* 8 (1991): 1-12.
88. Kelly, "Access Denied," 255.
89. Glen Fisher, *American Communication in a Global Society* (Norwood, N.J.: Ablex, 1987), 139.
90. David M. Abshire, "A New Dimension of Western Diplomacy," 40. Also see Allen C. Hansen, *USIA: Public Diplomacy in the Computer Age* (New York: Praeger, 1984).
91. Fisher, *American Communication,* 141.
92. Timothy J. McNulty, "Decisions at the Speed of Satellite," *Chicago Tribune,* December 22, 1991.

Readings

Berry, Nicholas O. *Foreign Policy and the Press: An Analysis of the New York Times' Coverage of U.S. Foreign Policy.* Westport, Conn.: Greenwood Press, 1990.

Evenson, Bruce J. *Truman, Palestine, and the Press: Shaping Conventional Wisdom at the Beginning of the Cold War.* Westport, Conn.: Greenwood Press, 1992.

Hachten, William A., with the collaboration of Harva Hachten. *The World News Prism: Changing Media of International Communication,* 3d ed. Ames: Iowa State University Press, 1992.

Hallin, Daniel C. *The 'Uncensored War': The Media and Vietnam.* New York: Oxford University Press, 1986.

Kern, Montague, Patricia Levering, and Ralph B. Levering. *The Kennedy Crises: The Press, the Presidency, and Foreign Policy.* Chapel Hill: University of North Carolina Press, 1983.

McPhail, Thomas L. *Electronic Colonialism: The Future of International Broadcasting and Communication,* 2d ed. Beverly Hills, Calif.: Sage, 1987.

O'Heffernan, Patrick. *Mass Media and American Foreign Policy: Insider Perspectives on Global Journalism and the Foreign Policy Process.* Norwood, N.J.: Ablex, 1991.

Serfaty, Simon, ed. *The Media and Foreign Policy.* New York: St. Martin's Press, 1991.

Stevenson, Robert L., and Donald Lewis Shaw, eds. *Foreign News and the New World Information Order.* Ames: Iowa State University Press, 1984.

CHAPTER 12

Trends in Media Policy

In Shakespeare's *Julius Caesar* Brutus urges his fellow conspirators to act while the time is ripe:

> There is a tide in the affairs of men
> Which, taken at the flood, leads on to fortune;
> Omitted, all the voyage of their life
> Is bound in shallows and in miseries.
> On such a full sea are we now afloat;
> And we must take the current when it serves
> Or lose our ventures.[1]

Communications policy has been standing on just such a threshold in the waning years of the twentieth century. New technologies call for a rethinking of established policy directions, but they must interact with established social structures and cultural patterns. Hence, old policy concepts linger and make the future hostage to the past. Attempts to take control of the tides of change have faltered, thus far, diminishing the chance to reap the full benefits made possible by the communications revolution.

Both the forces pushing for new communications policies and the obstacles that lie in the way will be discussed in this chapter. We will explore some of the areas of disenchantment with mass media performance that have fueled demands for reform and the steps taken by dissatisfied communicators and audiences to improve and supplement the existing information supply. The potential impact of major new technologies on politics and policy alternatives will be examined. Finally, we will peer into the murky crystal ball to try to discern the shape of future communications policies that will guide the interaction between the mass media and the American political system in the twenty-first century.

Dissatisfaction with the Media

The 1960s and 1970s were decades of political disenchantment in the United States. Many people became dissatisfied with political institutions and blamed them for the ills of society. Vocal protesters have always been vastly outnumbered by the "silent majorities" whose silence is interpreted as approval of the political system or resignation to its unavoidable shortcomings. But even the silent have often felt that the times were out of joint, if only because of the increase in publicly voiced dissent.

The media, particularly television, have been frequent targets of protest. Although recent polls give high marks to newspapers and television, more than one hundred thousand complaints about television are registered annually at the Washington Broadcast Bureau of the Federal Communications Commission (FCC).[2] Most complaints concern the display of obscenity, excessive crime and violence, infringement of equal time and fairness provisions, the treatment of racial and religious matters, and the substance and amount of advertising.

Besides the formal complaints lodged with the FCC, a host of less formal criticisms have been made as well. Media critics call television a vast intellectual wasteland. They chide the networks for greedy pandering to mass audiences and blame shallow programming, lacking in background and context, and cheap appeals to human emotions on the desire to secure high ratings that will raise advertising income. They complain about the scant criticism of American society and politics and the mere parroting of easily obtainable "expert" guesses about unknowable future events. Similar complaints are voiced about print media. Newspapers are accused of superficial coverage, catering to their financial benefactors, and all-too-frequent mean-spirited excursions into sensationalism and sleaze. The press, says *Chicago Tribune* columnist Bill Granger, has become judge, jury, and executioner—the pitbull of politics.[3]

Media orientations toward politics have been criticized as both too liberal and too conservative. Sniping from the left about the media's subservience to the establishment and insensitivity to the concerns of the politically powerless and economically deprived has been balanced by criticism from the middle and the right. Conservatives accuse the media of demeaning the status of American business and labor and of respected professions such as medicine and law. The media, they argue, are unduly romantic about the woes and virtues of the poor, the disadvantaged, and the racially different. In the process the media allegedly undermine national security and hurt the nation's prestige at home and abroad. The media also have been accused by liberals and conservatives alike of invading individual privacy and impairing the fairness of the judicial process.

The gist of the charges is that the media do not serve "the public interest" and that they fail to nourish a viable democratic political order. These elusive concepts are always measured by political yardsticks of disputed accuracy and validity. What is important to an understanding of media policy making is the response to perceived media deficiencies. How do dissatisfied Americans cope with shortcomings in their information supply? They engage in various forms of informal criticism, expressed regularly and sporadically; they establish and use formal criticism mechanisms; and they use alternative media.

Informal Criticism

Informal criticism has come from within the journalism profession as well as from the general public. Specialized journals that frequently review media performance, such as the *Columbia Journalism Review,* publish criticism by media professionals. Many review journals have been short-lived because they could not maintain enough subscribers to pay their expenses. The degree of influence wielded by such journals is a matter of opinion. Within narrow circles, professional reputations may be affected. But the circulation of these reviews is so limited, and the pocketbook effects of adverse criticism are so negligible, that their pressure on the industry to alter journalistic practices is likely to be small.

More robust and probably more influential vehicles of criticism are critical essays by media analysts writing for television networks and high-circulation newspapers and news magazines. Columnists such as Bill Granger, reporters such as the *Chicago Tribune*'s James Warren, and television hosts such as Ted Koppel have become familiar gadflies of the news business and the journalism profession. Their work supplements the efforts of many academic experts who have written critical appraisals of the mass media in recent years. Authors Lance Bennett, Norman Isaacs, Tom Goldstein, Robert Entman, Michael Parenti, and Herbert Schiller belong in this group.[4] The media also routinely are scanned critically, if informally, at professional conventions of social scientists and journalists. Special workshops, such as the annual Aspen Conference on Communications and Society, have focused narrowly on specific problems of the media and have publicized reform proposals.

Informal criticism has also come from various public interest groups. In many cases these have been institutions organized for other purposes, such as the national Parent and Teacher Association or the American Medical Association. Special media action groups have voiced their concerns publicly. The National Citizens Committee for Broadcasting and the now defunct Children's Television Workshop, discussed in Chapter 2, are examples. Complaints by public interest and media action groups, like most other forms of informal criticism, have been largely ineffectual. The critics may disturb the news profession momentarily, but they rarely induce a change in media policies.

Formal Criticism

Formal protests about media performance can be lodged with the FCC, the government agency charged with supervision of the electronic media. As mentioned earlier, the FCC's Broadcast Bureau in Washington accepts citizen complaints. Interested parties also have a chance to present their perspectives on media policy at FCC hearings. The commission holds such hearings before granting broadcast licenses or when licenses have been challenged. They provide opportunities to counter the pressures brought by the media industry and balance the pro-industry biases that public regulatory bodies often develop.

Formal avenues for criticism and policy suggestions by the public are beneficial. However, a number of serious problems have diminished their usefulness. Most fundamental and least solvable is the problem of making sure that the complaints and suggestions thus aired represent widely shared beliefs. Advocates of mainstream positions are often conspicuously silent. The laudable desire to hear and heed dissenters may lead to inadequate concern about the merits of their claims, to the detriment of more general public interests.

A few examples of vociferous protests will illustrate the problem of determining what constitutes the "voice of the people." Some of these protests were ignored; others were heeded. The mini-series "Holocaust" that dramatized Nazi atrocities was loudly opposed by groups claiming that it generated anti-German feelings and hatred between Jews and gentiles. Yet it attracted between 38 and 48 million viewers nightly and was widely acclaimed. Similarly, between 30 and 40 million people watched and praised each episode of the "Godfather" series about Mafia ventures. Yet thousands of Italian-Americans denounced the show as slandering Italians. Stories about abortion, homosexuality, drug addiction, the activities of religious cults, or the successful ventures of discredited politicians have often been suppressed or toned down because of the flood of protests they might invite.

Lack of money can be a major barrier to challenging broadcasters effectively in an FCC hearing or before a court of law. In the past, the broadcast industry occasionally has voluntarily shouldered the legal fees of poor protest groups. This has encouraged them to sue rather than try to negotiate settlements. The FCC cannot pay the expenses of protest groups, as they have suggested, since Congress is unlikely to allocate special funds for this purpose.

Most lawsuits involving claims about harmful television programming have failed. A widely publicized example is the trial of Ronny Zamora, a teenager who was convicted by a Florida court for murdering an eighty-three-year-old woman. His parents sued the three networks for negligent programming, claiming that television shows had incited and taught their son how to murder. The suit was dismissed by a federal judge who ruled that the media had not been negligent.[5] In 1978 a California court likewise dismissed a negligence suit against NBC brought by the parents of a young rape victim. The rape had mimicked a scene from the movie "Born Innocent," which had been shown on television four days earlier.[6]

To enhance public influence on communications policy, there have been proposals to place ombudsmen—formal advocates of the public's interests—in various bodies that deal with communications policy. Alternatively, a central ombudsman office has been proposed to assist public interest groups and individuals in preparing and presenting their complaints and suggestions. Thus far, these proposals have not been implemented. However, several dozen newspapers have set up ombudsmen facilities to permit readers to challenge news policies.[7] Readers' concerns and ombudsmen's activities are regularly reported by these papers.

Elected or appointed bodies that hear and investigate complaints about mass media output—media councils—are another avenue for channeling criticism. These councils then publicize their findings, using the power of publicity to correct undesirable media practices. Generally, media councils lack power to enforce their recommendations. Media councils have been used in Great Britain and in some midwestern and western states and cities in the United States. The press has strongly opposed media councils, even though they appear to enhance media credibility and reduce the frequency of libel suits.[8] Journalists fear that councils will impair their editorial independence by publicizing appraisals of the merits of ongoing news policies. When a National News Council was set up in 1973, several news organizations gave space to its activities and reports. But it never became a major force in arbitrating questions of media ethics. It was dissolved in 1984.[9]

Alternative Media

Hundreds of specialized media address information needs neglected or poorly served by the regular media. They serve as a partial antidote to the concentrated ownership of the general mass media. Ethnic media, discussed in Chapter 10, are examples. Some specialized media, such as the *New Republic, Mother Jones,* the *National Review,* and, at times, the *New Yorker* are primarily devoted to political commentary. Recent simple and cheap technologies also enable many interest groups to publish and distribute their own magazines, newsletters, and audio and video tapes on controversial political issues. Antinuclear and environmental groups, for example, have created and distributed tapes either for individual use or for broadcast.[10] Supporters of candidates for political office have done the same.

Numerous professional and trade journals and newsletters are devoted to a multitude of concerns such as religion, sports, fine and popular arts, automobiles, health issues, and bird watching. If audiences numbering into thousands and even millions of people constitute a "mass," these are, by definition, mass media. Modern means of distributing information bridge the distances that physically separate these mass audiences that share specialized interests. The demand for targeted information has increased in recent years so that more than ten thousand magazines are now published in the United States.[11] The popularity of specialized magazines has led to the demise of broadly oriented publications such as *Look,* the original *Life,* and the *Saturday Evening Post,* which lost advertising revenues to these competitors.

For many people the term *alternative media* conjures up visions of the politically radical, iconoclastic, and counterculture newspapers that were plentiful in the late 1960s and early 1970s. Many Americans, particularly youths and minorities, opposed to the positions taken on the Vietnam War and other issues by the regular media, created the "underground press." These media carried on the flagrant opposition to government policy that is often forbidden in other countries, where such opposition media must hide from the police. Underground actually was a misnomer for the American media of protest because they were allowed to operate quite openly. But it gave them an aura of fighting the establishment at great personal risk.

Some underground publications went beyond rejecting the current political establishment and attacked the values and culture of American mainstream society. In this they differed from social responsibility journalism that supports basic American values and attacks only their violations. Politically, the underground media were generally left-wing in orientation: Communist, Socialist, or Anarchist. They attracted attention by being totally subjective and visually and verbally shocking. Pornographic pictures and profanity abounded because underground journalists felt that their assaults on American society must be sensational to succeed.

The rise of the underground press demonstrates that mass media can be started and operated with modest means. The media of the 1960s were financed mostly through advertising for things like counterculture records, music productions, pornographic movies, and classified advertisements requesting services such as sex partners, nude models, or hallucinogenic drugs. Staffs were paid meager salaries or no salaries at all.[12] They were assigned to write features rather than regular news stories. For daily news and some features they relied on the Underground Press Service (UPS), Liberation News Service (LNS), and other news service cooperatives. There were no set numbers of issues per year, no regular publication schedules, no business staffs or circulation departments. At the height of underground press popularity, readership was estimated at 10 million, with most issues used by several people.

Underground media in the 1960s were not limited to the comparatively unregulated print realm. They also flourished in the regulated broadcast field. Underground radio stations featured mostly rock music and disc jockeys who commented on society, sexual matters, the drug culture, and other counterculture interests. The FCC rarely interfered with their unconventional activities, except when they flouted the law too brazenly. For instance, when a Texas rock station tipped off the local drug community about a drug raid planned by police, there was an investigation into the sources from which the station had received the advance information.

The mushrooming of protest media in the 1960s and 1970s—at one time there were nearly one thousand underground newspapers and four hundred counterculture radio stations—attests to the vitality and flexibility of the mass media system.[13] The abrupt decline of underground media with the end of the Vietnam War—there are only a handful left, and most of them either have turned middle-class or have become predominantly pornographic—also shows that the system is able to prune its unneeded branches when the demand ends.

The tolerance of the government for underground media demonstrates that government control over media content, however offensive, has had a light touch. Few countries equal and none exceeds the freedom to express radical viewpoints enjoyed by American media. In fact, some of the causes pressed by underground news sources ultimately became part of the mainstream of politics. In the end waning public support rather than official censorship led to the steep decline in this genre of journalism. Neither technical nor legal barriers block a revival, should social or political conditions provide enough incentives.

The Impact of New Technologies

Marshall McLuhan, the television guru of the 1960s, predicted that the world would become a global village where humanity would share a global culture via television.[14] His vision of shared audio-visual news and entertainment has largely come to pass, but reality is far richer than even McLuhan imagined. The vast amounts of diverse information produced by new technologies permit people to create their own, individualized information diet. The new age of personalized mass media has arrived. In fact, as political scientist Russell Neuman has pointed out, we now "have the opportunity to design a new electronic and optical network that will blur the distinction between mass and interpersonal communications. . . ." A single high capacity digital network will combine "computing, telephony, broadcasting, motion pictures and publishing." [15] Audiences will be confronted with growing arrays of choices of program content, format, and timing, and with opportunities to respond privately or publicly to broadcast messages. With advertisers switching to the new information vehicles, lean days may be ahead for traditional mass media.

The store of information that is readily available to media audiences has grown by leaps and bounds.[16] Small as well as large communities share in this bounty, reducing the dangers of local monopoly control over information and opening up hitherto closed communication ghettos. Computers, communication satellites, video cassette recorders (VCRs), fiber optics, microwave, high-speed integrated circuits, digital compression, and other new technologies provide a virtually unlimited array of channels for electronic transmission of news and entertainment. Even newspapers can be printed and transmitted electronically. Cable television systems now in operation, or in the planning stage, project that they will offer broadcasts from forty to two hundred separate channels. The vast number of radio and television programs available from satellites can be received by television stations over the air or through cable channels. Individual consumers can tap directly into these offerings through backyard satellite dishes. Space for various types of electronic transmissions, including television, can be rented by public and private parties from the satellites' owners. Stations can even use satellites to supply other stations with live videos of stories that the station has covered locally. These offerings reduce dependence on current network programming and vastly expand television programming options.

Video recorders, video tapes, and video discs store electronic fare, allowing people to watch what they want when they want it. Annoying commercials can be readily suppressed. By 1988 nearly 40 million of America's 88 million households had at least one video recorder, a phenomenal growth spurt over a decade. Pay cable and pay over-the-air television provide special entertainment or special interest programs at moderate costs. People pay solely for those programs they choose to watch. Public access cable channels keep citizens in closer touch with various public institutions, policies, and problems.

Reprinted with permission of King Features Syndicate.

When programs are interactive, participants can communicate directly with each other, just like they would if they met in person. In fact, two-way channels on cable television have become commonplace. Viewers can interact with others while watching the same programs. Two-way communication technologies using radios, telephones, and computers have improved steadily. They have been useful in integrating outlying areas with social service systems in more populated centers. In Alaska and northern Canada, for example, these technologies deliver educational and health services and give people a greater voice in government.[17]

Thanks to the new technologies the mass media business has made noteworthy advances on three fronts: news gathering, news processing, and news dissemination.[18] Access to computer data bases and satellites has put an enormous store of usable information within reach of average newspeople wherever they may be. Even foreign countries kept off limits by hostile rulers can be explored by satellites, as can remote areas of the globe and even the private retreats of powerful elites. The ability to search data bases electronically for specific bits of information and to combine these data in a variety of ways opens up countless new possibilities for creating news stories. When it comes to distribution, the array of available channels for immediate or delayed transmission has multiplied far beyond the range deemed possible a scant twenty-five years ago.

Several serious problems created by the new broadcasting and narrowcasting technologies will require thoughtful new policies. High definition television (HDTV) is a case in point. Several incompatible technologies have been developed in Asia, the United States, and Europe to enhance the quality of television pictures and sounds. The technologies favored by the United States have the drawback of requiring consumers to buy expensive new television sets. Of course, the prospective vendors of the new sets, and the new taping and transmitting equipment that must be installed, are delighted by forecasts of billion dollar sales figures. Besides the domestic economic factors that the FCC must consider, there are foreign trade considerations as well. If the FCC authorizes a system developed and controlled by Europeans or Asians, the lion's share of profits will flow abroad.[19]

The FCC and Congress have proceeded at a snail's pace thus far on these issues, along with numerous other questions involving difficult policy choices and standardization problems. The FCC has promised to announce by the end of 1993 which HDTV system will be adopted for the United States. To avoid facing the issue of equipment obsolescence head-on, the FCC has also proposed a fifteen-year transition plan. The new technology and equipment would be introduced gradually with a dual system in operation until 2008. Thereafter, the old system would close down, making pre-HDTV equipment useless unless conversion technology becomes available. Whether the FCC's plans and its time table are realistic remains to be seen. If various new information transmission systems remain largely incompatible, nationally or internationally, consumers (including the news media) will be able to use only a small portion of the new information riches.

Safeguarding individual privacy also presents major hurdles. Ever smaller cameras and microphones permit reporters to spy with little chance for detection. Today computers can assemble scattered bits of information in seconds to derive a comprehensive portrait of an individual's past. Unless individual privacy becomes more fully protected, the computer age could well turn into an Orwellian nightmare of living in glass cages exposed to instant public scrutiny.[20] In the same way, the new information-gathering techniques will make it far more difficult to protect national security information from prying eyes. Congress and the courts will be hard put to strike a sound balance between a free press and a secure society. All this is happening at a time when the ease of disseminating information through private or public channels may make responsible journalism more difficult than ever before.

Barriers to Development

A look at technology may tell us what is possible rather than indicate what is likely to happen, particularly in the short run. A number of psychological, political, and economic barriers block the full development of new mass communication technologies. People are reluctant to change their media use habits, particularly when there are costs in time, attention, and effort to master new technologies. Many new developments never get off the ground because bureaucracies impose too many regulations to guard against abuses. Unrealistically high standards are frequently prescribed, raising costs beyond economically feasible levels. State and local rules, piled on top of federal regulations, complicate the picture even further. Not only do they add more requirements, but rules issued by various jurisdictions often conflict. Every major technological revolution—and the information transmission revolution is major—has brought about economic and political dislocations. Such massive changes are fought by those whose knowledge and equipment will be made obsolete by them. Communications technologies involve large investments so that their sudden obsolescence becomes a crushing financial blow. Business entrepreneurs often try to derail such changes.

Some of the new mass media offerings endanger current jobs. For instance, round-the-clock cable educational programs, structured like regular classrooms, threaten teachers' jobs. Medical programs that teach people better medical self-care methods may be unwelcome competition for the health profession. Televised programs featuring outstanding practitioners and facilities may establish standards for professional performance that average institutions cannot meet.

Early entrants in a technological field also develop a squatter's mentality about rights they have acquired, such as the right to use certain broadcast frequencies or particular technologies. Newcomers, on the other hand, are eager to reallocate facilities in line with their special interests. They want to mandate the use of more advanced technologies, even before they can guarantee that a market for these technologies and services will develop. This could wipe out proven interests in favor of new claimants whose prospects for success are uncertain. Obstacles also arise because competing new technologies benefit various groups unevenly. Power struggles, which may be prolonged, are fiercest before the status quo is determined. Meanwhile, technology continues its advance, raising new problems that further delay the green light for implementing new systems.

The Emergence of Cable Television

Cable television's rocky history in the United States illustrates the problems posed by technical innovations. It also illustrates the many political decisions that must be made to fit a new information technology into the existing legislative and administrative structure. Technological progress marches on relentlessly. The costly cable technology may be outmoded before it reaches maturity. Cheaper technologies, such as using direct broadcasting satellites to send programs to receiver dishes on earth or transmitting television over telephone wires, may be the wave of the future.

When cable television first became available in 1949, established broadcasters viewed it as a serious threat. They feared that the availability of numerous television channels would lead to a large menu of programs similar to the variety then offered by radio shows. This would splinter television audiences. Smaller audiences would mean smaller advertising revenues and smaller profits for existing stations. In turn, this might mean poorer programming because reduced revenue would necessitate curtailment of expenditures. Television networks were also concerned that cable operators would pirate, rather than buy, their signals and broadcast the programs they had produced at high cost. When satellite technology evolved, fears mounted. The networks might be destroyed entirely if stations could pick up programs directly from satellites and broadcast them nationwide via cable television.

The initial response of the FCC to cable technology was typical of regulatory agencies. The commission, prodded by established interests, protected the status quo with regulations that prevented the newcomers from harming these interests. These regulations sharply limited the types of programs that cable television stations could broadcast when they competed with established network services. Consequently, the growth of the cable industry was stunted.

Cable industry groups ultimately persuaded public officials that cable technology was needed because it could reach people in locations inaccessible to regular television signals. The idea of breaking the near monopoly enjoyed by the networks over broadcasting also became attractive. So did the possibility of opening up many new channels for broadcasting to groups hitherto shut out by a limited spectrum. By 1972 these pressures were sufficiently strong to convince the FCC to ease its regulations on the types of programs that cable television could broadcast. The cable system had a new lease on life. However, in what is also a typical move when new technologies arise, the FCC imposed a number of very costly regulations to force cable television to serve public needs that had never been met in the past. A minimum of twenty channels was required, including outlets for the general public, educational institutions, and local governments. There were also requirements for two-way capabilities and for carrying signals of local broadcasters.

When these rules turned out to be too burdensome to allow rapid development of cable television, they were eased in 1976. Service requirements imposed on the new industry were loosened further after successful legal challenges by cable operators who questioned the propriety of regulating cable television as if it were using scarce

Figure 12-1   The Cable TV Explosion

Year	Penetration rate (percent of households with cable)	Cable subscribers (in thousands)
1965	3.3	1,760
1970	7.5	4,498
1975	13.3	9,197
1980	22.6	17,671
1981	28.3	23,219
1982	35.0	29,341
1983	40.5	33,794
1984	43.7	37,291
1986	47.4	41,000
1988	53.8	48,600
1990	54.9	54,900
1991	60.6	55,800

Source: Compiled from *Television and Cable Factbook,* 1991.

airwaves when cable transmission channels were plentiful.[21] In 1979 the FCC issued a lengthy research report on the economic impact of cable broadcasting. It concluded—erroneously as it turned out—that cable was only a minor economic threat to the established television industry and that it did not endanger the industry's "ability to perform in the public interest." In the wake of these findings, the federal shackles were removed from the industry, one by one.[22] With the passage of the Cable Communications Policy Act of 1984, deregulation was complete.[23] The act deregulated rates and made renewal of cable franchises nearly automatic in areas with ready access to over-the-air television—roughly 90 percent of the cabled areas.

Meanwhile, the resistance of the established industries to this new competition had gradually softened. In fact, a number of them, heeding the old adage "If you can't lick 'em, join 'em," invested heavily in cable facilities once the FCC eased controls regarding crossownership and admission of the networks to the cable market. Figure 12-1 illustrates the rapid explosion of the cable industry in the 1970s and 1980s. By 1992, 61 percent of the nation's television households were linked to

Table 12-1   Ownership of Top Fifty Cable Systems

Category of owner	Number of systems	Percentage of systems	Percentage of cable homes
Broadcasters	23	46	30
Newspaper/magazine publishers	17	34	25
Film producers and distributors	6	12	9
Independents	19	38	25
Other	3	6	5

Source: Adapted from Herbert H. Howard, "An Update on Cable TV Ownership: 1985," *Journalism Quarterly* 63 (Winter 1986): 709. Reprinted by permission of the Association for Education in Journalism and Mass Communication, publishers of *Journalism Quarterly.*
Note: Includes only the fifty largest multiple-system organizations. Totals exceed N of 50 and 100 percent because many owners do business in more than one category. Ownership may be full or partial.

cable systems, and network television had lost nearly 20 percent of its prime-television audience.

Today the old-line media enterprises see cable largely as a new delivery system for the news and entertainment programs that they already produce. Satellites that orbit the earth carry programs from more than seventy cable channels to more than 8,000 cable systems in the United States. Table 12-1 shows the media industry's heavy investment in the new technology and the consolidation of ownership in the industry. In fact, by 1985 the fifty systems analyzed in Table 12-1 served 60 percent of the nation's cable television audience. The top ten in the group served 43 percent. According to FCC reports, by 1990 concentration had increased so that four companies controlled 47 percent of all cable subscribers. Small independent companies were rapidly vanishing from the market.[24] If present trends continue, including the escalation of costs for entering the cable business and surviving the initial years, oligopoly may become the dominant cable pattern. In recognition of that fact, Congress provided for cable rate regulation in 1992 to protect consumers from price gouging. Cable rates had risen by more than 60 percent in the preceding five-year period.[25]

The FCC's willingness to let old-line media buy cable systems contrasts sharply with its nearly total prohibition of telephone company activity in the cable field. Telephone companies are allowed to serve only remote areas that cable cannot profitably reach. Should the telephone companies receive permission to freely enter the cable business, the estimates for growth of the cable audience will rise sharply because existing telephone wiring could then be adapted. Fears that AT&T, the giant telephone enterprise, might monopolize the cable scene led to its initial exclusion from the cable market.[26] The court-ordered break-up of the company in 1984 has lessened that fear. Given the FCC's eagerness to promote competition in the cable industry, it was no surprise when local telephone companies were authorized in 1992 to package and transmit television programs over their new fiber-optic lines.[27]

FCC rules and the opposition of the established industries have not been the only hurdles faced by the cable industry. There are numerous local political hurdles as well. Laying of cables requires permission from local authorities. To avoid undue duplication of facilities, franchises must be granted. Usually these have gone to a single company only. The franchising process has been highly political, in terms of both the selection of a particular company and the determination of the conditions of the franchise. Many small enterprises have been squeezed out because they have been unable to pay the costs of bidding for a contract, to grease the wheels of politics, or to finance initial red-ink years. Like most public utility companies, the survivors enjoy monopoly status within the cable field. Since consumers benefit when they can choose among competing services, the FCC has been trying to strengthen cable's competitors in various ways. For instance, it has recommended that cable companies pay networks for the right to broadcast network programs that cable has hitherto obtained free of charge. Satellite and microwave competition would be boosted by receiving compulsory access to programs produced by cable companies.[28]

In the absence of national rules, local franchising policies have been diverse.[29] Franchisers and franchisees must agree on the time to be allowed for constructing the system and the life of the franchise (usually fifteen years). They also must agree on requirements regarding public service and open-access channels and service for outlying areas where costs will exceed profits temporarily or permanently. Service to rural areas may pose insurmountable economic problems, particularly in the western plains and the Rocky Mountain states. Alternatives to cable, such as microwave relays, satellite broadcasts, or transmission over telephone wires, may have to be considered. Difficult decisions have to be made in choosing appropriate government agencies to supervise the execution of cable contracts and to ensure that programming serves the public interest. Finally, major controversies need to be settled regarding the nature of the fee structure and the manner in which government exacts its tribute.

Regulatory Options

Governments have several policy options for dealing with emerging broadcast systems. First, they can play a hands-off, *laissez-faire* role, allowing the system to develop as its private owners please.[30] This is the policy advocated in various proposals to revise the Communications Act of 1934. The precedent for this policy is the traditional stance of government toward the print media. If one believes that government should regulate information supply only when transmission channels are scarce, as happened with early radio and television, then it makes sense to leave the current rich crop of information transmission systems unregulated. When broadcast and narrowcast outlets are plentiful, market forces presumably come into play so that necessary services will be supplied in a far more flexible way than is possible when government regulations intervene. The only restraints that may be needed are safeguards to protect national security and maintain social norms and privacy.

Second, information transmission systems can be treated as *common carriers*, like the telephone or rail and bus lines. Common carrier status makes transmission facilities available to everyone on a first-come, first-served basis. Under common carrier rules, the owners of cable facilities would not broadcast their own programs as they do now. Instead they would lease their channels to various broadcasters for fees regulated by government or by market forces. As common carriers they would not be allowed to selectively exclude certain programs.

The FCC and many local governments like the common carrier concept. It has been adopted for dealing with communications satellites. But the U.S. Supreme Court decided in 1979 that cable could not be considered a common carrier under federal laws.[31] However, the ruling does not bar state and local authorities from imposing common carrier status on the industry. Congress, too, has repeatedly imposed some common carrier features on the cable television industry. In the mid-1960s, for instance, it ordered cable systems to broadcast all local over-the-air programs. The industry brought suit and won judgments in 1985 and again in 1987 that the "must carry rule" violated the First Amendment rights of cable companies.[32] The victory for cable systems was a defeat for champions of broad public access rights to the media.

There is a third regulatory option. The government can confer *public trustee* status on communication enterprises. Owners would have full responsibility for programming, but they would be required to meet certain public service obligations. These might include adherence to equal time provisions and limitations on materials unsuitable for children or offensive to community standards of morality. They might also encompass rules about access to broadcast facilities to ensure availability of public and government channels, including facilities to broadcast public education, public safety, and medical and social service programs.

The rationale for conferring trustee status on broadcasters has been twofold. The scarcity argument has been powerful in the past, but has lost validity. The other argument for trustee status is that television is a highly influential medium. There must be assurance that valuable programs are broadcast and harmful ones avoided and that canons of fairness are observed. This is a powerful argument with strong support in much of the world. It is the argument that Third World nations have made so persuasively, as discussed in the previous chapter. But it is not the primary argument on which the American system was built, and it may clash with the First Amendment.

Paying the Piper

Whether new technologies are treated like any private enterprise, like a common carrier, or like a trustee, their costs have to be paid. There are three possibilities for financing, each with different policy consequences: advertiser support, audience payments, and government subsidies. Various combinations are also used. Print media, for example, are financed by their audiences, supplemented by advertisements and some mailing subsidies.

Advertiser support requires programming that has mass appeal. Such programming is bound to share the strengths and weaknesses of current mass media. Sponsor influence may increase in the age of medium proliferation because competition for sponsors becomes keener when media multiply. Many outlets—particularly those with small audiences or audiences that lack attraction for advertisers because they represent small markets—may even find it difficult to attract enough sponsors to pay for their operations.

While advertising revenues have been growing, many new broadcast facilities, such as cable television, rely heavily on *audience payments*. These have generally taken the form of a monthly service charge for the facilities, to which an installation or equipment charge has often been added. Additional programming may be available for a flat monthly rate or on a per program basis. Service charge financing for broadcasting has been quite popular in many foreign countries. In the United States, however, it initially met with resistance because good broadcast services are available throughout the United States free of charge.

By the mid-1980s much of the initial resistance to paying for television had been overcome. Half of America's households had been cabled, and many were paying for special programs in addition to their standard monthly fees. Although a number of programming services had succumbed to competition and some new cable ventures were in financial difficulties, the industry as a whole was thriving. Some of its services, like around-the-clock live coverage of major news happenings provided by Cable News Network, had become highly influential. These largely unedited broadcasts supplied up-to-the-minute information to mass audiences, as well as to government officials, lobbyists, and to other news professionals. Moreover, the worst fears of old-line broadcasting entrepreneurs had not materialized. The number of viewers had dropped measurably but not catastrophically. The networks were ailing financially, but had high hopes for capturing new audiences and advertisers by tailoring their programs to carefully selected audiences.[33] As had been the case with past innovations, the new media had not mortally wounded their predecessors.

A major social drawback of service charges for broadcasts is that poor families who most need many of the specialized programs are least able to pay. Middle-income families who already enjoy many social advantages benefit most. The information resources made available to them through cable and other programs enhance their status, leaving lower class people farther behind.[34] This problem could be reduced through *government subsidies* paid to the cable industry on a basis similar to financing public television, or through government subsidies paid to the poor. The latter system seems preferable to avoid making cable financially dependent on the government, thereby endangering cablecasters' freedom of action.

The Shape of the Future

Regulation versus Deregulation

New communications technologies require a complete rethinking of the scope and purpose of federal regulation of broadcast media. The Communications Act of 1934 was passed because transmission facilities were scarce; Congress wanted to make certain that the limited number of franchises served broad public interests and were parceled out equitably. Nearly sixty years later the basic regulatory framework remains intact although its ostensible raison d'être has largely vanished. Despite mushrooming broadcast outlets that have vastly expanded the number of broadcasts within reach of average Americans, total deregulation and reliance on traditional First Amendment values are still distant goals. The difference in treatment between the unregulated print media and the regulated electronic media has become highly controversial. Whereas competition has been rising among broadcasters, it has been falling among daily newspapers. Average Americans are generally limited to one local newspaper. The high cost of starting a paper and a finite advertising pool discourage would-be competitors. One can argue, therefore, that television and radio are far more competitive than the unregulated newspaper business and should be freed from all controls. Such arguments have been quite prominent in the perennial debates surrounding efforts to revise the Communications Act of 1934.

Opponents of extensive deregulation have argued that the age of electronic plenty remains a still far-off vision. Multiplying channels available for broadcasting does not automatically mean more diversity. Most channels are likely to use the traditional sources of programs to fill air time, as happened in cable systems where cable operators drew heavily on materials produced by other broadcasters.[35] Finally, it has been argued that the impact of television on public life in America is so profound that the public interest requires continued controls. Even when competition is ample, it may be necessary to mandate access to neglected viewpoints and provide programming for neglected audiences, such as children.

Even though full-scale attempts to rewrite the Communications Act of 1934 are doomed to rough legislative sailing, the trends toward deregulation that they have exhibited have been strong enough to find expression in the rules and regulations issued by the FCC, as discussed in Chapter 2. However, the strong moves toward deregulation in the Reagan years are facing reversals in the 1990s. Dissatisfaction with the services supplied by private entrepreneurs, including complaints about price gouging, has fueled opposition to deregulation. In fact, current pressures for restoring abandoned controls are strong. The wave of mergers in the 1980s, which placed most established and emerging networks under the control of big corporations, rekindled fears that the media might become the mouthpieces of special interests, and that financial returns would be their programming lodestar. Plummeting revenues and sharp cuts in news division staffs heightened these fears. Regulation, rather than deregulation, is once again becoming the battle cry for champions of a free press. "The issue is whether there are possible negative effects of failing to regulate expression. If so, maximizing free expression (that is, an absolutist First Amendment stand) becomes a value to weigh against those effects, not the basis for cutting off discussion on the issue." [36]

At the international level pressures also are mounting for increasing government control and responsibility for media performance. This is happening at a time when the lines between unregulated print and regulated electronic media are blurring. The price of progress in electronic transmission of printed news may be the loss of freedom from government regulation. A great challenge faces broadcast policy makers. They can yield to domestic and international pressures and make government the arbiter of what is good and safe news and entertainment for the public, or they can leave that role in private hands, at the mercy of nonelected media tycoons. Given these alternatives, this author casts her vote for the latter option, believing with Thomas Jefferson that "error of opinion may be tolerated where reason is left free to combat it." [37]

Two-Way Communication and Televotes

Another important area of public concern is two-way electronic communication. This feature of the communications revolution has been hailed as the gateway to genuine direct democracy, especially at the local level. In the future public business presumably can be conducted in front of the television set. Citizens can watch the proceedings of legislative bodies and cast votes of approval or disapproval.

Several pilot projects have been conducted in the United States and abroad.[38] In San José, California, for example, school board meetings were televised. All sides of controversial school issues were aired, and the televised discussion was supplemented by newspaper articles. The public was then given a chance to vote on policy suggestions through two-way cable or through ballots printed in the local newspapers. Unfortunately, participation was uneven. In San José, as in most of the other "televote" projects, the bulk of votes came from middle-income people. Most lower-income people, though they liked the idea of interactivity, did not participate.

Another problem has been the reluctance of public officials to implement policies supported by televotes. There are several reasons. On the national level, electronic voting raises important constitutional issues. The United States is a representative democracy that holds elections at regular intervals. Between elections, officials make decisions they consider to be in the public interest. The Constitution did not provide for direct democracy governed by a series of plebiscites. Hence direct democracy may be unconstitutional. Quite aside from legal questions, the merits of direct democracy at various government levels in the United States remain highly controversial. Widespread adoption of electronic plebiscites, with or without extensive prior information campaigns, is therefore unlikely in the future.

The possibility of using the two-way circuitry for educational programs, particularly those that would improve the status of disadvantaged groups, is less controversial. Available technologies include television and radio call-in shows, electronic computer bulletin boards, and cable public access channels.[39] Their growth rates have been phenomenal. For example, there were 45,000 electronic bulletin boards worldwide in 1991, with a user community estimated at five million people. Again the major obstacle, beyond funding and making new technologies available, is motivating disadvantaged populations to use them. Both successes and failures have been recorded.

Spartanburg, South Carolina, for example, experimented with interactive cablecasts of high school subjects to permit adults to earn high school diplomas without leaving home. Sixty-two percent of the adults in the area lacked a high school diploma. For people who took the course, results were as good as those obtained from actual classroom attendance. But the program had to be discontinued because too few people were enrolled to keep the per-pupil cost within reasonable limits.[40]

By contrast, a senior citizen program in Reading, Pennsylvania, that linked three senior citizen centers was highly successful. The program connected the centers to public schools, the city council, and other public places. Participants in the three centers could interact with people at the public facilities and with each other. All programs were produced and conducted by senior citizens. Potentially shut-in and shut-out adults were thus reintegrated into the community. They became more aware of their mutual problems and problems of the community at large. The community benefited from hearing senior citizens' views about public policies.[41]

Two-way cable has offered a variety of programs to general audiences, but they have been sharply curtailed because they were less popular than expected. Warner Amex Cable Communications' QUBE system, which served 350,000 viewers in Columbus, Cincinnati, Pittsburgh, Dallas, Houston, and St. Louis suburbs, rarely attained more than 2 percent participation for its interactive programs. These included talent contests, astrology shows, exercise classes, interactive games, football games, town meetings, and public hearings involving federal agencies. The reasons for the disappointing results may have been the audience's reluctance to participate, unattractive program formats, and technical difficulties in responding when several viewers were watching one television set.

Fragmentation of the Broadcast Audience

The multitude of broadcast channels and the even broader options created by video tape technology have prompted fears that the national political consensus will become fragmented. When people turn to specialized fare in news and entertainment, their attention to politics may diminish. Without national media, there may be no national political consensus.[42] As discussed in Chapter 7, nationwide dissemination of similar news has fostered shared political socialization. When news becomes fragmented, people are likely to be socialized in disparate ways. If political programming becomes available only on channels dedicated to politics, will people choose to watch it? Will government leaders be able to convey their messages to the public? A music fan, tuned in to an all-music station, may watch music programs only; an African-American or Hispanic person may tune in only to stations concerned with African-American and Hispanic affairs. Many citizens thus may become prisoners of their special interests and may miss out on happenings in the broader culture.

On the positive side of the ledger, specialization raises the possibility of a better fit between audience needs and public messages. Government programs may operate more successfully, given ampler opportunities for one- and two-way communication with selected audiences. The electoral chances of minority candidates and parties may improve with increased ability to target their messages to selected audiences. The possibilities for change are staggering, but too undefined as yet to hazard predictions.

Fears that fragmentation of the broadcast audience will lead to political fragmentation are not shared by everyone, of course.[43] Many people point out that the national consensus was not ruptured when alternative media were used in the past. They argue that fragmented interests create the demand for fragmented media rather than the reverse. If there is political and social consensus, people will seek out information pertaining to the larger community. Others point out that commercially oriented media will always try to attract large audiences by offering programs with wide appeal. That means sticking to the same tried and true formulas. Programming on cable television, which has become very uniform and similar to network television, is an example. Even if the new media increase fragmentation, many people do not find this objectionable, believing that pluralism is preferable to the traditional melting-pot ideals.

Media pluralism may herald more local programming. Most local governments are eager to use cable channels to broadcast local political news. Local school systems and police and fire departments have also sought access to cable to air their concerns. If publicity means power, the new communications media may enhance the power of local institutions, possibly at the expense of national ones. The two-way capacity may make programming attractive to local audiences even when it lacks the polish of professional programs.[44] The new communications media therefore may allow local organizations to reach much larger constituencies than was hitherto possible. Many thousands of hours of community programming are broadcast each week on community access channels. No audience figures are available, but they probably are modest considering the mixed quality of the broadcasts.

While the possibilities for strengthening local communities through increased publicity are good, the new narrowcasting technologies also can deflect interest away from the local scene and produce global villages of like-minded people. National cable television networks, such as CNN and C-SPAN, and the new Fox television network, are examples of movement in this direction.

Public Television

Yet another issue brought to the fore by the coming age of broadcast plenty is the fate of public television. As discussed in Chapter 2, public television was organized to provide an alternative to the typical programming available on the commercial networks. It also was intended to be an outlet for programs geared to minorities. These are the very services that cable television and other narrowcasting services presumably will perform on a commercial basis. Since public television has always depended on public subsidies, and its audiences, except for children's programs, have been quite limited, pressures to abandon it may become strong.

Of course, the hitch in this argument is the presumption that the mushrooming commercial television enterprises will be willing and able to fill the niche occupied by the public broadcasting system. A glance at any weekly television schedule raises serious doubts. Most of the new outlets provide clones of the offerings that are familiar from network television.[45] Sophisticated cultural and educational programming is scarce and has not been commercially viable because audiences have remained small. The difficulty of keeping the public broadcasting system solvent may spell its death knell, nonetheless. The European practice of funding public broadcasting principally through consumer fees has never been considered a realistic option in the United States.

The Consequences of Change

The concerns outlined thus far are undoubtedly not the only ones ahead. Many others will require decisions that go far beyond solving technical issues. The direction of communications policy is at stake and with it the tone and possibly the direction of American politics generally. John M. Eger, a former director of the White House Office of Telecommunications Policy, has remarked that this is indeed a time of decision. "For as we are moving into a future rich in innovation and in social change, we are also moving into a storm center of new world problems." The new technologies are "a force for change throughout the world that simply will not be stopped, no matter how it is resisted." And then he asks, "Are we ready for the consequences of this change? Are we prepared to consider the profound social, legal, economic, and political effects of technology around the world? " [46]

Currently, the answer is "no." In the communications field the structure for policy making at all government levels is fragmented and ill-suited to deal with the existing problems, to say nothing of those that must be anticipated.[47] Policies are improvised when pressures become strong, yielding in a crazy-quilt pattern to various industry concerns, to public interest groups, to domestic or foreign policy considerations, to the pleas of engineers and lawyers, and to the suggestions of political scientists and economists. Narrow issues are addressed, but the full scope of the situation is ignored.[48] As Russell Neuman notes, "the concept of a comprehensive industrial policy or even a broadly focused reformulation of communications policy for the information age is political anathema in the centers of power."[49]

Neither Congress nor the executive branch is willing to enter this thicket of controversy when so many other battles must be fought. It is not likely that policy leadership will emerge. "Muddling through," the watchphrase for the 1970s and 1980s, is likely to remain the watchphrase for the 1990s as well.

Summary

Many people are dissatisfied with the performance of the mass media, especially television. They can and do air their dissatisfaction through various formal and informal channels, but criticism usually has had limited success in changing media content. To fill the gaps left by the major mass media, many alternative media have been created. These media are organized either to serve demographically distinct populations or to cater to particular substantive concerns or political orientations.

Among alternative media the underground press is especially interesting. During the 1960s it demonstrated that the government will tolerate a journalism that attacks major domestic and foreign policies, even in wartime. The mushrooming of underground print and broadcast media during the Vietnam War era also showed that, in a business dominated by giants, small enterprises can operate successfully on a shoestring budget. The limited demand by the general public for published radical dissent, however, makes it difficult to sustain such publications over long periods of time.

In this chapter we also explored the social and political consequences of technological advances in mass media and outlined the areas where new public policies are needed. We briefly described some of the new electronic tools and sketched their capabilities in bringing about the age of broadcast plenty and of two-way communication. Their impact on life and politics in the United States could be enormous were it not for the fact that most people, most of the time, are disinclined to spend time and effort to find special-interest information or entertainment. Two-way circuitry has been hailed as the gateway to genuine direct democracy and as a great educational tool. However, electronic plebiscites are as yet too controversial to be adopted widely. Fragmentation of the broadcast audience has raised fears of political fragmentation and breakdown of the national political consensus that has been deemed essential for successful democratic government. But the extent and implications of the danger remain disputed.

Various changes in regulatory policy will be required to integrate the new broadcast and narrowcast technologies into the existing mass media regulatory structure. More importantly, major policy changes could arrive, almost unannounced, if the political impact of new technologies is not considered and guided carefully. By using electronic transmission facilities, the print media could be subject to the same government regulations as electronic media. The forces favoring greater government control of media content are strong at a time when most types of media use some form of electronic transmission. Whether the mass media are regulated more tightly or given freer rein, deliberate choice rather than drift should be the basis for the decisions. In that choice the perceptive comment of the *Washington Post*'s Alan Barth should be remembered: "If you want a watchdog to warn you of intruders you must put up with a certain amount of mistaken barking." [50]

Notes

1. *Julius Caesar,* act 4, scene 3, line 218.
2. David Gergen, "The Message to the Media," *Public Opinion* 7 (April/May 1984): 5-8; Andrew Randolph, "What Credibility Problem?" *Editor & Publisher* 119 (January 18, 1986): 12-13; Michael Robinson, "Pressing Opinion," *Public Opinion* 9 (September/October 1986): 56-59; and Philip Meyer, "Credibility: And Now the Good News," *Presstime* 7 (June 1985): 26-27.
3. Bill Granger, "Sleazy Does It: Decency and Fair Play Take a Holiday in the New-New Journalism," *Chicago Tribune Magazine,* January 3, 1988, 4. Also see Norman E. Isaacs, *Untended Gates: The Mismanaged Press* (New York: Columbia University Press, 1986).
4. Isaacs, *Untended Gates;* Tom Goldstein, *The News at Any Cost: How Journalists Compromise Their Ethics to Shape the News* (New York: Simon and Schuster, 1985); W. Lance Bennett, *News: The Politics of Illusion,* 2d ed. (New York: Longman, 1988); Robert M. Entman, *Democracy without Citizens: Media and the Decay of American Politics* (New York: Oxford University Press, 1989); Michael Parenti, *Inventing Reality: The Politics of the Mass Media* (New York: St. Martin's Press, 1986); and Herbert Schiller, *Communication and Cultural Domination* (New York: International Arts and Sciences Press, 1976).
5. *Zamora et al. v. Columbia Broadcasting System et al.,* 480 F. Supp. 199 (S. D. Fla. 1979). See also Robert E. Drechsel, "Media Tort Liability for Physical Harm," *Journalism Quarterly* 64 (Spring 1987): 99-105; and Juliet Lusbough Dee, "Media Accountability for Real-Life Violence: A Case of Negligence or Free Speech?" *Journal of Communication* 37 (Spring 1987):

106-138.

6. *Olivia N. (a minor) v. National Broadcasting Company,* 74 Cal. App. 3d 383 (1978), 126 Cal. App. 3d 488 (1981).

7. Donald T. Mogavero, "The American Press Ombudsman," *Journalism Quarterly* 59 (Winter 1982): 548-553, 580.

8. Ronald Farrar, "News Councils and Libel Actions," *Journalism Quarterly* 63 (Autumn 1986): 509-516.

9. Jonathan Friendly, "National News Council Will Dissolve," *New York Times,* March 23, 1984. Media critic Norman Isaacs has proposed ombudsmen as the best alternative to news councils. See Isaacs, *Untended Gates,* 132-146.

10. Erik Barnouw, "Historical Survey of Communications Breakthroughs," in *The Communications Revolution in Politics,* ed. Gerald Benjamin (New York: The Academy of Political Science, 1982), 20.

11. Ray Eldon Hiebert, Donald F. Ungurait, and Thomas W. Bohn, *Mass Media V: An Introduction to Modern Communication* (New York: Longman, 1988), 73.

12. John W. Johnstone, Edward J. Slawski, and William W. Bowman, *The Newspeople* (Urbana, Ill.: University of Illinois Press, 1976), 157-179.

13. They are described more fully in Johnstone, Slawski, and Bowman, *The Newspeople,* 157-181; Laurence Leamer, *The Paper Revolutionaries: The Rise of the Underground Press* (New York: Simon and Schuster, 1972); and Jack A. Nelson, "The Underground Press," in *Readings in Mass Communication,* ed. Michael C. Emery and Ted Curtis Smythe (Dubuque, Iowa: W. C. Brown, 1972), 212-226.

14. Marshall McLuhan, *Understanding Media: The Extensions of Man* (New York: McGraw-Hill, 1964); and Marshall McLuhan and Quentin Fiore, *The Medium Is the Message: An Inventory of Effects* (New York: Bantam Books, 1967).

15. Russell Neuman, *The Future of the Mass Audience* (New York: Cambridge University Press, 1991), ix-x.

16. Ithiel de Sola Pool, *Technologies of Freedom* (Cambridge, Mass.: Harvard University Press, 1983), 152-156; and James G. Webster, "Assessing Exposure to the New Media," in *Media Use in the Information Age: Emerging Patterns of Adoption and Consumer Use,* ed. Jerry L. Salvaggio and Jennings Bryant (Hillsdale, N.J.: Erlbaum, 1989), 7-19; and Leo Bogart, "Toward a National Media Policy," *Media Studies Journal* 6 (Spring 1992): 73-92.

17. Heather E. Hudson, "Implications for Development Communications," *Journal of Communication* 29 (Winter 1979): 179-186. Also see Carrie Heeter, "Implications of New Interactive Technologies for Conceptualizing Communication," in Salvaggio and Bryant, eds., *Media Use in the Information Age,* 217-233.

18. U.S. Congress, Office of Technology Assessment, *Science, Technology, and the First Amendment,* OTA-CIT-369 (Washington, D.C.: Government Printing Office, 1988), 1-33.

19. Denise Claveloux, "TV Technology Sparks a Global Feud," *Chicago Tribune,* March 30, 1989.

20. Vincent Mosco, "Une Drôle de Guerre," *Media Studies Journal* 6 (Spring 1992): 57-58.

21. *Home Box Office, Inc. v. FCC,* 567 F. 2d 9 (D.C. Cir.), *cert. denied,* 434 U.S. 829 (1977); and *FCC v. Midwest Video Corp.,* 440 U.S. 689 (1979).

22. Pay television had been freed from federal controls in 1977. Remaining federal controls were dropped by 1979. Benjamin M. Compaine, Christopher H. Sterling, Thomas Guback, and J. Kendrick Noble, Jr., *Who Owns the Media? Concentration and Ownership in the Mass Communications Industry,* 2d ed. (White Plains, N.Y.: Knowledge Industry Publications, 1982), 381, 407.
23. "Cable TV," *Consumer Reports* 52 (September 1987): 547-554.
24. Herbert H. Howard, "An Update on Cable TV Ownership: 1985," *Journalism Quarterly* 63 (Winter 1986): 706-709; and Patricia Aufderheide, "Cable Television and the Public Interest," *Journal of Communication* 42 (Winter 1992): 52-65. Also see *Television and Cable Factbook* (Washington, D.C.: Warren, 1990).
25. Edmund L. Andrews, "Hopes of Cable Industry Ride on Veto by Bush," *New York Times,* July 25, 1992.
26. Compaine et al., *Who Owns the Media?* 390-393.
27. Edmund L. Andrews, "Telephone Companies to Get Right to Transmit Television," *New York Times,* July 16, 1992.
28. Andrews, "Hopes of Cable Industry."
29. FCC regulations prevail over conflicting state regulations. *Capital Cities Cable v. Crisp,* 104 U.S. 2694 (1984). Federal law may preempt state laws. See William E. Hanks and Stephen E. Coran, "Federal Preemption of Obscenity Law Applied to Cable Television," *Journalism Quarterly* 63 (Spring 1986): 43-47.
30. Henry Geller, "Mass Communications Policy: Where We Are and Where We Should Be Going," in *Democracy and the Mass Media,* ed. Judith Lichtenberg (New York: Cambridge University Press, 1990), 290-329.
31. *FCC v. Midwest Video Corp.,* 440 U.S. 689 (1979).
32. "Cable TV," *Consumer Reports,* 555.
33. Bill Carter, "Broadcasters Take a Bite Out of Cable in the Ratings," *New York Times,* March 9, 1992.
34. Mosco, "Une Drôle de Guerre," 56-60.
35. Don R. LeDuc, "Deregulation and the Dream of Diversity," *Journal of Communication* 32 (Autumn 1982): 171.
36. Robert M. Entman and Steven S. Wildman, "Reconciling Economic and Non-Economic Perspectives in Media Policy: Transcending the 'Marketplace of Ideas,' " *Journal of Communication* 42 (Winter 1992): 5-19.
37. First inaugural address, March 4, 1801. See Andrew A. Lipscomb, ed., *The Writings of Thomas Jefferson,* vol. 3 (Washington, D.C.: Thomas Jefferson Memorial Association, 1905), 319.
38. Richard Hollander, *Video Democracy: The Vote-from-Home Revolution* (Mt. Airy, Md.: Lomond, 1985). Public access cable television may also spur political participation. For examples see Aufderheide, "Cable Television and the Public Interest," 58-63.
39. Features of various technologies are discussed by Heeter, "Implications of New Interactive Technologies."
40. William A. Lucas, "Telecommunications Technologies and Services," in *Communication for Tomorrow,* 248.
41. See Red Burns and Lynne Elton, "Reading, Pa.: Programming for the Future"; Eileen Connell, "Reading, Pa.: Training Local People"; and Mitchell L. Moss, "Reading, Pa.: Research on Community Uses," all in *Journal of Communication* 28 (Spring 1978): 148-167.
42. James G. Webster, "Audience Behavior in the New Media Environment,"

Journal of Communication 36 (Summer 1986): 77-91.
43. See Neuman, "The Future of the Mass Audience," 40; and Aufderheide, "Cable Television and the Public Interest," 58-63.
44. Use of cable television is compared with use of other media in Gerald L. Grotta and Doug Newsom, "How Does Cable Television in the Home Relate to Other Media Use Patterns?" *Journalism Quarterly* 59 (Winter 1982): 588-591, 609. Also see "Cable TV," *Consumer Reports*.
45. The reasons for this situation are explained by David Waterman, "The Failure of Cultural Programming on Cable TV: An Economic Interpretation," *Journal of Communication* 36 (Summer 1986): 92-107. Also see Entman and Wildman, "Reconciling Economic and Non-Economic Perspectives."
46. John M. Eger, "A Time of Decision," *Journal of Communication* 29 (Winter 1979): 204-207.
47. Lucas, "Telecommunications Technologies and Services," 248.
48. Ithiel de Sola Pool, "The Problems of WARC," *Journal of Communication* 29 (Winter 1979): 187-196.
49. Neuman, "The Future of the Mass Audience," x.
50. Alan Barth, "If the Press Didn't Tell Us, Who Would?" (Chicago: Sigma Delta Chi, 1987).

Readings

Arterton, F. Christopher. *Teledemocracy: Can Technology Protect Democracy?* Beverly Hills, Calif.: Sage, 1987.

Bennett, W. Lance. *News: The Politics of Illusion.* 2d ed. New York: Longman, 1988.

Isaacs, Norman E. *Untended Gates: The Mismanaged Press.* New York: Columbia University Press, 1986.

Kessler, Lauren. *The Dissident Press: Alternative Journalism in American History.* Beverly Hills, Calif.: Sage, 1984.

McKibben, Bill. *The Age of Missing Information.* New York: Random House, 1992.

Neuman, W. Russell. *The Future of the Mass Audience.* New York: Cambridge University Press, 1991.

Newberg, Paula R., ed. *New Directions in Communications Policy.* 2 vols. Durham, N.C.: Duke University Press, 1989.

Pool, Ithiel de Sola. *Technologies without Boundaries: On Telecommunication in a Global Age.* Eli M. Noam, ed. Cambridge, Mass.: Harvard University Press, 1990.

Tehranian, Majid. *Technologies of Power: Information Machines and Democratic Prospects.* Norwood, N.J.: Ablex, 1990.

INDEX

ABC network. *See also* Capital Cities/ABC
  "Arson for Profit" show, 175-176
  coverage of government branches, 289-291
  nuclear war broadcast, 15, 191
  ownership of, 43
  polls, 255
Abortion issue
  court cases, 329
  media interpretation, 9-10, 134
Accuracy in Media (AIM), 31n14, 58
Action for Children's Television (ACT), 58
Adams, William C., 392
Advertising
  on children's shows, 54
  cigarette, 70, 93
  and fairness doctrine, 69-70
  and news pressures, 354
  for policy issues, 74
  political, 248-249
  and program content, 56-57, 115, 419
AFL-CIO, 328
African-Americans. *See also* Minorities
  and civil rights coverage, 7
  as media executives, 103
  media exposure, 209-210
  newspapers, 337
  program access, 73
  television image of, 3, 221, 242n59
  TV license challenges by, 57
Agence France-Presse, 363, 365, 392
Agenda building
  defined, 182
  media role, 216-217
  and political scandal, 183-184

science policy, 184-187
  social movements, 187-190
  by subnational officials, 338
AIDS (acquired immune deficiency syndrome), 57, 72
Ailes, Roger, 256
AIM (Accuracy in Media), 31n14, 58
Alabama Education Television Network, 72
Alaska earthquake, 153
Albosta, Donald J., 19
Alternative press, 336-337, 407-409
Altheide, David, 378
American Bar Association, 328
American Civil Liberties Union, 194, 328
American Express Company, 56
American Independent party, 265
American Journalist, The, 103
American Medical Association, 59, 406
American Newspaper Publishers Association (ANPA), 56
American Research Bureau, 116
American Telephone and Telegraph Company (AT&T), 56, 416
American Voter, The, 13
"Amerika," 57
Amin, Idi, 376
Anderson, Jack, 161
Anderson, John, 255, 265, 270, 274
Annenberg School of Communications, 221
ANPA (American Newspaper Publishers Association), 56
Antenne Duex, 38
AP. *See* Associated Press (AP)
Apple, R. W., 251
Aquino, Corazón, 396
Arledge, Roone, 182